THE WESLEYAN EDITION OF THE
WORKS OF HENRY FIELDING

———

# THE HISTORY OF TOM JONES

## A FOUNDLING

Hogarth's Portrait of Fielding. From A. Murphy, *Works of Henry Fielding, Esq.*
(1762)

HENRY FIELDING

---

*The History of*
# TOM JONES
A FOUNDLING
*VOLUME I*

---

WITH AN INTRODUCTION AND
COMMENTARY BY
MARTIN C. BATTESTIN

THE TEXT EDITED BY
FREDSON BOWERS

WESLEYAN UNIVERSITY PRESS
1975

Printed in Great Britain
at the University Press, Oxford
by Vivian Ridler
Printer to the University

# TO RUTHE

What you do
Still betters what is done.

# PREFACE

THE Wesleyan edition of *Tom Jones* is designed to furnish a reliable text of the novel and to provide all other materials relevant to the history and essential meaning of the text. The principles and procedures followed in preparing the text and its apparatus are described in the Textual Introduction; the Appendices supply detailed records of editorial emendations to the copy-text and of substantive variation within the four editions of the novel published during Fielding's lifetime, as well as bibliographical descriptions of these four editions and of the *cancellanda* in the Rothschild copy of the first, now preserved at Trinity College, Cambridge, and in the recently acquired British Museum copy. After reviewing the personal circumstances in which Fielding wrote the novel and to which he frequently alludes in the narrative itself, the General Introduction defines the period of composition, traces in full the printing and publication of the four original editions, and rehearses the early reception of the book, emphasizing evidence that has come to light in the course of nearly half a century that has passed since F. T. Blanchard's important study. *Tom Jones*, furthermore, however timeless its appeal, is a highly topical and learned work, Fielding's allusions ranging from the classics of ancient and modern literature to those contemporary events, issues, books, people that mattered to him. Accompanying the text at the foot of the page, the explanatory annotations will assist the reader in identifying Fielding's references and in recovering the contexts of his thought and humour.

From the editors' point of view certainly, the story of the making of the Wesleyan *Tom Jones* is fraught with enough scoundrels and Samaritans, cross-accidents and fortunate discoveries, to furnish the materials for a modest 'comic romance' in its own right. One episode of that story, at least, was tragical enough to wring a sympathetic tear from even an unsentimental reader. After three years of intensive research, the commentary was finished in the summer of 1967, only to fall victim to a pair of latter-day highwaymen who rifled the editor's car in Washington, D.C. This misadventure is the principal reason why the

edition has been so long in preparation, but it is worth mentioning here chiefly for the sake of two German scholars whose
helpfulness in solving specific problems of annotation I wish to
acknowledge, but whose names were lost to me when the manuscript was stolen. At the start the task of annotation was expedited
by the kindness of Philip B. Daghlian, who made available to me
the notes of his friend and colleague, the late James A. Work:
before his death in 1961, Professor Work had agreed to provide
the commentary for the Wesleyan *Tom Jones* and had made
substantial progress in identifying many of Fielding's classical
allusions. There were other helping hands to lend incidental
assistance along the way in clearing obstacles and pointing
directions: in particular, I wish to thank Hugh Amory, James L.
Clifford, Miss M. Dunbar, Irvin Ehrenpreis, David Foxon,
Arthur Friedman, Edward Kessler, William Kinsley, Lewis M.
Knapp, the Lord Lyon, C. J. Rawson, and Mrs. William Talman.
Like Fielding's own peripatetic heroes in their progress home-
ward, I had my special benefactors who generously contributed
their time and energy to help bring the edition to a satisfactory
conclusion. Louis Landa and Henry K. Miller read the General
Introduction and the commentary with great care and offered
valuable suggestions for revision; and Mrs. Adelaide K. Morris,
then well along in her study of Wallace Stevens's poetry, found it
'diverting' (as she put it) to spend hours collating editions of *Tom
Jones*. It would be impossible to name here the many librarians
and archivists on both sides of the Atlantic who have assisted me,
patiently and skilfully, but thanks are due particularly to the
staffs of the British Museum, the Bodleian Library, the Morgan
Library, and the libraries of the University of Virginia, Rice
University, Yale University, and to the Master and Fellows of
Trinity College, Cambridge, and the Librarian of the British
Museum, for permission to publish the unique *cancellanda*
readings of their copies.

Preparation of the General Introduction and annotations was
made possible largely through the generous financial support of
several institutions, here gratefully acknowledged. A Fellowship
from the Guggenheim Foundation in 1964–5 enabled me to do
most of the research and to sketch out a first rough draft of the
notes. Summer grants from the University of Virginia (1966)
and the American Council of Learned Societies (1967) enabled

me to complete the research and to write the (temporarily!) final form of the manuscript. Much of the lost material was rewritten in the summer of 1968, thanks to a grant from Rice University. Two separate collations of the four editions were made for Professor Bowers by graduate students supported by the Research Committee of the University of Virginia and by the Work-Study Program sponsored by the University.

Finally, it should be said that this work is dedicated to Ruthe Rootes Battestin for far more than merely sentimental reasons. As wife to one of the editors and as friend to both, she gave self-lessly of her time and of her own considerable talents as a scholar to help perfect the present edition. She collated the text (twice), read proof, checked citations, tracked down references, and more than once—in determined sallies into such formidable documentary repositories as Somerset House, Stationers' Hall, the Middle Temple, the Westminster History Collection, the Middlesex Guildhall—she uncovered new facts that have appreciably enhanced our knowledge of Fielding and our understanding of his masterpiece. It is more justice than hyperbole to declare that, in many ways, the Wesleyan *Tom Jones* is as much her work as mine.

M. C. B.

*Charlottesville, Virginia*
*December 1971*

# LIST OF CONTENTS

# LIST OF PLATES

## Volume I

Hogarth's Portrait of Fielding (1762). Photograph Bodleian Library

*frontispiece*

## Volume II
### (at end)

1. *Morning*, from Hogarth's *The Four Times of the Day* (1738)
2. Hogarth's *A Harlot's Progress* (1732), Plate 3
3. Hogarth's *A Harlot's Progress* (1732), Plate 4
4. Margaret Cecil, Countess of Ranelagh, after Kneller
5. Hortense Mancini, Duchess of Mazarin, after Lely
6. From Charles LeBrun's *Porus before Alexander*

Photographs by courtesy of the Trustees of the British Museum

## MAP

The Geography of *Tom Jones*

# GENERAL INTRODUCTION

HENRY FIELDING's masterpiece, *The History of Tom Jones, a Foundling*, was published in February 1749. Seven years earlier, in reaction to *Pamela*, Fielding had founded, as he put it, 'a new Province of Writing', introducing into English letters the 'Comic Epic-Poem in Prose'. In *Joseph Andrews* (February 1742), he had turned away from the brooding, claustrophobic world of Richardson's beleaguered virgins to follow Cervantes along the open road—a way cheerful and panoramic, leading not merely through Georgian England, but, because his eye was steadily fixed on 'Nature', which is ever the same, through a timeless country. In this sense, as he remarked of the author of *Don Quixote*, Fielding's subject was 'the History of the World in general'; for he described 'not Men, but Manners; not an Individual, but a Species' (III. i). *Tom Jones* fulfilled the promise of that ambitious, splendid beginning. It is, as few books have managed to be, the realization of a particular form and conception of literary art.

In his Dedication to Lyttelton and in those prefatory chapters that serve as a kind of poetics for his art, Fielding reaffirmed and greatly elaborated the fictional programme he had enunciated in *Joseph Andrews*. His purpose, he declared, was 'to recommend Goodness and Innocence'; his manner, like that of Horace, was genial, to 'speak Truth with a smiling Countenance' (XI. i). And his subject was nothing less than 'HUMAN NATURE' (I. i), not as it is represented by romance-writers and historians, who deal in 'the marvellous' or 'the possible', but as Aristotle had said the poet sees it, whose province is 'the probable'—that higher reality, Truth in her universal aspect (VIII. i).

Although our present purpose is historical rather than critical—not to ascertain the 'meaning' of the novel, but to illuminate those particular biographical and topical circumstances in which the book itself was made—yet it is well to acknowledge at the start what most readers have found to be the essential quality of *Tom Jones*: that in it Fielding shaped the materials of his private experience into a fable of universal significance. The process of his art was the continual transformation of the local and idiosyncratic into the timeless and typical. In its 'main Design' (x. i)

—and in many of its parts: the episode of gypsies, for example (XII. xii)[1]—*Tom Jones* may more profitably be read not merely as a quaint reflection of its author's life and times, nor even (solely) as the festive entertainment he promises and provides, but rather as a work whose deepest impulse is poetic—or perhaps, for want of a more precise term, allegorical, where allegory is to be broadly understood as the embodiment of a coherent, moral interpretation of human life in a narrative action whose characters, while interesting in and for themselves, bear a conceptual significance larger than themselves. In this sense, Fielding offers not merely the story of one wayward young man's pursuit of happiness and his true identity, but, through this action, a paradigm of the human comedy. For, according to a cherished metaphor of the Christian humanist tradition which he inherited, the drama of life was, in the profoundest sense, a comedy—to be seen as an ordered progress, contrived and presided over by a wise and benevolent Providence, who, like Fielding's own omniscient narrator, conducts the actor-worldings through complications of their own and others' making toward that final catastrophe when the cosmic equivalent of poetic justice will be meted out to one and all.

Stated more abstractly, this is the confident, comfortable doctrine behind the most famous philosophic poem of the age:

> All Nature is but Art, unknown to thee;
> All Chance, Direction, which thou canst not see;
> All Discord, Harmony, not understood;
> All partial Evil, universal Good. . . .

The world of *Tom Jones*, like that of the *Essay on Man*, is characterized not only by Energy, but by Order. 'Art', ultimately, is what Fielding celebrates: with respect to the universe at large, the controlling hand of Providence, 'the Art of God', is the source of harmony; with respect to the little world of man, Prudence—that practical, rational virtue which Fielding, following Cicero, called 'the Art of Life'[2]—is the essential moral quality leading to the possession of Wisdom herself. According to the philosophers and divines of the Christian humanist

---

[1] See Battestin, 'Tom Jones and "His *Egyptian* Majesty": Fielding's Parable of Government', *PMLA*, lxxxii (1967), 68–77.
[2] *Amelia* (1751), I. i.

tradition, Providence and Prudence were the analogous attributes of the macrocosm and microcosm; they are also the principal themes of Fielding's novel, his own 'great Creation' (x. i).[1] In *Tom Jones* these complementary motifs are rendered in the story of the hero's pursuit of Sophia and in the wonderful architecture of the book's formal design, in which, through the method of the omniscient narrator and a careful symmetry of structure, Fielding's form acquires an ontological significance, implying the similar attributes of his universe. Viewed in this way, *Tom Jones* appears as the last and the consummate literary expression of an ethos peculiarly 'Augustan'.

Although Fielding as a novelist was thus ultimately concerned with larger matters, with the timeless pattern of the human comedy as he saw it, yet *Tom Jones* is also a very personal book, the product of those private and public circumstances in which it was written. Appropriately, it is 'Experience' whom Fielding invokes as the last of those patron deities essential to the novelist (xiii. i). His own experiences during the period in which he was composing *Tom Jones* affected the novel in various, and at times surprising, ways. They are reflected in countless allusions to his friends and antagonists and to contemporary political, philosophic, and literary issues; and often they are the materials which determined not only the details of characterization, but also the pattern of particular episodes and the content of individual essays. If the effort to reconstruct these circumstances can be tiresome, it is nonetheless indispensable to an appreciation of Fielding's method and his achievement.

I. CIRCUMSTANCES OF COMPOSITION

Aurélien Digeon has described Fielding's *Miscellanies*, published in April 1743 after a series of delays, as 'une liquidation de son passée littéraire'.[2] What is remarkable is that Fielding, having

---

[1] For a discussion of these twin themes, see Battestin, 'Fielding's Definition of Wisdom: Some Functions of Ambiguity and Emblem in *Tom Jones*', *ELH*, xxxv (1968), 188–217; and '*Tom Jones*: The Argument of Design', in H. K. Miller, E. Rothstein, and G. Rousseau (edd.), *The Augustan Milieu: Essays Presented to Louis A. Landa* (Oxford, 1970), pp. 289–319.

[2] *Les Romans de Fielding* (Paris, 1923), p. 118. The statement is correct in the main: so far as is known, the only unpublished pieces Fielding failed to include in this collection were *The Fathers: or, The Good-Natur'd Man*, the comedy produced by Sheridan in 1778,

thus disposed of his literary wares, seems to have resolved at this juncture to terminate a rather lucrative career as 'hackney Author' and to devote himself exclusively to the law—a profession which, from his admission to the Bar (June 1740) until his appointments to the magistracy (1748–9), he never found very rewarding. Despite the popular success of *Joseph Andrews* and the generosity of the subscribers to the *Miscellanies*—which, together with his other productions, brought him over £1,000 during 1742–3[1]—Fielding published nothing for more than a year. When, in July 1744,[2] he did appear again in print, it was chiefly to affirm this fact and, what is more, to declare his disinclination to resume the 'Trade', as he once called it, of authorship.

In the Preface he contributed to the second edition of *David Simple*, Fielding thus indignantly denied the rumour that he was the author not only of his sister's novel, but of *The Causidicade*

---

and two autograph poems recently discovered by Miss Isobel Grundy among the papers of Lady Mary Wortley Montagu. (See 'New Verse by Henry Fielding', *PMLA*, lxxxvii [1972], 213–45). Fielding's wish to exclude the poems is understandable—one (written *c.* 1729) being a fragmentary and clumsy parody of Pope's *Dunciad*, in which Fielding champions Walpole against the Scriblerus group; the other being an epistle to Lyttelton (1733) defending Lady Mary against the aspersions of Pope. By 1743 Fielding was on friendly terms with Pope, and he had acquired a reputation as Walpole's adversary.

[1] According to his formal agreement with Andrew Millar, dated 13 April 1742, Fielding received £199. 6s. for *Joseph Andrews*, *A Full Vindication of the Dutchess Dowager of Marlborough*, and *Miss Lucy in Town* (see *Joseph Andrews*, ed. Battestin [Oxford and Middletown, Conn., 1967], pp. xxx–xxxi). The subscription to the *Miscellanies* grossed another 770 guineas, and from the two benefit nights of his unsuccessful comedy, *The Wedding Day* (performed 17 February 1743), he received something les sthan £50 (see Henry K. Miller, *Essays on Fielding's 'Miscellanies'* [Princeton, N.J., 1961], pp. 8–9, 15). Presumably, he would have received additional sums from the published version of the play, from his satire, *Some Papers Proper to be Read before the R[oya]l Society* (16 February 1743), and from his collaboration with William Young on the translation of Aristophanes' *Plutus* (31 May 1742). On the other side of the ledger, during the same period Fielding had to settle a debt for £197 which he owed to one Joseph King (see Wilbur L. Cross, *The History of Henry Fielding* [New Haven, Conn., 1918], i. 376), and of course there were the printers of the *Miscellanies* to be paid—an expense, if one may extrapolate from Strahan's charges for printing the first of the three volumes, amounting to some £90 (see Strahan's account book [B.M. Add. MSS. 48800] for 2 April 1743, where the charges for printing Vol. I are given as £29. 16s.). The income from his publications and from the production of *The Wedding Day* should have been more than sufficient to meet these expenses. But, to judge from his constant complaints of impecuniosity, Fielding's improvidence with money was formidable.

[2] The second edition of Sarah Fielding's *David Simple*, to which her brother contributed a preface, was published on 13 July 1744. (See *The General Advertiser*, 13–14, 16–19 July 1744).

(1743), a scandalous satire directed against certain prominent members of the legal profession, 'to which', he protested, 'I have applied with so arduous and intent a Diligence, that I have had no Leisure, if I had Inclination, to compose any thing of this kind'. Affecting to despise the insubstantial favours of the Muse, he continued:

Indeed I am very far from entertaining such an Inclination; I know the Value of the Reward, which Fame confers on Authors, too well, to endeavour any longer to obtain it; nor was the World ever more unwilling to bestow the glorious, envied Prize of the Laurel or Bays, than I should now be to receive any such Garland or Fool's Cap. There is not, I believe, (and it is bold to affirm) a single *Free Briton* in this Kingdom, who hates his Wife more heartily than I detest the Muses.

To be sure, much of this is bluster—a pose struck to assuage those influential lawyers who, had they believed Fielding had reverted to writing novels and lampoons, might be indisposed to assist him in his profession. Yet there is no reason to doubt the sincerity of Fielding's intention to disown his Muse: what the Preface to *David Simple* makes clear is that as late as the summer of 1744 he had no plans to write another novel, or, indeed, to resume his literary activities in any capacity. Since he had not been taken at his word, he now felt at liberty to revoke his promise (made in the Preface to the *Miscellanies*) not to publish any anonymous work. But in doing so, he was careful to reassure his readers that this gesture was more a matter of principle than a declaration of authorial intent: 'I shall now', he asserted, 'look upon myself at full Liberty to publish an anonymous Work, without any Breach of Faith. For tho' probably I shall never make any use of this Liberty, there is no reason why I should be under a Restraint, for which I have not enjoyed the purposed Recompence.'

Except for the important Preface to *David Simple*—which, as we have seen, was written in part as a public repudiation of his Muse—Fielding published nothing during a long period of nineteen months (from the publication of the *Miscellanies* in April 1743 to the appearance of *An Attempt towards a Natural History of the Hanover Rat* in November 1744). Determined to make his way in the law, he had apparently found that the character of a 'Poet' was no recommendation for a barrister; perhaps, as Mr. Wilson learned in *Joseph Andrews* (III. iii), there were too many prospective clients who feared he would turn their deeds into plays. It now seems clear that, in order to allay such fears and to demonstrate his competence in his profession, Fielding during this time was applying himself, with a 'Diligence' sufficiently 'arduous and intent', to the preparation of an ambitious work on Crown Law, based on the notes of his maternal grandfather, Sir Henry Gould.[1] This work, entitled 'An Institute of the Pleas of the Crown', in two folio volumes, was never printed, though by February 1745 it was far enough advanced for Fielding and his bookseller to announce that its publication was imminent.[2] The reasons why this promise was never fulfilled are obscure, but Fielding's 'Law-Book' remained a lively topic with his enemies. As late as 1748–9 the 'weakly' scribblers of the Opposition press were still affecting impatience as they awaited this prodigy of legal erudition from a writer of novels and the impresario of a puppet-show.[3]

Presumably, the effort to complete this difficult work demanded most of his energies during the winter of 1744–5. But if Fielding supposed he could escape from the drudging indignities of authorship by applying himself to the law, the events of this same period proved disillusioning. In November, to assist his friends in Opposition, he published anonymously *An Attempt towards a Natural History of the Hanover Rat*,[4] a stinging satire against the ministry; and, though the precise moment cannot be fixed, not long after the turn of the year he had probably begun work on *Tom Jones*.[5]

It is a tribute to Fielding's powers of detachment that in tone and spirit neither the pamphlet nor the novel betrays the gloom of what must have been the darkest winter of his life. On 14 November 1744 the great bell of St. Martin's-in-the-Fields tolled the death of his beloved wife Charlotte, who was buried in the chancel vault. The loss of this lovely woman moved Fielding

[1] See William B. Coley, 'Henry Fielding's "Lost" Law Book', *MLN*, lxxvi (1961), 408–13.

[2] See the advertisements in *The General Evening-Post*, 26–8 February, 5–7, 12–14 March 1745; *The Daily Post*, 25, 29 March 1745; and *The London Evening-Post*, 2–4 April 1745.

[3] See *Old England*, 3 September 1748; 7 January, 5, 26 August, 25 November 1749.

[4] On Fielding's authorship of this pamphlet, see Gerard E. Jensen, 'A Fielding Discovery', *Yale University Library Gazette*, x (1935), 23–32.

[5] See below, pp. xxxviii ff.

deeply: she was, as he said, 'one from whom I draw all the solid Comfort of my Life',[1] and he was to preserve her image in the heroines of his fiction, Sophia Western and Amelia Booth. But Fielding's history was not quite the romance invented by his biographers, who have supposed that Charlotte's death plunged him into a paralysing depression which only the shock of the Jacobite uprising could dispel. Improvident he may have been, but he was not an impractical man. His wife's final illness coincided with a political crisis in which Fielding's friends in Opposition—Lyttelton, Pitt, Dodington, Chesterfield—were very much concerned. These men, having engineered Walpole's fall from power in February 1742, were now again pressing for the dismissal of the King's favourite minister, John Carteret, Lord Granville. To this end they held Granville responsible for the disastrous conduct of the war with France (formally declared in March 1744), and they continued to denounce his unpopular policy of using English funds to subsidize the Hanoverian forces. This issue, the depredations of the omnivorous 'Hanover rat', became Fielding's theme in a satiric anatomy performed in parody of the transactions of the Royal Society. The pamphlet was published on 23 November,[2] scarcely a fortnight after his wife's death; on the day following publication—though it would be quixotic to suppose a causal relationship between the two events—Granville resigned. Before Parliament adjourned for the Christmas recess, a new 'Broad-Bottom' government had been formed, a coalition in which the 'Old Whigs' under Henry Pelham, his brother the Duke of Newcastle, and Lord Hardwicke, joined with the Chesterfield–Cobham faction for whom Fielding had been working.[3] From this moment he never wavered in his allegiance to the ministry. Though in the past he had been willing on occasion to draw his pen in defence of Walpole,[4] for the

---

[1] See the Preface to the *Miscellanies* (1743).

[2] See *The General Advertiser*, 23-4 November 1744.

[3] For an authoritative analysis of these events, see John B. Owen, *The Rise of the Pelhams* (1957), esp. ch. vi.

[4] Together with such other evidence as his Dedication to *The Modern Husband* (1732), the recent discovery of Fielding's unfinished satire against the Scriblerus group (*c.* 1729) clearly reveals that early in his career he was prepared to enlist himself on Walpole's side against the formidable wits of the Tory Opposition (see above, p. xix, n. 2). For the argument that later, after leaving *The Champion* in June 1741, Fielding also offered his services to Walpole, see Battestin, 'Fielding's Changing Politics and *Joseph Andrews*', *PQ*, xxxix (1960), 39–55.

most part, in his dramatic satires and in *The Champion*, he had been with Lyttelton and the 'Patriots', the gadfly of the Opposition. Now, his friends at last in power, he would soon emerge as the government's most dutiful and effective apologist. The change in roles was not made, to be sure, without a certain awkwardness: in *Tom Jones* it is no longer Fielding, but the fatuous, ale-swilling Tory, Squire Western, who blusters against the '*Hannover* Rats' (VI. xiv).

By February 1745, when the first advertisements began to appear, Fielding's 'Law-Book' was apparently in the final stages of preparation. At what must have been about this time, with the necessary leisure at his disposal and with Lyttelton to encourage him,[1] Fielding began work on his masterpiece, pressing on with the narrative during the spring and summer until, by the time the rebellion drew him to more urgent concerns, he had completed roughly one third of the novel. If he needed an incentive to spur him on, it was supplied by an act of generosity which greatly embarrassed him financially. On 14 June 1745, in order to prevent Arthur Collier from being committed to Marshalsea Prison, Fielding and James Harris became surety for a debt of £400, plus £40 in damages, which their friend had contracted some years earlier.[2] In November, Fielding twice appealed to delay the execution of the judgement, but he succeeded only in adding £20. 1s. to the cost of damages. On 4 June of the following year, the court ordered the money to be paid. Considering the weight of these pecuniary obligations, Fielding's invocation of his 'plumper' Dutch Muse (*Tom Jones*, XIII. i) was not entirely facetious. The state of his finances may also explain why he was prompted to make his own wry contribution to the medical controversy precipitated by Walpole's death in March 1745: in a flurry of pamphlets the several physicians who had attended the Great Man in his final illness engaged in an indecorous debate calculated to justify their own incompetency. This *cause célèbre*, in which Fielding's friend John Ranby was the central figure, is doubtless reflected in the dispute between Captain Blifil's physicians (*Tom Jones*, II. ix), and it elicited from Fielding an amusing satire entitled *The Charge to the Jury: or, The Sum of the*

---

[1] See the Dedication to *Tom Jones*.

[2] See J. Paul de Castro, 'Fielding and the Collier Family', *N & Q*, 12th Ser., ii (5 August 1916), 104–6.

*Evidence, on the Trial of A. B. C. D. and E. F. All M. D. For the Death of one Robert at Orfud* (2 July 1745).[1]

If we except the Preface to *David Simple*, this pamphlet was only the second publication—both of them fugitive, hackney pieces—to issue from Fielding's pen in two and a half years since the appearance of the *Miscellanies*. During this time he had been occupied with grander schemes: with his abortive work on Crown Law and, more recently, with the novel that would assure his immortality. In the autumn, however, the crisis of the rebellion interrupted him, demanding his energies on behalf of the Hanoverian Establishment. His career had entered a new phase in which, as journalist and pamphleteer, he would emerge over the next several years as the government's leading propagandist. In October 1745 he published in rapid succession three hortatory pamphlets designed to acquaint the public with the pernicious consequences of a Jacobite victory and to arouse them in defence of their Constitution and religion. These works, issued within a fortnight,[2] were *A Serious Address to the People of Great Britain*, *The History of the Present Rebellion*, and *A Dialogue between the Devil, the Pope, and the Pretender*. The same motives prompted him to undertake *The True Patriot*, a weekly journal which he conducted from 5 November 1745 to 17 June 1746. The winter of 1745–6 was indeed a dark and ominous moment in England's history, when the political and religious institutions Fielding cherished were in jeopardy. Engaged abroad in an unsuccessful war with France and stricken at home by a rebellion that penetrated deep into the kingdom, the nation was faltering at 'the very Brink of Ruin'.[3] It was a day, as he later recalled, 'far more terrible to all the Lovers of Liberty and the Protestant Religion, than this Age had ever seen before, or is, I hope, in any Danger of seeing again'.[4] When Fielding returned to *Tom Jones* after the crisis had passed, the events of the terrible winter of the

---

[1] For the date of publication, see *The General Advertiser*, 2 July 1745. To judge from advertisements in that paper for 24–8 June, the pamphlet was in the press during the last week of June. For the general background and the question of Fielding's authorship, see R. C. Jarvis, 'The Death of Walpole: Henry Fielding and a Forgotten *Cause Célèbre*', *MLR*, xli (1946), 113–30.

[2] As announced in *The Daily Advertiser*, the dates of publication of these pamphlets are, respectively, 3, 8, and 15 October 1745.

[3] *The True Patriot*, 22–9 April 1746.

[4] *The Jacobite's Journal*, 13 August 1748.

'Forty-Five' would provide the setting for his hero's journey through the heart of England. What is more, the political issues which had been settled in blood at Culloden (16 April 1746) would affect Fielding's conception of his characters and his choice of episodes—being reflected, for example, in the Jacobitical sympathies of Squire Western and Partridge; in the history of the Man of the Hill, who suffered in Monmouth's cause against James II (VIII. xiv); and in the curious episode of the gypsy king, whose government serves as an ironic parable of Toryism (XII. xii).

From the time he relinquished *The True Patriot* until the following June, when the impending Parliamentary elections required his services on behalf of the government, Fielding set politics aside in order, one supposes, to resume his professional and literary interests. In the summer, when he was not prevented by the gout, a painful and chronic affliction, he regularly rode the Western Circuit, attending the August Assizes at Southampton, Salisbury, Dorchester, Exeter, Bodmin, Wells, and Bristol. The summers, too, drew him to Bath—or, more precisely, to Twerton-on-Avon near Bath—where, according to Richard Graves, he worked on his novel and 'dined almost daily' with Ralph Allen at Prior Park.[1] In *Tom Jones*, it is Allen (together with Lyttelton) whose benevolence is reflected in the character of Squire Allworthy and whose handsome estate is imaged in the description of 'Paradise Hall'.[2]

Whatever may have been the extent of Allen's generosity to him at this time, it was apparently insufficient to rescue Fielding from the embarrassed circumstances in which he found himself after June 1746, when the court ruled that Arthur Collier's debts be paid. When he returned to London in the autumn, to the comfortable house he had leased in Boswell Court,[3] he was again obliged to write for money. It was an uncongenial role, if familiar enough, and on this occasion he was as cynically pragmatic about it as ever Defoe could have been. On 12 November,

---

[1] *The Triflers* (1806), p. 67.

[2] See the Dedication (p. 4, n. 1) and I. iv (p. 42, n. 1).

[3] Boswell Court was located between Carey Street and Butcher Row, on part of the site now occupied by the Royal Courts of Justice. Many lawyers resided in this quarter and Fielding, who lived there from 1744 to 1747, had one of the most expensive houses in it. According to the rate-books, he paid annual rents of £45 (1744–5) and £55 (1746–7). See J. Paul de Castro, 'Fielding at Boswell Court', *N & Q*, 12th Ser., i (1 April 1916), 264–5.

Fielding produced a tawdry six-penny pamphlet purporting (falsely) to be an authentic account of the brief, but certainly sensational, career of one Mary Hamilton—lesbian, transvestite, and impostor, who had been apprehended at Glastonbury on 13 September and tried at Taunton on 7 October. The nature of this anonymous *gagne pain* is clear from the title-page: *The Female Husband: or, The Surprising History of Mrs. Mary, Alias Mr. George Hamilton, Who was convicted of having married a Young Woman of Wells and lived with her as her Husband. Taken from Her own Mouth since her Confinement.* Despite the pretence of authenticity, Fielding's narrative is more fiction than fact, being based chiefly on the newspaper reports and on whatever secondhand information he may have received from his cousin, the Glastonbury lawyer Henry Gould, who was consulted in the case.[1] *The Female Husband* doubtless served its purpose: it had a lively sale.[2] Prudently enough, therefore, Fielding's other publication of the winter was equally amatory in its appeal. On 25 February 1747[3] appeared *Ovid's Art of Love Paraphrased, and Adapted to the Present Time*, Fielding's version of the *Ars Amatoria*, Book 1. In the Preface, Fielding hinted that this 'new Undertaking . . . might perhaps, if properly encouraged, be carried on with other *Latin* Poets'; but if he seriously hoped his Ovid would inaugurate a series of profitable translations of the classics, he was disappointed. The reason for this spurt of hackney writing at a time when his energies might better have been directed toward the completion of *Tom Jones* is possibly to be found in one of the letters which, together with a Preface, he contributed to his sister's novel, *Familiar Letters between the Principal Characters in David Simple*, published 10 April 1747.[4] There Fielding has Valentine explain the declining condition of English letters: 'I think I may affirm with Truth, that there is no one Patron of true Genius, nor the least Encouragement left for it in this Kingdom'

---

[1] See Sheridan Baker, 'Henry Fielding's *The Female Husband*: Fact and Fiction', *PMLA*, lxxiv (1959), 213–24.

[2] The ledgers of William Strahan, the printer, reveal that the original issue of 1,000 copies was supplemented later in the month by another 250 copies. (B.M. Add. MSS. 48800.)

[3] See *The General Advertiser*, 25–8 February, 2–3 March 1747.

[4] Ibid., 9–10 April 1747. As early as 24 January, the same paper carried notices that the work was in the press (see also the numbers for 26–30 January, 20–3 March 1747).

(Letter xl, dated 20 December [1746?]). If Fielding had enjoyed Allen's benefactions, it would appear that, in his present circumstances, they were inconsiderable. Since there was no one to encourage the productions of 'true Genius', he would trust instead the public's proven keenness for another sort of entertainment.

While he regretted the neglect of the arts, Valentine, advising David Simple in the same letter, was quite sanguine about the 'Administration of our public Affairs', which, he asserted, was 'at present in the Hands of the very Men, whom you, and every honest Person would wish to be intrusted with it'. Having weathered the storm of the rebellion and restored confidence in the economy, the Pelham administration had firmly established itself in power. What was especially soothing to Fielding, this 'Broad-Bottom' government included the 'very Men' whose friendship and patronage he had long enjoyed: Chesterfield as principal Secretary of State; Lyttelton as, under Pelham, one of the Lords of the Treasury; Dodington as Treasurer of the Navy; Pitt as Paymaster-General of the Forces; Hardwicke as Lord Chancellor; Bedford as First Lord of the Admiralty.[1] It is not at all surprising, therefore, that in the year and a half before he assumed his duties as magistrate and brought *Tom Jones* to completion, Fielding's only publications were of a political nature, written in support of the Ministry and its policies.

On 18 June 1747 Pelham, sensing the strength of his position, surprised the Opposition by dissolving Parliament and calling a general election. This action was not expected, for it was not legally required until the following year, but Fielding had obviously been forewarned: five days after the minister's announcement and four days before the Westminster elections began, he published *A Dialogue between a Gentleman of London, Agent for two Court Candidates, and an Honest Alderman of the Country Party. Wherein the Grievances under which the Nation at present* groans *are fairly and impartially laid open and considered.*

---

[1] With the curious exception of Chesterfield, who resigned his office in February 1748, being replaced by Bedford, all these men are specifically complimented in *Tom Jones*: Lyttelton, of course, in the Dedication and in many other passages (see p. 3, n. 1); Pelham and Dodington in XI. ix (p. 612, nn. 1, 4); Pitt in XIV. i (p. 740, n. 2); Hardwicke in IV. vi (p. 172, n. 2); and Bedford in the Dedication (p. 5, n. 1). In the opening chapter, moreover, Fielding's allusion to 'the best Cook' of 'the present Age' is very probably a facetious compliment to Pelham's brother, the Duke of Newcastle, whose French chef was famous (p. 33, n. 2).

*Earnestly address'd to the Electors of Great-Britain.*[1] Despite the
ruse of the sub-title,[2] the pamphlet is, of course, a thoroughgoing
vindication of the Ministry, who are represented as the sole
protectors of Church and Constitution against the Tory Opposition. The *Dialogue*, in which Pelham's men, Sir John Protestant
and Mr. English, are preferred to the fatuous Jacobites, Sir
Thomas Leadenhead and Mr. Toastum, comprises an illuminating résumé of Fielding's political attitudes at a time when he
was well along in the composition of *Tom Jones*. His sincerity in
espousing the Whig cause need not, of course, be questioned; in
this he was constant from first to last. At the same time, however,
it seems clear that the *Dialogue* was written in part out of a sense
of personal obligation to Lyttelton and his other influential
friends, for on 20 June, three days before the pamphlet was
published, Fielding's name was included on the list of Com-
missioners of the Peace for the County of Middlesex, appointed
in the King's name 'by the discretion of the Lord Chancellor'.[3]
Though more than eighteen months would pass before he began
to function in this office, this was the first step in Fielding's
progress to the magistracy.

Fielding's habit of seeing the opponents of the Administration
as Jacobites in disguise was, to be sure, a somewhat disingenuous
strategy of his polemical writing. Towards the end of the year,
however, it did in fact appear that a 'Strange Spirit of Jacobitism'[4]
was in Staffordshire, at least, very much alive. When the races
began at Lichfield in September, Tory sympathizers, some

[1] Published, according to *The General Advertiser*, on 23 June 1747. Strahan's ledger
reveals that 3,500 copies of the *Dialogue* were distributed, followed in July by a second
printing of 1,000 copies (B.M. Add. MSS. 48800). These figures would seem to strengthen
the probability that the work was being underwritten by Fielding's friends in government.

[2] Thus a correspondent to *The General Advertiser* (29 June 1747) wrote that though he
was 'one, among many others, who have been deceived by the Title', the pamphlet had
'undeceived' him about the relative merits of the Court and Country parties: 'I wish with
all my Heart', he continued, 'the whole Nation may read this excellent Performance, since
I am certain it must convince every impartial and sensible Man, that all Clamours against
the Government at present are unjust, and raised for the worst of Purposes.'

[3] On Fielding's legal career, see Archibald B. Shepperson, 'Additions and Corrections to
Facts about Fielding', *MP*, li (1954), 217–24, and W. B. Coley, 'Fielding's Two Appoint-
ments to the Magistracy', *MP*, lxiii (1965), 144–9. According to Horace Walpole, Fielding
was appointed to the magistracy 'by the Interest of Mr. Lyttelton'. (See Coley, 'Henry
Fielding and the Two Walpoles', *PQ*, xlv [1966], 173; also Walpole's letter to George
Montagu, dated 18 May 1749, in the Yale Edition of Walpole's *Correspondence*, ed. W. S.
Lewis [New Haven, Conn., 1941], ix. 84.)

[4] *The Jacobite's Journal*, 5 November 1748.

flaunting the Stuart tartan and openly drinking the Pretender's health, demonstrated against the election of the court candidates, Richard Leveson Gower (brother-in-law of the Duke of Bedford) and Thomas Anson.[1] Partly 'to stop the Progress of this dangerous, epidemical Madness',[2] but mostly to provide the government with an effective advocate against the abusive essayists of the Opposition press, Fielding undertook the editorship of *The Jacobite's Journal*, which he continued weekly from 5 December 1747 until 5 November 1748. According to the anonymous author of *The Patriot Analized* (February 1748),[3] he had a more practical motive as well: he needed the money and his friends, by arranging to distribute 2,000 copies of each issue gratis through the Post Office, had guaranteed him a comfortable return for his trouble. Fielding's only other publication of this period was prompted, one may assume, by similar interests, though its specific occasion was an anti-ministerial tract purporting to be the posthumous autobiography of the politician, Thomas Winnington, who had died in 1746. By accusing most of the prominent Whigs of the age—from Godolphin and Marlborough to Walpole and the Pelhams—of secretly promoting the Jacobite cause, the author of this arch little book (published 30 November 1747) started a lively and vituperative controversy.[4] On 24 December[5] Fielding replied in *A Proper Answer to a Late Scurrilous Libel*,

[1] During October and November 1747, the political disturbances in Staffordshire evoked a spate of prints and ballads: e.g., as announced in *The General Advertiser*, 'A Sight of the Banging Bout at *Litchfield*, and their Meeting Cloathed in Plaid, for a General Day at Stag-Hunting' (7 October); 'The Litchfield Squabble' (15 October); 'The Lords Lamentation: or, Whittingdon's Defeat' (30 October); and 'The Plad-Hunting: A Ballad' (14 November).

[2] *The Jacobite's Journal*, 5 November 1748.

[3] Announced in *The General Advertiser*, 18 February 1748. For the relevant passages from this pamphlet, see Cross, ii. 75–6. See also Laurence Hanson, *Government and the Press, 1695–1763* (Oxford, 1936), p. 119. Despite the assistance of his friends and the various hackney projects in which he engaged, Fielding's reputation for impecuniosity persisted. Thus in an anonymous poem of 1748 entitled *A Sorrowful Ditty: or, The Lady's Lamentation for the Death of Her Favourite Cat* (B.M. Poems: C. 57. g. 7), the Muses are represented 'rocking poor supperless F[ie]ld[i]ng to sleep'.

[4] For the date of publication, see *The General Advertiser*, 30 November 1747. Besides Fielding's reply, other tracts relating to this controversy include: *A Free Comment on the late Mr. W——'s Apology for his Conduct* (21 December); *An Apologetical Discourse for a late Celebrated Apology* (22 January 1748); T. Manning, *A View of the late Mr. W——n's Conduct and Principles* (6 February); and *The Patriot Analized* (18 February).

[5] See *The General Advertiser*, 23–4 December 1747; the second edition was announced on 2 January 1748. Strahan's ledger reveals that 500 copies of each edition were issued (B.M. Add. MSS. 48800).

*Entitled, An Apology for the Conduct of a late celebrated Second-rate Minister.* Written as a brisk, polemical review of English politics since the Revolution, the pamphlet stands as Fielding's most vigorous defence of the Hanoverian Establishment.

During the final months in the composition of *Tom Jones*, Fielding had matters other than politics to occupy him—his marriage and the birth of a son, his resumption of the familiar role of theatrical manager (this time of a puppet show!), and finally, of course, his appointments to the magistracy. In one way or another, all of these concerns affected the novel he was writing. Since Charlotte's death in November 1744, her maid, Mary Daniel, had remained with him as housekeeper and as nurse for his two children.[1] Having got this good woman with child, Fielding married her quietly on 27 November 1747, his friend Lyttelton attending, according to contemporary report, to give the bride away.[2] In order that his wife might pass the final months of her pregnancy in suitable retirement, Fielding leased a pair of rooms in Twickenham,[3] and there in the latter part of February his son William was born (baptized 25 February 1748).

Now more than ever in need of money, Fielding soon hit upon an amusing scheme to supplement his income from the journal. On 7 March *The General Advertiser* had heard 'that the Town will shortly be entertained with *a Puppet Show after the Ancient manner*; in which the true Humour of that most diverting Entertainment will be restored'. Promoting this enterprise was Fielding himself, who, under the guise of 'Madame de la Nash', proprietress of a theatrical 'Breakfasting-Room' in Panton Street, was about to revive the satiric antics of Punch and Joan.[4]

[1] These were his daughter Harriet (1737–66) and, as recent research has disclosed, his son Henry (1742–50). On the latter see T. C. Duncan Eaves and B. D. Kimpel, *N & Q*, N.S. xv (June 1968), 212.

[2] Smollett's imputation to this effect in the first edition of *Peregrine Pickle* (1751), iv. 123, would seem to be supported by Horace Walpole, who, with a characteristic snigger, recorded the following anecdote, recently found among his unpublished papers: 'some Gentlemen commending Mr. L[yttelton] for having tho a Ld of the Treasury, voted against the Ministry in the Bedwin-Election, Fielding started up, & striking his Breast, cried, If you talk of Virtue, here's a Virtue! I married my Whore yesterday.—He had; Lyttelton made Him.' (Quoted in W. B. Coley, 'Henry Fielding and the Two Walpoles', *PQ*, xlv [1966], 173.)

[3] See R. S. Cobbett, *Memorials of Twickenham* (1872), pp. 52, 358–9.

[4] See Battestin, 'Fielding and "Master Punch" in Panton Street', *PQ*, xlv (1966), 191–208.

Attended by 'Persons of the politest Taste', the little theatre had a successful season from 28 March to 2 June and doubtless served to ease the strain on Fielding's finances. More important to our present purpose, it provides a colourful background for that curious episode in *Tom Jones* (XII. v–vi) in which Fielding's hero defends his 'old Acquaintance Master *Punch*' against the Cibberian aspersions of a travelling puppet-master. Incidentally, several passages in the latter books of the novel reflect 'the Comical Humours of the Town'—'Drums . . . Hoops, Plaid Wastecoats, Criticizing, Whisk-Learning, Muffle-Boxing'[1]— which Fielding was satirizing on stage in Panton Street.

By summer Fielding's personal fortunes had brightened materially. In the opinion of one who mattered—his bookseller Andrew Millar—the manuscript of his novel was sufficiently far along, and sufficiently promising, to warrant a generous advance of £600, given on 11 June in payment for the copyright.[2] On 30 July, furthermore, the date of the fiat appointing him to the magistracy of the city and borough of Westminster, he at last enjoyed the reward of his years of 'Diligence' in his profession— or rather of his friendship with Lyttelton and his services to the Broad-Bottom government. He did not undertake this office, however, until his return to London in the autumn. To interpret certain changes in the quality and content of *The Jacobite's Journal*, it seems probable that, from mid-July to mid-September, Fielding had left town as usual, entrusting the paper to an assistant.[3] Perhaps during August he was again riding the circuit, though his recent elevation to the bench would presumably have relieved him from such barrister's business. Perhaps, too, this was the occasion on which he joined Lyttelton and Pitt in a visit to Sanderson Miller at Radway Grange. There, according to a tradition in the Miller family, Fielding read aloud from *Tom*

---

[1] See the advertisement in *The General Advertiser*, 14 April 1748.

[2] See below, p. xliv.

[3] After the issue of 16 July, Fielding dropped one of the notable topical features of the journal, the series of literary articles entitled, 'Proceedings at the Court of Criticism'. Similarly, from that date until the number for 17 September the editorial comments on the news items are markedly less frequent. The leaders during this same period become shorter and more perfunctory—the one for 6 August, for example, consisting of an essay reprinted from Addison's *Freeholder*; Fielding may have written them all before leaving town. There is some support for this speculation in Ursula Fielding's letter of 25 October 1748, which implies that her brother had been away for the summer (see J. Paul de Castro, *N & Q*, 15th Ser., xx [9 March 1940], 164–7).

*Jones* to sound the company's opinion of the manuscript before submitting it to the printers.[1]

The winter of 1748–9 marks the culmination of Fielding's literary and legal careers: the publication of his masterpiece and the commencement of his tenure as magistrate. When he returned to town in the autumn, he temporarily leased a house in Brownlow Street, near Drury Lane, later removing briefly to Meard's Court, St. Anne's; in December, finally, he was established in Bow Street, Covent Garden, in the house formerly occupied by the famous justice, Sir Thomas De Veil.[2] Some weeks earlier he had seen the first two volumes of *Tom Jones* through the press,[3] and had begun to administer justice for the district of Westminster. On 2 November, three days before the final issue of *The Jacobite's Journal*, he was signing recognizances at the court in Bow Street, committing criminals to the Gatehouse Prison[4]—

---

[1] See George Miller, *Rambles Round Edge Hills and in the Vale of the Red Horse* (Banbury, 1896), pp. 16–17. Miller here states that Fielding read the manuscript to this distinguished company for their opinion 'before it was printed'. In a later edition (1900) of his book, however, Miller altered this to read: 'before he [Fielding] offered it to the publishers' (p. 30). The change is significant as far as dating the occasion is concerned, since Fielding had certainly submitted the novel to his bookseller before June 1748, when Millar paid him for the copyright, whereas the printers probably did not have the manuscript until the autumn. Although the meeting at Radway might easily have occurred earlier, the summer of 1748 seems the most likely time. In late August, Pitt was visiting Lyttelton at Hagley Park (see his letter of 21 August to William Lyttelton, in R. Phillimore [ed.], *Memoirs and Correspondence of George Lord Lyttelton, from 1734 to 1773* [1845], i. 265–6); together they may well have made the short journey across country to see Miller, a close mutual friend. According to the newspapers, furthermore, before the publication of *Tom Jones*, Pitt, as well as Lyttelton, had seen the manuscript and was eagerly 'puffing' it about town (see *Old England*, 27 May 1749).

[2] In a letter of 25 October 1748, Ursula Fielding informed a friend in Salisbury that her brother and his family 'are come to Town for the winter, and have taken a house in Brownlow Street, near Drury Lane, where he intends to administer justice' (see de Castro, *N & Q*, 15th Ser., xx [9 March 1940], 164–7). Brownlow Street was renamed Betterton Street in 1877. Apparently Fielding did not remain there long. In reporting a case brought before him on 30 November, *The General Advertiser* (2 December 1748) gave his address as 'Meard's-Court, St. Anne's'. By 9 December, however, he is said to be living in 'Bow-Street, Covent-Garden, formerly Sir Thomas De Veil's' (see *The General Advertiser* for 10, 12 December 1748). De Castro erred, however, in stating that Fielding replaced John Poulson (d. 17 December 1748) as occupant of this house. Though Poulson did live in Bow Street, it is clear from *The General Advertiser* (31 October 1748) that not he but another justice, John Green, was the previous occupant; cases in which Green was active continue to be reported in that paper until 14 November 1748.

[3] In a letter of 20 November 1748, the Countess of Hertford indicated to Lady Luxborough that she had read 'the two first Volumes of the *Foundling*, written by Mr. FIELDING, but not to be published till the 22d of January' (see below, p. xlv).

[4] See above, p. xxix, n. 3.

where, one may remark, Tom Jones was to pass his most melancholy hours (XVI. x). Owing, however, to Fielding's inability to
satisfy the property requirement for the Middlesex magistracy,
his commission, announced as long ago as June 1747, had
remained ineffective. In order to qualify for this office, Fielding
on 13 December 1748 appealed to the Duke of Bedford, whose
kindness he had previously enjoyed and acknowledged in the
Dedication to *Tom Jones*. Bedford granted the favour, leasing him
various houses collectively worth the necessary £100. Shortly
after the turn of the year, Fielding was sitting as justice for both
the city of Westminster and the county of Middlesex, and the
remaining volumes of *Tom Jones* were in the press.

At a time when criticism has stressed (most usefully) the
essentially dramatic and impersonal nature of Augustan literature,
this review of the biographical contexts of Fielding's novel may
seem naïve and supererogatory. Yet, as Wayne Booth has
observed,[1] the most important 'character' in *Tom Jones* is the
narrator himself, whose voice, as he relates the story to his 'good-
natured' and (one trusts) 'sagacious' reader, sounds very like
Fielding's own. More than any other novelist of the period,
Fielding—or, if one prefers, that heightened and idealized pro-
jection of him which has been called his 'second self'[2]—is im-
manent in his book. His themes and characters, his episodes and
opinions, reveal the pressure of his personal circumstances and
the climate of life and thought in which he wrote.

The world in which Tom Jones lives and through which he
moves in the perilous autumn of 1745 is a world in which fiction
and actuality coalesce. Like Joyce's Dublin, it is populated both by
characters of the author's imagination and by living people of his
own acquaintance—by inn-keepers and dancing-masters, actors
and attorneys, doctors and divines, coachmen and mantua-makers.
Its events, whether trivial or momentous, are often those Fielding
had experienced: in discordant strains the Westerns harp on the
Court and on the war with France, and Jones marches north
against the Jacobites. Sophia attends the riotous first night of
Edward Moore's new comedy (XIII. xi), and Partridge at a performance of *Hamlet* prefers the acting of 'Billy' Mills to that of
Garrick (XVI. v). Sophia is moved by the tender passages in *David*

---

[1] *The Rhetoric of Fiction* (Chicago, Ill., 1961), pp. 215–18.
[2] Ibid., pp. 71 ff.

*Simple* (vi. v), and, in her sentiments and demeanour, Fielding
invites us to compare his heroine with her rival, Richardson's
Clarissa (xv. iii, xvi. v, xviii. ix). What is more, the moral and
religious issues that define his characters are those that mattered
to their author. Against the Methodistical cant of Captain Blifil,
Allworthy, echoing Tillotson and Barrow, refutes the doctrine of
absolute reprobation and defines true charity (ii. ii, v). The deist
Square mouths the ineffectual platitudes of Shaftesbury, Tindal,
and Chubb (iii. iii), and in his conversion endorses the arguments
Warburton and Lyttelton had used to assert the Christian doctrine of immortality (xviii. iv).

Through allusion, analogy, parody Fielding in such passages
deepens and complicates the meaning of his book, moving
reciprocally from the public to the private, from the species to the
individual, from manners to men. Though *Tom Jones* is, after all,
'the History of the World in general', the epic comedy of
'HUMAN NATURE', it is equally its author's own story and the
mirror of mid-Georgian England.

## 2. DATE OF COMPOSITION

From our present scant and uncertain knowledge of Fielding's
affairs, it is impossible to say exactly when he began to write *Tom
Jones*. July 1744—when, in the Preface to the second edition of
*David Simple*, he publicly disowned the Muses—may be taken
as the *terminus a quo*: by his own declaration he then had neither
leisure nor inclination to undertake another work of fiction.[1] From
this time more than three years elapsed before the earliest known
reference to the novel in November 1747, when William Strahan
recorded in his ledger the printing of 250 'Receipts for Mr
Fielding's Foundling'[2]—a curious notation, suggesting that
Fielding's original intention was, as in the lucrative instance of the
*Miscellanies*, to publish the work by subscription. Though it
would not be without precedent in the period for such receipts to
be distributed for works that, as Mr. Wilson remarked in *Joseph
Andrews* (iii. iii), were 'not writ, nor ever intended', yet it is clear
that Fielding's novel was quite far advanced by the late autumn of
1747. In a letter of 19 January 1748, Thomas Birch, an avid and

[1] See above, pp. xx–xxi.   [2] B.M. Add. MSS. 48800.

usually reliable literary gossip, observed to Lord Orrery that 'Mr.
Fielding is printing three volumes of Adventures under the title
of *The Foundling*'.[1] The statement is tantalizing. Was Birch
repeating information given in the receipts, no copy of which has
survived? If so, it is possible that Fielding was then well enough
satisfied with half of his manuscript to have thought of submitting
it to the printer. It is certain, at least, that he had progressed far
enough with the novel to merit his patron's praise of his ingenious handling of the plot: 'Mr. Littleton,' Birch continued,
'who has read the manuscript, commends the performance to me
as an excellent one, and abounding with strong and lively painting of characters, and a very copious and happy invention in the
conduct of the story.'

Though they raise more questions than they answer, these
references to the novel by Strahan and Birch are the only bits of
external evidence early enough or substantial enough to be of any
help in fixing the period of composition. To construct a more
useful, if entirely hypothetical, account of the evolution of the
manuscript, one must rely on clues to be found within the text
itself. This method, of course, is regrettably tenuous. For one
thing—though topical references abound in the novel, many of
them to events that may be precisely dated—such allusions
provide a *terminus a quo* only for the particular passages in which
they occur; they need not have been written at, or even very near,
the time of the event to which they refer. For another thing,
Fielding's habit of revising his works so as to enliven dull
material is well known from, for example, the alterations and
additions he made for the second edition of *Joseph Andrews*, or
from the similar changes he made in preparing the *Miscellanies*
for publication.[2] The printer's records for *Tom Jones*, furthermore, indicate that Fielding was tampering with the manuscript
even while it was in the press.[3] All one can safely conclude about

---

[1] See *The Orrery Papers*, ed. Countess of Cork and Orrery (1903), ii. 14.

[2] See *Joseph Andrews*, ed. Battestin (Oxford and Middletown, Conn., 1967), Appendix I;
and the *Miscellanies*, Vol. I, ed. H. K. Miller (Oxford and Middletown, Conn., 1972),
the General Introduction: Date of Composition.

[3] Strahan's entry for the first edition refers to 'many Alterations', made presumably
while the work was in press (see below, p. xlviii). Similarly, his ledger records charges for
'Extraordinary Corrections' in the printing of several of Fielding's other works: e.g., *A
Charge Delivered to the Grand Jury* (July 1749), *An Enquiry into the Causes of the Late
Increase of Robbers* (January 1751), *Amelia* (December 1751), *A Proposal for Making an
Effectual Provision for the Poor* (January 1753). Henry Woodfall, the printer of the first

a datable allusion in a work as extensive and as long in the making as *Tom Jones*, therefore, is that the allusion itself must postdate the event to which it refers; the chapter in which it appears may well have been composed months or even years earlier. Finally, there is the further problem of the prolegomenous essays prefixed to the several books of the novel. By his own admission, Fielding could 'with less Pains write one of the Books of this History, than the Prefatory Chapter to each of them' (xvi. i). Rather than interrupt the flow of his narrative to compose these essays, he quite probably reserved this chore for some later time.

Untroubled by such considerations, Fielding's biographers have too confidently asserted that he began *Tom Jones* in the summer of 1746, after the rebellion had been conquered and he felt at liberty to discontinue *The True Patriot*.[1] Even at first glance there is a certain presumption against this view, since it supposes a period of composition shorter than Fielding's own statements imply. In his Dedication (which, since the first volumes of the novel were published by mid-November 1748, could not have been written much later than the preceding month) Fielding twice refers to the length of time his book had been in the making: 'So many Years', he recalled, had passed since Lyttelton first encouraged him to write the novel; again, he states, these were 'the Labours of some Years' of his life. The phrasing suggests a period of composition substantially longer than the two years and four months that Cross allows.

A still stronger presumption against dating the commencement of the work as late as June 1746 is the fact that nowhere during the course of the first six books and ten chapters of his narrative does Fielding allude to the rebellion; nor, with the exception of an oblique reference to the controversy surrounding the trial of the Jacobite lords (ii. vi), does he in the same space allude to any of the events associated with it. This is true even though Fielding's time-scheme requires that the action after Book v, Chapter vi, be set in November 1745.[2] Thus, when Jones encounters the company of soldiers at Hambrook (vii. xi),

edition of *Joseph Andrews*, also noted 'alterations' made in press (see Battestin ed., p. xxix). According to tradition, Fielding stopped the press while *Tom Jones* was printing in order to insert in his book a compliment to his friend Mrs. Hussey (see below, p. 538, n. 1).

[1] See Cross, ii. 100–8, and Dudden, ii. 584–92.

[2] The reasons for this dating are given in the notes to the text: see, esp., p. 368, n. 1; p. 435, n. 1.

Fielding first establishes his chronology, with a coy apology for having omitted to do so earlier: 'the Reader may perceive (a Circumstance which we have not thought necessary to communicate before) that this was the very Time when the late Rebellion was at the highest; and indeed the Banditti were now marched into *England*, intending, as it was thought, to fight the King's Forces, and to attempt pushing forward to the Metropolis.' If Fielding had had this scheme in mind earlier, it is curious that he should have neglected every opportunity of alluding to it. There are, for example, numerous references to the war with France (v. vii, xi, xii; vi. ii, iv; vii. iii), but none at all to the rebellion then presumably sweeping the north. When, on a day in late November 1745, Mrs. Western rejoices that 'Things look so well in the North' (vi. iv), she is thinking of the state of affairs in Europe, not in England. And when Jones, having been expelled from Paradise Hall, seeks some meaningful direction to give his life, he can think of none, in despair choosing at last to go to sea (vii. ii), not to defend his country against the rebels then, as it soon appears, in full march toward the capital. Fielding, moreover, makes no allusion even to Western's Jacobite sympathies until v. ii, when we learn that the squire's favourite horse is named 'the *Chevalier*'. Since, however, the threat of a French invasion in support of the Pretender had been felt as early as March 1744, Western's Jacobitism need not connote his author's awareness of the fact of 'the Forty-Five'.

On the contrary, what the evidence does suggest is that when Fielding was composing the first six books (and more) of his narrative, he was unaware of the rebellion because it had not yet occurred. One may infer, therefore, that he had completed roughly one third of *Tom Jones* before August 1745, when news that Charles Edward had landed in Scotland first reached London. The plan of setting his central narrative in November 1745, 'the very Time when the late Rebellion was at the highest', was consequently an after-thought.[1] At least one sign that Fielding did alter an original chronology still survives in the text. In v. x, a point in the narrative just three weeks before that chill November day when Jones volunteers to march against the rebels, Fielding introduces his hero's amorous adventure with Molly Seagrim by

[1] The earliest reference to this time-scheme occurs in vii. vii, where Honour advises Sophia to 'consider how cold the Nights are now, we shall be frozen to Death'.

observing: 'It was now a pleasant Evening in the latter End of
*June.*' An error of five months in narrative chronology is not
characteristic of Fielding, but the discrepancy is understandable
in terms of the hypothesis here proposed:[1] that Fielding had
progressed far into his novel by 'the latter End of *June*' 1745;
that he had completed another book and more of the narrative
before news of the rebellion interrupted him in the late summer;
and that, when he returned to *Tom Jones* after this most critical
period in England's recent history had passed, he adjusted his
original time-scheme so as to accommodate this event within the
developing action of the novel.

Against this interpretation it may be objected that the first six
books of *Tom Jones* contain several allusions to events that may
be dated, with more or less confidence, in the months following
August 1745. Clearest of these are Fielding's two facetious
references to John Freke's *Essay to Shew the Cause of Electricity*
(II. iv, IV. ix), published 11 October 1746, and his glance at
those 'late Writers' (II. vi) who in the summer of the same year
were urging the condign punishment of the Jacobite lords. Other
possible allusions in the narrative proper (for reasons already
advanced it is futile to consider the prefatory chapters in this
regard) are to the death of Lyttelton's wife (I. ii) on 19 January
1747 and to Thomas Carte's *General History of England* (I. iii),
published 1 January 1748; but no one, surely, would propose that
Fielding was only just beginning his novel quite as tardily as this.
Such discrepancies are too infrequent and incidental to discredit
the hypothesis set forth above. Given Fielding's habits of revision,
they are easily accounted for by the likely speculation that, upon
returning to his book after the rebellion, he retouched the manuscript so as to make it more timely. Indeed, if the allusions to
Lyttelton's wife and to Carte were actually intended, they are so
late as to suggest he made such revisions more than once.

To have completed one third of *Tom Jones* by the late summer
of 1745, Fielding must have begun writing the novel some
months earlier, no later, certainly, than the spring of the year. It
is impossible to fix the time more narrowly.

In the long stretch of narrative from Book VII to the end of
Book XI there is scarcely a clue to the time of composition.

[1] A similar interpretation of this inconsistency in Fielding's chronology was advanced
in the last century by Thomas Keightley, *N & Q*, 3rd Ser., iii (30 May 1863), 424–5.

Datable references abound, but they are not very useful. In VII. xiii, for example, the landlady protests, somewhat anachronistically: 'Why now there is above forty Shillings for Window-lights, and yet we have stopt up all we could; we have almost blinded the House I am sure.' This particular complaint could not have been made until after 25 March 1747, when the government's revision of the window tax took effect, and probably long enough after that event for Fielding to have had some experience of those who, like the landlady and like 'Humphry Gubbins' of *The Jacobite's Journal* (13 February 1748), were trying to reduce payments by bricking up their windows. But the passage occurs so early in the middle third of the novel that one must suppose either that it is a later interpolation or that Fielding, having completed his first six books before the rebellion, was unable to resume the narrative until the spring of 1747. Such are the difficulties preventing any very certain analysis of his chronological progress through the novel.

In Books XII–XIII, however, a suggestive concentration of parallels occurs between passages in the novel and certain topics and events which drew Fielding's attention during the early months of 1748. In XII. v–vi, for example, Tom Jones's defence of 'Master *Punch*' against the travelling puppet-master may reflect his author's own motives in undertaking the theatre in Panton Street, announced in the newspapers on 7 March but doubtless projected before then. In the following book, moreover, Fielding in the space of two chapters (XIII. iv–v) alludes to three of 'the Comical Humours of the Town'—namely, 'Hoops', 'Whisk-Learning', and 'Muffle-Boxing'—which he began to satirize in his puppet-show on 14 April 1748. The references to 'Muffle-Boxing', at least, must have been made at approximately the same time: in XIII. v Fielding explains a cryptic allusion to 'all the muffled Graduates of Mr. *Broughton's* School' by quoting the notice of the opening of this manly academy in *The Daily Advertiser* for 1 February 1748. The passage, then, could not have been written earlier than this, and, taken together with the other parallels to his concerns in the puppet theatre, it suggests that as late as the first quarter of 1748 Fielding had only just entered upon the final third of his novel. Later in the same book (XIII. ix, xi) this inference is strengthened by another probable anachronism in Fielding's time-scheme, as Sophia is made to attend the uproarious first night of Edward Moore's comedy, *The Foundling*, produced at Drury Lane on 13 February 1748.

From this point to the end of the novel the only signs that Fielding was, in 1748, still composing the final books of *Tom Jones* are several oblique allusions to Richardson's *Clarissa* (xv. iii, xvi. v, xviii. iv)—all of them apparently to the first two volumes of that work, published 1 December 1747. Finally, if, as seems likely, Fielding's mention of 'the late War' in xv. iii refers not to the conflict in which England had been engaged since 1740, but to the War of the Spanish Succession, one may surmise that he had passed this stage in his narrative some time before October 1748, when the Treaty of Aix-la-Chapelle was signed. To judge from the few contemporary observations on the progress of the work, he expected to have finished the novel by that time, but he was disappointed. On 30 September 1748, Thomas Birch advised Lord Orrery that *Tom Jones* would be published by the middle of November.[1] A month later, however, on 25 October, Ursula Fielding was apologizing to a friend for her brother's procrastination: the novel, she regretted, would not be ready 'till after Christmas, for that rogue Tom Jones will follow his own will and pleasure'.[2]

In the dim light of such evidence as this, it is impossible to trace the stages in the novel's composition in any detail or with very much confidence. If the assumption is correct that Fielding, had he been aware of the rebellion, would not have composed the first six books of *Tom Jones* so sedulously avoiding any mention of that crucial and disturbing event, then we may take it that he began the work some time in the early months of 1745. This inference, as we have seen, makes better sense of his own statement that the novel represented 'the Labours of some Years' of his life, and it conveniently explains the jarring inconsistency in the time-scheme of Books v–vii. Presumably, after the suppression of the rebellion had left him with the leisure and inclination for less urgent pursuits, he returned to his manuscript in the latter part of 1746, reviewing what he had already written and pressing ahead with his central narrative. By the winter of 1747–8, however, he appears to have had the entire last third of the work still before him; considering his other

[1] *The Orrery Papers* (1903), ii. 43.
[2] J. P. de Castro, *N & Q*, 15th Ser., xx (9 March 1940), 164.

enterprises of the same period—*The Jacobite's Journal* and the theatre in Panton Street—the demands on his wit and energies must have been formidable. In January 1749 at the latest, the final pages of copy were with the printer.

### 3. HISTORY OF PUBLICATION

*Tom Jones* was brought out by Andrew Millar early in February 1749. In his friendly association with this man, who published all his novels and much of his other work, Fielding was especially fortunate.[1] Millar, a Scotsman, early distinguished himself among the members of the London trade both by his canny promotion of the books he published and by his liberal treatment of authors. Writing to Aaron Hill at the very time *Tom Jones* was in press, Richardson, though he disapproved of Fielding, could thus declare the esteem in which he held his publisher: 'I think him to be a fair, honest, open Man, and one who loves to deal generously by Authors . . . none of whom, who understand their own Interests, ever leave him, after once acquainted with him . . . . He has great Business, and is in a Way of promoting the Sale of what he engages in.'[2] Millar's role in the publishing history of *Tom Jones* is a notable instance of the justice of these remarks. In the absence of any 'one Patron of true Genius' in the kingdom, Fielding could take some comfort in the knowledge that he had attached himself to one who, in Johnson's phrase, was the true 'Maecenas of the age'.

The nature of Fielding's original arrangements with Millar are curious and obscure. At first glance it would appear that he planned to publish *Tom Jones* by subscription, no doubt with Millar, as in the case of the *Miscellanies*, backing the project and

[1] After arriving in London from Edinburgh in 1728, Millar (1706–68) enjoyed a prosperous career as a bookseller, publishing Thomson's *Seasons*, the histories of Robertson and Hume, and, with others, Johnson's *Dictionary*. His first publication for Fielding was *Joseph Andrews* (February 1742). From that time until the publication of *Tom Jones*, Millar also brought out *A Full Vindication of the Dutchess Dowager of Marlborough* (1742), *Miss Lucy in Town* (1742), *The Wedding-Day* (1743), the so-called 'second edition' of the *Miscellanies* (1743), and *Ovid's Art of Love Paraphrased* (1747). Thereafter, with few exceptions, he published all of Fielding's works. The relations between the two men were more than merely professional. (See Austin Dobson, 'Fielding and Andrew Millar', *The Library*, 3rd Ser., vii [1916], 177–90.)

[2] Letter of January 1749, quoted in William M. Sale, Jr., *Samuel Richardson: Master Printer* (Ithaca, N.Y., 1950), p. 331.

serving as intermediary with the public, taking in the receipts and distributing the printed books. Such is the inference to be drawn from the ledgers of the printer, William Strahan, who in November 1747 made the following entry under Millar's account:

Receipts for M^r Fielding's Foundling
N°. 250 with Paper                                                    –/7/6[1]

The profits Fielding had gleaned from the *Miscellanies* might well have encouraged him to publish his novel in the same manner. But the number of receipts issued is strangely small. Surely he would have anticipated a sale at least as brisk as the *Miscellanies* enjoyed, for which there had been 427 subscribers. When in the following year, for example, his sister planned to publish *The Lives of Cleopatra and Octavia* by subscription, Millar arranged for the printing of 600 receipts.[2] The number of receipts for *Tom Jones* does, however, exactly correspond to Millar's usual order for *de luxe* sets of works, such as Fielding's *Miscellanies* or *Works* (1762),[3] which he planned to issue in two forms and at two prices: that is, a larger quantity of cheaper, coarse-paper sets, and a smaller quantity of more expensive sets on fine paper. Fielding, then, may never have intended to publish *Tom Jones* by subscription only. Instead, with Millar's co-operation, he may have planned to realize an immediate return on the book[4] by soliciting subscriptions to a limited, fine-paper edition. Regrettably, there is no firm evidence to dispel this mystery. No copy of the receipts has survived, and, if proposals or advertisements for such an edition were ever printed, they too have been lost—unless, perhaps, one may hear an echo of them in Thomas Birch's cryptic mention of a three-volume edition of the novel which Fielding was allegedly 'printing' in January 1748.[5] Whatever Fielding's purpose may have been in printing these receipts, it seems clear, at least, that no copy of a special subscription issue of *Tom Jones* was ever published.[6]

---

[1] B.M. Add. MSS. 48800.          [2] See Strahan's ledger, June 1748.

[3] The ledgers of Strahan and William Bowyer reveal that for the *Miscellanies* Millar ordered 1,000 sets on coarse paper and 250 on fine (see H. K. Miller, *Essays on Fielding's 'Miscellanies'* [Princeton, N.J., 1961], pp. 12–13). For the *Works*, 500 sets of the cheaper octavo edition were printed, 250 of the quarto (see Strahan's ledger, 7 April 1762).

[4] As in the case of the *Miscellanies*, the usual practice was for half the price to be paid upon subscribing, the other upon publication (see Miller, p. 4).     [5] See above, p. xxxvi.

[6] There is evidence, however, that some readers of the novel received preferential treatment and that some paid more for their copies of the six-volume editions than the advertised

Within a few months Fielding had sold the rights to his book to Millar for £600—at £100 per volume, a rate somewhat higher than he had received for *Joseph Andrews*.[1] Signed on 11 June 1748, the agreement reads as follows:

> June 11 1748
>
> Recd of M^r. Andrew Millar Six hundred Pounds being in full for the sole Copy Right of a Book called The History of a Foundling in Eighteen Books, and in Consideration of the said Six Hundred Pounds I promise to assign over the said Book to the said Andrew Millar his Executors and assigns for ever when I shall be thereto demanded.
>
> £          s          d.
>
> £: 600,    00,    00:                                   Hen: Fielding
>
> The said book to contain six Volumes in Duodecimo.[2]

The amount was generous for the time, and, according to Horace Walpole, Millar gave Fielding another hundred pounds after he found the book 'sell so greatly'.[3] A liberal gesture, to be sure, but as Joseph Spence shrewdly observed at the height of the novel's popularity, Fielding 'might probably have got 5 times as much [as £600] by it, had he kept the right in his own hands: but authors at first dont know, whether their works are good or bad; much less, whether they will sell or not.'[4]

By the end of the summer it was common knowledge in town that the long-awaited publication of Fielding's *Foundling* was imminent. With typically puerile sarcasm against the government's man, one contributor to *Old England* (3 September 1748) was dismayed to find that Fielding 'boasts so loud . . . of his being

price of eighteen shillings. The Countess of Hertford had received and read the first two volumes as early as 20 November 1748 (see below, p. xlv). And the author of *An Apology for the Life of Mr. Bampfylde-Moore Carew* ('2nd ed.', 1751) assured his readers that 'great Numbers . . . have purchased [*Tom Jones*] at one Pound one Shilling, and thought it well worth their Money, for indeed it is a most *profitable Book*' (p. 16). If true, however, this statement may merely reflect a certain inflation in the bookstalls owing to the initial keen demand for the novel. The difference in price between coarse- and fine-paper editions of a work was usually much greater than three shillings; in the case of the *Miscellanies*, for example, the difference was a full guinea (see Miller, p. 4).

[1] For *Joseph Andrews*, in two volumes, Fielding was paid £183. 11s.

[2] Transcribed from the original document in the J. P. Morgan Library, New York.

[3] Letter to George Montagu, 18 May 1749, in Walpole's *Correspondence*, ed. W. S. Lewis (New Haven, Conn., 1941), ix. 84.

[4] Letter of 15 April 1749 to William Burrell Massingberd; quoted in Austin Wright, *Joseph Spence: A Critical Biography* (Chicago, Ill., 1950), p. 232, n. 29.

to be brought to Bed soon of a Law-Book, begoten upon himself by the *Notes of an old Judge*, which is to be published at the same Time with Six Volumes of his Novels, spick and span new, fronted with spe[c]ial Dedications'. Though Fielding need not have done his 'boasting' in print, the jargon of these remarks might well be a parody of some recent advertisement supplying details of the projected publication of his novel and his abortive work on Crown Law. Again, however, no such advertisement has come to light. At the end of the month Thomas Birch, who had heard Lyttelton speak of the manuscript 'in terms of high appro- bation', assured Lord Orrery that *Tom Jones* and the last volumes of *Clarissa* would be appearing together 'about the middle of November'.[1] The public eagerly awaited both events, sensing what would in fact prove to be the case: that Fielding and Richardson, for the better part of a decade acknowledged rivals in the art of fiction, were about to produce their masterpieces. Regrettably for those who delight in the coincidences of literary history, Birch erred (though not by very much) in predicting a simultaneous publication for these two books, the greatest comic novel and the only tragic novel of the age. The final volumes of *Clarissa* were issued on 6 December; and by the middle of November only the first two volumes of *Tom Jones* were in print. Thus on the 20th of that month the Countess of Hertford, who had received pre-publication copies, wrote from Percy Lodge to her friend Lady Luxborough: 'I have been very well enter- tained lately with the two first Volumes of the *Foundling*, written by Mr. FIELDING, but not to be published till the 22d of *January*; if the same Spirit runs through the whole Work, I think it it [*sic*] will be much preferable to JOSEPH ANDREWS.'[2] A month later, the projected date of publication to which the countess refers appears to have remained firm—so Birch implies in writing to Lord Orrery on 20 December: 'Mr. Fielding's novel, called the

---

[1] Letter of 30 September 1748, *The Orrery Papers* (1903), ii. 43.

[2] Thomas Hull (ed.), *Select Letters between the Late Duchess of Somerset, Lady Lux- borough . . . and others* (1778), i. 85. Apparently, the Richardsonians who read (or did not read) the novel before publication were less admiring. On 19 January 1749 Thomas Edwards, who seems to have cordially disliked Fielding, wrote to Philip Yorke praising *Clarissa* but doubting he would have time for *Tom Jones*: 'as for Justice Dingo's voluminous Novel, unless it is, as I hear, thin spread, I know not whether I shall be able to compass it or no, for I beleive I must make a short visit there [i.e. to London] this year' (Bodl. MSS. 1011, p. 98). For a possible allusion to Edwards in *Tom Jones*, see p. 790, n. 1.

*Foundling*, in 6 Volumes, was expected before this time, but will not be published before the middle, or perhaps end, of next month. Humour is the chief characteristic of it, though I am told by my friends, who have seen it, that it is not destitute of the instructive and pathetic.'[1]

Much of the impatience with which the public suffered these repeated postponements of the novel's publication—from mid-November, 'till after Christmas',[2] till the latter part of January— may be explained by the fact that expectations had been raised to a fever pitch, owing chiefly to the friendly ministrations of George Lyttelton, who, as Fielding gratefully acknowledged in his Dedication, had first encouraged him to write the book and then, having read the manuscript, 'warmly' recommended it to his acquaintance. Birch's letters of 19 January and 30 September 1748 attest to these good offices of Fielding's patron,[3] and they were remarked as well in a less amicable quarter. Fielding's enemies, who could not conceal their dismay that *Tom Jones* had prospered, sneeringly attributed the fact not to any merit in the work, but rather to Lyttelton's assiduity in 'puffing' it. Thus 'Aretine' of *Old England* (27 May 1749) taunted Lyttelton for his obstetrical dexterity in ushering the *Foundling* into the world:

> Not only the Dedication, but common Fame is full of the warm Commendations you have given of the afore-mentioned *Romance* [.] You have run up and down the Town, and made Visits, and wrote Letters merely for that Purpose. You puffed it up so successfully about Court, and among Placemen and Pensioners, that, having catched it from you, they thought it incumbent upon them to echo it about the Coffeehouses; insomuch, that all the Women laboured under the Burthen of Expectation, 'till it was midwived into the World by your all-auspicious Hand, and proclaimed by them to be the goodest Book that was ever read.[4]

Lyttelton's enthusiastic approbation of the novel, echoed about town in coffeehouse and parlour, helped to precipitate one of the most unusual episodes in the publishing history of the period: the public demand for *Tom Jones* was so keen that the

[1] *The Orrery Papers* (1903), ii. 49.
[2] See Ursula Fielding's letter of 25 October 1748, quoted above, p. xli.
[3] See above, pp. xxxv–xxxvi, xlv.
[4] Resuming 'Aretine's' metaphor, a writer in *Old England* for 16 December 1749 recalled that Lyttelton had 'midwived the *Brat* into the World, with as many Commendations as any Gossip at a Christening could utter'. Cf. also the Preface to *The History of Tom Jones the Foundling, in His Married State* (Dublin, 1749), sig. A3r.

entire first edition was sold out before the announced date of publication, 10 February 1749. For the benefit of those who, like Lady Hertford, were expecting to have the remaining volumes of the novel by 22 January, Millar on the preceding day ran the following advertisement in *The Whitehall Evening-Post* (Thursday, 19 January, to Saturday, 21 January 1749), announcing still another delay in publication:

*Friday, Feb.* 10, *will be published,* | *In* SIX VOLUMES, Twelves, | [Price bound 18 s.] | THE History of *Tom Jones,* a Foundling. | BY | HENRY FIELDING, *Esq;* | '—Mores hominum multorum vidit.' | Printed for A. Millar, opposite to Katherine-street in the Strand.[1]

Despite such assurances, it was not until the last day of February that publication notices for the novel began to appear in the newspapers, Millar cannily taking the opportunity to apologize to his clients for being unable to have sets bound fast enough to satisfy the demand.[2]

These advertisements have led Fielding's biographers to the mistaken conclusion that *Tom Jones* was originally issued on 28 February.[3] It is now clear, however, that what Millar was announcing on that date was in fact the *second* edition of the novel. What had happened to obviate any earlier notice on the promised date of 10 February was, as Joseph Spence observed, 'perhaps an unheard-of case'. Writing to William Burrell Massingberd on 15 April 1749, Spence vividly recalled the extraordinary circumstances surrounding the publication of the first edition:

---

[1] See also *The Whitehall Evening-Post* for 21–4 January 1749; *The London Evening-Post,* 19–21, 21–4 January 1749; *The Daily Advertiser,* 23, 25, 27 January 1749; and *The General Advertiser,* 23, 24, 25 January 1748/9.

[2] See *The General Advertiser* for Tuesday, 28 February 1748/9; *The Daily Advertiser,* 28 February 1749; *The London Evening-Post,* 25–8 February, 28 February–2 March, 2–4 March 1749; and *The Whitehall Evening-Post,* 25–8 February 1749. Millar's note reads as follows: 'It being impossible to get Sets bound fast enough to answer the Demand for them, such Gentlemen and Ladies as please, may have them sew'd in Blue Paper and Boards, at the Price of 16s. a Set, of A. Millar over-against Catherine-street in the Strand'. This advertisement was continued in *The General Advertiser* and *The Whitehall Evening-Post* until 4 March.

[3] See Cross, ii. 117–18, iii. 317, and Dudden, ii. 584, 1131. In 1937 Gerard E. Jensen's hypothesis concerning the dates of publication of the first three editions was essentially correct (see 'Proposals for a Definitive Edition of Fielding's *Tom Jones*', *The Library,* 4th Ser., xviii [1937], esp. pp. 316–17); but, like Dudden, recent editors of the novel have perpetuated Cross's errors (see, for example, R. P. C. Mutter's 1966 Penguin edition, p. 29).

Tom Jones is my old acquaintance, now; for I read it, before it was publisht: & read it with such rapidity, that I began & ended within the compass of four days; tho' I took a Journey to S$^t$ Albans, in y$^e$ same time. He is to me extreamly entertaining; & will be so, I believe, to you. A set of 2500 Copies was sold, before it was publisht; which is perhaps an unheard-of case. That I may not seem to write Riddles, you must know that the way here generally is, to send in their number of Books to each of the Booksellers they deal with, four or five days before the Publication; that they may oblige people, who are eager for a new thing. In y$^s$ case, the 10th of Febr$^y$ was fixt for y$^e$ Publication; & by the 10th, all the books were disposed of.[1]

In all essential respects, Spence's account is certainly correct. An entry in Strahan's ledgers, for example, reveals that the first edition was through the press in January, well before the expected date of publication:

Janry [1749]          Foundling 81 Sheets N°. 2000
                with many Alterations, @ £1:15
                                141/15/–

In February, moreover, Strahan's only reference to the work is to the second edition, so designated:

Febry [1749]          Foundling 2$^d$ Edit. 18 Sheets N°.
                1500 @ £1:6:0 p Sheet          23/8/–[2]

One last piece of evidence may be adduced confirming the fact that *Tom Jones* was printed and ready for publication nearly a month sooner than has been supposed: on 3 February 1748/9 Millar entered the novel in the Stationers' Register, wherein it is noted that nine copies had been received.[3] We may assume, then,

[1] Quoted in Austin Wright, *Joseph Spence: A Critical Biography* (Chicago, Ill., 1950), p. 232, n. 29. See also P. D. Mundy, *N & Q*, 15th Ser., i (28 December 1935), 456; and xxx (16 June 1945), 252–5. Spence's account of the early demand for *Tom Jones* may be compared with the following remark of Élie C. Fréron in a review of La Place's translation of the novel: 'An Englishman told me that the first edition was sold with the leaves still wet, and was followed by three others that enriched both author and bookseller. The latter was seen to purchase an equipage.' (Lettre I, 6 July 1751, *Lettres sur quelques écrits de ce tems* [1751], v. 3–22; trans. R. Paulson and T. Lockwood [edd.], *Henry Fielding: The Critical Heritage* [1969], p. 281.)

[2] B.M. Add. MSS. 48800. To judge from the number of sheets for which Strahan was responsible, Millar employed more than one printer to prepare this edition, a circumstance which helps to account for its rapid progress through the press.

[3] Records of the Stationers Hall, Registry of Copyrights. Entries of Copies 1746–1773, p. 55. One may note that Millar entered *Amelia* in the register on 19 December 1751, also the date of publication for that novel (see p. 107). That all six volumes of *Tom Jones* were available well before 28 February is a certain inference from the long synopsis of the novel

that the first edition of *Tom Jones* was ready for distribution on
that date and that, owing to the keen demand for the book, the
entire issue was exhausted before a week had passed. The advertisements on 28 February refer to the publication of the second
edition, not the first.

Some time in the following month a third edition of 3,000
copies, completely reset in small pica and reduced from six to four
volumes duodecimo, was through Strahan's presses. The entry in
his ledger reads:

> March [1749]      Foundling 3ᵈ Edit. Small Pica,
> 55 Sheets Nº. 3000 @ £2:6: p Sheet
> 126/10/–

Before releasing this new edition for sale, however, Millar
prudently required Fielding to prepare and sign the formal copyright agreement, which, in acknowledging Millar's payment
of £600 on 11 June 1748, Fielding had promised to do upon
demand. Written throughout in Fielding's hand and witnessed by
his clerk, Joshua Brogden, the full text of the agreement, dated
25 March 1749, is as follows:

KNOW ALL MEN BY THESE PRESENTS that I Henry Fielding of Sᵗ Paul's
Covent Garden in the County of Middlesex Esqʳ. for & in consideration of
the Sum of Six hundred Pounds of lawful Money of Great Britain to me in
hand paid by Andrew Millar of Sᵗ Mary le Strand in the County aforesᵈ.
Bookseller, the Receipt whereof is hereby acknowledged and of which I do
Acquit the sᵈ. Andrew Millar his Executors & Assigns, have bargained sold
delivered assigned & set over all that my Title Right and Property in & to a
certain Book printed in Six Volumes, known & called by the Name &
Title of The History of Tom Jones, a Foundling, in [6 volˢ.] written by me
the sᵈ. Henry Fielding, with all Improvements, Additions or Alterations
whatsoever which now are or hereafter shall at any time be made by me the
sᵈ. Henry Fielding, or any one else by my authority to the sᵈ. Book To Have
and to Hold the sᵈ. bargained Premises unto the sᵈ. Andrew Millar, his
Exõrs Admõrs or Assigns for ever And I do hereby covenant to & with the
sᵈ. Andrew Millar his Exõrs Admõrs & Assigns that I the sᵈ. Henry Fielding
the Author of the sᵈ. bargained Premises have not at any time heretofore
done committed or suffered any Act or thing whatsoever by means whereof
the sᵈ. bargained Premises or any part thereof is or shall be impeached or
encumbered in any wise. And I the sᵈ. Henry Fielding for myself my Exõrs

given in the February number of *The London Magazine* (pp. 51–5), published, according
to *The General Advertiser*, on 1 March 1749.

# General Introduction

Admōrs and Assigns shall warrant & defend the s^d. bargained Premises for ever against all Persons whatsoever claiming under me my Exōrs Admōrs or Assigns—

> In Witness whereof I have hereunto set my hand & Seal this twenty fifth day of March, One thousand seven hundred & forty nine,
>
> H Fielding [seal]
>
> Signed sealed & delivered by the within named Henry Fielding the day & year within mentioned, in the presence of,
>
> Jos. Brogden[1]

Although copies of the second edition continued to be available well into October,[2] Millar wished to publish the new and cheaper edition without delay. The earliest public reference to it occurs in *The General Advertiser* for 7 April, where it is promised '*In a few Days . . . (Price sew'd in Blue Paper Half a Guinea, or Bound 12s.)*'.[3] In due course, the third edition, designated only as 'New' in the advertisements, was released to the public on Wednesday, 12 April (or possibly a day earlier).[4]

That the demand for the novel continued brisk is clear from another entry in Strahan's ledger indicating that a fourth edition of 3,500 copies was through the presses in September:

> Sep^r. 1749     Foundling 4th Edition 55 Sheets
> N°. 3500 @ £2:11:– p Sheet     140/5/–

This edition brought the total number of copies printed during the first nine months of 1749 to 10,000, a figure testifying plainly enough to the immediacy and scope of the novel's popularity. This supply, however, was sufficient to satisfy the public for many years to come, a fifth edition not being called for until 1763. Before publishing the fourth edition, Millar waited to dispose of stock already on hand. Notices in the newspapers for 25–8 November promise publication '*Next Week*',[5] but it was not to

---

[1] Transcribed from the original document in the J. P. Morgan Library, New York.

[2] See the notices in *The General Advertiser*, 2, 7, 17 October 1749.

[3] See also *The General Advertiser* for 10 April; *The Whitehall Evening-Post*, 6–8, 8–11 April.

[4] The notice in *The General Advertiser* for 12 April begins '*This Day is published*'; this declaration does not appear in the advertisement in the same paper a day earlier. Publication was announced in *The London Evening-Post* and *The Whitehall Evening-Post* for 11–13 April. See also *The General Advertiser*, 13, 14, 15 April; *The Whitehall Evening-Post* 13–15, 15–18, 18–20, 20–2 April; *The London Evening-Post*, 15–18, 18–20, 22–5 April.

[5] See *The Whitehall Evening-Post* and *The London Evening-Post*, 25–8, 28–30 November, 30 November–2 December.

appear in the stalls until Monday, 11 December.[1] Like the third, the fourth edition is described in the advertisements simply as 'New', but in view of the confusion that has prevailed concerning the relative authority of these texts, it is worth remarking that only the notices for the fourth edition contain the further important declaration that the work has been 'Carefully revis'd and corrected / *By* HENRY FIELDING, *Esq*.'. Though Fielding had for the third edition extensively rewritten certain passages in the Man-of-the-Hill's section (VIII. xiii–xv) so as to reinforce the attack on Jacobitism, it is now clear that only the fourth edition was in any general way 'revised and corrected' by him—the most curious of these changes being the deliberate restoration of the revised chapters in Book VIII to their original form.[2] It is the

---

[1] See *The General Advertiser*, 11, 12, 13 December; and *The London Evening-Post* and *The Whitehall Evening-Post*, 9–12, 12–14, 14–16 December. Other advertisements for the edition appear in these papers during December.

[2] See Professor Bowers's Textual Introduction to the present edition, esp. pp. lxiv ff. In setting the fourth edition, the compositor followed throughout a copy of the third edition that Fielding had marked for revision—the single exception being gathering N of volume II, the sheet containing the extensive changes Fielding, in III, had introduced into the Man-of-the-Hill's narrative. At this point, the compositor deliberately reverted to the first edition for his copy, thereby restoring the revised passages in III to their original form. That he did so on Fielding's instructions is suggested not only by the bibliographical evidence Professor Bowers has adduced, but also by a comparison of the aesthetic effectiveness of the two versions.

From this point of view, what is surprising is not that Fielding cancelled the revisions, but that he had the questionable judgement to make them in the first place. The principal changes in III are of two kinds: (1) in VIII. xiv a long interpolation accentuating the Man-of-the-Hill's attack on Jacobitism and defending his participation in Monmouth's rebellion, especially for religious reasons; (2) in VIII. xv the deletion of three paragraphs characterizing the Man-of-the-Hill's misanthropy in colourful detail. What Fielding on second thought came to see is what any careful reader of the two versions will readily acknowledge to be the case: that the loss of enlivening strokes in the comedy and in the characterization of the Man-of-the-Hill was in no way compensated for by the heightened intensity of his fulminations against the Jacobites.

In basic import the two versions of ch. xiv are much the same, since, in both, the Man-of-the-Hill and Jones approve Monmouth's rebellion against James II, a tyrannical and 'Popish' prince, while at the same time they decry the uprisings of 1715 and 1745 against the Hanoverian Establishment. The revision in III elaborates James's efforts to subvert 'our Religion and Liberties', and it justifies his expulsion from the throne by emphasizing that the event was providentially ordained. The revision, moreover, distinguishes between the rebellion against James II and that against George II on religious grounds, George, champion of Protestantism and of liberty under the Constitution, being represented as the favourite and agent of Providence. The restrained monitory tone of the original passage has become in the revision angrier and more pious, verging, indeed, upon the strident and superstitious. Reviewing the passage in a cooler moment, Fielding may have sensed that his propagandizing had become too heavy-handed, and he may also have doubted the fourth edition—and not, as has been supposed, the third[1]—which represents Fielding's final conception of his masterpiece.

Shortly after the turn of the year, *Tom Jones* had begun to make its way abroad, translations of the novel appearing in French, Dutch, and German during 1750. Superficially, the earliest of these would seem to be the Dutch version by P. Le Clercq, published in three volumes at Amsterdam (vols. I–II dated 1749, vol. III 1750). But a careful comparison of the illustrations common to both the Dutch and the French translations has established that the distinction of priority belongs to the latter.[2] This work, by Pierre-Antoine de la Place, went through three editions in the twelve-month period from February 1750 to January 1751,[3] and, for extra-literary reasons, it is easily the most notable of the foreign renditions of the novel.

advisability of justifying *any* rebellion by appeals to Providence—the followers of James, after all, professed to believe that he was God's own anointed, ruler of Britain by 'divine right'. Fielding, we may also suppose, would certainly have regretted the fact that, in revising, he had sacrificed some of the essential, vivifying features of his narrative—the Man-of-the-Hill's comic astonishment at the folly of the English Jacobites, for instance ('the old Gentleman started up . . . he walked several Turns about the Room, in a profound Silence, then cried, then laughed, and, at last, fell down on his Knees, and blessed God, in a loud Thanksgiving-Prayer, for having delivered him from all Society with Human Nature, which could be capable of such monstrous Extravagances'); or his characterization of Watson's 'different Motives' for joining him in Monmouth's cause ('for the Spirit of a Gamester will carry a Man as far upon such an Occasion as the Spirit of Patriotism'). In III this entire section remains largely abstract, sombre, hortatory, unrelieved by wit or drama, the lively elements of Fielding's comic art.

On aesthetic grounds the deletion of three paragraphs in ch. xv was still more damaging to the narrative, since it involved the loss of important features delineating the Man-of-the-Hill's misanthropy. In the first two of these paragraphs he had likened his experience of foreign nations to that of a spectator passing through 'a Croud at a Shew, jostling to get by them, holding my Nose with one Hand, and defending my Pockets with the other . . .', grudgingly preferring Turks to Christians, and Hottentots to Frenchmen. In the last of the omitted paragraphs he had supplied fresh insights into his strange manner of life—his delight in solitude; his ancient housekeeper, who performs her duties in silence and is charged with warding off all intruders; his habit of roaming the hills at night, like 'a Ghost or a Hobgoblin'. As he revised his novel for the fourth edition, Fielding's judgement in restoring these chapters to their original form was quite sound.

[1] See Aurélien Digeon, *Le Texte des romans de Fielding* (Paris, 1923), pp. 70–7; G. E. Jensen, *The Library*, 4th Ser., xviii (1937), 314–30; and, most recently, R. P. C. Mutter's edition of the novel (1966), p. 29.

[2] See T. C. Duncan Eaves, 'The Publication of the First Translations of Fielding's *Tom Jones*', *The Library*, 4th ser., xxvi (1946), 189–90.

[3] La Place's *Histoire de Tom Jones, ou l'enfant trouvé* in 4 vols. was published in February 1750, anonymously and with the place of publication falsely given as London, 'Chez Jean Nourse'. A second edition, still anonymous, was published in April at Amsterdam; the third edition, signed, was published in Paris the following January.

In order to accommodate *Tom Jones* to the French taste, and doubtless to spare himself some weeks of trouble, La Place pitilessly mutilated the book, compressing the narrative at will and, of course, excising '*toute espèce de Digressions, de Dissertations, ou de Traité de Morale*'.[1] The *Histoire de Tom Jones* is, therefore, a very different work from the original; nevertheless, it was through this version, handsomely illustrated by Gravelot, that most European readers formed their estimate of Fielding's powers as a novelist.[2] Despite the depredations of the translator, La Place's book had 'a vast run' in France, as M. Defreval assured Samuel Richardson, who pressed him for confirmation of a report that Fielding's novel had been suppressed by the French authorities as an immoral work.[3] Gleefully circulated by Fielding's enemies,[4] this rumour had only a slight basis in fact: the now famous *Arrêt du Conseil* of 24 February 1750 was directed not against *Tom Jones*, but against La Place's bookseller, Jacques Rollin, who had published the work without due license.[5] Presumably, Rollin made his apologies and paid the fine, for the *Arrêt* seems never to have been enforced. A second edition of La Place's translation appeared in April and a third the following January. On the whole, as the Marquis d'Argenson observed, Fielding's novel prospered in France as only the most celebrated works of English fiction had done: 'Tout le monde lit aujourd'hui ce livre à Paris, comme on faisait de *Gulliver* et de *Paméla* dans leur temps.'[6]

At home, as the publishing history of the novel attests, *Tom Jones* was a splendid and instantaneous success. The four editions published within the year together amounted to 10,000 copies— not to mention the unauthorized Dublin edition published in three volumes by John Smith. As even Fielding's enemies were compelled to admit, *Tom Jones* was 'in every Hand, from the

[1] See the 'Traduction d'une Lettre' prefixed to vol. i. (See Paulson and Lockwood, No. 89.)

[2] It was the basis, for example, of the Italian translation (1756–7).

[3] See Defreval's letter of 17 April 1751, in Anna Laetitia Barbauld (ed.), *The Correspondence of Samuel Richardson* (1804), v. 276–7.

[4] See, for example, *Old England* (7 April 1750); *The Gentleman's Magazine*, xx (March 1750), 118 n.; *The Monthly Review*, ii (March 1750), 432—the note appears at the end of a notice of the *Memoirs of Fanny Hill*!

[5] For an authoritative discussion of the incident, see B. P. Jones, 'Was There a Temporary Suppression of *Tom Jones* in France ?', *MLN*, lxxvi (1961), 495–8.

[6] Marquis d'Argenson, *Journal et Mémoires* (Paris, 1857–8), v. 111–12.

liv *General Introduction*

beardless Youth, up to the hoary Hairs of Age'.[1] There is no need
here to rehearse at length the story of the book's reception so
fully told by F. T. Blanchard;[2] most of the documentary materials,
indeed, have been conveniently collected by Ronald Paulson and
Thomas Lockwood.[3] It is appropriate, however, to mark the
salient features of that story, and to supply certain details that
have come to light in the course of nearly half a century since
Blanchard's study appeared.

The brisk sale *Tom Jones* enjoyed is the surest, but by no means
the only, sign of its vogue. The immediate public response may be
gauged from the earliest notice of the novel, a lengthy synopsis
published in *The London Magazine* for February 1749 and
reprinted some months later in *The Penny London Post*.[4] *Tom
Jones*, the reviewer begins, has already '*given great Amusement,
and, we hope, Instruction to the polite Part of the Town*'; and he
concludes with assurances that the abstract of '*this pretty novel*' he
has supplied is intended only '*as an incitement to those, that have not
yet had the pleasure of reading it*'. It appears, however, that except
for those who contemned the book out of personal animus towards the author—Richardson, for example, or his friend Thomas
Edwards—there were not many so incurious as to deny themselves the pleasure the reviewer speaks of. Though a contributor
to *The British Magazine* might commend the empress Eusebia
for preferring 'hard, sound, and honest Greek philosophy' to the
'Tom Jones's, or Clarissa's' of her time,[5] it is clear that in this
year of the reign of George Augustus, Fielding and Richardson
divided the world of letters between them.

The delight readers took in *Tom Jones* expressed itself in a
variety of ways, some as frivolous as amusing. When the races
began at Epsom in April, for example, two of the horses com-
peting were 'Mr. Shaftoe's Chestnut Horse, *Joseph Andrews*;

---

[1] *An Apology for the Life of Bampfylde-Moore Carew*, '2nd ed.' (1751), p. 2.
[2] See *Fielding the Novelist: A Study in Historical Criticism* (New Haven, Conn., 1926),
pp. 26–78 and *passim*.
[3] See their edition, *Henry Fielding: The Critical Heritage* (1969).
[4] See *The London Magazine*, xviii (February 1749), 51–5; and *The Penny London Post*,
10–12, 12–15, 15–17 May 1749. (See Paulson and Lockwood, No. 57.)
[5] *The British Magazine*, iv (March 1749), 87. In the June number of this periodical, the
author of a '*Dissertation on* Halfpenny Grubs' regrets that news bulletins are 'generally
condemned by the society of the *Belles Lettres* at *George*'s coffee-house, who prefer to these
true novels the lying history of *Tom Jones, Lettice Pilkington*, and *Roderick Random*; people
who either never existed at all, or never in the characters they are drawn in' (p. 234).

and Mr. Greswood's Bay Horse, *Tom Jones'*, a competition won, somewhat unprophetically, by 'Joseph Andrews'.¹ Nor was it very long before Fielding's characters, whimsically translated, began to appear in drawing-rooms as well: thus, referring to a romantic fad that Lady Bradshaigh had also remarked with impatience, *Old England* hoped that 'Orbilius's' *Examen* of the novel would 'have such an Effect on some forward *Petticoats*, that they will hardly fur [*sic*] the future be so very fond of calling their *Pensioners* by the Name of *Tom Jones*, nor the *Fribbles* their Harlots by that of *Sophia*'.² In a friendlier spirit, one provincial versifier, imitating Pope, recounted the rape of his heroine's prized possession, an ornamental fan on which is depicted a number of the most affecting scenes from *Tom Jones*: 'She lov'd the Toy, because she lov'd the Tale.'³ The heroine of this clever piece may be regarded as typical of those young women who took Fielding's novel to heart: 'The Foundling's Story touch'd the tender Dame, / The Foundling's Story then was all her Theme' (p. 6). In an apostrophe, the poet asks:

> Say, happy *Fielding*, can thy laurell'd Brow
> Give half that Joy, as *Lydia* gives thee now?
> Say, could you hope thy Scenes would leave behind
> Such deep Impression, and so touch the Mind?
> When Female Sense and Female Softness meet
> To praise thy Work, thy Work is sure compleat.  (p. 9)

What the author finds most engaging about *Tom Jones* are not its comic, but its 'tender' aspects, its theme of benevolence and romantic love. What he finds most remarkable about the art of the novel is Fielding's iconographic skill in rendering his scenes: though Lydia's fan is imaginary, he hopes it may show 'what a rich Fund, for the Pencil, there is in the Scenes of *Tom Johns* [*sic*]: No weak Argument for their Beauty, when they still please, though stript of Words. I hope this will prove a Hint to some ingenious Artist' (p. iii). No artist seems to have taken this advice, but before the year was out Fielding's profitable book had

¹ *The London Evening-Post*, 2–4 May 1749.
² *Old England* (16 December 1749). For Lady Bradshaigh's letter [November 1749] on the same subject, see Anna Laetitia Barbauld (ed.), *The Correspondence of Samuel Richardson* (1804), iv. 280–1. (See Paulson and Lockwood, No. 79.)
³ *The Fan: A Heroi-Comical Poem in Three Cantos* (Norwich, 1749). The relevant excerpts from this poem are reprinted in Alan D. McKillop, 'An Iconographic Poem on *Tom Jones*', *PQ*, xvii (1938), 403–6. (See Paulson and Lockwood, No. 58.)

served to inspire another sort of imitator. This was the author of the spurious sequel to the novel, entitled *The History of Tom Jones the Foundling, in His Married State*—a dull performance, but one that achieved the end for which it was written, a second, expanded edition of the work being called for within the month.[1]

Though *Tom Jones* prospered in the months immediately following its publication, for the most part it was hailed with abuse by the hackney critics of the age. Exasperated by the book's popularity, Fielding's enemies read him with a lust to misapply, attacking both the novel and its author with a malevolent zeal surpassing even their usual impressive talents for invective. To 'Aretine' of *Old England* (27 May 1749) the 'Performance' was 'beneath the Dignity of regular Criticism', yet he could not in conscience refrain from damning 'this motley History of Bastardism, Fornication and Adultery', a book 'so truly profligate, of such evil Tendency, and offensive to every chaste Reader, so discouraging to Virtue and detrimental to Religion!' The scribblers of *Old England* sounded monotonous variations on this theme for months to come; indeed, when earthquakes shook the capital in 1750, it seemed self-evident to one of this pious crew that these seismic prodigies were signs of God's wrath at the enthusiastic reception accorded Fielding's lewd romance.[2] Before enlisting Providence against him, however, Fielding's antagonists had found a mortal champion in 'Orbilius', who laboured and early in December 1749 produced one of the genuine monuments of ultracrepidarian criticism, *An Examen of the History of Tom Jones, a Foundling*.[3] Starting with the Dedication and proceeding chapter by chapter through the novel, this egregious performance is a notable exercise in the systematic annihilation of a work of art. Its aim—ultimately altruistic, of course—is perhaps best summarized in the advertisement carried in *The General Advertiser* (16 December): 'An Examen of the History of Tom Jones, a Foundling. In which the bad Morals, unnatural Descriptions,

---

[1] The work was originally published on 4 November 1749; the second edition, '*corrected, with an additional Chapter by Mr.* Allworthy, *&c. relating to Plays in general, and the* French *Play-House in particular*', appeared on 6 December. (See *The General Advertiser* for these dates.) For an appropriately uncomplimentary notice of the book, see *The Monthly Review*, ii (November 1749), 25–6.

[2] See *Old England* (7 April 1750); earlier criticisms of the novel appear in the numbers for 5, 26 August and 16 December 1749. (See Paulson and Lockwood, Nos. 66, 93.)

[3] For an abridgement of this work, see Paulson and Lockwood, No. 82.

Inconsistencies, Improbabilities, impertinent Shew of Learning and false Pretensions to Wit, of that Droll Performance, are exploded. Designed to rescue true Taste from the Sophistry of the farcical Author.' It is fitting to note that this piece of invective was itself condemned in *The Monthly Review* for the same month.[1]

Such were the public manifestations of taste and judgement that greeted Fielding's masterpiece in the year of its publication. One looks for some reasoned criticism of the work; one finds only personal effusions of pleasure or spite. In the famous *Rambler* essay of the following spring (31 March 1750), however, the weight of Samuel Johnson's heavy moralism fell upon the book, among those other 'familiar histories'—*Roderick Random*, for example—whose profligate, but good-natured heroes he regarded as too seductively attractive.[2] It was not, indeed, until 1751 that Fielding found an advocate and imitator at all worthy of his achievement: in February of that year Francis Coventry published his sprightly *History of Pompey the Little*, cordially acknowledging his indebtedness to Fielding's '*Epic Poem in Prose*' (1. i) and proclaiming its founder 'King of *Biographers*' (11. i); and in the following month it was perhaps Coventry again who produced *An Essay on the New Species of Writing founded by Mr. Fielding*, a sane and salutary, if not a very profound, appreciation of Fielding's art that serves as a welcome antidote to the venomous performances of 'Orbilius' and the author of *Bampfylde-Moore Carew*.[3]

The immediate reaction to *Tom Jones* is not, of course, to be

---

[1] See Paulson and Lockwood, No. 83.

[2] Ibid., No. 92.

[3] Ibid., Nos. 98–9, 134. Among the early imitations prompted by Fielding's success, the following escaped Blanchard's notice: *The Adventures of the Rd. Mr. Judas Hawke, the Rd. Mr. Nathan Briggs, Miss Lucretia Briggs, &c. Late Inhabitants of the Island of Querumania. After the Manner of Joseph Andrews* (1751): B.M. 17714. This humourless, ill-written book bears little resemblance to its model, though in Briggs and Hawkes it contains characters vaguely reminiscent of Parson Adams and Jonathan Wild. Despite his dependence on Fielding, the author at one point adds his own voice to the chorus of those who disparaged *Tom Jones*. From his general condemnation of contemporary 'memorialists', who lose the reader in a maze of irrelevant circumstances, he ironically exempts 'the author of Tom Jones, who, (like Job's messenger, shall alone escape the slaughter of the critics, to tell the world, that he can spin a web to catch every fly—and, that the most triffling of triffles may be drawn out by him to whatever length he thinks proper, without the reader's being in the least dissatisfied at his not having confined his subject to a less [more ?] limited compass.)' (p. 26).

estimated solely from published notices of the book, but also from
those more private expressions of delight or dismay that survive
in the epistolary gossip of the period. Despite Fielding's compliments to him on the occasion of *Clarissa*,[1] Richardson persisted in
his haughty refusal to read *Tom Jones*, which, however, did not
deter him from summarily damning the book and its 'vicious'
author.[2] To review Richardson's correspondence on this subject,
already presented at length by Blanchard, would be as depressing
as it is unnecessary. In this, as in most things, Thomas Edwards
shared his friend's opinion and followed his example in neglecting
to read the novel. Anticipating a trip to town, where *Tom Jones*
had been the principal topic of conversation for some months, he
wrote to the Reverend Lewis Crusius on 3 May 1749:

> Yet I am almost afraid of coming, for what a figure shall I make there
> who have not seen Tom Jones? but though I have not seen, I have heard a
> great deal of him; some give, though not so judicious a character of that
> work as you do, yet such a one as confirms your opinion of it; others cry it up
> to the skies, but they are such as do not relish my favorite Clarissa, and who
> look more to the head than the heart; and indeed from what I know of the
> Man, both from his conversation and his works, I am sure he is not capable
> of going higher than you say he has gone; in short I am every day more con-
> vinced that he who would write perfectly on a moral subject must be a
> moral man; Is it not the same in every other science? Can he who is no
> Mathematician write like Sir Isaac Newton?
>
> I always thought that in his other pieces whenever he touched upon those
> sort of subjects there was an aukwardness, and a stiffness which shew'd he
> was not in his element, and that what he wrote was the effect of reasoning or
> observation, and not the dictates of the heart.[3]

A similarly unfavourable opinion of the novel was expressed by an
equally biased judge, Tobias Smollett, who in *Roderick Random*
(1748) had set up as Fielding's rival in the art of fiction and who,
in the first edition of *Peregrine Pickle* (1751), would not scruple
to asperse his character.[4] But Smollett, at least, had read the
book. Writing on 1 October 1749 to his compatriot, the Reverend

---

[1] See *The Jacobite's Journal* (2 January, 5 March 1748) and Fielding's letter to Richardson, dated 15 October 1748.

[2] For an account of Richardson's correspondence on the subject of *Tom Jones*, see
Blanchard, pp. 60–70. (See Paulson and Lockwood, Nos. 71, 73–4, 85, 121–2.)

[3] Bodl. MSS. 1011, pp. 130–1. For a possible allusion to Edwards in *Tom Jones*, see
p. 790, n. 1.

[4] See above, p. xxxi, n. 2.

Mr. Alexander Carlyle, he agreed that *Tom Jones* was a flawed performance, Fielding having attempted in it an unfortunate compromise between his mercenary interests and his Muse:

If I should pretend to set up in Defence of Tom Jones, in those particulars where he is affected by your Censure, you would easily discover my affectation and be justly offended at my feigned Candour. I will therefore own that the same observations occurred to me which you have communicated, and are indeed obvious to every reader of discernment; even the Author's most sanguine Adherents confess that there is an Evident Difference between that part of his Book which he wrote for the Town, and that which was composed for the Benefit of his Bookseller.[1]

It is not true, however, that 'every reader of discernment' reacted to *Tom Jones* with this characteristically Smollettian mixture of condescension and scorn. Writing to Lady Luxborough on 7 April 1749, William Shenstone, for one, acknowledged that Fielding had wit, which he found 'ty'd up in Bundles at yᵉ beginning of every *Book*', and he remarked that the naturalness and humour of Squire Western were of such a high order as to have had a therapeutic efficacy: Western 'made me *laugh*; & yᵗ is a great Point gain'd, when one is in danger of losing yᵗ *Faculty* thro' Disuse'.[2] Though yielding to none in her admiration of *Clarissa*, Elizabeth Carter wrote on 20 June to Catherine Talbot, scolding her friend for being 'so outrageous about poor Tom Jones': with all her 'partiality' to Richardson, 'I am afraid', she insists, 'it must be confessed, that Fielding's book is the most natural representation of what passes in the world, and of the bizarreries which arise from the mixture of good and bad which makes up the composition of most folks.'[3] The most charming testimony of the novel's power to please came, however, from Astraea and Minerva Hill, devoted Richardsonians both, who on 27 July responded in a most unexpected way to his request to hear their opinion of Fielding's 'coarse' performance. Instead of roundly damning *Tom Jones*, as Richardson required, the young ladies exercised a judgement and clemency worthy of

---

[1] See Lewis M. Knapp (ed.), *The Letters of Tobias Smollett* (Oxford, 1970), p. 11. (See Paulson and Lockwood, No. 78.)

[2] *Letters of William Shenstone*, ed. Duncan Mallam (1939), p. 140. (See Paulson and Lockwood, No. 63.)

[3] *A Series of Letters between Mrs. Elizabeth Carter and Miss Catherine Talbot* (1808), i. 207. (See Paulson and Lockwood, No. 67.)

their namesakes; they forgave Fielding his 'bantering Levity' and 'ironic satire', which were enlisted, after all, in the service of truth, and they praised him for 'a double merit, both of Head, and *Heart*'—commending the book's artful and 'regular Design', its truth to life, and, especially, its 'Humanity'.[1]

Two other letters recently come to light will further serve to redress the balance of contemporary opinion, which on the whole, at least among articulate readers of *Tom Jones*, did not tip in Fielding's favour. Like Messrs. Crusius and Carlyle, the recipient of the first of these was a clergyman, a circumstance which may in part account for the writer's restraint in commending so low and licentious a work as *Tom Jones*. On 30 March 1749, John Blair wrote to John Douglas, later Bishop of Salisbury, at Leipzig. After regretting the sad decline of the English stage, Blair was encouraged that the 'Genius' of his nation had found expression in a new mode, the novels of Richardson and Fielding:

The three last Volumes of Clarissa are inimitably well & Fieldings new Piece of Tom Jones reads not badly—it is ray$^r$ inferior to Joseph Andrews & has no Character half so diverting as Abraham Adams however it is in higher Life, & contains many good Scenes & quaint Witticisms which do well enough now & then There is a droll Contrast betw$^n$ y$^s$ last Piece of his & Joseph Andrews. For as he had been condemn'd by many Criticks even of y$^e$ Fair Sex for y$^e$ immaculate Chastity of Joseph, he has now given his Hero Tom Jones a violent & constant Passion for a young Lady & without lessening y$^t$ makes him at y$^e$ same time lye w$^{th}$ every Woman y$^t$ comes in his Way. It has so great a Run y$^t$ I believe five or six thousand Copys of it are already sold. . . .[2]

Besides offering further testimony of the vogue of Fielding's novel, Blair's remarks are of special interest to the critic, for in drawing the wry comparison between the situations of *Joseph Andrews* and *Tom Jones*, they point toward a significant development in Fielding's conception of his art, both in characterization and in the strategies of conveying his moral meaning.

To the party (apparently small) of those who joined with Lyttelton in hailing the novel as a masterpiece may be added the names of Welbore Ellis and a certain Captain Lewis Thomas. In Carlisle on 3 April 1749, Captain Thomas, having finished

---

[1] Forster MSS., XV. ii. ff. 74–7. (See Paulson and Lockwood, No. 72.)

[2] B.M. MSS. Egerton 2185 (Press 524. H), ff. 9–10. I am indebted to Professor James L. Clifford for calling this letter to my attention.

reading *Tom Jones*, hastened to assure his friend, later Baron
Mendip, that he shared his high opinion of the book, which was,
he declared, a triumph not only of art and humour, but of
morality:

I am just got up from a very Amazing entertainment; to use a Metaphor
in the Foundling, I have been these four or five days last past a fellow traveller
of Harry Fieldings, & a very agreeable Journey I have had. Character,
Painting, Reflexion, Humour, excellent each in its Kind, in short I found
every thing there, You said I should find, when you gave me an Account of
the Writing. If my design had been to propagate virtue by appearing publickly in its defence, I should rather have been y^e Author of Tom Jones than
of five Folio Volumes of sermons.[1]

As we have seen, the Captain's concluding observation would
have struck many readers as wilful. Though *Tom Jones* incurred
the censure of prudes and the scornful indignation of its author's
enemies, it is pleasant to record that there were other, juster
voices to praise it.

[1] Quoted by J. P. Feil, *PQ*, xxxix (1960), 508–10. (See Paulson and Lockwood,
No. 62.)

# TEXTUAL INTRODUCTION

THIS edition offers a critical unmodernized text of *Tom Jones*. The text is critical in that it has been established by the application of analytical criticism to the evidence of the various documentary forms in which the novel appeared. It is unmodernized in that every effort has been made to present the text in as close a form to Fielding's own inscription and final revision as the surviving documents permit, subject only to normal editorial regulation.

## I. THE COPY-TEXT AND ITS TREATMENT

Since the formal assignment of copyright from Fielding to his publisher Millar is extant, no doubt can exist as to the authoritative nature of the manuscript of *Tom Jones* that was sent to the press. The first edition, therefore, must have been printed from holograph and in that respect remains the only text with an overall authority. Strahan's accounts for the printing set a price of £1. 15s. per sheet in contrast to the £1. 6s. charged for the second edition and mention 'with many Alterations'. These alterations seem to have been of two kinds. First, a full sheet of twelve cancellans leaves was printed but presumably charged for in the 81 sheets billed for the first edition.[1] Second, some of the regular text pages are excessively crowded whereas others are short, both suggesting changes made in proof that involved resetting. It seems probable that Fielding read proof on at least some if not most of the sheets before they were sent to the press and in the process considerably revised his work to create the 'many Alterations' that Strahan specifically noted and no doubt passed on in his charges. Despite this care, Fielding made up a list of 61 errata for the first five volumes. Although various of these correct printer's errors, perhaps a majority of the altered readings consist of further revisions. The distribution may be significant. In the first two volumes which Professor Battestin has shown were early printed, before all the copy for the novel had

---

[1] If Strahan had printed as economically as possible, the six volumes with cancellans sheet could have been managed in 80 sheets.

been received, eight alterations are requested for the first volume and seven for the second. However, the number jumps to thirteen for Volume III, and then to nineteen for Volume IV, before lowering to fourteen for Volume V. Although this errata list was printed among the preliminaries to the first volume and thus either as a very late or perhaps even as the final operation for the edition, no errata for Volume VI appear.[1] What is perhaps suggested by the considerable difference in the number of the errata items in the first two volumes as against those in the next three is that Fielding had been able to see the sheets of the first two through the press in a more leisurely way than was possible later when it became clear that the original publication date could not be met and pressure could have been felt to speed the operation. Thus we may expect more rewriting in proof to have been present in the first six books than in the remaining twelve where, in the last four volumes, Fielding would probably have been hastier in his survey of the proof-sheets and might even have been forced to skip the careful perusal of some of them.

One thing is clear, at any rate. It is not at all likely that Fielding attended the press during the actual machining of the sheets. The few press-variants that have been observed are not part of a systematic correction of any forme but instead appear sporadically one to a sheet and thus must have originated in the printing-house. With the exception of the significant substantive correction of 'scattered' to 'shattered' in II. 284. 15, and the addition of a necessary 'to' at I. 43. 8, these few alterations in press are concerned with simple mistakes in the punctuation or in the spelling. The confirmed variants are listed in the Emendations and are noted by copies in the bibliographical description of the first edition in Appendix V.

The second edition, printed before publication and perhaps even without notice to Fielding, is a paginal and substantially a line-for-line reprint of the first. Apart from a few obvious corrections

---

[1] On sig. A11ᵛ the catchword *'Nineteen'* and the following word on sig. A12 *'Nineteen'* in the Contents heading for Book III correct the reading *'Seventeen'* in the text according to the errata instructions, indicating that the errata, printed on final preliminary sig. c8ʳ, had been received before the early preliminaries were set up and printed. It is possible to conjecture that these preliminaries were printed before the return of Fielding's final survey of the Volume VI sheets in case he had submitted errata for the sixth volume, now lost. This re-survey that resulted, perhaps volume by volume, in the errata list was independent, of course, of his proof-reading the sheets before printing.

and the incorporation of the errata from the list printed in the preliminaries to Volume 1 of the first edition, the variants constitute printer's errors. It would seem to have been impossible for Fielding to have ordered any alterations, and hence no reading in the second edition can carry authority. This edition was not used as printer's copy for any subsequent text and thus is terminal, without influence on other editions.

The third edition, still in 1749, was the first of the cheaper editions reduced typographically into four volumes. Strahan rendered his account in March and thus the third edition followed by about a month the printing of the second and by less than two months the completion of printing of the first. The copy given to the compositors was the first edition with the errata corrected so that the third and the second editions both radiate from the first. The brief interval between the printing of the first three editions had not permitted Fielding to prepare revised copy. Hence with a single exception the third edition is an unauthoritative reprint of the first, its variant readings errors and sophistications not to be imputed to Fielding, mixed with a few necessary corrections that were wholly within any compositor's province.[1]

The single exception comes in Book VIII, Chapters xiii–xv (the second volume of the third edition), where in Chapter xiv Fielding rewrote one block of the Man-of-the-Hill's narrative (477.11–478.31), reducing the length of the text slightly but increasing the anti-Roman Catholic fervour and the re-enforcement of the parallel between the bloody suppression of the Duke of Monmouth's revolt against James II and the consequences to be expected if the '45 rebellion had succeeded. This block of rewritten copy was substituted in manuscript for printed material beginning in the first edition on sig. O5, line 24, and continuing to sig. O6ᵛ, line 18, occupying in the third edition sig. N5, line 9, to N6, line 5. However, Fielding's revisions were not confined to

---

[1] This view differs from that originally advanced by Aurélien Digeon in *Le Texte des romans de Fielding* (Paris, 1923), pp. 70–7, and followed by Gerard E. Jensen, 'Proposals for a Definitive Edition of Fielding's *Tom Jones*', *The Library*, 4th Ser., xviii (December 1937), 314–30. Both critics assumed that the third-edition revision of the Man-of-the-Hill's narrative required the minor variants in the rest of the text to have originated with Fielding. The bibliographical facts isolating this single block of revision to one first-edition gathering, the marked differences between the stylistic revisions in this sheet and the other third-edition alterations, and a critical survey of these other alterations as noted in the Historical Collation appended to the present edition effectively demonstrate the contrary.

this block of manuscript, for in addition he revised stylistically the text within the entire bibliographical unit of gathering O of the first edition (472.3–486.6) which comprised the latter part of Chapter xiii, Chapter xiv, and most of Chapter xv, occupying in the third edition sigs. N1$^v$, line 8, to N9$^v$, line 33, both before and after the central substitution of the manuscript material. Finally he made a substantial cut at 482.20–483.6, 483.10–27 affecting the characterization of the Man-of-the-Hill. These revisions were effected by annotation of the first-edition pages corrected from the errata so that the printer's copy remained the same as in the rest of the third edition except that in this sheet O of the first-edition copy Fielding had entered a number of alterations. Thereafter for the rest of the novel the third edition returns to reprinting the first from unrevised copy in the same manner as before the special situation of gathering O. The confinement of Fielding's revisions to the bibliographical unit of this sheet from the first edition is demonstrable. The first independent third-edition revision occurs on first edition sig. O1, line 24, where the I reading 'without being' (472.18–19) is altered in III (sig. N1$^v$, line 29) to 'where we were not'. The next stylistic alteration occurs at 474.19, sig. O2$^v$, lines 25–6, of I where for 'Principle of the Lawfulness of Self-Murder' III reads simply 'Practice' (sig. N3, line 15). Thereafter III revises I freely up to the final page O12$^v$ of I where the reading in line 18 'Time' is altered in III to 'Time only' (sig. N9$^v$). But starting with first-edition sig. P1, the III revisions cease and normality of reprinting is restored for the rest of the novel.

It is clear that Fielding felt so strongly at the time the desirability of the rather emotional revisions represented by his manuscript substitution that he made a singular effort to see that they were inserted in the third edition then printing. Apparently he secured a copy of the sheet of the first edition containing the passage he intended chiefly to revise, marked the substitution of the manuscript portion, and then took the opportunity to read over the rest of the sheet, which he revised with some copiousness by marginal annotation. The marked-up copy of this sheet O with its manuscript insertion was then utilized as copy for the third edition. So much is certain, that revision of two kinds—both for content and then for style—was confined to this special first-edition sheet O. It is also certain that this revision for the third edition was carried out before its sheet N had been set and printed and was not later inserted by a sheet cancel. The exact concurrence in positions of the running-titles of III sheet N, page by page with the corresponding pages of sheet L (just as the running-titles indicate that the skeleton-formes of sheet M were transferred to impose sheet O), demonstrates complete regularity of printing.[1]

It may be thought odd that Fielding did not content himself with sending the manuscript altered passage to Millar with instructions for its use but instead worked over the whole of a first-edition sheet O copy; and it might be conjectured that in fact he had already prepared this sheet as part of a complete revised edition for the future such as was produced in the fourth edition. But the bibliographical evidence discourages any such hypothesis. If such copy had been prepared, no reason exists why Fielding could not have taken the opportunity to send other revised sheets. However, the opportunity did not exist, apparently, for when Fielding prepared the revised fourth edition he seems to have marked up a copy of the third edition for the printer, not the first as represented by the I sheet O that was used for the third edition.[2] It would seem that his stylistic revisions marked in first-edition sheet O were inserted as a consequence of his abstraction of this sheet to send to the printer with the proper place marked for his substituted passage in manuscript. The revision in this single sheet of the third edition has misled critics

[1] In addition, and an important piece of evidence, the original fuller text of the first edition could not have been contained within the pages of this sheet, nor is there evidence for stretching out the text of the shorter third-edition version.

[2] One might speculate, on the contrary, that Fielding had instead prepared copy for a revised edition by marking sheets of I throughout, and that the subsequent revised fourth edition was prepared from these marked sheets by transferring in the printing shop the annotations from I to a copy of III in order to allow the compositor to set a largely paginal reprint of III. If sheet O had been abstracted from such a marked copy in order to revise the long passage in III, and incidentally the text around it, one could still return to the query why the earlier as well as the later marked sheets were not also used as copy for III. To answer this requires yet another conjecture, that Fielding did not know of the printing of the third edition until this place was reached and by sheer coincidence had not progressed further in his revision of I than sheet O so that more revised copy could not be provided. That the third edition was a surprise to him and that he insisted on the revision of the Monmouth passage by furnishing a sheet from his already revised I copy in order to produce a cancel sheet would probably fit better. But the fact remains that gathering N in III is not a cancel. For further discussion of the faulty hypothesis that Fielding could have prepared a revision by marking I sheets, see Appendix, pp. lxxx ff.

into the untenable hypothesis that the third edition was revised throughout. The facts are otherwise, as the record of variants published for the first time in the Historical Collation of the present edition will demonstrate.

Strahan's special charge of 12*s*. in June, 1749, for 'Composing a Sheet of the Foundling, an Imperfection' is gnomic in its import except that it can have no connection with the revised text in sheet N even though it must refer to the third edition. If one must guess, faults in a sheet were discovered in later bindings-up, and Strahan printed a new gathering to replace damaged copies or copies of sheets spoiled in the presswork. This sheet has not been identified.

Between the printing of the third edition in March and the printing of the fourth in September, Fielding engaged himself to his only revision of the text except for the isolated unit in the Man-of-the-Hill narrative revised for the third edition. For his purposes, unfortunately, he was given a copy of the third as a convenience for the printer in producing for the fourth edition a largely paginal and line-for-line reprint of the third. The revision, which Millar advertised, was chiefly stylistic and concerned itself specifically with purity of usage and with correcting careless grammatical modification. In the process Fielding was not aware of the variant readings in which III had strayed from its I copy, and thus he altered readings unauthoritatively initiated by III only when they were relatively obvious blunders. His revision was remarkably consistent throughout the whole text, and it is an important factor for the final language in which the novel was cast.

One anomaly occurs. The area in III from sigs. N1$^v$ to N9 that in III had been revised by annotation and manuscript sub-stitution appears in IV as a straight reprint of the first edition, whose sheet O in its original form—the errata uncorrected—was the printer's copy for this area in IV, although sigs. N1 and the upper part of N1$^v$, as well as the lower part of N9 and the rest of the gathering to N12$^v$, were printed from III copy that had been annotated and revised for the fourth edition. Once again demon-stration is possible for the relationship of the anomaly to the bibliographical unit of gathering O of I. On first-edition sig. N12$^v$, line 2, which is III and IV sig. N1, line 24 (471.26), appears quite normally the IV revision 'entirely' for I–III 'sincerely', the last for the moment of the series of IV revisions characteristic of the edition. However, on first-edition sig. O1, line 21—III sig. N1ᵛ, line 26, and IV sig. N1ᵛ, line 25—the I text reading 'Affronts' which in III had been corrected from the errata list to 'Affront' appears in its I form as 'Affronts', and a few lines down the III revision 'where we were not' (472.18–19) appears in IV in its I form 'without being'. It is also noteworthy that on sig. N1ᵛ after the start in line 8 of IV of the sheet O printer's copy from I, the IV compositor begins to set more tightly to save space. The line-for-line agreement with III breaks at line 10 where a four-line paragraph in III (472.3–5) is set in three lines, and though with the next paragraph the lineation of the two agrees for nine more lines, it breaks again at IV line 20 and thereafter the IV compositor starts with sig. N5 to set 38 lines to the page instead of the regular 36 and so continues until sig. N10 (which in line 31 marked the end of the I sheet O copy and the return of III copy). Finally he is able to end Book VIII, Chapter xv, with 35 lines on sig. N10ᵛ (corresponding to line 5 on III sig. N10ᵛ). Beginning on sig. N11, therefore, with the heading for Book ix, Chapter i, IV again becomes a generally line-for-line and page-for-page reprint of III in so far as the IV revisions permit. Throughout this area from IV N1ᵛ to N10—corresponding to I sheet O—not only is the rewriting in the III revision from manuscript ignored but also all III stylistic revisions are replaced by the original I versions, and another word in the I text corrected in the errata is faithfully preserved (481.7).

The conclusion is inescapable that the IV compositor was instructed to shift his copy at sig. N1ᵛ, line 8 from III and to set from sheet O of I, complete, returning to III copy only at III sig. N9ᵛ, line 33, at the phrase 'whose own Minds' (486.6) after the conclusion of I sheet O with 'but those'. Almost immediately, on III sig. N10, line 17, the IV revision of the III text resumes with 'having' for I–III 'his having' (486.19) and continues to the end of the novel with no further interruption. Since the compositor knew that his I copy was longer than the III text which it replaced, and that the start of Book ix on sig. N11 was the positively required place where he must resume his paginal setting from III, his efforts to make up space by resorting to the longer 38-line page from sigs. N5 to N10 indicate conclusively that the change in copy was planned, not fortuitous, and that the problems that resulted had been foreseen. (Indeed, the circumstances in which a sheet from I could have been accidentally inserted in III are difficult to conceive.) It follows that the only purpose of this change in copy was to remove the III religious and political revisions in favour of a return to the original text. That in a sense the baby got thrown out with the bath-water and the desirable III stylistic revisions were correspondingly sacrificed can scarcely have been designed and must have resulted from some accidental misinterpretation of whatever was the precise form of the instructions that Fielding gave. It is plausible to conjecture that Fielding did not himself provide the extra first-edition sheet O intercalated with the marked III copy he was sending to Millar for the fourth edition. Precise instructions, indeed, would have requested only the use of I copy to replace III starting, say, with the paragraph 'Events of this Nature' (477.7) on line 3 of III sig. N5, page 273, and continuing to line 5 and the end of a paragraph with 'Duke at *Bridgewater*' (478.28–9) on sig. N6, page 275, or at the most starting three lines lower with 'I escaped, together with Mr. *Watson*'. However, what instructions Fielding gave can never be known, for it is clear that whatever their nature Strahan seems to have misunderstood Millar's conjectured provision of first-edition sheet O and hence had it set up entire. (See Appendix, pp. lxxx ff.)

In a situation of this complexity textual critics recognize a double authority.[1] For an unmodernized edition the most authentic form of what are known as the 'accidentals' of a text—that is, the spelling, punctuation, capitalization, word-division, and such typographical matters as the use of italicized words—can be transmitted only in the document that lies nearest to the lost holograph, that is, in the first edition, the one printing that was set direct from manuscript. An editor will understand that the first edition by no means represented a diplomatic reprint of the manuscript and that in many respects the accidentals are a mixture of the author's and the compositor's. But whatever the relative impurity, the first edition stands nearest to the author's

---

[1] Sir Walter Greg, 'The Rationale of Copy-Text', *Studies in Bibliography*, iii (1950), 19–36, reprinted in *W. W. Greg: Collected Papers*, ed. J. C. Maxwell (Oxford, 1966), pp. 374–91, is the main authority. See also F. Bowers, 'Current Theories of Copy-Text, with an Illustration from Dryden', *MP*, xlviii (1950), 12–20; 'Established Texts and Definitive Editions', *PQ*, xli (1962), 1–17; and 'Textual Criticism', in *The Aims and Methods of Scholarship in Modern Languages and Literatures*, ed. J. Thorpe (Modern Language Association of America, 2nd ed., revised, 1970), pp. 29–54.

own characteristics and represents the only basic authority in these matters that has been preserved for the texture in which his words were originally clothed. It may be remarked that Fielding was accustomed, as authors still are, to the styling of his work by the press; but since we have evidence that he read proof for at least a good part of the *Tom Jones* first edition, he had the opportunity, if he chose to exercise it, to alter any compositorial intervention that did not suit his convictions.

On the other hand, when he sent the marked-up pages of the third edition to the press as copy for the revised fourth, there is no solid evidence that in any major respect or with any frequency he altered the accidentals that had passed his scrutiny in the original first-edition proof-sheets. The odds do not favour an author of the time tinkering extensively with the accidentals of printed copy so long as his meaning had not been altered as a result of house-styling, and all seemed reasonably in order. Thus despite the numerous authoritative changes that Fielding made in the words, or 'substantives', for the fourth edition, the few authoritative corrections or alterations in the accidental styling that evidence suggests actually took place do not alter the fact that the vast majority of the changes in the accidentals represent merely the normal compositorial differences characteristic of reprints of the time.

In this respect, in the fourth edition the authority of the substantives and of the accidentals splits. Given the thoroughgoing nature of the literary revision, almost all of the changes in the words must be accepted as authorial, whereas almost all of the changes in the accidental texture must be labelled as compositorial and hence unauthoritative. Under these circumstances Sir Walter Greg's classic theory of copy-text must hold. That is, a critical editor chooses as his copy-text—the basic authority for his old-spelling edition—that document which can be isolated as the supreme authority for the accidentals. In this respect, then, he comes as close as documentary evidence permits to the desirable reproduction of authorial characteristics in spelling, pointing, and the like. In this authoritative texture of the first edition, then, he inserts those verbal and accidental changes in later editions that in his estimate represent authorial correction or revision, and not compositorial variation and corruption. By this procedure an editor of *Tom Jones* does not substantially reproduce the exact marked copy that was given to the press for the fourth edition, for this was the third edition which is at one step removed from the authority of the first-edition accidentals. Instead, by choosing the first edition as copy-text and then substituting for its substantives those revisions in the fourth edition that are considered to be authorial, not compositorial, an editor attempts to reproduce what would have been the characteristics of the marked copy if Fielding had annotated the first instead of the third edition. That this procedure reconstructs a purely hypothetical printer's copy for the fourth edition is of no consequence in comparison to the virtues that are achieved in wedding the authority of the first-edition accidentals with the general authority of the revised fourth-edition substantives. This operation is a critical process almost exclusively in which the editor shoulders his proper responsibility to separate the author's intended alterations from the verbal corruption that inevitably accompanies the transmission of a text in a reprint. Unfortunately, there is no short cut. The fourth edition, although it represents Fielding's only substantial revision, cannot be the supreme authority for the substantives that the first edition represents for the accidentals. As the appendix Historical Collation demonstrates, Fielding almost invariably allowed the third edition verbal errors to stand in the fourth, and to these the IV compositors added their own share of corruption. Despite its authoritative new revisions, therefore, the fourth has numerically more verbal errors than any preceding edition.[1]

When the textual situation as in *Tom Jones* dictates this critical treatment of the copy-text, the main editorial problem centres on the identification of authorial revision. Here certain

[1] Earlier editors have been content to reprint either the third or the fourth edition. Reprints of the fourth present accidentals that are at two removes from those of the authoritative first edition and in the substantives faithfully follow not only the corruptions of the fourth-edition compositors but also the numerous unauthoritative substantive variants of the third edition repeated in the fourth. The day has long since passed when anyone could seriously argue that these had been 'approved' by Fielding since he failed to alter them back to the first-edition readings. Reprints of the third edition ignore the whole important range of Fielding's only major revision of the novel. The present edition is the first to appear that by a bibliographical and linguistic study of the relationship of the texts to authority attempts to segregate the authentic fourth-edition substantive revisions and to weed out the various errors in this important edition while at the same time presenting Fielding's purified substantive final text within the framework of the more authoritative first-edition accidentals.

logical rules of textual criticism are of assistance. That is, the part is always surveyed in relation to the whole so that the circumstances surrounding the production of any given edition can be used as evidence, or at least as suggesting an editorial 'climate of opinion', when an individual reading is under scrutiny. It is simple to discard automatically all substantive variants, other than necessary corrections, that originated in the third edition with which Fielding had nothing to do but which were inadvertently followed in the fourth. It is no longer possible to argue that by passing them without alteration Fielding in any sense 'approved' them and gave them authority. Correspondingly, since he never supervised the copy for the terminal second edition, all of its variants may be discarded that do not represent necessary corrections. Thus the careful and extensive revision of the fourth edition, as an entity, shifts the weight of critical opinion in favour of most of its altered readings. Since so many are manifestly authorial, the 'indifferent' variant is more likely to be the author's too, than a compositorial corruption. This would be especially true, of course, if Fielding had read proof on the sheets of the fourth edition, but we have no evidence that he did; indeed the possibility is remote and not to be considered seriously.

The present editor, therefore, has admitted all unique fourth-edition substantive variants as authorial save only recognizable printers' errors and indifferent variants like 'his' for the more definite 'this' that run counter to Fielding's normal style and to the current of revision in the opposite direction in IV of just such small matters of idiom or usage. A certain number of semi-orthographic variants have been admitted when they have appeared in the errata or are so consistent as to be improbable as stylistic variants to be imputed to a number of compositors and thus are taken to represent the author's changed ideas of purity of verbal forms; e.g. 'torn' for 'tore', 'borne' for 'bore', 'Counsel' for 'Council', 'arrant' for 'errant', 'art' for dialect 'at' in roman but not in italic, and the like. When variation is present in the text but Fielding's own forms are unknown and an insufficient number of appearances prevents an attempt to assess changes as the work of author or of compositors, the variation has been retained, as in 'desarts' and 'deserts'. There is no question in the editor's mind that in the fourth edition Fielding was concerned to modernize certain of his older-fashioned forms present in the first edition;

but it is also true that the general trend of reprints is towards modernization, and hence a distinct effort has been made to collect the available evidence and to bring its cumulative weight to bear on each individual case. For example, all evidence points towards Fielding's invariable use of the form 'hath'; the sporadic modernizations in IV to 'has' indicate not Fielding's modernization but the compositors' and thus have been rejected as unauthoritative fourth-edition departures from copy. In this process of decision the small amount of Fielding's own holograph writing preserved has been drawn on for suggestions. The critical and linguistic tests that have been applied to sift the unique fourth-edition variants may perhaps have excluded a handful of Fielding's changes for which adequate reasons were hard to find, but they have also succeeded in barring a larger number of printing-house errors, whether of sophistication or of inadvertence, that demonstrably plague the later transmission in print of any text, and which in *Tom Jones* cannot be imputed to Fielding's authority. On the whole, however, the treatment has been conservative and in cases of doubt the general authority of the fourth edition has been given the odds. The Wesleyan edition, therefore, offers an eclectic text that in its representation of the author's final intentions for his novel is as pure as the logic of textual criticism and a study of the substance and expression of Fielding's thought can produce within the capacities of the present editor.

Two further problems concern the copy-text. Since 1908 the bibliographical facts about twelve cancel leaves in the first edition have been known,[1] and although several descriptions of this edition have been published,[2] no further facts have been discovered. However, one recorded copy, no. 850 in the

---

[1] These were first printed in the anonymous 'News for Bibliophiles' in *The Nation*, lxxxvii (24 December 1908), 624.

[2] The most complete is David Randall's in *The Publisher's Weekly*, 21 March 1942, pp. 1200–2. The cancellans leaves and the area of their text within the page-line references are as follows:

VOLUME I, sigs. B9–10, pp. 17–20 (42.1–44.31) [CHAPTER IV . . . informed him].

VOLUME II, sigs. B4–5, pp. 7–10 (154.10–157.5) [from Nature . . . Dimple which the]; sig. N12, pp. 287–8 (302.24–303.20) [was he cured . . . Father of *Sophia*.].

VOLUME III, sigs. H8–10, pp. 147–52 (402.24–406.29) [with Assent...the Surprizing.']; sig. M3, pp. 233–4 (450.12–451.12) [Yearnings . . . This was pre-]; sig. Q11, pp. 345–6 (510.14–511.10) [It was . . . fine Gentlemen there.]. [*Note 2 continued overleaf*

Rothschild Library (now at Trinity College, Cambridge), preserves the slit leaves of the three *cancellanda* originals of sigs. H8–10 in Volume III.[1] A recently acquired copy in the British Museum preserves the slit *cancellandum* leaf sig. N8 in Volume v. The facts of both have been recorded in Appendix VI and, for the substantives, in the Historical Collation. The second problem touches the treatment of the sole authorial revisions in the third edition, made in sheet O of the first edition as printer's copy for the third, described above. According to the working hypothesis adopted by the present editor, in the revised fourth edition Fielding intended to remove as an injudicious substitute the long passage that he had written out in manuscript as a replacement in the third edition for the Man-of-the-Hill's religious and political opinions as initially printed in the first edition and to return to the first-edition version. Further, according to this hypothesis, through some misunderstanding of the instructions to replace this one passage, the printer instead reprinted in the fourth edition the whole of first-edition sheet O, thereby removing the various literary and stylistic revisions present in the revised copy of this sheet used for the third edition. It seems clear that these revisions had nothing to do with the major block passage that came to be questioned and that their removal in the fourth edition was an inadvertent error. Hence the editor has chosen the eclectic method of endeavouring to reproduce Fielding's intentions by respecting his decision to print the original first-edition Monmouth passage as in his revised fourth edition but also by restoring the separate third-edition stylistic revisions in this sheet that belong in Fielding's full revision of the *Tom Jones* text. That he intended to disown these is inconceivable. A problem is certainly raised whether what appears to be the intention to restore the first-edition text of the Monmouth passage applied as well to the restoration of the long cut made in III for purely literary reasons at 482.20–483.6, continued at 483.10–483.27. This cut in III removed the Old Man-of-the-Hill's crotchety comments

VOLUME IV, sig. B1, pp. 1–2 (523.1–525.6) [BOOK X . . . must acknowledge to].

VOLUME V, sig. N8, pp. 279–80 (824.5–825.8) [the rest . . . sur shee is].

[1] This copy was purchased at the sale of 27 April 1936 from Sotheby's *Catalogue of the Valuable Library Formed by the Late Frank L. James*, in which *cancellandum* sig. H10ᵛ was reproduced.

on his travels about foreign nations and softened some elements of misanthropy in his present life. Whether the first-edition version deepens his character or else the third-edition cuts remove elements of caricature may well be a matter of opinion. The question, then, is whether Fielding altered his mind about these cuts at the time that he chose to revert to the first edition for the political and religious situation. No certain answer to this question can be produced, for the cuts could have been restored as readily by accident as by design. Since the case is almost completely moot, the editor has opted for consistency in the treatment of the two major sets of revisions and has restored both to the first-edition original form, retaining only the stylistic revisions of the third edition as in keeping with the intentions elsewhere of the fourth. Something may be said for consistency in treating the two blocks of third-edition alterations in this manner. The rise in the emotional fervour of the revised political-religious material in the third is accompanied by a decrease in the Old Man's eccentricity caused by the cuts; thus when the tenor of the original is restored for the Monmouth passage in the fourth edition, it can be argued that, as a balance, the cuts should also be restored.

As the final operation in the recovery of this Fielding text the editor has corrected the accidentals of the first-edition copy-text whenever the change has seemed desirable as restoring Fielding's general stylistic habits (so far as these can be determined) and achieving some logical uniformity from the inconsistent treatment given the manuscript by at least four and perhaps more partly identifiable compositors of varying habits. Whenever the second, third, or fourth editions restored what in the opinion of the editor was a close approximation of the assumed manuscript reading, the emendation has been noted from its earliest source, even though the accidentals—like the substantives—of the second and third editions can have no authority. Some few accidental changes have been adopted from the fourth edition which may hypothetically represent Fielding's own corrections but if not are at least desirable and even necessary. These changes have been made cautiously and in some small part with the convenience of the reader in view when marked anomalies might have distracted the attention, particularly in the case of the highly erratic punctuation of dialogue in the first and indeed in all the early editions. Correspondingly, on his own authority the editor has made some alterations to remove patent error or striking inconsistency which had been allowed to stand in the early editions, so long as the changes conform to Fielding's usual characteristics or to the general standards of the copy-text itself. In this process the editor has not tried to achieve an unnatural consistency in spelling, capitalization, or punctuation that would involve real rewriting: wanting the manuscript, no editor could determine whether in many cases the compositors or Fielding himself was responsible for the casual variation that is normal in the period. On the other hand, as has been remarked, the extremely erratic punctuation of dialogue has been normalized in respect to the use and placement of quotation marks according to what has seemed to be the best compositorial usage in the copy-text, the position of other punctuation to round brackets and to dashes has also been made uniform to correspond to the majority usage, occasional questions of hyphenated word-division have been adjusted according to the prevailing mode of the copy-text, and the relatively few appearances of the spelling 'Hero' have been changed to the common 'Heroe', which is also a spelling blessed by Fielding's holograph.[1]

With certain exceptions, all accidental as well as substantive alterations have been recorded in the List of Emendations so that a critic may reconstruct the copy-text in essential detail except for the purely formal matters that may be thought of most properly as typographical. The following editorial changes have been made silently. (1) The running quotation marks in the left margin have been omitted and quotations have been indicated according to the modern custom. Throughout, missing opening or closing quotation marks have been supplied silently but all other added quotation marks, especially about indirect discourse and other dialogue have always been noted when the running marginal quotation marks have not suggested their presence. The few double quotation marks have been silently made into the prevailing single but single have been made into double when they occur within single quotation marks. The faulty placement of quotation marks, especially in the work of one compositor who was inclined to add them after the indication of the speaker, has been corrected. (2) The placement of punctuation in relation to

[1] This important poetic holograph was reprinted by Isabel Grundy, 'New Verse by Henry Fielding', *PMLA*, lxxxvii (1972), 213-45.

quotation marks has been normalized according to the usual practice of the copy-text, and full stops have been silently supplied at the ending of sentences before dashes when the construction was obvious. Doubtful cases of sentence ending have been noted as emendations. (3) The lengths of dashes, whether as one-em or as two-em, have been made uniform according to their function and, likewise according to their function, the spacing about dashes has been silently normalized. (4) The copy-text apostrophe-s genitive in roman has been altered to italic when present in italicized names. (5) Accents in the Latin have been removed and abbreviations expanded. Unjoined 'oe' and 'ae' have been treated as digraphs. (6) The usual abbreviations such as 'Chap.' for 'Chapter' have been expanded and full stops after headings removed. (7) The fount of punctuation is normalized without regard for the variable practice of the original. Pointing within an italic passage is italicized; but pointing following an italicized word that is succeeded by roman text is silently placed in roman. All wrong-fount punctuation is silently corrected.

The intent has been throughout to contrive a reading text by removal of typographical and purely formal anomalies while yet preserving every essential feature of the old-spelling copy-text.

## 2. THE APPARATUS

All the textual apparatus is placed in appendices where it may be consulted at leisure by those who wish to analyse the total evidence on which the present text has been established. In the List of Emendations all alterations in the copy-text not noted as in the categories of silent changes are presented. Since the purpose of this list is to present at a view the editorial departures from the copy-text first edition, only the earliest source of the adopted variant is recorded together with the history of the copy-text reading up to its accepted emendation in the earliest source. The subsequent history of all substantive variants will be found in the Historical Collation. As early sources of emendation, only the second, third, and fourth editions are listed. Other emendations are assigned to W, representing the present edition, whether or not they may have originated here or with some preceding editor. The basic note provides, first, the page-line reference (all lines on the page save for the running-titles being counted) and the precise form of the emended reading in the present text, except that succeeding punctuation when not part of the emendation is ignored. Following the square bracket comes the identification of the earliest source of the emendation in the editions collated. A semicolon succeeds this notation, and following this appears the rejected copy-text reading with the sigla of the editions that provide its history up to the point of emendation. Arbitrary symbols and other sigla are described in the head-note to the List. An asterisk preceding the page-line number indicates that the emendation (or failure to emend when the notation *stet* appears) is discussed in the Textual Notes.

The second Appendix contains a brief series of Textual Notes that discuss certain of the emendations or else decisions to retain the copy-text readings.

The third Appendix provides the critic with the means of reconstructing certain questions of word-division. The first list enables a reader to quote the copy-text form with confidence in all cases when the Wesleyan edition has broken a hyphenated compound, or possible compound, at the end of its line. In short, in the present edition all hyphenated words broken at the end of a line of text are to be read as single words unless specifically noted in this list as hyphenated in the copy-text. The second list notes the editorial decision that has been made about the hyphenation or non-hyphenation of compounds broken at the end of a line in the copy-text. Whether or not these are to be read as hyphenated forms may involve editorial decision that verges on emendation and it should not be made silently.

The Historical Collation forming the fourth Appendix keys its readings to the present edited text, not to the precise readings of the first-edition copy-text, and is confined to the four editions published in Fielding's lifetime. No later edition has any authority. This collation contains (1) all rejected first-edition substantive and semi-substantive readings listed as Emendations in the first Appendix, with the record carried through to the fourth edition. (2) All rejected substantive and semi-substantive variants in the second, third, and fourth editions. Excluded here are typographical misprints. Included, however, are all rejected substantive readings in the three *cancellanda* leaves H8–10 in the third volume of the first edition within the range of 402.24–406.29, and of the similar leaf N8 in the fifth volume (824.5–825.8). In this Historical Collation the reading of a collated edition is to be taken as agreeing with that of the present text to the left of the bracket unless a variant is specifically recorded for it following the bracket. The accidental form of the word to the left of the bracket is that of the present edited text which in the case of emendation will usually represent the form of the word in the edition from which it was drawn if it agrees with the custom of the first edition. To the right of the bracket the accidental form of the reading will be that of the earliest edition noted: variation in the accidentals of later editions from this are not recorded. In all cases only punctuation that is part of the variation itself is recorded along with the verbal reading.

In the fifth Appendix appear the bibliographical descriptions of the four collated editions, with a note on the Murphy edition of 1762.

Finally, all variations from the first-edition cancellans leaves of Volume III, sigs. H8–10, in the original *cancellanda* of the Rothschild unique example at Trinity College, Cambridge, are listed in the sixth Appendix, including a deleted anecdote about Vanbrugh's *Relapse*, as well as the rewritten *cancellandum* leaf N8 in Volume v in the British Museum copy.

### 3. COLLATION

In the preparation of the present text the following four copies of the first edition have been collated: British Museum (C. 71. cc. 7), Yale University (Fielding Coll., 749h 1949), University of Virginia (McG E. 1749. F54. 285141), and University of Virginia (PR 3454. H5. 1749. 590763). The last two were compared on the Hinman Collator, the first two by sight against photographs. The second edition was collated against the first from photographs of Harvard University's copy (EC 85 T3255. 22. 749f), the third from photographs of the British Museum copy (12604. aa. 11), and the fourth from photographs of the British Museum copy (1206. b. 5–8). The second edition was independently collated against the first on three occasions by different persons, the third against the first similarly, and the fourth against the first four times by four different persons. The few press-variants discovered in the collation of the four copies of the first edition have been listed under Emendations, with full details of provenience added in Appendix V.

#### 4. APPENDIX

Instead of the hypothesis presented above (p. lxix), a purely mechanical explanation for the undoubted anomaly of the use of unmarked sheet O from I in its entirety in setting up IV would certainly be preferable, but none can be advanced that does not create fatal objections. For example, as remarked above, one could speculate that before the third-edition sheet N was printed Fielding had indeed revised a copy of I, and that these annotations were later transferred in the printing shop to a copy of III in order to permit the compositors of IV to set a paginal reprint of III. One could then speculate that he had earlier abstracted sheet O from this revision and sent it to Millar to make in III what he regarded as the urgent alterations in the political and religious discourse of the Man-of-the-Hill's narrative. Then when the revised copy was required for the fourth edition, he gave Millar his revised I sheets, expecting that the annotated sheet O used for setting III would be inserted. But, as commonly happened, this sheet had been destroyed after the printing of III and hence was not available. In these circumstances, finally, one could then conjecture that, coming upon the missing sheet O in the revised I copy that was being used to mark up a set of the III sheets, Strahan simply substituted a spare sheet of O from the first edition. Such a hypothesis would neatly explain on a mechanical basis the sudden appearance of unrevised copy in IV. It would have important textual and critical consequences, also, since it would upset the hypothesis above that the return to the original version of the religious matter was designed by Fielding and it would substitute an inadvertent error to explain the unintentional appearance in IV of the original text. The speculation is indeed so tempting that it is a pity it will not stand up under scrutiny. The first weakness is the need to assume that by March of 1749, perhaps little more than a month after writing Book XVIII, Fielding had revised copy at least as far as the end of Book VIII and perhaps further. The second weakness is the need to assume that (*a*) Fielding did not know of the start of the third edition until it was well along and then troubled himself to send Millar only a single revised sheet, or (*b*) Fielding had a preliminary revision under way but preferred to finish and perfect it for a fully revised fourth edition (except for the urgently wanted

Monmouth revision) instead of improving the third edition with the revisions already available. This last is possible, of course, although the extensive stylistic changes in sheet O as printed in III fail to encourage a view that Fielding had not revised sheets of I with sufficient thoroughness to wish them printed in III. One would be forced to the alternative position that he had not completed the revision and preferred to wait, except for the Man-of-the-Hill passage, to present a complete new edition to the public. Again this is possible; Fielding was concerned with his literary reputation even though there is no indication that he would profit financially above the copyright payment by making a revision.

Still, one serious logical difficulty remains. We know from the bibliographical evidence of the compression of the text in sheet N of the fourth edition that the IV compositor had to take special measures to fit the text of the original sheet O of I into the III paginal pattern so as to resume page-for-page setting from III with Book ix. If, as hypothesized, in preparing the copy for IV by transferring the annotations from I to a copy of III, Strahan's workman had come to the missing sheet O, the thought-process is obscure that would lead him to insert an un-marked sheet O from I into the marked III copy for the com-positors. The almost inevitable thing to do, it would seem, would be merely to omit any annotation of the III sheet N at this point (no copy being available for the purpose) and to resume the transfer of revisions with I sheet P. This is the real sticking point, for it seems impossible to conceive why Millar or Strahan would deliberately create difficulties when there would seem to be no virtue in following unmarked sheet O of I instead of the sheet N copy of III. (Bibliographical evidence forbids the most improbable speculation that I sheet O was collated against the III text and its variants transferred to III. In this section the printer's copy for IV is definitely I.)

Under these circumstances the present editor takes it that fewer logical difficulties are encountered in the hypothesis that Fielding designed a return to the I text for the lengthy passage because of the critical reasons adduced by Professor Battestin, and that through some misunderstanding a copy of the I sheet O was used throughout instead of for the N5–6 III passage alone. Against a mechanical explanation, no matter how tempting, is the pyramiding of hypotheses that would force one of necessity to conjecture, first, that Fielding started to revise his work in the first edition (not using third-edition copy) and had progressed almost half-way through the task in about a month; second, that he failed to supply more than one sheet of this revision for the third edition (although this is a matter that can be rationalized); and, thirdly, that under inexplicable circumstances, because the originally revised sheet O was not available when, conjecturally, Millar or Strahan's people were transferring the I annotations to third-edition copy, an uncorrected sheet of O was substituted as printer's copy. Yet human aberration can take extreme forms and it is well if the case need not rest on probability, no matter how strong this probability may appear. Hence another consideration may be advanced. In fact, small but sufficient evidence is present that Fielding himself was marking the third-edition copy used to set the fourth edition and that annotations from the first were not being transferred in the shop to make up printer's copy for IV. Since there is no argument about the fact that generally an annotated copy of III was the printer's copy for IV, the usual bibliographical links signify nothing. That is, whether or not III disagreed with I it would pass its printed reading on to IV in all cases where its pages had not been annotated. The exception, of course, would be typographical errors and misprints so obvious that the IV correction of these back to their original I reading could be attributed to the compositor and not necessarily to Fielding's own annotation of the III copy. That is, when in IV the III misprint 'at' for 'as' is returned to I 'as' at II. 14. 25, or III 'betry' to 'betray' at II. 106. 22, or III 'she is one the best of Women' to 'one of the best' at v. 177. 6, no evidence is provided to identify the corrector, whether Fielding or the IV compositor. We cannot take it that any workman charged with transferring handwritten annotations from sheets of I to III would be reading the text of III in search of printed errors. Thus if there had been this transfer of annotations, at I. 146. 3 we should need to conjecture that it was the IV compositor who correctly guessed that III 'Adversity' should read 'Adversary' and that it was not Fielding correcting the error in the III copy; and so with III 'this' for 'his' at II. 57. 23, and so on. These readings can scarcely be used as bibliographical evidence since they are so completely subject to personal opinion about the probabilities that a compositor would recognize them as errors. This caveat holds as well for such a situation as at v. 21. 2 where III reads 'Mrs. *Fitzpatrick* made many Apologies for early, abrupt Visit' and IV reads 'an early, abrupt Visit' whereas the original I was 'this early, abrupt Visit'.

The only readings that may be allowed as evidence are those unique III corruptions that make such sufficient sense as to lead with general conviction to the view that IV variants returning to I must necessarily represent Fielding's own corrections of the III copy since a compositor would be expected to pass them without alteration. The III variants rejected by IV are almost exclusively confined to obvious misprints owing to the almost universal acceptance by IV of the III corruptions that made sufficient sense. Thus there are only two cases—and we are fortunate to have these—in which IV altered in an authoritative way a III unique variant by returning to the I printed reading when little or no question could obtain that the III reading seemed quite acceptable. The first of these is not wholly demonstrable as evidence because of the remote possibility that a compositor might also interfere with the grammar at vi. 194. 27 and might as well as Fielding alter III 'I would yet be wanting to my Duty' in IV so that it fortuitously agreed with I 'I should yet be wanting'. But earlier on the same page occurs a reading that makes perfect sense in either version and would have required the hand of the author to set right. Here, at vi. 194. 13, in Thwackum's letter to Allworthy III reads, 'I am not at all surprized at hearing from your worthy Nephew a fresh Instance of the Villany of Mr. *Jones* the Atheist's young Pupil. I shall not wonder at any Murders he may commit.' Here both I and IV read 'the Villany of Mr. *Square* the Atheist's young Pupil'. The sophistication of the III compositor is a natural one since he assumed that 'the Atheist's young Pupil' was the phrase that was in apposition to the name, in which case '*Square*' would be an error. However, it is clear to us that I is right (in some part aided perhaps by the lack of a comma after '*Square*'), that only 'the Atheist's' is in apposition to '*Square*', and that the sense is *the villainy of the young pupil of Mr. Square the atheist.* But the lack of parenthetical commas about 'the Atheist's' makes the phrase ambiguous and readily misunderstood, and the alteration in III of the fancied wrong name is natural enough, the result creating perfect sense. It would be difficult indeed to argue that the IV compositor reading the III text here would take it upon himself to re-order the syntax and restore the name of *'Square'* when *'Jones'* would seem to be the perfectly natural reference. In short, only an author—in this case recalling what he had originally written—would make the return change from III *'Jones'* to I *'Square'*, and on this evidence for the authorial annotation of III, perhaps supplemented by the alteration mentioned at vi. 194. 27, the case may comfortably rest. This being so, the hypothesis that Fielding revised I sheets but that his annotations were transferred in the printing house to III printer's copy collapses, and with it collapses any possibility of the otherwise reasonably plausible mechanical explanation for the sudden appearance in the III printer's copy for IV of the unrevised sheet O from I. The hypothesis given in the text above for the misunderstanding of Fielding's instructions about a return to the I version, reducing the religious polemics that had been intensified by revision in III, would appear to be vindicated and with it is vindicated Professor Battestin's critical explanation for Fielding's reasons behind the return to the I version of the text.

FREDSON BOWERS

# THE

# HISTORY

## OF

# TOM JONES,

## A

# FOUNDLING.

In SIX VOLUMES.

By HENRY FIELDING, Eſq;

——*Mores hominum multorum vidit.*——

LONDON:

Printed for A. MILLAR, over-againſt
Catharine-ſtreet in the Strand.
MDCCXLIX.

To the HONOURABLE

# George Lyttleton, *Esq*;[1]

## One of the Lords Commissioners of
## the TREASURY

SIR,

NOTWITHSTANDING your constant Refusal, when I have asked Leave to prefix your Name to this Dedication, I must still insist on my Right to desire your Protection of this Work.

To you, Sir, it is owing that this History[2] was ever begun. It was by your Desire that I first thought of such a Composition.

---

[1] *Note to title-page.* Horace, *Ars Poetica*, 141–2: 'Sing, Muse, for me the man who on Troy's fall / Saw the wide world, its ways and cities all'—trans. H. R. Fairclough, Loeb Classical Library (1929). Advising the poet to begin his work simply and modestly, Horace here cites the example of Homer, paraphrasing the exordium of the *Odyssey*. Fielding used the same motto in *The Champion* (20 March 1739/40).

[1] George Lyttelton (1709–73) of Hagley Park, Worcestershire; later first Baron Lyttelton (1757). When the Pelham administration was formed in 1744, Lyttelton was appointed to the Treasury. An appropriate model for Squire Allworthy, he was widely esteemed for his piety, benevolence, and taste. Though Lyttelton was himself an author of modest abilities—e.g., *Letters from a Persian in England* (1735), *Observations on the Conversion and Apostleship of St. Paul* (1747), *Dialogues of the Dead* (1760)—in letters he is perhaps best remembered as the friend of Pope and the patron of Thomson and Fielding. His close and lasting association with Fielding probably began at Eton in the early 1720s; certainly, they were on the friendliest terms in 1733, the year of Fielding's unpublished poem, 'An Epistle to Mr. Lyttelton', censuring Pope for his satire of Lady Mary Wortley Montagu (see Isobel Grundy, 'New Verse by Henry Fielding', *PMLA*, lxxxvii (1972), 213–45). Together with Pitt, Chesterfield, and Dodington—to name only the most prominent of those who befriended Fielding—Lyttelton was a member of the Opposition during Walpole's last years as prime minister, when Fielding was supporting the 'Patriot' cause in his plays and in *The Champion* (1739–41). Throughout this period, if one may judge from Fielding's compliments to Lyttelton in the poems 'Of True Greatness' (1741) and 'Liberty' (1743, in *Miscellanies*, i), relations between the two men remained cordial.

In the months preceding the publication of *Tom Jones*, Fielding's obligations to Lyttelton, whom he praised in *The Jacobite's Journal* (16 July 1748) as 'almost the only Patron which the Muses at present can boast of among the Great', were widely known and jeeringly remarked by their enemies. The writers of *Old England* (5 March, 12 November 1748) asserted that Lyttelton had hired his friend to edit *The Jacobite's Journal* as an administration organ and had arranged to distribute the paper gratis throughout the kingdom. According to Horace Walpole, it was owing to Lyttelton's influence that Fielding was

*Notes 1 and 2 continued overleaf.*

So many Years have since past, that you may have, perhaps,
forgotten this Circumstance: But your Desires are to me in the
Nature of Commands; and the Impression of them is never to
be erased from my Memory.

Again, Sir, without your Assistance this History had never
been completed. Be not startled at the Assertion. I do not intend
to draw on you the Suspicion of being a Romance Writer. I mean
no more than that I partly owe to you my Existence during great
Part of the Time which I have employed in composing it:
another Matter which it may be necessary to remind you of; since
there are certain Actions of which you are apt to be extremely
forgetful; but of these I hope I shall always have a better Memory
than yourself.

Lastly, it is owing to you that the History appears what it now
is. If there be in this Work, as some have been pleased to say, a
stronger Picture of a truly benevolent Mind than is to be found
in any other, who that knows you, and a particular Acquaintance
of yours,[1] will doubt whence that Benevolence hath been copied?
The World will not, I believe, make me the Compliment of
thinking I took it from myself. I care not: This they shall own,

appointed Justice of the Peace for Middlesex (see the General Introduction, p. xxix, n. 3).
And it was Lyttelton's enthusiastic commendation of *Tom Jones* that stimulated public
interest in the novel before it was published (see the General Introduction, p. xlvi).

For further discussion of Lyttelton and his relations with Fielding, see Rose Mary Davis,
*The Good Lord Lyttelton* (Bethlehem, Pa., 1939). For other allusions to Lyttelton in *Tom
Jones*, see below, pp. 405, n. 2; 687; 925, n. 2.

[2] On Fielding's association of his new species of fiction with the genre of history, see
below, p. 489, n. 2.

[1] Ralph Allen (1693–1764) of Bath, philanthropist and patron of letters. Though of
humble birth, Allen made a fortune by improving the system of cross-country posts in
England and Wales, and then purchased the valuable stone quarries at Combe Down. With
this stone Allen and the architect John Wood transformed Bath into a new Roman city and
built Allen's own magnificent Palladian mansion at Prior Park, Widcombe (see p. 42, n. 1;
613, n. 1). For his various charities—especially his donations to hospitals, such as the
General Hospital at Bath and the Foundling Hospital and St. Bartholomew's in London—
Allen was celebrated as the very type of 'the Benevolent Man'. (See, for example, the anonymous poem 'Of the Characters of Men. An Epistle to Ralph Allen, Esq.' [1750].) Among
men of letters, Pope and Richardson were his good friends; but from the time of their first
meeting in 1741, Allen took a particular beneficent interest in Fielding and his family.
Fielding, in turn, warmly acknowledged these favours, praising Allen in *Joseph Andrews*
(1742; III. i, vi), *A Journey from This World to the Next* (1743; I. v), and *The Covent-
Garden Journal* (11 April 1752), and to Allen he dedicated his last novel, *Amelia* (1751).
For an authoritative biography, see Benjamin Boyce, *The Benevolent Man: A Life of Ralph
Allen of Bath* (Cambridge, Mass., 1967). For other allusions to Allen in *Tom Jones*, see
below, pp. 38, n. 1; 42, n. 1; 403–4; 613, n. 1; 687.

that the two Persons from whom I have taken it, that is to say, two of the best and worthiest Men in the World, are strongly and zealously my Friends. I might be contented with this, and yet my Vanity will add a third to the Number; and him one of the greatest and noblest, not only in his Rank, but in every public and private Virtue. But here whilst my Gratitude for the princely Benefactions of the Duke of *Bedford*[1] bursts from my Heart, you must forgive my reminding you, that it was you who first recommended me to the Notice of my Benefactor.

And what are your Objections to the Allowance of the Honour which I have sollicited? Why, you have commended the Book so warmly, that you should be ashamed of reading your Name before the Dedication. Indeed, Sir, if the Book itself doth not make you ashamed of your Commendations, nothing that I can here write will, or ought. I am not to give up my Right to your Protection and Patronage, because you have commended my Book: For though I acknowledge so many Obligations to you, I do not add this to the Number; in which Friendship, I am convinced, hath so little Share: Since that can neither biass your Judgment, nor pervert your Integrity. An Enemy may at any Time obtain your Commendation by only deserving it; and the utmost which the

---

[1] John Russell (1710–71), fourth Duke of Bedford, succeeded to the dukedom in 1732. He had been associated with Lyttelton in Opposition, working at first against Walpole and then, after the Minister's resignation in 1742, against the Hanoverian policies of Carteret. When the Broad-Bottom coalition was formed in December 1744, Bedford was appointed First Lord of the Admiralty; on 12 February 1748 he replaced Chesterfield as Secretary of State for the Southern Department, an office which he held until 1751. He was Lord Justice in 1745, 1748, 1750, and in 1746 was appointed Warden of the New Forest (see below, p. 259, n. 4). Among his public benefactions, Bedford was Head of the Corporation of the Foundling Hospital, receiving the royal charter from Captain Coram in 1739 (see below, p. 761, n. 3).

The personal favours he bestowed upon Fielding began at least as early as 1743, when Bedford's name appeared among the subscribers to the *Miscellanies*. The 'princely Benefactions' to which the novelist refers in the present passage were doubtless more substantial and of more recent date. Since, however, the first two volumes of *Tom Jones* had been issued as early as November 1748, the reference here—contrary to what most scholars have assumed—could not be to the best-known instance of Bedford's generosity to Fielding: not until 13 December did Fielding write to his patron requesting the lease of certain properties having a rental value of £100, the gift of which made it possible for him to qualify as Justice of the Peace for Middlesex (see Cross, ii. 96–8). Some years later, in the Introduction to the *Journal of a Voyage to Lisbon* (1755), Fielding acknowledged further obligations to his 'great Patron', who granted him a yearly pension out of the public service-money. For complimentary references to Bedford, see also *The Jacobite's Journal* (30 January and 20 February 1748).

Faults of your Friends can hope for is your Silence; or, perhaps,
if too severely accused, your gentle Palliation.

In short, Sir, I suspect, that your Dislike of public Praise is
your true Objection to granting my Request. I have observed,
that you have, in common with my two other Friends, an Unwillingness to hear the least Mention of your own Virtues; that,
as a great Poet says of one of you, (he might justly have said it
of all three) you

*Do Good by stealth, and blush to find it Fame.*[1]

If Men of this Disposition are as careful to shun Applause, as
others are to escape Censure, how just must be your Apprehension of your Character falling into my Hands; since what would
not a Man have Reason to dread, if attacked by an Author who
had received from him Injuries equal to my Obligations to you!

And will not this Dread of Censure increase in Proportion to
the Matter which a Man is conscious of having afforded for it?
If his whole Life, for Instance, should have been one continued
Subject of Satire, he may well tremble when an incensed Satyrist
takes him in Hand. Now, Sir, if we apply this to your modest
Aversion to Panegyric, how reasonable will your Fears of me
appear!

Yet surely you might have gratified my Ambition, from this
single Confidence, that I shall always prefer the Indulgence of
your Inclinations to the Satisfaction of my own. A very strong
Instance of which I shall give you in this Address; in which I
am determined to follow the Example of all other Dedicators, and
will consider not what my Patron really deserves to have written,
but what he will be best pleased to read.

Without further Preface then, I here present you with the
Labours of some Years of my Life. What Merit these Labours
have is already known to yourself. If, from your favourable Judgment, I have conceived some Esteem for them, it cannot be imputed to Vanity; since I should have agreed as implicitly to
your Opinion, had it been given in Favour of any other Man's
Production. Negatively, at least, I may be allowed to say, that

[1] Pope's famous, if somewhat condescending, compliment to Ralph Allen in *Epilogue to
the Satires. Dialogue I* (1738), 135–6: 'Let humble ALLEN, with an aukward Shame, / Do
good by stealth, and blush to find it Fame.' Later in *Tom Jones* (p. 404, n. 4). Fielding
seems again to allude to these lines, this time betraying his irritation at the inadequacy of
Pope's praise.

had I been sensible of any great Demerit in the Work, you are the last Person to whose Protection I would have ventured to recommend it.

From the Name of my Patron, indeed, I hope my Reader will be convinced, at his very Entrance on this Work, that he will find in the whole Course of it nothing prejudicial to the Cause of Religion and Virtue; nothing inconsistent with the strictest Rules of Decency, nor which can offend even the chastest Eye in the Perusal. On the contrary, I declare, that to recommend Goodness and Innocence hath been my sincere Endeavour in this History. This honest Purpose you have been pleased to think I have attained: And to say the Truth, it is likeliest to be attained in Books of this Kind; for an Example is a Kind of Picture, in which Virtue becomes as it were an Object of Sight, and strikes us with an Idea of that Loveliness, which *Plato* asserts[1] there is in her naked Charms.

Besides displaying that Beauty of Virtue which may attract the Admiration of Mankind, I have attempted to engage a stronger Motive to Human Action in her Favour, by convincing Men, that their true Interest directs them to a Pursuit of her. For this Purpose I have shewn, that no Acquisitions of Guilt can compensate the Loss of that solid inward Comfort of Mind, which is the sure Companion of Innocence and Virtue; nor can in the least balance the Evil of that Horror and Anxiety which, in their Room, Guilt introduces into our Bosoms. And again, that as these Acquisitions are in themselves generally worthless, so are the Means to attain them not only base and infamous, but at best incertain, and always full of Danger. Lastly, I have endeavoured strongly to inculcate, that Virtue and Innocence can scarce ever be injured but by Indiscretion; and that it is this alone which often betrays them into the Snares that Deceit and Villainy spread for them. A Moral which I have the more industriously laboured, as the teaching it is, of all others, the likeliest to be attended with

---

[1] Cf. *Phaedrus*, 250d: 'wisdom would arouse terrible love, if such a clear image of it were granted as would come through sight' (trans. H. N. Fowler, Loeb Classical Library, 1914). See also Cicero, *De Finibus*, II. xvi, and *De Officiis*, I. v; and Seneca, *Epistulae Morales*, cxv. 6. The specific notion of the naked charms of Virtue, imaged as a beautiful woman, is only implicit in Plato. Fielding was especially fond of this commonplace: see, for example, *The Champion* (24, 26 January 1739/40) and the essays 'On Conversation' and 'On the Knowledge of the Characters of Men'—both in the *Miscellanies* (1743). For a later allusion in *Tom Jones*, see below, p. 537, n. 1.

Success; since, I believe, it is much easier to make good Men wise, than to make bad Men good.

For these Purposes I have employed all the Wit and Humour of which I am Master in the following History; wherein I have endeavoured to laugh Mankind out of their favourite Follies and Vices. How far I have succeeded in this good Attempt, I shall submit to the candid Reader, with only two Requests: First, That he will not expect to find Perfection in this Work; and Secondly, That he will excuse some Parts of it, if they fall short of that little Merit which I hope may appear in others.

I will detain you, Sir, no longer. Indeed I have run into a Preface, while I professed to write a Dedication. But how can it be otherwise? I dare not praise you; and the only Means I know of to avoid it, when you are in my Thoughts, are either to be entirely silent, or to turn my Thoughts to some other Subject.

Pardon, therefore, what I have said in this Epistle, not only without your Consent, but absolutely against it; and give me at least Leave, in this public Manner, to declare, that I am, with the highest Respect and Gratitude,

*SIR,*

*Your most Obliged,*

*Obedient Humble Servant,*

Henry Fielding

# CONTENTS OF THE
# FIRST VOLUME

# BOOK III

*Containing the most memorable Transactions which passed in the Family of Mr. Allworthy, from the Time when Tommy Jones arrived at the Age of Fourteen, till he attained the Age of Nineteen. In this Book the Reader may pick up some Hints concerning the Education of Children.*

# CONTENTS OF THE
# SECOND VOLUME

## BOOK IV

*Containing the Time of a Year.*

# Contents

# CONTENTS OF THE
# THIRD VOLUME

## BOOK VII
### *Containing three Days.*

# BOOK IX

## *Containing twelve Hours.*

# CONTENTS OF THE
# FOURTH VOLUME

# Contents

# CONTENTS OF THE FIFTH VOLUME

## BOOK XIII

*Containing the Space of Twelve Days.*

# Contents

## BOOK XIV

*Containing two Days.*

## BOOK XV

*In which the History advances about two Days.*

# CONTENTS OF THE
# SIXTH VOLUME

## BOOK XVI
### Containing the Space of Five Days.

## BOOK XVII
### Containing three Days.

## BOOK XVIII

### Containing about Six Days.

# Contents

# THE HISTORY OF
# A FOUNDLING

## BOOK I

*Containing as much of the Birth of the Foundling as is necessary or proper to acquaint the Reader with in the Beginning of this History.*

### CHAPTER I

*The Introduction to the Work, or Bill of Fare to the Feast.*

AN Author ought to consider himself, not as a Gentleman who gives a private or eleemosynary Treat, but rather as one who keeps a public Ordinary, at which all Persons are welcome for their Money. In the former Case, it is well known, that the Entertainer provides what Fare he pleases; and tho' this should be very indifferent, and utterly disagreeable to the Taste of his Company, they must not find any Fault; nay, on the contrary, Good-Breeding forces them outwardly to approve and to commend whatever is set before them. Now the contrary of this happens to the Master of an Ordinary. Men who pay for what they eat, will insist on gratifying their Palates, however nice and whimsical these may prove; and if every Thing is not agreeable to their Taste, will challenge a Right to censure, to abuse, and to d—n their Dinner without Controul.

To prevent therefore giving Offence to their Customers by any such Disappointment, it hath been usual, with the honest and well-meaning Host, to provide a Bill of Fare, which all Persons may peruse at their first Entrance into the House; and, having thence acquainted themselves with the Entertainment which they may expect, may either stay and regale with what is provided for them, or may depart to some other Ordinary better accommodated to their Taste.

As we do not disdain to borrow Wit or Wisdom from any Man who is capable of lending us either, we have condescended to take a Hint from these honest Victuallers, and shall prefix not only a general Bill of Fare to our whole Entertainment, but shall likewise give the Reader particular Bills to every Course which is to be served up in this and the ensuing Volumes.

The Provision then which we have here made is no other than HUMAN NATURE. Nor do I fear that my sensible Reader, though most luxurious in his Taste, will start, cavil, or be offended, because I have named but one Article. The Tortoise, as the Alderman of *Bristol*,[1] well learned in eating, knows by much Experience, besides the delicious *Calibash* and *Calipee*, contains many different Kinds of Food;[2] nor can the learned Reader be ignorant, that in *Human Nature*, tho' here collected under one general Name, is such prodigious Variety, that a Cook will have sooner gone through all the several Species of animal and vegetable Food in the World, than an Author will be able to exhaust so extensive a Subject.

An Objection may perhaps be apprehended from the more delicate, that this Dish is too common and vulgar; for what else is the Subject of all the Romances, Novels, Plays and Poems, with which the Stalls abound. Many exquisite Viands might be rejected by the Epicure, if it was a sufficient Cause for his contemning of them as common and vulgar, that something was to be found in the most paultry Alleys under the same Name. In reality, true Nature is as difficult to be met with in Authors, as the *Bayonne* Ham or *Bologna* Sausage is to be found in the Shops.

[1] Owing to the extravagant feasts consumed on such civic occasions as the Lord Mayor's Day, the gluttony of aldermen was proverbial (see, for example, the anonymous poem, *Bath* [1748], p. 18). By mid-century, turtle, imported to Bristol and London from the West Indies, was considered a great delicacy. Perhaps the best gloss on the passage occurs in Lyttelton's *Dialogues of the Dead* (1760), xix, in which Apicius remarks: 'I am credibly informed, that they [turtles] are now as plentiful in England as sturgeons. There are turtle-boats that go regularly to London and Bristol from the West Indies. I have just received this information from a fat alderman, who died in London last week, of a surfeit he got at a turtle-feast in that city.' (Lyttelton's *Works*, ed. G. E. Ayscough, 3rd ed. [1776], ii. 263–4.)

[2] Calipash and calipee are the edible substances found, respectively, under the upper shell and inside the lower shell of a turtle. According to William Verral, who learned to cook under the Duke of Newcastle's celebrated French chef, M. de St. Clouet (see p. 33, n. 2), a turtle made 'a pretty first-course' of seven dishes—'the calliopash and calliopee at top and bottom, soup in the middle, and the other four [i.e., fins, head, tripe, and innards] the corners'. (See Verral's *Complete System of Cookery* [1759], p. 240.)

But the whole, to continue the same Metaphor, consists in the Cookery of the Author; for, as Mr. *Pope* tells us,

True Wit is Nature to Advantage drest,
What oft' was thought, but ne'er so well exprest.[1]

The same Animal which hath the Honour to have some Part of his Flesh eaten at the Table of a Duke, may perhaps be degraded in another Part, and some of his Limbs gibbeted, as it were, in the vilest Stall in Town. Where then lies the Difference between the Food of the Nobleman and the Porter, if both are at Dinner on the same Ox or Calf, but in the seasoning, the dressing, the garnishing, and the setting forth. Hence the one provokes and incites the most languid Appetite, and the other turns and palls that which is the sharpest and keenest.

In like manner, the Excellence of the mental Entertainment consists less in the Subject, than in the Author's Skill in well dressing it up. How pleased therefore will the Reader be to find, that we have, in the following Work, adhered closely to one of the highest Principles of the best Cook[2] which the present Age, or perhaps that of *Heliogabalus*,[3] hath produced. This great Man,

[1] *Essay on Criticism* (1711), 297–8.

[2] Not, as Cross surmised (ii. 105), a reference to Lebeck, proprietor of a tavern in the Strand, who flourished much earlier (*c*. 1690–1710). In the preceding paragraph Fielding's mention of 'the Table of a Duke' provides the clue to what is doubtless a facetious compliment to Thomas Pelham-Holles (1693–1768), Duke of Newcastle and since 1744 Secretary of State in the government headed by his brother, Henry Pelham (see below, p. 612, n. 1). During the 1740s the most famous cook in England was Newcastle's French chef, M. de St. Clouet, known as 'Cloe'. For several contemporary references to him, see Walpole's letters to Horace Mann (7 July 1742), to Sir Charles Hanbury Williams (6 August 1745), and to Lady Hervey (17 October 1758); see also Print No. 3378 ('A Scene in Hell, or the Infernal Jubilee'), *Catalogue of Prints and Drawings in the British Museum*, Division I (Political and Personal Satires), Vol. iii, Pt. ii (1877). A satiric print of 1745 (No. 2684, 'The Duke of N—tle, and his Cook') depicts Newcastle and 'Cloe' and suggests how closely they were associated in the public mind. For a character of 'Cloe' and an admiring description—with recipes—of his culinary arts, see William Verral, *A Complete System of Cookery* (1759).

[3] Elagabalus, emperor of Rome (A.D. 218–22), was notorious for his licentiousness and gluttony. His lavish banquets, which sometimes lasted for days, are reported in detail by Lampridius, *Scriptores Historiae Augustae*, xviii. 4–xxxiii. In *The True Patriot* (3 December 1745) Fielding anticipated the present analogy between the two feasts, gastronomic and literary. Posing as the epicure 'Heliogabalus', he addressed a letter to himself, observing 'that you had cooked up the Entertainment you *serve* to the Public with much Propriety: You give us first a Dish of substantial Food, when our Appetites are brisk and keen; you then *serve up* several *petit Plats* from the News Papers; and lastly, send us away with a *Bon Bouche* of your own.' Among Fielding's contemporaries Horace Walpole, at least, would not have been puzzled by the juxtaposition of allusions to Elagabalus and the Duke of Newcastle (see above, n. 2): writing in 1756, Walpole described the Duke as having 'the

as is well known to all Lovers of polite eating, begins at first by setting plain Things before his hungry Guests, rising afterwards by Degrees, as their Stomachs may be supposed to decrease, to the very Quintessence of Sauce and Spices. In like manner, we shall represent Human Nature at first to the keen Appetite of our Reader, in that more plain and simple Manner in which it is found in the Country, and shall hereafter hash and ragoo it with all the high *French* and *Italian* Seasoning of Affectation and Vice which Courts and Cities afford. By these Means, we doubt not but our Reader may be rendered desirous to read on for ever, as the great Person, just above-mentioned, is supposed to have made some Persons eat.

Having premised thus much, we will now detain those, who like our Bill of Fare, no longer from their Diet, and shall proceed directly to serve up the first Course of our History, for their Entertainment.

## CHAPTER II

*A short Description of Squire* Allworthy, *and a fuller Account of Miss* Bridget Allworthy *his Sister.*

IN that Part of the western Division of this Kingdom, which is commonly called *Somersetshire*, there lately lived (and perhaps lives still) a Gentleman whose Name was *Allworthy*, and who might well be called the Favourite of both Nature and Fortune;[1] for both of these seem to have contended which should bless and enrich him most. In this Contention, Nature may seem to some to have come off victorious, as she bestowed on him many Gifts; while Fortune had only one Gift in her Power; but in pouring forth this, she was so very profuse, that others perhaps may think this single Endowment to have been more than equivalent to all the various Blessings which he enjoyed from Nature. From the former of these, he derived an agreeable Person, a sound Constitution, a solid Understanding, and a benevolent Heart; by the latter, he was decreed to the Inheritance of one of the largest Estates in the County.

monkey disposition of Heliogabalus' (see *Memoirs of the Reign of King George the Second*, ed. Lord Holland, 2nd ed. [1847], i. 373).

  [1] Cf. 'Liberty. To George Lyttleton, Esq.;' (1743), in which Fielding paid a similar compliment to his friend and patron—one 'Whom Nature vy'd with Fortune to adorn!'

This Gentleman had, in his Youth, married a very worthy and beautiful Woman, of whom he had been extremely fond: By her he had three Children, all of whom died in their Infancy. He had likewise had the Misfortune of burying this beloved Wife herself, about five Years before the Time in which this History chuses to set out. This Loss, however great, he bore like a Man of Sense and Constancy; tho' it must be confest, he would often talk a little whimsically on this Head: For he sometimes said, he looked on himself as still married, and considered his Wife as only gone a little before him, a Journey which he should most certainly, sooner or later, take after her; and that he had not the least Doubt of meeting her again, in a Place where he should never part with her more.[1] Sentiments for which his Sense was arraigned by one Part of his Neighbours, his Religion by a second, and his Sincerity by a third.

He now lived, for the most Part, retired in the Country, with one Sister, for whom he had a very tender Affection. This Lady was now somewhat past the Age of 30,[2] an Æra, at which, in the Opinion of the malicious, the Title of Old Maid may, with no Impropriety, be assumed. She was of that Species of Women, whom you commend rather for good Qualities than Beauty, and who are generally called by their own Sex, very good Sort of

---

[1] The sentiments which comfort Allworthy were commonplaces of the Christian *consolatio*: thus in his 'Consolatory Discourse' (1660) Simon Patrick observed that 'my friend is not gone, but gone before. . . . He hath taken a journey into a far Country, and there I may go to see him' (quoted in H. K. Miller, *Essays on Fielding's 'Miscellanies'* [Princeton, N.J., 1961], p. 246, n. 137). But the present passage may glance specifically at Lyttelton, whose wife died on 19 January 1747. Lyttelton's monody on her death (published 30 October 1747) closes with an expectation similar to Allworthy's that his wife awaits him in heaven. Still closer to the squire's sentiments are those Lyttelton expressed to Doddridge shortly after the death of Thomson: 'It often occurs to my mind that the death of our friends is one of the most powerfull ordinary means made use of by Providence to detach our affections and hopes from this world, and convince us that we have here *no enduring city, but are to look for a better*. By that time we have run half our course, those who set out with us, and of whose company we are most fond, are parted from us, and got to the end of their journey. If we were never to meet again, to what purpose has nature implanted in us such strong, such bitter, such lasting regrets at this separation; these affections are not in vain, they are not fixed upon what is no more; they are intimations and notices of a life to come, and are designed to carry our views, our wishes, I could almost say our passions, on to that life.' (Letter from Hagley, 30 September 1748; R. Phillimore, ed. *Memoirs and Correspondence of George Lord Lyttelton, from 1734 to 1773* [1845], i. 407.) Cf. also, *Tom Jones*, p. 117.

[2] Later in this Book (ch. viii) Bridget Allworthy is said to be approaching forty years of age.

Women—as good a Sort of Woman, Madam, as you would wish to know. Indeed she was so far from regretting Want of Beauty, that she never mention'd that Perfection (if it can be called one) without Contempt; and would often thank God she was not as handsome as Miss such a one, whom perhaps Beauty had led into Errors, which she might have otherwise avoided. Miss *Bridget Allworthy* (for that was the Name of this Lady) very rightly conceived the Charms of Person in a Woman to be no better than Snares for herself, as well as for others, and yet so discreet was she in her Conduct, that her Prudence[1] was as much

---

[1] The first occurrence in *Tom Jones* of the idea of *prudence* (and of the more or less synonymous term, *discretion*), the dominant ethical theme of the novel. Prudence in *Tom Jones* is an ambiguous concept, shifting in connotation from pejorative to positive according to the context, which Fielding carefully controls. In the present instance Bridget Allworthy's prudence suggests the usual modern understanding of the term, a certain self-protective caution and mean-spirited sense of expediency. (In this sense the word is also used to describe a host of other characters: e.g. Deborah Wilkins [I. v, vi], Jenny Jones [I. ix], Mrs. Seagrim [IV. viii], Mrs. Western [VI. xiv], Partridge [VIII. ix], Mrs. Honour [X. ix], Lady Bellaston [XIII. iii, xv. ix].) Yet in the penultimate paragraph of the novel, Tom Jones is said to be a fit partner for Sophia only because he has 'by Reflexion on his past Follies, acquired a Discretion and Prudence very uncommon in one of his lively Parts'; prudence in this sense is the indispensable requisite of the moral man—'the Duty', as Allworthy puts it, 'which we owe to ourselves' (XVIII. x). In still another sense, prudence is the summarizing attribute of Blifil, the villain of the piece.

   In *Tom Jones* this single term thus carries with it at least three distinct meanings. (1) In the Christian humanist tradition, two kinds of wisdom were distinguished: *sophia*, or speculative wisdom, and *prudentia*, or practical wisdom. (See Cicero, *De Officiis*, I. xliii.) *Prudentia*, the chief of the cardinal virtues, is the rational ability to distinguish between goods real and only apparent and, by the proper use of the intellectual faculties of memory, judgement, and foresight, to estimate the future consequences of present actions and events. (See Cicero, *De Inventione*, II. liii. 160; *De Natura Deorum*, III. xv. 38; *De Finibus*, V. vi. 16.) This is the *ars vivendi*, or, as Fielding has it in *Amelia* (I. i), 'the Art of Life'—the virtue which Tom Jones, like the *vir honestus*, must acquire. (2) On the other hand, in *Tom Jones*, 'prudence' may signify the false wisdom of this world, the self-interested cunning of a Blifil: it is 'wisdom [*prudentia*]', Cicero writes, 'which cunning [*malitia*] seeks to counterfeit' (*De Officiis*, III. xxv, trans. W. Miller, Loeb Classical Library, 1913; see also ibid., II. iii, III. xvii). (3) By the eighteenth century, however, the concept of *prudentia* had suffered from reinterpretation by writers of bromidic conduct books addressed chiefly to a middle-class audience of shopkeepers and schoolboys. In the process, ironically, its counterfeit and shadow came to be taken for the thing itself: self-discipline, discretion, foresight, expediency came to be valued for mercenary reasons—not as the way to self-knowledge and virtuous conduct, but as the surest means of prospering in the world. (See, for example, William de Britaine, *Humane Prudence* [1680]; Balthazar Gracian, *The Art of Prudence* [English trans. 1685]; Thomas Fuller, *Introductio ad Prudentiam*, 3rd ed. [1731]; Nathaniel Lardner, *Counsels of Prudence for the Use of Young People* [1735].) Thus the hard-earned wisdom of the *vir honestus* had become—if in name only—the property of the *vir œconomicus*, of a Robinson Crusoe or a Pamela, or in *Tom Jones* of Bridget Allworthy and a crowded gallery of meretricious and self-interested characters from every rank of society.

on the Guard, as if she had all the Snares to apprehend which
were ever laid for her whole Sex. Indeed, I have observed (tho'
it may seem unaccountable to the Reader) that this Guard of
Prudence, like the Trained Bands,[1] is always readiest to go on
Duty where there is the least Danger. It often basely and cowardly
deserts those Paragons for whom the Men are all wishing, sighing, dying, and spreading every Net in their Power; and constantly attends at the Heels of that higher Order of Women, for
whom the other Sex have a more distant and awful Respect, and
whom (from Despair, I suppose, of Success) they never venture
to attack.

Reader, I think proper, before we proceed any farther together,
to acquaint thee, that I intend to digress, through this whole
History, as often as I see Occasion: Of which I am myself a
better Judge than any pitiful Critic whatever; and here I must
desire all those Critics to mind their own Business, and not to
intermeddle with Affairs, or Works, which no ways concern
them: For, till they produce the Authority by which they are
constituted Judges,[2] I shall plead to their Jurisdiction.

CHAPTER III

*An odd Accident which befel Mr.* Allworthy, *at his Return home.
The decent Behaviour of Mrs.* Deborah Wilkins *, with some proper
Animadversions on Bastards.*

I HAVE told my Reader, in the preceding Chapter, that Mr.
*Allworthy* inherited a large Fortune; that he had a good Heart,
and no Family. Hence, doubtless, it will be concluded by many,

By using the same term to convey these antithetical meanings, Fielding's rhetorical
strategy in *Tom Jones* requires the reader to exercise his own prudential faculties, to distinguish between true wisdom and false. The reader, too, is implicated, as it were, in Tom
Jones's awkward progress toward the acquisition of prudence. For a full discussion of this
theme, see Battestin, 'Fielding's Definition of Widsom: Some Functions of Ambiguity and
Emblem in *Tom Jones*', *ELH*, xxxv (1968), 188–217. See also below, pp. 141, n. 1; 770,
n. 3).

1 Companies of citizen soldiers. For an earlier ironic allusion to their courage, see *Joseph
Andrews* (1742), II. vii.

2 Sarcasm at the expense of critics recurs throughout *Tom Jones*. Implicit in the present
passage is an etymological joke later developed at length in XI. i: the derivation of *critic*
from the Greek word signifying a judge (see below, p. 566, n. 2). For a discussion of
Fielding's estimate of critics, see R. C. Beatty, *PMLA*, xlix (1934), 1095–1100.

that he lived like an honest Man, owed no one a Shilling, took
nothing but what was his own, kept a good House, entertained
his Neighbours with a hearty Welcome at his Table, and was
charitable to the Poor, *i.e.* to those who had rather beg than work,
by giving them the Offals from it; that he dy'd immensely rich,
and built an Hospital.

And true it is, that he did many of these Things; but, had he
done nothing more, I should have left him to have recorded his
own Merit on some fair Free-Stone over the Door of that Hospital.[1] Matters of a much more extraordinary Kind are to be the
Subject of this History, or I should grossly mispend my Time in
writing so voluminous a Work; and you, my sagacious Friend,
might, with equal Profit and Pleasure, travel through some Pages,
which certain droll Authors have been facetiously pleased to call
*The History of England.*[2]

Mr. *Allworthy* had been absent a full Quarter of a Year in
*London*, on some very particular Business, tho' I know not what
it was; but judge of its Importance, by its having detained him so
long from home, whence he had not been absent a Month at a
Time during the Space of many Years. He came to his House
very late in the Evening, and after a short Supper with his Sister,
retired much fatigued to his Chamber. Here, having spent some

---

[1] Doubtless a compliment to Ralph Allen (see above, p. 4, n. 1), for whom hospitals
were a favourite public charity. In a very particular sense Allen 'built' the General Hospital
at Bath, completed in 1742: the building was constructed entirely of the 'fair Free-Stone'
from Allen's quarries, which he donated free of charge. Allen similarly contributed to the
building of St. Bartholomew's Hospital in London.

[2] Fielding was both exasperated and amused at the inaccuracies of contemporary
historians, who distorted the facts according to personal or political bias. In *Joseph
Andrews* (1742; III. i) he distinguished between the true 'history' or 'biography' he was
writing and the 'romances' of such English historians as Clarendon, Echard, Whitelocke,
and Rapin, who, he insisted, were not historians at all, but rather mere 'Topographers or
Chorographers'. The present passage, however, may point specifically at Thomas Carte's
*General History of England*, the first volume of which (published 1 January 1747/8)
revealed the author's Jacobital sympathies. Fielding ridiculed Carte in several numbers of
*The Jacobite's Journal* (20, 27 February, 12 March 1748), calling him a 'learned and
facetious Novelist', and urging him to issue the remaining volumes of his 'great Romance
. . . in the same manner with those true and delectable Histories of *Argalus* and *Parthenia*,
*Guy* Earl of *Warwick*, the *Seven Champions*, &c. in which Form, at the Price of 1*d.* each,
when embellished by our Frontispiece, I make no doubt of assuring him as universal a
Sale, as the inimitable Adventures of *Robinson Crusoe* formerly had throughout this
Kingdom'. Other works hostile to Carte's *History* were published in 1748, among them the
anonymous *Remarks upon Mr. Carte's Specimen of His General History of England* and the
pseudonymous *Letter to John Trot-Plaid, Esq; Author of the Jacobite's Journal, concerning
Mr. Carte's General History of England* by 'Duncan MacCarte a Highlander'.

Minutes on his Knees, a Custom which he never broke through on any Account, he was preparing to step into Bed, when, upon opening the Cloaths, to his great Surprize, he beheld an Infant, wrapt up in some coarse Linnen, in a sweet and profound Sleep, between his Sheets. He stood some Time lost in Astonishment at this Sight; but, as Good-nature[1] had always the Ascendant in his Mind, he soon began to be touched with Sentiments of Compassion for the little Wretch before him. He then rang his Bell, and ordered an elderly Woman Servant to rise immediately and come to him, and in the mean Time was so eager in contemplating the Beauty of Innocence, appearing in those lively Colours with which Infancy and Sleep always display it, that his Thoughts were too much engaged to reflect that he was in his Shirt, when the Matron came in. She had indeed given her Master sufficient Time to dress himself; for out of Respect to him, and Regard to Decency, she had spent many Minutes in adjusting her Hair at the Looking-glass, notwithstanding all the Hurry in which she had been summoned by the Servant, and tho' her Master, for ought she knew, lay expiring in an Apoplexy, or in some other Fit.

It will not be wondered at, that a Creature, who had so strict a Regard to Decency in her own Person, should be shocked at the least Deviation from it in another. She therefore no sooner opened the Door, and saw her Master standing by the Bedside in his Shirt, with a Candle in his Hand, than she started back in a most terrible Fright, and might perhaps have swooned away, had he not now recollected his being undrest, and put an End to her Terrors, by desiring her to stay without the Door till he had thrown some Cloaths over his Back, and was become incapable of shocking the pure Eyes of Mrs. *Deborah Wilkins*, who, tho'

---

[1] 'Good-nature' is the distinguishing characteristic of all Fielding's moral men—of Parson Adams, Heartfree, Allworthy, Jones, Captain Booth, Dr. Harrison. It signifies those benevolent, social affections which lead us to empathic involvement in the concerns of others and which prompt us to charitable actions. In his poem, 'Of Good-Nature' (1743), Fielding calls this virtue 'the glorious Lust of doing Good'. In 'An Essay on the Knowledge of the Characters of Men' (1743) he is more specific: Good-Nature is that benevolent and amiable Temper of Mind which disposes us to feel the Misfortunes, and enjoy the Happiness of others; and consequently pushes us on to promote the latter, and prevent the former; and that without any abstract Contemplation on the Beauty of Virtue, and without the Allurements or Terrors of Religion.' For discussion of this concept in Fielding, and of its genesis in the theories of the latitudinarian divines, see Battestin, *The Moral Basis of Fielding's Art* (Middletown, Conn., 1959), pp. 14–19, 54–63, 65–81, and Miller, *Essays on Fielding's 'Miscellanies'*, pp. 54–88.

in the 52d Year of her Age, vowed she had never beheld a
Man without his Coat. Sneerers and prophane Wits may perhaps
laugh at her first Fright, yet my graver Reader, when he considers the Time of Night, the Summons from her Bed, and the
Situation in which she found her Master, will highly justify and
applaud her Conduct; unless the Prudence, which must be supposed to attend Maidens at that Period of Life at which Mrs.
*Deborah* had arrived, should a little lessen his Admiration.

When Mrs. *Deborah* returned into the Room, and was acquainted by her Master with the finding the little Infant, her Consternation was rather greater than his had been; nor could she
refrain from crying out with great Horror of Accent as well as
Look, 'My good Sir! what's to be done?' Mr. *Allworthy* answered,
she must take care of the Child that Evening, and in the Morning
he would give Orders to provide it a Nurse. 'Yes, Sir,' says she,
'and I hope your Worship will send out your Warrant to take
up the Hussy its Mother (for she must be one of the Neighbourhood) and I should be glad to see her committed to *Bridewel*,
and whipt at the Cart's Tail.[1] Indeed such wicked Sluts cannot be
too severely punished. I'll warrant 'tis not her first, by her Impudence in laying it to your Worship.' 'In laying it to me,
*Deborah*,' answered *Allworthy*, 'I can't think she hath any such
Design. I suppose she hath only taken this Method to provide for
her Child; and truly I am glad she hath not done worse.' 'I
don't know what is worse,' cries *Deborah*, 'than for such wicked
Strumpets to lay their Sins at honest Men's Doors; and though
your Worship knows your own Innocence, yet the World is
censorious; and it hath been many an honest Man's Hap to pass
for the Father of Children he never begot; and if your Worship
should provide for the Child, it may make the People the apter to
believe: Besides, why should your Worship provide for what the
Parish is obliged to maintain?[2] For my own Part, if it was an
honest Man's Child indeed; but for my own part, it goes against
me to touch these misbegotten Wretches, whom I don't look

[1] According to 7 James I, cap. 4, the mother of a bastard child chargeable to the parish
(see below, n. 2) could be committed by order of two justices to the house of correction,
there to be corporally punished and set to work for the term of one year. (See Theodore
Barlow, *The Justice of the Peace* [1745], s.v. 'Bastards', p. 55.)

[2] According to the provisions of the Elizabethan Poor Law (43 Elizabeth, cap. 2), each
parish was taxed in order to provide shelter and sustenance for its impotent poor, such as
foundling infants.

upon as my Fellow Creatures. Faugh, how it stinks! It doth not
smell like a Christian. If I might be so bold to give my Advice,
I would have it put in a Basket, and sent out and laid at the
Church-Warden's Door.[1] It is a good Night, only a little rainy
and windy; and if it was well wrapt up, and put in a warm Basket,
it is two to one but it lives till it is found in the Morning. But
if it should not, we have discharged our Duty in taking proper
care of it; and it is, perhaps, better for such Creatures to die in a
state of Innocence, than to grow up and imitate their Mothers;
for nothing better can be expected of them.'

There were some Strokes in this Speech which, perhaps, would
have offended Mr. *Allworthy*, had he strictly attended to it; but
he had now got one of his Fingers into the Infant's Hand, which
by its gentle Pressure, seeming to implore his Assistance, had
certainly out-pleaded the Eloquence of Mrs. *Deborah*, had it
been ten times greater than it was. He now gave Mrs. *Deborah*
positive Orders to take the Child to her own Bed, and to call up a
Maid-servant to provide it Pap and other things against it waked.
He likewise ordered that proper Clothes should be procured for it
early in the Morning, and that it should be brought to himself as
soon as he was stirring.

Such was the Discernment of Mrs. *Wilkins*, and such the
Respect she bore her Master, under whom she enjoyed a most
excellent Place, that her Scruples gave way to his peremptory
Commands; and she took the Child under her Arms, without
any apparent Disgust at the Illegality of its Birth; and declaring
it was a sweet little Infant, walked off with it to her own Chamber.

*Allworthy* here betook himself to those pleasing Slumbers,
which a Heart that hungers after Goodness, is apt to enjoy, when
thoroughly satisfied. As these are possibly sweeter than what are
occasioned by any other hearty Meal, I should take more Pains
to display them to the Reader, if I knew any Air to recommend
him to for the procuring such an Appetite.

---

[1] Churchwardens were among those overseers of the poor whose duty it was to levy a
'poor's rate' and to care for the impotent poor of the parish.

## CHAPTER IV

*The Reader's Neck brought into Danger by a Description, his Escape,
and the great Condescension of Miss Bridget Allworthy.*

THE *Gothick* Stile of Building could produce nothing nobler
than Mr. *Allworthy*'s House.[1] There was an Air of Grandeur in it, that struck you with Awe, and rival'd the Beauties of
the best *Grecian* Architecture; and it was as commodious within,
as venerable without.

It stood on the South-east Side of a Hill, but nearer the Bottom
than the Top of it, so as to be sheltered from the North-east by
a Grove of old Oaks, which rose above it in a gradual Ascent of
near half a Mile, and yet high enough to enjoy a most charming
Prospect of the Valley beneath.

In the midst of the Grove was a fine Lawn sloping down towards the House, near the Summit of which rose a plentiful
Spring, gushing out of a Rock covered with Firs, and forming a
constant Cascade of about thirty Foot, not carried down a regular
Flight of Steps, but tumbling in a natural Fall over the broken
and mossy Stones, till it came to the bottom of the Rock; then

---

[1] Appropriately enough, the description of Allworthy's seat—the place of Tom Jones's
birth and the home of his spiritual father—is an imaginative synthesis of details associated
primarily with Sharpham Park, Fielding's own birthplace and the home of his maternal
grandfather, Sir Henry Gould, and secondarily with Hagley Park and Prior Park, the
estates, respectively, of Fielding's patrons, George Lyttelton and Ralph Allen (see above,
pp. 3, n. 1; 4, n. 1). From the threshold at Sharpham Park, Fielding would have looked
across the moors at Glastonbury and Tor Hill. The prospect from Allworthy's Paradise
Hall corresponds in general to the view westward from atop Tor Hill (see Cross, ii. 165).
The 'Stile' of Paradise Hall itself doubtless compliments a mutual friend of Fielding's and
Lyttelton's, Sanderson Miller (1717–80), amateur architect and pioneer of the Gothic
revival. In 1747–8 and 1749–50 Lyttelton erected a ruined castle and a rotunda of Miller's
design at Hagley Park; indeed, until his second wife disapproved, he had wanted Miller to
build him a Gothic house. Like Allworthy's mansion, furthermore, Hagley Hall is situated
on the south side of a hill, nearer the bottom than the top, yet high enough to command a
pleasant view of the valley. And, what is especially noteworthy, many of the details in
Fielding's description echo Thomson's celebration of Hagley Park in 'Spring', ll. 900–58
(*Seasons*, 1744 ed.); with Fielding's introduction of Allworthy later in this chapter, compare, too, Thomson's description of Lyttelton, strolling through Hagley and delighting
both in the natural scene and in the thoughts of benevolence which the season inspires. At
the same time, in the third paragraph of the chapter, Fielding does not forget Ralph Allen,
whose house, an example of 'the best *Grecian* Architecture', he had praised earlier in *Joseph
Andrews* (III. i, vi) and *A Journey from This World to the Next* (I. v): Allen's Palladian
mansion stands on the summit of a hill down which a stream falls into a lake which is
visible 'from every Room in the Front'.

running off in a pebly Channel, that with many lesser Falls
winded along, till it fell into a Lake at the Foot of the Hill, about
a quarter of a Mile below the House on the South Side, and which
was seen from every Room in the Front. Out of this Lake, which
filled the Center of a beautiful Plain, embellished with Groupes
of Beeches and Elms, and fed with Sheep, issued a River, that
for several Miles was seen to meander through an amazing
Variety of Meadows and Woods, till it emptied itself into the
Sea, with a large Arm of which, and an Island beyond it, the
Prospect was closed.

On the right of this Valley opened another of less Extent,
adorned with several Villages, and terminated by one of the
Towers of an old ruined Abbey, grown over with Ivy, and Part
of the Front which remained still entire.

The left Hand Scene presented the View of a fine Park, composed of very unequal Ground, and agreeably varied with all
the Diversity that Hills, Lawns, Wood and Water, laid out with
admirable Taste, but owing less to Art than to Nature,[1] could
give. Beyond this the Country gradually rose into a Ridge of wild
Mountains, the Tops of which were above the Clouds.

It was now the Middle of *May*, and the Morning was remarkably serene, when Mr. *Allworthy* walked forth on the Terrace,
where the Dawn opened every Minute that lovely Prospect we
have before described to his Eye. And now having sent forth
Streams of Light, which ascended the blue Firmament before
him as Harbingers preceding his Pomp, in the full Blaze of his
Majesty, up rose the Sun; than which one Object alone in this
lower Creation could be more glorious, and that Mr. *Allworthy*
himself presented; a human Being replete with Benevolence,
meditating in what manner he might render himself most acceptable to his Creator, by doing most good to his Creatures.

Reader, take care, I have unadvisedly led thee to the Top of as

---

[1] The observation would apply equally to the estates of both Fielding's patrons.
Influenced principally by the example of William Kent, who broke with continental
theories of the classic, formal garden, Lyttelton developed Hagley Park—his '*British
Tempe*', as Thomson called it—into one of the monuments of the natural school of English
landscape gardening. (See R. M. Davis, *Good Lord Lyttelton*, Pt. III, ch. iii.) At Prior Park,
too, nature, as Fielding remarks later in *Tom Jones* (XI. ix), seemed 'to triumph' over art.
In September 1746, on his first visit to Allen's estate, Charles Yorke was similarly impressed:
'The natural beauties of wood, water, prospect, hill and vale, wildness and cultivation,
make it one of the most delightful spots I ever saw, without adding any thing from art.'
(Quoted in B. Boyce, *Benevolent Man*, p. 169.)

high a Hill as Mr. *Allworthy's*, and how to get thee down without breaking thy Neck, I do not well know. However, let us e'en venture to slide down together, for Miss *Bridget* rings her Bell, and Mr. *Allworthy* is summoned to Breakfast, where I must attend, and, if you please, shall be glad of your Company.

The usual Compliments having past between Mr. *Allworthy* and Miss *Bridget*, and the Tea being poured out, he summoned Mrs. *Wilkins*, and told his Sister he had a Present for her; for which she thanked him, imagining, I suppose, it had been a Gown or some Ornament for her Person. Indeed, he very often made her such Presents, and she in Complacence to him spent much time in adorning herself. I say, in Complacence to him, because she always exprest the greatest Contempt for Dress, and for those Ladies who made it their Study.

But if such was her Expectation, how was she disappointed, when Mrs. *Wilkins*, according to the Order she had receiv'd from her Master, produced the little Infant. Great Surprises, as hath been observed,[1] are apt to be silent, and so was Miss *Bridget*, till her Brother began and told her the whole Story, which as the Reader knows it already, we shall not repeat.

Miss *Bridget* had always exprest so great a regard for what the Ladies are pleased to call Virtue, and had herself maintained such a Severity of Character, that it was expected, especially by *Wilkins*, that she would have vented much Bitterness on this Occasion, and would have voted for sending the Child, as a kind of noxious Animal, immediately out of the House; but on the contrary, she rather took the good-natur'd side of the question, intimated some Compassion for the helpless little Creature, and commended her Brother's Charity in what he had done.

Perhaps the Reader may account for this Behaviour from her Condescension to Mr. *Allworthy*, when we have informed him, that the good Man had ended his Narrative with owning a Resolution to take care of the Child, and to breed him up as his own; for, to acknowledge the Truth, she was always ready to oblige her Brother, and very seldom, if ever, contradicted his

---

[1] Cf. the proverbial observation that great joys, like great griefs, are silent—to which Fielding alludes below, pp. 228.3–4, 978.10–12. (For examples from Seneca, Shakespeare, and Shackerley Marmion, see Stevenson's *Book of Quotations Classical and Modern* [n.d.], pp. 842, 1018; and the *Oxford Dictionary of Quotations*, 2nd ed. [Oxford, 1953], pp. 331, 468.)

Sentiments; she would indeed sometimes make a few Observations, as, that Men were headstrong and must have their own way, and would wish she had been blest with an independent Fortune; but these were always vented in a low Voice, and at the most amounted only to what is called Muttering.

However, what she withheld from the Infant, she bestowed with the utmost Profuseness on the poor unknown Mother, whom she called an impudent Slut, a wanton Hussy, an audacious Harlot, a wicked Jade, a vile Strumpet, with every other Appellation with which the Tongue of Virtue never fails to lash those who bring a Disgrace on the Sex.

A Consultation was now entered into, how to proceed in order to discover the Mother. A Scrutiny was first made into the Characters of the female Servants of the House, who were all acquitted by Mrs. *Wilkins*, and with apparent Merit; for she had collected them herself, and perhaps it would be difficult to find such another Set of Scarecrows.

The next Step was to examine among the Inhabitants of the Parish; and this was referred to Mrs. *Wilkins*, who was to enquire with all imaginable Diligence, and to make her Report in the Afternoon.

Matters being thus settled, Mr. *Allworthy* withdrew to his Study, as was his Custom, and left the Child to his Sister, who, at his Desire, had undertaken the Care of it.

## CHAPTER V

*Containing a few common Matters, with a very uncommon Observation upon them.*

WHEN her Master was departed, Mrs. *Deborah* stood silent, expecting her Cue from Miss *Bridget*; for as to what had past before her Master, the prudent Housekeeper by no means relied upon it, as she had often known the Sentiments of the Lady in her Brother's Absence to differ greatly from those which she had expressed in his Presence. Miss *Bridget* did not, however, suffer her to continue long in this doubtful Situation; for having looked some time earnestly at the Child, as it lay asleep in the Lap of Mrs. *Deborah*, the good Lady could not forbear giving it a hearty Kiss, at the same time declaring herself wonderfully pleased with its Beauty and Innocence. Mrs. *Deborah* no sooner observed this, than she fell to squeezing and kissing with as great Raptures as sometimes inspire the sage Dame of forty and five towards a youthful and vigorous Bridegroom, crying out in a shrill Voice, 'O the dear little Creature, the dear, sweet, pretty Creature! well, I vow, it is as fine a Boy as ever was seen!'

These Exclamations continued till they were interrupted by the Lady, who now proceeded to execute the Commission given her by her Brother, and gave Orders for providing all Necessaries for the Child, appointing a very good Room in the House for his Nursery. Her Orders were indeed so liberal, that had it been a Child of her own, she could not have exceeded them; but lest the virtuous Reader may condemn her for shewing too great Regard to a base-born Infant, to which all Charity is condemned by Law as irreligious,[1] we think proper to observe, that she concluded the whole with saying, 'Since it was her Brother's Whim to adopt the little Brat, she supposed little Master must be treated with great Tenderness; for her part, she could not help thinking it was an Encouragement to Vice; but that she knew too much of the Obstinacy of Mankind to oppose any of their ridiculous Humours.'

With Reflections of this nature, she usually, as hath been hinted, accompany'd every Act of Compliance with her Brother's Inclinations; and surely nothing could more contribute to heighten the Merit of this Compliance, than a Declaration that she knew at the same time the Folly and Unreasonableness of those Inclinations to which she submitted. Tacit Obedience implies no Force upon the Will, and consequently may be easily, and without any Pains, preserved; but when a Wife, a Child, a Relation, or a Friend, performs what we desire, with Grumbling, and Reluctance, with Expressions of Dislike and Dissatisfaction, the manifest Difficulty which they undergo, must greatly enhance the Obligation.

[1] Fielding's remark appears to be ironical. The Poor Law (43 Elizabeth, cap. 4) specifically provided for the efficient management of all 'Lands, Goods, and Stocks of Money' donated to the uses of the poor, including foundling infants. In 1739, furthermore, the Foundling Hospital 'for the Maintenance and Education of Exposed and Deserted Young Children' was granted the royal charter (see below, p. 761, n. 3). Perhaps, however, Fielding alludes to the legal *status* of bastards, who were prevented by law from inheriting property by descent (see below, p. 79, n. 3).

As this is one of those deep Observations which very few Readers can be supposed capable of making themselves, I have thought proper to lend them my Assistance; but this is a Favour rarely to be expected in the Course of my Work. Indeed I shall seldom or never so indulge him, unless in such Instances as this, where nothing but the Inspiration with which we Writers are gifted, can possibly enable any one to make the Discovery.


## CHAPTER VI

*Mrs.* Deborah *is introduced into the Parish, with a Simile. A short Account of* Jenny Jones, *with the Difficulties and Discouragements which may attend young Women in the Pursuit of Learning.*

MRS. *Deborah,* having disposed of the Child according to the Will of her Master, now prepared to visit those Habitations which were supposed to conceal its Mother.

Not otherwise than when a Kite, tremendous Bird, is beheld by the feathered Generation soaring aloft, and hovering over their Heads, the amorous Dove, and every innocent little Bird spread wide the Alarm, and fly trembling to their Hiding-places: He proudly beats the Air, conscious of his Dignity, and meditates intended Mischief.

So when the Approach of Mrs. *Deborah* was proclaimed through the Street, all the Inhabitants ran trembling into their Houses, each Matron dreading lest the Visit should fall to her Lot. She with stately Steps proudly advances over the Field, aloft she bears her tow'ring Head, filled with Conceit of her own Pre-eminence, and Schemes to effect her intended Discovery.

The sagacious Reader will not, from this Simile, imagine these poor People had any Apprehension of the Design with which Mrs. *Wilkins* was now coming towards them; but as the great Beauty of the Simile may possibly sleep these hundred Years, till some future Commentator shall take this Work in hand, I think proper to lend the Reader a little Assistance in this Place.

It is my Intention therefore to signify, that as it is the Nature of a Kite to devour little Birds, so is it the Nature of such Persons as Mrs. *Wilkins,* to insult and tyrannize over little People. This being indeed the Means which they use to recompense to themselves their extreme Servility and Condescension to their

Superiors; for nothing can be more reasonable, than that Slaves
and Flatterers should exact the same Taxes on all below them,
which they themselves pay to all above them.

Whenever Mrs. *Deborah* had Occasion to exert any extraordinary Condescension to Miss *Bridget*, and by that means had
a little sowered her natural Disposition, it was usual with her to
walk forth among these People, in order to refine her Temper,
by venting, and, as it were, purging off all ill Humours; on which
Account, she was by no means a welcome Visitant; to say the
Truth, she was universally dreaded and hated by them all.

On her Arrival in this Place, she went immediately to the
Habitation of an elderly Matron; to whom, as this Matron had
the good Fortune to resemble herself in the Comeliness of her
Person, as well as in her Age, she had generally been more
favourable than to any of the rest. To this Woman she imparted
what had happened, and the Design upon which she was come
thither that Morning. These two began presently to scrutinize
the Characters of the several young Girls, who lived in any of
those Houses, and at last fixed their strongest Suspicion on one
*Jenny Jones*, who they both agreed was the likeliest Person to
have committed this Fact.

This *Jenny Jones* was no very comely Girl, either in her Face
or Person; but Nature had somewhat compensated the Want of
Beauty with what is generally more esteemed by those Ladies,
whose Judgment is arrived at Years of perfect Maturity; for she
had given her a very uncommon Share of Understanding. This
Gift *Jenny* had a good deal improved by Erudition. She had lived
several Years a Servant with a Schoolmaster, who discovering a
great Quickness of Parts in the Girl, and an extraordinary Desire
of learning, (for every leisure Hour she was always found reading
in the Books of the Scholars) had the Good-nature, or Folly (just
as the Reader pleases to call it,) to instruct her so far, that she
obtained a competent Skill in the Latin Language, and was perhaps as good a Scholar as most of the young Men of Quality of
the Age. This Advantage, however, like most others of an extraordinary Kind, was attended with some small Inconveniencies:
For as it is not to be wondered at, that a young Woman so well
accomplished should have little Relish for the Society of those
whom Fortune had made her Equals, but whom Education had
rendered so much her Inferiors; so is it Matter of no greater

Astonishment, that this Superiority in *Jenny*, together with that Behaviour which is its certain Consequence, should produce among the rest some little Envy and Ill-will towards her; and these had perhaps secretly burnt in the Bosoms of her Neighbours, ever since her Return from her Service.

Their Envy did not however display itself openly, till poor *Jenny*, to the Surprize of every Body, and to the Vexation of all the young Women in these Parts, had publickly shone forth on a *Sunday* in a new Silk Gown, with a laced Cap, and other proper Appendages to these.

The Flame, which had before lain in Embrio, now burst forth. *Jenny* had, by her Learning, encreased her own Pride, which none of her Neighbours were kind enough to feed with the Honour she seemed to demand; and now, instead of Respect and Adoration, she gained nothing but Hatred and Abuse, by her Finery. The whole Parish declared she could not come honestly by such Things; and Parents, instead of wishing their Daughters the same, felicitated themselves that their Children had them not.

Hence perhaps it was, that the good Woman first mentioned the Name of this poor Girl to Mrs. *Wilkins*; but there was another Circumstance that confirmed the latter in her Suspicion: For *Jenny* had lately been often at Mr. *Allworthy's* House. She had officiated as Nurse to Miss *Bridget*, in a violent Fit of Illness, and had sat up many Nights with that Lady; besides which, she had been seen there the very Day before Mr. *Allworthy's* Return, by Mrs. *Wilkins* herself, tho' that sagacious Person had not at first conceived any Suspicion of her on that Account: For, as she herself said, 'She had always esteemed *Jenny* as a very sober Girl, (tho' indeed she knew very little of her) and had rather suspected some of those wanton Trollops, who gave themselves Airs because, forsooth, they thought themselves handsome.'

*Jenny* was now summoned to appear in Person before Mrs. *Deborah*, which she immediately did: When Mrs. *Deborah*, putting on the Gravity of a Judge, with somewhat more than his Austerity, began an Oration with the Words 'You audacious Strumpet,' in which she proceeded rather to pass Sentence on the Prisoner, than to accuse her.

Tho' Mrs. *Deborah* was fully satisfied of the Guilt of *Jenny*, from the Reasons above shewn, it is possible Mr. *Allworthy* might have required some stronger Evidence to have convicted her; but she saved her Accusers any such Trouble, by freely confessing the whole Fact with which she was charged.

This Confession, tho' delivered rather in Terms of Contrition, as it appeared, did not at all mollify Mrs. *Deborah*, who now pronounced a second Judgment against her, in more opprobrious Language than before; nor had it any better Success with the Bye-standers, who were now grown very numerous. Many of them cried out, 'They thought what Madam's Silk Gown would end in;' others spoke sarcastically of her Learning. Not a single Female was present, but found some Means of expressing her Abhorrence of poor *Jenny*; who bore all very patiently, except the Malice of one Woman, who reflected upon her Person, and, tossing up her Nose, said, 'The Man must have a good Stomach, who would give Silk Gowns for such Sort of Trumpery.' *Jenny* replied to this, with a Bitterness which might have surprized a judicious Person, who had observed the Tranquility with which she bore all the Affronts to her Chastity; but her Patience was perhaps tired out: For this is a Virtue which is very apt to be fatigued by Exercise.

Mrs. *Deborah*, having succeeded beyond her Hopes in her Enquiry, returned with much Triumph, and at the appointed Hour made a faithful Report to Mr. *Allworthy*, who was much surprized at the Relation; for he had heard of the extraordinary Parts and Improvements of this Girl, whom he intended to have given in Marriage, together with a small Living, to a neighbouring Curate. His Concern therefore on this Occasion, was at least equal to the Satisfaction which appeared in Mrs. *Deborah*, and to many Readers may seem much more reasonable.

Miss *Bridget* blessed herself, and said, 'For her Part, she should never hereafter entertain a good Opinion of any Woman:' For *Jenny* before this had the Happiness of being much in her good Graces also.

The prudent Housekeeper was again dispatched to bring the unhappy Culprit before Mr. *Allworthy*, in order, not, as it was hoped by some and expected by all, to be sent to the House of Correction; but to receive wholesome Admonition and Reproof, which those who relish that kind of instructive Writing, may peruse in the next Chapter.

## CHAPTER VII

*Containing such grave Matter, that the Reader cannot laugh once through the whole Chapter, unless peradventure he should laugh at the Author.*

WHEN *Jenny* appeared, Mr. *Allworthy* took her into his Study, and spoke to her as follows:

'You know, Child, it is in my Power, as a Magistrate, to punish you very rigorously for what you have done;[1] and you will perhaps be the more apt to fear I should execute that Power, because you have, in a manner, laid your Sins at my Door.

'But perhaps this is one Reason which hath determined me to act in a milder Manner with you: For, as no private Resentment should ever influence a Magistrate, I will be so far from considering your having deposited the Infant in my House, as an Aggravation of your Offence, that I will suppose, in your Favour, this to have proceeded from a natural Affection to your Child; since you might have some Hopes to see it thus better provided for, than was in the Power of yourself, or its wicked Father, to provide for it. I should indeed have been highly offended with you, had you exposed the little Wretch in the Manner of some inhuman Mothers, who seem no less to have abandoned their Humanity, than to have parted with their Chastity. It is the other Part of your Offence therefore upon which I intend to admonish you, I mean the Violation of your Chastity. A Crime, however lightly it may be treated by debauched Persons, very heinous in itself, and very dreadful in its Consequences.

'The heinous Nature of this Offence must be sufficiently apparent to every Christian, inasmuch as it is committed in Defiance of the Laws of our Religion, and of the express Commands of him who founded that Religion.

'And here its Consequences may well be argued to be dreadful; for what can be more so, than to incur the divine Displeasure, by the Breach of the divine Commands; and that in an Instance, against which the highest Vengeance is specifically denounced.

'But these Things, tho' too little, I am afraid, regarded, are so plain, that Mankind, however they may want to be reminded,

---

[1] See above, p. 40, n. 1.

can never need Information on this Head. A Hint therefore to awaken your Sense of this Matter shall suffice; for I would inspire you with Repentance, and not drive you to Desperation.

'There are other Consequences, not indeed so dreadful or replete with Horror as this; and yet such, as if attentively considered, must, one would think, deter all, of your Sex at least, from the Commission of this Crime.

'For by it you are rendered infamous, and driven, like Lepers of old, out of Society; at least from the Society of all but wicked and reprobate Persons; for no others will associate with you.

'If you have Fortunes, you are hereby rendered incapable of enjoying them; if you have none, you are disabled from acquiring any, nay almost of procuring your Sustenance; for no Persons of Character will receive you into their Houses. Thus you are often driven by Necessity itself into a State of Shame and Misery, which unavoidably ends in the Destruction of both Body and Soul.

'Can any Pleasure compensate these Evils? Can any Temptation have Sophistry and Delusion strong enough to persuade you to so simple a Bargain? Or can any carnal Appetite so overpower your Reason, or so totally lay it asleep, as to prevent your flying with Affright and Terror from a Crime which carries such Punishment always with it?

'How base and mean must that Woman be, how void of that Dignity of Mind, and decent Pride, without which we are not worthy the Name of human Creatures, who can bear to level herself with the lowest Animal, and to sacrifice all that is great and noble in her, all her Heavenly Part, to an Appetite which she hath in common with the vilest Branch of the Creation! For no Woman sure, will plead the Passion of Love for an Excuse. This would be to own herself the meer Tool and Bubble of the Man. Love, however barbarously we may corrupt and pervert its Meaning, as it is a laudable, is a rational Passion, and can never be violent, but when reciprocal; for though the Scripture bids us love our Enemies,[1] it means not with that fervent Love,

---

[1] Cf. Matthew 5: 44, Luke 6: 27, 35. 'FORGIVE THE ACTS OF YOUR ENEMIES', Fielding remarked in 'An Essay on the Knowledge of the Characters of Men' (1743), 'hath been thought the highest Maxim of Morality'. In *The Champion* (27 March 1740) he insisted that 'this excellent Doctrine' was distinctively Christian, teaching 'us something beyond what the Religion of Nature and Philosophy could arrive at' (see also *The Champion*, 5 April 1740).

which we naturally bear towards our Friends; much less that we should sacrifice to them our Lives, and what ought to be dearer to us, our Innocence. Now in what Light, but in that of an Enemy, can a reasonable Woman regard the Man, who solicits her to entail on herself, all the Misery I have described to you, and who would purchase to himself a short, trivial, contemptible Pleasure, so greatly at her Expence! For by the Laws of Custom the whole Shame, with all its dreadful Consequences, falls entirely upon her. Can Love, which always seeks the Good of its Object, attempt to betray a Woman into a Bargain, where she is so greatly to be the Loser? If such Corrupter, therefore, should have the Impudence to pretend a real Affection for her, ought not the Woman to regard him, not only as an Enemy, but as the worst of all Enemies; a false, designing, treacherous, pretended Friend, who intends not only to debauch her Body, but her Understanding at the same Time?'

Here *Jenny* expressing great Concern, *Allworthy* paused a Moment, and then proceeded: 'I have talked thus to you, Child, not to insult you for what is past, and irrevocable, but to caution and strengthen you for the future. Nor should I have taken this Trouble, but from some Opinion of your good Sense, notwithstanding the dreadful Slip you have made; and from some Hopes of your hearty Repentance, which are founded on the Openness and Sincerity of your Confession. If these do not deceive me, I will take care to convey you from this Scene of your Shame, where you shall, by being unknown, avoid the Punishment which, as I have said, is allotted to your Crime in this World; and I hope by Repentance, you will avoid the much heavier Sentence denounced against it in the other. Be a good Girl the rest of your Days, and Want shall be no Motive to your going astray: And believe me, there is more Pleasure, even in this World, in an innocent and virtuous Life,[1] than in one debauched and vicious.

'As to your Child, let no Thoughts concerning it, molest you;

[1] Hobbes and the Calvinists having asserted the essential selfishness and depravity of human nature, the latitudinarian divines answered this cynical view by accommodating what Professor Crane called 'a strain of egoistic hedonism' within the system of benevolism —the notion that virtuous behaviour was attended with a 'Self-approving Joy'. For Tillotson, 'There is no sensual Pleasure in the World comparable to the Delight and Satisfaction that a good Man takes in doing good.' (See Crane, 'Suggestions toward a Genealogy of the "Man of Feeling" ', *ELH*, i (1934), esp. 227–9.) For other instances of this concept in *Tom Jones*, see pp. 96, n. 1; 659.

I will provide for it in a better manner than you can ever hope. And now nothing remains, but that you inform me who was the wicked Man that seduced you; for my Anger against him will be much greater than you have experienced on this Occasion.'

*Jenny* now first lifted her Eyes from the Ground, and with a modest Look, and decent Voice, thus began:

'To know you, Sir, and not love your Goodness, would be an Argument of total want of Sense or Goodness in any one. In me it would amount to the highest Ingratitude, not to feel, in the most sensible manner, the great Degree of Goodness you have been pleased to exert on this Occasion. As to my Concern for what is past, I know you will spare my Blushes the Repetition. My future Conduct will much better declare my Sentiments, than any Professions I can now make. I beg leave to assure you, Sir, that I take your Advice much kinder, than your generous Offer with which you concluded it. For as you are pleased to say, Sir, it is an Instance of your Opinion of my Understanding—' Here her Tears flowing apace, she stopped a few Moments, and then proceeded thus, 'Indeed, Sir, your Kindness overcomes me; but I will endeavour to deserve this good Opinion; for if I have the Understanding you are so kindly pleased to allow me, such Advice cannot be thrown away upon me. I thank you, Sir, heartily, for your intended Kindness to my poor helpless Child; he is innocent, and I hope will live to be grateful for all the Favours you shall shew him. But now, Sir, I must on my Knees intreat you, not to persist in asking me to declare the Father of my Infant. I promise you faithfully, you shall one Day know; but I am under the most solemn Ties and Engagements of Honour, as well as the most religious Vows and Protestations, to conceal his Name at this Time. And I know you too well to think you would desire I should sacrifice either my Honour, or my Religion.'

Mr. *Allworthy*, whom the least Mention of those sacred Words was sufficient to stagger, hesitated a Moment before he replied, and then told her she had done wrong to enter into such Engagements to a Villain; but since she had, he could not insist on her breaking them. He said, it was not from a Motive of vain Curiosity he had enquired, but in order to punish the Fellow; at least, that he might not ignorantly confer Favours on the Undeserving.

As to these Points, *Jenny* satisfied him by the most solemn Assurances, that the Man was entirely out of his Reach, and was neither subject to his Power, nor in any probability of becoming an Object of his Goodness.

The Ingenuity of this Behaviour, had gained *Jenny* so much Credit with this worthy Man, that he easily believed what she told him: For as she had disdained to excuse herself by a Lie, and had hazarded his farther Displeasure in her present Situation, rather than she would forfeit her Honour, or Integrity, by betraying another, he had but little Apprehension that she would be guilty of Falshood towards himself.

He therefore dismissed her with Assurances, that he would very soon remove her out of the Reach of that Obloquy she had incurred, concluding with some additional Documents, in which he recommended Repentance, saying, 'Consider, Child, there is one still to reconcile yourself to, whose Favour is of much greater Importance to you than mine.'

## CHAPTER VIII

*A Dialogue between Mesdames* Bridget, *and* Deborah; *containing more Amusement, but less Instruction than the former.*

WHEN Mr. *Allworthy* had retired to his Study with *Jenny Jones*, as hath been seen, Miss *Bridget*, with the good Housekeeper, had betaken themselves to a Post next adjoining to the said Study; whence, through the Conveyance of a Key-hole, they sucked in at their Ears the instructive Lecture delivered by Mr. *Allworthy*, together with the Answers of *Jenny*, and indeed every other Particular which passed in the last Chapter.

This Hole in her Brother's Study Door, was indeed as well known to Miss *Bridget*, and had been as frequently applied to by her, as the famous Hole in the Wall was by *Thisbe*¹ of old. This served to many good Purposes. For by such Means Miss *Bridget* became often acquainted with her Brother's Inclinations, without giving him the Trouble of repeating them to her. It is true, some Inconveniencies attended this Intercourse, and she had sometimes Reason to cry out with *Thisbe*, in *Shakespear*,² 'O wicked, wicked Wall!' For as Mr. *Allworthy* was a Justice of Peace, certain

---

¹ See Ovid, *Metamorphoses*, iv. 55–166.
² In fact, it is Pyramus who cries out—*A Midsummer Night's Dream*, v. i.

Things occurred in Examinations concerning Bastards, and such like, which are apt to give great Offence to the chaste Ears of Virgins, especially when they approach the Age of forty,[1] as was the Case of Miss *Bridget*. However, she had, on such Occasions, the Advantage of concealing her Blushes from the Eyes of Men, and *De non apparentibus, et non existentibus eadem est ratio*.[2] In *English*: 'When a Woman is not seen to blush, she doth not blush at all.'

Both the good Women kept strict Silence during the whole Scene between Mr. *Allworthy* and the Girl; but as soon as it was ended, and that Gentleman was out of hearing, Mrs. *Deborah* could not help exclaiming against the Clemency of her Master, and especially against his suffering her to conceal the Father of the Child, which she swore she would have out of her before the Sun set.

At these Words Miss *Bridget* discomposed her Features with a Smile (a Thing very unusual to her.) Not that I would have my Reader imagine, that this was one of those wanton Smiles, which *Homer* would have you conceive came from *Venus*, when he calls her the laughter-loving Goddess;[3] nor was it one of those Smiles, which Lady *Seraphina* shoots from the Stage-Box, and which *Venus* would quit her Immortality to be able to equal. No, this was rather one of those Smiles, which might be supposed to have come from the dimpled Cheeks of the august *Tysiphone*,[4] or from one of the Misses her Sisters.

With such a Smile then, and with a Voice, sweet as the Evening Breeze of *Boreas*[5] in the pleasant Month of *November*, Miss *Bridget* gently reproved the Curiosity of Mrs. *Deborah*, a Vice with which it seems the latter was too much tainted, and which the former inveighed against with great Bitterness, adding, 'that among all her Faults, she thanked Heaven, her Enemies could not accuse her of prying into the Affairs of other People.'

She then proceeded to commend the Honour and Spirit with which *Jenny* had acted. She said, she could not help agreeing with her Brother, that there was some Merit in the Sincerity of her

[1] Earlier Bridget was said to be 'somewhat past the Age of 30' (see above, p. 35).
[2] 'That which is not seen must be treated as if it did not exist'—a legal maxim found in Sir Edward Coke's *Reports* (1658), v. 343. Fielding quotes it again in *The Covent-Garden Journal* (7 January 1752). [3] *Iliad*, iii. 424.
[4] One of the Erinyes or Furies of classical mythology.
[5] The north wind.

Confession, and in her Integrity to her Lover. That she had always thought her a very good Girl, and doubted not but she had been seduced by some Rascal, who had been infinitely more to blame than herself, and very probably had prevailed with her by a Promise of Marriage, or some other treacherous Proceeding.

This Behaviour of Miss *Bridget* greatly surprized Mrs. *Deborah*; for this well-bred Woman seldom opened her Lips either to her Master or his Sister, till she had first sounded their Inclinations, with which her Sentiments were always strictly consonant. Here, however, she thought she might have launched forth with Safety; and the sagacious Reader will not perhaps accuse her of want of sufficient Forecast in so doing, but will rather admire with what wonderful Celerity she tacked about, when she found herself steering a wrong Course.

'Nay, Madam,' said this able Woman, and truly great Politician, 'I must own I cannot help admiring the Girl's Spirit, as well as your Ladyship. And, as your Ladyship says, if she was deceived by some wicked Man, the poor Wretch is to be pitied. And to be sure, as your Ladyship says, the Girl hath always appeared like a good, honest, plain Girl, and not vain of her Face, forsooth, as some wanton Husseys in the Neighbourhood are.'

'You say true, *Deborah*,' said Miss *Bridget*, 'if the Girl had been one of those vain Trollops, of which we have too many in the Parish, I should have condemned my Brother for his Lenity towards her. I saw two Farmers Daughters at Church, the other Day, with bare Necks. I protest they shock'd me. If Wenches will hang out Lures for Fellows, it is no matter what they suffer. I detest such Creatures; and it would be much better for them, that their Faces had been seamed with the Small-Pox; but I must confess, I never saw any of this wanton Behaviour in poor *Jenny*; some artful Villain, I am convinced, hath betrayed, nay perhaps forc'd her; and I pity the poor Wretch with all my Heart.'

Mrs. *Deborah* approved all these Sentiments, and the Dialogue concluded with a general and bitter Invective against Beauty, and with many compassionate Considerations for all honest, plain Girls, who are deluded by the wicked Arts of deceitful Men.

## CHAPTER IX

*Containing Matters which will surprize the Reader.*

*JENNY* returned home well pleased with the Reception she had met with from Mr. *Allworthy*, whose Indulgence to her she industriously made public; partly perhaps as a Sacrifice to her own Pride, and partly from the more prudent Motive of reconciling her Neighbours to her, and silencing their Clamours.

But though this latter View, if she indeed had it, may appear reasonable enough, yet the Event did not answer her Expectation; for when she was convened before the Justice, and it was universally apprehended, that the House of Correction would have been her Fate; tho' some of the young Women cry'd out, 'it was good enough for her,' and diverted themselves with the Thoughts of her beating Hemp in a Silk Gown;[1] yet there were many others who began to pity her Condition: But when it was known in what manner Mr. *Allworthy* had behaved, the Tide turned against her. One said, 'I'll assure you, Madam hath had good Luck.' A second cry'd, 'See what it is to be a Favourite.' A third, 'Ay, this comes of her Learning.' Every Person made some malicious Comment or other, on the Occasion; and reflected on the Partiality of the Justice.

The Behaviour of these People, may appear impolitic, and ungrateful to the Reader, who considers the Power, and the Benevolence of Mr. *Allworthy*: But as to his Power, he never used it; and as to his Benevolence, he exerted so much, that he had thereby disobliged all his Neighbours: For it is a Secret well known to great Men, that by conferring an Obligation, they do not always procure a Friend, but are certain of creating many Enemies.

*Jenny* was, however, by the Care and Goodness of Mr. *Allworthy*, soon removed out of the Reach of Reproach; when Malice, being no longer able to vent its Rage on her, began to seek another Object of its Bitterness, and this was no less than Mr. *Allworthy* himself; for a Whisper soon went abroad, that he himself was the Father of the foundling Child.

---

[1] The activity and attire of Kate Hackabout in Plate 4 of Hogarth's *Harlot's Progress* 1732). For references to Hogarth in *Tom Jones*, see below, p. 66, n. 1.

This Supposition so well reconciled his Conduct to the general Opinion, that it met with universal Assent; and the Outcry against his Lenity soon began to take another Turn, and was changed into an Invective against his Cruelty to the poor Girl. Very grave and good Women exclaimed against Men who begot Children and then disowned them. Nor were there wanting some, who, after the Departure of *Jenny*, insinuated, that she was spirited away with a Design too black to be mentioned, and who gave frequent Hints, that a legal Inquiry ought to be made into the whole Matter, and that some People should be forced to produce the Girl.

These Calumnies might have probably produced ill Consequences (at the least might have occasioned some Trouble) to a Person of a more doubtful and suspicious Character than Mr. *Allworthy* was blessed with; but in his Case they had no such Effect; and, being heartily despised by him, they served only to afford an innocent Amusement to the good Gossips of the Neighbourhood.

But as we cannot possibly divine what Complexion our Reader may be of, and as it will be some Time before he will hear any more of *Jenny*, we think proper to give him a very early Intimation, that Mr. *Allworthy* was, and will hereafter appear to be, absolutely innocent of any criminal Intention whatever. He had indeed committed no other than an Error in Politics, by tempering Justice with Mercy, and by refusing to gratify the good-natured Disposition of the Mob,* with an Object for their Compassion to work on in the Person of poor *Jenny*, whom, in order to pity, they desired to have seen sacrificed to Ruin and Infamy by a shameful Correction in a *Bridewel*.¹

So far from complying with this their Inclination, by which all Hopes of Reformation would have been abolished, and even the

---

* Whenever this Word occurs in our Writings, it intends Persons without Virtue, or Sense, in all Stations, and many of the highest Rank are often meant by it.

---

1 '*Bridewel*'—after Bridewell Hospital in London, rebuilt in 1720, the name given to any house of correction, wherein minor offenders, such as whores and vagabonds, were set to work beating hemp and supported on a penny-loaf of bread a day. In Fielding's opinion, commitment to these prisons was a severe punishment which, instead of reforming prisoners, generally confirmed them in the practice of vice. During his own tenure as magistrate he, like Squire Allworthy, refused to commit any but the most hardened offenders to Bridewell. (See *An Enquiry into the Causes of the Late Increase of Robbers* [1751], section iv, and *The Covent-Garden Journal* [1 August 1752].)

Gate shut against her, if her own Inclinations should ever hereafter lead her to chuse the Road of Virtue, Mr. *Allworthy* rather
chose to encourage the Girl to return thither by the only possible
Means; for too true I am afraid it is, that many Women have
become abandoned, and have sunk to the last Degree of Vice
by being unable to retrieve the first Slip. This will be, I am afraid,
always the Case while they remain among their former Acquaintance; it was therefore wisely done by Mr. *Allworthy*, to remove
*Jenny* to a Place where she might enjoy the Pleasure of Reputation, after having tasted the ill Consequences of losing it.

To this Place therefore, wherever it was, we will wish her a
good Journey, and for the present take leave of her, and of the
little Foundling her Child, having Matters of much higher Importance to communicate to the Reader.

## CHAPTER X

*The Hospitality of Allworthy; with a short Sketch of the Characters of*
*two Brothers, a Doctor, and a Captain, who were entertained by that*
*Gentleman.*

NEITHER Mr. *Allworthy's* House, nor his Heart, were shut
against any Part of Mankind, but they were both more particularly open to Men of Merit. To say the Truth, this was the only
House in the Kingdom where you was sure to gain a Dinner by
deserving it.

Above all others, Men of Genius and Learning shared the
principal Place in his Favour; and in these he had much Discernment: For though he had missed the Advantage of a learned
Education, yet being blest with vast natural Abilities, he had so
well profited by a vigorous, though late Application to Letters,
and by much Conversation with Men of Eminence in this Way,
that he was himself a very competent Judge in most Kinds of
Literature.

It is no Wonder that in an Age when this Kind of Merit is so
little in Fashion, and so slenderly provided for, Persons possessed
of it should very eagerly flock to a Place where they were sure
of being received with great Complaisance; indeed where they
might enjoy almost the same Advantages of a liberal Fortune as if

they were entitled to it in their own Right; for Mr. *Allworthy* was not one of those generous Persons, who are ready most bountifully to bestow Meat, Drink, and Lodging on Men of Wit and Learning, for which they expect no other Return but Entertainment, Instruction, Flattery, and Subserviency; in a Word, that such Persons should be enrolled in the Number of Domestics, without wearing their Master's Cloaths, or receiving Wages.

On the contrary, every Person in this House was perfect Master of his own Time: and as he might at his Pleasure satisfy all his Appetites within the Restrictions only of Law, Virtue and Religion; so he might, if his Health required, or his Inclination prompted him to Temperance, or even to Abstinence, absent himself from any Meals, or retire from them whenever he was so disposed, without even a Solicitation to the contrary: For indeed, such Solicitations from Superiors always savour very strongly of Commands. But all here were free from such Impertinence, not only those whose Company is in all other Places esteemed a Favour from their Equality of Fortune, but even those whose indigent Circumstances make such an eleemosynary Abode convenient to them, and who are therefore less welcome to a great Man's Table because they stand in need of it.

Among others of this Kind was Dr. *Blifil*, a Gentleman who had the Misfortune of losing the Advantage of great Talents by the Obstinacy of a Father, who would breed him to a Profession he disliked. In Obedience to this Obstinacy the Doctor had in his Youth been obliged to study Physick, or rather to say he studied it; for in reality Books of this Kind were almost the only ones with which he was unacquainted; and unfortunately for him, the Doctor was Master of almost every other Science but that by which he was to get his Bread; the Consequence of which was, that the Doctor at the Age of Forty had no Bread to eat.

Such a Person as this was certain to find a Welcome at Mr. *Allworthy's* Table, to whom Misfortunes were ever a Recommendation when they were derived from the Folly or Villany of others, and not of the unfortunate Person himself. Besides this negative Merit, the Doctor had one positive Recommendation. This was a great Appearance of Religion. Whether his Religion was real, or consisted only in Appearance, I shall not presume to say, as I am not possessed of any Touch-stone, which can distinguish the true from the false.

If this Part of his Character pleased Mr. *Allworthy*, it delighted Miss *Bridget*. She engaged him in many religious Controversies; on which Occasions she constantly expressed great Satisfaction in the Doctor's Knowledge, and not much less in the Compliments which he frequently bestowed on her own. To say the Truth, she had read much *English* Divinity, and had puzzled more than one of the neighbouring Curates. Indeed her Conversation was so pure, her Looks so sage, and her whole Deportment so grave and solemn, that she seemed to deserve the Name of Saint equally with her Name-sake,[1] or with any other Female in the *Roman* Kalendar.

As Sympathies of all Kinds are apt to beget Love, so Experience teaches us that none have a more direct Tendency this Way than those of a religious Kind between Persons of different Sexes. The Doctor found himself so agreeable to Miss *Bridget*, that he now began to lament an unfortunate Accident which had happened to him about ten Years before; namely, his Marriage with another Woman, who was not only still alive, but what was worse, known to be so by Mr. *Allworthy*. This was a fatal Bar to that Happiness which he otherwise saw sufficient Probability of obtaining with this young Lady; for as to criminal Indulgencies, he certainly never thought of them. This was owing either to his Religion, as is most probable, or to the Purity of his Passion, which was fixed on those Things, which Matrimony only, and not criminal Correspondence, could put him in Possession of, or could give him any Title to.

He had not long ruminated on these Matters before it occurred to his Memory that he had a Brother who was under no such unhappy Incapacity. This Brother he made no doubt would succeed; for he discerned, as he thought, an Inclination to Marriage in the Lady; and the Reader perhaps, when he hears the Brother's Qualifications, will not blame the Confidence which he entertained of his Success.

This Gentleman was about 35 Years of Age. He was of a middle Size, and what is called well built. He had a Scar on his Forehead, which did not so much injure his Beauty, as it denoted his Valour (for he was a half-pay Officer.) He had good Teeth,

---

[1] St. Brigid (*c.* 451–525), patroness of Ireland, whose feast day in the Roman calendar is 1 February. Not only Bridget Allworthy, but Bridewell Hospital, the house of correction for loose women, was named after St. Brigid (or St. Bride).

and something affable, when he pleased, in his Smile; though naturally his Countenance, as well as his Air and Voice, had much of Roughness in it, yet he could at any Time deposite this, and appear all Gentleness and good Humour. He was not ungenteel, nor entirely void of Wit, and in his Youth had abounded in Spriteliness, which, though he had lately put on a more serious Character, he could, when he pleased, resume.

He had, as well as the Doctor, an Academic Education; for his Father had, with the same Paternal Authority we have mentioned before, decreed him for holy Orders; but as the old Gentleman died before he was ordained, he chose the Church Military, and preferred the King's Commission to the Bishop's.

He had purchased the Post of Lieutenant of Dragoons, and afterwards came to be a Captain; but having quarrelled with his Colonel, was by his Interest obliged to sell; from which Time he had entirely rusticated himself, had betaken himself to studying the Scriptures, and was not a little suspected of an Inclination to *Methodism.*[1]

[1] The Methodist movement had begun in the late 1730s under the leadership of the great evangelists, John Wesley (1703–91) and George Whitefield (1714–70). Its purpose was to reform the Church of England, both the worldliness of the clergy and the rationalistic, Pelagian tendencies of the latitudinarian divines. From the first, however, Fielding distrusted the movement and repeatedly attacked the fiery, calvinistic bias of Whitefield in particular, who, as Parson Adams declares in *Joseph Andrews* (1. xvii), was calling 'Nonsense and Enthusiasm to his Aid' and preaching the 'pernicious' doctrine of justification by faith and grace alone, without regard to good works. The latitudinarian divines whom Fielding admired—Barrow, Tillotson, and Hoadly, for example—stressed an opposite doctrine, denouncing emotionalism and mystery in religion and making salvation conditional upon an active charity. Whereas Whitefield condemned Tillotson and his followers for disregarding the calvinistic tenor of the Articles of the Church and for transforming Christianity into a mere moral system, little preferable to deism or to the stoicism of Cicero or Seneca, Fielding in turn decried the Antinomian implications of Whitefield's theology. Virtually repeated by Parson Adams, the popular rendering of Whitefield's position was, 'So you say you believe in the Lord Jesus Christ, you may live the life of devils.' After incidental allusions to Whitefield in *The Champion* (5 April, 24 May 1740), Fielding vigorously began his campaign against the new 'sect' in *Shamela* (1741), where, with the aid of Whitefield's works, Fielding's heroine rationalizes her frequent fornication and the hypocritical Parson Williams is made to parrot Whitefield's sermons. In *The Female Husband* (1746) Mary Hamilton is said to have been first corrupted by a recent convert to Methodism, and in *Amelia* (1. iv), the Methodist Cooper preaches the 'cant' doctrine of grace versus works and ends by picking Booth's pocket. As may be seen from his representation of Shamela and Mary Hamilton, Fielding suspected that the enthusiastical behaviour of the Methodists was often a convenient cover for sexual licence. For other derogatory allusions to Whitefield and his 'Sect' in *Tom Jones*, see below, pp. 430, 726, 980; also pp. 79, n. 4; 93, n. 1; 96, n. 2. A discussion of the subject may be found in Battestin, *The Moral Basis of Fielding's Art*, pp. 22–5, 81–4.

It seemed therefore not unlikely that such a Person should succeed with a Lady of so Saint-like a Disposition, and whose Inclinations were no otherwise engaged than to the married State in general; but why the Doctor, who certainly had no great Friendship for his Brother, should for his Sake think of making so ill a Return to the Hospitality of *Allworthy*, is a Matter not so easy to be accounted for.

Is it that some Natures delight in Evil, as others are thought to delight in Virtue? Or is there a Pleasure in being accessary to a Theft when we cannot commit it ourselves? Or Lastly, (which Experience seems to make probable) have we a Satisfaction in aggrandizing our Families, even tho' we have not the least Love or Respect for them?

Whether any of these Motives operated on the Doctor we will not determine; but so the Fact was. He sent for his Brother, and easily found Means to introduce him at *Allworthy's* as a Person who intended only a short Visit to himself.

The Captain had not been in the House a Week before the Doctor had Reason to felicitate himself on his Discernment. The Captain was indeed as great a Master of the Art of Love as *Ovid*[1] was formerly. He had besides received proper Hints from his Brother, which he failed not to improve to the best Advantage.

## CHAPTER XI

*Containing many Rules, and some Examples, concerning falling in love: Descriptions of Beauty, and other more prudential Inducements to Matrimony.*

IT hath been observed by wise Men or Women, I forget which, that all Persons are doomed to be in Love once in their Lives. No particular Season is, as I remember, assigned for this; but the Age at which Miss *Bridget* was arrived seems to me as proper a Period as any to be fixed on for this Purpose: It often indeed

---

[1] In late February 1747, Fielding published his own version of Ovid's *Ars Amatoria*, Book I, entitled *Ovid's Art of Love Paraphras'd and Adapted to the Present Times*. See *The Jacobite's Journal* (12 March 1748), where Fielding recommends this work to the 'unlearn'd Reader'.

happens much earlier; but when it doth not, I have observed, it
seldom or never fails about this Time. Moreover, we may remark
that at this Season Love is of a more serious and steady Nature
than what sometimes shews itself in the younger Parts of Life.
The Love of Girls is uncertain, capricious, and so foolish that
we cannot always discover what the young Lady would be at;
nay, it may almost be doubted, whether she always knows this
herself.

Now we are never at a Loss to discern this in Women about
Forty; for as such grave, serious and experienced Ladies well
know their own Meaning, so it is always very easy for a Man of
the least Sagacity to discover it with the utmost Certainty.

Miss *Bridget* is an Example of all these Observations. She
had not been many Times in the Captain's Company before she
was seized with this Passion. Nor did she go pining and moping
about the House, like a puny foolish Girl, ignorant of her Distemper: She felt, she knew, and she enjoyed, the pleasing
Sensation, of which, as she was certain it was not only innocent
but laudable, she was neither afraid nor ashamed.

And to say the Truth, there is in all Points, great Difference
between the reasonable Passion which Women at this Age conceive towards Men, and the idle and childish Liking of a Girl to a
Boy, which is often fixed on the Outside only, and on Things of
little Value and no Duration; as on Cherry Cheeks, small Lily-
white Hands, slow-black Eyes, flowing Locks, downy Chins,
dapper Shapes, nay sometimes on Charms more worthless than
these, and less the Party's own; such are the outward Ornaments
of the Person, for which Men are beholden to the Taylor, the
Laceman, the Perriwigmaker, the Hatter, and the Milliner, and
not to Nature. Such a Passion Girls may well be ashamed, as
they generally are, to own either to themselves or to others.

The Love of Miss *Bridget* was of another Kind. The Captain
owed nothing to any of these Fop-makers in his Dress, nor was
his Person much more beholden to Nature. Both his Dress and
Person were such as, had they appeared in an Assembly, or a
Drawing-room, would have been the Contempt and Ridicule of
all the fine Ladies there. The former of these was indeed neat,
but plain, coarse, ill-fancied, and out of Fashion. As for the latter,
we have expressly described it above. So far was the Skin on his
Cheeks from being Cherry-coloured, that you could not discern

what the natural Colour of his Cheeks was, they being totally
overgrown by a black Beard, which ascended to his Eyes. His
Shape and Limbs were indeed exactly proportioned, but so large,
that they denoted the Strength rather of a Ploughman than any
other. His Shoulders were broad, beyond all Size, and the Calves
of his Legs larger than those of a common Chairman. In short,
his whole Person wanted all that Elegance and Beauty, which is
the very reverse of clumsy Strength, and which so agreeably
sets off most of our fine Gentlemen; being partly owing to the
high Blood of their Ancestors, *viz.* Blood made of rich Sauces
and generous Wines, and partly to an early Town Education.

Tho' Miss *Bridget* was a Woman of the greatest Delicacy of
Taste; yet such were the Charms of the Captain's Conversation,
that she totally overlooked the Defects of his Person. She imagined,
and perhaps very wisely, that she should enjoy more agreeable
Minutes with the Captain, than with a much prettier Fellow;
and forewent the Consideration of pleasing her Eyes, in order
to procure herself much more solid Satisfaction.

The Captain no sooner perceived the Passion of Miss *Bridget*,
in which Discovery he was very quick-sighted, than he faithfully
returned it. The Lady, no more than her Lover, was remarkable
for Beauty. I would attempt to draw her Picture; but that is done
already by a more able Master, Mr. *Hogarth* himself, to whom she
sat many Years ago, and hath been lately exhibited by that Gentleman in his Print of a Winter's Morning,[1] of which she was no
improper Emblem, and may be seen walking (for walk she doth
in the Print) to *Covent-Garden* Church, with a starved Foot-boy
behind carrying her Prayer-book.

The Captain likewise very wisely preferred the more solid

---

[1] See 'Morning' from Hogarth's *The Four Times of the Day* (1738); the print is reproduced
as Plate I of this edition. Fielding's great admiration for the works of his good friend
William Hogarth (1697–1764) is amply attested. In a famous passage in *The Champion*
(10 June 1740) he pronounced 'the ingenious Mr. *Hogarth*' to be 'one of the most useful
Satyrists any Age hath produced'. In the Preface to *Joseph Andrews* Fielding refers to his
friend's works in order to illustrate the distinction between comic art and caricature; and in
*Tom Jones*, besides the allusion to 'Morning' in the present passage, Fielding directs his
readers to other specific paintings by Hogarth in order to clarify the description of Mrs.
Partridge (II. iii) and Thwackum (III. vi). Compliments to Hogarth also appear in *The
Vernon-iad* (1741), 'An Essay on Conversation' (1743), the Preface to Sarah Fielding's
*Familiar Letters* (1747), *Amelia* (1751; I. vi, III. iii, xii), *The Covent-Garden Journal* (21
January, 30 June 1752), and *The Journal of a Voyage to Lisbon* (1755). For other references
in *Tom Jones*, see below, pp. 82, 138, 282, 555, 742.

Enjoyments he expected with this Lady, to the fleeting Charms of Person. He was one of those wise Men, who regard Beauty in the other Sex as a very worthless and superficial Qualification; or, to speak more truly, who rather chuse to possess every Convenience of Life with an ugly Woman, than a handsome one without any of those Conveniencies. And having a very good Appetite, and but little Nicety, he fancied he should play his Part very well at the matrimonial Banquet, without the Sauce of Beauty.

To deal plainly with the Reader, the Captain, ever since his Arrival, at least from the Moment his Brother had proposed the Match to him, long before he had discovered any flattering Symptoms in Miss *Bridget,* had been greatly enamoured; that is to say, of Mr. *Allworthy's* House and Gardens, and of his Lands, Tenements and Hereditaments; of all which the Captain was so passionately fond, that he would most probably have contracted Marriage with them, had he been obliged to have taken the Witch of *Endor*¹ into the Bargain.

As Mr. *Allworthy* therefore had declared to the Doctor, that he never intended to take a second Wife, as his Sister was his nearest Relation, and as the Doctor had fished out that his Intentions were to make any Child of hers his Heir, which indeed the Law, without his Interposition, would have done for him;² the Doctor and his Brother thought it an Act of Benevolence to give Being to a human Creature, who would be so plentifully provided with the most essential Means of Happiness. The whole Thoughts therefore of both the Brothers, were how to engage the Affections of this amiable Lady.

But Fortune, who is a tender Parent, and often doth more for her favourite Offspring than either they deserve or wish, had been so industrious for the Captain, that whilst he was laying Schemes to execute his Purpose, the Lady conceived the same Desires with himself, and was on her Side contriving how to give the Captain proper Encouragement, without appearing too forward; for she was a strict Observer of all Rules of Decorum. In

¹ See 1 Samuel 28: 7–25.

² Since Allworthy has no children of his own to survive him, upon his death his estate would pass by law to the person who is '*next of Kin* in the *Collateral* Line of the whole Blood (tho' never so Remote)'—in this case, to his sister and her children. (See Thomas Wood, *An Institute of the Laws of England,* 7th ed. [1745], p. 228.)

this, however, she easily succeeded; for as the Captain was always on the Look-out, no Glance, Gesture, or Word, escaped him.

The Satisfaction which the Captain received from the kind Behaviour of Miss *Bridget,* was not a little abated by his Apprehensions of Mr. *Allworthy*; for, notwithstanding his disinterested Professions, the Captain imagined he would, when he came to act, follow the Example of the rest of the World, and refuse his Consent to a Match, so disadvantageous in point of Interest, to his Sister. From what Oracle he received this Opinion, I shall leave the Reader to determine; but, however he came by it, it strangely perplexed him how to regulate his Conduct so, as at once to convey his Affection to the Lady, and to conceal it from her Brother. He, at length, resolved to take all private Opportunities of making his Addresses; but in the Presence of Mr. *Allworthy* to be as reserved, and as much upon his Guard as was possible; and this Conduct was highly approved by the Brother.

He soon found Means to make his Addresses, in express Terms, to his Mistress, from whom he receiv'd an Answer in the proper Form; *viz.* The Answer which was first made some thousands of Years ago, and which hath been handed down by Tradition from Mother to Daughter ever since. If I was to translate this into Latin, I should render it by these two Words, *Nolo Episcopari*;[1] a Phrase likewise of immemorial Use on another Occasion.

The Captain, however he came by his Knowledge, perfectly well understood the Lady; and very soon after repeated his Application with more Warmth and Earnestness than before, and was again, according to due Form, rejected; but as he had encreased in the Eagerness of his Desires, so the Lady, with the same Propriety, decreased in the Violence of her Refusal.

Not to tire the Reader, by leading him through every Scene of this Courtship, (which, tho' in the Opinion of a certain great Author,[2] it is the pleasantest Scene of Life to the Actor, is perhaps as dull and tiresome as any whatever to the Audience) the

[1] 'I do not wish to be made a bishop'—the formal (and entirely perfunctory) reply traditionally made upon the royal offer of a bishopric. Cf. *A Journey from This World to the Next* (I. ix.).

[2] Joseph Addison in *The Spectator*, No. 261 (29 December 1711): 'The pleasantest Part of a Man's Life is generally that which passes in Courtship, provided his Passion be sincere, and the Party beloved kind with Discretion. Love, Desire, Hope, all the pleasing Motions of the Soul rise in the Pursuit.'

Captain made his Advances in Form, the Citadel was defended in Form, and at length, in proper Form, surrendered at Discretion.

During this whole Time, which filled the Space of near a Month, the Captain preserved great Distance of Behaviour to his Lady, in the Presence of the Brother, and the more he succeeded with her in private, the more reserved was he in public. And as for the Lady, she had no sooner secured her Lover, than she behaved to him before Company with the highest Degree of Indifference; so that Mr. *Allworthy* must have had the Insight of the Devil (or perhaps some of his worse Qualities) to have entertained the least Suspicion of what was going forward.

## CHAPTER XII

*Containing what the Reader may perhaps expect to find in it.*

IN all Bargains, whether to fight, or to marry, or concerning any other such Business, little previous Ceremony is required, to bring the Matter to an Issue, when both Parties are really in earnest. This was the Case at present, and in less than a Month the Captain and his Lady were Man and Wife.

The great Concern now was to break the Matter to Mr. *Allworthy*; and this was undertaken by the Doctor.

One Day then as *Allworthy* was walking in his Garden, the Doctor came to him, and with great Gravity of Aspect, and all the Concern which he could possibly affect in his Countenance, said, 'I am come, Sir, to impart an Affair to you of the utmost Consequence; but how shall I mention to you, what it almost distracts me to think of!' He then launched forth into the most bitter Invectives both against Men and Women; accusing the former of having no Attachment but to their Interest, and the latter of being so addicted to vicious Inclinations, that they could never be safely trusted with one of the other Sex. 'Could I,' said he, 'Sir, have suspected, that a Lady of such Prudence, such Judgment, such Learning, should indulge so indiscreet a Passion; or could I have imagined that my Brother—why do I call him so? He is no longer a Brother of mine.——'

'Indeed but he is,' said *Allworthy*, 'and a Brother of mine too.' ——'Bless me, Sir,' said the Doctor, 'do you know the shocking

Affair?'—— 'Look'ee, Mr. *Blifil,*' answered the good Man, 'it
hath been my constant Maxim in Life, to make the best of all
Matters which happen. My Sister, tho' many Years younger than
I, is at least old enough to be at the Age of Discretion. Had he
imposed on a Child, I should have been more averse to have forgiven him; but a Woman upwards of thirty must certainly be
supposed to know what will make her most happy. She hath
married a Gentleman, tho' perhaps not quite her Equal in Fortune; and if he hath any Perfections in her Eye, which can make
up that Deficiency, I see no Reason why I should object to her
Choice of her own Happiness; which I, no more than herself,
imagine to consist only in immense Wealth. I might, perhaps,
from the many Declarations I have made, of complying with
almost any Proposal, have expected to have been consulted on
this Occasion; but these Matters are of a very delicate Nature,
and the Scruples of Modesty perhaps are not to be overcome. As
to your Brother, I have really no Anger against him at all. He
hath no Obligations to me, nor do I think he was under any
Necessity of asking my Consent, since the Woman is, as I have
said, *Sui Juris,*[1] and of a proper Age to be entirely answerable
only to herself for her Conduct.'

The Doctor accused Mr. *Allworthy* of too great Lenity, repeated his Accusations against his Brother, and declared that he
should never more be brought either to see, or to own him for his
Relation. He then launched forth into a Panegyric on *Allworthy's*
Goodness, into the highest Encomiums on his Friendship; and
concluded, by saying, He should never forgive his Brother for
having put the Place which he bore in that Friendship, to a
Hazard.

*Allworthy* thus answer'd: 'Had I conceived any Displeasure
against your Brother, I should never have carried that Resentment to the Innocent: But, I assure you, I have no such Displeasure. Your Brother appears to me to be a Man of Sense and
Honour. I do not disapprove the Taste of my Sister; nor will I
doubt but that she is equally the Object of his Inclinations. I
have always thought Love the only Foundation of Happiness in
a married State; as it can only produce that high and tender
Friendship, which should always be the Cement of this Union;
and, in my Opinion, all those Marriages which are contracted

[1] 'Of one's own right'—the state of being able to exercise one's legal rights.

from other Motives, are greatly criminal; they are a Profanation of a most holy Ceremony, and generally end in Disquiet and Misery: For surely we may call it a Profanation, to convert this most sacred Institution into a wicked Sacrifice to Lust, or Avarice: And what better can be said of those Matches to which Men are induced merely by the Consideration of a beautiful Person, or a great Fortune!

'To deny that Beauty is an agreeable Object to the Eye, and even worthy some Admiration, would be false and foolish. Beautiful is an Epithet often used in Scripture, and always mentioned with Honour. It was my own Fortune to marry a Woman, whom the World thought handsome, and I can truly say, I liked her the better on that Account. But, to make this the sole Consideration of Marriage, to lust after it so violently, as to overlook all Imperfections for its Sake, or to require it so absolutely as to reject and disdain Religion, Virtue, and Sense, which are Qualities, in their Nature of much higher Perfection, only because an Elegance of Person is wanting; this is surely inconsistent either with a wise Man, or a good Christian. And it is, perhaps, being too charitable to conclude that such Persons mean any thing more by their Marriage, than to please their carnal Appetites, for the Satisfaction of which we are taught it was not ordained.

'In the next Place, with respect to Fortune. Worldly Prudence perhaps exacts some Consideration on this Head; nor will I absolutely and altogether condemn it. As the World is constituted, the Demands of a married State, and the Care of Posterity, require some little Regard to what we call Circumstances. Yet this Provision is greatly encreased beyond what is really necessary, by Folly and Vanity, which create abundantly more Wants than Nature. Equipage for the Wife, and large Fortunes for the Children, are by Custom enrolled in the List of Necessaries; and, to procure these, every thing truly solid and sweet, and virtuous, and religious, are neglected and overlooked.

'And this in many Degrees; the last and greatest of which seems scarce distinguishable from Madness. I mean, where Persons of immense Fortunes contract themselves to those who are, and must be, disagreeable to them; to Fools and Knaves, in order to encrease an Estate, already larger even than the Demands of their Pleasures. Surely such Persons, if they will not be thought mad, must own, either that they are incapable of tasting the

Sweets of the tenderest Friendship, or that they sacrifice the greatest Happiness of which they are capable, to the vain, uncertain, and senseless Laws of vulgar Opinion, which owe as well their Force, as their Foundation, to Folly.'

Here *Allworthy* concluded his Sermon, to which *Blifil* had listened with the profoundest Attention, tho' it cost him some Pains to prevent now and then a small Discomposure of his Muscles. He now praised every Period of what he had heard, with the Warmth of a young Divine who hath the Honour to dine with a Bishop the same Day in which his Lordship hath mounted the Pulpit.

## CHAPTER XIII

*Which concludes the first Book, with an Instance of Ingratitude, which we hope will appear unnatural.*

THE Reader, from what hath been said, may imagine that the Reconciliation (if indeed it could be so called) was only Matter of Form; we shall therefore pass it over, and hasten to what must surely be thought Matter of Substance.

The Doctor had acquainted his Brother with what had past between Mr. *Allworthy* and him; and added with a Smile. 'I promise you, I paid you off; nay, I absolutely desired the good Gentleman not to forgive you: For you know, after he had made a Declaration in your Favour, I might, with Safety, venture on such a Request with a Person of his Temper; and I was willing, as well for your Sake as for my own, to prevent the least Possibility of a Suspicion.'

Captain *Blifil* took not the least Notice of this, at that Time; but he afterwards made a very notable Use of it.

One of the Maxims which the Devil, in a late Visit upon Earth, left to his Disciples, is, when once you are got up, to kick the Stool from under you. In plain *English*, when you have made your Fortune by the good Offices of a Friend, you are advised to discard him as soon as you can.

Whether the Captain acted by this Maxim, I will not positively determine; so far we may confidently say, that his Actions may be fairly derived from this diabolical Principle; and indeed it is difficult to assign any other Motive to them: For no sooner was he possessed of Miss *Bridget*, and reconciled to *Allworthy*, than he began to shew a Coldness to his Brother, which encreased daily; till at length it grew into Rudeness, and became very visible to every one.

The Doctor remonstrated to him privately concerning this Behaviour, but could obtain no other Satisfaction than the following plain Declaration: 'If you dislike any thing in my Brother's House, Sir, you know you are at Liberty to quit it.' This strange, cruel, and almost unaccountable Ingratitude in the Captain, absolutely broke the poor Doctor's Heart: For Ingratitude never so thoroughly pierces the human Breast, as when it proceeds from those in whose Behalf we have been guilty of Transgressions. Reflections on great and good Actions, however they are received or returned by those in whose Favour they are performed, always administer some Comfort to us; but what Consolation shall we receive under so biting a Calamity as the ungrateful Behaviour of our Friend, when our wounded Conscience at the same Time flies in our Face, and upbraids us with having spotted it in the Service of one so worthless?

Mr. *Allworthy* himself spoke to the Captain in his Brother's Behalf, and desired to know what Offence the Doctor had committed; when the hard-hearted Villain had the Baseness to say, that he should never forgive him for the Injury which he had endeavoured to do him in his Favour; which, he said, he had pumped out of him, and was such a Cruelty, that it ought not to be forgiven.

*Allworthy* spoke in very high Terms upon this Declaration, which, he said, became not a human Creature. He expressed, indeed, so much Resentment against an unforgiving Temper, that the Captain at last pretended to be convinced by his Arguments, and outwardly professed to be reconciled.

As for the Bride, she was now in her Honey-moon, and so passionately fond of her new Husband, that he never appeared, to her, to be in the wrong; and his Displeasure against any Person, was a sufficient Reason for her Dislike to the same.

The Captain, at Mr. *Allworthy's* Instance, was outwardly, as we have said, reconciled to his Brother, yet the same Rancour remained in his Heart; and he found so many Opportunities of giving him private Hints of this, that the House at last grew insupportable to the poor Doctor; and he chose rather to submit to any Inconveniencies which he might encounter in the World, than longer to bear these cruel and ungrateful Insults, from a Brother for whom he had done so much.

He once intended to acquaint *Allworthy* with the whole; but he could not bring himself to submit to the Confession, by which he must take to his Share so great a Portion of Guilt. Besides, by how much the worse Man he represented his Brother to be, so much the greater would his own Offence appear to *Allworthy*, and so much the greater, he had Reason to imagine, would be his Resentment.

He feigned, therefore, some Excuse of Business for his Departure, and promised to return soon again; and took leave of his Brother with so well-dissembled Content, that, as the Captain played his Part to the same Perfection, *Allworthy* remained well satisfied with the Truth of the Reconciliation.

The Doctor went directly to *London*, where he died soon after of a broken Heart; a Distemper which kills many more than is generally imagined, and would have a fair Title to a Place in the Bill of Mortality,[1] did it not differ in one Instance from all other Diseases, *viz*. That no Physician can cure it.

Now, upon the most diligent Enquiry into the former Lives of these two Brothers, I find, besides the cursed and hellish Maxim of Policy above-mentioned, another Reason for the Captain's Conduct: The Captain, besides what we have before said of him, was a Man of great Pride and Fierceness, and had always treated his Brother, who was of a different Complexion, and greatly deficient in both those Qualities, with the utmost Air of Superiority. The Doctor, however, had much the larger Share of Learning, and was by many reputed to have the better Understanding. This the Captain knew, and could not bear. For, tho' Envy is at best a very malignant Passion, yet is its Bitterness greatly heightened by mixing with Contempt towards the same Object; and very much afraid I am, that whenever an Obligation is joined to these two, Indignation, and not Gratitude, will be the Product of all three.

---

[1] Since 1592, when plague broke out, the Company of Parish Clerks had published weekly records of deaths (and later of births and baptisms) occurring in 109 parishes in and around London.

# BOOK II

*Containing Scenes of matrimonial Felicity in different Degrees of Life; and various other Transactions during the first two Years after the Marriage between Captain* Blifil, *and* Miss *Bridget Allworthy.*

## CHAPTER I

*Shewing what Kind of a History this is; what it is like, and what it is not like.*

THO' we have properly enough entitled this our Work, a History, and not a Life; nor an Apology for a Life, as is more in Fashion;[1] yet we intend in it rather to pursue the Method of those Writers who profess to disclose the Revolutions of Countries, than to imitate the painful and voluminous Historian, who to preserve the Regularity of his Series thinks himself obliged to fill up as much Paper with the Detail of Months and Years in which nothing remarkable happened, as he employs upon those notable Æras when the greatest Scenes have been transacted on the human Stage.

Such Histories as these do, in reality, very much resemble a News-Paper, which consists of just the same Number of Words,

---

[1] Doubtless another hit at Colley Cibber (1671–1757), actor, playwright, and poet laureate. Cibber's autobiography, *An Apology for the Life of Mr. Colley Cibber, Comedian* (1740), was a favourite target of Fielding's satire: see, especially, *The Champion* (1, 15, 22, 29 April, 3, 6, 17 May 1740), *Shamela* (1741)—the full title of which parodies Cibber's own—*Joseph Andrews* (1742; I. i), and *Jonathan Wild* (1743; I. xiii). For a full sketch of Fielding's relations with Cibber, see the notes to the Wesleyan Edition of *Joseph Andrews*. While *Tom Jones* was nearing completion, moreover, other writers followed Cibber's example by publishing autobiographical 'apologies'. On 30 November 1747 appeared *An Apology for the Conduct of a late celebrated Second-rate Minister,* a spurious work purporting to disclose the unscrupulous politics of Thomas Winnington, recently deceased, and incidentally accusing Fielding's Whig friends in the government of being Jacobites in disguise; Fielding's *Proper Answer to a Late Scurrilous Libel* (24 December 1747) was written to refute this pamphlet. In April 1748 the scandalous 'Con' Phillips began to issue her own *Apology*, to which Fielding alludes in *Amelia* (1751; IV. i). This Cibberian device continued to be 'fashionable' after the publication of *Tom Jones*: late in 1749 there appeared the popular *Apology for the Life of Mr. Bampfylde-Moore Carew, Commonly call'd The King of the Beggars.*

whether there be any News in it or not. They may likewise be
compared to a Stage-Coach, which performs constantly the same
Course, empty as well as full. The Writer, indeed, seems to think
himself obliged to keep even Pace with Time, whose Amanuensis
he is; and, like his Master, travels as slowly through Centuries
of monkish Dulness, when the World seems to have been
asleep, as through that bright and busy Age so nobly distinguished
by the excellent *Latin* Poet.[1]

> *Ad confligendum venientibus undique pœnis;*
> *Omnia cum belli trepido concussa tumultu*
> *Horrida contremuere sub altis ætheris auris:*
> *In dubioque fuit sub utrorum regna cadendum*
> *Omnibus humanis esset, terraque marique.*

Of which, we wish we could give our Reader a more adequate
Translation than that by Mr. *Creech*.[2]

> When dreadful *Carthage* frighted *Rome* with Arms,
> And all the World was shook with fierce Alarms;
> Whilst undecided yet, which Part should fall,
> Which Nation rise the glorious Lord of all.

Now it is our Purpose in the ensuing Pages, to pursue a contrary Method. When any extraordinary Scene presents itself (as
we trust will often be the Case) we shall spare no Pains nor Paper
to open it at large to our Reader; but if whole Years should pass
without producing any thing worthy his Notice, we shall not be
afraid of a Chasm in our History; but shall hasten on to Matters of
Consequence, and leave such Periods of Time totally unobserved.
      These are indeed to be considered as Blanks in the grand
Lottery of Time. We therefore who are the Registers of that Lottery, shall imitate those sagacious Persons who deal in that which
is drawn at *Guild-Hall*,[3] and who never trouble the Public with

---

[1] Lucretius, *De Rerum Natura*, iii. 833–7. Fielding apparently followed the Creech text
of 1717 (in his library), which differs in several readings from the text of the Loeb Classical
Library edition (trans. W. H. D. Rouse, 1924), here cited.

[2] Thomas Creech (1659–1700), whose popular translation of Lucretius was first published in 1682.

[3] From 1694 to 1826 state lotteries were held at intervals to raise money for such purposes
as the construction of Westminster Bridge and the establishment of the British Museum.
Draws were held in November–December at the Guildhall, the Hall of the Corporation of
the City of London. The lottery system, which encouraged gambling even among the
poor and which led to profiteering by unscrupulous ticket-mongers, was often satirized by

the many Blanks they dispose of; but when a great Prize happens to be drawn, the News-Papers are presently filled with it, and the World is sure to be informed at whose Office it was sold: Indeed, commonly two or three different Offices lay claim to the Honour of having disposed of it; by which I suppose the Adventurers are given to understand that certain Brokers are in the Secrets of Fortune, and indeed of her Cabinet-Council.

My Reader then is not to be surprised, if in the Course of this Work, he shall find some Chapters very short, and others altogether as long; some that contain only the Time of a single Day, and others that comprise Years; in a word, if my History sometimes seems to stand still, and sometimes to fly. For all which I shall not look on myself as accountable to any Court of Critical Jurisdiction whatever: For as I am, in reality, the Founder of a new Province of Writing, so I am at liberty to make what Laws I please therein.[1] And these Laws, my Readers, whom I consider as my Subjects, are bound to believe in and to obey; with which that they may readily and chearfully comply, I do hereby assure them that I shall principally regard their Ease and Advantage in all such Institutions: For I do not, like a *jure divino* Tyrant,[2]

Fielding, most notably in his ballad-opera, *The Lottery* (1732), and in *The Champion* (29 December 1739, 3 January 1739/40). Incidental jibes at the lottery and at the 'Puffs' of 'Lottery-Mongers' occur in *The True Patriot* (12, 19, 26 November 1745). In the present passage, however, Fielding may allude specifically to the advertisements of two well-known brokers, Francis Wilson and J. Hazard: on 24 December 1746 and 4 December 1747 both these men claimed in the newspapers to have sold identical tickets, prizes of £5,000 and £500, respectively. (See *The General Advertiser*, 24 December 1746, and *The Penny London Post*, 24–6 December 1746; and *The Daily Advertiser*, 4 December 1747.)

[1] An echo of the famous critical axiom enunciated by Le Bossu in the opening chapter of his *Traité du poëme épique* (Paris, 1675). Dryden paraphrases as follows: 'That all excellent arts, and particularly that of poetry, have been invented and brought to perfection by men of a transcendent genius; and that, therefore, they, who practise afterwards the same arts, are obliged to tread in their footsteps, and to search in their writings the foundation of them; for it is not just that new rules should destroy the authority of the old' ('Preface to *Troilus and Cressida* [1679], containing The Grounds of Criticism in Tragedy'; in W. P. Ker, ed. *Essays of John Dryden* [New York, 1961], i. 211).

[2] The political metaphor developed in this passage is the first of many anti-Jacobitical strokes in *Tom Jones*. Specifically, Fielding's argument recalls Locke's *Two Treatises of Government* (1690), which maintained the principles of a limited, constitutional monarchy against the doctrine of absolutism propounded by Sir Robert Filmer in *Patriarcha* (1680). Filmer's view that the king ruled *jure divino*, by divine right, provided the ideological basis of Jacobitism. Locke, on the other hand, was the great apologist for the Revolution Settlement of 1689, insisting that the supreme power resided in the legislature, which governs only by consent of the governed. Fielding always subscribed to this view (cf. 'Liberty' [1743], l. 79, where he ironically reflects on 'the strange Divinity of Kings'); but from

imagine that they are my Slaves or my Commodity. I am, indeed, set over them for their own Good only, and was created for their Use, and not they for mine. Nor do I doubt, while I make their Interest the great Rule of my Writings, they will unanimously concur in supporting my Dignity, and in rendering me all the Honour I shall deserve or desire.

## CHAPTER II

*Religious Cautions against shewing too much Favour to Bastards; and a great Discovery made by Mrs.* Deborah Wilkins.

EIGHT Months after the Celebration of the Nuptials between Captain *Blifil* and Miss *Bridget Allworthy*, a young Lady of great Beauty, Merit, and Fortune,[1] was Miss *Bridget*, by reason of a Fright, delivered of a fine Boy. The Child, was indeed, to all Appearance, perfect; but the Midwife discovered, it was born a Month before its full Time.

Tho' the Birth of an Heir by his beloved Sister was a Circumstance of great Joy to Mr. *Allworthy*, yet it did not alienate his Affections from the little Foundling, to whom he had been Godfather, had given his own Name of *Thomas*, and whom he had hitherto seldom failed of visiting at least once a Day, in his Nursery.

He told his Sister, if she pleased, the new-born Infant should be bred up together with little *Tommy*, to which she consented, tho' with some little Reluctance: For she had truly a great Complacence for her Brother; and hence she had always behaved towards the Foundling with rather more Kindness than Ladies of

the time of the Jacobite uprising in 1745 he was especially outspoken in applying Lockean principles to defend the Hanoverian Establishment. In *A Serious Address to the People of Great Britain* (1745) he represents James II as a king whose 'Mind was strongly tainted with all the Notions of absolute Power. Passive Obedience, and Non-resistance on the Part of the Subject, and a *dispensing Power* in the Crown, with an indefeasible Hereditary Right, *Jure Divino*, were as much Articles of his political Creed, as the Supremacy of the Pope, or Transubstantiation, were of his religious one . . .' (p. 5). Later, in the third number of *The Jacobite's Journal* (19 December 1747), Fielding cited the doctrine of the king's rule *jure divino* as the fundamental 'Mystery' of Jacobitism.

  1 The phrasing parodies the fulsome and pretentious language of wedding-notices in the newspapers, a subject which Fielding frequently ridiculed in his journals. See below, p. 705, n. 1, where the hyperbole here applied to Bridget Allworthy reappears verbatim in a similar satire from *The Jacobite's Journal* (13 February 1748).

rigid Virtue can sometimes bring themselves to shew to these Children, who, however innocent, may be truly called the living Monuments of Incontinence.

The Captain could not so easily bring himself to bear what he condemned as a Fault in Mr. *Allworthy*. He gave him frequent Hints, that to adopt the Fruits of Sin was to give countenance to it. He quoted several Texts (for he was well read in Scripture) such as, *He visits the Sins of the Fathers upon the Children*;[1] and, *the Fathers have eaten sour Grapes, and the Children's Teeth are set on edge,*[2] &c. Whence he argued the Legality of punishing the Crime of the Parent on the Bastard. He said, 'Tho' the Law did not positively allow the destroying such base-born Children, yet it held them to be the Children of no body; that the Church considered them as the Children of no body;[3] and that at the best, they ought to be brought up to the lowest and vilest Offices of the Commonwealth.'

Mr. *Allworthy* answered[4] to all this and much more which the

---

[1] The second commandment (Exodus 20: 5, Deuteronomy 5: 9): 'Thou shalt not bow down thyself to them [graven images], nor serve them: for I the LORD thy God *am* a jealous God, visiting the iniquity of the fathers upon the children unto the third and fourth *generation* of them that hate me.'

[2] Ezekiel 18: 2–3: 'What mean ye, that ye use this proverb concerning the land of Israel, saying, The fathers have eaten sour grapes, and the children's teeth are set on edge ?/ *As* I live, saith the Lord GOD, ye shall not have *occasion* any more to use this proverb in Israel.' (Cf. Jeremiah 31: 29–30 and Numbers 14: 18.)

[3] 'A *Bastard* is he that is born out of Marriage. He shall never inherit or be Heir to any one. He cannot be of kin to one. For in Law he is *Quasi nullius Filius*, and no Man's Issue.' (Wood, *Institutes*, 7th ed. [1745], p. 67.) Since 1160 the position of the Church had been that children born out of wedlock should be considered legitimate; but in 1235 (20 Henry III, cap. 9) the secular courts denied the bishops' plea to this effect. (Edmund Gibson, *Codex Juris Ecclesiastici Anglicani* [1713], ii. 1129–30.)

[4] Though ostensibly a question of the guilt or innocence of bastards, the dispute between Captain Blifil and Allworthy is actually a rehearsal of contemporary arguments for and against the theological doctrine of absolute reprobation. Blifil, 'not a little suspected of an Inclination to *Methodism*' (p. 63, n. 1), echoes the harsh Calvinistic views of George Whitefield, who cited the same scriptural texts as the captain in asserting the doctrines of original sin and justification by grace and faith alone. Thus in his sermon, 'The Potter and the Clay', Whitefield promised that those who attended to his message 'will then no longer have any thing to say against the doctrine of *Original Sin*; or charge the Almighty foolishly, for suffering our first parents to be prevailed on to eat such sour grapes, and permitting thereby their children's teeth to be set on edge'. (Sermon xiii, *Works* [1771–2], v. 214.) It was Whitefield's belief in absolute reprobation that caused him to break with Wesley, whose Methodism was milder and more Arminian in character. (See Whitefield's 'Letter to the Reverend Mr. John Wesley: In Answer to his Sermon, Entituled, Free-Grace' [24 December 1740]; ibid., iv. 67 and *passim*.)

On the other hand, Allworthy's refutation of Blifil closely follows the arguments of John

Captain had urged on this Subject, 'That however guilty the
Parents might be, the Children were certainly innocent. That
as to the Texts he had quoted, the former of them was a particular
Denunciation against the *Jews* for the Sin of Idolatry, of relin-
quishing and hating their heavenly King; and the latter was
parabolically spoken,[1] and rather intended to denote the certain
and necessary Consequences of Sin, than any express Judgment
against it. But to represent the Almighty as avenging the Sins
of the Guilty on the Innocent, was indecent, if not blasphemous,
as it was to represent him acting against the first Principles of
natural Justice, and against the original Notions of Right and
Wrong, which he himself had implanted in our Minds; by which
we were to judge not only in all Matters which were not revealed,
but even of the Truth of Revelation itself. He said, he knew
many held the same Principles with the Captain on this Head;
but he was himself firmly convinced to the contrary, and would
provide in the same Manner for this poor Infant, as if a legitimate
Child had had the Fortune to have been found in the same Place.'

While the Captain was taking all Opportunities to press these
and such like Arguments to remove the little Foundling from Mr.
*Allworthy's*, of whose Fondness for him he began to be jealous,

Tillotson (see below, p. 145), Archbishop of Canterbury and leader of the latitudinarians.
In his sermon, 'The goodness of God', for example, Tillotson vehemently denounced 'the
doctrine of absolute reprobation: by which I mean the decreeing the greatest part of
mankind to eternal misery and torment, without any consideration or respect to their sin
and fault.... GOD is infinitely better than the best of men, and yet none can possibly think
that man a good man, who should absolutely resolve to disinherit and destroy his children,
without the foresight and consideration of any fault to be committed by them. We may
talk of the goodness of GOD; but it is not an easy matter to devise to say any thing worse
than this of the devil.' (Sermon cxlv, *Works* [1757], viii. 277–9.) To assert this view of the
Deity, Tillotson elsewhere declared, is 'little less than a horrid and dreadful blasphemy'.
(Sermon cxxxvi, 'The wisdom, glory, and sovereignty of GOD', ibid., viii. 124.) The text
Allworthy applies to Blifil's position, furthermore, had been recommended by Tillotson in
rejecting the doctrine of reprobation. In Sermon cxv, 'The sins of men not chargeable upon
GOD; but upon themselves', Tillotson insisted that 'one of the surest ways of reasoning in
religion' is 'from the natural notions which men have of GOD. . . . And if any thing be,
upon good grounds in reason, received for a divine revelation, (as the holy scriptures are
amongst christians) no man ought to be regarded, who from thence pretends to maintain
any doctrine contrary to the natural notions, which men have of GOD; such as clearly
contradict his holiness, or goodness, or justice, or do by plain and undeniable consequence
make GOD the author of sin, or the like; because the very attempt to prove any such thing
out of the scripture, does strike at the divine authority of those books' (ibid., vii. 93–5).

[1] According to William Warburton, Origen was the first to offer a parabolical interpretation of the texts cited by Captain Blifil. (See *The Divine Legation of Moses Demonstrated*,
ii [1741], 460–1.)

Mrs. *Deborah* had made a Discovery, which in its Event threatned at least to prove more fatal to poor *Tommy*, than all the Reasonings of the Captain.

Whether the insatiable Curiosity of this good Woman had carried her on to that Business, or whether she did it to confirm herself in the good Graces of Mrs. *Blifil*, who, notwithstanding her outward Behaviour to the Foundling, frequently abused the Infant in private, and her Brother too for his Fondness to it, I will not determine; but she had now, as she conceived, fully detected the Father of the Foundling.

Now as this was a Discovery of great Consequence, it may be necessary to trace it from the Fountain-head. We shall therefore very minutely lay open those previous Matters by which it was produced; and for that Purpose, we shall be obliged to reveal all the Secrets of a little Family, with which my Reader is at present entirely unacquainted; and of which the Oeconomy was so rare and extraordinary, that I fear it will shock the utmost Credulity of many married Persons.

## CHAPTER III

*The Description of a domestic Government founded upon Rules directly contrary to those of* Aristotle.[1]

MY Reader may please to remember he hath been informed that *Jenny Jones* had lived some Years with a certain Schoolmaster, who had, at her earnest Desire, instructed her in *Latin*, in which, to do justice to her Genius, she had so improved herself, that she was become a better Scholar than her Master.

Indeed, tho' this poor Man had undertaken a Profession to which Learning must be allowed necessary, this was the least of his Commendations. He was one of the best-natured Fellows in the World, and was at the same time Master of so much Pleasantry and Humour that he was reputed the Wit of the Country; and all the neighbouring Gentlemen were so desirous of his Company, that as denying was not his Talent, he spent much

---

[1] Cf. *Politics*, i. v. 1–2, where Aristotle states that the husband is by nature meant to govern his wife and family.

Time at their Houses, which he might with more Emolument have spent in his School.

It may be imagined, that a Gentleman so qualified, and so disposed, was in no danger of becoming formidable to the learned Seminaries of *Eton* or *Westminster*. To speak plainly, his Scholars were divided into two Classes. In the upper of which was a young Gentleman, the Son of a neighbouring Squire, who at the Age of Seventeen was just entered into his Syntaxis;[1] and in the lower was a second Son of the same Gentleman, who, together with seven Parish-boys, was learning to read and write.

The Stipend arising hence would hardly have indulged the Schoolmaster in the Luxuries of Life, had he not added to this Office those of Clerk and Barber, and had not Mr. *Allworthy* added to the whole an Annuity of Ten Pound, which the poor Man received every Christmas, and with which he was enabled to chear his Heart during that sacred Festival.

Among his other Treasures, the Pedagogue had a Wife whom he had married out of Mr. *Allworthy's* Kitchen, for her Fortune, *viz.* Twenty Pound, which she had there amassed.

This Woman was not very amiable in her Person. Whether she sat to my Friend *Hogarth*,[2] or no, I will not determine; but she exactly resembled the young Woman who is pouring out her Mistress's Tea in the third Picture of the Harlot's Progress. She was besides a profest Follower of that notable Sect founded by *Xantippe*[3] of old; by means of which, she became more formidable in the School than her Husband: for to confess the Truth, he was never Master there, or any where else, in her Presence.

Tho' her Countenance did not denote much natural Sweetness of Temper, yet this was perhaps somewhat soured by a Circumstance which generally poisons matrimonial Felicity. For Children are rightly called the Pledges of Love; and her Husband, tho' they had been married nine Years, had given her no such Pledges; a Default for which he had no Excuse, either from Age or Health,

---

[1] The construction of grammar—usually the second stage in the teaching of Latin.

[2] See above, p. 66, n. 1. Plate 3 of Hogarth's *A Harlot's Progress* (1732) is reproduced as Plate 2. For this satiric series and for the later *Rake's Progress* (1735) Fielding had the highest praise: 'I almost dare affirm', he remarked in *The Champion* (10 June 1740), that these two works 'are calculated more to serve the Cause of Virtue, and for the Preservation of Mankind, than all the *Folio's* of Morality which have been ever written'.

[3] The shrewish wife of Socrates.

being not yet thirty Years old, and, what they call a jolly, brisk, young Man.

Hence arose another Evil which produced no little Uneasiness to the poor Pedagogue, of whom she maintained so constant a Jealousy, that he durst hardly speak to one Woman in the Parish; for the least Degree of Civility, or even Correspondence with any Female, was sure to bring his Wife upon her Back, and his own.

In order to guard herself against matrimonial Injuries in her own House, as she kept one Maid Servant, she always took Care to chuse her out of that Order of Females, whose Faces are taken as a Kind of Security for their Virtue; of which Number *Jenny Jones*, as the Reader hath been before informed, was one.

As the Face of this young Woman might be called pretty good Security of the before-mentioned Kind, and as her Behaviour had been always extremely modest; which is the certain Consequence of Understanding in Women; she had passed above four Years at Mr. *Partridge's*, (for that was the Schoolmaster's Name) without creating the least Suspicion in her Mistress. Nay, she had been treated with uncommon Kindness, and her Mistress had permitted Mr. *Partridge* to give her those Instructions, which have been before commemorated.

But it is with Jealousy, as with the Gout. When such Distempers are in the Blood, there is never any Security against their breaking out; and that often on the slightest Occasions, and when least suspected.

Thus it happened to Mrs. *Partridge*, who had submitted four Years to her Husband's teaching this young Woman, and had suffered her often to neglect her Work, in order to pursue her Learning. For passing by one Day, as the Girl was reading, and her Master leaning over her, the Girl, I know not for what Reason, suddenly started up from her Chair; and this was the first Time that Suspicion ever entered into the Head of her Mistress.

This did not, however, at that Time, discover itself, but lay lurking in her Mind, like a concealed Enemy, who waits for a Reinforcement of additional Strength, before he openly declares himself, and proceeds upon hostile Operations; and such additional Strength soon arrived to corroborate her Suspicion: For not long after, the Husband and Wife being at Dinner, the Master said to his Maid, *Da mihi aliquid Potum*;[1] upon which the

---

[1] Partridge tries to say, 'Give me something to drink.'

poor Girl smiled, perhaps at the Badness of the Latin, and when her Mistress cast her Eyes on her, blushed, possibly with a Consciousness of having laughed at her Master. Mrs. *Partridge*, upon this, immediately fell into a Fury, and discharged the Trencher on which she was eating, at the Head of poor *Jenny*, crying out, 'You impudent Whore, do you play Tricks with my Husband before my Face?' and, at the same Instant, rose from her Chair, with a Knife in her Hand, with which, most probably, she would have executed very tragical Vengeance, had not the Girl taken the Advantage of being nearer the Door than her Mistress, and avoided her Fury, by running away; for, as to the poor Husband, whether Surprize had rendered him motionless, or Fear (which is full as probable) had restrained him from venturing at any Opposition, he sat staring and trembling in his Chair; nor did he once offer to move or speak, till his Wife returning from the Pursuit of *Jenny*, made some defensive Measures necessary for his own Preservation; and he likewise was obliged to retreat, after the Example of the Maid.

This good Woman was, no more than *Othello*,[1] of a Disposition,

> ———To make a Life of Jealousy,
> And follow still the Changes of the Moon
> With fresh Suspicions———

with her, as well as him;

> ———To be once in doubt
> Was once to be resolved———

she therefore ordered *Jenny* immediately to pack up her Alls, and be gone; for that she was determined she should not sleep that Night within her Walls.

Mr. *Partridge* had profited too much, by Experience, to interpose in a Matter of this Nature. He therefore had Recourse to his usual Recipe of Patience; for, tho' he was not a great Adept in Latin, he remembered and well understood the Advice contained in these Words:

> ———*Leve fit, quod bene fertur Onus.*[2]

In English: 'A Burden becomes lightest, when it is well borne.'

---

[1] *Othello*, III. iii.
[2] Ovid, *Amores*, I. ii. 10. Cf. *Amelia* (1751), III. x.

Which he had always in his Mouth, and of which, to say the Truth, he had often Occasion to experience the Truth.

*Jenny* offered to make Protestations of her Innocence; but the Tempest was too high for her to be heard. She then betook herself to the Business of Packing, for which a small Quantity of brown Paper sufficed; and, having received her small Pittance of Wages, she returned home.

The Schoolmaster and his Consort pass'd their Time unpleasantly enough that Evening; but something or other happened before the next Morning, which a little abated the Fury of Mrs. *Partridge*; and she at length admitted her Husband to make his Excuses. To which she gave the readier Belief, as he had, instead of desiring her to recall *Jenny*, professed a Satisfaction in her being dismissed, saying, She was grown of little Use as a Servant, spending all her Time in reading, and was become, moreover, very pert and obstinate: For indeed she and her Master had lately had frequent Disputes in Literature; in which, as hath been said, she was become greatly his Superior. This, however, he would by no means allow; and, as he called her persisting in the Right, Obstinacy, he began to hate her with no small Inveteracy.

CHAPTER IV

*Containing one of the most bloody Battles, or rather Duels, that were ever recorded in Domestic History.*

FOR the Reasons mentioned in the preceding Chapter, and from some other matrimonial Concessions, well known to most Husbands; and which, like the Secrets of Free Masonry,[1]

---

[1] Incidental satire directed against the esotericism of Freemasonry occurs in several of Fielding's publications during 1747: e.g. in *Ovid's Art of Love Paraphrased*, in the Preface to Sarah Fielding's *Familiar Letters*, and in the three first numbers of *The Jacobite's Journal* (5, 12, 19 December 1747), where a facetious comparison is drawn between the 'mysterious' doctrines of Freemasonry and Jacobitism. This, indeed, may be the connection that prompted Fielding's sarcasm. As may be seen in James Anderson's *Constitutions of the Free-Masons* (1723; 2nd ed., 1738) the brothers took a special pride in claiming the Stuart kings for their fraternity; in particular, Anderson praised James I as 'a *Mason* King' who, by patronizing 'our *great Master-Mason* INIGO JONES', became 'the *First* Prince in the World that recover'd the *Roman* Architecture from the Ruins of *Gothick* Ignorance' (see L. Vibert, ed. [1923], pp. 38–41). According to the constitution of

should be divulged to none who are not Members of that honourable Fraternity; Mrs. *Partridge* was pretty well satisfied, that she had condemned her Husband without Cause, and endeavoured, by Acts of Kindness, to make him Amends for her false Suspicion. Her Passions were, indeed, equally violent, which ever Way they inclined: for, as she could be extremely angry, so could she be altogether as fond.

But tho' these Passions ordinarily succeeded each other, and scarce twenty-four Hours ever passed in which the Pedagogue was not, in some Degree, the Object of both; yet, on extraordinary Occasions, when the Passion of Anger had raged very high, the Remission was usually longer, and so was the Case at present; for she continued longer in a State of Affability, after this Fit of Jealousy was ended, than her Husband had ever known before: And, had it not been for some little Exercises, which all the Followers of *Xantippe* are obliged to perform daily, Mr. *Partridge* would have enjoyed a perfect Serenity of several Months.

Perfect Calms at Sea are always suspected by the experienced Mariner to be the Forerunners of a Storm: And I know some Persons, who, without being generally the Devotees of Superstition, are apt to apprehend, that great and unusual Peace or Tranquility, will be attended with its opposite: For which Reason the Antients used, on such Occasions, to sacrifice to the Goddess *Nemesis*; a Deity who was thought by them to look with an invidious Eye on human Felicity, and to have a peculiar Delight in overturning it.

As we are very far from believing in any such Heathen Goddess, or from encouraging any Superstition, so we wish Mr. *John Fr——*,[1] or some other such Philosopher, would bestir

the Order, furthermore, no brother could be expelled from a lodge merely for being a rebel, a stipulation designed to accommodate powerful Jacobite elements in the fraternity (ibid., pp. xxix, 50). For a later reference to Freemasonry in *Tom Jones*, see below, p. 236, n. 1.

[1] John Freke (1688–1756), F.R.S. and Surgeon at St. Bartholomew's Hospital, London. In 1746 the publication of William Watson's *Experiments and Observations* generated considerable popular and scientific interest in electricity and electrical phenomena. Freke entered the controversy in mid October, publishing an absurdly theoretical and pretentious work entitled, *An Essay to Shew the Cause of Electricity; and Why Some Things are Non-Electricable . . . In a Letter to Mr. William Watson, F.R.S.* (The first edition was announced in *The Daily Advertiser*, 11 October 1746; the second edition appeared on 3 November 1746—see *The Daily Advertiser* and *The London Courant* for that date.) Freke's claims for his pamphlet were extravagant, to say the least. His subject, he declared, *'can, with more Nobleness and Dignity employ the Mind of Man, than any I can think of relating to the sub-*

himself a little, in order to find out the real Cause of this sudden Transition, from good to bad Fortune, which hath been so often remarked, and of which we shall proceed to give an Instance; for it is our Province to relate Facts, and we shall leave Causes to Persons of much higher Genius.

Mankind have always taken great Delight in knowing and descanting on the Actions of others. Hence there have been, in all Ages, and Nations, certain Places set apart for public Rendezvous, where the Curious might meet, and satisfy their mutual Curiosity. Among these, the Barbers Shops have justly borne the Pre-eminence. Among the *Greeks*, Barbers News was a proverbial Expression,[1] and *Horace*, in one of his Epistles,[2] makes honourable Mention of the *Roman* Barbers in the same Light.

Those of *England* are known to be no wise inferior to their *Greek* or *Roman* Predecessors. You there see foreign Affairs discussed in a Manner little inferior to that with which they are handled in the Coffee-houses; and domestick Occurrences are much more largely and freely treated in the former, than in the latter. But this serves only for the Men. Now, whereas the Females of this Country, especially those of the lower Order, do associate themselves much more than those of other Nations, our Polity would be highly deficient, if they had not some Place set apart likewise for the Indulgence of their Curiosity, seeing they are in this no way inferior to the other half of the Species.

In enjoying, therefore, such Place of Rendezvous, the *British* Fair ought to esteem themselves more happy than any of their foreign Sisters; as I do not remember either to have read in

*lunary Part of the World. For by it you may be acquainted with the immediate Officer of* God Almighty, *which he seems to send to all Things living. Nay, this Power, according to my Conception, seems to be the Cause, under* HIM, *both of Life and Death*' (pp. v–vi). Having discovered the '*Flamma Vitalis*' (p. 4) of the ancient philosophers, he saw himself enshrined among the Harveys and Newtons of modern science (pp. vii–viii). Others besides Fielding were amused by Freke's hobby-horsical performance. In *Remarks on a Rhapsody of Adventures of a Modern Knight-Errant in Philosophy* (Bath, 1746), Benjamin Martin likened Freke to a scientific Don Quixote performing 'Feats of *Electrical Chivalry*' (p. 25). For a later allusion to Freke's essay in *Tom Jones*, see below, p. 187, n. 1.

1 Cf. Plutarch, 'De Garrulitate', *Moralia*, 509; also Lucian, *How to Write History*, 24. But Fielding may be allowed his own gloss on the passage: in a note to his and William Young's translation of Aristophanes' *Plutus, the God of Riches* (1742; II. iii), he describes barber shops as 'the Coffee-Houses of the Antients. . . . They were Assemblies of all idle gossipping Fellows, who there assembled to vent their Malignity against their Betters. The Barbers themselves were likewise the most talkative and impertinent of all People.'

2 Fielding probably means Horace's *Satires*, I. vii. 2–3.

History, or to have seen in my Travels, any thing of the like Kind.

This Place then is no other than the Chandler's Shop; the known Seat of all the News; or, as it is vulgarly called, Gossiping, in every Parish in *England*.

Mrs. *Partridge* being one Day at this Assembly of Females, was asked by one of her Neighbours, if she had heard no News lately of *Jenny Jones*. To which she answered in the negative. Upon this, the other replied, with a Smile, That the Parish was very much obliged to her for having turned *Jenny* away as she did.

Mrs. *Partridge*, whose Jealousy, as the Reader well knows, was long since cured, and who had no other Quarrel to her Maid, answered boldly, She did not know any Obligation the Parish had to her on that Account, for she believed *Jenny* had scarce left her Equal behind her.

'No, truly,' said the Gossip, 'I hope not, tho' I fancy we have Sluts enow too. Then you have not heard, it seems, that she hath been brought to bed of two Bastards; but as they are not born here, my Husband, and the other Overseer, says we shall not be obliged to keep them.'[1]

'Two Bastards!' answered Mrs. *Partridge* hastily, 'you surprize me. I don't know whether we must keep them; but I am sure they must have been begotten here, for the Wench hath not been nine Months gone away.'

Nothing can be so quick and sudden as the Operations of the Mind, especially when Hope, or Fear, or Jealousy to which the two others are but Journeymen, set it to work. It occurred instantly to her, that *Jenny* had scarce ever been out of her own House, while she lived with her. The leaning over the Chair, the sudden starting up, the Latin, the Smile, and many other Things rushed upon her all at once. The Satisfaction her Husband expressed in the Departure of *Jenny*, appeared now to be only dissembled; again, in the same Instant, to be real; but yet to confirm her Jealousy, proceeding from Satiety, and a hundred other bad Causes. In a Word, she was convinced of her Husband's Guilt, and immediately left the Assembly in Confusion.

[1] A bastard child was considered to be settled in, and therefore chargeable to, the parish in which it was born, even though it was conceived elsewhere. (See Michael Dalton, *The Country Justice* [1746], p. 172.)

As fair *Grimalkin*, who, though the youngest of the Feline Family, degenerates not in Ferosity from the elder Branches of her House, and, though inferior in Strength, is equal in Fierceness to the noble Tyger himself, when a little Mouse, whom it hath long tormented in Sport, escapes from her Clutches for a while, frets, scolds, growls, swears; but if the Trunk, or Box, behind which the Mouse lay hid, be again removed, she flies like Lightning on her Prey, and, with envenomed Wrath, bites, scratches, mumbles, and tears the little Animal.

Not with less Fury did Mrs. *Partridge* fly on the poor Pedagogue. Her Tongue, Teeth, and Hands, fell all upon him at once. His Wig was in an Instant torn from his Head, his Shirt from his Back, and from his Face descended five Streams of Blood, denoting the Number of Claws with which Nature had unhappily armed the Enemy.

Mr. *Partridge* acted for some Time on the defensive only; indeed he attempted only to guard his Face with his Hands; but as he found that his Antagonist abated nothing of her Rage, he thought he might, at least, endeavour to disarm her, or rather to confine her Arms; in doing which, her Cap fell off in the Struggle, and her Hair being too short to reach her Shoulders, erected itself on her Head; her Stays likewise, which were laced through one single Hole at the Bottom, burst open, and her Breasts, which were much more redundant than her Hair, hung down below her Middle; her Face was likewise marked with the Blood of her Husband; her Teeth gnashed with Rage; and Fire, such as sparkles from a Smith's Forge, darted from her Eyes. So that, altogether, this Amazonian Heroine might have been an Object of Terror to a much bolder Man than Mr. *Partridge*.

He had, at length, the good Fortune, by getting Possession of her Arms, to render those Weapons, which she wore at the Ends of her Fingers, useless; which she no sooner perceived, than the Softness of her Sex prevailed over her Rage, and she presently dissolved in Tears, which soon after concluded in a Fit.

That small Share of Sense which Mr. *Partridge* had hitherto preserved through this Scene of Fury, of the Cause of which he was hitherto ignorant, now utterly abandoned him. He ran instantly into the Street, hollowing out, that his Wife was in the Agonies of Death, and beseeching the Neighbours to fly with the utmost Haste to her Assistance. Several good Women obeyed his

Summons, who entering his House, and applying the usual Remedies on such Occasions, Mrs. *Partridge* was, at length, to the great Joy of her Husband, brought to herself.

As soon as she had a little recollected her Spirits, and somewhat composed herself with a Cordial, she began to inform the Company of the manifold Injuries she had received from her Husband; who, she said, was not contented to injure her in her Bed; but, upon her upbraiding him with it, had treated her in the cruelest Manner imaginable; had torn her Cap and Hair from her Head, and her Stays from her Body, giving her, at the same Time, several Blows, the Marks of which she should carry to the Grave.

The poor Man, who bore on his Face many more visible Marks of the Indignation of his Wife, stood in silent Astonishment at this Accusation; which the Reader will, I believe, bear Witness for him, had greatly exceeded the Truth; for indeed he had not struck her once; and this Silence being interpreted to be a Confession of the Charge, by the whole Court, they all began at once, *una voce*, to rebuke and revile him, repeating often, that none but a Coward ever struck a Woman.

Mr. *Partridge* bore all this patiently; but when his Wife appealed to the Blood on her Face, as an Evidence of his Barbarity, he could not help laying Claim to his own Blood, for so it really was; as he thought it very unnatural, that this should rise up (as we are taught[1] that of a murdered Person often doth) in Vengeance against him.

To this the Women made no other Answer, than that it was Pity it had not come from his Heart, instead of his Face; all declaring, that if their Husbands should lift their Hands against them, they would have their Heart's Bloods out of their Bodies.

After much Admonition for what was past, and much good Advice to Mr. *Partridge* for his future Behaviour, the Company, at length, departed, and left the Husband and Wife to a personal Conference together, in which Mr. *Partridge* soon learned the Cause of all his Sufferings.

[1] Cf. Genesis 4: 10. Fielding alludes to this text in the introduction to *Examples of the Interposition of Providence in the Detection and Punishment of Murder* (1752).

## CHAPTER V

*Containing much Matter to exercise the Judgment and Reflection of the Reader.*

I BELIEVE it is a true Observation, that few Secrets are divulged to one Person only; but certainly, it would be next to a Miracle, that a Fact of this Kind should be known to a whole Parish, and not transpire any farther.

And, indeed, a very few Days had past, before the Country, to use a common Phrase, rung of the Schoolmaster of *Little Baddington*; who was said to have beaten his Wife in the most cruel Manner. Nay, in some Places, it was reported he had murdered her; in others, that he had broke her Arms; in others, her Legs; in short, there was scarce an Injury which can be done to a human Creature, but what Mrs. *Partridge* was somewhere or other affirmed to have received from her Husband.

The Cause of this Quarrel was likewise variously reported; for, as some People said that Mrs. *Partridge* had caught her Husband in Bed with his Maid, so many other Reasons, of a very different Kind, went abroad. Nay, some transferred the Guilt to the Wife, and the Jealousy to the Husband.

Mrs. *Wilkins* had long ago heard of this Quarrel; but, as a different Cause from the true one had reached her Ears, she thought proper to conceal it; and the rather, perhaps, as the Blame was universally laid on Mr. *Partridge*; and his Wife, when she was Servant to Mr. *Allworthy*, had in something offended Mrs. *Wilkins*, who was not of a very forgiving Temper.

But Mrs. *Wilkins*, whose Eyes could see Objects at a Distance, and who could very well look forward a few Years into Futurity, had perceived a strong Likelihood of Captain *Blifil's* being hereafter her Master; and, as she plainly discerned, that the Captain bore no great Good-will to the little Foundling, she fancied it would be rendering him an agreeable Service, if she could make any Discoveries that might lessen the Affection which Mr. *Allworthy* seemed to have contracted for this Child, and which gave visible Uneasiness to the Captain; who could not entirely conceal it even before *Allworthy* himself; though his Wife, who acted her Part much better in public, frequently recommended to him her own Example, of conniving at the Folly of her Brother,

which, she said, she at least as well perceived, and as much resented as any other possibly could.

Mrs. *Wilkins* having therefore, by Accident, gotten a true
Scent of the above Story, though long after it had happened, failed
not to satisfy herself thoroughly of all the Particulars, and then
acquainted the Captain, that she had at last discovered the true
Father of the little Bastard, which she was sorry, she said, to see
her Master lose his Reputation in the Country, by taking so much
Notice of.

The Captain chid her for the Conclusion of her Speech, as an
improper Assurance in judging of her Master's Actions: For if his
Honour, or his Understanding, would have suffered the Captain
to make an Alliance with Mrs. *Wilkins*, his Pride would by no
means have admitted it. And, to say the Truth, there is no Conduct less politic, than to enter into any Confederacy with your
Friend's Servants, against their Master. For, by these Means,
you afterwards become the Slave of these very Servants; by
whom you are constantly liable to be betrayed. And this Consideration, perhaps, it was which prevented Captain *Blifil* from
being more explicit with Mrs. *Wilkins*; or from encouraging the
Abuse which she had bestowed on *Allworthy*.

But though he declared no Satisfaction to Mrs. *Wilkins* at this
Discovery, he enjoyed not a little from it in his own Mind, and
resolved to make the best Use of it he was able.

He kept this Matter a long Time concealed within his own
Breast, in Hopes that Mr. *Allworthy* might hear it from some
other Person; but Mrs. *Wilkins*, whether she resented the Captain's Behaviour, or whether his Cunning was beyond her, and
she feared the Discovery might displease him, never afterwards
opened her Lips about the Matter.

I have thought it somewhat strange, upon Reflection, that the
House-keeper never acquainted Mrs. *Blifil* with this News, as
Women are more inclined to communicate all Pieces of In-
telligence to their own Sex, than to ours. The only Way, as it
appears to me, of solving this Difficulty, is, by imputing it to
that Distance which was now grown between the Lady and the
House-keeper: Whether this arose from a Jealousy in Mrs.
*Blifil*, that *Wilkins* shewed too great a Respect to the Foundling;
for while she was endeavouring to ruin the little Infant, in order
to ingratiate herself with the Captain, she was every Day more

and more commending it before *Allworthy*, as his Fondness for it every Day encreased. This, notwithstanding all the Care she took at other Times to express the direct contrary to Mrs. *Blifil*, perhaps offended that delicate Lady, who certainly now hated Mrs. *Wilkins*; and though she did not, or possibly could not, absolutely remove her, from her Place, she found, however, the Means of making her Life very uneasy. This Mrs. *Wilkins*, at length, so resented, that she very openly shewed all Manner of Respect and Fondness to little *Tommy*, in Opposition to Mrs. *Blifil*.

The Captain, therefore, finding the Story in Danger of perishing, at last took an Opportunity to reveal it himself.

He was one Day engaged with Mr. *Allworthy* in a Discourse on Charity:[1] In which the Captain, with great Learning, proved

[1] In their 'Discourse on Charity' which Fielding develops over the next several paragraphs, Captain Blifil again reveals his Methodistical inclinations while Allworthy, in answering him, draws upon one of Fielding's favourite latitudinarian divines, Isaac Barrow. Blifil begins by echoing Whitefield (see pp. 63, n. 1; 79, n. 4; 96, n. 2; 430, n. 1; 929, n. 1). In his sermon on 1 Corinthians 13, 'The great Duty of Charity recommended' (1740), Whitefield replied to those critics who, he said, had falsely accused him of denying the efficacy of moral actions. Nevertheless, the definition of charity he proposed makes it a much less practical virtue than that recommended by the latitudinarians. Most commentators agree that the Greek word *agape*, translated as 'charity' in the King James version, is more accurately rendered as 'spiritual love'; thus Whitefield, referring to St. Paul, informs his congregation 'what the apostle means by charity; and that is, LOVE' (Sermon xlvii, *Works* [1771–2], vi. 228). Though he does not quite disparage almsgiving, he denies that St. Paul intended us 'to hurt ourselves or our families' by an imprudent generosity (ibid., vi. 227) and he further declares that charity is 'much more valuable ... when it extends to the souls of men' (ibid., vi. 233) than when it ministers to their bodies only. For Whitefield, true charity is the 'grace of love' (ibid., vi. 237), not the mere performance of good works:

'It is not the leading of a moral life, being honest, and paying every man his just due; this is not a proof of your being in a state of grace, or of being born again, and renewed in the spirit of your minds: No, you may die honest, just, charitable, and yet not be in a state of salvation.

'It is not the preaching of that morality, which most of our pulpits now bring forth, that is sufficient to bring you from sin unto GOD. . . .

'Therefore, let me advise you to be charitable to the souls of one another; that is, by advising them with all love and tenderness, to follow after CHRIST, and the things which belong to their immortal peace, before they be for ever hid from their eyes.' (Ibid., vi. 234–5.)

For Whitefield as for Captain Blifil, the latitudinarians, in preaching the doctrine of works, were feeding their flocks 'only with the dry husks of dead morality' (Sermon xxxviii, 'The Indwelling of the Spirit, the Common Privilege of All Believers', ibid., vi. 95): 'My dear brethren,' he admonished, '*Seneca, Cicero, Plato*, or any of the heathen philosophers, would have given as good a definition as this' (Sermon ix, 'The Folly and Danger of Being Not Righteous Enough', ibid., v. 126).

to Mr. *Allworthy*, that the Word *Charity*, in Scripture, no where means Beneficence, or Generosity.

'The Christian Religion,' he said, 'was instituted for much nobler Purposes, than to enforce a Lesson which many Heathen Philosophers had taught us long before, and which, though it might, perhaps, be called a moral Virtue, savoured but little of that sublime Christian-like Disposition, that vast Elevation of Thought, in Purity approaching to angelic Perfection, to be attained, expressed, and felt only by Grace. Those (he said) came nearer to the Scripture Meaning, who understood by it Candour, or the forming of a benevolent Opinion of our Brethren, and passing a favourable Judgment on their Actions; a Virtue much higher, and more extensive in its Nature, than a pitiful Distribution of Alms, which, though we would never so much prejudice, or even ruin our Families, could never reach many; whereas Charity, in the other and truer Sense, might be extended to all Mankind.'

He said, 'Considering who the Disciples were, it would be absurd to conceive the Doctrine of Generosity, or giving Alms, to have been preached to them. And, as we could not well imagine this Doctrine should be preached by its divine Author to Men who could not practise it, much less shall we think it understood so by those who can practise it, and do not.

'But though,' continued he, 'there is, I am afraid, little Merit in these Benefactions; there would, I must confess, be much Pleasure in them to a good Mind, if it was not abated by one Consideration. I mean, that we are liable to be imposed upon, and to confer our choicest Favours often on the Undeserving, as you must own was your Case in your Bounty to that worthless Fellow *Partridge*: For two or three such Examples must greatly lessen the inward Satisfaction, which a good Man would otherwise find in Generosity; nay, may even make him timorous in bestowing, lest he should be guilty of supporting Vice, and encouraging the Wicked; a Crime of a very black Dye, and for which it will by no means be a sufficient Excuse, that we have not actually intended such an Encouragement; unless we have used the utmost Caution in chusing the Objects of our Beneficence. A Consideration which, I make no Doubt, hath greatly checked the Liberality of many a worthy and pious Man.'

Mr. *Allworthy* answered,[1] 'He could not dispute with the Captain in the *Greek* Language, and therefore could say nothing as to the true Sense of the Word, which is translated *Charity*; but that he had always thought it was interpreted to consist in Action, and that giving Alms constituted at least one Branch of that Virtue.

'As to the meritorious Part,' he said, 'he readily agreed with the Captain; for where could be the Merit of barely discharging a Duty; which (he said) let the Word Charity have what Construction it would, it sufficiently appeared to be from the whole Tenor of the New Testament. And as he thought it an indispensable Duty, enjoined both by the Christian Law, and by the Law of Nature itself; so was it withal so pleasant, that if any Duty could be said to be its own Reward, or to pay us while we are discharging it, it was this.

[1] If Allworthy is unsure about the true signification of *agape*, his author had no such doubts. In *The Champion* (5 April 1740) Fielding offered his own interpretation of 1 Corinthians 13, declaring that the word *agape*, 'which some Versions, render Charity, is better rendered by others Love'. Like Allworthy, however, he further insists that this is above all an active virtue, 'not confined to our Wishes merely, but our Actions, under which Head I shall introduce Liberality. . . . By this Virtue, which is generally called Charity itself, (and perhaps it is the chief Part of it) is not meant the ostentatious giving a penny to a Beggar in the Street . . . as if Charity was Change for Sixpence, but the relieving the Wants and Sufferings of one another to the utmost of our Abilities. It is to be limited by our Power, I say, only.'
The arguments Allworthy adduces in defence of an active charity may be found in countless homilies by the latitudinarian divines. (See, for example, R. S. Crane, *ELH*, i [1934], esp. 208–13; and Battestin, *Moral Basis of Fielding's Art*, pp. 17–22.) But in the succeeding paragraphs his particular emphasis on the 'Duty' and 'Reward' of Beneficence, and his notion of the 'epicurean' pleasures which the charitable man enjoys, point to a specific source for the passage in Isaac Barrow's 'The Duty and Reward of Bounty to the Poor', a classic charity sermon of the period. Fielding's admiration for 'our favourite Dr. Barrow' (1630–77) is well attested by complimentary references in *Amelia* (1751; VI. vii; XII. v), where Booth is saved from infidelity by perusing Barrow's works, and in *The Covent-Garden Journal* (14 January, 24 March, 11 April, 16 May, 2 June, 4 November 1752), in which Barrow's sermon is frequently quoted. With Allworthy's view that charity consists principally in action, not, as Captain Blifil asserts, merely in 'Candour', compare Barrow: 'And of charity, works of bounty and mercy are both the chief instances, and the plainest signs: for whereas all charity doth consist either in mental desire, or in verbal signification, or in effectual performance of good to our neighbour; this last is the end, the completion, and the assurance of the rest. Good-will is indeed the root of charity; but that lies under ground, and out of sight; nor can we conclude its being or life without visible fruits of beneficence. Good words are at best but fair leaves thereof, such as may (and too often do) proceed from a weak and barren disposition of mind. . . . It is to decline spending their goods, or their pains, that men forge and feign; pretending to make up in wishing well, the defect of doing so, and paying words instead of things' (Sermon xxxi, *Works*, 5th ed. [1741], i. 308–9).

'To confess the Truth,' said he, 'there is one Degree of Generosity, (of Charity I would have called it) which seems to have some Shew of Merit, and that is, where from a Principle of Benevolence, and Christian Love, we bestow on another what we really want ourselves; where, in order to lessen the Distresses of another, we condescend to share some Part of them by giving what even our own Necessities cannot well spare. This is, I think, meritorious; but to relieve our Brethren only with our Superfluities; to be charitable (I must use the Word) rather at the Expence of our Coffers than ourselves; to save several Families from Misery rather than hang up an extraordinary Picture in our Houses, or gratify any other idle, ridiculous Vanity, this seems to be only being Christians, nay indeed, only being human Creatures. Nay, I will venture to go farther, it is being in some degree Epicures:[1] For what could the greatest Epicure wish rather than to eat with many Mouths instead of one; which I think may be predicated of any one who knows that the Bread of many is owing to his own Largesses.

'As to the Apprehension of bestowing Bounty on such as may hereafter prove unworthy Objects, because many have proved such; surely it can never deter a good Man from Generosity: I do not think a few or many Examples of Ingratitude can justify a Man's hardening his Heart against the Distresses of his Fellow-Creatures; nor do I believe it can ever have such Effect on a truly benevolent Mind. Nothing less than a Persuasion of universal Depravity can lock up the Charity of a good Man; and this Persuasion must lead him, I think, either into Atheism, or Enthusiasm;[2] but surely it is unfair to argue such universal

---

[1] Cf. Barrow, 'The Duty and Reward of Bounty to the Poor': Nature has 'made the communication of benefits to others to be accompanied with a very delicious relish upon the mind of him that practices it; nothing indeed carrying with it a more pure and savoury delight than beneficence. A man may be virtuously voluptuous, and a laudable epicure by doing much good; for to receive good, even in the judgment of *Epicurus* himself, (the great patron of pleasure) is no wise so pleasant as to do it' (Sermon xxxi, op. cit., i. 322). In *The Covent-Garden Journal* (11 April 1752) Fielding quotes this passage from 'my beloved Author Dr. Barrow'.

[2] The cynical view of human nature that Allworthy here rejects, Fielding attributed chiefly to the 'atheistical' philosophies of Hobbes and Mandeville, on the one hand (see below, p. 268, n. 2), and to Whitefield and the Calvinists, on the other. In his sermon, 'The Folly and Danger of being not righteous enough', Whitefield thus assured his congregation that 'There is no difference between you, by nature, and the greatest malefactor that ever was executed at *Tyburn*: the difference made, is all owing to the free, the rich, the undeserved grace of GOD'(Sermon ix, op. cit., v. 137). His insistence that 'we must feel that

Depravity from a few vicious Individuals; nor was this, I believe, ever done by a Man, who upon searching his own Mind found one certain Exception to the general Rule.' He then concluded by asking who that *Partridge* was whom he had called a worthless Fellow.

'I mean,' said the Captain, '*Partridge*, the Barber, the School-master, what do you call him? *Partridge*, the Father of the little Child which you found in your Bed.'

Mr. *Allworthy* exprest great Surprise at this Account, and the Captain as great at his Ignorance of it: For he said, he had known it above a Month, and at length recollected with much Difficulty that he was told it by Mrs. *Wilkins*.

Upon this, *Wilkins* was immediately summoned, who having confirmed what the Captain had said, was by Mr. *Allworthy*, by and with the Captain's Advice, dispatched to *Little Badding-ton* to inform herself of the Truth of the Fact: For the Captain exprest great Dislike at all hasty Proceedings in criminal Matters, and said he would by no means have Mr. *Allworthy* take any Resolution either to the Prejudice of the Child or its Father, before he was satisfied that the latter was guilty: For tho' he had privately satisfied himself of this from one of *Partridge's* Neigh-bours, yet he was too generous to give any such Evidence to Mr. *Allworthy*.

## CHAPTER VI

*The Trial of* Partridge, *the Schoolmaster, for Incontinency; The Evidence of his Wife; A short Reflection on the Wisdom of our Law; with other grave Matters, which those will like best who understand them most.*

IT may be wondered that a Story so well known, and which had furnished so much Matter of Conversation, should never have been mentioned to Mr. *Allworthy* himself, who was perhaps the only Person in that Country who had never heard of it.

To account in some measure for this to the Reader, I think proper to inform him that there was no one in the Kingdom less

Spirit upon our hearts' encouraged displays of religious fervour amongst Whitefield's followers which his critics condemned as 'enthusiasm and madness' (ibid., v. 125).

interested in opposing that Doctrine concerning the Meaning of the Word Charity, which hath been seen in the preceding Chapter, than our good Man. Indeed, he was equally intitled to this Virtue in either Sense: For as no Man was ever more sensible of the Wants, or more ready to relieve the Distresses of others, so none could be more tender of their Characters, or slower to believe any thing to their Disadvantage.

Scandal, therefore, never found any Access to his Table: For as it hath been long since observed that you may know a Man by his Companions;[1] so I will venture to say, that by attending to the Conversation at a great Man's Table, you may satisfy yourself of his Religion, his Politics, his Taste, and indeed of his entire Disposition: For tho' a few odd Fellows will utter their own Sentiments in all Places, yet much the greater Part of Mankind have enough of the Courtier to accommodate their Conversation to the Taste and Inclination of their Superiors.

But to return to Mrs. *Wilkins*, who having executed her Commission with great Dispatch, tho' at fifteen Miles Distance, brought back such a Confirmation of the Schoolmaster's Guilt, that Mr. *Allworthy* determined to send for the Criminal, and examine him *viva voce*. Mr. *Partridge*, therefore, was summoned to attend, in order to his Defence (if he could make any) against this Accusation.

At the Time appointed, before Mr. *Allworthy* himself, at *Paradise-Hall*, came as well the said *Partridge*, with *Anne* his Wife, as Mrs. *Wilkins*, his Accuser.

And now Mr. *Allworthy* being seated in the Chair of Justice, Mr. *Partridge* was brought before him. Having heard his Accusation from the Mouth of Mrs. *Wilkins*, he pleaded, Not guilty, making many vehement Protestations of his Innocence.

Mrs. *Partridge* was then examined, who, after a modest Apology for being obliged to speak the Truth against her Husband, related all the Circumstances with which the Reader hath already been acquainted; and at last concluded with her Husband's Confession of his Guilt.

Whether she had forgiven him or no, I will not venture to determine: But it is certain, she was an unwilling Witness in this Cause, and it is probable, from certain other Reasons would never have been brought to depose as she did, had not Mrs. *Wilkins*,

---

[1] Cf. the proverb, 'Noscitur a socio', cited pp. 119, 542.

with great Art, fished all out of her, at her own House, and had
she not indeed made Promises in Mr. *Allworthy's* Name, that the
Punishment of her Husband should not be such as might any
wise affect his Family.

*Partridge* still persisted in asserting his Innocence, tho' he
admitted he had made the above-mentioned Confession; which
he however endeavoured to account for, by protesting that he
was forced into it by the continued Importunity she used, who
vowed, that as she was sure of his Guilt, she would never leave
tormenting him till he had owned it, and faithfully promised, that
in such Case, she would never mention it to him more. Hence,
he said, he had been induced falsely to confess himself guilty,
tho' he was innocent; and that he believed he should have confest
a Murder from the same Motive.

Mrs. *Partridge* could not bear this Imputation with Patience;
and having no other Remedy, in the present Place but Tears,
she called forth a plentiful Assistance from them, and then
addressing herself to Mr. *Allworthy*, she said, (or rather cried)
'May it please your Worship, there never was any poor Woman so
injured as I am by that base Man: For this is not the only Instance
of his Falshood to me. No, may it please your Worship, he hath
injured my Bed many's the good time and often. I could have
put up with his Drunkenness and Neglect of his Business, if he
had not broke one of the sacred *Commandiments*. Besides, if it had
been out of Doors I had not mattered it so much; but with my
own Servant, in my own House, under my own Roof; to defile
my own chaste Bed, which to be sure he hath with his beastly
stinking Whores. Yes, you Villain, you have defiled my own
Bed, you have; and then you have charged me with *bullocking*
you into owning the Truth. It is very likely, an't please your
Worship, that I should *bullock* him.—I have Marks enow about
my Body to shew of his Cruelty to me. If you had been a Man,
you Villain, you would have scorned to injure a Woman in that
Manner. But you an't half a Man, you know it.—Nor have you
been half a Husband to me. You need run after Whores, you need,
when I'm sure——And since he provokes me, I am ready, an't
please your Worship, to take my bodily Oath, that I found them
a-bed together. What, you have forgot, I suppose, when you beat
me into a Fit, and made the Blood run down my Forehead,
because I only civilly taxed you with your Adultery! but I can

prove it by all my Neighbours. You have almost broke my Heart,
you have, you have.'

Here Mr. *Allworthy* interrupted, and begged her to be pacified,
promising her that she should have Justice; then turning to
*Partridge*, who stood aghast, one half of his Wits being hurried
away by Surprise and the other half by Fear, he said, he was sorry
to see there was so wicked a Man in the World. He assured him,
that his prevaricating and lying backward and forward was a
great Aggravation of his Guilt: For which, the only Attonement
he could make was by Confession and Repentance. He exhorted
him, therefore, to begin by immediately confessing the Fact, and
not to persist in denying what was so plainly proved against him,
even by his own Wife.

Here, Reader, I beg your Patience a Moment, while I make a
just Compliment to the great Wisdom and Sagacity of our Law,
which refuses to admit the Evidence of a Wife for or against her
Husband. This, says a certain learned Author,[1] who, I believe,
was never quoted before in any but a Law-book, would be the
Means of creating an eternal Dissention between them. It would,
indeed, be the Means of much Perjury, and of much Whipping,
Fining, Imprisoning, Transporting, and Hanging.

*Partridge* stood a while silent, till being bid to speak, he said,
he had already spoken the Truth, and appealed to Heaven for his
Innocence, and lastly, to the Girl herself, whom he desired his
Worship immediately to send for; for he was ignorant, or at least
pretended to be so, that she had left that Part of the Country.

Mr. *Allworthy*, whose natural Love of Justice, joined to his
Coolness of Temper, made him always a most patient Magistrate
in hearing all the Witnesses which an accused Person could produce in his Defence, agreed to defer his final Determination of
this Matter, till the Arrival of *Jenny*, for whom he immediately
dispatched a Messenger; and then having recommended Peace
between *Partridge* and his Wife (tho' he addressed himself chiefly
to the wrong Person) he appointed them to attend again the third
Day: For he had sent *Jenny* a whole Day's Journey from his own
House.

1 Sir Edward Coke (1552–1634) in his *Commentary upon Littleton*, I. i: 'It hath been
resolved by the Justices, That a Wife cannot be produced either against or for her Husband,
*quia sunt duae animae in una carne*; and it might be a Cause of implacable Discord and
Dissension between the Husband and the Wife, and a Means of great Inconvenience' (11th
ed. [1719], p. 6).

At the appointed Time the Parties all assembled, when the Messenger returning brought word, that *Jenny* was not to be found: For that she had left her Habitation a few Days before, in company with a recruiting Officer.

Mr. *Allworthy* then declared, that the Evidence of such a Slut as she appeared to be, would have deserved no Credit; but he said he could not help thinking that had she been present, and would have declared the Truth, she must have confirmed what so many Circumstances, together with his own Confession, and the Declaration of his Wife, that she had caught her Husband in the Fact, did sufficiently prove. He therefore once more exhorted *Partridge* to confess; but he still avowing his Innocence, Mr. *Allworthy* declared himself satisfied of his Guilt, and that he was too bad a Man to receive any Encouragement from him. He therefore deprived him of his Annuity, and recommended Repentance to him, on account of another World, and Industry to maintain himself and his Wife in this.

There were not, perhaps, many more unhappy Persons, than poor *Partridge*. He had lost the best Part of his Income by the Evidence of his Wife, and yet was daily upbraided by her for having, among other Things, been the Occasion of depriving her of that Benefit; but such was his Fortune, and he was obliged to submit to it.

Tho' I called him, poor *Partridge*, in the last Paragraph, I would have the Reader rather impute that Epithet to the Compassion in my Temper, than conceive it to be any Declaration of his Innocence. Whether he was innocent or not, will perhaps appear hereafter; but if the Historic-Muse[1] hath entrusted me with any Secrets, I will by no means be guilty of discovering them till she shall give me leave.

Here therefore, the Reader must suspend his Curiosity. Certain it is, that whatever was the Truth of the Case, there was Evidence more than sufficient to convict him before *Allworthy*; indeed much less would have satisfied a Bench of Justices on an Order of Bastardy;[2] and yet, notwithstanding the Positiveness of Mrs. *Partridge*, who would have taken the Sacrament upon the Matter,

[1] Clio.

[2] By order of two justices of the parish (one being of the quorum), the mother and father of a bastard child could be punished and compelled to provide for the care of the child, which would otherwise become chargeable to the parish. (See Dalton, *The Country Justice* [1746], p. 33.)

there is a Possibility that the Schoolmaster was entirely innocent: For tho' it appeared clear, on comparing the Time when *Jenny* departed from *Little Baddington*, with that of her Delivery, that she had there conceived this Infant, yet it by no means followed, of Necessity, that *Partridge* must have been its Father: For, to omit other Particulars, there was in the same House a Lad near Eighteen, between whom, and *Jenny*, there had subsisted sufficient Intimacy to found a reasonable Suspicion; and yet, so blind is Jealousy, this Circumstance never once entered into the Head of the enraged Wife.

Whether *Partridge* repented or not, according to Mr. *Allworthy's* Advice, is not so apparent. Certain it is, that his Wife repented heartily of the Evidence she had given against him; especially when she found Mrs. *Deborah* had deceived her, and refused to make any Application to Mr. *Allworthy* on her Behalf. She had, however, somewhat better Success with Mrs. *Blifil*, who was, as the Reader must have perceived, a much better-tempered Woman; and very kindly undertook to solicit her Brother to restore the Annuity. In which, tho' Good-nature might have some Share, yet a stronger and more natural Motive will appear in the next Chapter.

These Solicitations were nevertheless unsuccessful: For tho' Mr. *Allworthy* did not think, with some late Writers,[1] that Mercy consists only in punishing Offenders; yet he was as far from thinking that it is proper to this excellent Quality to pardon great Criminals wantonly, without any Reason whatever.[2] Any Doubtfulness of the Fact, or any Circumstance of Mitigation, was never disregarded; but the Petitions of an Offender, or the Inter-

---

[1] In the summer of 1746, the question of whether or not mercy should be shown to the defeated rebels occasioned a heated controversy in the newspapers which may be followed in the pages of *The Gentleman's Magazine*, xvi (June–October). A certain Andrew Horne was most vehement in urging the severest punishment (see *The General Evening-Post*, 22 July and 21 August 1746). Others, however, advocated clemency and applauded the king's decision to pardon the Earl of Cromarty, one of three Jacobite lords sentenced to be executed on 18 August.

[2] Cf. Fielding in *An Enquiry into the Causes of the Late Increase of Robbers* (1751), section x: 'To speak out fairly and honestly, tho' Mercy may appear more amiable in a Magistrate, Severity is a more wholesome Virtue; nay Severity to an Individual may, perhaps, be in the End the greatest Mercy, not only to the Public in general . . . but to many Individuals.' When confronted with villainy, Fielding continues, 'the Passions of the Man are to give Way to the Principles of the Magistrate. Those may lament the Criminal, but these must condemn him.' Contrast, in different circumstances, Jones's leniency towards the highwayman (XII. xiv) with Allworthy's sternness towards Black George (XVIII. xi).

cessions of others, did not in the least affect him. In a word, he never pardoned, because the Offender himself, or his Friends, were unwilling that he should be punished.

*Partridge* and his Wife were therefore both obliged to submit to their Fate; which was indeed severe enough: For so far was he from doubling his Industry on the account of his lessened Income, that he did in a manner abandon himself to despair; and as he was by Nature indolent, that Vice now increased upon him, by which means he lost the little School he had; so that neither his Wife nor himself would have had any Bread to eat, had not the Charity of some good Christian interposed, and provided them with what was just sufficient for their Sustenance.

As this Support was conveyed to them by an unknown Hand, they imagined, and so, I doubt not, will the Reader, that Mr. *Allworthy* himself was their secret Benefactor; who, though he would not openly encourage Vice, could yet privately relieve the Distresses of the Vicious themselves, when these became too exquisite and disproportionate to their Demerit. In which Light, their Wretchedness appeared now to Fortune herself; for she at length took pity on this miserable Couple, and considerably lessened the wretched State of *Partridge*, by putting a final end to that of his Wife, who soon after caught the Small-Pox, and died.

The Justice which Mr. *Allworthy* had executed on *Partridge*, at first met with universal Approbation; but no sooner had he felt its Consequences, than his Neighbours began to relent, and to compassionate his Case; and presently after, to blame that as Rigour and Severity, which they before called Justice. They now exclaimed against punishing in cold Blood, and sang forth the Praises of Mercy and Forgiveness.

These Cries were considerably increased by the Death of Mrs. *Partridge*, which, tho' owing to the Distemper above mentioned which is no Consequence of Poverty or Distress, many were not ashamed to impute to Mr. *Allworthy's* Severity, or, as they now termed it, Cruelty.

*Partridge*, having now lost his Wife, his School, and his Annuity, and the unknown Person having now discontinued the last-mentioned Charity, resolved to change the Scene, and left the Country, where he was in Danger of starving with the universal Compassion of all his Neighbours.

## CHAPTER VII

*A short Sketch of that Felicity which prudent Couples may extract from Hatred; with a short Apology for those People who overlook Imperfections in their Friends.*

THO' the Captain had effectually demolished poor *Partridge*, yet had he not reaped the Harvest he hoped for, which was to turn the Foundling out of Mr. *Allworthy's* House.

On the contrary, that Gentleman grew every Day fonder of little *Tommy*, as if he intended to counterbalance his Severity to the Father with extraordinary Fondness and Affection towards the Son.

This a good deal soured the Captain's Temper, as did all the other daily Instances of Mr. *Allworthy's* Generosity: For he looked on all such Largesses to be Diminutions of his own Wealth.

In this, we have said, he did not agree with his Wife; nor indeed, in any thing else: For tho' an Affection placed on the Understanding is by many wise Persons thought much more durable than that which is founded on Beauty, yet it happened otherwise in the present Case. Nay, the Understandings of this Couple were their principal Bone of Contention, and one great Cause of many Quarrels which from time to time arose between them; and which at last ended, on the Side of the Lady, in a sovereign Contempt for her Husband, and on the Husband's, in an utter Abhorrence of his Wife.

As these had both exercised their Talents chiefly in the Study of Divinity, this was, from their first Acquaintance, the most common Topic of Conversation between them. The Captain, like a well-bred Man, had, before Marriage, always given up his Opinion to that of the Lady; and this, not in the clumsy, aukward Manner of a conceited Blockhead, who, while he civilly yields to a Superiour in an Argument, is desirous of being still known to think himself in the Right. The Captain, on the contrary, tho' one of the proudest Fellows in the World, so absolutely yielded the Victory to his Antagonist, that she, who had not the least Doubt of his Sincerity, retired always from the Dispute with an Admiration of her own Understanding, and a Love for his.

But tho' this Complaisance to one whom the Captain thoroughly despised, was not so uneasy to him, as it would have been, had any Hopes of Preferment made it necessary to shew the same Submission to a *Hoadley*,[1] or to some other of great Reputation in the Science, yet even this cost him too much to be endured without some Motive. Matrimony, therefore, having removed all such Motives, he grew weary of this Condescention, and began to treat the Opinions of his Wife with that Haughtiness and Insolence, which none but those who deserve some Contempt themselves can bestow, and those only who deserve no Contempt can bear.

When the first Torrent of Tenderness was over, and when in the calm and long Interval between the Fits, Reason began to open the Eyes of the Lady, and she saw this Alteration of Behaviour in the Captain, who at length answered all her Arguments only with Pish and Pshaw, she was far from enduring the Indignity with a tame Submission. Indeed, it at first so highly provoked her, that it might have produced some tragical Event, had it not taken a more harmless Turn, by filling her with the utmost Contempt for her Husband's Understanding, which somewhat qualified her Hatred towards him; tho' of this likewise, she had a pretty moderate Share.

The Captain's Hatred to her was of a purer Kind: For as to any Imperfections in her Knowledge or Understanding, he no more despised her for them than for her not being six Feet high. In his Opinion of the female Sex, he exceeded the Moroseness of *Aristotle* himself.[2] He looked on a Woman as on an Animal of domestic Use, of somewhat higher Consideration than a Cat, since her Offices were of rather more Importance; but the Difference between these two, was in his Estimation so small, that in his Marriage contracted with Mr. *Allworthy's* Lands and

[1] Benjamin Hoadly (1676–1761), Bishop of Winchester and the chief contemporary spokesman for the latitudinarians. Hoadly's famous sermon, 'The Nature of the Kingdom, or the Church, of Christ' (1717), began the Bangorian controversy by asserting that, since religion was a matter of sincerity and not of external forms of worship, the true Church was the whole community of Christians. In 1735 Hoadly's *Plain Account of the Nature and End of the Sacrament of the Lord's Supper*—a rational, mystery-dispelling analysis of the eucharist —involved him in another dispute with a host of more strictly orthodox clergymen. In *Joseph Andrews* (1742; I. xvii) Parson Adams praises this work, whose author Fielding himself had commended in *Of True Greatness* (1741) as the exemplary divine. For Fielding's use of Hoadly's sermon against the Jacobites, see below, p. 671, n. 1.

[2] Several passages in the *Politics* attest to Aristotle's belief that, with respect to virtue, women were by nature inferior to men (e.g., I. v and II. vi).

Tenements, it would have been pretty equal which of them he had taken into the Bargain. And yet so tender was his Pride, that it felt the Contempt which his Wife now began to express towards him; and this, added to the Surfeit he had before taken of her Love, created in him a Degree of Disgust and Abhorrence, perhaps hardly to be exceeded.

One Situation only of the married State is excluded from Pleasure; and that is, a State of Indifference; but as many of my Readers, I hope, know what an exquisite Delight there is in conveying Pleasure to a beloved Object, so some few, I am afraid, may have experienced the Satisfaction of tormenting one we hate. It is, I apprehend, to come at this latter Pleasure, that we see both Sexes often give up that Ease in Marriage, which they might otherwise possess, tho' their Mate was never so disagreeable to them. Hence the Wife often puts on Fits of Love and Jealousy, nay, even denies herself any Pleasure, to disturb and prevent those of her Husband; and he again, in return, puts frequent Restraints on himself, and stays at home in Company which he dislikes, in order to confine his Wife to what she equally detests. Hence too must flow those Tears[1] which a Widow sometimes so plentifully sheds over the Ashes of a Husband with whom she led a Life of constant Disquiet and Turbulency, and whom now she can never hope to torment any more.

But if ever any Couple enjoyed this Pleasure, it was at present experienced by the Captain and his Lady. It was always a sufficient Reason to either of them to be obstinate in any Opinion, that the other had previously asserted the contrary. If the one proposed any Amusement, the other constantly objected to it. They never loved or hated, commended or abused the same Person. And for this Reason, as the Captain looked with an evil Eye on the little Foundling, his Wife began now to caress it almost equally with her own Child.

The Reader will be apt to conceive, that this Behaviour between the Husband and Wife did not greatly contribute to Mr. *Allworthy's* Repose, as it tended so little to that serene Happiness which he had designed for all three, from this Alliance; but the Truth is, though he might be a little disappointed in his sanguine Expectations, yet he was far from being acquainted with the whole Matter: For, as the Captain was, from certain obvious

[1] See below, p. 415, n. 3.

Reasons, much on his Guard before him, the Lady was obliged, for fear of her Brother's Displeasure, to pursue the same Conduct. In fact, it is possible for a third Person to be very intimate, nay even to live long in the same House, with a married Couple, who have any tolerable Discretion, and not even guess at the sour Sentiments which they bear to each other: For though the whole Day may be sometimes too short for Hatred, as well as for Love; yet the many Hours which they naturally spend together, apart from all Observers, furnish People of tolerable Moderation with such ample Opportunity for the Enjoyment of either Passion, that, if they love, they can support being a few Hours in Company, without toying, or if they hate, without spitting in each other's Faces.

It is possible, however, that Mr. *Allworthy* saw enough to render him a little uneasy; for we are not always to conclude, that a wise Man is not hurt, because he doth not cry out and lament himself, like those of a childish or effeminate Temper. But indeed it is possible he might see some Faults in the Captain, without any Uneasiness at all: For Men of true Wisdom and Goodness are contented to take Persons and Things as they are, without complaining of their Imperfections, or attempting to amend them. They can see a Fault in a Friend, a Relation, or an Acquaintance, without ever mentioning it to the Parties themselves, or to any others; and this often without lessening their Affection. Indeed unless great Discernment be tempered with this overlooking Disposition, we ought never to contract Friendship but with a Degree of Folly which we can deceive: For I hope my Friends will pardon me, when I declare I know none of them without a Fault; and I should be sorry if I could imagine I had any Friend who could not see mine. Forgiveness, of this Kind, we give and demand in Turn. It is an Exercise of Friendship, and, perhaps, none of the least pleasant. And this Forgiveness we must bestow, without Desire of Amendment. There is, perhaps, no surer Mark of Folly, than an Attempt to correct the natural Infirmities of those we love. The finest Composition of human Nature, as well as the finest China, may have a Flaw in it; and this, I am afraid, in either Case, is equally incurable; though, nevertheless, the Pattern may remain of the highest Value.

Upon the whole then, Mr. *Allworthy* certainly saw some Imperfections in the Captain; but, as this was a very artful Man, and eternally upon his Guard before him, these appeared to him no more than Blemishes in a good Character; which his Goodness made him overlook, and his Wisdom prevented him from discovering to the Captain himself. Very different would have been his Sentiments, had he discovered the whole; which, perhaps, would, in Time, have been the Case, had the Husband and Wife long continued this Kind of Behaviour to each other; but this kind Fortune took effectual Means to prevent, by forcing the Captain to do that which rendered him again dear to his Wife, and restored all her Tenderness and Affection towards him.

## CHAPTER VIII

*A Receipt to regain the lost Affections of a Wife, which hath never been known to fail in the most desperate Cases.*

THE Captain was made large Amends for the unpleasant Minutes which he passed in the Conversation of his Wife (and which were as few as he could contrive to make them) by the pleasant Meditations he enjoyed when alone.

These Meditations were entirely employed on Mr. *Allworthy's* Fortune; for first, he exercised much Thought in calculating, as well as he could, the exact Value of the whole; which Calculations he often saw Occasion to alter in his own Favour: And secondly, and chiefly, he pleased himself with intended Alterations in the House and Gardens, and in projecting many other Schemes, as well for Improvement of the Estate, as of the Grandeur of the Place. For this Purpose he applied himself to the Studies of Architecture and Gardening, and read over many Books on both these Subjects; for these Sciences, indeed, employed his whole Time, and formed his only Amusement. He at last completed a most excellent Plan; and very sorry we are, that it is not in our Power to present it to our Reader, since even the Luxury of the present Age, I believe, would hardly match it. It had, indeed, in a superlative Degree, the two principal Ingredients which serve to recommend all great and noble Designs of this Nature: For it required an immoderate Expence to execute, and a vast Length of Time to bring it to any Sort of Perfection. The former of these, the immense Wealth of which the

Captain supposed Mr. *Allworthy* possessed, and which he thought himself sure of inheriting, promised very effectually to supply; and the latter, the Soundness of his own Constitution, and his Time of Life, which was only what is called Middle Age, removed all Apprehension of his not living to accomplish.

Nothing was wanting to enable him to enter upon the immediate Execution of this Plan, but the Death of Mr. *Allworthy*; in calculating which he had employed much of his own Algebra; besides purchasing every Book extant that treats of the Value of Lives, Reversions,[1] *&c.* From all which, he satisfied himself, that as he had every Day a Chance of this happening, so had he more than an even Chance of its happening within a few Years.

But while the Captain was one Day busied in deep Contemplations of this Kind, one of the most unlucky, as well as unseasonable Accidents, happened to him. The utmost Malice of Fortune could indeed have contrived nothing so cruel, so mal-a-propos, so absolutely destructive to all his Schemes. In short, not to keep the Reader in long Suspence, just at the very Instant when his Heart was exulting in Meditations on the Happiness which would accrue to him by Mr. *Allworthy's* Death, he himself—died of an Apoplexy.

This unfortunately befel the Captain as he was taking his Evening Walk by himself, so that no Body was present to lend him any Assistance, if indeed any Assistance could have preserved him. He took, therefore, Measure of that Proportion of Soil, which was now become adequate to all his future Purposes, and he lay dead on the Ground, a great (though not a living) Example of the Truth of that Observation of *Horace*:[2]

> Tu secanda marmora
> Locas sub ipsum funus: et sepulchri
> Immemor, struis domos.

Which Sentiment, I shall thus give to the *English* Reader: 'You provide the noblest Materials for Building, when a Pick-ax and a Spade are only necessary; and build Houses of five hundred by a hundred Feet, forgetting that of six by two.'

[1] See below, p. 748, n. 1; also p. 278. 6.
[2] *Odes*, II. xviii. 17–19: 'yet thou on the grave's verge dost contract for the cutting of marble slabs, and, forgetful of the tomb, dost rear a palace' (trans. C. E. Bennett, Loeb Classical Library, 1914).

## CHAPTER IX

*A Proof of the Infallibility of the foregoing Receipt, in the Lamenta-*
*tions of the Widow; with other suitable Decorations of Death, such as*
*Physicians, &c. and an Epitaph in the true Stile.*

MR. *Allworthy*, his Sister, and another Lady, were assembled
at the accustomed Hour in the Supper Room, where having
waited a considerable Time longer than usual, Mr. *Allworthy*
first declared he began to grow uneasy at the Captain's Stay (for
he was always most punctual at his Meals,) and gave Orders that
the Bell should be rung without the Doors, and especially towards
those Walks which the Captain was wont to use.

All these Summons proving ineffectual, (for the Captain had,
by perverse Accident, betaken himself to a new Walk that Evening) Mrs. *Blifil* declared she was seriously frightned. Upon which
the other Lady, who was one of her most intimate Acquaintance,
and who well knew the true State of her Affections, endeavoured
all she could to pacify her; telling her—To be sure she could not
help being uneasy; but that she should hope the best. That,
perhaps, the Sweetness of the Evening had enticed the Captain
to go farther than his usual Walk, or he might be detained at some
Neighbour's. Mrs. *Blifil* answered, No; she was sure some Accident had befallen him; for that he would never stay out without
sending her Word, as he must know how uneasy it would make
her. The other Lady, having no other Arguments to use, betook
herself to the Entreaties usual on such Occasions, and begged
her not to frighten herself, for it might be of very ill Consequence
to her own Health; and, filling out a very large Glass of Wine,
advised, and at last prevailed with, her to drink it.

Mr. *Allworthy* now returned into the Parlour; for he had been
himself in Search after the Captain. His Countenance sufficiently
shewed the Consternation he was under, which indeed had a good
deal deprived him of Speech; but as Grief operates variously on
different Minds, so the same Apprehension which depressed his
Voice, elevated that of Mrs. *Blifil*. She now began to bewail
herself in very bitter Terms, and Floods of Tears accompanied
her Lamentations, which the Lady, her Companion, declared
she could not blame; but at the same Time dissuaded her from
indulging; attempting to moderate the Grief of her Friend, by

philosophical Observations on the many Disappointments to which human Life is daily subject, which, she said, was a sufficient Consideration to fortify our Minds against any Accidents, how sudden or terrible soever. She said, her Brother's Example ought to teach her Patience, who, though indeed he could not be supposed as much concerned as herself, yet was doubtless very uneasy, though his Resignation to the Divine Will had restrained his Grief within due Bounds.

'Mention not my Brother,' said Mrs. *Blifil*, 'I alone am the Object of your Pity. What are the Terrors of Friendship to what a Wife feels on these Occasions? O he is lost! Somebody hath murdered him—I shall never see him more.'——Here a Torrent of Tears had the same Consequence with what the Suppression had occasioned to Mr. *Allworthy*, and she remained silent.

At this Interval, a Servant came running in, out of Breath, and cried out, the Captain was found; and, before he could proceed farther, he was followed by two more, bearing the dead Body between them.

Here the curious Reader may observe another Diversity in the Operations of Grief: For as Mr. *Allworthy* had been before silent, from the same Cause which had made his Sister vociferous; so did the present Sight, which drew Tears from the Gentleman, put an entire Stop to those of the Lady; who first gave a violent Scream, and presently after fell into a Fit.

The Room was soon full of Servants, some of whom, with the Lady visitant, were employed in Care of the Wife, and others, with Mr. *Allworthy*, assisted in carrying off the Captain to a warm Bed, where every Method was tried, in order to restore him to Life.

And glad should we be, could we inform the Reader that both these Bodies had been attended with equal Success; for those who undertook the Care of the Lady, succeeded so well, that after the Fit had continued a decent Time, she again revived, to their great Satisfaction; but as to the Captain, all Experiments of bleeding, chafing, dropping, &c. proved ineffectual. Death, that inexorable Judge, had passed Sentence on him, and refused to grant him a Reprieve, though two Doctors who arrived, and were fee'd at one and the same Instant, were his Counsel.

These two Doctors, whom, to avoid any malicious Applications, we shall distinguish by the Names of Dr. *Y*. and Dr. *Z*., having felt his Pulse; to wit, Dr. *Y*. his right Arm, and Dr. *Z*. his left, both agreed that he was absolutely dead; but as to the Distemper, or Cause of his Death, they differed, Dr. *Y*. holding that he had died of an Apoplexy, and Dr. *Z*. of an Epilepsy.

Hence arose a Dispute between the learned Men, in which each delivered the Reasons of their several Opinions. These were of such equal Force, that they served both to confirm either Doctor in his own Sentiments, and made not the least Impression on his Adversary.

To say the Truth, every Physician, almost, hath his favourite Disease, to which he ascribes all the Victories obtained over human Nature. The Gout, the Rheumatism, the Stone, the Gravel, and the Consumption, have all their several Patrons in the Faculty; and none more than the nervous Fever, or the Fever on the Spirits.[1] And here we may account for those Disagreements in Opinion, concerning the Cause of a Patient's Death; which sometimes occur between the most learned of the College;[2] and which have greatly surprized that Part of the World who have been ignorant of the Fact we have above asserted.

The Reader may, perhaps, be surprized, that instead of en-

---

[1] Otherwise known as the vapours, hypo, or the spleen, this was a hysteric disorder to which 'weak and tender Women' were most susceptible. One prominent 'Patron', as Fielding says, of this disease was Sir Richard Manningham, who in November 1745 published a popular treatise on the subject, entitled *The Symptoms, Nature, Causes, and Cure of the Febricula, or Little Fever: Commonly Called the Nervous or Hysteric Fever; the Fever on the Spirits; Vapours, Hypo, or Spleen*. The narrator of *A Journey from This World to the Next* (1743) believes he has died from this malady, but he searches in vain for it in the City of Diseases (I. iii). In *Amelia* (1751; III. vii), however, Fielding seems to have considered the distemper very real indeed, for his heroine suffers from it. See also *Tom Jones*, p. 579.

[2] The Royal College of Physicians, founded in 1518 and situated during the eighteenth century in Warwick Lane. Until 1858 no one except graduates of Oxford or Cambridge could legally practise medicine without a licence from the College.

Throughout this passage Fielding's amusement at learned doctors who dispute the cause of a patient's death recalls his earlier satire, *The Charge to the Jury: or, The Sum of the Evidence, on the Trial of A. B. C. D. and E. F. All M. D. for the Death of one Robert at Orfud, at a Special Commission of Oyer and Terminer held at Justice-College, in W[arwi]ck-Lane* (2 July 1745). After Walpole's death on 18 March 1745 the physicians who had attended him became embroiled in an unseemly public debate, defending their methods of treating the disease that killed him. On 10 April 1745 Fielding's friend John Ranby began the controversy by publishing his *Narrative* of Walpole's last illness. Ranby, who had correctly diagnosed the case, criticized his colleagues Drs. Jurin, Hulse, and Crowe for their incompetency and their reliance upon such questionable nostrums as the 'Lithontriptic Lixivium' prescribed by Jurin. For complimentary allusions to Ranby in *Tom Jones*, see below, pp. 468, 911.

deavouring to revive the Patient, the learned Gentlemen should fall immediately into a Dispute on the Occasion of his Death; but in reality, all such Experiments had been made before their Arrival: For the Captain was put into a warm Bed, had his Veins scarified, his Forehead chafed, and all Sorts of strong Drops applied to his Lips and his Nostrils.

The Physicians, therefore, finding themselves anticipated in every thing they ordered, were at a Loss how to employ that Portion of Time which it is usual and decent to remain for their Fee, and were therefore necessitated to find some Subject or other for Discourse; and what could more naturally present itself than that before-mentioned?

Our Doctors were about to take their Leave, when Mr. *Allworthy*, having given over the Captain, and acquiesced in the divine Will, began to enquire after his Sister, whom he desired them to visit before their Departure.

This Lady was now recovered of her Fit, and, to use the common Phrase, as well as could be expected for one in her Condition. The Doctors, therefore, all previous Ceremonies being complied with, as this was a new Patient, attended, according to Desire, and laid hold on each of her Hands, as they had before done on those of the Corpse.

The Case of the Lady was in the other Extreme from that of her Husband; for, as he was past all the Assistance of Physic, so, in reality, she required none.

There is nothing more unjust, than the vulgar Opinion by which Physicians are misrepresented, as Friends to Death. On the contrary, I believe, if the Number of those who recover by Physic could be opposed to that of the Martyrs to it, the former would rather exceed the latter. Nay, some are so cautious on this Head, that, to avoid a Possibility of killing the Patient, they abstain from all Methods of curing, and prescribe nothing but what can neither do good nor harm. I have heard some of these, with great Gravity, deliver it as a Maxim, That Nature should be left to do her own Work, while the Physician stands by, as it were to clap her on the Back, and encourage her when she doth well.

So little then did our Doctors delight in Death, that they discharged the Corpse after a single Fee; but they were not so disgusted with their living Patient; concerning whose Case they immediately agreed, and fell to prescribing with great Diligence.

Whether, as the Lady had at first persuaded her Physicians to believe her ill, they had now, in return, persuaded her to believe herself so, I will not determine; but she continued a whole Month with all the Decorations of Sickness. During this Time she was visited by Physicians, attended by Nurses, and received constant Messages from her Acquaintance, to enquire after her Health.

At length, the decent Time for Sickness and immoderate Grief being expired, the Doctors were discharged, and the Lady began to see Company; being altered only from what she was before by that Colour of Sadness in which she had dressed her Person and Countenance.

The Captain was now interred, and might, perhaps, have already made a large Progress towards Oblivion, had not the Friendship of Mr. *Allworthy* taken Care to preserve his Memory, by the following Epitaph, which was written by a Man of as great Genius as Integrity, and one who perfectly well knew the Captain.[1]

Here lies,
In Expectation of a joyful Rising,
The Body of
Captain JOHN BLIFIL.
LONDON
had the Honour of his Birth,
OXFORD
of his Education.
His Parts
were an Honour to his Profession
and to his Country.
His Life to his Religion
and human Nature.
He was a dutiful Son,
a tender Husband,

[1] With Fielding's opinion of '*the true Stile*' of epitaphs (as he ironically remarks in the heading to this chapter), compare Pope's definition in *The Dunciad* (1729), I. 41: 'Sepulchral lyes our holy walls to grace.' Epitaphs, Pope later observed in a letter to Ralph Allen (30 April 1736), were synonymous with 'flatteries and false history'. The true nature of this abused genre was the subject of an essay by Samuel Johnson in *The Gentleman's Magazine*, x (December 1740), 593–6. In the notes to a satiric elegy published not long after *Tom Jones*, a pseudonymous Oxonian expressed his delight in Fielding's mock-epitaph for Captain Blifil, wherein 'this prevailing Folly' is ridiculed 'with great Humour' (see 'Jo: Freinshemius', *Threnodia: or, An Elegy on the unexpected and unlamented Death of the M[aster] of B[alliol]* [Oxford, 1753], pp. 13–14).

an affectionate Father,
a most kind Brother,
a sincere Friend,
a devout Christian,
and a good Man.
His inconsolable Widow
hath erected this Stone,
The Monument of
His Virtues,
and Her Affection.

# BOOK III

*Containing the most memorable Transactions which passed in the Family of Mr.* Allworthy, *from the Time when* Tommy Jones *arrived at the Age of Fourteen, till he attained the Age of Nineteen. In this Book the Reader may pick up some Hints concerning the Education of Children.*

## CHAPTER I

*Containing little or nothing.*

THE Reader will be pleased to remember, that at the Beginning of the Second Book of this History, we gave him a Hint of our Intention to pass over several large Periods of Time, in which nothing happened worthy of being recorded in a Chronicle of this Kind.

In so doing, we do not only consult our own Dignity and Ease; but the Good and Advantage of the Reader: For besides, that by these Means we prevent him from throwing away his Time in reading either without Pleasure or Emolument, we give him at all such Seasons an Opportunity of employing that wonderful Sagacity, of which he is Master, by filling up these vacant Spaces of Time with his own Conjectures; for which Purpose, we have taken care to qualify him in the preceding Pages.

For Instance, what Reader but knows that Mr. *Allworthy* felt at first for the Loss of his Friend,[1] those Emotions of Grief, which on such Occasions enter into all Men whose Hearts are not composed of Flint, or their Heads of as solid Materials? Again, what Reader doth not know that Philosophy and Religion, in time, moderated, and at last extinguished this Grief? The former of these, teaching the Folly and Vanity of it, and the latter, correcting it, as unlawful, and at the same time

---

[1] Allworthy's grief on this occasion and his eventual triumph over it by attending to the precepts of philosophy and religion recall Fielding's consolatory essay, 'Of the Remedy of Affliction for the Loss of our Friends' (1743), written upon the death of his daughter Charlotte in March 1742. For a comprehensive discussion of this work and of its place in the Christian humanist tradition of the *consolatio*, see Miller, *Essays on Fielding's 'Miscellanies'*, pp. 228–71.

assuaging it by raising future Hopes and Assurances which enable
a strong and religious Mind to take leave of a Friend on his Death-
bed with little less Indifference than if he was preparing for a
long Journey;[1] and indeed with little less Hope of seeing him
again.

Nor can the judicious Reader be at a greater Loss on Account
of Mrs. *Bridget Blifil,* who, he may be assured, conducted herself through the whole Season in which Grief is to make its
Appearance on the Outside of the Body, with the strictest Regard
to all the Rules of Custom and Decency, suiting the Alterations
of her Countenance to the several Alterations of her Habit: For
as this changed from Weeds to Black, from Black to Grey, from
Grey to White, so did her Countenance change from Dismal to
Sorrowful, from Sorrowful to Sad, and from Sad to Serious, till
the Day came in which she was allowed to return to her former
Serenity.

We have mentioned these two as Examples only of the Task
which may be imposed on Readers of the lowest Class. Much
higher and harder Exercises of Judgment and Penetration may
reasonably be expected from the upper Graduates in Criticism.
Many notable Discoveries will, I doubt not, be made by such, of
the Transactions which happened in the Family of our worthy
Man, during all the Years which we have thought proper to
pass over: For tho' nothing worthy of a Place in this History
occurred within that Period; yet did several Incidents happen, of
equal Importance with those reported by the daily and weekly
Historians of the Age, in reading which, great Numbers of
Persons consume a considerable Part of their Time, very little,
I am afraid, to their Emolument. Now, in the Conjectures here
proposed, some of the most excellent Faculties of the Mind may
be employed to much Advantage, since it is a more useful
Capacity to be able to foretel the Actions of Men in any Circumstance from their Characters; than to judge of their Characters
from their Actions.[2] The former, I own, requires the greater
Penetration; but may be accomplished by true Sagacity, with
no less Certainty than the latter.

[1] See above, p. 35, n. 1.
[2] Cf. Fielding's 'Essay on the Knowledge of the Characters of Men' (1743) where,
however, he warns that a man's actions are 'a more infallible Guide' to his character than his
appearance or reputation.

As we are sensible that much the greatest Part of our Readers are very eminently possessed of this Quality, we have left them a Space of twelve Years to exert it in; and shall now bring forth our Heroe, at about fourteen Years of Age, not questioning that many have been long impatient to be introduced to his Acquaintance.

## CHAPTER II

*The Heroe of this great History appears with very bad Omens. A little Tale, of so* LOW *a Kind, that some may think it not worth their Notice. A Word or two concerning a Squire, and more relating to a Game-keeper, and a Schoolmaster.*

AS we determined when we first sat down to write this History, to flatter no Man; but to guide our Pen throughout by the Directions of Truth, we are obliged to bring our Heroe on the Stage in a much more disadvantageous Manner than we could wish; and to declare honestly, even at his first Appearance, that it was the universal Opinion of all Mr. *Allworthy's* Family, that he was certainly born to be hanged.

Indeed, I am sorry to say, there was too much Reason for this Conjecture. The Lad having, from his earliest Years, discovered a Propensity to many Vices, and especially to one, which hath as direct a Tendency as any other to that Fate, which we have just now observed to have been prophetically denounced against him. He had been already convicted of three Robberies, *viz.* of robbing an Orchard, of stealing a Duck out of a Farmer's Yard, and of picking Master *Blifil's* Pocket of a Ball.

The Vices of this young Man were moreover heightened by the disadvantageous Light in which they appeared, when opposed to the Virtues of Master *Blifil*, his Companion: A Youth of so different a Cast from little *Jones*, that not only the Family, but all the Neighbourhood resounded his Praises. He was indeed a Lad of a remarkable Disposition; sober, discreet, and pious beyond his Age. Qualities, which gained him the Love of every one who knew him, while *Tom Jones* was universally disliked, and many expressed their Wonder that Mr. *Allworthy* would suffer such a Lad to be educated with his Nephew, lest the Morals of the latter should be corrupted by his Example.

An Incident which happened about this Time, will set the Characters of these two Lads, more fairly before the discerning Reader, than is in the Power of the longest Dissertation.

*Tom Jones*, who, bad as he is, must serve for the Heroe of this History, had only one Friend among all the Servants of the Family; for, as to Mrs. *Wilkins*, she had long since given him up, and was perfectly reconciled to her Mistress. This Friend was the Game-keeper, a Fellow of a loose kind of Disposition, and who was thought not to entertain much stricter Notions concerning the Difference of *meum* and *tuum*, than the young Gentleman himself. And hence, this Friendship gave Occasion to many sarcastical Remarks among the Domestics, most of which were either Proverbs before, or at least are become so now; and indeed, the Wit of them all may be comprised in that short *Latin* Proverb, '*Noscitur a socio*,' which, I think, is thus expressed in *English*, 'You may know him by the Company he keeps.'

To say the Truth, some of that atrocious Wickedness in *Jones*, of which we have just mentioned three Examples, might perhaps be derived from the Encouragement he had received from this Fellow, who, in two or three Instances, had been what the Law calls an Accessary after the Fact. For the whole Duck, and great Part of the Apples, were converted to the Use of the Game-keeper and his Family. Tho' as *Jones* alone was discovered, the poor Lad bore not only the whole Smart, but the whole Blame; both which fell again to his Lot, on the following Occasion. Contiguous to Mr. *Allworthy's* Estate, was the Manor of one of those Gentlemen, who are called *Preservers of the Game*. This Species of Men, from the great Severity with which they revenge the Death of a Hare or a Partridge, might be thought to cultivate the same Superstition with the Bannians in *India*;[1] many of whom, we are told, dedicate their whole Lives to the Preservation and Protection of certain Animals; was it not that our *English* Bannians, while they preserve them from other Enemies, will most unmercifully slaughter whole Horse-loads themselves, so that they stand clearly acquitted of any such heathenish Superstition.

I have, indeed, a much better Opinion of this Kind of Men than is entertained by some, as I take them to answer the Order of Nature, and the good Purposes for which they were ordained

---

[1] A Hindu caste of merchants who, because they believe that all animal life is sacred, observe a strict vegetarian diet. See *The Champion* (22 March 1739/40).

in a more ample Manner than many others. Now, as *Horace* tells us,[1] that there are a Set of human Beings,

*Fruges consumere nati.*

'Born to consume the Fruits of the Earth.' So, I make no manner of Doubt but that there are others

*Feras consumere nati.*

'Born to consume the Beasts of the Field,' or, as it is commonly called, the Game; and none, I believe, will deny, but that those Squires fulfil this End of their Creation.

Little *Jones* went one Day a shooting with the Game-keeper; when, happening to spring a Covey of Partridges, near the Border of that Manor, over which Fortune, to fulfil the wise Purposes of Nature, had planted one of the Game-Consumers, the Birds flew into it, and were *marked* (as it is called) by the two Sportsmen, in some Furze Bushes, about two or three hundred Paces beyond Mr. *Allworthy's* Dominions.

Mr. *Allworthy* had given the Fellow strict Orders, on Pain of forfeiting his Place, never to trespass on any of his Neighbours, no more on those who were less rigid in this Matter, than on the Lord of this Manor. With regard to others, indeed, these Orders had not been always very scrupulously kept; but as the Disposition of the Gentleman with whom the Partridges had taken sanctuary, was well known, the Game-keeper had never yet attempted to invade his Territories. Nor had he done it now, had not the younger Sportsman, who was excessively eager to pursue the flying Game, over-persuaded him; but *Jones* being very importunate, the other, who was himself keen enough after the Sport, yielded to his Persuasions, entered the Manor, and shot one of the Partridges.

The Gentleman himself was at that time on horseback, at a little Distance from them; and hearing the Gun go off, he immediately made towards the Place, and discovered poor *Tom*: For the Game-keeper had leapt into the thickest Part of the Furze-brake, where he had happily concealed himself.

The Gentleman having searched the Lad, and found the Partridge upon him, denounced great Vengeance, swearing he would acquaint Mr. *Allworthy*. He was as good as his Word, for he rode immediately to his House, and complained of the Trespass on his Manor, in as high Terms, and as bitter Language, as if his House had been broken open, and the most valuable Furniture stole out of it. He added, that some other Person was in his Company, tho' he could not discover him: for that two Guns had been discharged almost in the same Instant. And, says he, 'we have found only this Partridge, but the Lord knows what Mischief they have done.'

At his Return home, *Tom* was presently convened before Mr. *Allworthy*. He owned the Fact, and alledged no other Excuse but what was really true, *viz.* that the Covey was originally sprung in Mr. *Allworthy's* own Manor.[1]

*Tom* was then interrogated who was with him, which Mr. *Allworthy* declared he was resolved to know, acquainting the Culprit with the Circumstance of the two Guns, which had been deposed by the Squire and both his Servants; but *Tom* stoutly persisted in asserting that he was alone; yet, to say the Truth, he hesitated a little at first, which would have confirmed Mr. *Allworthy's* Belief, had what the Squire and his Servants said, wanted any further Confirmation.

The Game-keeper being a suspected Person, was now sent for, and the Question put to him; but he, relying on the Promise which *Tom* had made him, to take all upon himself, very resolutely denied being in Company with the young Gentleman, or indeed having seen him the whole Afternoon.

Mr. *Allworthy* then turned towards *Tom*, with more than usual

---

[1] Legally, Tom and the gamekeeper would have been judged guilty of an offence only if they had trespassed on a game warren (i.e. a place especially privileged by the King's licence for the preservation of game). Earlier in this chapter the squire of this manor (identified as Western in III. ix) is ironically referred to as 'one of those Gentlemen, who are called *Preservers of the Game*'; but it seems unlikely that Fielding, who knew the law and therefore the significance of this point to the determination of Tom's guilt, would have neglected specifically to designate Western's estate a warren if he had meant the reader to think of it as such. The law is summarized as follows in Giles Jacob, *A New Law-Dictionary*, 4th ed. (1739), s.v. 'Game': 'An Action was brought against a Person for entering another Man's Warren; the Defendant pleaded that there was a Pheasant on his Land, and his Hawk pursued it into the Plaintiff's Ground; it was resolved that this doth not amount to a sufficient Justification, for in this Case he can only follow his Hawk and not take the *Game*. *Poph.* 162. though it is said to be otherwise where the Soil of the Plaintiff is not a Warren. 2 *Roll. Abr.* 567. If a Man in Hunting starts a Hare upon his own Ground, and follows and kills it on the Ground of another, yet still the Hare is his own, because of the fresh Suit. . . . *Cro. Car.* 553.' (Cf. Barlow, *The Justice of the Peace* [1745], s.v. 'Game'.)

Anger in his Countenance, and advised him to confess who was with him; repeating, that he was resolved to know. The Lad, however, still maintained his Resolution, and was dismissed with much Wrath by Mr. *Allworthy*, who told him, he should have to the next Morning to consider of it, when he should be questioned by another Person, and in another Manner.

Poor *Jones* spent a very melancholy Night, and the more so, as he was without his usual Companion: for Master *Blifil* was gone abroad on a Visit with his Mother. Fear of the Punishment he was to suffer was on this Occasion his least Evil; his chief Anxiety being, lest his Constancy should fail him, and he should be brought to betray the Game-keeper, whose Ruin he knew must now be the Consequence.

Nor did the Game-keeper pass his Time much better. He had the same Apprehensions with the Youth; for whose Honour he had likewise a much tenderer Regard than for his Skin.

In the Morning, when *Tom* attended the Reverend Mr. *Thwackum*, the Person to whom Mr. *Allworthy* had committed the Instruction of the two Boys, he had the same Questions put to him by that Gentleman, which he had been asked the Evening before, to which he returned the same Answers. The Consequence of this was, so severe a Whipping, that it possibly fell little short of the Torture with which Confessions are in some Countries extorted from Criminals.

*Tom* bore his Punishment with great Resolution; and tho' his Master asked him between every Stroke, whether he would not confess, he was contented to be flead rather than betray his Friend, or break the Promise he had made.

The Game-keeper was now relieved from his Anxiety, and Mr. *Allworthy* himself began to be concerned at *Tom's* Sufferings: For, besides that Mr. *Thwackum*, being highly enraged that he was not able to make the Boy say what he himself pleased, had carried his Severity much beyond the good Man's Intention, this latter began now to suspect that the Squire had been mistaken; which his extreme Eagerness and Anger seemed to make probable; and as for what the Servants had said in Confirmation of their Master's Account, he laid no great Stress upon that. Now, as Cruelty and Injustice were two Ideas, of which Mr. *Allworthy* could by no Means support the Consciousness a single Moment, he sent for *Tom*, and after many kind and friendly Exhortations, said, 'I am convinced, my dear Child, that my Suspicions have wronged you; I am sorry that you have been so severely punished on this Account.'—And at last gave him a little Horse to make him amends; again repeating his Sorrow for what had past.

*Tom's* Guilt now flew in his Face more than any Severity could make it. He could more easily bear the Lashes of *Thwackum*, than the Generosity of *Allworthy*. The Tears burst from his Eyes, and he fell upon his Knees, crying, 'Oh! Sir, you are too good to me. Indeed, you are. Indeed, I don't deserve it.' And at that very Instant, from the Fullness of his Heart, had almost betrayed the Secret; but the good Genius of the Game-keeper suggested to him what might be the Consequence to the poor Fellow, and this Consideration sealed his Lips.

*Thwackum* did all he could to dissuade *Allworthy* from shewing any Compassion or Kindness to the Boy, saying, 'He had persisted in an Untruth;' and gave some Hints, that a second Whipping might probably bring the Matter to Light.

But Mr. *Allworthy* absolutely refused to consent to the Experiment. He said, the Boy had suffered enough already, for concealing the Truth, even if he was guilty, seeing that he could have no Motive but a mistaken Point of Honour for so doing.

'Honour!' cry'd *Thwackum*, with some Warmth, 'mere Stubborness and Obstinacy! Can Honour teach any one to tell a Lie, or can any Honour exist independent of Religion?'

This Discourse happened at Table when Dinner was just ended; and there were present Mr. *Allworthy*, Mr. *Thwackum*, and a third Gentleman who now entered into the Debate, and whom, before we proceed any farther, we shall briefly introduce to our Reader's Acquaintance.

## CHAPTER III

*The Character of Mr.* Square *the Philosopher, and of Mr.* Thwackum *the Divine; with a Dispute concerning*————

THE Name of this Gentleman who had then resided some time at Mr. *Allworthy's* House, was Mr. *Square*.[1] His

---

[1] Fielding's biographers have rather too categorically identified Square with Thomas Chubb (1679–8 February 1747), tallow-chandler of Salisbury and the prolific author of deistical tracts. (See Cross, ii. 169–70, and Dudden, ii. 647–9.) Though Square's views

natural Parts were not of the first Rate, but he had greatly improved them by a learned Education. He was deeply read in the Antients, and a profest Master of all the Works of *Plato* and

correspond with Chubb's at several points (see below), in every other respect the two are diametrically different. Chubb, for example, was recognized even by his enemies as 'a Man of *uncommon* Genius, and *natural* Capacities', but who had not had the advantage of a learned education. Unlike Square, who 'was a comely Man' (III. vi) and attractive to the ladies, Chubb was short and portly, his appearance '*despicable* and *mean*'; and far from being a philanderer, as is the case with Square (V. v), he had a reputation for perfect chastity with respect to women, though his effeminate manner led his detractors to suspect him of being homosexual. Finally, whereas Square is converted to Christianity on his deathbed (XVIII. iv), Chubb died suddenly and without renouncing his heterodox views. (See the accounts of Chubb published shortly after his death: *A Short and Faithful Account of the Life and Character of the Celebrated Mr. Thomas Chubb* [1747] and the reply, *Memoirs of Mr. Thomas Chubb, Late of Salisbury* [1747].) Personally, indeed, Square and Chubb are so completely antithetical that one may suspect Fielding's character of being a sort of negative image of the man.

However that may be, Fielding clearly intended Square as a satire not on any one philosopher, but on the whole tribe of deists and free-thinkers who sought to base religion solely on the grounds of reason and natural law, neglecting the authority of divine revelation. In sum, Square epitomizes the two principal schools of contemporary deism: the school of 'moral sentiment', whose chief spokesman was Shaftesbury (see below, p. 217), and the 'intellectualist' school descended from the Cambridge Platonists through Samuel Clarke, Matthew Tindal, Chubb, and many others. (See A. R. Humphreys, ' "The Eternal Fitness of Things": An Aspect of Eighteenth-Century Thought', *MLR*, xlii [1947], 188–98—which, however, errs in identifying Square exclusively with the 'intellectualists'.) The distinction between these schools was widely recognized. In *Deism Revealed* (2nd ed., 1751) Dechaine thus defines 'the light of nature' as consisting of both *natural sentiment* and *reason*: the former is 'that perception of beauty in a good, and of deformity in a bad, action, which every man feels in himself'; the latter is 'that divine faculty of the mind, by which all men are enabled to judge and direct themselves in the choice of such means, as are necessary to bring about the ends suggested to them by their natural sentiments, to decide between them according to the fitness of things' (i. 40).

Square's 'favourite Phrase . . . *the natural Beauty of Virtue*' and his belief that 'Vice was a Deviation from our Nature in the same Manner as Deformity of Body is' may be traced ultimately to Shaftesbury, who maintained that the moral sense consisted 'in a real Antipathy or Aversion to *Injustice* or *Wrong*, and in a real Affection or Love towards *Equity* and *Right*, for its own sake, and on the account of its own natural Beauty and Worth' ('An Inquiry concerning Virtue or Merit', I. iii. 1; *Characteristicks*, 5th ed. [1732], ii. 42). In 'The Moralists' (III. ii) Shaftesbury had asked: 'Is there then . . . a natural Beauty of *Figures?* and is there not as natural a one of ACTIONS ? No sooner the Eye opens upon *Figures*, the Ear to *Sounds*, than straight *the Beautiful* results, and *Grace* and *Harmony* are known and acknowledg'd. No sooner are ACTIONS view'd, no sooner the *human Affections* and *Passions* discern'd . . . than straight *an inward* EYE distinguishes, and sees *the Fair* and *Shapely, the Amiable* and *Admirable*, apart from *the Deform'd, the Foul, the Odious*, or *the Despicable*. How is it possible therefore not to own, "That as these *Distinctions* have their Foundation *in Nature*, the Discernment it-self is *natural*, and from NATURE *alone?*" ' (ibid., ii. 414–15).

On the other hand, Square's method of measuring 'all Actions by the *unalterable Rule of Right* and the *eternal Fitness of Things*' derives from the 'intellectualists', who believed that

*Aristotle.* Upon which great Models he had principally form'd himself, sometimes according with the Opinion of the one, and sometimes with that of the other. In Morals he was a profest *Platonist*, and in Religion he inclined to be an *Aristotelian.*[1]

But tho' he had, as we have said, formed his Morals on the *Platonic* Model, yet he perfectly agreed with the Opinion of *Aristotle*, in considering that great Man rather in the Quality of a Philosopher or a Speculatist, than as a Legislator.[2] This Sentiment he carried a great way; indeed, so far, as to regard all Virtue as Matter of Theory only. This, it is true, he never affirmed, as I have heard, to any one; and yet upon the least Attention to his Conduct, I cannot help thinking, it was his real Opinion, as it will perfectly reconcile some Contradictions which might otherwise appear in his Character.

morality could be made into a rational science as systematic and as infallible as Euclidian geometry. Chubb, to choose only one among many possible exemplars of this school, insisted that natural religion was 'grounded upon the unalterable nature, and the eternal reason of things' and, as such, did not depend on the sanctions of 'any *divine revelation*, or any *promulged law*'; Christ, he maintained, taught nothing contradictory 'to the eternal rule of right and wrong' ('The Author's Farewell to his Readers', in *The Ground and Foundation of Morality Considered* [1745], pp. 40–1, 42). Indeed, Square's favourite phrases recur throughout Chubb's works: 'By moral duties', he explained, 'I understand the performance of such actions as are in themselves right and fit to be performed by every intelligent being, or moral agent, in equal circumstances; which fitness results solely from the nature and reason of things, when considered abstractedly from, and antecedent to any promulgated law, whether human or divine. And . . . there is such a fitness and unfitness arising from, and founded in the natural and essential differences in things' ('Some Reflections upon the comparative Excellency and Usefulness of moral and positive Duties', in *A Discourse concerning Reason, with regard to Religion and Divine Revelation* [1731], pp. 33–4; see also *The True Gospel of Jesus Christ Asserted* [1738], pp. 18, 38). But by mid century such formulas had become part of the common vocabulary of deism; they cannot with certainty be traced to any one author.

Perhaps the most useful gloss on Fielding's intentions with regard to Square is the first volume (1738) of Warburton's *Divine Legation of Moses*. Here, after addressing his work 'to the Free-Thinkers', Warburton proceeds in some detail to refute those authors who had recently flooded the bookstalls with 'a Deluge of Moral Systems, in which either the *Moral Sense*, or the *Essential Difference* makes the sole Foundation' (i. 41). His chief argument, to which Fielding would have subscribed, is that only the supreme authority of the divine will could render such abstract notions efficacious as a moral imperative. (On Warburton, see below, p. 687, n. 3.)

[1] Cf. Warburton on the ultimate sources of deism: 'And indeed, the following the antient Philosophers too servilely, has occasioned the Errors of modern Moralists, in unnaturally separating the Grounds of Obligation: *Plato* being the Patron of the *Moral Sense*; *Aristotle* of the *Essential Differences*; and the *Stoics* of *Arbitrary Will*' (*Divine Legation*, i [1738], 41, n. *e*).

[2] Cf. the general tenor of Aristotle's criticism of Plato's *Republic* and *Laws* (*Politics*, II. i–iii).

This Gentleman and Mr. *Thwackum* scarce ever met without a Disputation; for their Tenets were, indeed, diametrically opposite to each other. *Square* held human Nature to be the Perfection of all Virtue, and that Vice was a Deviation from our Nature in the same Manner as Deformity of Body is. *Thwackum*, on the contrary, maintained that the human Mind, since the Fall, was nothing but a Sink of Iniquity, till purified and redeemed by Grace. In one Point only they agreed, which was, in all their Discourses on Morality never to mention the Word *Goodness*. The favourite Phrase of the former, was *the natural Beauty of Virtue*; that of the latter, was the *divine Power of Grace*. The former measured all Actions by the *unalterable Rule of Right*, and the *eternal Fitness of Things*; the latter decided all Matters by Authority; but, in doing this, he always used the Scriptures and their Commentators, as the Lawyer doth his *Coke upon Lyttleton*,[1] where the Comment is of equal Authority with the Text.

After this short Introduction, the Reader will be pleased to remember, that the Parson had concluded his Speech with a triumphant Question, to which he had apprehended no Answer; *viz.* Can any Honour exist independent of Religion?

To this *Square* answered, that it was impossible to discourse philosophically concerning Words, till their Meaning was first established;[2] that there were scarce any two Words of a more

---

[1] Sir Edward Coke's commentary (1628) on the *Tenures* of Sir Thomas Littleton (*c.* 1422–81), a standard authority on real property law. (See above, p. 100, n. 1.)

[2] Rigid in his orthodoxy and morose in his Augustinian view of human nature, Thwackum throughout this chapter interprets 'Honour' as a 'Mode of divine Grace' strictly dependent on the Church of England. In attempting to refute this position, Square's method and argument, though in accord with the strategies of deism in general, correspond quite closely to those of Chubb in 'The Author's Farewell to His Readers' (1745). In this work Chubb methodically attacks 'the doctrine of *grace*, or *special grace*, as it is sometimes called' (ibid., p. 57), advocating instead a 'doctrine' of moral '*self-sufficiency*' (p. 62), our ability to perform moral actions being entirely natural to us and '*antecedent*' (p. 60) to any alleged (and in his view illusory) dispensation of divine grace. He further disposes of the narrow assumptions of religious sects that their beliefs alone are divinely authorized. Like Square, Chubb typically begins each division of his argument by 'fixing' his subject, defining his terms (e.g., pp. 47, 57). Keeping in mind Square's objections to Thwackum's orthodoxy, consider Chubb on '*religious parties*': 'I am sensible, that the doctrine of divine impressions has been adhered to, and maintained by *most*, if not *all*, *religious parties* in the world; but then they all seem inclined to *confine* the favour to their *own party*, or, at least, to think it is *chiefly*, and *more certainly* with them; and therefore, they are apt to *draw back*, and are unwilling to submit to what is dictated to them as a *divine oracle*, when it comes from any *other quarter*; and thus, a christian would scarce think himself *concerned*, much less *obliged* to attend to what may be delivered to him as the *produce* of *divine impression* by

vague and uncertain Signification, than the two he had mentioned: For that there were almost as many different Opinions
concerning Honour, as concerning Religion. 'But,' says he, 'if by
Honour you mean the true natural Beauty of Virtue, I will maintain it may exist independent of any Religion whatever. Nay
(added he) you yourself will allow it may exist independent of
all but one; so will a *Mahometan*, a *Jew*, and all the Maintainers of
all the different Sects in the World.'

*Thwackum* replied, This was arguing with the usual Malice
of all the Enemies to the true Church. He said, he doubted not
but that all the Infidels and Hereticks in the World would, if
they could, confine Honour to their own absurd Errors, and
damnable Deceptions; 'But Honour,' says he, 'is not therefore
manifold, because there are many absurd Opinions about it;
nor is Religion manifold, because there are various Sects and
Heresies in the World. When I mention Religion, I mean the
Christian Religion; and not only the Christian Religion, but the
Protestant Religion; and not only the Protestant Religion, but
the Church of *England*.¹ And, when I mention Honour, I mean
that Mode of divine Grace which is not only consistent with,
but dependent upon, this Religion; and is consistent with, and
dependent upon, no other. Now to say that the Honour I here
mean, and which was, I thought, all the Honour I could be supposed to mean, will uphold, much less dictate, an Untruth, is to
assert an Absurdity too shocking to be conceived.'

'I purposely avoided,' says *Square*, 'drawing a Conclusion which
I thought evident from what I have said; but if you perceived it,
I am sure you have not attempted to answer it. However, to
drop the Article of Religion, I think it is plain, from what you
have said, that we have different Ideas of Honour; or why do

---

a *Mahometan*; and the like of a *Mahometan*, by a christian' (pp. 55–6). Similarly, with
Square's rejection of Thwackum's Augustinianism, compare Chubb, who derisively
notices 'what is sometimes urged in *favour* of the doctrine of *special grace*, or rather of
what is urged *against* the doctrine of *self-sufficiency*, which seems to stand in *competition* with
it; namely, *first*, That it must be *great pride* and *arrogance* in man to consider himself as an
*independent, self-sufficient* creature, as one who can, *of himself*, do *many good* actions; whereas
man, especially *since* the *fall*, is most *corrupt, impotent,* and *weak*, who cannot, *of himself*, so
much as *think* a *good thought*, much less bring forth any thing that is good, without the
*special aid* of his Maker' (pp. 64–5).

¹ Thwackum's narrow and rigid orthodoxy should be contrasted with the latitudinarian-
ism of, for example, Bishop Hoadly (see above, p. 105).

we not agree in the same Terms of its Explanation? I have asserted, that true Honour and true Virtue are almost synonimous Terms, and they are both founded on the unalterable Rule of Right, and the eternal Fitness of Things; to which an Untruth being absolutely repugnant and contrary,[1] it is certain that true Honour cannot support an Untruth. In this, therefore, I think we are agreed; but that this Honour can be said to be founded on Religion, to which it is antecedent, if by Religion be meant any positive Law——'

'I agree,' answered *Thwackum*, with great Warmth, 'with a Man who asserts Honour to be antecedent to Religion!—Mr. *Allworthy*, did I agree——?'

He was proceeding, when Mr. *Allworthy* interposed, telling them very coldly, they had both mistaken his Meaning; for that he had said nothing of true Honour.—It is possible, however, he would not have easily quieted the Disputants, who were growing equally warm, had not another Matter now fallen out, which put a final End to the Conversation at present.


CHAPTER IV

*Containing a necessary Apology for the Author; and a childish Incident, which perhaps requires an Apology likewise.*

BEFORE I proceed farther, I shall beg leave to obviate some Misconstructions, into which the Zeal of some few Readers may lead them; for I would not willingly give Offence to any, especially to Men who are warm in the Cause of Virtue or Religion.

I hope, therefore, no Man will, by the grossest Misunderstanding, or Perversion, of my Meaning, misrepresent me, as endeavouring to cast any Ridicule on the greatest Perfections of Human Nature; and which do, indeed, alone purify and enoble the Heart of Man, and raise him above the Brute Creation. This, Reader, I will venture to say, (and by how much the better Man you are yourself, by so much the more will you be inclined to

---

[1] Again Square recalls Chubb, who argued that 'lying and deceiving' were invariably wrong because contrary to the 'essential *difference* in things' and because 'one thing or action is *preferable* to another in nature', as truth is preferable to a lie, or as a promise, once made, must be kept, not broken (*The True Gospel of Jesus Christ Asserted* [1738], p. 189).

believe me) that I would rather have buried the Sentiments of these two Persons in eternal Oblivion, than have done any Injury to either of these glorious Causes.

On the contrary, it is with a View to their Service that I have taken upon me to record the Lives and Actions of two of their false and pretended Champions. A treacherous Friend is the most dangerous Enemy; and I will say boldly, that both Religion and Virtue have received more real Discredit from Hypocrites, than the wittiest Profligates or Infidels could ever cast upon them: Nay farther, as these two, in their Purity, are rightly called the Bands of civil Society, and are indeed the greatest of Blessings; so when poisoned and corrupted with Fraud, Pretence and Affectation, they have become the worst of civil Curses, and have enabled Men to perpetrate the most cruel Mischiefs to their own Species.

Indeed, I doubt not but this Ridicule will in general be allowed; my chief Apprehension is, as many true and just Sentiments often came from the Mouths of these Persons, lest the whole should be taken together, and I should be conceived to ridicule all alike. Now the Reader will be pleased to consider, that as neither of these Men were Fools, they could not be supposed to have holden none but wrong Principles, and to have uttered nothing but Absurdities; what Injustice, therefore, must I have done to their Characters, had I selected only what was bad, and how horridly wretched and maimed must their Arguments have appeared!

Upon the whole, it is not Religion or Virtue, but the Want of them which is here exposed. Had not *Thwackum* too much neglected Virtue, and *Square* Religion, in the Composition of their several Systems; and had not both utterly discarded all natural Goodness of Heart, they had never been represented as the Objects of Derision in this History; in which we will now proceed.

This Matter, then, which put an end to the Debate mentioned in the last Chapter, was no other than a Quarrel between Master *Blifil* and *Tom Jones*, the Consequence of which had been a bloody Nose to the former; for though Master *Blifil*, notwithstanding he was the younger, was in Size above the other's Match, yet *Tom* was much his Superior at the noble Art of Boxing.

*Tom*, however, cautiously avoided all Engagements with that

Youth: For besides that *Tommy Jones* was an inoffensive Lad amidst all his Roguery, and really loved *Blifil*; Mr. *Thwackum* being always the Second of the latter, would have been sufficient to deter him.

But well says a certain Author,[1] No Man is wise at all Hours; it is therefore no Wonder that a Boy is not so. A Difference arising at Play between the two Lads, Master *Blifil* called *Tom* a *Beggarly Bastard*. Upon which the latter, who was some-what passionate in his Disposition, immediately caused that Phænomenon in the Face of the former, which we have above remembred.

Master *Blifil* now, with his Blood running from his Nose, and the Tears galloping after from his Eyes, appeared before his Uncle, and the tremendous *Thwackum*. In which Court an Indict-ment of Assault, Battery, and Wounding, was instantly preferred against *Tom*; who in his Excuse only pleaded the Provocation, which was indeed all the Matter that Master *Blifil* had omitted.

It is indeed possible, that this Circumstance might have escaped his Memory; for, in his Reply, he positively insisted, that he had made Use of no such Appellation; adding, 'Heaven forbid such naughty Words should ever come out of his Mouth.'

*Tom*, though against all Form of Law,[2] rejoined in Affirmance of the Words. Upon which Master *Blifil* said, 'It is no Wonder. Those who will tell one Fib, will hardly stick at another. If I had told my Master such a wicked Fib as you have done, I should be ashamed to shew my Face.'

'What Fib, Child?' cries *Thwackum* pretty eagerly.

'Why, he told you that Nobody was with him a shooting when he killed the Partridge; but he knows, (here he burst into a Flood of Tears) yes, he knows; for he confessed it to me, that *Black George* the Game-keeper was there. Nay, he said,—Yes you did,—deny it if you can, That you would not have confest the Truth, though Master had cut you to Pieces.'

At this the Fire flashed from *Thwackum's* Eyes; and he cried out in Triumph: 'Oh ho! This is your mistaken Notion of

---

[1] See below, pp. 677, n. 3; 856.

[2] In this mock trial, the plaintiff, Blifil, has made his accusation and has been answered by the defendant, Tom, who 'pleaded the Provocation'. Blifil then makes his reply or *replication* and is answered by Tom's *rejoinder*, which, however, because merely a rehearsal of his original plea, would be disallowed in a court of law. (See Wood's *Institutes*, 7th ed. [1745], pp. 609-11.)

Honour! This is the Boy who was not to be whipped again!'
But Mr. *Allworthy*, with a more gentle Aspect, turned towards the
Lad, and said, 'Is this true, Child? How came you to persist so
obstinately in a Falshood?'

*Tom* said, 'He scorned a Lie as much as any one; but he thought
his Honour engaged him to act as he did; for he had promised
the poor Fellow to conceal him; which,' he said, 'he thought
himself farther obliged to, as the Game-keeper had begged him
not to go into the Gentleman's Manor, and had at last gone himself in Compliance with his Persuasions.' He said, 'this was the
whole Truth of the Matter, and he would take his Oath of it;'
and concluded with very passionately begging Mr. *Allworthy*,
'to have Compassion on the poor Fellow's Family, especially as
he himself only had been guilty, and the other had been very
difficultly prevailed on to do what he did.' 'Indeed Sir,' said he,
'it could hardly be called a Lie that I told; for the poor Fellow
was entirely innocent of the whole Matter. I should have gone
alone after the Birds; nay, I did go at first, and he only followed
me to prevent more Mischief. Do, pray, Sir, let me be punished,
take my little Horse away again; but pray, Sir, forgive poor
*George*.'

Mr. *Allworthy* hesitated a few Moments, and then dismissed
the Boys, advising them to live more friendly and peaceably
together.


## CHAPTER V

*The Opinions of the Divine and the Philosopher concerning the two*
*Boys; with some Reasons for their Opinions, and other Matters.*

IT is probable, that by disclosing this Secret, which had been
communicated in the utmost Confidence to him, young *Blifil*
preserved his Companion from a good Lashing: For the Offence
of the bloody Nose would have been of itself sufficient Cause for
*Thwackum* to have proceeded to Correction; but now this was
totally absorbed, in the Consideration of the other Matter; and
with Regard to this, Mr. *Allworthy* declared privately, he thought
the Boy deserved Reward rather than Punishment; so that
*Thwackum's* Hand was withheld by a general Pardon.

*Thwackum*, whose Meditations were full of Birch, exclaimed against this weak, and, as he said he would venture to call it, wicked Lenity. To remit the Punishment of such Crimes was, he said, to encourage them. He enlarged much on the Correction of Children, and quoted many Texts from *Solomon*,[1] and others; which being to be found in so many other Books, shall not be found here. He then applied himself to the Vice of Lying, on which Head he was altogether as learned as he had been on the other.

*Square* said, he had been endeavouring to reconcile the Behaviour of *Tom* with his Idea of perfect Virtue; but could not. He owned there was something which at first Sight appeared like Fortitude in the Action; but as Fortitude was a Virtue, and Falshood a Vice, they could by no Means agree or unite together. He added, that as this was in some measure to confound Virtue and Vice, it might be worth Mr. *Thwackum's* Consideration, whether a larger Castigation might not be laid on, upon that Account.

As both these learned Men concurred in censuring *Jones*, so were they no less unanimous in applauding Master *Blifil*. To bring Truth to light, was by the Parson asserted to be the Duty of every religious Man; and by the Philosopher this was declared to be highly conformable with the Rule of Right, and the eternal and unalterable Fitness of Things.

All this, however, weighed very little with Mr. *Allworthy*. He could not be prevailed on to sign the Warrant for the Execution of *Jones*. There was something within his own Breast with which the invincible Fidelity which that Youth had preserved, corresponded much better than it had done with the Religion of *Thwackum*, or with the Virtue of *Square*. He therefore strictly ordered the former of these Gentlemen to abstain from laying violent Hands on *Tom* for what had past. The Pedagogue was obliged to obey those Orders; but not without great Reluctance, and frequent Mutterings, that the Boy would be certainly spoiled.

Towards the Game-keeper the good Man behaved with more Severity. He presently summoned that poor Fellow before him, and after many bitter Remonstrances, paid him his Wages, and dismist him from his Service; for Mr. *Allworthy* rightly observed that there was a great Difference between being guilty of a

[1] e.g. Proverbs 13: 24, 19: 18, 22: 15, 23: 13–14, 29: 15.

Falsehood to excuse yourself, and to excuse another. He likewise urged, as the principal Motive to his inflexible Severity
against this Man, that he had basely suffered *Tom Jones* to
undergo so heavy a Punishment for his Sake, whereas he ought
to have prevented it by making the Discovery himself.

When this Story became public, many People differed from
*Square* and *Thwackum*, in judging the Conduct of the two Lads on
the Occasion. Master *Blifil* was generally called a sneaking Rascal,
a poor-spirited Wretch; with other Epithets of the like Kind;
whilst *Tom* was honoured with the Appellations of a brave Lad,
a jolly Dog, and an honest Fellow. Indeed his Behaviour to
*Black George* much ingratiated him with all the Servants; for
though that Fellow was before universally disliked, yet he was no
sooner turned away than he was as universally pitied; and the
Friendship and Gallantry of *Tom Jones* was celebrated by them
all with the highest Applause; and they condemned Master
*Blifil*, as openly as they durst, without incurring the Danger of
offending his Mother. For all this, however, poor *Tom* smarted in
the Flesh; for though *Thwackum* had been inhibited to exercise
his Arm on the foregoing Account; yet, as the Proverb says,[1] *It is
easy to find a Stick*, &c. So was it easy to find a Rod; and, indeed,
the not being able to find one was the only thing which could
have kept *Thwackum* any long Time from chastising poor Jones.

Had the bare Delight in the Sport been the only Inducement
to the Pedagogue, it is probable, Master *Blifil* would likewise
have had his Share; but though Mr. *Allworthy* had given him
frequent Orders to make no Difference between the Lads, yet
was *Thwackum* altogether as kind and gentle to this Youth, as
he was harsh, nay even barbarous, to the other. To say the Truth,
*Blifil* had greatly gained his Master's Affections; partly by the
profound Respect he always shewed his Person, but much more
by the decent Reverence with which he received his Doctrine;
for he had got by Heart, and frequently repeated his Phrases,
and maintained all his Master's religious Principles with a
Zeal which was surprising in one so young, and which greatly
endeared him to the worthy Preceptor.

*Tom Jones*, on the other hand, was not only deficient in outward
Tokens of Respect, often forgetting to pull off his Hat, or to

[1] 'It is easy to find a stick to beat a dog.' (See W. G. Smith and P. Harvey (edd.), *Oxford
Dictionary of English Proverbs*, 2nd ed. [Oxford, 1948], p. 617.)

bow at his Master's Approach; but was altogether as unmindful both of his Master's Precepts and Example. He was indeed a thoughtless, giddy Youth, with little Sobriety in his Manners, and less in his Countenance; and would often very impudently and indecently laugh at his Companion for his serious Behaviour.

Mr. *Square* had the same Reason for his Preference of the former Lad; for *Tom Jones* shewed no more Regard to the learned Discourses which this Gentleman would sometimes throw away upon him, than to those of *Thwackum*. He once ventured to make a Jest of the Rule of Right; and at another Time said, He believed there was no Rule in the World capable of making such a Man as his Father (for so Mr. *Allworthy* suffered himself to be called.)

Master *Blifil*, on the contrary, had Address enough at sixteen to recommend himself at one and the same Time to both these Opposites. With one he was all Religion, with the other he was all Virtue. And when both were present, he was profoundly silent, which both interpreted in his Favour and in their own.

Nor was *Blifil* contented with flattering both these Gentlemen to their Faces; he took frequent Occasions of praising them behind their Backs to *Allworthy*; before whom, when they two were alone, and his Uncle commended any religious or virtuous Sentiment, (for many such came constantly from him) he seldom fail'd to ascribe it to the good Instructions he had received from either *Thwackum* or *Square*: For he knew his Uncle repeated all such Compliments to the Persons for whose Use they were meant; and he found by Experience the great Impressions which they made on the Philosopher, as well as on the Divine: For, to say the Truth, there is no kind of Flattery so irresistible as this, at second Hand.

The young Gentleman, moreover, soon perceived how extremely grateful all those Panegyricks on his Instructors were to Mr. *Allworthy* himself, as they so loudly resounded the Praise of that singular Plan of Education which he had laid down:[1] For

---

[1] Like Parson Adams in *Joseph Andrews* (1742; III. v), Allworthy naïvely trusts in the superior moral efficacy of a private education over a public one. The 'Fault in the Plan', as Fielding remarks later in this chapter, had been stated by Joseph Andrews in his reply to Adams: 'I remember when I was in the Stable, if a young Horse was vicious in his Nature, no Correction would make him otherwise; I take it to be equally the same among Men: if a Boy be of a mischievous wicked Inclination, no School, tho' ever so private, will ever make him good; on the contrary, if he be of a righteous Temper, you may trust him to *London*,

this worthy Man having observed the imperfect Institution of our public Schools, and the many Vices which Boys were there liable to learn, had resolved to educate his Nephew, as well as the other Lad, whom he had in a Manner adopted, in his own House; where he thought their Morals would escape all that Danger of being corrupted, to which they would be unavoidably exposed in any public School or University.

Having therefore determined to commit these Boys to the Tuition of a private Tutor, Mr. *Thwackum* was recommended to him for that Office, by a very particular Friend, of whose Understanding Mr. *Allworthy* had a great Opinion, and in whose Integrity he placed much Confidence. This *Thwackum* was Fellow of a College, where he almost entirely resided; and had a great Reputation for Learning, Religion and Sobriety of Manners. And these were doubtless the Qualifications by which Mr. *Allworthy's* Friend had been induced to recommend him; tho' indeed this Friend had some Obligations to *Thwackum's* Family, who were the most considerable Persons in a Borough which that Gentleman represented in Parliament.

*Thwackum*, at his first Arrival, was extremely agreeable to *Allworthy*; and indeed he perfectly answered the Character which had been given of him. Upon longer Acquaintance, however, and more intimate Conversation, this worthy Man saw Infirmities in the Tutor, which he could have wished him to have been without; tho' as those seemed greatly over-ballanced by his good Qualities, they did not incline Mr. *Allworthy* to part with him; nor would they indeed have justified such a Proceeding: For the Reader is greatly mistaken, if he conceives that *Thwackum* appeared to Mr. *Allworthy* in the same Light as he doth to him in this History; and he is as much deceived, if he imagines, that the most intimate Acquaintance which he himself could have had with that Divine, would have informed him of those Things which we, from our Inspiration, are enabled to open and discover. Of Readers who from such Conceits as these, condemn the Wisdom or Penetration of Mr. *Allworthy*, I shall not scruple to say, that they make a very bad and ungrateful Use of that Knowledge which we have communicated to them.

or where-ever else you please, he will be in no danger of being corrupted.' This view, to which Fielding doubtless subscribed, is merely a paraphrase of Quintilian, *Institutio Oratoria*, I. ii. 4–5.

These apparent Errors in the Doctrine of *Thwackum*, served greatly to palliate the contrary Errors in that of *Square*, which our good Man no less saw and condemned. He thought indeed that the different Exuberancies of these Gentlemen, would correct their different Imperfections; and that from both, especially with his Assistance, the two Lads would derive sufficient Precepts of true Religion and Virtue. If the Event happened contrary to his Expectations, this possibly proceeded from some Fault in the Plan itself; which the Reader hath my Leave to discover, if he can: For we do not pretend to introduce any infallible Characters into this History; where we hope nothing will be found which hath never yet been seen in human Nature.

To return therefore; the Reader will not, I think, wonder that the different Behaviour of the two Lads above commemorated, produced the different Effects, of which he hath already seen some Instance; and besides this, there was another Reason for the Conduct of the Philosopher and the Pedagogue; but this being Matter of great Importance, we shall reveal it in the next Chapter.

## CHAPTER VI

*Containing a better Reason still for the before-mentioned Opinions.*

IT is to be known then, that those two learned Personages, who have lately made a considerable Figure on the Theatre of this History, had from their first Arrival at Mr. *Allworthy's* House, taken so great an Affection, the one to his Virtue, the other to his Religion, that they had meditated the closest Alliance with him.

For this Purpose they had cast their Eyes on that fair Widow, whom, tho' we have not for some Time made any Mention of her, the Reader, we trust, hath not forgot. Mrs. *Blifil* was indeed the Object to which they both aspired.

It may seem remarkable that of four Persons whom we have commemorated at Mr. *Allworthy's* House, three of them should fix their Inclinations on a Lady who was never greatly celebrated for her Beauty, and who was, moreover, now a little descended into the Vale of Years; but in reality Bosom Friends, and intimate Acquaintance, have a kind of natural Propensity to particular Females at the House of a Friend; *viz.* to his Grand-mother,

Mother, Sister, Daughter, Aunt, Niece or Cousin, when they are rich, and to his Wife, Sister, Daughter, Niece, Cousin, Mistress or Servant Maid, if they should be handsome.

We would not, however, have our Reader imagine, that Persons of such Characters as were supported by *Thwackum* and *Square*, would undertake a Matter of this Kind, which hath been a little censured by some rigid Moralists, before they had thoroughly examined it, and considered whether it was (as *Shakespear* phrases it)¹ 'Stuff o' th' Conscience' or no. *Thwackum* was encouraged to the Undertaking, by reflecting, that to covet your Neighbour's Sister is no where forbidden, and he knew it was a Rule in the Construction of all Laws, that '*Expressum facit cessare Tacitum*,'² the Sense of which is, 'When a Law-giver sets down plainly his whole Meaning, we are prevented from making him mean what we please ourselves.' As some Instances of Women, therefore, are mentioned in the divine Law, which forbids us to covet our Neighbours Goods, and that of a Sister omitted, he concluded it to be lawful. And as to *Square*, who was in his Person what is called a jolly Fellow, or a Widow's Man, he easily reconciled his Choice to the eternal Fitness of Things.

Now, as both these Gentlemen were industrious in taking every Opportunity of recommending themselves to the Widow, they apprehended one certain Method was, by giving her Son the constant Preference to the other Lad; and as they conceived the Kindness and Affection which Mr. *Allworthy* shewed the latter, must be highly disagreeable to her, they doubted not but the laying hold on all Occasions to degrade and villify him, would be highly pleasing to her; who, as she hated the Boy, must love all those who did him any Hurt. In this *Thwackum* had the Advantage; for while *Square* could only scarify the poor Lad's Reputation, he could flea his Skin; and indeed he considered every Lash he gave him as a Compliment paid to his Mistress; so that he could with the utmost Propriety repeat this old flogging Line, '*Castigo te non quod odio habeam, sed quod* AMEM;³ I chastize thee

¹ Iago's speech in *Othello*, I. ii: 'Though in the trade of Warre I have slaine men,/ Yet do I hold it very stuffe o' th' conscience/ To do no contriv'd Murder.'

² A legal maxim meaning literally: 'That which is expressed nullifies [i.e., causes to cease] that which is tacitly assumed.'

³ Cf. Proverbs 13: 24: 'He that spareth his rod hateth his son: but he that loveth him chasteneth him betimes.' Not only Thwackum apparently (see above, p. 132, n. 1), but also the Church fathers cited this text in defending the practice of corporal discipline (see

not out of Hatred, but out of Love.' And this indeed he often had in his Mouth, or rather, according to the old Phrase, never more properly applied, at his Fingers Ends.

For this Reason principally, the two Gentlemen concurred, as we have seen above, in their Opinion concerning the two Lads; this being indeed almost the only Instance of their concurring on any Point: For beside the Difference of their Principles, they had both long ago strongly suspected each other's Design, and hated one another with no little Degree of Inveteracy.

This mutual Animosity was a good deal increased by their alternate Successes: For Mrs. *Blifil* knew what they would be at long before they imagined it; or indeed intended she should: For they proceeded with great Caution lest she should be offended, and acquaint Mr. *Allworthy*; but they had no Reason for any such Fear. She was well enough pleased with a Passion of which she intended none should have any Fruits but herself. And the only Fruits she designed for herself were Flattery and Court-ship; for which Purpose, she soothed them by Turns, and a long Time equally. She was indeed rather inclined to favour the Parson's Principles; but *Square's* Person was more agreeable to her Eye; for he was a comely Man; whereas the Pedagogue did in Countenance very nearly resemble that Gentleman, who in the Harlot's Progress is seen correcting the Ladies in *Bridewel*.[1]

Whether Mrs. *Blifil* had been surfeited with the Sweets of Marriage, or disgusted by its Bitters, or from what other Cause it proceeded, I will not determine; but she could never be brought to listen to any second Proposals. However, she at last conversed with *Square*, with such a Degree of Intimacy, that malicious Tongues began to whisper Things of her, to which, as well for the Sake of the Lady, as that they were highly disagreeable to the Rule of Right, and the Fitness of Things, we will give no Credit; and therefore shall not blot our Paper with them. The Pedagogue, 'tis certain, whipt on without getting a Step nearer to his Journey's End.

Indeed he had committed a great Error, and that *Square* dis-covered much sooner than himself. Mrs. *Blifil* (as perhaps the

the Abbé Boileau, *Histoire des flagellans* [Amsterdam, 1701], pp. 162–3). Cf. the sadistic priest in *A Journey from This World to the Next* (1743; I. xv).

[1] Plate 4 of Hogarth's *A Harlot's Progress* (1732) is reproduced as Plate 3. See also above, pp. 58, 66, 82.

Reader may have formerly guess'd) was not over and above pleased with the Behaviour of her Husband; nay, to be honest, she absolutely hated him, till his Death at last a little reconciled him to her Affections. It will not be therefore greatly wondered at, if she had not the most violent Regard to the Offspring she had by him. And, in fact, she had so little of this Regard, that in his Infancy she seldom saw her Son, or took any Notice of him; and hence she acquiesced, after a little Reluctance, in all the Favours which Mr. *Allworthy* showered on the Foundling; whom the good Man called his own Boy, and in all Things put on an intire Equality with Master *Blifil*. This Acquiescence in Mrs. *Blifil* was considered by the Neighbours, and by the Family, as a Mark of her Condescension to her Brother's Humour, and she was imagined by all others, as well as *Thwackum* and *Square*, to hate the Foundling in her Heart; nay, the more Civility she shewed him, the more they conceived she detested him, and the surer Schemes she was laying for his Ruin: For as they thought it her Interest to hate him, it was very difficult for her to perswade them she did not.

*Thwackum* was the more confirmed in his Opinion, as she had more than once slily caused him to whip *Tom Jones*, when Mr. *Allworthy*, who was an Enemy to this Exercise, was abroad; whereas she had never given any such Orders concerning young *Blifil*. And this had likewise imposed upon *Square*. In reality, though she certainly hated her own Son; of which, however monstrous it appears, I am assured she is not a singular Instance, she appeared, notwithstanding all her outward Compliance, to be in her Heart sufficiently displeased with all the Favour shewn by Mr. *Allworthy* to the Foundling. She frequently complained of this behind her Brother's Back, and very sharply censured him for it, both to *Thwackum* and *Square*; nay, she would throw it in the Teeth of *Allworthy* himself, when a little Quarrel or Miff, as it is vulgarly called, arose between them.

However, when *Tom* grew up, and gave Tokens of that Gallantry of Temper which greatly recommends Men to Women, this Disinclination which she had discovered to him when a Child, by Degrees abated, and at last she so evidently demonstrated her Affection to him to be much stronger than what she bore her own Son, that it was impossible to mistake her any longer. She was so desirous of often seeing him, and discovered such Satisfaction and Delight in his Company, that before he was eighteen Years old, he was become a Rival to both *Square* and *Thwackum*; and what is worse, the whole Country began to talk as loudly of her Inclination to *Tom*, as they had before done of that which she had shewn to *Square*; on which Account the Philosopher conceived the most implacable Hatred for our poor Heroe.

## CHAPTER VII

*In which the Author himself makes his Appearance on the Stage.*

THO' Mr. *Allworthy* was not of himself hasty to see Things in a disadvantageous Light, and was a Stranger to the public Voice, which seldom reaches to a Brother or a Husband, tho' it rings in the Ears of all the Neighbourhood; yet was this Affection of Mrs. *Blifil* to *Tom*, and the Preference which she too visibly gave him to her own Son, of the utmost Disadvantage to that Youth.

For such was the Compassion which inhabited Mr. *Allworthy's* Mind, that nothing but the Steel of Justice could ever subdue it. To be unfortunate in any Respect was sufficient, if there was no Demerit to counterpoise it, to turn the Scale of that good Man's Pity, and to engage his Friendship, and his Benefaction.

When therefore he plainly saw Master *Blifil* was absolutely detested (for that he was) by his own Mother, he began, on that Account only, to look with an Eye of Compassion upon him; and what the Effects of Compassion are in good and benevolent Minds, I need not here explain to most of my Readers.

Henceforward, he saw every Appearance of Virtue in the Youth thro' the magnifying End, and viewed all his Faults with the Glass inverted, so that they became scarce perceptible. And this perhaps the amiable Temper of Pity may make commendable; but the next Step the Weakness of human Nature alone must excuse: For he no sooner perceived that Preference which Mrs. *Blifil* gave to *Tom*, than that poor Youth, (however innocent) began to sink in his Affections as he rose in hers. This, it is true, would of itself alone never have been able to eradicate *Jones* from his Bosom; but it was greatly injurious to him, and prepared Mr. *Allworthy's* Mind for those Impressions, which afterwards produced the mighty Events, that will be contained hereafter in this History; and to which, it must be confest, the unfortunate Lad, by his own Wantonness, Wildness, and Want of Caution, too much contributed.

In recording some Instances of these, we shall, if rightly understood, afford a very useful Lesson to those well-disposed Youths, who shall hereafter be our Readers: For they may here find that Goodness of Heart, and Openness of Temper, tho' these may give them great Comfort within, and administer to an honest Pride in their own Minds, will by no Means, alas! do their Business in the World. Prudence[1] and Circumspection are necessary even to the best of Men. They are indeed as it were a Guard to Virtue, without which she can never be safe. It is not enough that your Designs, nay that your Actions are intrinsically good, you must take Care they shall appear so. If your Inside be never so beautiful, you must preserve a fair Outside also. This must be constantly looked to, or Malice and Envy will take Care to blacken it so, that the Sagacity and Goodness of an *Allworthy* will not be able to see through it, and to discern the Beauties within. Let this, my young Readers, be your constant Maxim, That no Man can be good enough to enable him to neglect the Rules of Prudence; nor will Virtue herself look beautiful, unless she be bedecked with the outward Ornaments of Decency and Decorum. And this Precept, my worthy Disciples, if you read with due Attention, you will, I hope, find sufficiently enforced by Examples in the following Pages.

I ask Pardon for this short Appearance, by Way of Chorus on

---

[1] See above, p. 36, n. 1. Most contemporary discussions of prudence stressed the importance of one's preserving the appearance, at least, of virtue. In *The Art of Prudence* (1702) Gracián had warned that 'THINGS are not taken for what they really are, but for what they appear to be. . . . It is not enough to have a good Intention, if the Action look ill' (maxim xcix; see also cxxx), and Fuller's apothegms similarly emphasize that 'a fair Reputation' is necessary to all men (*Introductio ad Prudentiam*, 3rd ed. [1731], Nos. 1425, 1590). As may be seen from *The Champion* (22 November 1739), Fielding agreed with this much at least of the worldly wisdom inculcated by the writers of conduct books, though, unlike them, he took care to distinguish a proper sense of discretion from a hypocritical dissimulation: 'I would . . . by no Means recommend to Mankind to cultivate Deceit, or endeavour to appear what they are not; on the contrary, I wish it were possible to induce the World to make a diligent Enquiry into Things themselves, to withold them from giving too hasty a Credit to the outward Shew and first Impression; I would only convince my Readers, *That it is not enough to have Virtue, without we also take Care to preserve, by a certain Decency and Dignity of Behaviour, the outward Appearance of it also.*' Cf. also Mrs. Raffler in *The Universal Gallant* (1735), II. i.

the Stage. It is in Reality for my own Sake, that while I am discovering the Rocks on which Innocence and Goodness often split, I may not be misunderstood to recommend the very Means to my worthy Readers, by which I intend to shew them they will be undone. And this, as I could not prevail on any of my Actors to speak, I myself was obliged to declare.

## CHAPTER VIII

*A childish Incident, in which, however, is seen a good-natur'd Disposition in* Tom Jones.

THE Reader may remember, that Mr. *Allworthy* gave *Tom Jones* a little Horse, as a kind of smart Money for the Punishment, which he imagined he had suffered innocently.

This Horse *Tom* kept above half a Year, and then rode him to a neighbouring Fair, and sold him.

At his Return, being questioned by *Thwackum*, what he had done with the Money for which the Horse was sold, he frankly declared he would not tell him.

'Oho!' says *Thwackum*, 'you will not! then I will have it out of your Br—h;' that being the Place to which he always applied for Information, on every doubtful Occasion.

*Tom* was now mounted on the Back of a Footman, and every Thing prepared for Execution, when Mr. *Allworthy* entering the Room, gave the Criminal a Reprieve, and took him with him into another Apartment; where being alone with *Tom*, he put the same Question to him which *Thwackum* had before asked him.

*Tom* answered, He could in Duty refuse him nothing; but as for that tyrannical Rascal, he would never make him any other Answer than with a Cudgel, with which he hoped soon to be able to pay him for all his Barbarities.

Mr. *Allworthy* very severely reprimanded the Lad, for his indecent and disrespectful Expressions concerning his Master; but much more for his avowing an Intention of Revenge. He threatened him with the entire Loss of his Favour, if he ever heard such another Word from his Mouth; for he said, he would never support or befriend a Reprobate. By these and the like Declarations, he extorted some Compunction from *Tom*, in which that

Youth was not over sincere: For he really meditated some Return for all the smarting Favours he had received at the Hands of the Pedagogue. He was, however, brought by Mr. *Allworthy* to express a Concern for his Resentment against *Thwackum*; and then the good Man, after some wholesome Admonition, permitted him to proceed, which he did, as follows.

'Indeed, my dear Sir, I love and honour you more than all the World; I know the great Obligations I have to you, and should detest myself, if I thought my Heart was capable of Ingratitude. Could the little Horse you gave me speak, I am sure he could tell you how fond I was of your Present: For I had more Pleasure in feeding him, than in riding him. Indeed, Sir, it went to my Heart to part with him; nor would I have sold him upon any other Account in the World than what I did. You yourself, Sir, I am convinced, in my Case, would have done the same: For none ever so sensibly felt the Misfortunes of others. What would you feel, dear Sir, if you thought yourself the Occasion of them?—Indeed, Sir, there never was any Misery like theirs.'—'Like whose, Child,' says *Allworthy*, 'what do you mean?' 'Oh, Sir,' answered *Tom*, 'your poor Game-keeper, with all his large Family, ever since your discarding him, have been perishing with all the Miseries of Cold and Hunger. I could not bear to see these poor Wretches naked and starving, and at the same Time know myself to have been the Occasion of all their Sufferings.—I could not bear it, Sir, upon my Soul, I could not.' (Here the Tears run down his Cheeks, and he thus proceeded) 'It was to save them from absolute Destruction, I parted with your dear Present, notwithstanding all the Value I had for it.—I sold the Horse for them, and they have every Farthing of the Money.'

Mr. *Allworthy* now stood silent for some Moments, and before he spoke, the Tears started from his Eyes. He at length dismissed *Tom* with a gentle Rebuke, advising him for the future to apply to him in Cases of Distress, rather than to use extraordinary Means of relieving them himself.

This Affair was afterwards the Subject of much Debate between *Thwackum* and *Square*. *Thwackum* held, that this was flying in Mr. *Allworthy's* Face, who had intended to punish the Fellow for his Disobedience. He said, in some Instances, what the World called Charity appeared to him to be opposing the Will of the Almighty, which had marked some particular Persons for

Destruction; and that this was in like manner acting in Opposition
to Mr. *Allworthy*; concluding, as usual, with a hearty Recommendation of Birch.

*Square* argued strongly, on the other Side, in Opposition perhaps to *Thwackum*, or in Compliance with Mr. *Allworthy*, who
seemed very much to approve what *Jones* had done. As to what
he urged on this Occasion, as I am convinced most of my Readers
will be much abler Advocates for poor *Jones*, it would be impertinent to relate it. Indeed it was not difficult to reconcile to
the *Rule of Right*, an Action which it would have been impossible
to deduce from the *Rule of Wrong*.

## CHAPTER IX

*Containing an Incident of a more heinous Kind, with the Comments of*
Thwackum *and* Square.

IT hath been observed by some Man of much greater Reputation for Wisdom than myself, that Misfortunes seldom come
single. An Instance of this may, I believe, be seen in those Gentlemen who have the Misfortune to have any of their Rogueries
detected: For here Discovery seldom stops till the whole is come
out. Thus it happened to poor *Tom*; who was no sooner pardoned
for selling the Horse, than he was discovered to have some time
before sold a fine Bible which Mr. *Allworthy* gave him, the Money
arising from which Sale he had disposed of in the same Manner.
This Bible Master *Blifil* had purchased, though he had already
such another of his own, partly out of Respect for the Book, and
partly out of Friendship to *Tom*, being unwilling that the Bible
should be sold out of the Family at half Price. He therefore
disbursed the said half Price himself; for he was a very prudent
Lad, and so careful of his Money, that he had laid up almost every
Penny which he had received from Mr. *Allworthy*.

Some People have been noted to be able to read in no Book but
their own.[1] On the contrary, from the Time when Master *Blifil*
was first possessed of this Bible, he never used any other. Nay,
he was seen reading in it much oftner than he had before been

[1] Said proverbially of the Parson of Saddleworth. (See John Ray's *Collection of English Proverbs* [1670].)

in his own. Now, as he frequently asked *Thwackum* to explain difficult Passages to him, that Gentleman unfortunately took Notice of *Tom's* Name, which was written in many Parts of the Book. This brought on an Enquiry, which obliged Master *Blifil* to discover the whole Matter.

*Thwackum* was resolved, a Crime of this Kind, which he called Sacrilege, should not go unpunished. He therefore proceeded immediately to Castigation; and not contented with that, he acquainted Mr. *Allworthy*, at their next Meeting, with this monstrous Crime, as it appeared to him; inveighing against *Tom* in the most bitter Terms, and likening him to the Buyers and Sellers who were driven out of the Temple.[1]

*Square* saw this Matter in a very different Light. He said, He could not perceive any higher Crime in selling one Book, than in selling another. That to sell Bibles was strictly lawful by all Laws both divine and human, and consequently there was no Unfitness in it. He told *Thwackum* that his great Concern on this Occasion brought to his Mind the Story of a very devout Woman, who out of pure Regard to Religion, stole *Tillotson's* Sermons[2] from a Lady of her Acquaintance.

This Story caused a vast Quantity of Blood to rush into the Parson's Face, which of itself was none of the palest; and he was going to reply with great Warmth and Anger, had not Mrs. *Blifil*, who was present at this Debate, interposed. That Lady declared herself absolutely of Mr. *Square's* Side. She argued, indeed, very learnedly in Support of his Opinion; and concluded with saying, If *Tom* had been guilty of any Fault, she must confess her own Son appeared to be equally culpable; for that she could see no Difference between the Buyer and the Seller; both of whom were alike to be driven out of the Temple.

Mrs. *Blifil* having declared her Opinion, put an End to the Debate. *Square's* Triumph would almost have stopt his Words,

[1] Cf. Matthew 21: 12–13, Mark 11: 15–17, John 2: 14–16.

[2] John Tillotson (1630–94), Archbishop of Canterbury and a leader of the latitudinarians. Because of his 'natural and easy' style, Tillotson's sermons were much admired. (See, for example, Henry Felton, *A Dissertation on Reading the Classics, and Forming a Just Style*, 5th ed. [1753], pp. 178–9.) In *Tom Jones* Allworthy apparently draws upon Tillotson's works in disputing a theological point with Captain Blifil (see above, p. 79, n. 4). Indeed, complimentary allusions to this distinguished divine occur frequently in Fielding's writings: see, for example, *The Champion* (22 January, 15 March 1739/40), *Joseph Andrews* (1742; I. xvi), *The Covent-Garden Journal* (14 January 1752), and *A Proposal for Making an Effectual Provision for the Poor* (1753).

had he needed them; and *Thwackum*, who, for Reasons before-mentioned, durst not venture at disobliging the Lady, was almost choaked with Indignation. As to Mr. *Allworthy*, he said, Since the Boy had been already punished, he would not deliver his Sentiments on the Occasion; and whether he was, or was not angry with the Lad, I must leave to the Reader's own Conjecture.

Soon after this, an Action was brought against the Game-keeper by Squire *Western* (the Gentleman in whose Manor the *Partridge* was killed) for Depredations of the like Kind. This was a most unfortunate Circumstance for the Fellow, as it not only of itself threatened his Ruin, but actually prevented Mr. *All-worthy* from restoring him to his Favour: For as that Gentleman was walking out one Evening with Master *Blifil* and young *Jones*, the latter slily drew him to the Habitation of *Black George*; where the Family of that poor Wretch, namely, his Wife and Children, were found in all the Misery with which Cold, Hunger, and Nakedness, can affect human Creatures: For as to the Money they had received from *Jones*, former Debts had consumed almost the whole.

Such a Scene as this could not fail of affecting the Heart of Mr. *Allworthy*. He immediately gave the Mother a couple of Guineas, with which he bid her cloath her Children. The poor Woman burst into Tears at this Goodness, and while she was thanking him, could not refrain from expressing her Gratitude to *Tom*; who had, she said, long preserved both her and hers from starving. We have not, says she, had a Morsel to eat, nor have these poor Children had a Rag to put on, but what his Good-ness hath bestowed on us: For indeed, besides the Horse and the Bible, *Tom* had sacrificed a Night-gown and other Things to the Use of this distressed Family.

On their Return home, *Tom* made use of all his Eloquence to display the Wretchedness of these People, and the Penitence of *Black George* himself; and in this he succeeded so well, that Mr. *Allworthy* said, He thought the Man had suffered enough for what was past; that he would forgive him, and think of some Means of providing for him and his Family.

*Jones* was so delighted with this News, that though it was dark when they returned home, he could not help going back a Mile in a Shower of Rain to acquaint the poor Woman with the glad Tidings; but, like other hasty Divulgers of News, he only brought on himself the Trouble of contradicting it: For the Ill-fortune of *Black George* made use of the very Opportunity of his Friend's Absence to overturn all again.

## CHAPTER X

*In which Master* Blifil *and* Jones *appear in different Lights.*

MASTER *Blifil* fell very short of his Companion in the amiable Quality of Mercy; but he as greatly exceeded him in one of a much higher Kind, namely, in Justice: In which he followed both the Precepts and Example of *Thwackum* and *Square*; for though they would both make frequent Use of the Word *Mercy*, yet it was plain, that in reality *Square* held it to be inconsistent with the Rule of Right; and *Thwackum* was for doing Justice, and leaving Mercy to Heaven. The two Gentlemen did indeed somewhat differ in Opinion concerning the Objects of this sublime Virtue; by which *Thwackum* would probably have destroyed one half of Mankind, and *Square* the other half.

Master *Blifil* then, though he had kept Silence in the Presence of *Jones*, yet when he had better considered the Matter, could by no Means endure the Thoughts of suffering his Uncle to confer Favours on the Undeserving. He therefore resolved immediately to acquaint him with the Fact which we have above slightly hinted to the Readers. The Truth of which was as follows:

The Game-keeper, about a Year after he was dismissed from Mr. *Allworthy's* Service, and before *Tom's* selling the Horse, being in Want of Bread, either to fill his own Mouth, or those of his Family, as he passed through a Field belonging to Mr. *Western*, espied a Hare sitting in her Form. This Hare he had basely and barbarously knocked on the Head, against the Laws of the Land, and no less against the Laws of Sportsmen.

The Higler to whom the Hare was sold, being unfortunately taken many Months after with a Quantity of Game upon him, was obliged to make his Peace with the Squire by becoming Evidence against some Poacher.[1] And now *Black George* was

[1] According to the Game Laws (viz. 5 Anne [Session 2], cap. 14), any higgler or other unauthorized person found to have game in his possession could be prosecuted. If convicted within three months of the offence, he was liable to a fine of £5 for each bird, etc.,

pitched upon by him as being a Person already obnoxious to Mr. *Western*, and one of no good Fame in the Country. He was, besides, the best Sacrifice the Higler could make, as he had supplied him with no Game since; and by this Means the Witness had an Opportunity of screening his better Customers: For the Squire, being charmed with the Power of punishing *Black George*, whom a single Transgression was sufficient to ruin, made no further Enquiry.

Had this Fact been truly laid before Mr. *Allworthy*, it might probably have done the Game-keeper very little Mischief. But there is no Zeal blinder than that which is inspired with the Love of Justice against Offenders. Master *Blifil* had forgot the Distance of the Time. He varied likewise in the Manner of the Fact; and, by the hasty Addition of the single Letter S, he considerably altered the Story; for he said that *George* had wired Hares. These Alterations might probably have been set right, had not Master *Blifil* unluckily insisted on a Promise of Secrecy from Mr. *Allworthy*, before he revealed the Matter to him; but by that Means, the poor Game-keeper was condemned, without having any Opportunity to defend himself: For as the Fact of killing the Hare, and of the Action brought, were certainly true, Mr. *Allworthy* had no Doubt concerning the rest.

Short-lived then was the Joy of these poor People; for Mr. *Allworthy* the next Morning declared he had fresh Reason, without assigning it, for his Anger, and strictly forbad *Tom* to mention *George* any more; though as for his Family, he said, he would endeavour to keep them from starving; but as to the Fellow himself, he would leave him to the Laws, which nothing could keep him from breaking.

*Tom* could by no Means divine what had incensed Mr. *Allworthy*: For of Master *Blifil* he had not the least Suspicion. However, as his Friendship was to be tired out by no Disappointments, he now determined to try another Method of preserving the poor Game-keeper from Ruin.

*Jones* was lately grown very intimate with Mr. *Western*. He

or, if unable to pay the money, he could be imprisoned. By supplying evidence leading to the conviction of some other offender within three months of the offence, he would, however, not only escape punishment himself, but be rewarded with half the amount of all fines paid. (See Wood's *Institutes*, 7th ed. [1745], pp. 462–3.) As Hugh Amory has noticed, however, in 1728 and 1738 the King's Bench had held that the higgler's interest in the conviction disqualified him as a witness.

had so greatly recommended himself to that Gentleman, by leaping over five-barred Gates, and by other Acts of Sportsmanship, that the Squire had declared *Tom* would certainly make a great Man, if he had but sufficient Encouragement. He often wished he had himself a Son with such Parts; and one Day very solemnly asserted at a drinking Bout, that *Tom* should hunt a Pack of Hounds for a thousand Pound of his Money with any Huntsman in the whole Country.

By such kind of Talents he had so ingratiated himself with the Squire, that he was a most welcome Guest at his Table, and a favourite Companion in his Sport: Every Thing which the Squire held most dear; to wit, his Guns, Dogs, and Horses, were now as much at the Command of *Jones*, as if they had been his own. He resolved therefore to make use of this Favour on Behalf of his Friend *Black George*, whom he hoped to introduce into Mr. *Western's* Family in the same Capacity in which he had before served Mr. *Allworthy*.

The Reader, if he considers that this Fellow was already obnoxious to Mr. *Western*, and if he considers farther the weighty Business by which that Gentleman's Displeasure had been incurred, will perhaps condemn this as a foolish and desperate Undertaking; but if he should not totally condemn young *Jones* on that Account, he will greatly applaud him for strengthening himself with all imaginable Interest on so arduous an Occasion.

For this Purpose then *Tom* applied to Mr. *Western's* Daughter, a young Lady of about seventeen Years of Age, whom her Father, next after those necessary Implements of Sport just beforementioned, loved and esteemed above all the World. Now as she had some Influence on the Squire, so *Tom* had some little Influence on her. But this being the intended Heroine of this Work, a Lady with whom we ourselves are greatly in Love, and with whom many of our Readers will probably be in Love too before we part, it is by no Means proper she should make her Appearance in the End of a Book.

*The End of the* First Volume.

# BOOK IV

## Containing the Time of a Year.

### CHAPTER I

#### Containing five Pages of Paper.

AS Truth distinguishes our Writings, from those idle Romances which are filled with Monsters, the Productions, not of Nature, but of distempered Brains;[1] and which have been therefore recommended by an eminent Critic[2] to the sole Use of the Pastry-cook: So, on the other hand, we would avoid any Resemblance to that Kind of History which a celebrated Poet seems to think is no less calculated for the Emolument of the Brewer, as the reading it should be always attended with a Tankard of good Ale.

> While—History with her Comrade Ale,
> Sooths the sad Series of her serious Tale.[3]

For as this is the Liquor of modern Historians, nay, perhaps

---

[1] See also *Tom Jones* (IX. i) and *Joseph Andrews* (1742; III. i), where Fielding similarly distinguishes between the confused and unnatural productions of romance-writers and the 'true histories' of authors such as Cervantes and LeSage, 'who are contented to copy Nature'.

[2] Cf. the Preface to *The Journal of a Voyage to Lisbon* (1755), where Fielding tentatively identifies this critic as Joseph Addison (1672–1719). Fielding's memory, however, seems to have failed him in this instance, for, though both Addison and Steele facetiously allude to the pastry-cooks, who used the sheets of ephemeral books and pamphlets to line pie plates, they do not specifically recommend that romances be dismembered for this purpose. (See *The Spectator*, No. 85 [7 June 1711] and No. 304 [18 February 1712].) Closer to the present context are two passages from Shaftesbury which Fielding may have confused: in 'Advice to an Author' (III. iii), Shaftesbury deplores the contemporary taste for novels and romances, 'Things the most *unnatural* and *monstrous*'; in his 'Miscellaneous Reflections' (chap. ii), he takes comfort in the fact that another kind of fugitive literature, the works of polemical pamphleteers, 'have been long since paying their attendance to the *Pastry-cooks*'. (See *Characteristicks*, 5th ed. [1732], i. 347, iii. 14.) Cf. *The Covent-Garden Journal* (21 January 1752), where Fielding offers the following translation of the epigraph from Martial: '*How many fear the Moth's and Bookworm's Rage,/ And Pastry-Cooks, sole Buyers in this Age?*'

[3] Fielding imperfectly recalls a couplet from the original version of Pope's *Dunciad* (1728), III. 171–2: '*While happier Hist'ry with her comrade Ale,/ Sooths the sad series of her tedious tale.*' The lines are part of the passage beginning, 'each *Science* by its modern type/ Stands known' (III. 167–8). See also below, p. 684. 10–11.

their Muse, if we may believe the Opinion of *Butler*,[1] who attributes Inspiration to Ale, it ought likewise to be the Potation
of their Readers; since every Book ought to be read with the
same Spirit, and in the same Manner, as it is writ.[2] Thus the
famous Author of *Hurlothrumbo*[3] told a learned Bishop, that
the Reason his Lordship could not taste the Excellence of his
Piece, was, that he did not read it with a Fiddle in his Hand;
which Instrument he himself had always had in his own, when
he composed it.

That our Work, therefore, might be in no Danger of being
likened to the Labours of these Historians, we have taken every
Occasion of interspersing through the whole sundry Similes,
Descriptions, and other kind of poetical Embellishments. These
are, indeed, designed to supply the Place of the said Ale, and to
refresh the Mind, whenever those Slumbers which in a long
Work are apt to invade the Reader as well as the Writer, shall
begin to creep upon him. Without Interruptions of this Kind,
the best Narrative of plain Matter of Fact must overpower every
Reader; for nothing but the everlasting Watchfulness, which
*Homer* hath ascribed[4] only to *Jove* himself, can be Proof against a
News-Paper of many Volumes.

---

[1] In Part I of *Hudibras* (1663), Samuel Butler (1613–80) invokes the nameless Muse who
> . . . with Ale, or viler Liquors,
> Didst inspire *Withers*, *Pryn*, and *Vickars*,
> And force them, though it were in spight
> Of nature and their stars, to write. . . .
>                               (I. i. 639–42; ed. J. Wilders [Oxford, 1967].)
For other allusions to Butler and *Hudibras* in *Tom Jones*, see below, pp. 178, 399, 561.

[2] Cf. Pope's *Essay on Criticism* (1711), 233–4: 'A perfect Judge will *read* each Work of
Wit/ With the same Spirit that its Author *writ*. . . .' Cf. also the Preface to Swift's *Tale of a
Tub* (1704), where the author lays down the following 'general Maxim' for the benefit of
those readers with 'the Taste of Wit' who would fully sound the depths of that sublime
work: 'Whatever Reader desires to have a thorow Comprehension of an Author's Thoughts,
cannot take a better Method, than by putting himself into the Circumstances and Postures
of Life, that the Writer was in, upon every important Passage as it flow'd from his Pen; For
this will introduce a Parity and strict Correspondence of Idea's between the Reader and the
Author.'

[3] *Hurlothrumbo: or, The Super-Natural*, a heroic extravaganza by Samuel Johnson
(1691–1773), dancing-master of Cheshire, had a spectacular run when it was first produced
at the Haymarket in 1729. Johnson, who took the part of Lord Flame, fiddled and danced
and ranted his way through the role. Fielding alludes facetiously to Johnson and his
nonsensical drama in *The Author's Farce* (1730; I. v and III), in the Preface to *Tom Thumb*
(1730), in *Pasquin* (1736; V. i), and in *The Champion* (19 February 1739/40, 15 April 1740).

[4] *Iliad*, ii. 1–2. For an earlier reference, see Fielding's note to *A Journey from This
World to the Next* (1743), I. ii.

We shall leave to the Reader to determine with what Judgment we have chosen the several Occasions for inserting those ornamental Parts of our Work. Surely it will be allowed that none could be more proper than the present; where we are about to introduce a considerable Character on the Scene; no less, indeed, than the Heroine of this Heroic, Historical, Prosaic Poem. Here, therefore, we have thought proper to prepare the Mind of the Reader for her Reception, by filling it with every pleasing Image, which we can draw from the Face of Nature. And for this Method we plead many Precedents. First, this is an Art well known to, and much practised by, our Tragic Poets; who seldom fail to prepare their Audience for the Reception of their principal Characters.

Thus the Heroe is always introduced with a Flourish of Drums and Trumpets,[1] in order to rouse a martial Spirit in the Audience, and to accommodate their Ears to Bombast and Fustian, which Mr. *Lock's* blind Man[2] would not have grossly erred in likening to the Sound of a Trumpet. Again, when Lovers are coming forth, soft Music often conducts them on the Stage, either to sooth the Audience with the Softness of the tender Passion, or to lull and prepare them for that gentle Slumber in which they will most probably be composed by the ensuing Scene.

And not only the Poets, but the Masters of these Poets, the Managers of Playhouses, seem to be in this Secret; for, besides the aforesaid Kettle Drums, &c. which denote the Heroe's Approach, he is generally ushered on the Stage by a large Troop of half a dozen Scene-shifters; and how necessary these are imagined to his Appearance, may be concluded from the following Theatrical Story.

King *Pyrrhus*[3] was at Dinner at an Alehouse bordering on the

---

[1] Facetious allusions to this dramatic convention occur earlier in *The Tragedy of Tragedies* (1731), I. i and note k, and in *Jonathan Wild* (1743), I. iii.

[2] John Locke (1632–1704) in *An Essay concerning Human Understanding* (1690), III. iv 11: 'A studious blind Man, who had mightily beat his Head about visible Objects, and made use of the Explication of his Books and Friends, to understand those Names of Light and Colours, which often came in his way; bragged one Day, That he now understood what *Scarlet* signified. Upon which his Friend demanding, what *Scarlet* was? The blind Man answered, it was like the Sound of a Trumpet' (12th ed. [1741], ii. 29). See also *Tom Jones*, p. 271.

[3] Barton Booth (1681–1733), the celebrated tragedian, who first acted the part of Pyrrhus in Ambrose Philips's *The Distrest Mother* (1712). From 1711 Booth was associated with Cibber and Robert Wilks (1665–1732) in the management of Drury Lane.

Theatre, when he was summoned to go on the Stage. The Heroe, being unwilling to quit his Shoulder of Mutton, and as unwilling to draw on himself the Indignation of Mr. *Wilks*, (his Brother Manager) for making the Audience wait, had bribed these his Harbingers to be out of the Way. While Mr. *Wilks*, therefore, was thundering out, 'Where are the Carpenters to walk on before King *Pyrrhus*,' that Monarch very quietly eat his Mutton, and the Audience, however impatient, were obliged to entertain themselves with Music in his Absence.

To be plain, I much question whether the Politician, who hath generally a good Nose, hath not scented out somewhat of the Utility of this Practice. I am convinced that awful Magistrate my Lord Mayor contracts a good deal of that Reverence which attends him through the Year, by the several Pageants which precede his Pomp.[1] Nay, I must confess, that even I myself, who am not remarkably liable to be captivated with Show, have yielded not a little to the Impressions of much preceding State. When I have seen a Man strutting in a Procession, after others whose Business was only to walk before him, I have conceived a higher Notion of his Dignity, than I have felt on seeing him in a common Situation. But there is one Instance which comes exactly up to my Purpose. This is the Custom of sending on a Basket-woman,[2] who is to precede the Pomp at a Coronation, and to strew the Stage with Flowers, before the great Personages begin their Procession. The Antients would certainly have invoked the Goddess *Flora* for this Purpose, and it would have been no Difficulty for their Priests or Politicians to have persuaded the People of the real Presence of the Deity, though a plain Mortal had personated her, and performed her Office. But we have no such

[1] Occurring annually in late October, the day on which the new Lord Mayor of London took the oaths of office was an occasion of much pomp and pageantry. The following account is from *The General Advertiser* (29 October 1748): 'This Day the new Lord-Mayor, accompanied by the late Lord-Mayor, Aldermen, Recorder, and Sheriffs in their Scarlet Gowns, will go in their Coaches to the Water-Side, the Sword and Mace carried before them, and the City Officers attending, and from thence proceed in the City Barge, attended by the several Companies in their respective Barges, adorned with Streamers and Pendants to Westminster; and after having walked round the Hall and solemnly Saluted all the Courts, they will go to the Exchequer-Bar, and the Lord-Mayor will there take the Oaths appointed, and having recorded Warrants of Attorney in the proper Courts, they will return by Water to Black-Fryars, and from thence in Coaches with the usual Solemnity to Guildhall; where a magnificent Entertainment will be provided for them. . . .'

[2] This convention is alluded to in *Pasquin* (1736), III. i.

Design of imposing on our Reader, and therefore those who object to the Heathen Theology, may, if they please, change our Goddess into the above-mentioned Basket-woman. Our Intention, in short, is to introduce our Heroine with the utmost Solemnity in our Power, with an Elevation of Stile, and all other Circumstances proper to raise the Veneration of our Reader. Indeed we would, for certain Causes, advise those of our Male Readers who have any Hearts, to read no farther, were we not well assured, that how amiable soever the Picture of our Heroine will appear, as it is really a Copy from Nature,[1] many of our fair Countrywomen will be found worthy to satisfy any Passion, and to answer any Idea of Female Perfection, which our Pencil will be able to raise.

And now, without any further Preface, we proceed to our next Chapter.

## CHAPTER II

*A short Hint of what we can do in the Sublime, and a Description of Miss Sophia Western.*

HUSHED be every ruder Breath. May the Heathen Ruler of the Winds[2] confine in iron Chains the boisterous Limbs of noisy *Boreas*, and the sharp-pointed Nose of bitter-biting *Eurus*. Do thou, sweet *Zephyrus*, rising from thy fragrant Bed, mount the western Sky, and lead on those delicious Gales, the Charms of which call forth the lovely *Flora* from her Chamber, perfumed with pearly Dews, when on the first of *June*, her Birth-day, the blooming Maid, in loose Attire, gently trips it over the verdant Mead, where every Flower rises to do her Homage, till the whole Field becomes enamelled, and Colours contend with Sweets which shall ravish her most.

So charming may she now appear; and you the feather'd Choristers of Nature, whose sweetest Notes not even *Handel*[3] can

---

[1] See below, p. 156, n. 3.

[2] Aeolus. The names that follow are those, respectively, of the north, east, and west winds.

[3] George Frideric Handel (1685–1759), the celebrated composer, had been residing in England since 1712. Fielding, who delighted in 'the enchanting Harmony' of his music (see *The Champion*, 10 June 1740), paid frequent compliments to Handel: see, for example,

excel, tune your melodious Throats, to celebrate her Appearance. From Love proceeds your Music, and to Love it returns. Awaken therefore that gentle Passion in every Swain: for lo! adorned with all the Charms in which Nature can array her; bedecked with Beauty, Youth, Sprightliness, Innocence, Modesty, and Tenderness, breathing Sweetness from her rosy Lips, and darting Brightness from her sparkling Eyes, the lovely *Sophia* comes.

Reader, perhaps thou hast seen the Statue of the *Venus de Medicis*.[1] Perhaps too, thou hast seen the Gallery of Beauties at *Hampton-Court*.[2] Thou may'st remember *each bright* Churchill *of the Gallaxy*,[3] and all the Toasts of the *Kit-Cat*.[4] Or if their Reign was before thy Times, at least thou hast seen their Daughters, the no less dazling Beauties of the present Age; whose Names, should we here insert, we apprehend they would fill the whole Volume.

Now if thou hast seen all these, be not afraid of the rude Answer which Lord *Rochester* once gave[5] to a Man, who had seen

---

*Of True Greatness* (1741), *The True Patriot* (5 November 1745, 28 January–4 February 1746), Letter xl of Sarah Fielding's *Familiar Letters* (1747), *The Jacobite's Journal* (19 March 1748), *Amelia* (1751; IV. ix), and *The Covent-Garden Journal* (16 September 1752). See also below, p. 169.

[1] Done by a follower of Praxiteles, this famous statue now stands in the Uffizi Gallery, Florence. According to Joseph Spence, the body of the Venus de Medici 'will ever be the standard of all female beauty and softness' (*Polymetis* [1747], p. 66). Burlington placed a copy of the statue in the Rotunda at Chiswick, and prints of it were very popular in England (see, for example, the advertisements in *The General Advertiser*, 4–6 February 1746/7).

[2] The 'Hampton Court Beauties' were the series of eight portraits by Godfrey Kneller (1649?–1723) representing the principal ladies who attended upon Queen Mary. Completed in 1691, the series hung first in the Water Gallery and then in the Eating Room at Hampton Court. Engravings were made by John Faber.

[3] Cf. *The Dispensary* (1699), iv. 280, by Samuel Garth (1661–1719): 'And each fair Churchill of the galaxy.' The four daughters of John and Sarah Churchill, Duke and Duchess of Marlborough, were celebrated for their beauty. In his *Apology* (1740), Cibber complimented the Duchess on having 'given the World four of the loveliest Daughters, that ever were gaz'd on', who were 'the reigning Toasts of every Party of Pleasure' (2nd ed., pp. 59–60). Fielding alludes to these 'fair' ladies again in his poem, 'To a Friend on the Choice of a Wife' (1743). See also Pope's *Epistle to Mr. Jervas* (1716), ll. 46, 59, on the beauty of '*Churchill's* race'.

[4] The Kit-Cat Club (*fl.* 1700–20) was composed of the most eminent Whig statesmen and wits of the day—Garth (see n. 3 above), Robert Walpole, Vanbrugh, Congreve, Addison, and Steele. The name presumably derives from one Christopher Cat, a pastry-cook at whose house the members originally met. It was the club's custom to toast the fair ladies of their acquaintance—the Churchill 'galaxy' among them—in glasses inscribed with appropriate verses. See 'Verses Written for the Toasting-Glasses of the Kit-kat Club, in the Year 1703' in Tonson's *Miscellany Poems*, v (1716), [60–70].

[5] John Wilmot (1648–80), second Earl of Rochester. Fielding refers to the poem 'To all

many Things. No. If thou hast seen all these without knowing what Beauty is, thou hast no Eyes; if without feeling its Power, thou hast no Heart.

Yet is it possible, my Friend, that thou mayest have seen all these without being able to form an exact Idea of *Sophia*: for she did not exactly resemble any of them. She was most like the Picture of Lady *Ranelagh*;[1] and I have heard more still to the famous Dutchess of *Mazarine*;[2] but most of all, she resembled one whose Image never can depart from my Breast,[3] and whom, if thou dost remember, thou hast then, my Friend, an adequate Idea of *Sophia*.

But lest this should not have been thy Fortune, we will endeavour with our utmost Skill to describe this Paragon, though we are sensible that our highest Abilities are very inadequate to the Task.

*Sophia* then, the only Daughter of Mr. *Western*, was a middle-sized Woman; but rather inclining to tall. Her Shape was not only exact, but extremely delicate; and the nice Proportion of her Arms promised the truest Symmetry in her Limbs. Her Hair, which was black, was so luxuriant, that it reached her Middle, before she cut it, to comply with the modern Fashion; and it was now curled so gracefully in her Neck, that few could believe it to be her own. If Envy could find any Part of the Face which demanded less Commendation than the rest, it might possibly think her Forehead might have been higher without Prejudice to her. Her Eye-brows were full, even, and arched beyond the Power of Art to imitate. Her black Eyes had a Lustre in them, which all her Softness could not extinguish. Her Nose was exactly regular, and her Mouth, in which were two Rows of Ivory, exactly answered Sir *John Suckling's* Description[4] in those Lines,

Curious Criticks and Admirers of Metre', which, though probably not in fact by Rochester, originally appeared in his *Poems* (1680) and continued to be attributed to him. Organized in a manner similar to Fielding's preceding paragraph, the poem proceeds through a series of questions—'Have you seen' a ship tossed by a storm, a jealous bull, fairies dancing, etc. ?—to a rude conclusion: 'If you have seen all this, then kiss mine A[rs]e.'

[1] Margaret Cecil (1673–1727), Countess of Ranelagh, was one of the 'Hampton Court Beauties' painted by Kneller (see above, p. 155, n. 2, and Plate 4).

[2] Hortense Mancini (1646–99), Duchess of Mazarin, was a famous beauty who, after emigrating to England from France in 1676, was taken into the court of Charles II. Sir Peter Lely (1618–80) painted her portrait several times, from which engravings were made. One of these prints is reproduced as Plate 5.

[3] Charlotte Cradock, Fielding's first wife, who died in November 1744.

[4] 'A Ballad upon a Wedding', ll. 61–3, by Sir John Suckling (1609–42).

> *Her Lips were red, and one was thin,*
> *Compar'd to that was next her Chin.*
> *Some Bee had stung it newly.*

Her Cheeks, were of the oval Kind; and in her right she had a Dimple which the least Smile discovered. Her Chin had certainly its Share in forming the Beauty of her Face; but it was difficult to say it was either large or small, tho' perhaps it was rather of the former Kind. Her Complexion had rather more of the Lilly than of the Rose; but when Exercise, or Modesty, encreased her natural Colour, no Vermilion could equal it. Then one might indeed cry out with the celebrated Dr. *Donne*,[1]

> ——*Her pure and eloquent Blood*
> *Spoke in her Cheeks, and so distinctly wrought,*
> *That one might almost say her Body thought.*

Her Neck was long and finely turned; and here, if I was not afraid of offending her Delicacy, I might justly say, the highest Beauties of the famous *Venus de Medicis* were outdone. Here was Whiteness which no Lillies, Ivory, nor Alabaster could match. The finest Cambric might indeed be supposed from Envy to cover that Bosom, which was much whiter than itself,—It was indeed,

> *Nitor splendens Pario marmore purius.*[2]

'A Gloss shining beyond the purest Brightness of *Parian* Marble.'

Such was the Outside of *Sophia*; nor was this beautiful Frame disgraced by an Inhabitant unworthy of it. Her Mind was every way equal to her Person; nay, the latter borrowed some Charms from the former: For when she smiled, the Sweetness of her Temper diffused that Glory over her Countenance, which no Regularity of Features can give. But as there are no Perfections of the Mind which do not discover themselves, in that perfect Intimacy, to which we intend to introduce our Reader, with this charming young Creature; so it is needless to mention them here: Nay, it is a Kind of tacit Affront to our Reader's Understanding, and may also rob him of that Pleasure which he will receive in forming his own Judgment of her Character.

[1] John Donne (*c.* 1572–1631), Dean of St. Paul's from 1621. The passage describing Elizabeth Drury from Donne's *Second Anniversarie*, ll. 244–6, had been quoted by Steele in *Spectator*, No. 41 (17 April 1711), who used the lines to praise the charms of 'Statira'.

[2] Horace, *Odes*, I. xix. 5–6: 'urit me Glycerae nitor,/ splendentis Pario marmore purius' ('I am enamoured of Glycera's beauty, more dazzling than Parian marble'—trans. C. E. Bennett, Loeb Classical Library, 1914).

It may however, be proper to say, that whatever mental Accomplishments she had derived from Nature, they were somewhat improved and cultivated by Art: for she had been educated under the Care of an Aunt, who was a Lady of great Discretion, and was thoroughly acquainted with the World, having lived in her Youth about the Court, whence she had retired some Years since into the Country. By her Conversation and Instructions, *Sophia* was perfectly well-bred, though perhaps she wanted a little of that Ease in her Behaviour, which is to be acquired only by Habit, and living within what is called the polite Circle. But this, to say the Truth, is often too dearly purchased; and though it hath Charms so inexpressible, that the *French*, perhaps, among other Qualities, mean to express this, when they declare they know not what it is,[1] yet its Absence is well compensated by Innocence; nor can good Sense, and a natural Gentility ever stand in need of it.

## CHAPTER III

*Wherein the History goes back to commemorate a trifling Incident that happened some Years since; but which, trifling as it was, had some future Consequences.*

THE amiable *Sophia* was now in her eighteenth Year, when she is introduced into this History. Her Father, as hath been said, was fonder of her than of any other human Creature. To her, therefore, *Tom Jones* applied, in order to engage her Interest on the Behalf of his Friend the Game-keeper.

But before we proceed to this Business, a short Recapitulation of some previous Matters may be necessary.

Though the different Tempers of Mr. *Allworthy*, and of Mr. *Western* did not admit of a very intimate Correspondence, yet they

---

[1] The French phrase, *je ne sais quoi*, was commonly used by aestheticians to denote that indefinable quality of grace which lies, as Pope put it, 'beyond the Reach of Art' (*An Essay on Criticism* [1711], l. 155). Thus Shaftesbury advised his author to 'fix his Eye upon that consummate *Grace*, that Beauty of *Nature*, and that *Perfection* of Numbers, which the rest of Mankind, feeling only the Effect, whilst ignorant of the Cause, term the *Je-ne-sçay-quoy*, the unintelligible, or the I know not what; and suppose to be a kind of *Charm*, or *Inchantment*, of which the Artist himself can give no account' ('Soliloquy: or, Advice to an Author', in *Characteristicks*, 5th ed. [1732], i. 332).

lived upon what is called a decent Footing together; by which Means the young People of both Families had been acquainted from their Infancy; and as they were all near of the same Age, had been frequent Play-mates together.

The Gaiety of *Tom's* Temper suited better with *Sophia*, than the grave and sober Disposition of Master *Blifil*. And the Preference which she gave the former of these, would often appear so plainly, that a Lad of a more passionate Turn than Master *Blifil* was, might have shewn some Displeasure at it.

As he did not, however, outwardly express any such Disgust, it would be an ill Office in us to pay a Visit to the inmost Recesses of his Mind, as some scandalous People search into the most secret Affairs of their Friends, and often pry into their Closets and Cupboards, only to discover their Poverty and Meanness to the World.

However, as Persons who suspect they have given others Cause of Offence, are apt to conclude they are offended; so *Sophia* imputed an Action of Master *Blifil*, to his Anger, which the superior Sagacity of *Thwackum* and *Square* discerned to have arisen from a much better Principle.

*Tom Jones*, when very young, had presented *Sophia* with a little Bird, which he had taken from the Nest, had nursed up, and taught to sing.

Of this Bird, *Sophia*, then about thirteen Years old, was so extremely fond, that her chief Business was to feed and tend it, and her chief Pleasure to play with it. By these Means little *Tommy*, for so the Bird was called, was become so tame, that it would feed out of the Hand of its Mistress, would perch upon her Finger, and lie contented in her Bosom, where it seemed almost sensible of its own Happiness; tho' she always kept a small String about its Leg, nor would ever trust it with the Liberty of flying away.

One Day, when Mr. *Allworthy* and his whole Family, dined at Mr. *Western's*, Master *Blifil*, being in the Garden with little *Sophia*, and observing the extreme Fondness that she shewed for her little Bird, desired her to trust it for a Moment in his Hands. *Sophia* presently complied with the young Gentleman's Request, and after some previous Caution, delivered him her Bird; of which he was no sooner in Possession, than he slipt the String from its Leg, and tossed it into the Air.

The foolish Animal no sooner perceived itself at Liberty, than forgetting all the Favours it had received from *Sophia*, it flew directly from her, and perched on a Bough at some Distance.

*Sophia*, seeing her Bird gone, screamed out so loud, that *Tom Jones*, who was at a little Distance, immediately ran to her Assistance.

He was no sooner informed of what had happened, than he cursed *Blifil* for a pitiful, malicious Rascal, and then immediately stripping off his Coat, he applied himself to climbing the Tree to which the Bird escaped.

*Tom* had almost recovered his little Name-sake, when the Branch, on which it was perched, and that hung over a Canal, broke, and the poor Lad plumped over Head and Ears into the Water.

*Sophia's* Concern now changed its Object. And as she apprehended the Boy's Life was in Danger, she screamed ten times louder than before; and indeed Master *Blifil* himself now seconded her with all the Vociferation in his Power.

The Company, who were sitting in a Room next the Garden, were instantly alarmed, and came all forth; but just as they reached the Canal, *Tom*, (for the Water was luckily pretty shallow in that Part) arrived safely on shore.

*Thwackum* fell violently on poor *Tom*, who stood dropping and shivering before him, when Mr. *Allworthy* desired him to have Patience, and turning to Master *Blifil*, said, Pray, Child, what is the Reason of all this Disturbance?

Master *Blifil* answered, 'Indeed, Uncle, I am very sorry for what I have done; I have been unhappily the Occasion of it all. I had Miss *Sophia's* Bird in my Hand, and thinking the poor Creature languished for Liberty, I own, I could not forbear giving it what it desired: for I always thought there was something very cruel in confining any Thing. It seemed to me against the Law of Nature, by which every Thing hath a Right to Liberty; nay, it is even unchristian; for it is not doing what we would be done by: But if I had imagined Miss *Sophia* would have been so much concerned at it, I am sure I would never have done it; nay, if I had known what would have happened to the Bird itself: for when Master *Jones*, who climbed up that Tree after it, fell into the Water, the Bird took a second Flight, and presently a nasty Hawk carried it away.'

Poor *Sophia*, who now first heard of her little *Tommy's* Fate; (for her Concern for *Jones* had prevented her perceiving it when it happened) shed a Shower of Tears. These Mr. *Allworthy* endeavoured to assuage, promising her a much finer Bird; but she declared she would never have another. Her Father chid her for crying so for a foolish Bird; but could not help telling young *Blifil*, if he was a Son of his, his Backside should be well flea'd.

*Sophia* now returned to her Chamber, the two young Gentlemen were sent home, and the rest of the Company returned to their Bottle; where a Conversation ensued on the Subject of the Bird, so curious, that we think it deserves a Chapter by itself.


## CHAPTER IV

*Containing such very deep and grave Matters, that some Readers, perhaps, may not relish it.*


*SQUARE* had no sooner lighted his Pipe, than addressing himself to *Allworthy*, he thus began: 'Sir, I cannot help congratulating you on your Nephew; who, at an Age when few Lads have any Ideas but of sensible Objects, is arrived at a Capacity of distinguishing Right from Wrong. To confine any thing, seems to me against the Law of Nature, by which every thing hath a Right to Liberty.[1] These were his Words; and the Impression hey have made on me is never to be eradicated. Can any Man have a higher Notion of the Rule of Right, and the Eternal Fitness of Things? I cannot help promising myself from such a

---

[1] The hypocritical intent of Blifil's words is clear enough. What may be obscure is that his statement of the 'law of nature' would have been regarded by most authorities on the subject—Grotius (1583–1645) and Pufendorf (1632–94), for example—as excessively libertarian, blurring the distinction between the conditions of life in a 'state of nature' and in society. To Grotius, the possession of wild creatures was 'certainly *Natural* . . . now *Property* is Establish'd'; for, he continued, 'Nature gives all these to him who *finds*, and lays hold on 'em *first*' (*Of the Rights of War and Peace* [1715], ii. 196, 199). Since the formation of societies, when the 'law of nations' superseded the 'law of nature' in certain crucial respects, not even human beings could consider that they were exempt from being the subjects or property of others: men, he remarked, are '*by Nature* in a State of *Freedom* [;] *by Nature* is to be understood the *Right of Nature*, as 'tis antecedent to all Human Acts to the contrary; and the *Freedom* there meant is a *Freedom* in a *private*, and not a *Contradictory* Sense, that is, tho' a Man be not *by Nature* a *Slave* or *subject* to any, yet from thence he cannot derive a Right of being always exempted from *Slavery* and *Subjection*, for in this Sense no body living is *Free*' (ibid., ii. 580).

Dawn, that the Meridian of this Youth will be equal to that of either the elder or the younger *Brutus*.'[1]

Here *Thwackum* hastily interrupted, and spilling some of his Wine, and swallowing the rest with great Eagerness, answered, 'From another Expression he made use of, I hope he will resemble much better Men. The Law of Nature is a Jargon of Words, which means nothing. I know not of any such Law, nor of any Right which can be derived from it. To do as we would be done by, is indeed a Christian Motive, as the Boy well expressed himself, and I am glad to find my Instructions have born such good Fruit.'

'If Vanity was a thing fit (says *Square*) I might indulge some on the same Occasion; for whence only he can have learnt his Notions of Right or Wrong, I think is pretty apparent. If there be no Law of Nature, there is no Right nor Wrong.'

'How! (says the Parson) do you then banish Revelation? Am I talking with a Deist or an Atheist?'

'Drink about, (says *Western*) Pox of your Laws of Nature. I don't know what you mean either of you, by Right and Wrong. To take away my Girl's Bird was wrong in my Opinion; and my Neighbour *Allworthy* may do as he pleases; but to encourage Boys in such Practices, is to breed them up to the Gallows.'

*Allworthy* answered, 'that he was sorry for what his Nephew had done; but could not consent to punish him, as he acted rather from a generous than unworthy Motive.' He said, 'if the Boy had stolen the Bird, none would have been more ready to vote for a severe Chastisement than himself; but it was plain that was not his Design:' And, indeed, it was as apparent to him, that he could have no other View but what he had himself avowed. (For as to

---

[1] See also p. 163. According to tradition, Lucius Junius Brutus was one of the first two Roman consuls (*c*. 509 B.C.). After having liberated Rome from the Tarquins, he put to death his own two sons for conspiring to restore that tyrannical regime. In *An Enquiry into the Causes of the late Increase of Robbers* (1751), section x, Fielding calls him 'a worthy Pattern' of the maxim that, for the good of society, the tenderness of the man must give way to the rigour of the magistrate. (See also *The Jacobite's Journal*, 26 March 1748.) From selfless motives of patriotism Marcus Junius Brutus (78 ?–42 B.C.) led the conspiracy to assassinate Caesar (44 B.C.), even though he was under the strongest personal obligations to the dictator. In the Preface to the *Miscellanies* (1743), Fielding cites Brutus, together with Socrates, as a rare example of the great and good man, the '*true Sublime* in Human Nature'. In *The Jacobite's Journal* (11 June 1748) the two Brutuses are again linked to illustrate the observation that the motives even of those 'deserving our highest Commendation' may be misconstrued.

that malicious Purpose which *Sophia* suspected, it never once entered into the Head of Mr. *Allworthy*.) He, at length, concluded with again blaming the Action as inconsiderate, and which, he said, was pardonable only in a Child.

*Square* had delivered his Opinion so openly, that if he was now silent, he must submit to have his Judgment censured. He said, therefore, with some Warmth, 'that Mr. *Allworthy* had too much Respect to the dirty Consideration of Property. That in passing our Judgments on great and mighty Actions, all private Regards should be laid aside; for by adhering to those narrow Rules, the younger *Brutus* had been condemned of Ingratitude, and the elder of Parricide.'

'And if they had been hanged too for those Crimes,' cried *Thwackum*, 'they would have had no more than their Deserts. A couple of heathenish Villains! Heaven be praised, we have no *Brutus's* now-a-days. I wish, Mr. *Square*, you would desist from filling the Minds of my Pupils with such Antichristian Stuff: For the Consequence must be, while they are under my Care, its being well scourged out of them again. There is your Disciple *Tom* almost spoiled already. I overheard him the other Day disputing with Master *Blifil*, that there was no Merit in Faith without Works. I know that is one of your Tenets, and I suppose he had it from you.'

'Don't accuse me of spoiling him,' says *Square*. 'Who taught him to laugh at whatever is virtuous and decent, and fit and right in the Nature of Things? He is your own Scholar, and I disclaim him. No, no, Master *Blifil* is my Boy. Young as he is, that Lad's Notions of moral Rectitude I defy you ever to eradicate.'

*Thwackum* put on a contemptuous Sneer at this, and replied, 'Ay, ay, I will venture him with you. He is too well grounded for all your philosophical Cant to hurt. No, no, I have taken Care to instil such Principles into him——'

'And I have instilled Principles into him too,' cries *Square*. 'What but the sublime Idea of Virtue could inspire a human Mind with the generous Thought of giving Liberty? And I repeat to you again, if it was a fit thing to be proud, I might claim the Honour of having infused that Idea——'

'And if Pride was not forbidden,' said *Thwackum*, 'I might boast of having taught him that Duty which he himself assigned as his Motive.'

'So between you both,' says the Squire, 'the young Gentleman hath been taught to rob my Daughter of her Bird. I find I must take Care of my Partridge Mew. I shall have some virtuous, religious Man or other set all my Partridges at Liberty.' Then slapping a Gentleman of the Law, who was present, on the Back, he cried out, 'What say you to this, Mr. Counsellor? Is not this against Law?'

The Lawyer, with great Gravity, delivered himself as follows: 'If the Case be put of a Partridge, there can be no Doubt but an Action would lie: For though this be *feræ Naturæ*, yet being reclaimed, Property vests;[1] but being the Case of a Singing Bird, though reclaimed, as it is a Thing of base Nature, it must be considered as *nullius in Bonis*.[2] In this Case, therefore, I conceive the Plaintiff must be nonsuited; and I should disadvise the bringing any such Action.'

'Well, (says the Squire) if it be *nullus Bonus*, let us drink about, and talk a little of the State of the Nation, or some such Discourse that we all understand; for I am sure I don't understand a Word of this. It may be Learning and Sense for aught I know; but you shall never persuade me into it. Pox! you have neither of you mentioned a Word of that poor Lad who deserves to be commended. To venture breaking his Neck to oblige my Girl, was a generous spirited Action; I have Learning enough to see that. D—n me, here's *Tom's* Health, I shall love the Boy for it the longest Day I have to live.'

Thus was this Debate interrupted; but it would probably have been soon resumed, had not Mr. *Allworthy* presently called for his Coach, and carried off the two Combatants.

Such was the Conclusion of this Adventure of the Bird, and of

---

[1] In law, *feræ naturæ* signified wild beasts and birds (as opposed to domestic), which no one could claim as his 'absolute real *Property*'; if, however, such beasts were reclaimed—i.e. 'inclosed and made Tame'—then 'there may be a qualified and possessory *Property* in them.' (See Giles Jacob, *New Law Dictionary*, 4th ed. [1739], s.v. 'Feræ Naturæ' and 'Property'.)

[2] *Nullius in bonis*: literally, 'among the goods of nobody'—i.e. nobody's natural property. In this case the law does not admit the possibility of larceny where there can be no motive of personal gain. Cf. Wood's *Institutes*, 7th ed. (1745): 'Besides, The Law does not presume, that any one would Steal such Things that are of no Value or Use to any one but the Owner. The Personal Goods also must not be of a *Base Nature*, as Dogs or Cats, if They may be said to be One's Personal Goods. Some Things that are *Wild* by Nature, and made Tame, cannot be Taken away feloniously as Personal Goods; as (for Example) . . . Singing Birds, &c.' (p. 386).

the Dialogue occasioned by it, which we could not help recounting to our Reader, though it happened some Years before
that Stage, or Period of Time, at which our History is now
arrived.


CHAPTER V

*Containing Matter accommodated to every Taste.*

*PARVA leves capiunt Animos,*[1] 'Small Things affect light
Minds,' was the Sentiment of a great Master of the Passion
of Love. And certain it is, that from this Day *Sophia* began to
have some little Kindness for *Tom Jones,* and no little Aversion
for his Companion.

Many Accidents from time to time improved both these
Passions in her Breast; which, without our recounting, the Reader
may well conclude, from what we have before hinted of the
different Tempers of these Lads, and how much the one suited
with her own Inclinations more than the other. To say the Truth,
*Sophia,* when very young, discerned that *Tom,* though an idle,
thoughtless, rattling Rascal, was no-body's Enemy but his own;
and that Master *Blifil,* though a prudent, discreet, sober young
Gentleman, was at the same Time strongly attached to the Interest only of one single Person; and who that single Person was,
the Reader will be able to divine without any Assistance of ours.

These two Characters are not always received in the World
with the different Regard which seems severally due to either;
and which one would imagine Mankind, from Self-interest,
should shew towards them. But perhaps there may be a political
Reason for it: In finding one of a truly benevolent Disposition,
Men may very reasonably suppose, they have found a Treasure,
and be desirous of keeping it, like all other good Things, to
themselves. Hence they may imagine, that to trumpet forth the
Praises of such a Person, would, in the vulgar Phrase, be crying
*Roast-meat;*[2] and calling in Partakers of what they intend to apply
solely to their own Use. If this Reason doth not satisfy the Reader,
I know no other Means of accounting for the little Respect which

[1] Ovid, *Ars Amatoria,* i. 159.
[2] Foolishly proclaiming a piece of private good fortune. (See W. G. Smith and P.
Harvey (eds.), *Oxford Dictionary of English Proverbs,* 2nd ed. [Oxford, 1948], p. 121.)

I have commonly seen paid to a Character which really doth great Honour to Human Nature, and is productive of the highest Good to Society. But it was otherwise with *Sophia*. She honoured *Tom Jones*, and scorned Master *Blifil*, almost as soon as she knew the Meaning of those two Words.

*Sophia* had been absent upwards of three Years with her Aunt; during all which Time she had seldom seen either of these young Gentlemen. She dined, however, once together with her Aunt, at Mr. *Allworthy's*. This was a few Days after the Adventure of the Partridge, before commemorated. *Sophia* heard the whole Story at Table, where she said nothing; nor indeed could her Aunt get many Words from her, as she returned home; but her Maid, when undressing her, happening to say, 'Well, Miss, I suppose you have seen young Master *Blifil* to Day.' She answered with much Passion, 'I hate the Name of Master *Blifil*, as I do whatever is base and treacherous; and I wonder Mr. *Allworthy* would suffer that old barbarous Schoolmaster to punish a poor Boy so cruelly for what was only the Effect of his Good-nature.' She then recounted the Story to her Maid, and concluded with Saying— 'Don't you think he is a Boy of a noble Spirit?'

This young Lady was now returned to her Father; who gave her the Command of his House, and placed her at the upper End of his Table, where *Tom* (who for his great Love of Hunting was become a great Favourite of the Squire) often dined. Young Men of open, generous Dispositions are naturally inclined to Gallantry, which, if they have good Understandings, as was in reality *Tom's* Case, exerts itself in an obliging, complaisant Behaviour to all Women in general. This greatly distinguished *Tom* from the boisterous Brutality of mere Country Squires on the one hand; and from the solemn, and somewhat sullen, Deportment of Master *Blifil* on the other: And he began now, at Twenty, to have the Name of a pretty Fellow among all the Women in the Neighbourhood.

*Tom* behaved to *Sophia* with no Particularity, unless, perhaps, by shewing her a higher Respect than he paid to any other. This Distinction her Beauty, Fortune, Sense, and amiable Carriage, seemed to demand; but as to Design upon her Person he had none; for which we shall at present suffer the Reader to condemn him of Stupidity; but perhaps we shall be able indifferently well to account for it hereafter.

*Sophia*, with the highest Degree of Innocence and Modesty, had a remarkable Sprightliness in her Temper. This was so greatly encreased whenever she was in Company with *Tom*, that, had he not been very young and thoughtless, he must have observed it; or had not Mr. *Western's* Thoughts been generally either in the Field, the Stable, or the Dog-kennel, it might have, perhaps, created some Jealousy in him; but so far was the good Gentleman from entertaining any such Suspicions, that he gave *Tom* every Opportunity with his Daughter which any Lover could have wished. And this *Tom* innocently improved to better Advantage, by following only the Dictates of his natural Gallantry and Good-nature, than he might, perhaps, have done, had he had the deepest Designs on the young Lady.

But, indeed, it can occasion little Wonder, that this Matter escaped the Observation of others, since poor *Sophia* herself never remarked it, and her Heart was irretrievably lost before she suspected it was in Danger.

Matters were in this Situation, when *Tom* one Afternoon finding *Sophia* alone, began, after a short Apology, with a very serious Face, to acquaint her, that he had a Favour to ask of her, which he hoped her Goodness would comply with.

Though neither the young Man's Behaviour, nor indeed his Manner of opening this Business, were such as could give her any just Cause of suspecting he intended to make Love to her; yet, whether Nature whispered something into her Ear, or from what Cause it arose I will not determine, certain it is, some Idea of that Kind must have intruded itself; for her Colour forsook her Cheeks, her Limbs trembled, and her Tongue would have faultered, had *Tom* stopped for an Answer: But he soon relieved her from her Perplexity, by proceeding to inform her of his Request, which was to sollicit her Interest on Behalf of the Gamekeeper, whose own Ruin, and that of a large Family, must be, he said, the Consequence of Mr. *Western's* pursuing his Action against him.

*Sophia* presently recovered her Confusion, and with a Smile full of Sweetness, said, 'Is this the mighty Favour you asked with so much Gravity. I will do it with all my Heart. I really pity the poor Fellow, and no longer ago than Yesterday sent a small Matter to his Wife.' This small Matter was one of her Gowns, some Linnen, and ten Shillings in Money, of which *Tom* had heard, and it had, in reality, put this Solicitation into his Head.

Our Youth, now emboldened with his Success, resolved to push the Matter farther; and ventured even to beg her Recommendation of him to her Father's Service; protesting that he thought him one of the honestest Fellows in the Country, and extremely well qualified for the Place of a Game-keeper, which luckily then happened to be vacant.

*Sophia* answered, 'Well, I will undertake this too; but I cannot promise you as much Success as in the former Part, which I assure you I will not quit my Father without obtaining. However, I will do what I can for the poor Fellow, for I sincerely look upon him and his Family as Objects of great Compassion.—And now, Mr. *Jones*, I must ask you a Favour——'

'A Favour, Madam, (cries *Tom*) if you knew the Pleasure you have given me in the Hopes of receiving a Command from you, you would think by mentioning it you did confer the greatest Favour on me; for by this dear Hand I would sacrifice my Life to oblige you.'

He then snatched her Hand, and eagerly kissed it, which was the first Time his Lips had ever touched her. The Blood, which before had forsaken her Cheeks, now made her sufficient Amends, by rushing all over her Face and Neck with such Violence, that they became all of a scarlet Colour. She now first felt a Sensation to which she had been before a Stranger, and which, when she had Leisure to reflect on it, began to acquaint her with some Secrets, which the Reader, if he doth not already guess them, will know in due Time.

*Sophia*, as soon as she could speak, (which was not instantly) informed him, that the Favour she had to desire of him, was not to lead her Father through so many Dangers in Hunting; for that, from what she had heard, she was terribly frightened every Time they went out together, and expected some Day or other to see her Father brought Home with broken Limbs. She therefore begged him, for her Sake, to be more cautious; and, as he well knew Mr. *Western* would follow him, not to ride so madly, nor to take those dangerous Leaps for the future.

*Tom* promised faithfully to obey her Commands; and after thanking her for her kind Compliance with his Request, took his Leave, and departed highly charmed with his Success.

Poor *Sophia* was charmed too; but in a very different Way. Her Sensations, however, the Reader's Heart (if he or she have any) will better represent than I can, if I had as many Mouths as ever Poet wished for,[1] to eat, I suppose, those many Dainties with which he was so plentifully provided.

It was Mr. *Western's* Custom every Afternoon, as soon as he was drunk, to hear his Daughter play on the Harpsichord: for he was a great Lover of Music, and perhaps, had he lived in Town, might have passed for a Connoisseur: for he always excepted against the finest Compositions of Mr. *Handel.*[2] He never relished any Music but what was light and airy; and indeed his most favourite Tunes, were *Old Sir* Simon *the King, St.* George *he was for* England, *Bobbing* Joan,[3] and some others.

His Daughter, though she was a perfect Mistress of Music, and would never willingly have played any but *Handel's*, was so devoted to her Father's Pleasure, that she learnt all those Tunes to oblige him. However, she would now and then endeavour to lead him into her own Taste, and when he required the Repetition of his Ballads, would answer with a 'Nay, dear Sir,' and would often beg him to suffer her to play something else.

This Evening, however, when the Gentleman was retired from his Bottle, she played all his Favourites three Times over, without any Solicitation. This so pleased the good Squire, that he started from his Couch, gave his Daughter a Kiss, and swore her Hand was greatly improved. She took this Opportunity to execute her Promise to *Tom*, in which she succeeded so well, that the Squire

[1] Cf. *Iliad*, ii. 489, where Homer wishes for ten tongues and ten mouths.

[2] See above, p. 154, n. 3. Early in 1745 Handel's popularity, always precarious at best, sank to a new low, chiefly owing to the opposition of the opera party led by the Earl of Middlesex. A certain fashionable lady (probably Lady Brown) carried her hostility to the composer so far as to give a 'drum' or 'rout' whenever Handel was to perform. Subscribers to his oratorio concerts were so few that Handel publicly lamented 'the loss of the publick Favour' and sadly predicted his 'Ruin' (see *The Daily Advertiser*, 17 January 1745). His friends rallied to his aid, complaining that the neglect of so great a genius was a 'National Disgrace' (see the poem 'To Mr. Handel' in *The Daily Advertiser*, 21 January 1745), but their efforts were ineffectual. On 2 April 1745 Mrs. Elizabeth Carter summarized the situation in a letter to Catherine Talbot: 'Handel, once so crowded, plays to empty walls in that opera house [i.e. the King's Theatre in the Haymarket], where there used to be a constant *audience* as long as there were any dancers to be *seen*. Unfashionable that I am, I was I own highly delighted the other night at his last oratorio.' (See O. E. Deutsch, *Handel: A Documentary Biography* [1955], pp. 602–10.)

[3] These old tunes, especially popular during the Restoration period, are discussed in W. Chappell, *Old English Popular Music*, ed. H. Ellis Wooldridge (1893), i. 280–2, 312; ii. 102–4.

declared, if she would give him t'other Bout of old Sir *Simon*, he would give the Game-keeper his Deputation[1] the next Morning. Sir *Simon* was played again and again, till the Charms of the Music soothed Mr. *Western* to sleep. In the Morning *Sophia* did not fail to remind him of his Engagement, and his Attorney was immediately sent for, and ordered to stop any further Proceedings in the Action, and to make out the Deputation.

*Tom's* Success in this Affair soon began to ring over the Country, and various were the Censures past upon it. Some greatly applauding it as an Act of good Nature, others sneering, and saying, 'No Wonder that one idle Fellow should love another.' Young *Blifil* was greatly enraged at it. He had long hated *Black George* in the same Proportion as *Jones* delighted in him; not from any Offence which he had ever received, but from his great Love to Religion and Virtue: For *Black George* had the Reputation of a loose kind of a Fellow. *Blifil* therefore represented this as flying in Mr. *Allworthy's* Face; and declared with great Concern, that it was impossible to find any other Motive for doing Good to such a Wretch.

*Thwackum* and *Square* likewise sung to the same Tune: They were now (especially the latter) become greatly jealous of young *Jones* with the Widow: For he now approached the Age of Twenty-one,[2] was really a fine young Fellow; and that Lady, by her Encouragements to him, seemed daily more and more to think him so.

*Allworthy* was not, however, moved with their Malice. He declared himself very well satisfied with what *Jones* had done. He said, the Perseverance and Integrity of his Friendship was highly commendable, and he wished he could see more frequent Instances of that Virtue.

But Fortune, who seldom greatly relishes such Sparks as my Friend *Tom*, perhaps because they do not pay more ardent Addresses to her, gave now a very different Turn to all his Actions, and shewed them to Mr. *Allworthy* in a Light far less agreeable than that Gentleman's Goodness had hitherto seen them in.

---

[1] According to 9 Anne, cap. 25, the appointment of a game-keeper by the Lord of the Manor had to be formally recorded and certified by the clerk of the parish. (See Dalton, *The Country Justice* [1746], p. 108.)

[2] Emended from 'Twenty'. In all editions Fielding here overlooked the fact that in the errata to the first edition he had earlier in this chapter changed Jones's age from nineteen to twenty (see above, p. 166.32).

## CHAPTER VI

*An Apology for the Insensibility of Mr.* Jones, *to all the Charms of the lovely* Sophia; *in which possibly we may, in a considerable Degree, lower his Character in the Estimation of those Men of Wit and Gallantry, who approve the Heroes in most of our modern Comedies.*

THERE are two Sorts of People, who I am afraid, have already conceived some Contempt for my Heroe, on Account of his Behaviour to *Sophia*. The former of these will blame his Prudence in neglecting an Opportunity to possess himself of Mr. *Western's* Fortune; and the latter will no less despise him for his Backwardness to so fine a Girl, who seemed ready to fly into his Arms, if he would open them to receive her.

Now, though I shall not perhaps be able absolutely to acquit him of either of these Charges; (for Want of Prudence admits of no Excuse; and what I shall produce against the latter Charge, will, I apprehend, be scarce satisfactory;) yet as Evidence may sometimes be offered in Mitigation, I shall set forth the plain Matter of Fact, and leave the whole to the Reader's Determination.

Mr. *Jones* had Somewhat about him, which, though I think Writers are not thoroughly agreed in its Name,[1] doth certainly

---

[1] The usual name for the moral faculty to which Fielding here refers is, of course, the 'conscience'—an important corollary of his concept of 'good-nature' (see above, p. 39, n. 1). As he defines the functions of this 'active Principle' in the ensuing paragraphs, Fielding may be seen to side with those Christian philosophers and divines who opposed Locke's attempt to discredit the doctrine of innate knowledge. Traditionally, the conscience was regarded not as an acquired, but as a natural, faculty which enabled men to recognize God's laws and which prompted them to do good and to eschew evil. In theological terms, it comprised two distinct, yet complementary, departments: *synteresis*, which functions as a guide for conduct, directing one's actions towards virtuous ends; and *syneidesis*, which passes judgement on actions already performed, signalling approval or disapproval. This theory, therefore, placed the foundation of morality in the very nature of man.

A useful gloss on Fielding's account of the conscience is supplied by Richard Carpenter, who describes synteresis as the 'treasury of morall principles, and of sacred rules wherewith the practicall understanding is furnished, for the saving direction of us in all actions'; it is 'a nobel and diuine power and faculty, planted of God in the substance of mans soule, working vpon itself by reflection, and taking exact notice, as a Scribe or Register, and determining as Gods Viceroy and deputy, Judge of all that is in the mind, will, affections, actions, and whole life of man' (*The Conscionable Christian* [1623], pp. [2], 41). Similarly, in Thomas Nabbes's moral masque, *Microcosmus* (1637), v, Conscience is represented in ways that suggest Fielding's general agreement with this pre-Lockean tradition:

inhabit some human Breasts; whose Use is not so properly to distinguish Right from Wrong, as to prompt and incite them to the former, and to restrain and with-hold them from the latter.

This Somewhat may be indeed resembled to the famous Trunk-maker in the Playhouse:[1] for whenever the Person who is possessed of it doth what is right, no ravished or friendly Spectator is so eager, or so loud in his Applause; on the contrary, when he doth wrong, no Critic is so apt to hiss and explode him.

To give a higher Idea of the Principle I mean, as well as one more familiar to the present Age; it may be considered as sitting on its Throne in the Mind, like the LORD HIGH CHANCELLOR[2] of this Kingdom in his Court; where it presides, governs, directs, judges, acquits and condemns according to Merit and Justice; with a Knowledge which nothing escapes, a Penetration which nothing can deceive, and an Integrity which nothing can corrupt.

> Conscience the judge of actions
> Is neither power, nor habit, but an act;
> To wit an application of that knowledge
> That shewes the difference. Its Synteresis,
> Or purer part, is th'instigation
> Of will to good and honest things, and seates
> The mind in a rich throne of endlesse quiet.

For a discussion of this theory and of Locke's opposition to it, see J. W. Yolton, *John Locke and the Way of Ideas* (Oxford, 1956), pp. 30–5, 55–7. For 'An Account of the Nature and Measures of Conscience' with which Fielding was certainly familiar, see Robert South's two sermons by that title (1691–2). In the latter, South to a degree anticipates Fielding's metaphor of 'the Lord High Chancellor' by characterizing the conscience as 'the vicegerent of God', remarking 'the extraordinary quickness and sagacity of its sight' and 'its great and rigorous impartiality' which no 'power, rhetoric, or riches' can corrupt (see *Sermons Preached upon Several Occasions* [1865], i. 195–6, 200–1).

[1] See *The Spectator*, No. 235 (29 November 1711). The *'Trunk-maker'*, who stationed himself in the upper-gallery and expressed his approbation of the play by loud knocks upon the benches and wainscot, is represented by Addison as the type of the true critic: 'his Stroaks are always just, and his Admonitions seasonable; he does not deal about his Blows at Random, but always hits the right Nail upon the Head.' In his essay on trunks in *The Champion* (31 May 1740), Fielding refers again to this 'great Judge of Dramatic Poetry'.

[2] Philip Yorke (1690–1764), Baron Hardwicke, was Lord Chancellor from 1737 to 1756; in the summer of 1746 he presided over the trials of the Jacobite lords. Fielding frequently expressed his admiration for 'this Great Man', whose 'Ability, Clemency and Justice' in the administration of his office had 'made the inferior Branches to regard him in the Light of a Father' (*The True Patriot*, 11–18 February 1746). In 1751 Fielding dedicated *An Enquiry into the Causes of the late Increase of Robbers* to Hardwicke. Other compliments to him may be found in *The Jacobite's Journal* (23 January, 12 March 1748) and in *A True State of the Case of Bosavern Penlez* (1749). With the present passage, compare Fielding's characterization of the conscience in the Preface to the *Miscellanies* (1743): 'there is still a Judge in every Man's Breast, which none can cheat nor corrupt. . . .'

This active Principle may perhaps be said to constitute the most essential Barrier between us, and our Neighbours the Brutes; for if there be some in the human Shape, who are not under any such Dominion, I chuse rather to consider them as Deserters from us to our Neighbours; among whom they will have the Fate of Deserters, and not be placed in the first Rank.

Our Heroe, whether he derived it from *Thwackum* or *Square* I will not determine, was very strongly under the Guidance of this Principle: for though he did not always act rightly, yet he never did otherwise without feeling and suffering for it. It was this which taught him, that to repay the Civilities and little Friendships of Hospitality by robbing the House where you have received them, is to be the basest and meanest of Thieves. He did not think the Baseness of this Offence lessened by the Height of the Injury committed; on the contrary, if to steal another's Plate deserved Death and Infamy,[1] it seemed to him difficult to assign a Punishment adequate to the robbing a Man of his whole Fortune, and of his Child into the Bargain.

This Principle therefore prevented him from any Thought of making his Fortune by such Means (for this, as I have said, is an active Principle, and doth not content itself with Knowledge or Belief only.) Had he been greatly enamoured of *Sophia*, he possibly might have thought otherwise; but give me Leave to say, there is great Difference between running away with a Man's Daughter from the Motive of Love,[2] and doing the same Thing from the Motive of Theft.

Now though this young Gentleman was not insensible of the Charms of *Sophia*; tho' he greatly liked her Beauty, and esteemed all her other Qualifications, she had made, however, no deep Impression on his Heart: For which, as it renders him liable to the Charge of Stupidity, or at least of Want of Taste, we shall now proceed to account.

The Truth then is, his Heart was in the Possession of another Woman. Here I question not, but the Reader will be surprized at our long Taciturnity as to this Matter; and quite at a Loss to

---

[1] Grand larceny was defined as the theft of personal goods 'above the Value of Twelve Pence' and was punishable by death. (See Wood's *Institutes*, 7th ed. [1745], p. 383.)

[2] On two occasions in his youth Fielding seems to have done just this: in 1725 he attempted to 'abduct' Sarah Andrew, an attractive girl of fifteen with whom he was in love; and in 1734 he married Charlotte Cradock, apparently after eloping with her. (See Cross, i. 51, 169.)

divine who this Woman was; since we have hitherto not dropt a Hint of any one likely to be a Rival to *Sophia*: For as to Mrs. *Blifil*, though we have been obliged to mention some Suspicions of her Affection for *Tom*, we have not hitherto given the least Latitude for imagining that he had any for her; and, indeed, I am sorry to say it, but the Youth of both Sexes are too apt to be deficient in their Gratitude, for that Regard with which Persons more advanced in Years are sometimes so kind to honour them.

That the Reader may be no longer in Suspence, he will be pleased to remember, that we have often mentioned the Family of *George Seagrim*, commonly called *Black George*, the Game-keeper, which consisted at present of a Wife and five Children.

The second of these Children was a Daughter, whose Name was *Molly*, and who was esteemed one of the handsomest Girls in the whole Country.

*Congreve* well says,[1] *There is in true Beauty something which vulgar Souls cannot admire*; so can no Dirt or Rags hide this Something from those Souls which are not of the vulgar Stamp.

The Beauty of this Girl made, however, no Impression on *Tom*, till she grew towards the Age of Sixteen, when *Tom*, who was near three Years older, began first to cast the Eyes of Affection upon her. And this Affection he had fixed on the Girl long before he could bring himself to attempt the Possession of her Person: for tho' his Constitution urged him greatly to this, his Principles no less forcibly restrained him. To debauch a young Woman, however low her Condition was, appeared to him a very heinous Crime; and the Good-will he bore the Father, with the Compassion he had for his Family, very strongly corroborated all such sober Reflections; so that he once resolved to get the better of his Inclinations, and he actually abstained three whole Months without ever going to *Seagrim's* House, or seeing his Daughter.

Now though *Molly* was, as we have said, generally thought a very fine Girl, and in reality she was so, yet her Beauty was not of the most amiable Kind. It had indeed very little of Feminine in it, and would have become a Man at least as well as a Woman;

[1] In *The Old Batchelour* (1693), IV. iii. When Belinda and Araminta unmask, Sharper declares: 'There is in true Beauty, as in Courage, somewhat, which narrow Souls cannot dare to admire.'

for, to say the Truth, Youth and florid Health had a very considerable Share in the Composition.

Nor was her Mind more effeminate than her Person. As this
was tall and robust, so was that bold and forward. So little had
she of Modesty, that *Jones* had more Regard for her Virtue than
she herself. And as most probably she liked *Tom* as well as he
liked her, so when she perceived his Backwardness, she herself
grew proportionably forward; and when she saw he had entirely
deserted the House, she found Means of throwing herself in his
Way, and behaved in such a Manner, that the Youth must have
had very much, or very little of the Heroe, if her Endeavours had
proved unsuccessful. In a Word, she soon triumphed over all
the virtuous Resolutions of *Jones*: For though she behaved at
last with all decent Reluctance, yet I rather chuse to attribute
the Triumph to her: Since, in Fact, it was her Design which
succeeded.

In the Conduct of this Matter, I say, *Molly* so well played her
Part, that *Jones* attributed the Conquest entirely to himself, and
considered the young Woman as one who had yielded to the
violent Attacks of his Passion. He likewise imputed her yielding,
to the ungovernable Force of her Love towards him; and this the
Reader will allow to have been a very natural and probable Supposition, as we have more than once mentioned the uncommon
Comeliness of his Person: And indeed he was one of the handsomest young Fellows in the World.

As there are some Minds whose Affections, like Master
*Blifil's*, are solely placed on one single Person, whose Interest
and Indulgence alone they consider on every Occasion; regarding
the Good and Ill of all others as merely indifferent, any farther
than as they contribute to the Pleasure or Advantage of that
Person: So there is a different Temper of Mind which borrows a
Degree of Virtue even from Self-love; such can never receive any
kind of Satisfaction from another, without loving the Creature to
whom that Satisfaction is owing, and without making its Well-
being in some sort necessary to their own Ease.

Of this latter Species was our Heroe. He considered this poor
Girl as one whose Happiness or Misery he had caused to be dependent on himself. Her Beauty was still the Object of Desire,
though greater Beauty, or a fresher Object, might have been
more so; but the little Abatement which Fruition had occasioned

to this, was highly over-ballanced by the Considerations of the
Affection which she visibly bore him, and of the Situation into
which he had brought her. The former of these created Gratitude,
the latter Compassion; and both together with his Desire for her
Person, raised in him a Passion, which might, without any great
Violence to the Word, be called *Love*; though, perhaps, it was
at first not very judiciously placed.

This then was the true Reason of that Insensibility which he
had shewn to the Charms of *Sophia*, and that Behaviour in her,
which might have been reasonably enough interpreted as an
Encouragement to his Addresses: For as he could not think of
abandoning his *Molly*, poor and destitute as she was, so no more
could he entertain a Notion of betraying such a Creature as
*Sophia*. And surely, had he given the least Encouragement to any
Passion for that young Lady, he must have been absolutely
guilty of one or other of those Crimes; either of which would,
in my Opinion, have very justly subjected him to that Fate,
which at his first Introduction into this History, I mentioned to
have been generally predicted as his certain Destiny.


CHAPTER VII

*Being the shortest Chapter in this Book.*

HER Mother first perceived the Alteration in the Shape of
*Molly*, and in order to hide it from her Neighbours, she
foolishly clothed her in that Sack which *Sophia* had sent her.
Though indeed that young Lady had little Apprehension, that
the poor Woman would have been weak enough to let any of her
Daughters wear it in that Form.

*Molly* was charmed with the first Opportunity she ever had of
shewing her Beauty to Advantage; for though she could very well
bear to contemplate herself in the Glass, even when drest in
Rags; and though she had in that Dress conquered the Heart of
*Jones*, and perhaps of some others; yet she thought the Addition
of Finery would much improve her Charms, and extend her
Conquests.

*Molly*, therefore, having dressed herself out in this Sack, with
a new laced Cap, and some other Ornaments which *Tom* had given

her, repairs to Church with her Fan in her Hand the very next
*Sunday*. The Great are deceived, if they imagine they have appropriated Ambition and Vanity to themselves. These noble
Qualities flourish as notably in a Country Church, and Church-
yard, as in the Drawing-Room, or in the Closet. Schemes have
indeed been laid in the Vestry, which would hardly disgrace the
Conclave. Here is a Ministry, and here is an Opposition. Here
are Plots and Circumventions, Parties and Factions, equal to
those which are to be found in Courts.

Nor are the Women here less practised in the highest Feminine
Arts than their fair Superiors in Quality and Fortune. Here are
Prudes and Coquettes. Here are Dressing and Ogling, Falshood,
Envy, Malice, Scandal; in short, every Thing which is common to
the most splendid Assembly, or politest Circle. Let those of high
Life, therefore, no longer despise the Ignorance of their In-
feriors; nor the Vulgar any longer rail at the Vices of their Betters.

*Molly* had seated herself some time before she was known by
her Neighbours. And then a Whisper ran through the whole
Congregation, 'Who is she?' But when she was discovered, such
sneering, gigling, tittering, and laughing, ensued among the
Women, that Mr. *Allworthy* was obliged to exert his Authority
to preserve any Decency among them.


## CHAPTER VIII

*A Battle sung by the Muse in the* Homerican *Stile, and which none
but the classical Reader can taste.*

MR. *Western* had an Estate in this Parish; and as his House
stood at little greater Distance from this Church than from
his own, he very often came to divine Service here; and both he
and the charming *Sophia* happened to be present at this Time.

*Sophia* was much pleased with the Beauty of the Girl, whom
she pitied for her Simplicity, in having dressed herself in that
Manner, as she saw the Envy which it had occasioned among her
Equals. She no sooner came home, than she sent for the Game-
keeper, and ordered him to bring his Daughter to her; saying,
She would provide for her in the Family, and might possibly place
the Girl about her own Person, when her own Maid, who was now
going away, had left her.

Poor *Seagrim* was thunderstruck at this; for he was no Stranger to the Fault in the Shape of his Daughter. He answered, in a stammering Voice, 'That he was afraid *Molly* would be too aukward to wait on her Ladyship, as she had never been at Service.' 'No matter for that,' says *Sophia*, 'she will soon improve. I am pleased with the Girl, and am resolved to try her.'

*Black George* now repaired to his Wife, on whose prudent Council he depended to extricate him out of this Dilemma; but when he came thither, he found his House in some Confusion. So great Envy had this Sack occasioned, that when Mr. *Allworthy* and the other Gentry were gone from Church, the Rage, which had hitherto been confined, burst into an Uproar, and, having vented itself at first in opprobrious Words, Laughs, Hisses, and Gestures, betook itself at last to certain missile Weapons; which, though from their plastic Nature they threatened neither the Loss of Life or of Limb, were however sufficiently dreadful to a well-dressed Lady. *Molly* had too much Spirit to bear this Treatment tamely. Having therefore——But hold, as we are diffident of our own Abilities, let us here invite a superior Power to our Assistance.

Ye Muses then, whoever ye are, who love to sing Battles, and principally thou, who whileom didst recount the Slaughter in those Fields where *Hudibras* and *Trulla* fought,[1] if thou wert not starved with thy Friend *Butler*,[2] assist me on this great Occasion. All things are not in the Power of all.[3]

As a vast Herd of Cows[4] in a rich Farmer's Yard, if, while they

[1] See Butler's *Hudibras*, I. iii. 769 ff.

[2] Even though Samuel Butler had in 1677 been granted a royal pension of £100 a year, the legend grew that he had been allowed to starve to death in a garret, and so in the eighteenth century Butler became the very type of the neglected genius. Erected in 1721, the monument to him in Westminster Abbey was inscribed with the following verses: 'The Poets Fate is here in Emblem shown:/ He asked for Bread and he received a Stone.' Among the innumerable contemporary allusions to the tradition, see Oldham's *Satire against Poetry*; Dryden's *Hind and the Panther*, iii. 247–50; and Bayle's *General Dictionary, Historical and Critical* (1734–41), s.v. 'Hudibras'. Earlier references in Fielding occur in *Eurydice Hiss'd* (1737), *The Champion* (27 November 1739), and 'Epitaph on Butler's Monument' (*Miscellanies*, 1743).

[3] Cf. Virgil's *Eclogues*, viii. 63. See below, pp. 414, 543.

[4] Molly's battle in the churchyard burlesques the *Iliad*, iv–v, Homer's account of the first battle between the Greek and Trojan armies. With the present paragraph compare, specifically, the *Iliad*, iv. 433–49, which describes the war-cry of the Trojans and introduces the conflict. Pope translates as follows:

> Not so the *Trojans*, from their Host ascends
> A gen'ral Shout that all the Region rends.

are milked, they hear their Calves at a Distance, lamenting the Robbery which is then committing, roar and bellow: So roared forth the *Somersetshire* Mob an Hallaloo, made up of almost as many Squawls, Screams, and other different Sounds, as there were Persons, or indeed Passions, among them: Some were inspired by Rage, others alarmed by Fear, and others had nothing in their Heads but the Love of Fun; but chiefly Envy, the Sister of *Satan*, and his constant Companion, rushed among the Crowd, and blew up the Fury of the Women; who no sooner came up to *Molly*, than they pelted her with Dirt and Rubbish.

*Molly*, having endeavoured in vain to make a handsome Retreat, faced about; and laying hold of ragged *Bess*, who advanced in the Front of the Enemy, she at one Blow felled her to the Ground. The whole Army of the Enemy (though near a hundred in Number) seeing the Fate of their General, gave back many Paces, and retired behind a new-dug Grave; for the Church-yard was the Field of Battle, where there was to be a Funeral that very Evening. *Molly* pursued her Victory, and catching up a Skull which lay on the Side of the Grave, discharged it with such Fury, that having hit a Taylor on the Head, the two Skulls sent equally forth a hollow Sound at their Meeting, and the Taylor took presently measure of his Length on the Ground, where the Skulls lay side by side, and it was doubtful which was the more valuable of the two. *Molly* then taking a Thigh Bone in her

> As when the fleecy Flocks unnumber'd stand
> In wealthy Folds, and wait the Milker's Hand,
> The hollow Vales incessant Bleating fills,
> The Lambs reply from all the neighb'ring Hills:
> Such Clamours rose from various Nations round,
> Mix'd was the Murmur, and confus'd the Sound.
> Each Host now joins, and each a God inspires,
> These *Mars* incites, and those *Minerva* fires.
> Pale *Flight* around, and dreadful *Terror* reign;
> And *Discord* raging bathes the purple Plain:
> *Discord!* dire Sister of the slaught'ring Pow'r,
> Small at her Birth, but rising ev'ry Hour,
> While scarce the Skies her horrid Head can bound,
> She stalks on Earth, and shakes the World around;
> The Nations bleed, where-e'er her Steps she turns,
> The Groan still deepens, and the Combat burns.
>   Now Shield with Shield, with Helmet Helmet clos'd,
> To Armour Armour, Lance to Lance oppos'd,
> Host against Host with shadowy Squadrons drew,
> The sounding Darts in Iron Tempests slew. . . .   (iv. 490–511)

Hand,[1] fell in among the flying Ranks, and dealing her Blows with great Liberality on either Side, overthrew the Carcass of many a mighty Heroe and Heroine.

Recount, O Muse, the Names of those who fell on this fatal Day. First *Jemmy Tweedle* felt on his hinder Head the direful Bone. Him the pleasant Banks of sweetly winding *Stower* had nourished,[2] where he first learnt the vocal Art, with which, wandring up and down at Wakes and Fairs, he cheered the rural Nymphs and Swains, when upon the Green they interweav'd the sprightly Dance; while he himself stood fidling and jumping to his own Music. How little now avails his Fiddle? He thumps the verdant Floor with his Carcass. Next old *Echepole*,[3] the Sow-gelder, received a Blow in his Forehead from our Amazonian Heroine, and immediately fell to the Ground. He was a swinging fat Fellow, and fell with almost as much Noise as a House. His Tobacco-box dropt at the same Time from his Pocket, which *Molly* took up as lawful Spoils. Then *Kate* of the Mill tumbled unfortunately over a Tombstone, which catching hold of her un-gartered Stocking, inverted the Order of Nature, and gave her Heels the Superiority to her Head.[4] *Betty Pippin*, with young *Roger* her Lover, fell both to the Ground. Where, O perverse

[1] Cf. Judges 15: 15–16—Samson's slaying a thousand Philistines with the jawbone of an ass.

[2] Cf. *Iliad*, iv. 473–6—'Fair *Simoïsius*, whom his Mother bore/ Amid the Flocks on silver *Simois*' Shore . . .' (Pope's trans., iv. 544–5).

[3] Cf. *Iliad*, iv. 457–66—the death of Echepolus:

> The bold *Antilochus* the Slaughter led,
> The first who strook a valiant *Trojan* dead:
> At great *Echepolus* the Lance arrives,
> Raz'd his high Crest, and thro' his Helmet drives,
> Warm'd in the Brain the brazen Weapon lies,
> And Shades Eternal settle o'er his Eyes.
> So sinks a Tow'r, that long Assaults had stood
> Of Force and Fire; its Walls besmear'd with Blood.
> Him, the bold Leader of th' *Abantian* Throng
> Seiz'd to despoil. . . . (Pope's trans., iv. 522–31.)

[4] Cf. *Iliad*, v. 582–3, 585–6—the fate and posture of the fallen Mydon:

> . . . From his numb'd Hand the Iv'ry-studded Reins
> Dropt in the Dust are trail'd along the Plains.
> . . . He groans in Death, and pondrous sinks to Ground:
> Deep drove his Helmet in the Sands, and there
> The Head stood fix'd, the quiv'ring Legs in Air. . . .
> (Pope's trans., v. 713–14, 716–18.)

Fate, she salutes the Earth, and he the Sky.[1] *Tom Freckle*,[2] the
Smith's Son, was the next Victim to her Rage. He was an ingen-
ious Workman, and made excellent Pattins; nay the very Pattin
with which he was knocked down was his own Workmanship.
Had he been at that Time singing Psalms in the Church, he
would have avoided a broken Head. Miss *Crow*, the Daughter of
a Farmer; *John Giddish*, himself a Farmer; *Nan Slouch*, *Esther
Codling*, *Will Spray*, *Tom Bennet*; the three Misses *Potter*, whose
Father keeps the Sign of the *Red Lion*; *Betty Chambermaid*, *Jack
Ostler*, and many others of inferior Note, lay rolling among the
Graves.

Not that the strenuous Arm of *Molly* reached all these; for
many of them in their Flight overthrew each other.

But now Fortune, fearing she had acted out of Character,
and had inclined too long to the same Side, especially as it was
the right Side, hastily turned about: For now Goody *Brown*,
whom *Zekiel Brown* caressed in his Arms; nor he alone, but half
the Parish besides; so famous was she in the Fields of *Venus*, nor
indeed less in those of *Mars*. The Trophies of both these, her
Husband always bore about on his Head and Face; for if ever
human Head did by its Horns display the amorous Glories of a
Wife, *Zekiel's* did; nor did his well-scratched Face less denote her
Talents (or rather Talons) of a different Kind.

No longer bore this Amazon the shameful Flight of her
Party. She stopt short, and calling aloud to all who fled, spoke as

---

[1] Cf. Virgil's *Aeneid*, ix. 444–5—where Nisus, slain, falls upon his dead friend Euryalus:
> Dying, he slew; and stagg'ring on the Plain,
> With swimming Eyes he sought his Lover slain:
> Then quiet on his bleeding Bosom fell;
> Content in Death, to be reveng'd so well.
>                         (Dryden's trans., ix. 593–6.)

[2] Cf. *Iliad*, v. 59–64—the death of Phereclus:
> Next artful *Phereclus* untimely fell;
> Bold *Merion* sent him to the Realms of Hell.
> Thy Father's Skill, O *Phereclus*, was thine,
> The graceful Fabrick and the fair Design;
> For lov'd by *Pallas*, *Pallas* did impart
> To him the Shipwright's and the Builder's Art.
> Beneath his Hand the Fleet of *Paris* rose,
> The fatal Cause of all his Country's Woes,
> But he, the mystick Will of Heav'n unknown,
> Nor saw his Country's Peril, nor his own.
>                         (Pope's trans., v. 75–84.)

follows:[1] 'Ye *Somersetshire* Men, or rather ye *Somersetshire* Women,
are ye not ashamed, thus to fly from a single Woman; but if no
other will oppose her, I myself and *Joan Top* here will have the
Honour of the Victory.' Having thus said, she flew at *Molly Seagrim*,
and easily wrenched the Thigh Bone from her Hand, at the same
Time clawing off her Cap from her Head. Then laying hold of
the Hair of *Molly*, with her Left Hand, she attacked her so
furiously in the Face with the Right, that the Blood soon began
to trickle from her Nose. *Molly* was not idle this while. She soon
removed the Clout from the Head of Goody *Brown*, and then
fastening on her Hair with one Hand, with the other she caused
another bloody Stream to issue forth from the Nostrils of the
Enemy.

When each of the Combatants had borne off sufficient Spoils
of Hair from the Head of her Antagonist, the next Rage was
against the Garments. In this Attack they exerted so much
Violence, that in a very few Minutes, they were both naked to
the middle.

It is lucky for the Women, that the Seat of Fistycuff-War is not
the same with them as among Men; but though they may seem
a little to deviate from their Sex, when they go forth to Battle, yet
I have observed they never so far forget, as to assail the Bosoms of
each other; where a few Blows would be fatal to most of them.
This, I know, some derive from their being of a more bloody
Inclination than the Males. On which Account they apply to
the Nose, as to the Part whence Blood may most easily be drawn;
but this seems a far-fetched, as well as ill-natured Supposition.

Goody *Brown* had great Advantage of *Molly* in this Particular;
for the former had indeed no Breasts, her Bosom (if it may be
so called) as well in Colour as in many other Properties, exactly
resembling an antient Piece of Parchment, upon which any one
might have drummed a considerable while, without doing her any
great Damage.

*Molly*, beside her present unhappy Condition, was differently

[1] Cf. *Iliad*, v. 785–7—Stentor's hortatory speech to the Greeks: Hera
   . . . shouts, in *Stentor's* sounding Voice, aloud:
   *Stentor* the strong, endu'd with Brazen Lungs,
   Whose Throat surpass'd the Force of fifty Tongues.
   Inglorious *Argives!* to your Race a Shame,
   And only Men in Figure and in Name!
                              (Pope's trans., v. 977–81.)

formed in those Parts, and might, perhaps, have tempted the
Envy of *Brown* to give her a fatal Blow, had not the lucky Arrival
of *Tom Jones* at this Instant put an immediate End to the bloody
Scene.

This Accident was luckily owing to Mr. *Square*; for he, Master
*Blifil*, and *Jones*, had mounted their Horses, after Church, to
take the Air, and had ridden about a Quarter of a Mile, when
*Square*, changing his Mind, (not idly, but for a Reason which we
shall unfold as soon as we have Leisure) desired the young
Gentlemen to ride with him another Way than they had at first
purposed. This Motion being complied with, brought them of
Necessity back again to the Church-yard.

Master *Blifil*, who rode first, seeing such a Mob assembled,
and two Women in the Posture in which we left the Combatants,
stopt his Horse to enquire what was the Matter. A Country
Fellow, scratching his Head, answered him; 'I don't know
Measter un't I; an't please your Honour, here hath been a
Vight, I think, between Goody *Brown* and *Mol Seagrim*.' 'Who,
who?' cries *Tom*; but without waiting for an Answer, having discovered the Features of his *Molly* through all the Discomposure
in which they now were, he hastily alighted, turned his Horse
loose, and leaping over the Wall, ran to her. She now, first bursting into Tears, told him how barbarously she had been treated.
Upon which, forgetting the Sex of Goody *Brown*, or perhaps not
knowing it, in his Rage; for, in reality, she had no feminine
Appearance, but a Petticoat, which he might not observe, he
gave her a Lash or two with his Horsewhip; and then flying at
the Mob, who were all accused by *Molly*, he dealt his Blows so
profusely on all Sides, that unless I would again invoke the
Muse, (which the good-natured Reader may think a little too
hard upon her, as she hath so lately been violently sweated) it
would be impossible for me to recount the Horsewhipping of that
Day.

Having scoured the whole Coast of the Enemy, as well as any
of *Homer's* Heroes ever did, or as *Don Quixotte*,[1] or any Knight
Errant in the World could have done, he returned to *Molly*,
whom he found in a Condition, which must give both me and
my Reader Pain, was it to be described here. *Tom* raved like a
Madman, beat his Breast, tore his Hair, stamped on the Ground,

<hr>

[1] For Fielding's opinion of Cervantes, see below, p. 686, n. 1.

and vowed the utmost Vengeance on all who had been concerned. He then pulled off his Coat, and buttoned it round her, put his Hat upon her Head, wiped the Blood from her Face as well as he could with his Handkerchief, and called out to the Servant to ride as fast as possible for a Side-saddle, or a Pillion, that he might carry her safe home.

Master *Blifil* objected to the sending away the Servant, as they had only one with them; but as *Square* seconded the Order of *Jones*, he was obliged to comply.

The Servant returned in a very short Time with the Pillion, and *Molly*, having collected her Rags as well as she could, was placed behind him. In which Manner she was carried home, *Square*, *Blifil*, and *Jones*, attending.

Here *Jones*, having received his Coat, given her a sly Kiss, and whispered her that he would return in the Evening, quitted his *Molly*, and rode on after his Companions.

## CHAPTER IX

*Containing Matter of no very peaceable Colour.*

*MOLLY* had no sooner apparelled herself in her accustomed Rags, than her Sisters began to fall violently upon her; particularly her eldest Sister, who told her she was well enough served. 'How had she the Assurance to wear a Gown which young Madam *Western* had given to Mother! If one of us was to wear it, I think,' says she, 'I myself have the best Right; but I warrant you think it belongs to your Beauty. I suppose you think yourself more handsomer than any of us.' 'Hand her down the Bit of Glass from over the Cupboard,' cries another, 'I'd wash the Blood from my Face before I tauked of my Beauty.' 'You'd better have minded what the Parson says,' cries the eldest, 'and not a harkened after Men Voke.' 'Indeed, Child, and so she had,' says the Mother sobbing, 'she hath brought a Disgrace upon us all. She's the vurst of the Vamily that ever was a Whore.' 'You need not upbraid me with that, Mother,' cries *Molly*, 'you your-self was brought to-bed of Sister there within a Week after you was married.' 'Yes, Hussy,' answered the enraged Mother, 'so

I was, and what was the mighty Matter of that? I was made an honest Woman then; and if you was to be made an honest Woman, I should not be angry; but you must have to be doing with a Gentleman, you nasty Slut, you will have a Bastard, Hussy, you will; and that I defy any one to say of me.'

In this Situation *Black George* found his Family, when he came home for the Purpose before mentioned. As his Wife and three Daughters were all of them talking together, and most of them crying, it was some time before he could get an Opportunity of being heard; but as soon as such an Interval occurred, he acquainted the Company with what *Sophia* had said to him.

Goody *Seagrim* then began to revile her Daughter afresh. 'Here,' says she, 'you have brought us into a fine Quandary indeed. What will Madam say to that big Belly? Oh that ever I should live to see this Day.'

*Molly* answered with great Spirit, 'And what is this mighty Place which you have got for me, Father?' (for he had not well understood the Phrase used by *Sophia* of being about her Person) 'I suppose it is to be under the Cook; but I shan't wash Dishes for any Body. My Gentleman will provide better for me. See what he hath given me this Afternoon; he hath promised I shall never want Money; and you shan't want Money neither, Mother, if you will hold your Tongue, and know when you are well.' And so saying, she pulled out several Guineas, and gave her Mother one of them.

The good Woman no sooner felt the Gold within her Palm, than her Temper began (such is the Efficacy of that *Panacea*) to be mollified. 'Why Husband,' says she, 'would any but such a Blockhead as you not have enquired what Place this was before he had accepted it! Perhaps, as *Molly* says, it may be in the Kitchin, and truly I don't care my Daughter should be a Scullion Wench: For poor as I am, I am a Gentlewoman. And thof I was obliged, as my Father, who was a Clergyman, died worse than nothing, and so could not give me a Shilling of *Potion*, to undervalue myself, by marrying a poor Man, yet I would have you to know, I have a Spirit above all *them* Things. Marry come up, it would better become Madam *Western* to look at Home, and remember who her own Grandfather was. Some of my Family, for ought I know, might ride in their Coaches, when the Grandfathers of some Voke walked a-voot. I warrant she fancies she did a mighty Matter, when she sent us that old *Gownd*; some of my Family would not have picked up such Rags in the Street; but poor People are always trampled upon.—The Parish need not have been in such a Fluster with *Molly*.—You might have told them, Child, your Grandmother wore better Things new out of the Shop.'

'Well but, consider,' cried *George*, 'What Answer shall I make to Madam?' 'I don't know what Answer,' says she, 'You are always bringing your Family into one Quandary or other. Do you remember when you shot the Partridge, the Occasion of all our Misfortunes? Did not I advise you never to go into Squire *Western's* Manor? Did not I tell you many a good Year ago what would come of it? but you would have your own headstrong Ways; yes, you would, you Villain——'

*Black George* was, in the main, a peaceable kind of Fellow, and nothing *choleric*, *nor rash*, yet did he bear about him some thing of what the Antients called the *Irascible*, and which his Wife, if she had been endowed with much *Wisdom, would have feared*.[1] He had long experienced, that when the Storm grew very high Arguments were but Wind, which served rather to increase than to abate it. He was therefore seldom unprovided with a small Switch, a Remedy of wonderful Force, as he had often essayed, and which the Word Villain served as a Hint for his applying.

No sooner, therefore, had this Symptom appeared, than he had immediate Recourse to the said Remedy, which though, as it is usual in all very efficacious Medicines, it at first seemed to heighten and inflame the Disease, soon produced a total Calm, and restored the Patient to perfect Ease and Tranquility.

This is, however, a kind of Horse-medicine, which requires a very robust Constitution to digest, and is therefore proper only for the Vulgar, unless in one single Instance, *viz.* where Superiority of Birth breaks out; in which Case, we should not think it very improperly applied by any Husband whatever, if the Application was not, in itself so base, that, like certain Applications of the Physical Kind which need not be mentioned, it so much degrades and contaminates the Hand employed in it, that

---

[1] Cf. Hamlet to Laertes (v. i):

> For, though I am not splenitive and rash,
> Yet have I in me something dangerous,
> Which let thy wisdom fear.

no Gentleman should endure the Thought of any Thing so low
and detestable.

The whole Family were soon reduced to a State of perfect
Quiet: For the Virtue of this Medicine, like that of Electricity,
is often communicated through one Person to many others,
who are not touched by the Instrument. To say the Truth, as
they both operate by Friction, it may be doubted whether there
is not something analogous between them, of which Mr. *Freke*[1]
would do well to enquire before he publishes the next Edition of
his Book.

A Council was now called, in which, after many Debates,
*Molly* still persisting that she would not go to Service, it was at
length resolved, that Goody *Seagrim* herself should wait on Miss
*Western*, and endeavour to procure the Place for her eldest
Daughter, who declared great Readiness to accept it; but Fortune, who seems to have been an Enemy of this little Family,
afterwards put a Stop to her Promotion.


## CHAPTER X

*A Story told by Mr.* Supple, *the Curate. The Penetration of Squire*
Western. *His great Love for his Daughter, and the Return to it made
by her.*


THE next Morning *Tom Jones* hunted with Mr. *Western*, and
was at his Return invited by that Gentleman to Dinner.

The lovely *Sophia* shone forth that Day with more Gaiety and
Sprightliness than usual. Her Battery was certainly levelled at our
Heroe; though, I believe, she herself scarce yet knew her own
Intention; but if she had any Design of charming him, she now
succeeded.

Mr. *Supple*, the Curate of Mr. *Allworthy's* Parish, made one of
the Company. He was a good-natured worthy Man; but chiefly
remarkable for his great Taciturnity at Table, though his
Mouth was never shut at it. In short, he had one of the best

---

[1] See above, p. 86, n. 1. In his *Essay to Shew the Cause of Electricity*, Freke had attempted to explain 'Why a Company of unelectrify'd Persons, who are joined together by their
holding each a Piece of iron Wire betwixt them, tho' they are ever so many, do all receive a
violent Blow or Concussion on their Bodies, when one of them touches a Piece of electrify'd
Iron' (pp. 36–7).

Appetites in the World. However, the Cloth was no sooner taken away, than he always made sufficient Amends for his Silence: For he was a very hearty Fellow; and his Conversation was often entertaining, never offensive.

At his first Arrival, which was immediately before the Entrance of the Roast-beef, he had given an Intimation that he had brought some News with him, and was beginning to tell, that he came that Moment from Mr. *Allworthy's*, when the Sight of the Roast-beef struck him dumb, permitting him only to say Grace, and to declare he must pay his Respect to the Baronet:[1] For so he called the Sirloin.

When Dinner was over, being reminded by *Sophia* of his News, he began as follows, 'I believe, Lady, your Ladyship observed a young Woman at Church yesterday at Even-song, who was drest in one of your outlandish Garments; I think I have seen your Ladyship in such a one. However, in the Country, such Dresses are

*Rara avis in Terris, nigroque simillima Cycno,*[2]

That is, Madam, as much as to say,

A rare Bird upon the Earth, and very like a black Swan.

'The Verse is in *Juvenal*: but to return to what I was relating. I was saying such Garments are rare Sights in the Country, and perchance too, it was thought the more rare, Respect being had to the Person who wore it, who, they tell me, is the Daughter of *Black George*, your Worship's Game-keeper, whose Sufferings I should have opined, might have taught him more Wit than to dress forth his Wenches in such gaudy Apparel. She created so much Confusion in the Congregation, that if Squire *Allworthy* had not silenced it, it would have interrupted the Service: For I was once about to stop in the Middle of the first Lesson. Howbeit, nevertheless, after Prayer was over, and I was departed home, this occasioned a Battle in the Church-yard, where, amongst other Mischief, the Head of a travelling Fidler was very much broken. This Morning the Fidler came to Squire *Allworthy* for a Warrant, and the Wench was brought before him. The Squire was inclined to have compounded Matters; when, lo! on a sudden, the

---

1 A 'baron of beef' was 'a joint consisting of two sirloins left uncut at the backbone' (*OED*).

2 Juvenal, *Satires*, vi. 165.

Wench appeared (I ask your Ladyship's Pardon) to be, as it were at the Eve of bringing forth a Bastard. The Squire demanded of her who was the Father; but she pertinaciously refused to make any Response. So that he was about to make her Mittimus to *Bridewel*, when I departed.'

'And is a Wench having a Bastard all your News, Doctor?' cries *Western*. 'I thought it might have been some public Matter, something about the Nation.'

'I am afraid it is too common, indeed,' answered the Parson, 'but I thought the whole Story all together deserved commemorating. As to National Matters, your Worship knows them best. My Concerns extend no farther than my own Parish.'

'Why ay,' says the Squire, 'I believe I do know a little of that Matter, as you say; but come, *Tommy*, drink about, the Bottle stands with you.'

*Tom* begged to be excused, for that he had particular Business; and getting up from Table, escaped the Clutches of the Squire who was rising to stop him, and went off with very little Ceremony.

The Squire gave him a good Curse at his Departure; and then turning to the Parson, he cried out, 'I smoke it, I smoke it. *Tom* is certainly the Father of this Bastard. Zooks, Parson, you remember how he recommended the Veather o'her to me——d—n un, what a sly B—ch 'tis. Ay, ay, as sure as Twopence, *Tom* is the Veather of the Bastard.'

'I should be very sorry for that,' says the Parson. 'Why sorry,' cries the Squire, 'Where is the mighty Matter o't? What, I suppose, dost pretend that thee hast never got a Bastard? Pox! more good Luck's thine: for I warrant hast a done *therefore* many's the good Time and often.' 'Your Worship is pleased to be jocular,' answered the Parson, 'but I do not only animadvert on the Sinfulness of the Action, though that surely is to be greatly deprecated; but I fear his Unrighteousness may injure him with Mr. *Allworthy*. And truly I must say, though he hath the Character of being a little wild, I never saw any Harm in the young Man; nor can I say I have heard any, save what your Worship now mentions. I wish, indeed he was a little more regular in his Responses at Church; but altogether he seems

*Ingenui vultus puer ingenuique pudoris.*[1]

[1] Juvenal, *Satires*, xi. 154.

'That is a classical Line, young Lady, and being rendered into *English* is, A Lad of an ingenuous Countenance and of an ingenuous Modesty: For this was a Virtue in great Repute both among the *Latins* and *Greeks*. I must say the young Gentleman (for so I think I may call him, notwithstanding his Birth) appears to me a very modest, civil Lad, and I should be sorry that he should do himself any Injury in Squire *Allworthy's* Opinion.'

'Poogh!' says the Squire, 'Injury with *Allworthy*! Why *Allworthy* loves a Wench himself. Doth not all the Country know whose Son *Tom* is? You must talk to another Person in that Manner. I remember *Allworthy* at College.'

'I thought,' said the Parson, 'he had never been at the University.'

'Yes, yes, he was,' says the Squire, 'and many a Wench have we two had together. As arrant a Whoremaster as any within five Miles o'un. No, no. It will do'n no Harm with he, assure your self; nor with any Body else. Ask *Sophy* there.—You have not the worse Opinion of a young Fellow for getting a Bastard, have you, Girl? No, no, the Women will like un the better for't.'

This was a cruel Question to poor *Sophia*. She had observed *Tom's* Colour change at the Parson's Story; and that, with his hasty and abrupt Departure, gave her sufficient Reason to think her Father's Suspicion not groundless. Her Heart now, at once, discovered the great Secret to her, which it had been so long disclosing by little and little; and she found herself highly interested in this Matter. In such a Situation, her Father's malapert Question rushing suddenly upon her, produced some Symptoms which might have alarmed a suspicious Heart; but to do the Squire Justice, that was not his Fault. When she rose therefore from her Chair, and told him, a Hint from him was always sufficient to make her withdraw, he suffered her to leave the Room; and then with great Gravity of Countenance remarked, 'that it was better to see a Daughter over-modest, than over-forward;' a Sentiment which was highly applauded by the Parson.

There now ensued between the Squire and the Parson, a most excellent political Discourse, framed out of News-papers, and political Pamphlets; in which they made a Libation of four Bottles of Wine to the Good of their Country; and then, the Squire being fast asleep, the Parson lighted his Pipe, mounted his Horse, and rode home.

When the Squire had finished his Half-hour's Nap, he sum-
moned his Daughter to her Harpsichord; but she begged to be
excused that Evening, on Account of a violent Head-ach. This
Remission was presently granted: For indeed she seldom had
Occasion to ask him twice, as he loved her with such ardent
Affection, that by gratifying her, he commonly conveyed the
highest Gratification to himself. She was really what he frequently
called her, his little Darling; and she well deserved to be so:
For she returned all his Affection in the most ample Manner.
She had preserved the most inviolable Duty to him in all Things;
and this her Love made not only easy, but so delightful, that
when one of her Companions laughed at her for placing so much
Merit in such scrupulous Obedience, as that young Lady called it,
*Sophia* answered, 'You mistake me, Madam, if you think I value
myself upon this Account: For besides that I am barely discharg-
ing my Duty, I am likewise pleasing myself. I can truly say, I
have no Delight equal to that of contributing to my Father's
Happiness; and if I value myself, my Dear, it is on having this
Power, and not on executing it.'

This was a Satisfaction, however, which poor *Sophia* was incapable of tasting this Evening. She therefore not only desired
to be excused from her Attendance at the Harpsichord, but likewise begged that he would suffer her to absent herself from
Supper. To this Request likewise the Squire agreed, though not
without some Reluctance; for he scarce ever permitted her to
be out of his Sight, unless when he was engaged with his Horses,
Dogs, or Bottle. Nevertheless he yielded to the Desire of his
Daughter, though the poor Man was, at the same Time, obliged
to avoid his own Company, (if I may so express myself) by sending for a neighbouring Farmer to sit with him.

## CHAPTER XI

*The narrow Escape of* Molly Seagrim, *with some Observations for
which we have been forced to dive pretty deep into Nature.*

*T*OM *JONES* had ridden one of Mr. *Western's* Horses that
Morning in the Chace: so that having no Horse of his own
in the Squire's Stable, he was obliged to go home on Foot. This

he did so expeditiously, that he ran upwards of three Miles within the half Hour.

Just as he arrived at Mr. *Allworthy's* outward Gate, he met the Constable and Company, with *Molly* in their Possession, whom they were conducting to that House where the inferior Sort of People may learn one good Lesson, *viz*. Respect and Deference to their Superiors. Since it must shew them the wide Distinction Fortune intends between those Persons who are to be corrected for their Faults, and those who are not; which Lesson, if they do not learn, I am afraid, they very rarely learn any other good Lesson, or improve their Morals, at the House of Correction.[1]

A Lawyer may, perhaps, think Mr. *Allworthy* exceeded his Authority a little in this Instance.[2] And, to say the Truth, I question, as here was no regular Information before him, whether his Conduct was strictly regular. However, as his Intention was truly upright, he ought to be excused in *Foro Conscientiæ*,[3] since so many arbitrary Acts are daily committed by Magistrates, who have not this Excuse to plead for themselves.

*Tom* was no sooner informed by the Constable, whither they were proceeding, (indeed he pretty well guessed it of himself) than he caught *Molly* in his Arms, and embracing her tenderly before them all, swore he would murder the first Man who offered to lay hold of her. He bid her dry her Eyes, and be comforted; for wherever she went, he would accompany her. Then turning to the Constable, who stood trembling with his Hat off, he desired him, in a very mild Voice, to return with him for a Moment only to his Father, (so he now called *Allworthy*) for he durst, he said, be assured, that when he had alledged what he had to say in her Favour, the Girl would be discharged.

The Constable, who, I make no Doubt, would have surrendered his Prisoner, had *Tom* demanded her, very readily consented to this Request. So back they all went into Mr. *Allworthy's* Hall;

---

[1] See above, p. 59, n. 1.

[2] Though the mother of a bastard child could be committed to the house of correction (see above, p. 40, n. 1), yet this could only be after she had been examined and the order of commitment signed by at least two justices, one being of the quorum. Furthermore, in order to prevent a possible miscarriage, it was unlawful for the justices to commit the woman, or even to summon her for examination, until one month after she had been delivered of the child. (See Barlow, *The Justice of the Peace* [1745], pp. 57–8, and Dalton, *The Country Justice* [1746], p. 34.)

[3] In a court of conscience. (See below, pp. 257.22, 676.24).

where *Tom* desired them to stay till his Return, and then went himself in Pursuit of the Good Man. As soon as he was found, *Tom* threw himself at his Feet, and having begged a patient Hearing, confessed himself to be the Father of the Child, of which *Molly* was then big. He entreated him to have Compassion on the poor Girl, and to consider, if there was any Guilt in the Case, it lay principally at his Door.

'If there is any Guilt in the Case!' answered *Allworthy* warmly, 'are you then so profligate and abandoned a Libertine, to doubt whether the breaking the Laws of God and Man, the corrupting and ruining a poor Girl, be Guilt? I own, indeed, it doth lie principally upon you, and so heavy it is, that you ought to expect it should crush you.'

'Whatever may be my Fate,' says *Tom*, 'let me succeed in my Intercessions for the poor Girl. I confess I have corrupted her; but whether she shall be ruined depends on you. For Heaven's Sake, Sir, revoke your Warrant, and do not send her to a Place which must unavoidably prove her Destruction.'

*Allworthy* bid him immediately call a Servant. *Tom* answered, there was no Occasion; for he had luckily met them at the Gate, and relying upon his Goodness, had brought them all back into his Hall, where they now waited his final Resolution, which, upon his Knees, he besought him might be in favour of the Girl; that she might be permitted to go home to her Parents, and not be exposed to a greater Degree of Shame and Scorn than must necessarily fall upon her. 'I know,' said he, 'that is too much. I know I am the wicked Occasion of it. I will endeavour to make Amends, if possible; and if you shall have hereafter the Goodness to forgive me, I hope I shall deserve it.'

*Allworthy* hesitated some Time, and at last said, 'Well, I will discharge my Mittimus.—You may send the Constable to me.' He was instantly called, discharged, and so was the Girl.

It will be believed, that Mr. *Allworthy* failed not to read *Tom* a very severe Lecture on this Occasion; but it is unnecessary to insert it here, as we have faithfully transcribed what he said to *Jenny Jones* in the first Book, most of which may be applied to the Men, equally with the Women. So sensible an Effect had these Reproofs on the young Man, who was no hardened Sinner, that he retired to his own Room, where he passed the Evening alone in much melancholy Contemplation.

*Allworthy* was sufficiently offended by this Transgression of *Jones*; for notwithstanding the Assertions of Mr. *Western*, it is certain this worthy Man had never indulged himself in any loose Pleasures with Women, and greatly condemned the Vice of Incontinence in others. Indeed, there is much Reason to imagine, that there was not the least Truth in what Mr. *Western* affirmed, especially as he laid the Scene of those Impurities at the University, where Mr. *Allworthy* had never been. In fact, the good Squire was a little too apt to indulge that Kind of Pleasantry which is generally called *Rodomontade*; but which may, with as much Propriety, be expressed by a much shorter Word; and, perhaps, we too often supply the Use of this little Monosyllable by others; since very much of what frequently passes in the World for Wit and Humour, should, in the strictest Purity of Language, receive that short Appellation, which, in Conformity to the well-bred Laws of Custom, I here suppress.

But whatever Detestation Mr. *Allworthy* had to this or to any other Vice, he was not so blinded by it, but that he could discern any Virtue in the guilty Person, as clearly, indeed, as if there had been no Mixture of Vice in the same Character. While he was angry, therefore, with the Incontinence of *Jones*, he was no less pleased with the Honour and Honesty of his Self-accusation. He began now to form in his Mind the same Opinion of this young Fellow which we hope our Reader may have conceived. And in ballancing his Faults with his Perfections, the latter seemed rather to preponderate.

It was to no Purpose, therefore, that *Thwackum*, who was immediately charged by Mr. *Blifil* with the Story, unbended all his Rancour against poor *Tom*. *Allworthy* gave a patient Hearing to these Invectives, and then answered coldly; 'That young Men of *Tom's* Complexion were too generally addicted to this Vice; but he believed that Youth was sincerely affected with what he had said to him on the Occasion, and he hoped he would not transgress again.' So that, as the Days of whipping were at an End, the Tutor had no other Vent but his own Mouth for his Gall, the usual poor Resource of impotent Revenge.

But *Square*, who was a less violent, was a much more artful Man; and as he hated *Jones* more, perhaps, than *Thwackum* himself did, so he contrived to do him more Mischief in the Mind of Mr. *Allworthy*.

The Reader must remember the several little Incidents of the Partridge, the Horse, and the Bible, which were recounted in the second Book. By all which *Jones* had rather improved than injured the Affection which Mr. *Allworthy* was inclined to entertain for him. The same, I believe, must have happened to him with every other Person who hath any Idea of Friendship, Generosity, and Greatness of Spirit; that is to say, who hath any Traces of Goodness in his Mind.

*Square* himself was not unacquainted with the true Impression which those several Instances of Goodness had made on the excellent Heart of *Allworthy*; for the Philosopher very well knew what Virtue was, though he was not always, perhaps, steady in its Pursuit; but as for *Thwackum*, from what Reason I will not determine, no such Thoughts ever entered into his Head. He saw *Jones* in a bad Light, and he imagined *Allworthy* saw him in the same, but that he was resolved, from Pride and Stubbornness of Spirit, not to give up the Boy whom he had once cherished, since, by so doing, he must tacitly acknowledge that his former Opinion of him had been wrong.

*Square* therefore embraced this Opportunity of injuring *Jones* in the tenderest Part, by giving a very bad Turn to all these before-mentioned Occurrences. 'I am sorry, Sir,' said he, 'to own I have been deceived as well as yourself. I could not, I confess, help being pleased with what I ascribed to the Motive of Friendship, though it was carried to an Excess, and all Excess is faulty, and vicious; but in this I made Allowance for Youth. Little did I suspect that the Sacrifice of Truth, which we both imagined to have been made to Friendship, was, in reality, a Prostitution of it to a depraved and debauched Appetite. You now plainly see whence all the seeming Generosity of this young Man to the Family of the Game-keeper proceeded. He supported the Father in order to corrupt the Daughter, and preserved the Family from starving, to bring one of them to Shame and Ruin. This is Friendship! this is Generosity! As Sir *Richard Steele* says,[1] Gluttons who give high Prices for Delicacies, are very worthy to be called generous. In short, I am resolved, from this Instance, never to give Way to the Weakness of Human Nature more, nor

---

[1] In *The Conscious Lovers* (1722), v. iii, Mr. Sealand scoffs when Indiana declares Bevil's generosity to her: 'Bounty! when Gluttons give high Prices for Delicates, they are prodigious Bountiful.'

to think any thing Virtue which doth not exactly quadrate with the unerring Rule of Right.'

The Goodness of *Allworthy* had prevented those Considerations from occurring to himself; yet were they too plausible to be absolutely and hastily rejected, when laid before his Eyes by another. Indeed what *Square* had said sunk very deeply into his Mind, and the Uneasiness which it there created was very visible to the other; though the good Man would not acknowledge this, but made a very slight Answer, and forcibly drove off the Discourse to some other Subject. It was well, perhaps, for poor *Tom*, that no such Suggestions had been made before he was pardoned; for they certainly stamped in the Mind of *Allworthy* the first bad Impression concerning *Jones*.


## CHAPTER XII

*Containing much clearer Matters; but which flowed from the same Fountain with those in the preceding Chapter.*

THE Reader will be pleased, I believe, to return with me to *Sophia*. She passed the Night, after we saw her last, in no very agreeable Manner. Sleep befriended her but little, and Dreams less. In the Morning, when Mrs. *Honour* her Maid attended her, at the usual Hour, she was found already up and drest.

Persons who live two or three Miles Distance in the Country are considered as next Door Neighbours, and Transactions at the one House fly with incredible Celerity to the other. Mrs. *Honour*, therefore, had heard the whole Story of *Molly's* Shame; which she, being of a very communicative Temper, had no sooner entered the Apartment of her Mistress, than she began to relate in the following Manner:

'La Ma'am, what doth your La'ship think? the Girl that your La'ship saw at Church on *Sunday*, whom you thought so handsome; though you would not have thought her so handsome neither, if you had seen her nearer; but to be sure she hath been carried before the Justice for being big with Child. She seemed to me to look like a confident Slut; and to be sure she hath laid the Child to young Mr. *Jones*. And all the Parish says Mr.

*Allworthy* is so angry with young Mr. *Jones,* that he won't see
him. To be sure, one can't help pitying the poor young Man,
and yet he doth not deserve much Pity neither, for demeaning
himself with such Kind of Trumpery. Yet he is so pretty a
Gentleman, I should be sorry to have him turned out of Doors.
I dares to swear the Wench was as willing as he; for she was
always a forward Kind of Body. And when Wenches are so
coming, young Men are not so much to be blamed neither; for
to be sure they do no more than what is natural. Indeed it is
beneath them to meddle with such dirty Draggle-tails, and whatever happens to them, it is good enough for them. And yet to be
sure the vile Baggages are most in Fault. I wishes, with all my
Heart, they were well to be whipped at the Cart's Tail; for it is
Pity they should be the Ruin of a pretty young Gentleman; and
no body can deny but that Mr. *Jones* is one of the most handsomest young Men that ever——'

She was running on thus, when *Sophia,* with a more peevish
Voice than she had ever spoken to her in before, cried, 'Prithee
why do'st thou trouble me with all this Stuff? What Concern have
I in what Mr. *Jones* doth? I suppose you are all alike. And you
seem to me to be angry it was not your own Case.'

'I, Ma'am!' answered Mrs. *Honour,* 'I am sorry your Ladyship should have such an Opinion of me. I am sure nobody can
say any such thing of me. All the young Fellows in the World may
go to the *Divil,* for me. Because I said he was a handsome Man!
Every body says it as well as I——To be sure, I never thought
as it was any Harm to say a young Man was handsome; but to be
sure I shall never think him so any more now; for handsome is
that handsome does. A Beggar Wench!——'

'Stop thy Torrent of Impertinence,' cries *Sophia,* 'and see
whether my Father wants me at Breakfast.'

Mrs. *Honour* then flung out of the Room, muttering much to
herself—of which—'Marry come up, I assure you,' was all that
could be plainly distinguished.

Whether Mrs. *Honour* really deserved that Suspicion, of which
her Mistress gave her a Hint, is a Matter which we cannot indulge our Reader's Curiosity by resolving. We will however make
him Amends, in disclosing what passed in the Mind of *Sophia.*

The Reader will be pleased to recollect, that a secret Affection
for Mr. *Jones* had insensibly stolen into the Bosom of this young

Lady. That it had there grown to a pretty great Height before she herself had discovered it. When she first began to perceive its Symptoms, the Sensations were so sweet and pleasing, that she had not Resolution sufficient to check or repel them; and thus she went on cherishing a Passion of which she never once considered the Consequences.

This Incident relating to *Molly*, first opened her Eyes. She now first perceived the Weakness of which she had been guilty; and though it caused the utmost Perturbation in her Mind, yet it had the Effect of other nauseous Physic, and for the Time expelled her Distemper. Its Operation indeed was most wonderfully quick; and in the short Interval, while her Maid was absent, so entirely removed all Symptoms, that when Mrs. *Honour* returned with a Summons from her Father, she was become perfectly easy, and had brought herself to a thorough Indifference for Mr. *Jones*.

The Diseases of the Mind do in almost every Particular imitate those of the Body. For which Reason, we hope, That learned Faculty, for whom we have so profound a Respect, will pardon us the violent Hands we have been necessitated to lay on several Words and Phrases,[1] which of Right belong to them, and without which our Descriptions must have been often unintelligible.

Now there is no one Circumstance in which the Distempers of the Mind bear a more exact Analogy to those which are called Bodily, than that Aptness which both have to a Relapse. This is plain, in the violent Diseases of Ambition and Avarice. I have known Ambition, when cured at Court by frequent Disappointments, (which are the only Physic for it) to break out again in a Contest for Foreman of the Grand Jury at an Assizes; and have heard of a Man who had so far conquered Avarice, as to give away many a Sixpence, that comforted himself, at last, on his Death-bed, by making a crafty and advantagious Bargain concerning his ensuing Funeral, with an Undertaker who had married his only Child.

In the Affair of Love, which out of strict Conformity with the Stoic Philosophy, we shall here treat as a Disease,[2] this Proneness

---

[1] Cf. *The Champion* (17 January 1739/40): 'every particular Profession seems to have laid violent Hands on, some certain Syllables which they use *ad Libitum* without conveying any Idea whatsoever.'

[2] For the stoic doctrine that the passions 'are but the diseases of Fools', see Anthony LeGrand, *Man without Passion: or, The Wise Stoick, According to the Sentiments of Seneca,*

to relapse is no less conspicuous. Thus it happened to poor *Sophia*; upon whom, the very next Time she saw young *Jones*, all the former Symptoms returned, and from that Time cold and hot Fits alternately seized her Heart.

The Situation of this young Lady was now very different from what it had ever been before. That Passion, which had formerly been so exquisitely delicious, became now a Scorpion in her Bosom. She resisted it therefore with her utmost Force, and summoned every Argument her Reason (which was surprizingly strong for her Age) could suggest, to subdue and expel it. In this she so far succeeded, that she began to hope from Time and Absence a perfect Cure. She resolved therefore to avoid *Tom Jones*, as much as possible; for which Purpose she began to conceive a Design of visiting her Aunt, to which she made no Doubt of obtaining her Father's Consent.

But Fortune, who had other Designs in her Head, put an immediate Stop to any such Proceeding, by introducing an Accident, which will be related in the next Chapter.

## CHAPTER XIII

*A dreadful Accident which befel* Sophia. *The gallant Behaviour of* Jones, *and the more dreadful Consequence of that Behaviour to the young Lady; with a short Digression in Favour of the Female Sex.*

MR. *Western* grew every Day fonder and fonder of *Sophia*, insomuch that his beloved Dogs themselves almost gave Place to her in his Affections; but as he could not prevail on himself to abandon these, he contrived very cunningly to enjoy their Company, together with that of his Daughter, by insisting on her riding a hunting with him.

*Sophia*, to whom her Father's Word was a Law, readily complied with his Desires, though she had not the least Delight in a Sport, which was of too rough and masculine a Nature to suit with her Disposition. She had, however, another Motive, beside

---

trans. G. R. (1675). LeGrand is especially severe with those 'lascivious *Poets*' who refuse to 'learn from Reason that that Love whose frequent Victories you proclaim is but the destemper [*sic*] of Mad-men' (p. 135).

her Obedience, to accompany the old Gentleman in the Chace; for by her Presence she hoped in some Measure to restrain his Impetuosity, and to prevent him from so frequently exposing his Neck to the utmost Hazard.

The strongest Objection was that which would have formerly been an Inducement to her, namely, the frequent Meeting with young *Jones*, whom she had determined to avoid; but as the End of the hunting Season now approached, she hoped, by a short Absence with her Aunt, to reason herself entirely out of her unfortunate Passion; and had not any Doubt of being able to meet him in the Field the subsequent Season without the least Danger.

On the second Day of her Hunting, as she was returning from the Chace, and was arrived within a little Distance from Mr. *Western's* House, her Horse, whose mettlesome Spirit required a better Rider, fell suddenly to prancing and capering, in such a Manner, that she was in the most eminent Peril of falling. *Tom Jones*, who was at a little Distance behind, saw this, and immediately galloped up to her Assistance. As soon as he came up, he leapt from his own Horse, and caught hold of her's by the Bridle. The unruly Beast presently reared himself an End on his hind Legs, and threw his lovely Burthen from his Back, and *Jones* caught her in his Arms.

She was so affected with the Fright, that she was not immediately able to satisfy *Jones*, who was very sollicitous to know whether she had received any Hurt. She soon after, however, recovered her Spirits, assured him she was safe, and thanked him for the Care he had taken of her. *Jones* answered, 'If I have preserved you, Madam, I am sufficiently repaid; for I promise you, I would have secured you from the least Harm, at the Expence of a much greater Misfortune to myself, than I have suffered on this Occasion.'

'What Misfortune,' replied *Sophia*, eagerly, 'I hope you have come to no Mischief?'

'Be not concerned, Madam,' answered *Jones*, 'Heaven be praised, you have escaped so well, considering the Danger you was in. If I have broke my Arm, I consider it as a Trifle, in Comparison of what I feared upon your Account.'

*Sophia* then screamed out, 'Broke your Arm! Heaven forbid.'

'I am afraid I have, Madam,' says *Jones*, 'but I beg you will suffer me first to take Care of you. I have a Right-hand yet at your Service, to help you into the next Field, whence we have but a very little Walk to your Father's House.'

*Sophia* seeing his left Arm dangling by his Side, while he was using the other to lead her, no longer doubted of the Truth. She now grew much paler than her Fears for herself had made her before. All her Limbs were seized with a Trembling, insomuch that *Jones* could scarce support her; and as her Thoughts were in no less Agitation, she could not refrain from giving *Jones* a Look so full of Tenderness, that it almost argued a stronger Sensation in her Mind, than even Gratitude and Pity united can raise in the gentlest female Bosom, without the Assistance of a third more powerful Passion.

Mr. *Western*, who was advanced at some Distance when this Accident happened, was now returned, as were the rest of the Horsemen. *Sophia* immediately acquainted them with what had befallen *Jones*, and begged them to take Care of him. Upon which, *Western*, who had been much alarmed by meeting his Daughter's Horse without its Rider, and was now overjoyed to find her unhurt, cried out, 'I am glad it is no worse; if *Tom* hath broken his Arm, we will get a Joiner to mend un again.'

The Squire alighted from his Horse, and proceeded to his House on foot, with his Daughter and *Jones*. An impartial Spectator, who had met them on the Way, would, on viewing their several Countenances, have concluded *Sophia* alone to have been the Object of Compassion: For as to *Jones*, he exulted in having probably saved the Life of the young Lady, at the Price only of a broken Bone; and Mr. *Western*, though he was not unconcerned at the Accident which had befallen *Jones*, was, however, delighted in a much higher Degree with the fortunate Escape of his Daughter.

The Generosity of *Sophia's* Temper construed this Behaviour of *Jones* into great Bravery; and it made a deep Impression on her Heart: For certain it is, that there is no one Quality which so generally recommends Men to Women as this; proceeding, if we believe the common Opinion, from that natural Timidity of the Sex; which is, says Mr. *Osborne*,[1] so great, that a Woman is

---

[1] Francis Osborne (1592–1659) was something of a misogynist. Though the words Fielding attributes to him do not occur in Osborne's works, the sentiment may be illustrated from his most popular book, *Advice to a Son* (1656–8), wherein he remarks as follows on the folly of affecting false characters: it remains, Osborne writes, '*equally rare,*

'the most cowardly of all the Creatures God ever made.' A Sentiment more remarkable for its Bluntness, than for its Truth. *Aristotle*, in his Politics,¹ doth them, I believe, more Justice, when he says, 'The Modesty and Fortitude of Men differ from those Virtues in Women; for the Fortitude which becomes a Woman, would be Cowardice in a Man; and the Modesty which becomes a Man, would be Pertness in a Woman.' Nor is there, perhaps, more of Truth in the Opinion of those who derive the Partiality which Women are inclined to shew to the Brave, from this Excess of their Fear. Mr. *Bayle*² (I think, in his Article of *Helen*) imputes this, and with greater Probability, to their violent Love of Glory; for the Truth of which, we have the Authority of him, who, of all others, saw farthest into human Nature; and who introduces the Heroine of his Odyssey,³ the great Pattern of matrimonial Love and Constancy, assigning the Glory of her Husband as the only Source of her Affection towards him.*

However this be, certain it is that the Accident operated very strongly on *Sophia*; and, indeed, after much Enquiry into the Matter, I am inclined to believe, that at this very Time, the

---

* The *English* Reader will not find this in the Poem: For the Sentiment is entirely left out in the Translation.

---

to find a *starched and Complemental Man wise*, as *a woman Valiant*: the most serious *Endeavours* of them both being to *captivate the ignorant Beholders*. And though this may pass but for a *blemish* in *Youth*, it becomes an *Ugly deformity* in *Age*: *asserting* their *Opinion* who have formerly thought *Apes* to be of the extraction of *Cham*, or some other *By-blow* of *Human Generation*, by their too near *approaching* towards the nature of *women*' (*Works*, 8th ed. [1682], pp. 147–8).

¹ Cf. *Politics*, I. v. 8.
² Pierre Bayle (1647–1706), French rationalist philosopher and author of the influential *Dictionnaire historique et critique* (1697–1702). The observation to which Fielding alludes occurs in Bayle's article on the Duke of Guise: 'It is granted that the Ladies love courageous men, and valiant admirers; but it's not because they are brave in all respects; it is rather on account of the exalted fame that is inseparable from bravery, and which reflects an honour on the mistresses of those who have acquired so great a renown. Therefore, when Women prefer Warriors to those of a peaceable profession, and Warriors of distinguished bravery to those who are otherwise, this arises more from pride than from lewdness. They think it is more glorious to captivate a man of exalted courage than to ensnare one of a pacifick disposition' (*A General Dictionary, Historical and Critical* [1734–41], v. 643, n. *o*). Bayle then cites the story of Paris and Helen, a circumstance which may explain Fielding's mistake in locating the passage. See also *Amelia* (1751; XII. iii).
³ Cf. Penelope in the *Odyssey*, i. 343–4: 'So dear a head do I ever remember with longing, even my husband, whose fame [κλέος] is wide through Hellas and mid-Argos' (trans. A. T. Murray, Loeb Classical Library, 1919). For Pope's rendering of these lines, see his translation (1725–6), i. 437–40.

charming *Sophia* made no less Impression on the Heart of *Jones*;
to say Truth, he had for some Time become sensible of the irresistible Power of her Charms.

## CHAPTER XIV

*The Arrival of a Surgeon. His Operations, and a long Dialogue
between* Sophia *and her Maid.*

WHEN they arrived in Mr. *Western's* Hall, *Sophia*, who had
totter'd along with much Difficulty, sunk down in a
Chair; but by the Assistance of Hartshorn and Water, she was
prevented from fainting away, and had pretty well recovered her
Spirits, when the Surgeon, who was sent for to *Jones*, appeared.
Mr. *Western*, who imputed these Symptoms in his Daughter to
her Fall, advised her to be presently blooded by way of Preven-
tion. In this Opinion he was seconded by the Surgeon, who gave
so many Reasons for bleeding, and quoted so many Cases where
Persons had miscarried for want of it, that the Squire became very
importunate, and indeed insisted peremptorily that his Daughter
should be blooded.

*Sophia* soon yielded to the Commands of her Father, though
entirely contrary to her own Inclinations: For she suspected, I
believe, less Danger from the Fright, than either the Squire or
the Surgeon. She then stretched out her beautiful Arm, and the
Operator began to prepare for his Work.

While the Servants were busied in providing Materials; the
Surgeon, who imputed the Backwardness which had appeared in
*Sophia* to her Fears, began to comfort her with Assurances that
there was not the least Danger; for no Accident, he said, could
ever happen in Bleeding, but from the monstrous Ignorance of
Pretenders to Surgery, which he pretty plainly insinuated was not
at present to be apprehended. *Sophia* declared she was not under
the least Apprehension; adding, 'if you open an Artery, I
promise you I'll forgive you.' 'Will you,' cries *Western*, 'D—n
me, if I will; if he does thee the least Mischief, d—n me, if I
don't ha' the Heart's Blood o'un out.' The Surgeon assented to
bleed her upon these Conditions, and then proceeded to his
Operation, which he performed with as much Dexterity as he had

promised; and with as much Quickness: For he took but little Blood from her, saying, it was much safer to bleed again and again, than to take away too much at once.

*Sophia,* when her Arm was bound up, retired: For she was not willing (nor was it, perhaps, strictly decent) to be present at the Operation on *Jones.* Indeed one Objection which she had to Bleeding, (tho' she did not make it) was the Delay which it would occasion to setting the broken Bone. For *Western,* when *Sophia* was concerned, had no Consideration, but for her; and as for *Jones* himself, he 'sat like Patience on a Monument smiling at Grief'.[1] To say the Truth, when he saw the Blood springing from the lovely Arm of *Sophia,* he scarce thought of what had happened to himself.

The Surgeon now ordered his Patient to be stript to his Shirt, and then entirely baring the Arm, he began to stretch and examine it, in such a Manner, that the Tortures he put him to, caused *Jones* to make several wry Faces; which the Surgeon observing, greatly wondered at, crying, 'What is the Matter, Sir? I am sure it is impossible I should hurt you.' And then holding forth the broken Arm, he began a long and very learned Lecture of Anatomy, in which simple and double Fractures were most accurately considered, and the several Ways in which *Jones* might have broken his Arm were discussed, with proper Annotations, shewing how many of these would have been better, and how many worse than the present Case.

Having at length finish'd his laboured Harangue, with which the Audience, tho' it had greatly raised their Attention and Admiration, were not much edified, as they really understood not a single Syllable of all he had said, he proceeded to Business, which he was more expeditious in finishing, than he had been in beginning.

*Jones* was then ordered into a Bed, which Mr. *Western* compelled him to accept at his own House, and Sentence of Water-Gruel was passed upon him.

Among the good Company which had attended in the Hall during the Bone-setting, Mrs. *Honour* was one; who being summoned to her Mistress as soon as it was over, and asked by her how the young Gentleman did, presently launched into extravagant Praises on the *Magnimity,* as she called it, of his Behaviour,

---

[1] *Twelfth Night,* II. iv—Viola describing to the Duke her 'sister's' silent love.

which, she said, 'was so charming in so pretty a Creature.' She then burst forth into much warmer Encomiums on the Beauty of his Person; enumerating many Particulars, and ending with the Whiteness of his Skin.

This Discourse had an Effect on *Sophia's* Countenance, which would not perhaps have escaped the Observance of the sagacious Waiting-woman, had she once looked her Mistress in the Face, all the Time she was speaking; but as a Looking-glass, which was most commodiously placed opposite to her, gave her an Opportunity of surveying those Features, in which, of all others, she took most Delight, so she had not once removed her Eyes from that amiable Object during her whole Speech.

Mrs. *Honour* was so entirely wrapped up in the Subject on which she exercised her Tongue, and the Object before her Eyes, that she gave her Mistress Time to conquer her Confusion; which having done, she smiled on her Maid, and told her, 'She was certainly in Love with this young Fellow.' 'I in Love, Madam!' answers she, 'upon my Word, Ma'am, I assure you, Ma'am, upon my Soul, Ma'am, I am not.' 'Why if you was,' cries her Mistress, 'I see no Reason that you should be ashamed of it; for he is certainly a pretty Fellow.'—'Yes, Ma'am,' answered the other, 'That he is, the most handsomest Man I ever saw in my Life. Yes, to be sure, that he is, and, as your Ladyship says, I don't know why I should be ashamed of loving him, though he is my Betters. To be sure gentle Folks are but Flesh and Blood no more than us Servants. Besides, as for Mr. *Jones*, thof Squire *Allworthy* hath made a Gentleman of him, he was not so good as myself by Birth: For thof I am a poor Body, I am an honest Person's Child, and my Father and Mother were married, which is more than some People can say, as high as they hold their Heads. Marry, come up! I assure you, my dirty Cousin! thof his Skin be so white, and to be sure, it is the most whitest that ever was seen, I am a Christian as well as he, and no-body can say that I am base born, my grand-father was a Clergyman,* and

---

* This is the second Person of low Condition whom we have recorded in this History, to have sprung from the Clergy. It is to be hoped such Instances will, in future Ages, when some Provision is made for the Families of the inferior Clergy, appear stranger than they can be thought at present.[1]

---

[1] From the time of *The Champion* (29 March, 5, 12, 19 April 1740) Fielding endeavoured in his writings to improve the condition of the inferior clergy and to remove from them and

would have been very angry, I believe, to have thought any of his Family should have taken up with *Molly Seagrim's* dirty Leavings.'

Perhaps *Sophia* might have suffered her Maid to run on in this Manner, from wanting sufficient Spirits to stop her Tongue, which the Reader may probably conjecture was no very easy Task: For, certainly there were some Passages in her Speech, which were far from being agreeable to the Lady. However, she now checked the Torrent, as there seemed no End of its Flowing. 'I wonder,' says she, 'at your Assurance in daring to talk thus of one of my Father's Friends. As to the Wench, I order you never to mention her Name to me. And, with Regard to the young Gentleman's Birth, those who can say nothing more to his Disadvantage, may as well be silent on that Head, as I desire you will be for the future.'

'I am sorry, I have offended your Ladyship,' answered Mrs. *Honour*, 'I am sure I hate *Molly Seagrim* as much as your Ladyship can, and as for abusing Squire *Jones*, I can call all the Servants in the House to witness, that whenever any Talk hath been about Bastards, I have always taken his Part: 'For which of you,' says I to the Footmen, 'would not be a Bastard, if he could, to be made a Gentleman of? and,' says I, 'I am sure he is a very fine Gentleman; and he hath one of the whitest Hands in the World:' For to be sure so he hath; 'and' says I, 'one of the sweetest temperedest, best naturedest Men in the World he is, and' says I, 'all the Servants and Neighbours all round the Country loves him.' And, to be sure, I could tell your Ladyship something, but that I am afraid it would offend you.'—'What could you tell me, *Honour?*' says *Sophia*. 'Nay, Ma'am, to be sure he meant nothing by it, therefore I would not have your Ladyship be offended.' —'Prithee tell me,' says *Sophia*,—'I will know it this Instant.' 'Why, Ma'am,' answered Mrs. *Honour*, 'he came into the Room, one Day last Week when I was at Work, and there lay your Ladyship's Muff on a Chair, and to be sure he put his Hands into it, that very Muff your Ladyship gave me but yesterday; 'La,' says I, 'Mr. *Jones*, you will stretch my Lady's Muff and

their families that 'contempt' which they suffered in large part because of their poverty. (See Battestin, *The Moral Basis of Fielding's Art*, ch. vii.) In 1748 he devoted several numbers of *The Jacobite's Journal* (23 April, 18, 25 June, 2, 9 July 1748) to urging the establishment 'of a charitable Provision for the Widows and Children of the poor Clergy', who, he declared, 'are, of all others, most the Objects of Compassion'. See also *The Covent-Garden Journal* (6 June 1752).

spoil it;' but he still kept his Hands in it, and then he kissed it—
to be sure, I hardly ever saw such a Kiss in my Life as he gave it.'
—'I suppose he did not know it was mine,' reply'd *Sophia*.
'Your Ladyship shall hear, Ma'am. He kissed it again and again,
and said it was the prettiest Muff in the World. 'La! Sir,' says I,
'you have seen it a hundred Times.'—'Yes, Mrs. *Honour*,' cry'd
he; 'but who can see any thing beautiful in the Presence of your
Lady but herself:' Nay, that's not all neither, but I hope your
Ladyship won't be offended, for to be sure he meant nothing:
One Day as your Ladyship was playing on the Harpsicord to my
Master, Mr. *Jones* was sitting in the next Room, and methought
he looked melancholy. 'La!' says I, 'Mr. *Jones*, what's the Matter?
A Penny for your Thoughts,' says I; 'Why, Hussy,' says he,
starting up from a Dream, 'what can I be thinking of when that
Angel your Mistress is playing?' And then squeezing me by the
Hand—'Oh! Mrs. *Honour*,' says he, 'how happy will that Man
be!'—and then he sighed; upon my Troth, his Breath is as sweet
as a Nosegay—but to be sure he meant no Harm by it. So I
hope your Ladyship will not mention a Word: For he gave me a
Crown never to mention it, and made me swear upon a Book, but
I believe, indeed, it was not the Bible.'

Till something of a more beautiful Red than Vermilion be
found out, I shall say nothing of *Sophia's* Colour on this Occasion. '*Ho—nour*,' says she, 'I—if you will not mention this any
more to me,—nor to any Body else, I will not betray you—I
mean I will not be angry; but I am afraid of your Tongue. Why,
my Girl, will you give it such Liberties?' 'Nay, Ma'am,' answered
she, 'to be sure, I would sooner cut out my Tongue than offend
your Ladyship—to be sure, I shall never mention a Word that
your Ladyship would not have me.'—'Why I would not have
you mention this any more,' said *Sophia*, 'for it may come to my
Father's Ears, and he would be angry with Mr. *Jones*, tho' I
really believe, as you say, he meant nothing. I should be very
angry myself if I imagined——' 'Nay, Ma'am,' says *Honour*,
'I protest I believe he meant nothing. I thought he talked as if
he was out of his Senses; nay, he said he believed he was beside
himself when he had spoken the Words. 'Ay, Sir,' says I, 'I
believe so too.' 'Yes,' says he, '*Honour*,—' but I ask your Ladyship's Pardon; I could tear my Tongue out for offending you.'
'Go on,' says *Sophia*, 'you may mention any thing you have not

told me before.' 'Yes, *Honour*,' says he, (this was some time afterwards when he gave me the Crown) 'I am neither such a Coxcomb, or such a Villain as to think of her, in any other *Delight*,
but as my Goddess; as such I will always worship and adore her
while I have Breath.' This was all, Ma'am, I will be sworn, to the
best of my Remembrance; I was in a Passion with him, myself,
till I found he meant no Harm.' 'Indeed, *Honour*,' says *Sophia*,
'I believe you have a real Affection for me; I was provoked the
other Day when I gave you Warning; but if you have a Desire
to stay with me, you shall.' 'To be sure, Ma'am,' answered Mrs.
*Honour*, 'I shall never desire to part with your Ladyship. To be
sure, I almost cried my Eyes out when you gave me Warning.
It would be very ungrateful in me, to desire to leave your Ladyship; because as why, I should never get so good a Place again. I
am sure I would live and die with your Ladyship—for, as poor
Mr. *Jones* said, happy is the Man——'

Here the Dinner-bell interrupted a Conversation which had
wrought such an Effect on *Sophia*, that she was, perhaps, more
obliged to her bleeding in the Morning, than she, at the time, had
apprehended she should be. As to the present Situation of her
Mind, I shall adhere to a Rule of *Horace*,[1] by not attempting to
describe it, from Despair of Success. Most of my Readers will
suggest it easily to themselves, and the few who cannot, would
not understand the Picture, or at least would deny it to be natural,
if ever so well drawn.

---

[1] *Ars Poetica*, 149–50: 'et quae / desperat tractata nitescere posse, relinquit' ('and what he
fears he cannot make attractive with his touch he abandons'—trans. H. R. Fairclough,
Loeb Classical Library, 1929).

# BOOK V

*Containing a Portion of Time, somewhat longer than Half a Year.*

## CHAPTER I

*Of* The SERIOUS *in writing; and for what Purpose it is introduced.*

PERADVENTURE there may be no Parts in this prodigious Work which will give the Reader less Pleasure in the perusing, than those which have given the Author the greatest Pains in composing. Among these probably may be reckoned those initial Essays which we have prefixed to the historical Matter contained in every Book; and which we have determined to be essentially necessary to this kind of Writing, of which we have set ourselves at the Head.

For this our Determination we do not hold ourselves strictly bound to assign any Reason; it being abundantly sufficient that we have laid it down as a Rule necessary to be observed in all Prosai-comi-epic Writing. Who ever demanded the Reasons of that nice Unity of Time or Place[1] which is now established to be

[1] By the middle decades of the seventeenth century, the French critics, following certain hints in Aristotle and his Italian commentators, had established the doctrine of the dramatic unities as an essential article of neoclassical orthodoxy. To Aristotle's insistence upon the unity of dramatic action, the French added the unities of time and place. In order to achieve a heightened sense of verisimilitude in the drama, they required a close correspondence between dramatic time and place and the actual circumstances of representation in the theatre; the action of the play was to be narrowly limited to one specific locale and to a single day in the hero's life. Though formulated earlier by Richelieu and the French Academy, this rigidly mechanistic theory of dramatic imitation was firmly established by Boileau (*Art poétique*, 1674) and by such other influential critics as René Rapin (*Réflexions sur la poétique et les poètes*, 1674), Père Bossu (*Traité du poème épique*, 1675), and André Dacier (trans. Aristotle's *Poetics*, 1692).

In England the arguments of Crites and Lisideus in Dryden's *Essay of Dramatic Poesy* (1666) gave currency to these ideas, which were approved and rigorously applied to the drama by such critics as Thomas Rymer (*The Tragedies of the Last Age, Considered and Examined*, 1678), the Earl of Mulgrave (*An Essay upon Poetry*, 1682), Jeremy Collier (*A Short View of the Immorality and Prophaneness of the English Stage*, 1698), Charles Gildon (*Complete Art of Poetry*, 1718), John Dennis (*The Characters and Conduct of Sir John Edgar*, 1720), and Joseph Trapp (*Lectures on Poetry*, 1742). Although the theory was not effectively so essential to dramatick Poetry? What Critick hath been ever asked why a Play may not contain two Days as well as one, or why the Audience (provided they travel like Electors, without any Expence) may not be wafted Fifty Miles as well as five! Hath any Commentator well accounted for the Limitation which an ancient Critic[1] hath set to the Drama, which he will have contain neither more nor less than five Acts; or hath any one living attempted to explain, what the modern Judges of our Theatres mean by that Word *low*; by which they have happily succeeded in banishing all Humour from the Stage,[2] and have made the Theatre as dull as a Drawing-Room? Upon all these Occasions, the World seems to have embraced a Maxim of our Law, viz. *Cuicunque in Arte sua perito credendum est*:[3] For it seems, perhaps, difficult to conceive that any one should have had enough of Impudence, to lay down dogmatical Rules in any Art or Science without the least Foundation. In such Cases, therefore, we are apt to conclude there are sound and good Reasons at the Bottom, tho' we are unfortunately not able to see so far.

Now, in Reality, the World have paid too great a Compliment to Critics, and have imagined them Men of much greater Profundity than they really are. From this Complaisance, the Critics have been emboldened to assume a Dictatorial Power, and have so far succeeded that they are now become the Masters, and have the Assurance to give Laws to those Authors, from whose Predecessors they originally received them.

exploded until Johnson's famous attack in the *Preface to Shakespeare* (1765), others besides Fielding had repudiated it much earlier. After Collier had condemned *The Relapse* for violating the unities of time and place—the action taking up most of a week and the setting being 'stroll'd Fifty Miles off' from London, where the play began—Farquhar rose to the defence in *A Discourse upon Comedy in Reference to the English Stage* (1702). Others who anticipated Fielding's liberal views include Sir Robert Howard (Prefaces to *Four New Plays* [1665] and *The Great Favourite* [1668]), Dryden (the arguments of Eugenius and Neander in *An Essay of Dramatic Poesy*, 1666), Leonard Welsted (*Dissertation concerning the Perfection of the English Language, the State of Poetry. &c.*, 1724).

[1] Horace, *Ars Poetica*, 189. Though he may not have 'well accounted' for Horace's rule, the Earl of Roscommon offered the following explanation in a footnote to his translation: 'Plays of three Acts have the Defect which *Aristotle* finds in little Objects. The Sight is confounded, and they are either naked of, or loaded with Incidents. Plays of six or seven *Acts* would have the Defect of great Objects. The Spectators would lose the Idea of the whole, on Account of its excessive Bigness, wherefore the just Medium lies in the five *Acts*' (*Horace's Treatise Concerning the Art of Poetry* [Dublin, 1733], pp. 68–70).

[2] See below, p. 638, n. 1.

[3] 'Whoever is skilled in his profession should be believed' (cf. *Coke upon Littleton*, 125a).

The Critic, rightly considered, is no more than the Clerk, whose Office it is to transcribe the Rules and Laws laid down by those great Judges, whose vast Strength of Genius hath placed them in the Light of Legislators in the several Sciences over which they presided. This Office was all which the Critics of old aspired to, nor did they ever dare to advance a Sentence, without supporting it by the Authority of the Judge from whence it was borrowed.

But in Process of Time, and in Ages of Ignorance, the Clerk began to invade the Power and assume the Dignity of his Master. The Laws of Writing were no longer founded on the Practice of the Author, but on the Dictates of the Critic. The Clerk became the Legislator, and those very peremptorily gave Laws, whose Business it was, at first, only to transcribe them.

Hence arose an obvious, and, perhaps, an unavoidable Error: For these Critics being Men of shallow Capacities, very easily mistook mere Form for Substance. They acted as a Judge would, who should adhere to the lifeless Letter of Law, and reject the Spirit. Little Circumstances which were, perhaps, accidental in a great Author, were, by these Critics, considered to constitute his chief Merit, and transmitted as Essentials to be observed by all his Successors. To these Encroachments, Time and Ignorance, the two great Supporters of Imposture, gave Authority; and thus, many Rules for good Writing have been established, which have not the least Foundation in Truth or Nature; and which commonly serve for no other Purpose than to curb and restrain Genius, in the same Manner, as it would have restrained the Dancing-master, had the many excellent Treatises on that Art,[1] laid it down as an essential Rule, that every Man must dance in Chains.

To avoid, therefore, all Imputation of laying down a Rule for Posterity, founded only on the Authority of *ipse dixit*; for which,

[1] Fielding's analogy may have been inspired by Pope's famous lines in the *Essay on Criticism* (1711), 362–3: 'True Ease in Writing comes from Art, not Chance, / As those move easiest who have learn'd to Dance.' (See also below, p. 740, n. 1.) From the time of Queen Anne, several dancing-masters published treatises disclosing the mysteries of this necessary social art. Among these were essays, based on the French of Rameau and Feuillet, by Messrs. Isaac, Siris, Pemberton, Weaver, and Tomlinson. For Fielding, however, the dancing-master *par excellence* was John Essex (see below, p. 741, n. 1), author of *A Treatis of Chorography* (1710) and *The Dancing-Master: or, The Whole Art and Mystery of Dancing Explained* (2nd ed., 1731).

to say the Truth, we have not the profoundest Veneration; we shall here wave the Privilege above contended for, and proceed to lay before the Reader, the Reasons which have induced us, to intersperse these several digressive Essays, in the Course of this Work.

And here we shall of Necessity be led to open a new Vein of Knowledge, which, if it hath been discovered, hath not, to our Remembrance, been wrought on by any antient or modern Writer. This Vein is no other than that of Contrast,¹ which runs through all the Works of the Creation, and may probably have a large Share in constituting in us the Idea of all Beauty, as well natural as artificial: For what demonstrates the Beauty and Excellence of any thing, but its Reverse? Thus the Beauty of Day, and that of Summer, is set off by the Horrors of Night and Winter. And I believe, if it was possible for a Man to have seen only the two former, he would have a very imperfect Idea of their Beauty.

But to avoid too serious an Air: Can it be doubted, but that the finest Woman in the World would lose all Benefit of her Charms, in the Eye of a Man who had never seen one of another Cast? The Ladies themselves seem so sensible of this, that they are all industrious to procure Foils; nay, they will become Foils to themselves; for I have observed, (at *Bath* particularly) that they endeavour to appear as ugly as possible in the Morning, in order to set off that Beauty which they intend to shew you in the Evening.

¹ Far from opening a 'new Vein of Knowledge', Fielding here merely applies an old and quite familiar aesthetic principle to his own theory of prose fiction. Related ultimately to the classical notion of *concordia discors*, of cosmic harmony resulting from the reconciliation of opposite elements, the important role that variety and contrast play in the creation of beauty, both in nature and in art, had long been recognized by philosophers and aestheticians. (For thorough documentation of this point, see H. V. S. Ogden, 'The Principles of Variety and Contrast in Seventeenth Century Aesthetics, and Milton's Poetry', *JHI*, x [1949], 159–82. On the background of *concordia discors*, see Leo Spitzer, *Classical and Christian Ideas of World Harmony* [Baltimore, Md., 1963].) The 'World's Beauty', observed Shaftesbury, is 'founded thus *on Contrarietys*' ('The Moralists', I. iii; *Characteristicks*, 5th ed. [1732], ii. 214). And the same point was made more than a century earlier by Richard Ashley, who anticipated Fielding's own illustrations: 'we may say in all cases, that contraries when they are put neere one to the other, they appeare the more cleerly: Even as want maketh riches to be the more esteemed; and the obscuritie of darkenesse commendeth the cleernesse of light: The sweetnesse of the Springtime is more esteemed by the sharpnesse of Winter: the happinesse of peace, by the calamaties of warre; and faire weather after long rayne' (trans. of Louis LeRoy, *Of the Interchangeable Course or Variety of Things in the Whole World* [1594], fol. 6ʳ; quoted in Ogden, op. cit., p. 168).

Most Artists have this Secret in Practice, tho' some, perhaps, have not much studied the Theory. The Jeweller knows that the finest Brilliant requires a Foil; and the Painter, by the Contrast of his Figures, often acquires great Applause.

A great Genius among us, will illustrate this Matter fully. I cannot, indeed, range him under any general Head of common Artists, as he hath a Title to be placed among those

*Inventas, qui vitam excoluere per Artes.*[1]

Who by invented Arts have Life improv'd.

I mean here the Inventor of that most exquisite Entertainment, called the *English* Pantomime.[2]

This Entertainment consisted of two Parts, which the Inventor distinguished by the Names of *the Serious* and *the Comic*. The *Serious* exhibited a certain Number of Heathen Gods and Heroes, who were certainly the worst and dullest Company into which an Audience was ever introduced; and (which was a Secret

---

[1] *Aeneid*, vi. 663.

[2] John Rich (1682 ?–1761), from 1732 manager of the Covent-Garden Theatre. Rich was chiefly responsible for the great popularity of pantomimes and 'entertainments', in which he performed the part of Harlequin, astonishing audiences with spectacular tricks and stage effects. Thomas Davies provides an illuminating gloss on the present passage: 'Rich created a species of dramatic composition unknown to this, and, I believe, to any other country, which he called a pantomime. It consisted of two parts; one serious, and the other comic: by the help of gay scenes, fine habits, grand dances, appropriated music, and other decorations, he exhibited a story from Ovid's Metamorphosis, or some other fabulous history. Between the pauses or acts of this serious representation he interwove a comic fable consisting chiefly of the courtship of Harlequin and Columbine, with a variety of surprising adventures and tricks, which were produced by the magic wand of Harlequin; such as the sudden transformation of palaces and temples to huts and cottages; of men and women into wheel-barrows and joint-stools; of trees turned to houses; colonades to beds of tulips; and mechanics shops into serpents and ostriches' (*Memoirs of the Life of David Garrick, Esq.* [1780], i. 92). In Fielding's *Tumble-Down Dick* (1736) Rich is brought on stage as Mr. Machine, declaring the 'serious Nature' of his Ovidian entertainment: 'This', he assures the doubtful Fustian, 'has been the Serious, Sir.—the Sublime. The Serious in an Entertainment, answers to the Sublime in Writing.' Rich persisted in his strategy of using 'the Serious' to heighten 'the Comic' part of his entertainments despite criticism from those who agreed with Fielding that the change effected was only in degrees of dullness: 'the friggling Tricks of Mr. *Merryman*, the Harlequin, have too much of the Sameness; and the grave poetic Part does well enough—to cloy, but not to invite'—such was the judgement of the anonymous author of *A Letter to a Certain Patentee* [1747], p. 9. Dullness, as Pope had shown in *The Dunciad* (iii. 252–64), was indeed the essential characteristic of Rich's pantomimes. For other references to Rich in Fielding's writings, see *Pasquin* (1736), v, *The Champion* (22 April, 3, 24 May 1740), *Joseph Andrews* (1742; I. vii), and *The Covent-Garden Journal* (11 January, 18 November 1752). See also below, p. 666, n. 1.

known to few) were actually intended so to be, in order to contrast the *Comic* Part of the Entertainment, and to display the
Tricks of Harlequin to the better Advantage.

This was, perhaps, no very civil Use of such Personages; but
the Contrivance was nevertheless ingenious enough, and had its
Effect. And this will now plainly appear, if instead of *Serious* and
*Comic*, we supply the Words *Duller* and *Dullest*; for the *Comic*
was certainly duller than any thing before shewn on the Stage,
and could be set off only by that superlative Degree of Dulness,
which composed the *Serious*. So intolerably serious, indeed,
were these Gods and Heroes, that Harlequin (tho' the *English*
Gentleman of that Name is not at all related to the *French* Family,
for he is of a much more serious Disposition)[1] was always welcome
on the Stage, as he relieved the Audience from worse Company.

Judicious Writers have always practised this Art of Contrast,
with great Success. I have been surprized that *Horace* should
cavil at this Art in *Homer*; but indeed he contradicts himself in
the very next Line.

> *Indignor quandoque bonus dormitat* Homerus,
> *Verum Opere in longo fas est obrepere Somnum.*[2]

> I grieve if e'er great *Homer* chance to sleep,
> Yet Slumbers on long Works have right to creep.

For we are not here to understand, as, perhaps, some have, that
an Author actually falls asleep while he is writing. It is true that
Readers are too apt to be so overtaken; but if the Work was as
long as any of *Oldmixon*,[3] the Author himself is too well enter-

---

[1] Cf. Davies's observation that Rich's 'harlequinade' was 'very different from that
which is seen at the opera comique in Paris, where harlequin and all the characters speak,
and a kind of droll farce, full of ridiculous incidents, and certain bon mots, called naivetès,
keep the audience in continual laughter' (op. cit., i. 91).

[2] *Ars Poetica*, 359–60. Even in the eighteenth century Fielding's reading 'opere in
longo' was considered less correct, and less 'elegant', than 'operi longo'. (See Philip Francis,
trans. *The Works of Horace*, 2nd ed. [1747], iv. 254–5.) The verse translation appears to be
Fielding's own.

[3] John Oldmixon (1673–1742), commemorated for his dullness in *The Dunciad* (A, ii.
199–202; B, ii. 283–90), had an unhappy reputation as a 'laborious' poet, an injudicious
critic, and a 'virulent Party-writer for hire'. Written from a Whig bias, his voluminous
histories include *The Secret History of Europe* (1712–15), the *Critical History of England*
(1724–6), and *The History of England* from the time of the Stuarts until the reign of George
I (1729–35). Fielding apparently regarded him as the very type of the tedious, long-winded
hackney author: see *Ovid's Art of Love Paraphrased* (1747) and *The Covent-Garden*

tained to be subject to the least Drowsiness. He is, as Mr. *Pope* observes,

> *Sleepless himself to give his Readers Sleep.*[1]

To say the Truth, these soporific Parts are so many Scenes of *Serious* artfully interwoven, in order to contrast and set off the rest; and this is the true Meaning of a late facetious Writer,[2] who told the Public, that whenever he was dull, they might be assured there was a Design in it.

In this Light then, or rather in this Darkness, I would have the Reader to consider these initial Essays. And after this Warning, if he shall be of Opinion, that he can find enough of Serious in other Parts of this History, he may pass over these, in which we profess to be laboriously dull, and begin the following Books, at the second Chapter.

## CHAPTER II

*In which Mr.* Jones *receives many friendly Visits during his Confinement; with some fine Touches of the Passion of Love, scarce visible to the naked Eye.*

*T*OM *JONES* had many Visitors during his Confinement, tho' some, perhaps, were not very agreeable to him. Mr. *Allworthy* saw him almost every Day; but tho' he pitied *Tom's* Sufferings, and greatly approved the gallant Behaviour which had occasioned them, yet he thought this was a favourable Opportunity to bring him to a sober Sense of his indiscreet Conduct; and that wholsome Advice for that Purpose, could never be applied at a more proper Season than at the present; when the Mind was softened by Pain and Sickness, and alarmed by Danger; and when its Attention was unembarrassed with those turbulent Passions, which engage us in the Pursuit of Pleasure.

*Journal* (11 January 1752); see also the parody of Oldmixon's histories in that journal (29 February 1752).

  [1] *The Dunciad* (A), i. 92: 'While pensive Poets painful vigils keep, / Sleepless themselves, to give their readers sleep.'

  [2] Sir Richard Steele (1672–1729) in *The Tatler*, No. 38 (7 July 1709): '*It is to be noted, That when any Part of this Paper appears dull, there is a Design in it*' (1728 ed.). Fielding, who acknowledged Steele as his model in the art of the periodical essay, was particularly fond of this passage: see *The Champion* (22 May 1740), *The Jacobite's Journal* (2 July 1748), and *The Covent-Garden Journal* (4 January 1752).

At all Seasons, therefore, when the good Man was alone with the Youth, especially when the latter was totally at Ease, he took Occasion to remind him of his former Miscarriages, but in the mildest and tenderest Manner, and only in order to introduce the Caution, which he prescribed for his future Behaviour; 'on which alone' he assured him, 'would depend his own Felicity, and the Kindness which he might yet promise himself to receive at the Hands of his Father by Adoption unless he should hereafter forfeit his Good Opinion: For as to what had past,' he said, 'it should be all forgiven and forgotten.' He, therefore, advised him 'to make a good Use of this Accident, that so in the End it might prove a Visitation for his own Good.'

*Thwackum* was likewise pretty assiduous in his Visits; and he too considered a sick Bed to be a convenient Scene for Lectures. His Stile, however, was more severe than Mr. *Allworthy's*: He told his Pupil, 'that he ought to look on his broken Limb as a Judgment from Heaven on his Sins. That it would become him to be daily on his Knees, pouring forth Thanksgivings that he had broken his Arm only, and not his Neck; which latter,' he said, 'was very probably reserved for some future Occasion, and that perhaps, not very remote. For his Part,' he said, 'he had often wondered some Judgment had not overtaken him before; but it might be perceived by this, that divine Punishments, tho' slow, are always sure.' Hence likewise he advised him 'to foresee, with equal Certainty, the greater Evils which were yet behind, and which were as sure as this, of overtaking him in his State of Reprobacy. These are,' said he, 'to be averted only by such a thorough and sincere Repentance, as is not to be expected or hoped for, from one so abandoned in his Youth, and whose Mind, I am afraid, is totally corrupted. It is my Duty, however, to exhort you to this Repentance, tho' I too well know all Exhortations will be vain and fruitless. But *liberavi Animam meam*.[1] I can accuse my own Conscience of no Neglect; tho' it is, at the same time, with the utmost Concern, I see you travelling on to certain Misery in this World, and to as certain Damnation in the next.

*Square* talked in a very different Strain: He said, 'such Accidents as a broken Bone were below the Consideration of a wise

---

[1] 'I have delivered my soul'—a familiar formula, evidently derived from Ezekiel 3: 19. Cf. Epistle 371 of St. Bernard of Clairvaux.

Man. That it was abundantly sufficient to reconcile the Mind to any of these Mischances, to reflect that they are liable to befal the wisest of Mankind, and are undoubtedly for the Good of the whole.' He said, 'it was a mere Abuse of Words, to call those Things Evils, in which there was no moral Unfitness; that Pain, which was the worst Consequence of such Accidents, was the most contemptible thing in the World;' with more of the like Sentences, extracted out of the Second Book of *Tully's* Tusculan *Questions*,[1] and from the Great Lord *Shaftesbury*.[2] In pronouncing these he was one Day so eager, that he unfortunately bit his Tongue; and in such a Manner, that it not only put an End to his Discourse, but created much Emotion in him, and caused him to mutter an Oath or two: But what was worst of all, this Accident gave *Thwackum*, who was present, and who held all such Doctrine to be heathenish and atheistical, an Opportunity to clap a Judgment on his Back. Now this was done with so malicious a Sneer, that it totally unhinged (if I may so say) the Temper of the Philosopher, which the Bite of his Tongue had somewhat ruffled; and as he was disabled from venting his Wrath at his Lips, he had possibly found a more violent Method of revenging himself, had not the Surgeon, who was then luckily in the Room, contrary to his own Interest, interposed, and preserved the Peace.

Mr. *Blifil* visited his Friend *Jones* but seldom, and never alone. This worthy young Man, however, professed much Regard for him, and as great Concern at his Misfortune; but cautiously avoided any Intimacy, lest, as he frequently hinted, it might

[1] Cf. Cicero, *Tusculan Disputations*, II. v. 14 ff. Cicero here rejects as a mere quibble Zeno's refusal to consider pain an evil, a term the latter reserved exclusively for base and immoral acts (II. xii. 29). Yet, Cicero continues, since 'disgrace is worse than pain, pain is clearly of no account ... for either no virtue exists or all pain is to be despised' (II. xiii. 31— trans. J. E. King, Loeb Classical Library, 1927). As Fielding had remarked in his *Charge to the Jury* (1745), the contempt of pain was, of course, a fundamental tenet of the Stoic philosophers: in *Man without Passion: or, The Wise Stoick* (trans. G. R., 1675), Anthony LeGrand maintained '*That Tortures are not terrible but in opinion, and that Fools or Cowards only are affrighted at them*' (II. iii. 2). While in the stocks, Butler's Hudibras invokes this same stoic doctrine (Wilders ed., II. i. 183 ff.).

[2] Anthony Ashley Cooper (1671–1713), third Earl of Shaftesbury, whose *Characteristicks of Men, Manners, Opinions and Times* (1711) made him the most influential deist philosopher of the period. In 'An Inquiry concerning Virtue, or Merit' and 'The Moralists', Shaftesbury's constant theme is that 'there is no such thing as real ILL in the Universe, nothing ILL with respect to the Whole' (*Characteristicks*, 5th ed. [1732], ii. 9). The place of Shaftesburian ideas in Square's philosophy is discussed above, p. 124, n. See also the description of Mr. Wilson's club of '*Rule of Right-men*' in *Joseph Andrews* (1742; III. iii). For later references to Shaftesbury in *Tom Jones*, see below, pp. 398, n. 4; 736, n. 1.

contaminate the Sobriety of his own Character: For which Purpose, he had constantly in his Mouth that Proverb in which *Solomon* speaks against Evil Communication.[1] Not that he was so bitter as *Thwackum*; for he always expressed some Hopes of *Tom's* Reformation; 'which,' he said, 'the unparallelled Goodness shewn by his Uncle on this Occasion, must certainly effect, in one not absolutely abandoned;' but concluded, 'if Mr. *Jones* ever offends hereafter, I shall not be able to say a Syllable in his Favour.'

As to Squire *Western*, he was seldom out of the Sick Room; unless when he was engaged either in the Field, or over his Bottle. Nay, he would sometimes retire hither to take his Beer, and it was not without Difficulty, that he was prevented from forcing *Jones* to take his Beer too: For no Quack ever held his Nostrum to be a more general *Panacea*, than he did this; which, he said, had more Virtue in it than was in all the Physic in an Apothecary's Shop. He was, however, by much Entreaty, prevailed on to forbear the Application of this Medicine; but from serenading his Patient every Hunting Morning with the Horn under his Window, it was impossible to withhold him; nor did he ever lay aside that Hollow, with which he entered into all Companies, when he visited *Jones*, without any Regard to the sick Person's being at that Time either awake or asleep.

This boisterous Behaviour, as it meant no Harm, so happily it effected none, and was abundantly compensated to *Jones*, as soon as he was able to sit up, by the Company of *Sophia*, whom the Squire then brought to visit him; nor was it, indeed, long before *Jones* was able to attend her to the Harpsichord, where she would kindly condescend, for Hours together, to charm him with the most delicious Music, unless when the Squire thought proper to interrupt her, by insisting on *Old Sir Simon*,[2] or some other of his favourite Pieces.

Notwithstanding the nicest Guard which *Sophia* endeavoured to set on her Behaviour, she could not avoid letting some Appearances now and then slip forth: For Love may again be likened

[1] As 'Orbilius' gleefully pointed out in his *Examen* (1749; pp. 44–5) of *Tom Jones*, Fielding incorrectly identifies the source of the proverb, 'evil communications corrupt good manners', which is found in St. Paul (1 Corinthians 15: 33) and Menander (*Thais*, Fragment 2). Later, in *The Covent-Garden Journal* (4 February 1752), Fielding rectified his mistake. See also below, p. 630.

[2] See above, p. 169, n. 3.

to a Disease in this, that when it is denied a Vent in one Part, it will certainly break out in another. What her Lips therefore concealed, her Eyes, her Blushes, and many little involuntary Actions, betrayed.

One Day when *Sophia* was playing on the Harpsichord, and *Jones* was attending, the Squire came into the Room, crying, 'There, *Tom*, I have had a Battle for thee below Stairs with thick Parson *Thwackum*.—He hath been a telling *Allworthy*, before my Face, that the broken Bone was a Judgment upon thee. D—n it, says I, how can that be? Did not he come by it in Defence of a young Woman? A Judgment indeed! Pox, if he never doth any thing worse, he will go to Heaven sooner than all the Parsons in the Country. He hath more reason to glory in it, than to be ashamed of it.' 'Indeed, Sir,' says *Jones*, 'I have no Reason for either; but if it preserved Miss *Western*, I shall always think it the happiest Accident of my Life.'—'And to gu,' said the Squire, 'to zet *Allworthy* against thee vor it.—D—n un, if the Parson had unt had his Petticuoats on, I should ha lent un a Flick; for I love thee dearly, my Boy, and d—n me if there is any thing in my Power which I won't do for thee. Sha't take thy Choice of all the Horses in my Stable to-morrow Morning, except only the *Chevalier*¹ and Miss *Slouch*.' *Jones* thanked him, but declined accepting the Offer.—'Nay,' added the Squire, 'Sha't ha the sorrel Mare that *Sophy* rode. She cost me fifty Guineas, and comes six Years old this Grass.' 'If she had cost me a thousand,' cries *Jones* passionately, 'I would have given her to the Dogs.' 'Pooh! pooh!' answered *Western*, 'what because she broke thy Arm. Shouldst forget and forgive. I thought hadst been more a Man than to bear Malice against a dumb Creature.'—Here *Sophia* interposed, and put an End to the Conversation, by desiring her Father's Leave to play to him; a Request which he never refused.

The Countenance of *Sophia* had undergone more than one Change during the foregoing Speeches; and probably she imputed the passionate Resentment which *Jones* had expressed against the Mare to a different Motive from that from which her Father had derived it. Her Spirits were at this Time in a visible Flutter; and she played so intolerably ill, that had not *Western* soon fallen asleep, he must have remarked it. *Jones*, however,

¹ The name of Western's favourite horse is doubtless in honour of the Pretender, James Francis Edward Stuart (1688–1766), known as the Chevalier de St. Georges.

who was sufficiently awake, and was not without an Ear any more than without Eyes, made some Observations; which being joined to all which the Reader may remember to have passed formerly, gave him pretty strong Assurances, when he came to reflect on the whole, that all was not well in the tender Bosom of *Sophia*. An Opinion which many young Gentlemen will, I doubt not, extremely wonder at his not having been well confirmed in long ago. To confess the Truth, he had rather too much Diffidence in himself, and was not forward enough in seeing the Advances of a young Lady; a Misfortune which can be cured only by that early Town Education, which is at present so generally in Fashion.

When these Thoughts had fully taken Possession of *Jones*, they occasioned a Perturbation in his Mind, which, in a Constitution less pure and firm than his, might have been, at such a Season, attended with very dangerous Consequences. He was truly sensible of the great Worth of *Sophia*. He extremely liked her Person, no less admired her Accomplishments, and tenderly loved her Goodness. In Reality, as he had never once entertained any Thought of possessing her, nor had ever given the least voluntary Indulgence to his Inclinations, he had a much stronger Passion for her than he himself was acquainted with. His Heart now brought forth the full Secret, at the same Time that it assured him the adorable Object returned his Affection.

## CHAPTER III

*Which all, who have no Heart, will think to contain much ado about nothing.*

THE Reader will perhaps imagine, the Sensations which now arose in *Jones* to have been so sweet and delicious, that they would rather tend to produce a cheerful Serenity in the Mind, than any of those dangerous Effects which we have mentioned; but in fact, Sensations of this Kind, however delicious, are, at their first Recognition, of a very tumultuous Nature, and have very little of the Opiate in them. They were, moreover, in the present Case, embittered with certain Circumstances, which being mixed with sweeter Ingredients, tended altogether to compose a

Draught that might be termed *bitter-sweet*; than which, as nothing can be more disagreeable to the Palate, so nothing, in the metaphorical Sense, can be so injurious to the Mind.

For first, though he had sufficient Foundation to flatter himself in what he had observed in *Sophia*, he was not yet free from Doubt of misconstruing Compassion, or, at best, Esteem, into a warmer Regard. He was far from a sanguine Assurance that *Sophia* had any such Affection towards him, as might promise his Inclinations that Harvest, which, if they were encouraged and nursed, they would finally grow up to require. Besides, if he could hope to find no Bar to his Happiness from the Daughter, he thought himself certain of meeting an effectual Bar in the Father; who, though he was a Country Squire in his Diversions, was perfectly a Man of the World in whatever regarded his Fortune; had the most violent Affection for this only Daughter, and had often signified, in his Cups, the Pleasure he proposed in seeing her married to one of the richest Men in the County. *Jones* was not so vain and senseless a Coxcomb as to expect, from any Regard which *Western* had professed for him, that he would ever be induced to lay aside these Views of advancing his Daughter. He well knew that Fortune is generally the principal, if not the sole Consideration, which operates on the best of Parents in these Matters: For Friendship makes us warmly espouse the Interest of others; but it is very cold to the Gratification of their Passions. Indeed, to feel the Happiness which may result from this, it is necessary we should possess the Passion ourselves. As he had therefore no Hopes of obtaining her Father's Consent, so he thought to endeavour to succeed without it, and by such Means to frustrate the Great Point of Mr. *Western's* Life, was to make a very ill Use of his Hospitality, and a very ungrateful Return to the many little Favours received (however roughly) at his Hands. If he saw such a Consequence with Horror and Disdain, how much more was he shocked with what regarded Mr. *Allworthy*; to whom, as he had more than filial Obligations, so had he for him more than filial Piety. He knew the Nature of that good Man to be so averse to any Baseness or Treachery, that the least Attempt of such a Kind would make the sight of the guilty Person for ever odious to his Eyes, and his Name a detestable Sound in his Ears. The Appearance of such unsurmountable Difficulties was sufficient to have inspired him with Despair, however ardent his Wishes had been; but even these were controlled by Compassion for another Woman. The Idea of lovely *Molly* now intruded itself before him. He had sworn eternal Constancy in her Arms, and she had as often vowed never to outlive his deserting her. He now saw her in all the most shocking Postures of Death; nay, he considered all the Miseries of Prostitution to which she would be liable, and of which he would be doubly the Occasion; first by seducing, and then by deserting her; for he well knew the Hatred which all her Neighbours, and even her own Sisters, bore her, and how ready they would all be to tear her to Pieces. Indeed he had exposed her to more Envy than Shame, or rather to the latter by Means of the former: For many Women abused her for being a Whore, while they envied her her Lover and her Finery, and would have been themselves glad to have purchased these at the same Rate. The Ruin, therefore, of the poor Girl must, he foresaw, unavoidably attend his deserting her; and this Thought stung him to the Soul. Poverty and Distress seemed to him to give none a Right of aggravating those Misfortunes. The Meanness of her Condition did not represent her Misery as of little Consequence in his Eyes, nor did it appear to justify, or even to palliate, his Guilt, in bringing that Misery upon her. But why do I mention Justification; his own Heart would not suffer him to destroy a human Creature, who, he thought, loved him, and had to that Love sacrificed her Innocence. His own good Heart pleaded her Cause; not as a cold venal Advocate; but as one interested in the Event, and which must itself deeply share in all the Agonies its Owner brought on another.

When this powerful Advocate had sufficiently raised the Pity of *Jones*, by painting poor *Molly* in all the Circumstances of Wretchedness; it artfully called in the Assistance of another Passion, and represented the Girl in all the amiable Colours of Youth, Health, and Beauty; as one greatly the Object of Desire, and much the more so, at least to a good Mind, from being, at the same time, the Object of Compassion.

Amidst these Thoughts, poor *Jones* passed a long sleepless Night, and in the Morning the Result of the whole was to abide by *Molly*, and to think no more of *Sophia*.

In this virtuous Resolution he continued all the next Day till the Evening, cherishing the Idea of *Molly*, and driving *Sophia* from his Thoughts; but in the fatal Evening, a very trifling

Accident set all his Passions again on Float, and worked so total a Change in his Mind, that we think it decent to communicate it in a fresh Chapter.

## CHAPTER IV

*A little Chapter, in which is contained a little Incident.*

AMONG other Visitants, who paid their Compliments to the young Gentleman in his Confinement, Mrs. *Honour* was one. The Reader, perhaps, when he reflects on some Expressions which have formerly dropt from her, may conceive that she herself had a very particular Affection for Mr. *Jones*; but, in reality, it was no such thing. *Tom* was a handsome young Fellow; and for that Species of Men Mrs. *Honour* had some Regard; but this was perfectly indiscriminate: For having been crossed in the Love which she bore a certain Nobleman's Footman, who had basely deserted her after a Promise of Marriage, she had so securely kept together the broken Remains of her Heart, that no Man had ever since been able to possess himself of any single Fragment. She viewed all handsome Men with that equal Regard and Benevolence, which a sober and virtuous Mind bears to all the Good.—She might, indeed, be called a Lover of Men, as *Socrates* was a Lover of Mankind, preferring one to another for corporeal, as he for mental Qualifications; but never carrying this Preference so far as to cause any Perturbation in the philosophical Serenity of her Temper.

The Day after Mr. *Jones* had that Conflict with himself, which we have seen in the preceding Chapter, Mrs. *Honour* came into his Room, and finding him alone, began in the following Manner: 'La, Sir, where do you think I have been? I warrants you, you would not guess in fifty Years; but if you did guess, to be sure, I must not tell you neither.' 'Nay, if it be something which you must not tell me,' said *Jones*, 'I shall have the Curiosity to enquire, and I know you will not be so barbarous to refuse me.' 'I don't know,' cries she, 'why I should refuse you neither, for that Matter; for to be sure you won't mention it any more. And for that Matter, if you knew where I had been, unless you knew what I had been about, it would not signify much. Nay, I don't see why it should be kept a Secret, for my Part; for to be sure she is the best Lady in the World.' Upon this, *Jones* began to beg earnestly to be let into this Secret, and faithfully promised not to divulge it. She then proceeded thus. 'Why, you must know, Sir, my young Lady sent me to enquire after *Molly Seagrim*, and to see whether the Wench wanted any thing; to be sure, I did not care to go, methinks; but Servants must do what they are ordered.—How could you undervalue yourself so, Mr. *Jones*?—So my Lady bid me go, and carry her some Linnen, and other Things.—She is too good. If such forward Sluts were sent to *Bridewell*, it would be better for them. I told my Lady, says I, Madam, Your La'ship is encouraging Idleness——' 'And was my *Sophia* so good?' says *Jones*.—'My *Sophia*! I assure you, marry come up,' answered *Honour*. 'And yet if you knew all.—Indeed, if I was as Mr. *Jones*, I should look a little higher than such Trumpery as *Molly Seagrim*.' 'What do you mean by these Words,' replied *Jones*, 'If I knew all?' 'I mean what I mean,' says *Honour*. 'Don't you remember putting your Hands in my Lady's Muff once? I vow I could almost find in my Heart to tell, if I was certain my Lady would never come to the Hearing on't.'—*Jones* then made several solemn Protestations. And *Honour* proceeded— 'then, to be sure, my Lady gave me that Muff; and afterwards, upon hearing what you had done——' 'Then you told her what I had done!' interrupted *Jones*. 'If I did, Sir,' answered she, 'you need not be angry with me. Many's the Man would have given his Head to have had my Lady told, if they had known—for, to be sure, the biggest Lord in the Land might be proud—but, I protest, I have a great Mind not to tell you.' *Jones* fell to Entreaties, and soon prevailed on her to go on thus. 'You must know then, Sir, that my Lady had given this Muff to me; but about a Day or two after I had told her the Story, she quarrels with her new Muff, and to be sure it is the prettiest that ever was seen. '*Honour*,' says she,—'this is an odious Muff;—it is too big for me,—I can't wear it—till I can get another, you must let me have my old one again, and you may have this in the room on't'—for she's a good Lady, and scorns to give a Thing and take a Thing, I promise you that. So to be sure I fetched it her back again, and, I believe, she hath worn it upon her Arm almost ever since, and I warrants hath given it many a Kiss when nobody hath seen her.'

Here the Conversation was interrupted by Mr. *Western* himself, who came to summon *Jones* to the Harpsichord; whither the poor young Fellow went all pale and trembling. This *Western* observed, but, on seeing Mrs. *Honour*, imputed it to a wrong Cause; and having given *Jones* a hearty Curse between Jest and Earnest, he bid him beat abroad, and not poach up the Game in his Warren.

*Sophia* looked this Evening with more than usual Beauty, and we may believe it was no small Addition to her Charms, in the Eye of Mr. *Jones*, that she now happened to have on her Right Arm this very Muff.

She was playing one of her Father's favourite Tunes, and he was leaning on her Chair, when the Muff fell over her Fingers, and put her out. This so disconcerted the Squire, that he snatched the Muff from her, and with a hearty Curse threw it into the Fire. *Sophia* instantly started up, and with the utmost Eagerness recovered it from the Flames.

Though this Incident will probably appear of little Consequence to many of our Readers, yet, trifling as it was, it had so violent an Effect on poor *Jones*, that we thought it our Duty to relate it. In reality, there are many little Circumstances too often omitted by injudicious Historians, from which Events of the utmost Importance arise.[1] The World may indeed be considered as a vast Machine,[2] in which the great Wheels are originally set in Motion by those which are very minute, and almost imperceptible to any but the strongest Eyes.

Thus, not all the Charms of the incomparable *Sophia*; not all the dazzling Brightness, and languishing Softness of her Eyes;

[1] Several passages in *Tom Jones* attest to Fielding's keen interest in the intricacies of historical causation: in life, and hence necessarily in those fictive 'histories' in which life is truly imitated, a perceptive observer may discern a 'nice Train of little Circumstances' (p. 916) working to complete the 'main Design' (p. 524). One historian whom Fielding would have exempted from the censure of being injudicious in this regard was Livy, who 'gives us so just a Detail of all the Circumstances that preceded and produced [an event]' (*The True Patriot*, 24 December 1745).

[2] The metaphor of the universe as a vast and intricate machine implying the existence of God, the supreme Artificer, was a commonplace in the period. With the present passage compare, among many possible examples, John Spencer, *A Discourse concerning Prodigies* (1665), sig. (A): '*to shew how many wheels in some great Engine, move in subordination to the production of some great work, were [not] to obscure and eclipse the art of the Artificer.*' The figure was a favourite with Robert Boyle and may be found as well in Henry More, John Ray, Isaac Barrow, John Tillotson, Samuel Clarke, and many others.

the Harmony of her Voice, and of her Person; not all her Wit, good Humour, Greatness of Mind, or Sweetness of Disposition, had been able so absolutely to conquer and enslave the Heart of poor *Jones*, as this little Incident of the Muff. Thus the Poet sweetly sings of *Troy*.

> ———*Captique dolis lachrymisque coacti*
> *Quos neque Tydides, nec Larissæus Achilles,*
> *Non anni domuere decem, non mille Carinæ.*[1]

What *Diomede*, or *Thetis'* greater Son,
A thousand Ships, nor ten Years Siege had done,
False Tears, and fawning Words, the City won.

DRYDEN.

The Citadel of *Jones* was now taken by Surprize. All those Considerations of Honour and Prudence, which our Heroe had lately with so much military Wisdom placed as Guards over the Avenues of his Heart, ran away from their Posts, and the God of Love marched in in Triumph.

## CHAPTER V

*A very long Chapter, containing a very great Incident.*

BUT though this victorious Deity easily expelled his avowed Enemies from the Heart of *Jones*, he found it more difficult to supplant the Garrison which he himself had placed there. To lay aside all Allegory, the Concern for what must become of poor *Molly*, greatly disturbed and perplexed the Mind of the worthy Youth. The superior Merit of *Sophia*, totally eclipsed, or rather extinguished all the Beauties of the poor Girl; but Compassion instead of Contempt succeeded to Love. He was convinced the Girl had placed all her Affections, and all her Prospect of future Happiness in him only. For this he had, he knew, given sufficient Occasion, by the utmost Profusion of Tenderness towards her: A Tenderness which he had taken every Means to persuade her he would always maintain. She, on her Side, had assured him of her firm Belief in his Promise, and had with the most solemn

---

[1] *Aeneid*, ii. 196–8, with reference to the Trojan horse. The verse translation is Dryden's (ii. 261–3).

Vows declared, that on his fulfilling, or breaking these Promises, it depended, whether she should be the happiest, or the most miserable of Womankind. And to be the Author of this highest Degree of Misery to a human Being, was a Thought on which he could not bear to ruminate a single Moment. He considered this poor Girl as having sacrificed to him every Thing in her little Power; as having been at her own Expence the Object of his Pleasure; as sighing and languishing for him even at that very Instant. Shall then, says he, my Recovery, for which she hath so ardently wished; shall my Presence which she hath so eagerly expected, instead of giving her that Joy with which she hath flattered herself, cast her at once down into Misery and Dispair? Can I be such a Villain? Here, when the Genius of poor *Molly* seem'd triumphant, the Love of *Sophia* towards him, which now appeared no longer dubious, rushed upon his Mind, and bore away every Obstacle before it.

At length it occurred to him, that he might possibly be able to make *Molly* amends another Way; namely, by giving her a Sum of Money. This nevertheless, he almost despaired of her accepting, when he recollected the frequent and vehement Assurances he had received from her, that the World put in Ballance with him, would make her no Amends for his Loss. However, her extreme Poverty, and chiefly her egregious Vanity, (somewhat of which hath been already hinted to the Reader) gave him some little Hope, that notwithstanding all her avowed Tenderness, she might in Time be brought to content herself with a Fortune superiour to her Expectation, and which might indulge her Vanity, by setting her above all her Equals. He resolved therefore, to take the first Opportunity of making a Proposal of this Kind.

One Day accordingly, when his Arm was so well recovered, that he could walk easily with it slung in a Sash, he stole forth, at a Season when the Squire was engaged in his Field Exercises, and visited his Fair one. Her Mother and Sisters, whom he found taking their Tea, informed him first that *Molly* was not at Home; but afterwards, the eldest Sister acquainted him with a malicious Smile, that she was above Stairs a-bed. *Tom* had no Objection to this Situation of his Mistress, and immediately ascended the Ladder which led towards her Bed-Chamber; but when he came to the Top, he, to his great Surprize, found the Door fast; nor could he for some Time obtain any Answer from within; for *Molly*, as she herself afterwards informed him, was fast asleep.

The Extremes of Grief and Joy have been remarked to produce very similar Effects;[1] and when either of these rushes on us by Surprize, it is apt to create such a total Perturbation and Confusion, that we are often thereby deprived of the Use of all our Faculties. It cannot therefore be wondered at, that the unexpected Sight of Mr. *Jones* should so strongly operate on the Mind of *Molly*, and should overwhelm her with such Confusion, that for some Minutes she was unable to express the great Raptures, with which the Reader will suppose she was affected on this Occasion. As for *Jones*, he was so entirely possessed, and as it were enchanted by the Presence of his beloved Object, that he for a while forgot *Sophia*, and consequently the principal Purpose of his Visit.

This, however, soon recurred to his Memory; and after the first Transports of their Meeting were over, he found Means by Degrees to introduce a Discourse on the fatal Consequences which must attend their Amour, if Mr. *Allworthy*, who had strictly forbidden him ever seeing her more, should discover that he still carried on this Commerce. Such a Discovery, which his Enemies gave him Reason to think would be unavoidable, must, he said, end in his Ruin, and consequently in hers. Since, therefore, their hard Fates had determined that they must separate, he advised her to bear it with Resolution, and swore he would never omit any Opportunity through the Course of his Life, of shewing her the Sincerity of his Affection, by providing for her in a Manner beyond her utmost Expectation, or even beyond her Wishes, if ever that should be in his Power; concluding, at last, that she might soon find some Man who would marry her, and who would make her much happier than she could be by leading a disreputable Life with him.

*Molly* remained a few Moments in Silence, and then bursting into a Flood of Tears, she began to upbraid him in the following Words. 'And is this your Love for me, to forsake me in this Manner, now you have ruined me? How often, when I have told you that all Men are false and Perjury alike, and grow tired of us as soon as ever they have had their wicked Wills of us, how often have you sworn you would never forsake me? And can

[1] See above, p. 44, n. 1.

you be such a perjury Man after all? What signifies all the
Riches in the World to me without you, now you have gained my
Heart, so you have—you have—? Why do you mention another
Man to me? I can never love any other Man as long as I live.
All other Men are nothing to me. If the greatest Squire in all the
Country would come a suiting to me to-morrow, I would not
give my Company to him. No, I shall always hate and despise the
whole Sex for your Sake——'

She was proceeding thus, when an Accident put a Stop to her
Tongue, before it had run out half its Career. The Room, or
rather Garret, in which *Molly* lay, being up one Pair of Stairs,
that is to say, at the Top of the House, was of a sloping Figure,
resembling the great *Delta* of the *Greeks*. The *English* Reader
may, perhaps, form a better Idea of it, by being told, that it was
impossible to stand upright any where but in the Middle. Now,
as this Room wanted the Conveniency of a Closet, *Molly* had, to
supply that Defect, nailed up an old Rug against the Rafters of
the House, which enclosed a little Hole where her best Apparel,
such as the Remains of that Sack which we have formerly mentioned, some Caps, and other Things with which she had lately
provided herself, were hung up and secured from the Dust.

This inclosed Place exactly fronted the Foot of the Bed, to
which, indeed, the Rug hung so near, that it served, in a Manner,
to supply the Want of Curtains. Now, whether *Molly* in the
Agonies of her Rage, pushed this Rug with her Feet; or, *Jones*
might touch it; or whether the Pin or Nail gave way of its own
Accord, I am not certain; but as *Molly* pronounced those last
Words, which are recorded above, the wicked Rug got loose from
its Fastning, and discovered every thing hid behind it; where
among other female Utensils appeared—(with Shame I write it,
and with Sorrow will it be read)—the Philosopher *Square*, in a
Posture (for the Place would not near admit his standing upright) as ridiculous as can possibly be conceived.

The Posture, indeed, in which he stood, was not greatly unlike that of a Soldier who is tyed Neck and Heels; or rather resembling the Attitude in which we often see Fellows in the public
Streets of *London*, who are not suffering but deserving Punishment by so standing. He had a Night-cap belonging to *Molly*
on his Head, and his two large Eyes, the Moment the Rug fell,
stared directly at *Jones*; so that when the Idea of Philosophy was

added to the Figure now discovered, it would have been very difficult for any Spectator to have refrained from immoderate Laughter.

I question not but the Surprize of the Reader will be here equal to that of *Jones*; as the Suspicions which must arise from the Appearance of this wise and grave Man in such a Place, may seem so inconsistent with that Character, which he hath, doubtless, maintained hitherto, in the Opinion of every one.

But to confess the Truth, this Inconsistency is rather imaginary than real. Philosophers are composed of Flesh and Blood as well as other human Creatures; and however sublimated and refined the Theory of these may be, a little practical Frailty is as incident to them as to other Mortals. It is, indeed, in Theory only and not in Practice, as we have before hinted, that consists the Difference: For tho' such great Beings think much better and more wisely, they always act exactly like other Men. They know very well how to subdue all Appetites and Passions, and to despise both Pain and Pleasure; and this Knowledge affords much delightful Contemplation, and is easily acquired; but the Practice would be vexatious and troublesome; and, therefore, the same Wisdom which teaches them to know this, teaches them to avoid carrying it into Execution.

Mr. *Square* happened to be at Church, on that *Sunday* when, as the Reader may be pleased to remember, the Appearance of *Molly* in her Sack had caused all that Disturbance. Here he first observed her and was so pleased with her Beauty, that he prevailed with the young Gentlemen to change their intended Ride that Evening, that he might pass by the Habitation of *Molly*, and, by that Means, might obtain a second Chance of seeing her. This Reason, however, as he did not at that time mention to any, so neither did we think proper to communicate it then to the Reader.

Among other Particulars which constituted the Unfitness of Things in Mr. *Square's* Opinion, Danger and Difficulty were two. The Difficulty, therefore, which he apprehended there might be in corrupting this young Wench, and the Danger which would accrue to his Character on the Discovery, were such strong Dissuasives, that it is probable, he at first intended to have contented himself with the pleasing Ideas which the Sight of Beauty furnishes us with. These the gravest Men, after a full Meal of serious Meditation, often allow themselves by Way of Desert: For which Purpose, certain Books and Pictures find their Way into the most private Recesses of their Study, and a certain liquorish Part of natural Philosophy is often the principal Subject of their Conversation.

But when the Philosopher heard a Day or two afterwards, that the Fortress of Virtue had already been subdued, he began to give a larger Scope to his Desires. His Appetite was not of that squeamish Kind which cannot feed on a Dainty because another hath tasted it. In short, he liked the Girl the better for the Want of that Chastity, which, if she had possessed it, must have been a Bar to his Pleasures; he pursued, and obtained her.

The Reader will be mistaken, if he thinks *Molly* gave *Square* the Preference to her younger Lover: On the contrary, had she been confined to the Choice of one only, *Tom Jones* would, undoubtedly, have been, of the two, the victorious Person. Nor was it solely the Consideration that two are better than one (tho' this had its proper Weight) to which Mr. *Square* owed his Success; the Absence of *Jones* during his Confinement was an unlucky Circumstance; and in that Interval, some well chosen Presents from the Philosopher so softened and unguarded the Girl's Heart, that a favourable Opportunity became irresistable, and *Square* triumphed over the poor Remains of Virtue which subsisted in the Bosom of *Molly*.

It was now about a Fortnight since this Conquest, when *Jones* paid the above-mentioned Visit to his Mistress, at a time when she and *Square* were in Bed together. This was the true Reason why the Mother denied her as we have seen; for as the old Woman shared in the Profits arising from the Iniquity of her Daughter, she encouraged and protected her in it to the utmost of her Power; but such was the Envy and Hatred which the eldest Sister bore towards *Molly*, that, notwithstanding she had some Part of the Booty, she would willingly have parted with this to ruin her Sister, and spoil her Trade. Hence she had acquainted *Jones* with her being above Stairs in Bed, in Hopes that he might have caught her in *Square's* Arms. This, however, *Molly* found Means to prevent, as the Door was fastned; which gave her an Opportunity of conveying her Lover behind that Rug or Blanket where he now was unhappily discovered.

*Square* no sooner made his Appearance than *Molly* flung

herself back in her Bed, cried out she was undone, and abandoned herself to Despair. This poor Girl, who was yet but a Novice in her Business, had not arrived to that Perfection of Assurance which helps off a Town Lady in any Extremity; and either prompts her with an Excuse, or else inspires her to brazen out the Matter with her Husband; who from Love of Quiet, or out of Fear of his Reputation, and sometimes, perhaps, from Fear of the Gallant, who, like Mr. *Constant* in the Play,[1] wears a Sword, is glad to shut his Eyes, and contented to put his Horns in his Pocket: *Molly*, on the contrary, was silenced by this Evidence, and very fairly gave up a Cause which she had hitherto maintained with so many Tears, and with such solemn and vehement Protestations of the purest Love and Constancy.

As to the Gentleman behind the Arras, he was not in much less Consternation. He stood for a while motionless, and seemed equally at a Loss what to say, or whither to direct his Eyes. *Jones*, tho' perhaps the most astonished of the three, first found his Tongue; and, being immediately recovered from those uneasy Sensations, which *Molly* by her Upbraidings had occasioned, he burst into a loud Laughter, and then saluting Mr. *Square*, advanced to take him by the Hand, and to relieve him from his Place of Confinement.

*Square*, being now arrived in the Middle of the Room, in which Part only he could stand upright, looked at *Jones* with a very grave Countenance, and said to him, 'Well, Sir, I see you enjoy this mighty Discovery, and, I dare swear, taste great Delight in the Thoughts of exposing me; but if you will consider the Matter fairly, you will find you are yourself only to blame. I am not guilty of corrupting Innocence. I have done nothing for which that Part of the World which judges of Matters by the Rule of Right will condemn me. Fitness is governed by the Nature of Things, and not by Customs, Forms, or municipal Laws. Nothing is, indeed, unfit which is not unnatural.' 'Well reasoned, old Boy,' answered *Jones*; 'but why dost thou think I should desire to expose thee? I promise thee, I was never better pleased with thee in my Life; and unless thou hast a Mind to discover it thyself, this Affair may remain a profound Secret

---

1 In Vanbrugh's *The Provok'd Wife* (1697). When discovered in an intrigue with Lady Brute (v. ii), Constant hopes her husband will be assured that their relationship was innocent: 'If not—I wear a Sword, Sir, and so good b'uy to you' (1710 ed.).

for me.' 'Nay, Mr. *Jones*,' replied *Square*, 'I would not be thought
to undervalue Reputation. Good Fame is a Species of the K A L O N[1]
and it is by no Means fitting to neglect it. Besides to murder one's
own Reputation, is a kind of Suicide, a detestable and odious
Vice. If you think proper, therefore, to conceal any Infirmity of
mine; (for such I may have, since no Man is perfectly perfect)
I promise you I will not betray myself. Things may be fitting to
be done, which are not fitting to be boasted of: for by the perverse Judgment of the World, That often becomes the Subject
of Censure, which is, in Truth, not only innocent but laudable.'
'Right!' cries *Jones*, 'what can be more innocent than the In-
dulgence of a natural Appetite? or what more laudable than the
Propagation of our Species?' 'To be serious with you,' answered
*Square*, 'I profess they always appeared so to me.' 'And yet,' said
*Jones*, 'you was of a different Opinion when my Affair with this
Girl was first discovered.' 'Why, I must confess,' says *Square*, 'as
the Matter was misrepresented to me by that Parson *Thwackum*,
I might condemn the Corruption of Innocence: It was that,
Sir, it was that—and that—: For you must know, Mr. *Jones*, in
the Consideration of Fitness, very minute Circumstances, Sir,
very minute Circumstances cause great Alteration.'—'Well,' cries
*Jones*, 'be that as it will, it shall be your own Fault, as I have
promised you, if you ever hear any more of this Adventure. Behave kindly to the Girl, and I will never open my Lips concerning
the Matter to any one. And, *Molly*, do you be faithful to your
Friend, and I will not only forgive your Infidelity to me; but
will do you all the Service I can.' So saying, he took a hasty Leave,
and slipping down the Ladder, retired with much Expedition.

*Square* was rejoyced to find this Adventure was likely to have
no worse Conclusion; and as for *Molly*, being recovered from her
Confusion, she began at first to upbraid *Square* with having been
the Occasion of her Loss of *Jones*; but that Gentleman soon found
the Means of mitigating her Anger, partly by Caresses, and
partly by a small Nostrum from his Purse, of wonderful and
approved Efficacy in purging off the ill Humours of the Mind,
and in restoring it to a good Temper.

[1] Cf. Bishop Berkeley's definition in *Alciphron: or, The Minute Philosopher* (1732):
'Doubtless there is a beauty of the mind, a charm in virtue, a symmetry and proportion in
the moral world. This moral beauty was known to the ancients by the name of *honestum*, or
τὸ καλόν' (Fraser ed., *Works* [1901], ii. 127).

She then poured forth a vast Profusion of Tenderness towards her new Lover; turned all she had said to *Jones*, and *Jones* himself into Ridicule, and vowed, tho' he once had the Possession of her Person, that none but *Square* had ever been Master of her Heart.

## CHAPTER VI

*By comparing which with the former, the Reader may possibly correct some Abuse which he hath formerly been guilty of, in the Application of the Word* LOVE.

THE Infidelity of *Molly*, which *Jones* had now discovered, would, perhaps, have vindicated a much greater Degree of Resentment than he expressed on the Occasion; and if he had abandoned her directly from that Moment, very few, I believe, would have blamed him.

Certain, however, it is, that he saw her in the Light of Compassion; and tho' his Love to her was not of that Kind which could give him any great Uneasiness at her Inconstancy, yet was he not a little shocked on reflecting that he had himself originally corrupted her Innocence; for to this Corruption he imputed all the Vice, into which she appeared now so likely to plunge herself.

This Consideration gave him no little Uneasiness, till *Betty*, the eldest Sister, was so kind some time afterwards entirely to cure him by a Hint, that one *Will Barnes*, and not himself, had been the first Seducer of *Molly*; and that the little Child, which he had hitherto so certainly concluded to be his own, might very probably have an equal Title at least, to claim *Barnes* for its Father.

*Jones* eagerly pursued this Scent when he had first received it; and in a very short Time was sufficiently assured that the Girl had told him Truth, not only by the Confession of the Fellow, but, at last, by that of *Molly* herself.

This *Will Barnes* was a Country Gallant, and had acquired as many Trophies of this Kind as any Ensign or Attorney's Clerk in the Kingdom. He had, indeed, reduced several Women to a State of utter Profligacy, had broke the Hearts of some, and had the Honour of occasioning the violent Death of one poor Girl, who had either drowned herself, or, what was rather more probable, had been drowned by him.

Among other of his Conquests, this Fellow had triumphed over the Heart of *Betty Seagrim*. He had made love to her long before *Molly* was grown to be a fit Object of that Pastime; but had afterwards deserted her, and applied to her Sister, with whom he had almost immediate Success. Now *Will* had, in reality, the sole Possession of *Molly's* Affection, while *Jones* and *Square* were almost equally Sacrifices to her Interest, and to her Pride.

Hence had grown that implacable Hatred which we have before seen raging in the Mind of *Betty*; though we did not think it necessary to assign this Cause sooner, as Envy itself alone was adequate to all the Effects we have mentioned.

*Jones* was become perfectly easy by Possession of this Secret with Regard to *Molly*; but as to *Sophia*, he was far from being in a State of Tranquility; nay, indeed, he was under the most violent Perturbation: His Heart was now, if I may use the Metaphor, entirely evacuated, and *Sophia* took absolute Possession of it. He loved her with an unbounded Passion, and plainly saw the tender Sentiments she had for him; yet could not this Assurance lessen his Despair of obtaining the Consent of her Father, nor the Horrors which attended his Pursuit of her by any base or treacherous Method.

The Injury which he must thus do to Mr. *Western*, and the Concern which would accrue to Mr. *Allworthy*, were Circumstances that tormented him all Day, and haunted him on his Pillow at Night. His Life was a constant Struggle between Honour and Inclination, which alternately triumphed over each other in his Mind. He often resolved, in the Absence of *Sophia*, to leave her Father's House, and to see her no more; and as often, in her Presence, forgot all those Resolutions, and determined to pursue her at the Hazard of his Life, and at the Forfeiture of what was much dearer to him.

This Conflict began soon to produce very strong and visible Effects: For he lost all his usual Sprightliness and Gaiety of Temper, and became not only melancholy when alone, but dejected and absent in Company; nay, if ever he put on a forced Mirth, to comply with Mr. *Western's* Humour, the Constraint appeared so plain, that he seemed to have been giving the strongest Evidence of what he endeavoured to conceal by such Ostentation.

It may, perhaps, be a Question, whether the Art which he used to conceal his Passion, or the Means which honest Nature employed to reveal it, betrayed him most: For while Art made him more than ever reserved to *Sophia*, and forbad him to address any of his Discourse to her; nay, to avoid meeting her Eyes, with the utmost Caution; Nature was no less busy in counterplotting him. Hence, at the Approach of the young Lady, he grew pale; and if this was sudden, started. If his Eyes accidentally met hers, the Blood rushed into his Cheeks, and his Countenance became all over Scarlet. If common Civility ever obliged him to speak to her, as to drink her Health at Table, his Tongue was sure to faulter. If he touched her his Hand, nay his whole Frame trembled. And if any Discourse tended, however remotely, to raise the Idea of Love, an involuntary Sigh seldom failed to steal from his Bosom. Most of which Accidents Nature was wonderfully industrious to throw daily in his Way.

All these Symptoms escaped the Notice of the Squire; but not so of *Sophia*. She soon perceived these Agitations of Mind in *Jones*, and was at no Loss to discover the Cause; for indeed she recognized it in her own Breast. And this Recognition is, I suppose, that Sympathy which hath been so often noted in Lovers, and which will sufficiently account for her being so much quicker-sighted than her Father.

But, to say the Truth, there is a more simple and plain Method of accounting for that prodigious Superiority of Penetration which we must observe in some Men over the rest of the human Species, and one which will serve not only in the Case of Lovers, but of all others. From whence is it that the Knave is generally so quick-sighted to those Symptoms and Operations of Knavery which often dupe an honest Man of a much better Understanding? There surely is no general Sympathy among Knaves, nor have they, like Free Masons, any common Sign of Communication.[1] In reality, it is only because they have the same thing in their Heads, and their Thoughts are turned the same Way. Thus, that *Sophia* saw, and that *Western* did not see the plain Symptoms of Love in *Jones* can be no Wonder, when we con-

[1] See above, p. 85, n. 1. For the signs to which Fielding refers, see *The Secret History of the Free-Masons. . . . With a Short Dictionary of private Signs, or Signals* (2nd ed., 1725).

sider that the Idea of Love never entered into the Head of the Father, whereas the Daughter, at present, thought of nothing else.

When *Sophia* was well satisfied of the violent Passion which tormented poor *Jones*, and no less certain that she herself was its Object, she had not the least Difficulty in discovering the true Cause of his present Behaviour. This highly endeared him to her, and raised in her Mind two of the best Affections which any Lover can wish to raise in a Mistress. These were Esteem and Pity; for sure the most outragiously rigid among her Sex will excuse her pitying a Man, whom she saw miserable on her own Account; nor can they blame her for esteeming one who visibly from the most honourable Motives, endeavoured to smother a Flame in his own Bosom, which, like the famous *Spartan* Theft,[1] was preying upon, and consuming his very Vitals. Thus his Backwardness, his Shunning her, his Coldness and his Silence, were the forwardest, the most diligent, the warmest, and most eloquent Advocates; and wrought so violently on her sensible and tender Heart, that she soon felt for him all those gentle Sensations which are consistent with a virtuous and elevated female Mind— In short, all which Esteem, Gratitude and Pity, can inspire in such, towards an agreeable Man—Indeed, all which the nicest Delicacy can allow—In a Word,—she was in Love with him to Distraction.

One Day, this young Couple accidentally met in the Garden, at the End of two Walks, which were both bounded by that Canal in which *Jones* had formerly risqued drowning to retrieve the little Bird that *Sophia* had there lost.

This Place had been of late much frequented by *Sophia*. Here she used to ruminate, with a Mixture of Pain and Pleasure, on an Incident, which, however trifling in itself, had possibly sown the first Seeds of that Affection which was now arrived to such Maturity in her Heart.

Here then this young Couple met. They were almost close together before either of them knew any Thing of the other's Approach. A By-stander would have discovered sufficient Marks

---

[1] See Plutarch, *Life of Lycurgus*, xviii. 1: a Spartan youth who had stolen a fox and concealed it under his cloak, suffered the animal to tear out his bowels rather than have the theft discovered. Fielding alludes to the story again in *The Covent-Garden Journal* (22 August 1752).

of Confusion, in the Countenance of each; but they felt it too much themselves to make any Observation. As soon as *Jones* had a little recovered his first Surprize, he accosted the young Lady with some of the ordinary Forms of Salutation, which she in the same Manner returned, and their Conversation began, as usual, on the delicious Beauty of the Morning. Hence they past to the Beauty of the Place, on which *Jones* launched forth very high Encomiums. When they came to the Tree whence he had formerly tumbled into the Canal, *Sophia* could not help reminding him of that Accident, and said, 'I fancy, Mr. *Jones*, you have some little shuddering when you see that Water.' 'I assure you, Madam,' answered *Jones*, 'the Concern you felt at the Loss of your little Bird, will always appear to me the highest Circumstance in that Adventure. Poor little *Tommy*, there is the Branch he stood upon. How could the little Wretch have the Folly to fly away from that State of Happiness in which I had the Honour to place him? His Fate was a just Punishment for his Ingratitude.' 'Upon my Word, Mr. *Jones*,' said she, 'your Gallantry very narrowly escaped as severe a Fate. Sure, the Remembrance must affect you.' 'Indeed, Madam,' answered he, 'if I have any Reason to reflect with Sorrow on it, it is, perhaps, that the Water had not been a little deeper, by which I might have escaped many bitter Heart-achs, that Fortune seems to have in Store for me.' 'Fie, Mr. *Jones*,' replied *Sophia*, 'I am sure you cannot be in Earnest now. This affected Contempt of Life is only an Excess of your Complaisance to me. You would endeavour to lessen the Obligation of having twice ventured it for my Sake. Beware the third Time.'—She spoke these last Words with a Smile and a Softness inexpressible. *Jones* answered with a Sigh, 'He feared it was already too late for Caution,'—and then looking tenderly and stedfastly on her, he cry'd, 'Oh! Miss *Western*, —Can you desire me to live? Can you wish me so ill?'—*Sophia* looking down on the Ground, answered with some Hesitation, 'Indeed, Mr. *Jones*, I do not wish you ill.'—'Oh! I know too well that heavenly Temper,' cries *Jones*, 'that divine Goodness which is beyond every other Charm.' 'Nay, now,' answered she, 'I understand you not.—I can stay no longer,—I——.' 'I would not be understood,' cries he, 'nay, I can't be understood. I know not what I say. Meeting you here so unexpectedly—I have been unguarded—for Heaven's Sake pardon me, if I have

said any Thing to offend you—I did not mean it—indeed, I
would rather have died—nay, the very Thought would kill me.'
'You surprize me,' answered she,—'How can you possibly think
you have offended me?' 'Fear, Madam,' says he, 'easily runs into
Madness; and there is no Degree of Fear like that which I feel
of offending you. How can I speak then? Nay don't look angrily
at me, one Frown will destroy me.—I mean nothing—Blame my
Eyes, or blame those Beauties—What am I saying? Pardon me
if I have said too much. My Heart overflowed. I have struggled
with my Love to the utmost, and have endeavoured to conceal a
Fever which preys on my Vitals, and will, I hope, soon make it
impossible for me ever to offend you more.'

Mr. *Jones* now fell a trembling as if he had been shaken with
the Fit of an Ague. *Sophia*, who was in a Situation not very
different from his, answered in these Words: 'Mr. *Jones*, I will
not affect to misunderstand you; indeed I understand you too
well; but for Heaven's Sake, if you have any Affection for me, let
me make the best of my way into the House. I wish I may be
able to support myself thither.'

*Jones*, who was hardly able to support himself, offered her his
Arm, which she condescended to accept, but begged he would
not mention a Word more to her of this Nature at present. He
promised he would not, insisting only on her Forgiveness of what
Love, without the Leave of his Will, had forced from him: This,
she told him, he knew how to obtain by his future Behaviour;
and thus this young Pair tottered and trembled along, the Lover
not once daring to squeeze the Hand of his Mistress, tho' it
was locked in his.

*Sophia* immediately retired to her Chamber, where Mrs.
*Honour* and the Hartshorn were summoned to her Assistance. As
to poor *Jones*, the only Relief to his distempered Mind, was an
unwelcome Piece of News, which, as it opens a Scene of a different
Nature from those in which the Reader hath lately been conversant, will be communicated to him in the next Chapter.

## CHAPTER VII

### *In which Mr.* Allworthy *appears on a Sick-Bed.*

MR. *Western* was become so fond of *Jones*, that he was un-willing to part with him, tho' his Arm had been long since cured; and *Jones*, either from the Love of Sport, or from some other Reason, was easily persuaded to continue at his House, which he did sometimes for a Fortnight together without paying a single Visit at Mr. *Allworthy's*; nay, without ever hearing from thence.

Mr. *Allworthy* had been for some Days indisposed with a Cold, which had been attended with a little Fever. This he had, how-ever, neglected, as it was usual with him to do all Manner of Disorders which did not confine him to his Bed, or prevent his several Faculties from performing their ordinary Functions. A Conduct which we would by no Means be thought to approve or recommend to Imitation: For surely the Gentlemen of the *Æsculapian* Art are in the Right in advising, that the Moment the Disease is entered at one Door, the Physician should be introduced at the other; what else is meant by that old Adage: *Venienti occurrite Morbo?*[1] 'Oppose a Distemper at its first Ap-proach.' Thus the Doctor and the Disease meet in fair and equal Conflict; whereas, by giving Time to the latter, we often suffer him to fortify and entrench himself, like a *French* Army;[2] so that the learned Gentleman finds it very difficult, and some-times impossible to come at the Enemy. Nay sometimes by gain-ing Time, the Disease applies to the *French* military Politics,[3] and corrupts Nature over to his Side, and then all the Powers of Physick must arrive too late. Agreeable to these Observations was, I remember, the Complaint of the great Doctor *Misaubin*,[4]

---

[1] Persius, *Satires*, iii. 64.

[2] A correspondent in *The Jacobite's Journal* (26 December 1747) repeated the widespread opinion that the success of France in the War of the Austrian Succession was attributable in part to the skill of her military engineers, 'the greatest . . . which perhaps the World hath produced'. Fielding offered a similar appraisal in *A Dialogue between a Gentleman of London . . . and an honest Alderman* (1747). See below, p. 266.

[3] This was one popular explanation for the ineffectual conduct of the Dutch in the war with France: the English believed that Dutch legislators had been bribed into pressing for a Treaty of Neutrality (see below, p. 333, n. 1), and that the governors of certain fortified towns in Flanders had been paid to capitulate without a struggle (see below, p. 513, n. 1).

[4] The French physician John Misaubin (d. 1734) settled in London to practise medicine. Though a duly licensed member of the College of Physicians (1719), Misaubin's faith in

who used very pathetically to lament the late Applications which were made to his Skill: Saying, 'Bygar, me believe my Pation take me for de Undertaker: For dey never send for me till de Physicion have kill dem.'

Mr. *Allworthy's* Distemper, by Means of this Neglect, gained such Ground, that when the Increase of his Fever obliged him to send for Assistance, the Doctor at his first Arrival shook his Head, wished he had been sent for sooner, and intimated that he thought him in very imminent Danger. Mr. *Allworthy*, who had settled all his Affairs in this World, and was as well prepared, as it is possible for human Nature to be, for the other, received this Information with the utmost Calmness and Unconcern. He could, indeed, whenever he laid himself down to Rest, say with *Cato* in the tragical Poem,[1]

> ——*Let Guilt or Fear*
> *Disturb Man's Rest*, Cato *knows neither of them;*
> *Indifferent in his Choice, to sleep or die.*

In Reality, he could say this with ten times more Reason and Confidence than *Cato*, or any other proud Fellow among the ancient or modern Heroes: For he was not only devoid of Fear; but might be considered as a faithful Labourer, when at the End of Harvest, he is summoned to receive his Reward at the Hands of a bountiful Master.[2]

The good Man gave immediate Orders for all his Family to be summoned round him. None of these were then abroad, but Mrs.

---

the infallible efficacy of his pills, together with his foreign speech and arrogant manner, made him the target of ridicule. Hogarth satirized him on several occasions, in Plate V of *The Harlot's Progress* (1732), for example, and in another print in which Misaubin is shown pointing to the monument of one recently deceased and offering the belated advice, 'Prenez des Pilules, prenez des Pilules.' (See Print 1987, *A Catalogue of Prints and Drawings in the British Museum*, vol. ii, 1689–1733 [1873]; see also Print 1986.) Fielding's *The Mock Doctor* (1732) is ironically dedicated to Misaubin, who though others might call him 'an illiterate Empirick', deserves the warmest praise for inventing 'that *Little Pill*', an 'invaluable Remedy, to which so many owe their Health, their Pleasure, nay the very Preservation of their Being'. In the play itself, Gregory is made to impersonate Misaubin when he poses as a French physician, urging Dorcas to 'taka de Peel; me sal give you de litle Peel dat sal cure you'. For a later reference to Misaubin in *Tom Jones*, see below, p. 688.

1 Addison's *Cato. A Tragedy* (1713), v. i.
2 Cf. Matthew 20: 1–16. With Fielding's application of this parable in the present context, compare Bishop Hoadly's sermon xviii, 'The Parable of the Labourers in the Vineyard, explained: together with the great Danger of delaying Amendment' (*Works*, ed. John Hoadly [1773], iii. 611–19).

*Blifil,* who had been some Time in *London,* and Mr. *Jones,* whom the Reader hath just parted from at Mr. *Western's* and who received this Summons just as *Sophia* had left him.

The News of Mr. *Allworthy's* Danger (for the Servant told him he was dying) drove all Thoughts of Love out of his Head. He hurried instantly into the Chariot which was sent for him, and ordered the Coachman to drive with all imaginable Haste; nor did the Idea of *Sophia,* I believe, once occur to him on the Way.

And now, the whole Family, namely, Mr. *Blifil,* Mr. *Jones,* Mr. *Thwackum,* Mr. *Square,* and some of the Servants (for such were Mr. *Allworthy's* Orders) being all assembled round his Bed, the good Man sat up in it, and was beginning to speak, when *Blifil* fell to blubbering; and began to express very loud and bitter Lamentations. Upon this Mr. *Allworthy* shook him by the Hand, and said, 'Do not sorrow thus, my dear Nephew, at the most ordinary of all human Occurrences. When Misfortunes befal our Friends we are justly grieved: For those are Accidents which might often have been avoided, and which may seem to render the Lot of one Man, more peculiarly unhappy than that of others; but Death is certainly unavoidable, and is that common Lot, in which alone the Fortunes of all Men agree; nor is the Time when this happens to us very material. If the wisest of Men hath compared Life to a Span,[1] surely we may be allowed to consider it as a Day. It is my Fate to leave it in the Evening; but those who are taken away earlier, have only lost a few Hours, at the best little worth lamenting, and much oftner Hours of Labour and Fatigue, of Pain and Sorrow. One of the *Roman* Poets,[2] I remember, likens our leaving Life to our Departure from a Feast. A Thought which hath often occurred to me, when I have seen Men struggling to protract an Entertainment, and to enjoy the Company of their Friends a few Moments longer. Alas! how short is the most protracted of such Enjoyments! How immaterial the Difference between him who retires the soonest, and him who stays the latest! This is seeing Life in the best View, and this

[1] Cf. Psalm 39 as rendered in *The Book of Common Prayer,* where it is part of the liturgy for the Burial of the Dead: 'Behold, thou hast made my days as it were a span long.' Cf. *Amelia* (1751; VIII. x) and 'Of the Remedy of Affliction for the Loss of Our Friends' (1743), where Fielding attributes the saying to Solomon.

[2] Cf. Lucretius, *De Rerum Natura,* iii. 938–9: 'Why not like a banqueter fed full of life, withdraw with contentment and rest in peace' (trans. W. H. D. Rouse, Loeb Classical Library, 1924). The figure is repeated by Horace, *Satires,* I. i. 118; *Epistles,* II. ii. 215.

Unwillingness to quit our Friends is the most amiable Motive,
from which we can derive the Fear of Death; and yet the longest
Enjoyment which we can hope for of this Kind is of so trivial a
Duration, that it is to a wise Man truly contemptible. Few Men,
I own, think in this Manner: for, indeed, few Men think of
Death till they are in its Jaws. However gigantic and terrible an
Object this may appear when it approaches them, they are nevertheless incapable of seeing it at any Distance; nay, tho' they have
been ever so much alarmed and frightned when they have apprehended themselves in Danger of dying, they are no sooner
cleared from this Apprehension than even the Fears of it are
erased from their Minds. But alas! he who escapes from Death is
not pardoned, he is only reprieved, and reprieved to a short Day.

'Grieve, therefore, no more, my dear Child, on this Occasion;
an Event which may happen every Hour, which every Element,
nay almost every Particle of Matter that surrounds us is capable
of producing, and which must and will most unavoidably reach
us all at last, ought neither to occasion our Surprize, nor our
Lamentation.

'My Physician having acquainted me (which I take very kindly
of him) that I am in Danger of leaving you all very shortly, I
have determined to say a few Words to you at this our Parting,
before my Distemper, which I find grows very fast upon me,
puts it out of my Power.

'But I shall waste my Strength too much.—I intended to speak
concerning my Will, which tho' I have settled long ago, I
think proper to mention such Heads of it as concern any of you,
that I may have the Comfort of perceiving you are all satisfied
with the Provision I have there made for you.

'Nephew *Blifil,* I leave you the Heir to my whole Estate, except only 500 *l.* a Year which is to revert to you after the Death
of your Mother, and except one other Estate of 500 *l.* a Year,
and the Sum of 6000 *l.* which I have bestowed in the following
Manner.

'The Estate of 500 *l.* a Year I have given to you, Mr. *Jones.*
And as I know the Inconvenience which attends the Want of
ready Money, I have added 1000 *l.* in Specie. In this I know not
whether I have exceeded, or fallen short of your Expectation.
Perhaps you will think I have given you too little, and the World
will be as ready to condemn me for giving you too much; but the

latter Censure I despise, and as to the former, unless you should
entertain that common Error, which I have often heard in my
Life pleaded as an Excuse for a total Want of Charity; namely,
that instead of raising Gratitude by voluntary Acts of Bounty,
we are apt to raise Demands, which of all others are the most
boundless and most difficult to satisfy——Pardon me the bare
Mention of this, I will not suspect any such Thing.'

*Jones* flung himself at his Benefactor's Feet, and taking eagerly
hold of his Hand, assured him, his Goodness to him, both now,
and all other Times, had so infinitely exceeded not only his
Merit, but his Hopes, that no Words could express his Sense of
it. 'And I assure you, Sir,' said he, 'your present Generosity
hath left me no other Concern than for the present melancholy
Occasion.—Oh, my Friend! my Father!' Here his Words
choaked him, and he turned away to hide a Tear which was starting from his Eyes.

*Allworthy* then gently squeezed his Hand, and proceeded thus.
'I am convinced, my Child, that you have much Goodness,
Generosity and Honour in your Temper; if you will add Prudence[1]
and Religion to these, you must be happy: For the three former
Qualities, I admit, make you worthy of Happiness, but they are
the latter only which will put you in Possession of it.

'One thousand Pound I have given to you Mr. *Thwackum*; a
Sum, I am convinced, which greatly exceeds your Desires as well
as your Wants. However, you will receive it as a Memorial of my
Friendship; and whatever Superfluities may redound to you, that
Piety which you so rigidly maintain, will instruct you how to
dispose of them.

'A like Sum, Mr. *Square*, I have bequeathed to you. This, I
hope, will enable you to pursue your Profession with better
Success than hitherto. I have often observed with Concern, that
Distress is more apt to excite Contempt than Commiseration,
especially among Men of Business, with whom Poverty is understood to indicate Want of Ability. But the little I have been able
to leave you, will extricate you from those Difficulties with which
you have formerly struggled, and then I doubt not but you will
meet with sufficient Prosperity to supply what a Man of your
Philosophical Temper will require.

'I find myself growing faint, so I shall refer you to my Will for

[1] See above, p. 36, n. 1.

my Disposition of the Residue. My Servants will there find some
Tokens to remember me by, and there are a few Charities which,
I trust, my Executors will see faithfully performed. Bless you all.
I am setting out a little before you——'

Here a Footman came hastily into the Room, and said there
was an Attorney from *Salisbury*, who had a particular Message,
which he said he must communicate to Mr. *Allworthy* himself:
That he seemed in a violent Hurry, and protested he had so much
Business to do, that if he could cut himself into four Quarters,
all would not be sufficient.

'Go, Child,' said *Allworthy* to *Blifil*, 'see what the Gentleman
wants. I am not able to do any Business now, nor can he have any
with me, in which you are not at present more concerned than
myself. Besides I really am—I am incapable of seeing any one
at present, or of any longer Attention.' He then saluted them all,
saying, perhaps he should be able to see them again, but he should
be now glad to compose himself a little, finding that he had too
much exhausted his Spirits in Discourse.

Some of the Company shed Tears at their Parting; and even
the Philosopher *Square* wiped his Eyes, *albeit unused to the melting
Mood*. As to Mrs. *Wilkins*, she dropt her Pearls as fast *as the
Arabian Trees their Medicinal Gums*;[1] for this was a Ceremonial
which that Gentlewoman never omitted on a proper Occasion.

After this Mr. *Allworthy* again laid himself down on his Pillow,
and endeavoured to compose himself to Rest.

## CHAPTER VIII

*Containing Matter rather natural than pleasing.*

BESIDES Grief for her Master, there was another Source for
that briny Stream which so plentifully rose above the two
mountainous Cheek Bones of the House-keeper. She was no
sooner retired, than she began to mutter to herself in the following pleasant Strain. 'Sure Master might have made some Difference, methinks, between me and the other Servants. I suppose

---

[1] Cf. *Othello*, v. ii:    . . . of one whose subdu'd eyes,
                            Albeit unused to the melting mood,
                            Drop tears as fast as the Arabian trees
                            Their med'cinable gum.

he hath left me Mourning; but, i-fackins! if that be all, the Devil shall wear it for him for me. I'd have his Worship know I am no Beggar. I have saved five hundred Pound in his Service, and after all to be used in this Manner. It is a fine Encouragement to Servants to be honest; and to be sure, if I have taken a little Something now and then, others have taken ten times as much; and now we are all put in a Lump together. If so be that it be so, the Legacy may go to the Devil with him that gave it. No, I won't give it up neither, because that will please some Folks. No, I'll buy the gayest Gown I can get, and dance over the old Curmudgeon's Grave in it. This is my Reward for taking his Part so often, when all the Country have cried Shame of him for breeding up his Bastard in that Manner; but he is going now where he must pay for all. It would have becomed him better to have repented of his Sins on his Death-bed, than to glory in them, and give away his Estate out of his own Family to a mis-begotten Child. Found in his Bed, forsooth! A pretty Story! Ay, ay, those that hide know where to find. Lord forgive him, I warrant he hath many more Bastards to answer for, if the Truth was known. One Comfort is, they will all be known where he is a going now. 'The Servants will find some Token to remember me by.' Those were the very Words, I shall never forget them, if I was to live a thousand Years. Ay, ay, I shall remember you for huddling me among the Servants. One would have thought he might have mentioned my Name as well as that of *Square*; but he is a Gentleman forsooth, though he had not Clothes to his Back when he came hither first. Marry come up with such Gentlemen! though he hath lived here this many Years, I don't believe there is *arrow* Servant in the House ever saw the Colour of his Money. The Devil shall wait upon such a Gentleman for me.' Much more of the like kind she muttered to herself; but this Taste shall suffice to the Reader.

Neither *Thwackum* nor *Square* were much better satisfied with their Legacies. Tho' they breathed not their Resentment so loud, yet from the Discontent which appeared in their Countenances, as well as from the following Dialogue, we collect that no great Pleasure reigned in their Minds.

About an Hour after they had left the sick Room, *Square* met *Thwackum* in the Hall, and accosted him thus, 'Well, Sir, have you heard any News of your Friend since we parted from him?'

'If you mean Mr. *Allworthy*,' answered *Thwackum*, 'I think you might rather give him the Appellation of your Friend: For he seems to me to have deserved that Title.' 'The Title is as good on your Side,' replied *Square*, 'for his Bounty, such as it is, hath been equal to both.' 'I should not have mentioned it first,' cries *Thwackum*, 'but since you begin, I must inform you I am of a different Opinion. There is a wide Distinction between voluntary Favours and Rewards. The Duty I have done in his Family, and the Care I have taken in the Education of his two Boys, are Services for which some Men might have expected a greater Return. I would not have you imagine I am therefore dissatisfied; for St. *Paul* hath taught me[1] to be content with the little I have. Had the Modicum been less, I should have known my Duty. But though the Scripture obliges me to remain contented, it doth not enjoin me to shut my Eyes to my own Merit, nor restrain me from seeing, when I am injured by an unjust Comparison.' 'Since you provoke me,' returned *Square*, 'that Injury is done to me: Nor did I ever imagine Mr. *Allworthy* had held my Friendship so light, as to put me in Ballance with one who received his Wages: I know to what it is owing; it proceeds from those narrow Principles which you have been so long endeavouring to infuse into him, in Contempt of every Thing which is great and noble. The Beauty and Loveliness of Friendship is too strong for dim Eyes, nor can it be perceived by any other Medium, than that unerring Rule of Right which you have so often endeavoured to ridicule, that you have perverted your Friend's Understanding.' 'I wish,' cries *Thwackum*, in a Rage, 'I wish for the Sake of his Soul, your damnable Doctrines have not perverted his Faith. It is to this, I impute his present Behaviour so unbecoming a Christian. Who but an Atheist could think of leaving the World without having first made up his Account? without confessing his Sins, and receiving that Absolution which he knew he had one in the House duly authorised to give him? He will feel the Want of these Necessaries when it is too late. When he is arrived at that Place where there is Wailing and Gnashing of Teeth.[2] It is then he will find in what mighty Stead that Heathen Goddess, that Virtue which you and all other Deists of the Age adore, will stand him. He will then summon his Priest when there is none to be found,

---

[1] Cf. Philippians 4: 11, 1 Timothy 6: 6–8, Hebrews 13: 5.
[2] Cf. Matthew 8: 12, 13: 42, 50, etc.

and will lament the Want of that Absolution, without which no Sinner can be safe.' 'If it be so material,' says *Square*, 'Why don't you present it him of your own Accord?' 'It hath no Virtue,' cries *Thwackum*, 'but to those who have sufficient Grace to require it. But why do I talk thus to a Heathen and an Unbeliever? It is you that taught him this Lesson, for which you have been well rewarded in this World, as I doubt not your Disciple will soon be in the other.' 'I know not what you mean by Reward,' said *Square*, 'but if you hint at that pitiful Memorial of our Friendship, which he hath thought fit to bequeath me, I despise it, and nothing but the unfortunate Situation of my Circumstances should prevail on me to accept it.'

The Physician now arrived, and began to enquire of the two Disputants, *How we all did above Stairs?* 'In a miserable Way,' answered *Thwackum*. 'It is no more than I expected,' cries the Doctor; 'but pray what Symptoms have appeared since I left you?' 'No good ones, I am afraid,' replied *Thwackum*, 'after what past at our Departure, I think there were little Hopes.' The bodily Physician, perhaps, misunderstood the Curer of Souls, and before they came to an Explanation, Mr. *Blifil* came to them with a most melancholy Countenance, and acquainted them that he brought sad News: For that his Mother was dead at *Salisbury*. That she had been seized on the Road home with the Gout in her Head and Stomach, which had carried her off in a few Hours. 'Goodlack-a-day,' says the Doctor. 'One cannot answer for Events; but I wish I had been at Hand to have been called in. The Gout is a Distemper which it is difficult to treat, yet I have been remarkably successful in it.' *Thwackum* and *Square* both condoled with Mr. *Blifil* for the Loss of his Mother, which the one advised him to bear like a Man, and the other like a Christian. The young Gentleman said, he knew very well we were all mortal, and he would endeavour to submit to his Loss, as well as he could. That he could not, however, help complaining a little against the peculiar Severity of his Fate, which brought the News of so great a Calamity to him by Surprize, and that at a Time when he hourly expected the severest Blow he was capable of feeling from the Malice of Fortune. He said, the present Occasion would put to the Test those excellent Rudiments, which he had learnt from Mr. *Thwackum* and Mr. *Square*, and it would be entirely owing to them, if he was enabled to survive such Misfortunes.

It was now debated whether Mr. *Allworthy* should be informed of the Death of his Sister: This the Doctor violently op-
posed, in which, I believe, the whole College will agree with him;
but Mr. *Blifil* said he had received such positive and repeated
Orders from his Uncle never to keep any Secret from him, for
Fear of the Disquietude which it might give him, that he durst
not think of Disobedience, whatever might be the Consequence.
He said, for his Part, considering the religious and philosophic
Temper of his Uncle, he could not agree with the Doctor in his
Apprehensions. He was therefore resolved to communicate it to
him: For if his Uncle recovered (as he heartily prayed he might)
he knew he would never forgive an Endeavour to keep a Secret
of this Kind from him.

The Physician was forced to submit to these Resolutions which
the two other learned Gentlemen very highly commended. So
together moved Mr. *Blifil* and the Doctor towards the sick Room;
where the Physician first entered, and approached the Bed, in
order to feel his Patient's Pulse, which he had no sooner done,
than he declared he was much better, that the last Application
had succeeded to a Miracle, and had brought the Fever to inter-
mit. So that, he said, there appeared now to be as little Danger
as he had before apprehended there were Hopes.

To say the Truth, Mr. *Allworthy's* Situation had never been
so bad, as the great Caution of the Doctor had represented it;
but as a wise General never despises his Enemy, however inferior that Enemy's Force may be, so neither doth a wise Physician
ever despise a Distemper, however inconsiderable. As the former
preserves the same strict Discipline, places the same Guards,
and employs the same Scouts, tho' the Enemy be never so
weak; so the latter maintains the same Gravity of Countenance,
and shakes his Head with the same significant Air, let the Distemper be never so trifling. And both, among many other good
ones, may assign this solid Reason for their Conduct, that by
these Means the greater Glory redounds to them if they gain
the Victory, and the less Disgrace if by any unlucky Accident
they should happen to be conquered.

Mr. *Allworthy* had no sooner lifted up his Eyes, and thanked
Heaven for these Hopes of his Recovery, than Mr. *Blifil* drew
near with a very dejected Aspect, and having applied his
Handkerchief to his Eye, either to wipe away his Tears,

or to do as *Ovid* somewhere expresses himself on another Occasion,[1]

*Si nullus erit, tamen excute nullum.*

If there be none, then wipe away that none.

he communicated to his Uncle what the Reader hath been just before acquainted with.

*Allworthy* received the News with Concern, with Patience, and with Resignation. He dropt a tender Tear, then composed his Countenance, and at last cried, 'The Lord's Will be done in every Thing.'

He now enquired for the Messenger; but *Blifil* told him, it had been impossible to detain him a Moment; for he appeared by the great Hurry he was in to have some Business of Importance on his Hands: That he complained of being hurried, and driven and torn out of his Life, and repeated many Times, that if he could divide himself into four Quarters, he knew how to dispose of every one.

*Allworthy* then desired *Blifil* to take Care of the Funeral. He said, he would have his Sister deposited in his own Chapel; and as to the Particulars, he left them to his own Discretion, only mentioning the Person whom he would have employed on this Occasion.

## CHAPTER IX

*Which, among other Things, may serve as a Comment on that Saying of Æschines,[2] that* DRUNKENNESS SHEWS THE MIND OF A MAN, AS A MIRROUR REFLECTS HIS PERSON.

THE Reader may, perhaps, wonder at hearing nothing of Mr. *Jones* in the last Chapter. In fact, his Behaviour was so different from that of the Persons there mentioned, that we chose not to confound his Name with theirs.

---

[1] *Ars Amatoria*, i. 151: 'si nullus erit pulvis, tamen excute nullum.' Ovid advises the lover to affect a tender concern for his mistress, in this instance by pretending to brush away a fleck of dust from her garment.

[2] Aeschines (*c.* 390–330 B.C.), the famous Athenian orator and rival of Demosthenes. As in Stobæus, however, whose anthology of Greek aphorisms Fielding knew (see below, p. 257, n. 1), the saying should be attributed to Aeschylus (*Fragments*, 221 [393]): *Aes formæ speculum est, vinum mentis*: bronze is a mirror of the person, wine of the mind. (See

When the good Man had ended his Speech, *Jones* was the last who deserted the Room. Thence he retired to his own Apartment, to give Vent to his Concern; but the Restlessness of his Mind would not suffer him to remain long there; he slipped softly, therefore, to *Allworthy's* Chamber Door, where he listened a considerable Time without hearing any Kind of Motion within, unless a violent snoring, which at last his Fears misrepresented as Groans. This so alarmed him, that he could not forbear entering the Room; where he found the good Man in the Bed in a sweet composed Sleep, and his Nurse snoring in the above-mentioned hearty Manner, at the Bed's-Feet. He immediately took the only Method of silencing this thorough Bass, whose Music he feared might disturb Mr. *Allworthy*; and then sitting down by the Nurse, he remained motionless till *Blifil* and the Doctor came in together, and waked the sick Man; in order that the Doctor might feel his Pulse, and that the other might communicate to him that Piece of News, which, had *Jones* been apprized of it, would have had great Difficulty of finding its Way to Mr. *Allworthy's* Ear at such a Season.

When he first heard *Blifil* tell his Uncle this Story, *Jones* could hardly contain the Wrath which kindled in him at the other's Indiscretion, especially as the Doctor shook his Head, and declared his Unwillingness to have the Matter mentioned to his Patient. But as his Passion did not so far deprive him of all Use of his Understanding, as to hide from him the Consequences which any violent Expressions towards *Blifil* might have on the Sick, this Apprehension stilled his Rage, at the present; and he grew afterwards so satisfied with finding that this News had, in fact, produced no Mischief, that he suffered his Anger to die in his own Bosom, without ever mentioning it to *Blifil*.

The Physician dined that Day at Mr. *Allworthy's*; and having after Dinner visited his Patient, he returned to the Company, and told them, that he had now the Satisfaction to say, with

John Stobæus, *Sententiæ ex Thesauris Græcorum Delectæ* [Aureliæ Allobrogum, 1609], sermo xviii, 'De Incontinentia', p. 164.) Nevertheless, considering the context, Fielding may have wished to recall Aeschines. In *De Falsa Legatione*, Demosthenes called attention to his rival's drunken behaviour at a banquet in Macedonia, during which Aeschines was said to have cruelly abused a young woman who refused to drink with him: if the girl had not been rescued, Demosthenes declared, 'she would have perished, the victim of a drunken orgy, for the drunkenness of this blackguard is something terrible' (198—trans. C. A. and J. H. Vince, Loeb Classical Library, 1926).

Assurance, that his Patient was out of all Danger: That he had brought his Fever to a perfect Intermission, and doubted not by throwing in the Bark¹ to prevent its Return.

This Account so pleased *Jones*, and threw him into such immoderate Excess of Rapture, that he might be truly said to be drunk with Joy. An Intoxication which greatly forwards the Effects of Wine; and as he was very free too with the Bottle on this Occasion, (for he drank many Bumpers to the Doctor's Health, as well as to other Toasts) he became very soon literally drunk.

*Jones* had naturally violent animal Spirits. These being set on Float, and augmented by the Spirit of Wine, produced most extravagant Effects. He kissed the Doctor, and embraced him with the most passionate Endearments; swearing that, next to Mr. *Allworthy* himself, he loved him 'of all Men living.' 'Doctor,' added he, 'you deserve a Statue to be erected to you at the public Expence, for having preserved a Man, who is not only the Darling of all good Men who know him, but a Blessing to Society, the Glory of his Country, and an Honour to Human Nature. D—n me if I don't love him better than my own Soul.'

'More shame for you,' cries *Thwackum*. 'Though I think you have reason to love him, for he hath provided very well for you. And, perhaps, it might have been better for some Folks, that he had not lived to see just Reason of revoking his Gift.'

*Jones* now, looking on *Thwackum* with inconceivable Disdain, answered, 'And doth thy mean Soul imagine that any such Considerations could weigh with me? No, let the Earth open and swallow her own Dirt (if I had Millions of Acres I would say it) rather than swallow up my dear glorious Friend.'

> *Quis Desiderio sit Pudor aut modus*
> *Tam chari Capitis?*\*²

The Doctor now interposed, and prevented the Effects of a Wrath which was kindling between *Jones* and *Thwackum*; after

---

\* 'What Modesty, or Measure, can set Bounds to our Desire of so dear a Friend!' The Word *Desiderium* here cannot be easily translated. It includes our Desire of enjoying our Friend again, and the Grief which attends that Desire.

---

¹ The bark of the Cinchona tree, from which quinine is derived.

² Horace, *Odes*, I. xxiv. 1–2. The ode is addressed to Virgil on the death of their mutual friend, Quintilius.

which the former gave a Loose to Mirth, sang two or three amorous Songs, and fell into every frantic Disorder which unbridled Joy is apt to inspire; but so far was he from any Disposition to quarrel, that he was ten times better humoured, if possible, than when he was sober.

To say Truth, nothing is more erroneous than the common Observation, That Men who are ill-natured and quarrelsome when they are drunk, are very worthy Persons when they are sober: For Drink, in reality, doth not reverse Nature, or create Passions in Men, which did not exist in them before.[1] It takes away the Guard of Reason, and consequently forces us to produce those Symptoms, which many, when sober, have Art enough to conceal. It heightens and inflames our Passions (generally indeed that Passion which is uppermost in our Mind) so that the angry Temper, the amorous, the generous, the good-humoured, the avaricious, and all other Dispositions of Men, are in their Cups heightened and exposed.

And yet as no Nation produces so many drunken Quarrels, especially among the lower People, as *England*; (for, indeed, with them, to drink and to fight together are almost synonimous Terms) I would not, methinks, have it thence concluded that the *English* are the worst-natured People alive. Perhaps the Love of Glory only is at the Bottom of this; so that the fair Conclusion seems to be, that our Countrymen have more of that Love, and more of Bravery, than any other Plebeians. And this the rather, as there is seldom any thing ungenerous, unfair, or ill-natured, exercised on those Occasions: Nay, it is common for the Combatants to express Good-will for each other, even at the Time of the Conflict; and as their drunken Mirth generally ends in a Battle, so do most of their Battles end in Friendship.

But to return to our History. Tho' *Jones* had shewn no Design of giving Offence, yet Mr. *Blifil* was highly offended at a Behaviour which was so inconsistent with the sober and prudent Reserve of his own Temper. He bore it too with the greater Impatience, as it appeared to him very indecent at this Season; 'when,' as he said, 'the House was a House of Mourning, on the Account of his dear Mother; and if it had pleased Heaven to give them some Prospect of Mr. *Allworthy's* Recovery, it

[1] Cf. Seneca 'On Drunkenness', *Epistulae Morales*, lxxxiii. 19–20, and *Spectator*, No. 569 (19 July 1712).

would become them better to express the Exultations of their Hearts in Thanksgiving than in Drunkenness and Riots; which were properer Methods to encrease the divine Wrath, than to avert it.' *Thwackum*, who had swallowed more Liquor than *Jones*, but without any ill Effect on his Brain, seconded the pious Harangue of *Blifil*; but *Square*, for Reasons which the Reader may probably guess, was totally silent.

Wine had not so totally overpowered *Jones*, as to prevent his recollecting Mr. *Blifil's* Loss, the Moment it was mentioned. As no Person, therefore, was more ready to confess and condemn his own Errors, he offered to shake Mr. *Blifil* by the Hand, and begged his Pardon, saying, 'His excessive Joy for Mr. *Allworthy's* Recovery had driven every other Thought out of his Mind.'

*Blifil* scornfully rejected his Hand; and, with much Indignation, answered, 'It was little to be wondered at, if tragical Spectacles made no Impressions on the Blind; but, for his Part, he had the Misfortune to know who his Parents were, and consequently must be affected with their Loss.'

*Jones*, who, notwithstanding his good Humour, had some Mixture of the irascible in his Constitution, leaped hastily from his Chair, and catching hold of *Blifil's* Collar, cried out, 'D——n you for a Rascal, do you insult me with the Misfortune of my Birth?' He accompanied these Words with such rough Actions, that they soon got the better of Mr. *Blifil's* peaceful Temper; and a Scuffle immediately ensued, which might have produced Mischief, had it not been prevented by the Interposition of *Thwackum* and the Physician; for the Philosophy of *Square* rendered him superior to all Emotions, and he very calmly smoaked his Pipe, as was his Custom in all Broils, unless when he apprehended some Danger of having it broke in his Mouth.

The Combatants being now prevented from executing present Vengeance on each other, betook themselves to the common Resources of disappointed Rage, and vented their Wrath in Threats and Defiance. In this kind of Conflict, Fortune, which, in the personal Attack, seemed to incline to *Jones*, was now altogether as favourable to his Enemy.

A Truce, nevertheless, was at length agreed on, by the Mediation of the neutral Parties, and the whole Company again sat down at the Table; where *Jones* being prevailed on to ask Pardon,

and *Blifil* to give it, Peace was restored, and every thing seemed
in *Statu quo*.

But though the Quarrel was, in all Appearance, perfectly reconciled, the Good-humour which had been interrupted by it,
was by no means restored. All Merriment was now at an End,
and the subsequent Discourse consisted only of grave Relations
of Matters of Fact, and of as grave Observations upon them.
A Species of Conversation, in which, though there is much of
Dignity and Instruction, there is but little Entertainment. As we
presume, therefore, to convey only this last to the Reader, we shall
pass by whatever was said, till the rest of the Company having,
by Degrees, dropped off, left only *Square* and the Physician
together; at which Time the Conversation was a little heightened
by some Comments on what had happened between the two
young Gentlemen; both of whom the Doctor declared to be no
better than Scoundrels; to which Appellation the Philosopher,
very sagaciously shaking his Head, agreed.

## CHAPTER X

*Shewing the Truth of many Observations of* Ovid,[1] *and of other more
grave Writers, who have proved, beyond Contradiction, that Wine
is often the Fore-runner of Incontinency.*

*JONES* retired from the Company, in which we have seen
him engaged, into the Fields, where he intended to cool
himself by a Walk in the open Air, before he attended Mr.
*Allworthy*. There, whilst he renewed those Meditations on his
dear *Sophia*, which the dangerous Illness of his Friend and
Benefactor had for some time interrupted, an Accident happened,
which with Sorrow we relate, and with Sorrow, doubtless, will
it be read; however, that historic Truth to which we profess
so inviolable an Attachment, obliges us to communicate it to
Posterity.

It was now a pleasant Evening in the latter End of *June*,[2]
when our Heroe was walking in a most delicious Grove, where

---

[1] Cf. *Ars Amatoria*, i. 237.

[2] In revising the novel Fielding overlooked this vestige of an original time-scheme: in
VII. xi, a point in the narrative just three weeks later, the time is given as November 1745.
See below, p. 368, n. 1, and the General Introduction, pp. xxxvii ff.

the gentle Breezes fanning the Leaves, together with the sweet Trilling of a murmuring Stream, and the melodious Notes of Nightingales formed all together the most enchanting Harmony. In this Scene, so sweetly accommodated to Love, he meditated on his dear *Sophia*. While his wanton Fancy roved unbounded over all her Beauties, and his lively Imagination painted the charming Maid in various ravishing Forms, his warm Heart melted with Tenderness, and at length throwing himself on the Ground by the Side of a gently murmuring Brook, he broke forth into the following Ejaculation.

'O *Sophia*, would Heaven give thee to my Arms, how blest would be my Condition! Curst be that Fortune which sets a Distance between us. Was I but possessed of thee, one only Suit of Rags thy whole Estate, is there a Man on Earth whom I would envy! How contemptible would the brightest *Circassian* Beauty, drest in all the Jewels of the *Indies*, appear to my Eyes! But why do I mention another Woman? could I think my Eyes capable of looking at any other with Tenderness, these Hands should tear them from my Head. No, my *Sophia*, if cruel Fortune separates us for ever, my Soul shall doat on thee alone. The chastest Constancy will I ever preserve to thy Image. Tho' I should never have Possession of thy charming Person, still shalt thou alone have Possession of my Thoughts, my Love, my Soul. Oh! my fond Heart is so wrapt in that tender Bosom, that the brightest Beauties would for me have no Charms, nor would a Hermit be colder in their Embraces. *Sophia, Sophia* alone shall be mine. What Raptures are in that Name! I will engrave it on every Tree.'

At these Words he started up, and beheld—not his *Sophia*— no, nor a *Circassian* Maid richly and elegantly attired for the Grand Signior's Seraglio. No; without a Gown, in a Shift that was somewhat of the coarsest, and none of the cleanest, bedewed likewise with some odoriferous Effluvia, the Produce of the Day's Labour, with a Pitch-fork in her Hand, *Molly Seagrim* approached. Our Heroe had his Pen-knife in his Hand, which he had drawn for the before-mentioned Purpose, of carving on the Bark; when the Girl coming near him cry'd out with a Smile, 'You don't intend to kill me, Squire, I hope!' 'Why should you think I would kill you?' answered *Jones*. 'Nay,' replied she, 'after your cruel Usage of me when I saw you last, killing me would, perhaps, be too great Kindness for me to expect.'

Here ensued a Parly, which, as I do not think myself obliged to relate it, I shall omit. It is sufficient that it lasted a full Quarter of an Hour, at the Conclusion of which they retired into the thickest Part of the Grove.

Some of my Readers may be inclined to think this Event unnatural. However, the Fact is true; and, perhaps, may be sufficiently accounted for, by suggesting that *Jones* probably thought one Woman better than none, and *Molly* as probably imagined two Men to be better than one. Besides the before-mentioned Motive assigned to the present Behaviour of *Jones*, the Reader will be likewise pleased to recollect in his Favour, that he was not at this Time perfect Master of that wonderful Power of Reason, which so well enables grave and wise Men to subdue their unruly Passions, and to decline any of these prohibited Amusements. Wine now had totally subdued this Power in *Jones*. He was, indeed, in a Condition, in which if Reason had interposed, tho' only to advise, she might have received the Answer which one *Cleostratus*[1] gave many Years ago to a silly Fellow, who asked him if he was not ashamed to be drunk? 'Are not you,' said *Cleostratus*, 'ashamed to admonish a drunken Man?'—To say the Truth, in a Court of Justice, Drunkenness must not be an Excuse,[2] yet in a Court of Conscience it is greatly so; and therefore *Aristotle*, who commends the Laws of *Pittacus*,[3] by which drunken Men received double Punishment for their Crimes, allows there is more of Policy than Justice in that Law. Now, if there are any Transgressions pardonable from Drunkenness, they are certainly such as Mr. *Jones* was at present guilty of; on which Head I could pour forth a vast Profusion of Learning, if I imagined it would either entertain my Reader, or teach him any Thing more than he knows already. For his Sake, therefore, I shall keep my Learning to myself, and return to my History.

---

[1] The only source for this anecdote appears to be Stobæus' anthology, sermo xxxiv, 'De Tempestiva Oratione': '*Cleostratus ei qui dixerat, nŏ te pudet ebrietatis? respondit: Te verò non pudet ebrium admonere?*' (*Sententiæ ex Thesauris Græcorum Delectæ* [Aureliæ Allobrogum, 1609], p. 215; Fielding owned a copy of this edition.)

[2] In fact, drunkenness was legally considered to be an aggravation of the offence. (See Wood, *Institutes*, 7th ed. [1745], p. 14.)

[3] *Politics*, II. ix. 9. Pittacus of Mytilene (*c.* 650–570 B.C.), one of the 'Seven Sages' of Greece. Referring to this law in *An Enquiry into the Causes of the late Increase of Robbers* (1751), section ii ('Of Drunkenness'), Fielding remarked that he did not know 'a more excellent Institution'.

It hath been observed, that Fortune seldom doth Things by Halves. To say Truth, there is no End to her Freaks whenever she is disposed to gratify or displease. No sooner had our Heroe retired with his *Dido*, but

> *Speluncam* Blifil, *Dux et Divinus eandem*
> *Deveniunt.*———[1]

the Parson and the young Squire, who were taking a serious Walk, arrived at the Stile which leads into the Grove, and the latter caught a View of the Lovers, just as they were sinking out of Sight.

*Blifil* knew *Jones* very well, tho' he was at above a hundred Yards Distance, and he was as positive to the Sex of his Companion, tho' not to the individual Person. He started; blessed himself, and uttered a very solemn Ejaculation.

*Thwackum* express'd some Surprize at these sudden Emotions, and asked the Reason of them. To which *Blifil* answered, 'he was certain he had seen a Fellow and Wench retire together among the Bushes, which he doubted not was with some wicked Purpose.' As to the Name of *Jones* he thought proper to conceal it, and why he did so must be left to the Judgment of the sagacious Reader: For we never chuse to assign Motives to the Actions of Men, when there is any possibility of our being mistaken.

The Parson, who was not only strictly chaste in his own Person, but a great Enemy to the opposite Vice in all others, fired at this Information. He desired Mr. *Blifil* to conduct him immediately to the Place, which as he approached, he breathed forth Vengeance mixed with Lamentations; nor did he refrain from casting some oblique Reflections on Mr. *Allworthy*; insinuating that the Wickedness of the Country was principally owing to the Encouragement he had given to Vice, by having exerted such Kindness to a Bastard, and by having mitigated that just and wholsome Rigour of the Law, which allots a very severe Punishment to loose Wenches.

The Way, through which our Hunters were to pass in Pursuit of their Game, was so beset with Briars, that it greatly obstructed their Walk, and caused, besides, such a rustling that *Jones* had

---

[1] Fielding parodies the *Aeneid*, iv. 165–6. In a shower of rain Dido and Aeneas take shelter in a cave, where they consummate their love: 'speluncam Dido dux et Troianus eandem / deveniunt' ('To the same cave come Dido and the Trojan chief'—trans. H. R. Fairclough, Loeb Classical Library, 1916).

sufficient Warning of their Arrival, before they could surprize him; nay, indeed, so incapable was *Thwackum* of concealing his Indignation, and such Vengeance did he mutter forth every Step he took, that this alone must have abundantly satisfied *Jones*, that he was (to use the Language of Sportsmen) *found sitting*.


## CHAPTER XI

*In which a Simile in Mr.* Pope's *Period of a Mile,*[1] *introduces as bloody a Battle as can possibly be fought, without the Assistance of Steel or* cold *Iron.*


AS in the Season of RUTTING[2] (an uncouth Phrase, by which the Vulgar denote that gentle Dalliance, which in the well-wooded Forest* of *Hampshire*, passes between Lovers of the Ferine Kind) if while the lofty crested Stag meditates the amorous Sport, a Couple of Puppies, or any other Beasts of hostile Note, should wander so near the Temple of *Venus Ferina*, that the fair Hind should shrink from the Place, touched with that Somewhat, either of Fear or Frolic, of Nicety or Skittishness, with which Nature hath bedecked all Females, or hath, at least, instructed them how to put it on; lest, thro' the Indelicacy of Males, the *Samean* Mysteries[3] should be pryed into by un-hallowed Eyes: For at the Celebration of these Rites, the female

---

* This is an ambiguous Phrase, and may mean either a Forest well clothed with Wood, or well stript of it.[4]

---

[1] In *The Fourth Satire of Dr. John Donne, Dean of St. Paul's, Versifyed* (1733), l. 73, Pope alludes to Bishop Hoadly's long-windedness. When asked which writers he most esteems, the speaker replies: 'Swift, for closer Style, / And Ho[adl]y for a Period of a Mile.'
[2] With Fielding's account of the behaviour of stags in 'rutting' season (usually mid-September until mid-November), compare *The Gentleman's Recreation*, 6th ed. (1721), pp. 7, 52–4.
[3] Samos, an island in the Ionian Sea, was sacred to Juno, queen of the gods, whose function it was to preside over marriage and childbirth.
[4] The New Forest—of which Fielding's patron, the Duke of Bedford, was Warden (see above, p. 5, n. 1)—had fallen into decay under the Stuarts, who liberally awarded timber privileges to their favourites. In 1693, recognizing that 'the Forest was in danger of being destroyed', William III authorized the planting of 6,000 acres, but the devastation con-tinued virtually unchecked until the last decade of the eighteenth century. (See J. R. Wise, *The New Forest: Its History and its Scenery* [1863], pp. 43–5.)

Priestess cries out with her in *Virgil* (who was then probably hard at Work on such Celebration)

——*Procul, O procul este, profani;*
*Proclamat Vates, totoque absistite Luco.*[1]

——Far hence be Souls prophane,
The Sibyl cry'd, and from the Grove abstain.

DRYDEN.

If, I say, while these sacred Rites, which are in common to *Genus omne Animantium*,[2] are in Agitation between the Stag and his Mistress, any hostile Beasts should venture too near, on the first Hint given by the frighted Hind, fierce and tremendous rushes forth the Stag to the Entrance of the Thicket; there stands he Centinel over his Love, stamps the Ground with his Foot, and with his Horns brandished aloft in Air, proudly provokes the apprehended Foe to Combat.

Thus, and more terrible, when he perceived the Enemy's Approach, leap'd forth our Heroe. Many a Step advanced he forwards, in order to conceal the trembling Hind, and, if possible, to secure her Retreat. And now *Thwackum* having first darted some livid Lightning from his fiery Eyes, began to thunder forth, 'Fie upon it! Fie upon it! Mr. *Jones*. Is it possible you should be the Person!' 'You see,' answered *Jones*, 'it is possible I should be here.' 'And who,' said *Thwackum*, 'is that wicked Slut with you?' 'If I have any wicked Slut with me,' cries *Jones*, 'it is possible I shall not let you know who she is.' 'I command you to tell me immediately,' says *Thwackum*, 'and I would not have you imagine, young Man, that your Age, tho' it hath somewhat abridged the Purpose of Tuition, hath totally taken away the Authority of the Master. The Relation of the Master and Scholar is indelible, as, indeed, all other Relations are: For they all derive their Original from Heaven. I would have you think yourself, therefore, as much obliged to obey me now, as when I taught you your first Rudiments.' 'I believe you would,' cries *Jones*, 'but that will not happen, unless you had the same Birchen Argument to convince me.' 'Then I must tell you plainly,' said *Thwackum*, 'I am resolved

---

[1] *Aeneid*, vi. 258-9—as dogs howl and other ominous signs occur, the Cumaean Sibyl speaks these lines at the entrance to the underworld. For the translation, see Dryden's *Aeneis*, vi. 368-9.

[2] 'The whole race of living creatures.'

to discover the wicked Wretch.' 'And I must tell you plainly,' returned *Jones*, 'I am resolved you shall not.' *Thwackum* then offered to advance, and *Jones* laid hold of his Arms; which Mr. *Blifil* endeavoured to rescue, declaring 'he would not see his old Master insulted.'

*Jones* now finding himself engaged with two, thought it necessary to rid himself of one of his Antagonists as soon as possible. He, therefore, applied to the weakest first; and letting the Parson go, he directed a Blow at the young Squire's Breast, which luckily taking Place, reduced him to measure his Length on the Ground.

*Thwackum* was so intent on the Discovery, that the Moment he found himself at Liberty, he stept forward directly into the Fern, without any great Consideration of what might, in the mean Time, befal his Friend; but he had advanced a very few Paces into the Thicket, before *Jones* having defeated *Blifil*, overtook the Parson, and dragged him backward by the Skirt of his Coat.

This Parson had been a Champion in his Youth, and had won much Honour by his Fist, both at School and at the University. He had now, indeed, for a great Number of Years, declined the Practice of that noble Art; yet was his Courage full as strong as his Faith, and his Body no less strong than either. He was moreover, as the Reader may, perhaps, have conceived, somewhat irascible in his Nature. When he looked back, therefore, and saw his Friend stretched out on the Ground, and found himself at the same Time so roughly handled by one who had formerly been only passive in all Conflicts between them, (a Circumstance which highly aggravated the whole) his Patience at length gave Way; he threw himself into a Posture of Offence, and collecting all his Force, attacked *Jones* in the Front, with as much Impetuosity as he had formerly attacked him in the Rear.

Our Heroe received the Enemy's Attack with the most undaunted Intrepidity, and his Bosom resounded with the Blow. This he presently returned with no less Violence, aiming likewise at the Parson's Breast; but he dextrously drove down the Fist of *Jones*, so that it reached only his Belly, where two Pounds of Beef and as many of Pudding were then deposited, and whence consequently no hollow Sound could proceed. Many lusty Blows, much more pleasant as well as easy to have seen, than to read or describe, were given on both Sides; at last a violent Fall in which *Jones* had thrown his Knees into *Thwackum's* Breast, so weakened the latter, that Victory had been no longer dubious, had not *Blifil*, who had now recovered his Strength, again renewed the Fight, and, by engaging with *Jones*, given the Parson a Moment's Time to shake his Ears, and to regain his Breath.

And now both together attacked our Heroe, whose Blows did not retain that Force with which they had fallen at first; so weakened was he by his Combat with *Thwackum*: For tho' the Pedagogue chose rather to play *Solos* on the human Instrument, and had been lately used to those only, yet he still retained enough of his ancient Knowledge to perform his Part very well in a *Duet*.

The Victory, according to modern Custom, was like to be decided by Numbers,[1] when, on a sudden, a fourth Pair of Fists appeared in the Battle, and immediately paid their Compliments to the Parson; the Owner of them, at the same Time, crying out, 'Are not you ashamed and be d—nd to you, to fall two of you upon one?'

The Battle, which was of the Kind, that for Distinction's Sake is called ROYAL,[2] now raged with the utmost Violence during a few Minutes; till *Blifil* being a second Time laid sprawling by *Jones*, *Thwackum* condescended to apply for Quarter to his new Antagonist, who was now found to be Mr. *Western* himself: For in the Heat of the Action none of the Combatants had recognized him.

In Fact, that honest Squire, happening in his Afternoon's Walk with some Company, to pass through the Field where the bloody Battle was fought, and having concluded from seeing three Men engaged, that two of them must be on a Side, he hastened from his Companions, and with more Gallantry than Policy, espoused the Cause of the weaker Party. By which generous Pro-

[1] Fielding's constant theme during the disastrous war with France was that the French owed their victories not to the greater courage of their soldiers, but to their superiority in numbers. In *The True Patriot* (10 December 1745) and *A Dialogue between a Gentleman of London . . . and an honest Alderman* (1747) he put the ratio of French to Allied troops at three to one. Particularly relevant here, in view of the allusion which introduces the succeeding paragraph, is Fielding's facetious account in *The True Patriot* (28 January–4 February 1746, under 'Foreign History'), comparing the commencement of hostilities in the Low Countries to a 'Cock-Match'. After noting that 'one Lewis the Fifteenth, a great Cock-Merchant, threatens to bring above 200,000 Head into the Pit, on the other Side', he concludes: 'N. B. It is imagined most of the French are Shack-bags, and only depend on the Superiority of their Numbers, as there are to be several Battles Royal.' See also below, p. 679.

[2] In cock-fighting, a general battle between several combinations of birds. See above, n. 1.

ceeding, he very probably prevented Mr. *Jones* from becoming a Victim to the Wrath of *Thwackum*, and to the pious Friendship which *Blifil* bore his old Master: For besides the Disadvantage of such Odds, *Jones* had not yet sufficiently recovered the former Strength of his broken Arm. This Reinforcement, however, soon put an End to the Action, and *Jones* with his Ally obtained the Victory.

## CHAPTER XII

*In which is seen a more moving Spectacle, than all the Blood in the Bodies of* Thwackum *and* Blifil *and of Twenty other such, is capable of producing.*

THE rest of Mr. *Western's* Company were now come up, being just at the Instant when the Action was over. These were the honest Clergyman, whom we have formerly seen at Mr. *Western's* Table; Mrs. *Western* the Aunt of *Sophia*; and lastly, the lovely *Sophia* herself.

At this Time, the following was the Aspect of the bloody Field. In one Place, lay on the Ground, all pale and almost breathless, the vanquished *Blifil*. Near him stood the Conqueror *Jones*, almost covered with Blood, part of which was naturally his own, and part had been lately the Property of the Reverend Mr. *Thwackum*. In a third Place stood the said *Thwackum*, like King *Porus*,[1] sullenly submitting to the Conqueror. The last Figure in the Piece was *Western the Great*, most gloriously forbearing the vanquished Foe.

---

[1] The story of Alexander's victory over Porus (326 B.C.), the Indian king, is told in Plutarch, *Life of Alexander*, lx, and in Arrian, *Anabasis of Alexander*, v. viii ff. Fielding's mock-heroic description of this bloody scene recalls one of the most celebrated historical *tableaux* of the period: Plate VI of Charles LeBrun's magnificent series depicting the victories of Alexander. (See Plate 6.) Done in 1661–8 at the command of Louis XIV, LeBrun's paintings now hang in the Louvre. Copies of the official engravings by the Audrans were commissioned in England and published by Carington Bowles (British Museum Print Room: C. 293*). The series was much admired: see, for example, Farquhar's *Beaux' Stratagem* (1707), iv, and Charles Gildon, *The Complete Art of Poetry* (1718), i. 230. When Louis Laguerre was commissioned to commemorate Marlborough's victories over the French, he looked to LeBrun's *tableaux* for a model (see M. Whinney and O. Millar, *English Art, 1625–1744* [Oxford, 1957], pp. 305–6). King Porus also figured prominently in several operas based on Metastasio's libretto, *Alessandre nelle Indie*; one of these, with music by Lampugnani, was produced in London in 1746.

*Blifil*, in whom there was little Sign of Life, was at first the principal Object of the Concern of every one, and particularly of Mrs. *Western*, who had drawn from her Pocket a Bottle of Hartshorn, and was herself about to apply it to his Nostrils; when on a sudden the Attention of the whole Company was diverted from poor *Blifil*, whose Spirit, if it had any such Design, might have now taken an Opportunity of stealing off to the other World, without any Ceremony.

For now a more melancholy and a more lovely Object lay motionless before them. This was no other than the charming *Sophia* herself, who, from the Sight of Blood, or from Fear for her Father, or from some other Reason, had fallen down in a Swoon, before any one could get to her Assistance.

Mrs. *Western* first saw her, and screamed. Immediately two or three Voices cried out, 'Miss *Western* is dead.' Hartshorn, Water; every Remedy was called for, almost at one and the same Instant.

The Reader may remember, that in our Description of this Grove, we mentioned a murmuring Brook, which Brook did not come there, as such gentle Streams flow through vulgar Romances, with no other Purpose than to murmur. No; Fortune had decreed to enoble this little Brook with a higher Honour than any of those which wash the Plains of *Arcadia*, ever deserved.

*Jones* was rubbing *Blifil's* Temples: For he began to fear he had given him a Blow too much, when the Words, Miss *Western* and *Dead*, rushed at once on his Ear. He started up, left *Blifil* to his Fate, and flew to *Sophia*, whom, while all the rest were running against each other backward and forward looking for Water in the dry Paths, he caught up in his Arms, and then ran away with her over the Field to the Rivulet above-mentioned; where, plunging himself into the Water, he contrived to besprinkle her Face, Head, and Neck very plentifully.

Happy was it for *Sophia*, that the same Confusion which prevented her other Friends from serving her, prevented them likewise from obstructing *Jones*. He had carried her half ways before they knew what he was doing, and he had actually restored her to Life before they reached the Water-side: She stretched out her Arms, opened her Eyes, and cried, 'Oh, Heavens!' just as her Father, Aunt and the Parson came up.

*Jones*, who had hitherto held this lovely Burthen in his Arms, now relinquished his Hold; but gave her at the same Instant a tender Caress, which, had her Senses been then perfectly restored, could not have escaped her Observation. As she expressed, therefore, no Displeasure at this Freedom, we suppose she was not sufficiently recovered from her Swoon at the Time.

This tragical Scene was now converted into a sudden Scene of Joy. In this, our Heroe was, most certainly, the principal Character: For as he probably felt more extatic Delight in having saved *Sophia*, than she herself received from being saved; so neither were the Congratulations paid to her, equal to what were conferred on *Jones*, especially by Mr. *Western* himself, who, after having once or twice embraced his Daughter, fell to hugging and kissing *Jones*. He called him the Preserver of *Sophia*, and declared there was nothing, except her, or his Estate, which he would not give him; but upon Recollection, he afterwards excepted his Fox-hounds, the *Chevalier*, and Miss *Slouch* (for so he called his favourite Mare).

All Fears for *Sophia* being now removed, *Jones* became the Object of the Squire's Consideration. 'Come, my Lad,' says *Western*, '*D'off* thy *Quoat* and wash thy *Feace*: For *att* in a devilish Pickle, I promise thee. Come, come, wash thyself, and *shat* go *Huome* with me; and *wel zee* to *vind* thee another *Quoat*.'

*Jones* immediately complied; threw off his Coat, went down to the Water, and washed both his Face and Bosom: For the latter was as much exposed, and as bloody as the former: But tho' the Water could clear off the Blood, it could not remove the black and blue Marks which *Thwackum* had imprinted on both his Face and Breast, and which, being discerned by *Sophia*, drew from her a Sigh, and a Look full of inexpressible Tenderness.

*Jones* receiv'd this full in his Eyes, and it had infinitely a stronger Effect on him than all the Contusions which he had received before. An Effect, however, widely different; for so soft and balmy was it, that, had all his former Blows been Stabs, it would for some Minutes have prevented his feeling their Smart.

The Company now moved backwards, and soon arrived where *Thwackum* had got Mr. *Blifil* again on his Legs. Here we cannot suppress a pious Wish, that all Quarrels were to be decided by those Weapons only, with which Nature, knowing what is proper for us, hath supplied us; and that cold Iron was to be used in digging no Bowels, but those of the Earth. Then would War, the Pastime of Monarchs, be almost inoffensive, and Battles between great Armies might be fought at the particular Desire of several Ladies of Quality; who, together with the Kings themselves, might be actual Spectators of the Conflict. Then might the Field be this Moment well strewed with human Carcasses, and the next, the dead Men, or infinitely the greatest Part of them, might get up, like Mr. *Bayes's* Troops,[1] and march off either at the Sound of a Drum or Fiddle, as should be previously agreed on.

I would avoid, if possible, treating this Matter ludicrously, lest grave Men and Politicians, whom I know to be offended at a Jest, may cry Pish at it; but, in reality, might not a Battle be as well decided by the greater Number of broken Heads, bloody Noses, and black Eyes, as by the greater Heaps of mangled and murdered human Bodies? Might not Towns be contended for in the same Manner? Indeed, this may be thought too detrimental a Scheme to the *French* Interest, since they would thus lose the Advantage they have over other Nations, in the Superiority of their Engineers:[2] But when I consider the Gallantry and Generosity of that People, I am persuaded they would never decline putting themselves upon a Par with their Adversary; or, as the Phrase is, *making themselves his Match.*

But such Reformations are rather to be wished than hoped for; I shall content myself, therefore, with this short Hint, and return to my Narrative.

*Western* began now to enquire into the original Rise of this Quarrel. To which neither *Blifil* nor *Jones* gave any Answer; but *Thwackum* said surlily, 'I believe, the Cause is not far off; if you beat the Bushes well you may find her.' 'Find her!' replied *Western*, 'what, have you been fighting for a Wench?' 'Ask the Gentleman in his Wastecoat there,' said *Thwackum*, 'he best knows.' 'Nay, then,' cries *Western*, 'it is a Wench certainly.— Ah, *Tom, Tom*; thou art a liquorish Dog—but come, Gentlemen, be all Friends, and go home with me, and make final Peace over a Bottle.' 'I ask your Pardon, Sir,' says *Thwackum*, 'it is no such slight Matter for a Man of my Character to be thus injuriously treated, and buffetted by a Boy; only because I would have done

[1] Cf. *The Rehearsal* (1671), II. v—a hilarious burlesque of heroic drama by the Duke of Buckingham and others. Though fallen in battle, the soldiers in Bayes's play rise up 'at a certain Note . . . in *Effaut flat*, and fall a Dancing'.
[2] See above, p. 240, n. 2.

my Duty, in endeavouring to detect and bring to Justice a wanton
Harlot; but, indeed, the principal Fault lies in Mr. *Allworthy* and
yourself: For, if you put the Laws in Execution, as you ought to
do, you would soon rid the Country of these Vermin.'

'I would as soon rid the Country of Foxes,' cries *Western*. 'I
think we ought to encourage the recruiting those Numbers which
we are every Day losing in the War:[1] But where is she?—Prithee,
*Tom*, shew me.' He then began to beat about, in the same
Language, and in the same Manner, as if he had been beating for
a Hare, and at last cried out, 'Soho![2] Puss is not far off. Here's her
Form, upon my Soul; I believe I may cry *stole away*.' And indeed
so he might, for he had now discovered the Place whence the
poor Girl had, at the Beginning of the Fray, *stolen away*, upon
as many Feet as a Hare generally uses in travelling.

*Sophia* now desired her Father to return home; saying, she
found herself very faint, and apprehended a Relapse. The Squire
immediately complied with his Daughter's Request (for he was
the fondest of Parents). He earnestly endeavoured to prevail with
the whole Company to go and sup with him; but *Blifil* and
*Thwackum* absolutely refused; the former saying, There were
more Reasons than he could then mention, why he must decline
this Honour; and the latter declaring (perhaps rightly) that it
was not proper for a Person of his Function to be seen at any
Place in his present Condition.

*Jones* was incapable of refusing the Pleasure of being with his
*Sophia*. So on he marched with Squire *Western* and his Ladies,
the Parson bringing up the Rear. This had, indeed, offered to
tarry with his Brother *Thwackum*, professing, his Regard for the
Cloth would not permit him to depart; but *Thwackum* would not
accept the Favour, and, with no great Civility, pushed him after
Mr. *Western*.

Thus ended this bloody Fray; and thus shall end the fifth
Book of this History.

---

[1] The War of the Austrian Succession (1740–8), in which Britain, Austria, and Holland
were allied against Prussia (until 1745), France, Spain, and Bavaria. For Britain virtually
the only bright moment of the conflict was the early victory over the French at Dettingen
(June 1743). After war between France and England was formally declared in March 1744,
massive French armies invaded the Netherlands and defeated the Allied forces repeatedly in
a series of disastrous engagements, most notably at Fontenoy (May 1745).

[2] The huntsman's cry when a hare ('Puss') has been started.

# BOOK VI

*Containing about three Weeks.*

## CHAPTER I

*Of Love.*

IN our last Book we have been obliged to deal pretty much
with the Passion of Love; and, in our succeeding Book, shall
be forced to handle this Subject still more largely. It may not,
therefore, in this Place, be improper to apply ourselves to the
Examination of that modern Doctrine, by which certain Philosophers, among many other wonderful Discoveries, pretend to
have found out, that there is no such Passion in the human Breast.

Whether these Philosophers be the same with that surprizing
Sect, who are honourably mentioned by the late Dr. *Swift*;[1] as
having, by the mere Force of Genius alone, without the least
Assistance of any Kind of Learning, or even Reading, discovered
that profound and invaluable Secret, That there is no G——: or
whether they are not rather the same with those who, some Years
since, very much alarmed the World, by shewing that there were
no such things as Virtue or Goodness really existing in Human
Nature, and who deduced our best Actions from Pride,[2] I will

---

[1] See *An Argument to prove, That the Abolishing of Christianity in England, May, as
Things now Stand, be attended with some Inconveniencies, and perhaps, not produce those many
good Effects proposed thereby* (1711). Attacking the Free-thinkers, Swift ironically deplored
the curtailment of 'Liberty of Conscience' by the Church. In evidence he cited the 'severe
Instance' of two officers, 'young Gentlemen of great Hopes, bright Wit, and profound
Judgment, who upon a thorough Examination of Causes and Effects, and by the meer
Force of natural Abilities, without the least Tincture of Learning; having made a Discovery,
that there was no God, and generously communicating their Thoughts for the Good of the
Publick; were some Time ago, by an unparalleled Severity, and upon I know not what
*obsolete* Law, broke only for *Blasphemy*' (H. Davis [ed.], *Bickerstaff Papers and Pamphlets on
the Church* [Oxford, 1957], p. 28).

[2] Throughout his career as novelist and journalist, Fielding warmly denounced the
views of those 'Political Philosophers' who followed Hobbes (*Leviathan*, 1651) in representing human nature as 'depraved, and totally bad' (*The Champion*, 22 January 1739/40).
Among these, Rochefoucauld (*Sentences et maximes de morale*, 1664) and Esprit (*La
Fausseté des vertus humaines*, 1678) traced all human actions, even those of pity and love, to
self-interested motives. In Fielding's own century the most notorious exponent of this
cynical doctrine was Bernard Mandeville (1670–1733), who in several essays in *The Fable of*

not here presume to determine. In reality, I am inclined to suspect, that all these several Finders of Truth are the very identical Men, who are by others called the *Finders of Gold*.¹ The Method used in both these Searches after Truth and after Gold, being, indeed, one and the same; *viz.* the searching, rummaging, and examining into a nasty Place; indeed, in the former Instances, into the nastiest of all Places, A BAD MIND.

But though, in this Particular, and perhaps in their Success, the Truth-finder, and the Gold-finder, may very properly be compared together; yet in Modesty, surely, there can be no Comparison between the two; for who ever heard of a Gold-finder that had the Impudence or Folly to assert, from the ill Success of his Search, that there was no such thing as Gold in the World? Whereas the Truth-finder, having raked out that *Jakes* his own Mind, and being there capable of tracing no Ray of Divinity, nor any thing virtuous, or good, or lovely, or loving, very fairly, honestly, and logically concludes, that no such things exist in the whole Creation.²

To avoid, however, all Contention, if possible, with these Philosophers, if they will be called so; and to shew our own Disposition to accommodate Matters peaceably between us, we shall here make them some Concessions, which may possibly put an End to the Dispute.

---

*the Bees* (1714–34) dedicated himself to refuting Shaftesbury and to elaborating the proposition that 'the nearer we search into human Nature, the more we shall be convinced, that the Moral Virtues are the Political Offspring which Flattery begot upon Pride' ('An Enquiry into the Origin of Moral Virtue' [1714]; ed. F. B. Kaye [Oxford, 1924], i. 51). Accordingly, Fielding's sharpest criticism of this school was generally directed at 'that charming Fellow *Mandevil*', as Miss Matthews calls him in *Amelia* (1751; III. v): 'I hope you do not agree with *Mandevil* neither [Booth replies], who hath represented human Nature as a Picture of the highest Deformity. He hath left out of his System the best Passion which the Mind can possess, and attempts to derive the Effects or Energies of that Passion, from the base Impulses of Pride or Fear. Whereas, it is as certain that Love exists in the Mind of Man, as that its opposite Hatred doth, and the same Reasons will equally prove the Existence of the one as the Existence of the other.' See also *The Covent-Garden Journal* (14 March 1752), where 'Iago' agrees with 'that very wise Writer Dr. Mandevil' in tracing benevolence to motives of vanity.

¹ A slang phrase applied to those who cleaned out latrines. (See *The Champion*, 31 May 1740.)

² Thus Fielding usually explained and dismissed the arguments for universal depravity advanced by Whitefield and the Calvinists on the one hand (see above, pp. 79, n. 4; 96, n. 2) and by Hobbes and Mandeville on the other. See, for example, *The Champion* (11 December 1739), the Preface to the *Miscellanies* and 'An Essay on Conversation' (1743), *The True Patriot* (18–25 February 1746), and *Tom Jones*, below, p. 486.

First, we will grant that many Minds, and perhaps those of the Philosophers, are entirely free from the least Traces of such a Passion.

Secondly, That what is commonly called Love, namely, the Desire of satisfying a voracious Appetite with a certain Quantity of delicate white human Flesh, is by no Means that Passion for which I here contend. This is indeed more properly Hunger; and as no Glutton is ashamed to apply the Word Love to his Appetite, and to say he LOVES such and such Dishes; so may the Lover of this Kind, with equal Propriety say, he HUNGERS after such and such Women.

Thirdly, I will grant, which I believe will be a most acceptable Concession, that this Love for which I am an Advocate, though it satisfies itself in a much more delicate Manner, doth nevertheless seek its own Satisfaction as much as the grossest of all our Appetites.

And, Lastly, That this Love when it operates towards one of a different Sex, is very apt, towards its complete Gratification, to call in the Aid of that Hunger which I have mentioned above; and which it is so far from abating, that it heightens all its Delights to a Degree scarce imaginable by those who have never been susceptible of any other Emotions, than what have proceeded from Appetite alone.

In return to all these Concessions, I desire of the Philosophers to grant, that there is in some (I believe in many) human Breasts, a kind and benevolent Disposition, which is gratified by contributing to the Happiness of others.[1] That in this Gratification alone, as in Friendship, in parental and filial Affection, as indeed in general Philanthropy, there is a great and exquisite Delight. That if we will not call such Disposition Love, we have no Name for it. That though the Pleasures arising from such pure Love may be heightened and sweetened by the Assistance of amorous Desires, yet the former can subsist alone, nor are they destroyed by the Intervention of the latter. Lastly, That Esteem and Gratitude are the proper Motives to Love, as Youth and Beauty are to Desire; and therefore though such Desire may naturally cease, when Age or Sickness overtakes its Object, yet these can have no Effect on Love, nor ever shake or remove from a good Mind, that Sensation or Passion which hath Gratitude and Esteem for its Basis.

[1] See above, p. 39, n. 1.

To deny the Existence of a Passion of which we often see manifest Instances, seems to be very strange and absurd; and can indeed proceed only from that Self-Admonition which we have mentioned above: But how unfair is this? Doth the Man who recognizes in his own Heart no Traces of Avarice or Ambition, conclude therefore, that there are no such Passions in Human Nature? Why will we not modestly observe the same Rule in judging of the Good, as well as the Evil of others? Or why, in any Case, will we, as *Shakespear* phrases it, 'put the World in our own Person?'[1]

Predominant Vanity is, I am afraid, too much concerned here. This is one Instance of that Adulation which we bestow on our own Minds, and this almost universally. For there is scarce any Man, how much soever he may despise the Character of a Flatterer, but will condescend in the meanest Manner to flatter himself.[2]

To those, therefore, I apply for the Truth of the above Observations, whose own Minds can bear Testimony to what I have advanced.

Examine your Heart, my good Reader, and resolve whether you do believe these Matters with me. If you do, you may now proceed to their Exemplification in the following Pages; if you do not, you have, I assure you, already read more than you have understood; and it would be wiser to pursue your Business, or your Pleasures (such as they are) than to throw away any more of your Time in reading what you can neither taste nor comprehend. To treat of the Effects of Love to you, must be as absurd as to discourse on Colours to a Man born blind; since possibly your Idea of Love may be as absurd as that which we are told such blind Man once entertained of the Colour Scarlet: that Colour seemed to him to be very much like the Sound of a Trumpet;[3]

[1] From Benedick's speech in *Much Ado about Nothing* (II. i): 'It is the base (though bitter) disposition of Beatrice that puts the world into her person. . . .'

[2] Cf. 'Of True Greatness' (1741), ll. 43–4: 'Disdaining outward Flatterers to win,/Dost thou not feed a Flatterer within?'

[3] Cf. Steele in *Tatler*, No. 227 (19–21 September 1710): 'A man cannot have an idea of perfection in another which he was never sensible of in himself. Mr. Locke tells us, that upon asking a blind man, what he thought scarlet was, he answered, that he believed it was like the sound of a trumpet. He was forced to form his conceptions of ideas which he had not by those which he had' (G. A. Aitken, ed. [1899], iv. 166). For the passage from Locke's *Essay concerning Human Understanding*, see above, p. 152, n. 2.

and Love probably may, in your Opinion, very greatly resemble
a Dish of Soup, or a Sir-loin of Roast-beef.


## CHAPTER II

*The Character of Mrs.* Western. *Her great Learning and Knowledge of the World, and an Instance of the deep Penetration which she
derived from those Advantages.*

THE Reader hath seen Mr. *Western,* his Sister and Daughter,
with young *Jones,* and the Parson, going together to Mr.
*Western's* House, where the greater Part of the Company spent
the Evening with much Joy and Festivity. *Sophia* was indeed
the only grave Person: For as to *Jones,* though Love had now
gotten entire Possession of his Heart, yet the pleasing Reflection
on Mr. *Allworthy's* Recovery, and the Presence of his Mistress,
joined to some tender Looks which she now and then could not
refrain from giving him, so elevated our Heroe, that he joined
the Mirth of the other three, who were perhaps as good-humoured
People as any in the World.

*Sophia* retained the same Gravity of Countenance the next
Morning at Breakfast; whence she retired likewise earlier than
usual, leaving her Father and Aunt together. The Squire took
no Notice of this Change in his Daughter's Disposition. To say
the Truth, though he was somewhat of a Politician, and had been
twice a Candidate in the Country Interest[1] at an Election, he was
a Man of no great Observation. His Sister was a Lady of a different Turn. She had lived about the Court, and had seen the
World. Hence she had acquired all that Knowledge which the
said World usually communicates; and was a perfect Mistress
of Manners, Customs, Ceremonies, and Fashions; nor did her
Erudition stop here. She had considerably improved her Mind
by Study; she had not only read all the modern Plays, Operas,

---

[1] The Country Interest, or Country Party, was the name assumed by those Tories who
opposed the Pelham administration (formed December 1744), affecting to champion the
best interests of the country as a whole by resisting the selfish schemes of Whig placemen and
pensioners at Court. A staunch defender of the Pelham government, Fielding's views of
'the Country Party, as it is absurdly called', are presented at length in the electioneering
pamphlet, *A Dialogue between a Gentleman of London, Agent for Two Court Candidates, and
an Honest Alderman of the Country Party* (June 1747).

Oratorios, Poems and Romances; in all which she was a Critic;
but had gone thro' *Rapin's* History of *England*,[1] *Eachard's Roman
History*,[2] and many *French Memoires pour servir a l'Histoire*;[3] to
these she had added most of the political Pamphlets and Journals,
published within the last twenty Years. From which she had
attained a very competent Skill in Politics, and could discourse
very learnedly on the Affairs of *Europe*. She was moreover excellently well skilled in the Doctrine of Amour, and knew better
than any body who and who were together: A Knowledge which
she the more easily attained, as her Pursuit of it was never diverted
by any Affairs of her own; for either she had no Inclinations, or
they had never been sollicited; which last is indeed very probable:
For her masculine Person, which was near six Foot high, added
to her Manner and Learning, possibly prevented the other Sex
from regarding her, notwithstanding her Petticoats, in the Light

---

[1] *Histoire d'Angleterre* (1723–5) by the French Huguenot, Paul de Rapin de Thoyras
(1661–1725), who came to England in 1688 with William of Orange. Nicholas Tindal
translated the work into English (1726–31) and continued it to include the period from the
Revolution to the accession of George II (1745–7). Written from the Whig point of view,
Rapin's history came under attack from Tory writers who resented its representation of the
Stuart kings: see, for example, Thomas Salmon, *The History of Great Britain and Ireland
. . . With a Preface, wherein the Partiality of Mons. Rapin, and some other Republican
Historians, is Demonstrated* (2nd ed., 1725); anon., *A Vindication of the Royal Family of the
Stuarts, from the Aspersions Cast on them by Monsieur Rapin, Mr. Oldmixon, and Others*
(1734); and Thomas Carte, *A Defence of English History against the Misrepresentations of M.
Rapin de Thoyras* (1734). Though in *Joseph Andrews* (1742; III. i) Fielding ridiculed
Rapin's work along with other partisan histories, in *A Charge Delivered to the Grand Jury*
(1749) he referred to it approvingly. See also *The Champion* (13 September 1740) and *The
Covent-Garden Journal* (28 October 1752).

[2] *The Roman History* (vols. i–ii, 1695–8) by Laurence Echard (*c.* 1670–1730). This work
was continued by other hands and went through numerous editions. Among serious readers,
however, it was considered a most imperfect performance: in the Preface to his own Roman
history (1738) Fielding's friend Nathaniel Hooke (see below, p. 794, n. 2) observed that
Echard's work, 'though very useful for school-boys, has been thought by persons of riper
age and more curiosity, too dry, too brief and unsatisfactory' (i. A3ᵛ); and Goldsmith was
even more severe (*The Roman History* [1769], I. iii). In *A Journey from This World to the
Next* (1743; I. ix) Fielding has Livy himself express his contempt for Echard's work, and
later in *Tom Jones* (see below, p. 421) Echard's second volume turns up in the library of
Partridge, not a very reliable guide in scholarly matters.

[3] A formula often used in the titles of French works: e.g. C. Perrault, *Mémoires pour
servir à l'histoire naturelle des animaux* (1671); W. Theylis, *Mémoires pour servir à l'histoire
de Charles XII., roi de Suède* (1722); G. de Lamberty, *Mémoires pour servir à l'histoire du
XVIIIᵉ siècle* (2nd ed., 1731); etc. In *An Attempt towards a Natural History of the Hanover
Rat* (1744) Fielding facetiously alludes to one such work, *Mémoires pour servir à l'histoire des
insectes* by René A. F. de Réaumur (6 vols., Paris, 1734–42); he also probably knew *Mémoires
pour servir à l'histoire d'un genre de polypes* (Leyden, 1744) by A. Trembley, the author
and the subject ridiculed in *Some Papers Proper to be Read before the Royal Society* (1743).

of a Woman. However, as she had considered the Matter scientifically, she perfectly well knew, though she had never practised them, all the Arts which fine Ladies use when they desire to give Encouragement, or to conceal Liking, with all the long Appendage of Smiles, Ogles, Glances, &c. as they are at present practised in the Beau-monde. To sum the whole, no Species of Disguise or Affectation had escaped her Notice; but as to the plain simple Workings of honest Nature, as she had never seen any such, she could know but little of them.

By means of this wonderful Sagacity, Mrs. *Western* had now, as she thought, made a Discovery of something in the Mind of *Sophia*. The first Hint of this she took from the Behaviour of the young Lady in the Field of Battle; and the Suspicion which she then conceived, was greatly corroborated by some Observations which she had made that Evening, and the next Morning. However, being greatly cautious to avoid being found in a Mistake, she carried the Secret a whole Fortnight in her Bosom, giving only some oblique Hints, by Simperings, Winks, Nods, and now and then dropping an obscure Word, which indeed sufficiently alarmed *Sophia*, but did not at all affect her Brother.

Being at length, however, thoroughly satisfied of the Truth of her Observation, she took an Opportunity, one Morning, when she was alone with her Brother, to interrupt one of his Whistles in the following Manner.

'Pray, Brother, have you not observed something very extraordinary in my Niece lately?' 'No, not I,' answered *Western*; 'Is any thing the Matter with the Girl?' 'I think there is,' replies she, 'and something of much Consequence too.' 'Why she doth not complain of any Thing,' cries *Western*, 'and she hath had the Small Pox.' 'Brother,' returned she, 'Girls are liable to other Distempers besides the Small Pox, and sometimes possibly to much worse.' Here *Western* interrupted her with much Earnestness, and begged her, if any thing ailed his Daughter, to acquaint him immediately, adding, 'she knew he loved her more than his own Soul, and that he would send to the World's End for the best Physician to her.' 'Nay, nay,' answered she, smiling, 'the Distemper is not so terrible; but I believe, Brother, you are convinced I know the World, and I promise you I was never more deceived in my Life, if my Niece be not most desperately in Love.' 'How! in Love,' cries *Western*, in a Passion, 'in Love

without acquainting me! I'll disinherit her, I'll turn her out of
Doors, stark naked, without a Farthing. Is all my Kindness vor
'ur, and vondness o'ur come to this, to fall in Love without asking me Leave!' 'But you will not,' answered Mrs. *Western*, 'turn
this Daughter, whom you love better than your own Soul, out of
Doors, before you know whether you shall approve her Choice.
Suppose she should have fixed on the very Person whom you
yourself would wish, I hope you would not be angry then.'
'No, no,' cries *Western*, 'that would make a Difference. If she
marries the Man I would ha' her, she may love whom she pleases,
I shan't trouble my Head about that.' 'That is spoken,' answered
the Sister, 'like a sensible Man, but I believe the very Person
she hath chosen, would be the very Person you would chuse for
her. I will disclaim all Knowledge of the World if it is not so;
and I believe, Brother, you will allow I have some.' 'Why lookee,
Sister,' said *Western*, 'I do believe you have as much as any
Woman; and to be sure those are Women's Matters. You know
I don't love to hear you talk about Politics, they belong to us,
and Petticoats should not meddle: But come, Who is the Man?'
'Marry!' said she, 'you may find him out yourself, if you please.
You who are so great a Politician can be at no great Loss. The
Judgment which can penetrate into the Cabinets of Princes, and
discover the secret Springs which move the great State Wheels
in all the political Machines of *Europe*, must surely, with very little
Difficulty find out what passes in the rude uninformed Mind of a
Girl.' 'Sister,' cries the Squire, 'I have often warned you not to
talk the Court Gibberish to me. I tell you, I don't understand
the Lingo; but I can read a Journal, or the *London Evening-
Post*.[1] Perhaps indeed, there may be now and tan a Verse which
I can't make much of, because half the Letters are left out;[2] yet

---

[1] Founded in 1727, *The London Evening-Post* was one of the principal Opposition organs
of the period; from 1737 it had been under the editorship of John Meres (1698–1761),
printer and journalist of barely concealed Jacobite tendencies. Not surprisingly, therefore,
the paper became a prime target for Fielding's satire in *The Jacobite's Journal*, where it is
called 'the worst News-Paper that I believe was ever published': 'To spread Libels three
Times a Week over the whole Island, representing the Ministry as a Set of Persons who are
Enemies to the Public, and who are engaged in a Conspiracy to betray the Interest of their
Country; and, indeed, their Country itself, into the Hands of its Enemies, must produce, in
Time, very mischievous Consequences' (24 September 1748).

[2] Political journalists, and other authors who wished to escape prosecution for libel,
customarily deleted the vowels when printing the names of their victims. In *The Jacobite's
Journal* (5 December 1747) Fielding called this practice 'emvowelling' and he parodied

I know very well what is meant by that, and that our Affairs don't go so well as they should do, because of Bribery and Corruption.' 'I pity your Country Ignorance from my Heart,' cries the Lady. 'Do you?' answered *Western*, 'and I pity your Town Learning, I had rather be any Thing than a Courtier, and a Presbyterian, and a *Hannoverian* too, as some People, I believe, are.' 'If you mean me,' answered she, 'you know I am a Woman, Brother; and it signifies nothing what I am. Besides——' 'I do know you are a Woman,' cries the Squire, 'and it's well for thee, that art one; if hadst been a Man, I promise thee I had lent thee a *Flick* long ago.' 'Ay there,' said she, 'in that *Flick* lies all your fancied Superiority. Your Bodies, and not your Brains, are stronger than ours. Believe me, it is well for you that you are able to beat us, or such is the Superiority of our Understanding, we should make all of you what the brave, and wise, and witty, and polite are already,—our Slaves.' 'I am glad I know your Mind,' answered the Squire, 'but we'll talk more of this Matter another Time. At present, do tell me what Man is it you mean about my Daughter.' 'Hold a Moment,' said she, 'while I digest that sovereign Contempt I have for your Sex; or else I ought to be angry too with you. There— I have made a Shift to gulp it down. And now, good politic Sir, what think you of Mr. *Blifil*? Did she not faint away on seeing him lie breathless on the Ground? Did she not, after he was recovered, turn pale again the Moment we came up to that Part of the Field where he stood? And pray what else should be the Occasion of all her Melancholy that Night at Supper, the next Morning, and indeed ever since?' ''Fore *George*!' cries the Squire, 'now you mind me on't, I remember it all. It is certainly so, and I am glad on't with all my Heart. I knew *Sophy* was a good Girl, and would not fall in Love to make me angry. I was never more rejoiced in my Life: For nothing can lie so handy together as our two Estates. I had this

the absurd lengths to which Meres had carried it in *The London Evening-Post*: 'In this Dress [i.e. the tartan of the Jacobites] I intend to abuse the * * *, and the * * *, and the * * *. I intend to lash not only the M——stry, but EVERY MAN who *hath* any P—ce or P-ns—n from the G–v–rnm–nt, or who is *intrusted* with *any Degree of Power* or *Trust* under it, let his R–nk be never so *high*, his F–rt–n– never so *great*, or his Ch–r–ct–r never so *good*. For this Purpose I have provided myself with a vast Quantity of *Italian* Letter, and Astericks of all Sorts: And as for all the Words which I *embowel*, or rather *emvowel*, I will never so mangle them, but they shall be all as well known as if they retained every Vowel in them. This I promise my Readers, that when I have any Meaning, they shall understand it.' (See also the *Journal* for 11 June, 27 August 1748.)

Matter in my Head some Time ago; for certainly the two
Estates are in a Manner joined together in Matrimony already,
and it would be a thousand Pities to part them. It is true indeed,
there be larger Estates in the Kingdom, but not in this County,
and I had rather bate something, than marry my Daughter among
Strangers and Foreigners. Besides most o' zuch great Estates be
in the Hands of Lords, and I heate the very Name of *themmun*.
Well but, Sister, what would you advise me to do: For I tell
you Women know these Matters better than we do?' 'O, your
humble Servant, Sir,' answered the Lady, 'we are obliged to you
for allowing us a Capacity in any Thing. Since you are pleased
then, most politic Sir, to ask my Advice, I think you may propose
the Match to *Allworthy* yourself. There is no Indecorum in the
Proposal's coming from the Parent of either Side. King *Alcinous*,
in Mr. *Pope's* Odyssey,[1] offers his Daughter to *Ulysses*. I need
not caution so politic a Person not to say that your Daughter is in
Love; that would indeed be against all Rules.' 'Well,' said the
Squire, 'I will propose it; but I shall certainly, lend un a *Flick*,
if he should refuse me.' 'Fear not,' cries Mrs. *Western*, 'the
Match is too advantageous to be refused.' 'I don't know that,'
answered the Squire, '*Allworthy* is a queer B—ch, and Money
hath no Effect o'un.' 'Brother,' said the Lady, 'your Politics
astonish me. Are you really to be imposed on by Professions? Do
you think Mr. *Allworthy* hath more Contempt for Money than
other Men, because he professes more. Such Credulity would
better become one of us weak Women, than that wise Sex which
Heaven hath formed for Politicians. Indeed, Brother, you would
make a fine Plenipo to negotiate with the *French*. They would soon
persuade you, that they take Towns out of mere defensive Principles.' 'Sister,' answered the Squire, with much Scorn, 'Let
your Friends at Court answer for the Towns taken; as you are a
Woman, I shall lay no Blame upon you: For I suppose they are
wiser than to trust Women with Secrets.' He accompanied this
with so sarcastical a Laugh, that Mrs. *Western* could bear no
longer. She had been all this Time fretted in a tender Part (for she
was indeed very deeply skilled in these Matters, and very violent
in them) and therefore burst forth in a Rage, declared her Brother
to be both a Clown and a Blockhead, and that she would stay no
longer in his House.

[1] See Pope's *Odyssey* (1725–6), vii. 395–402.

The Squire, tho', perhaps, he had never read *Machiavel*,[1] was, however, in many Points, a perfect Politician. He strongly held all those wise Tenets, which are so well inculcated in that Politico-Peripatetic School of *Exchange-Alley*.[2] He knew the just Value and only Use of Money, *viz.* to lay it up. He was likewise well skilled in the exact Value of Reversions,[3] Expectations, *&c.* and had often considered the Amount of his Sister's Fortune, and the Chance which he or his Posterity had of inheriting it. This he was infinitely too wise to sacrifice to a trifling Resentment. When he found, therefore, he had carried Matters too far, he began to think of reconciling them; which was no very difficult Task, as the Lady had great Affection for her Brother, and still greater for her Niece; and tho' too susceptible of an Affront offered to her Skill in Politics, on which she much valued herself, was a Woman of a very extraordinary good and sweet Disposition.

Having first, therefore, laid violent Hands on the Horses, for whose Escape from the Stable no Place but the Window was left open; he next applied himself to his Sister, softened and soothed her, by unsaying all he had said, and by Assertions directly contrary to those which had incensed her. Lastly, he summoned the Eloquence of *Sophia* to his Assistance, who, besides a most graceful and winning Address, had the Advantage of being heard with great Favour and Partiality by her Aunt.

The Result of the whole was a kind Smile from Mrs. *Western*, who said, 'Brother, you are absolutely a perfect *Croat*;[4] but as those have their Use in the Army of the Empress Queen, so you likewise have some good in you. I will therefore once more sign a Treaty of Peace with you, and see that you do not infringe it on your Side; at least, as you are so excellent a Politician, I may expect you will keep your Leagues like the *French*,[5] till your Interest calls upon you to break them.'

---

[1] Niccolo di Bernardo dei Machiavelli (1469–1527), Florentine statesman and author of *Il Principe* (1513), the work which earned him his reputation as the master of unscrupulous power politics.

[2] A play on the so-called Peripatetic school of philosophy founded by Aristotle at the Lyceum. The coffee-houses in Exchange Alley, near the Royal Exchange, were a favourite resort of bankers, merchants, stock-jobbers, and speculators of all sorts.

[3] See below, p. 748, n. 1; also above, p. 109.10.

[4] In October 1740 Maria Theresa (1717–80) had become Queen of Hungary and ruler of the Austrian empire. Irregular Croatian troops in her army harassed Frederick of Prussia when he invaded Bohemia in 1744 and forced him to withdraw.

[5] Among their other grievances against France, Englishmen accused her of 'breaking the

## CHAPTER III

*Containing two Defiances to the Critics.*

THE Squire having settled Matters with his Sister, as we have seen in the last Chapter, was so greatly impatient to communicate the Proposal to *Allworthy*, that Mrs. *Western* had the utmost Difficulty to prevent him from visiting that Gentleman in his Sickness, for this Purpose.

Mr. *Allworthy* had been engaged to dine with Mr. *Western* at the Time when he was taken ill. He was, therefore, no sooner discharged out of the Custody of Physic, but he thought (as was usual with him on all Occasions, both the highest and the lowest) of fulfilling his Engagement.

In the Interval between the Time of the Dialogue in the last Chapter, and this Day of public Entertainment, *Sophia* had, from certain obscure Hints thrown out by her Aunt, collected some Apprehension that the sagacious Lady suspected her Passion for *Jones*. She now resolved to take this Opportunity of wiping out all such Suspicion, and for that Purpose to put an entire Constraint on her Behaviour.

First, she endeavoured to conceal a throbbing melancholy Heart with the utmost Sprightliness in her Countenance, and the highest Gayety in her Manner. Secondly, she addressed her whole Discourse to Mr. *Blifil*, and took not the least Notice of poor *Jones* the whole Day.

The Squire was so delighted with this Conduct of his Daughter, that he scarce eat any Dinner, and spent almost his whole Time in watching Opportunities of conveying Signs of his Approbation by Winks and Nods to his Sister; who was not at first altogether so pleased with what she saw as was her Brother.

Faith of All the Treaties she had made with All the Powers which she is now at War with' (*The General Advertiser*, 30 August 1746). Meant as a warning to the Allied ministers gathering at Breda for peace talks, a poem entitled 'King William's Advice' was published in *The General Advertiser* for 5 December 1746 to elaborate the point:

> As Spiders Nets and Cobwebs weave
> To catch a Prize and Flies deceive,
> So *Frenchmen* fine-spun Treaties make
> To hamper Dupes, then Bargains break—

In recent memory, the writer recalls, the French '*Proteus*' had violated the provisions of the Treaty of Utrecht and the Pragmatic Sanction.

In short, *Sophia* so greatly overacted her Part, that her Aunt was at first staggered, and began to suspect some Affectation in her Niece; but as she was herself a Woman of Great Art, so she soon attributed this to extreme Art in *Sophia*. She remembered the many Hints she had given her Niece concerning her being in Love, and imagined the young Lady had taken this Way to rally her out of her Opinion, by an overacted Civility; a Notion that was greatly corroborated by the excessive Gaiety with which the whole was accompanied. We cannot here avoid remarking that this Conjecture would have been better founded, had *Sophia* lived ten Years in the Air of *Grosvenor-square*, where young Ladies do learn a wonderful Knack of rallying and playing with that Passion, which is a mighty serious Thing in Woods and Groves a hundred Miles distant from *London*.

To say the Truth, in discovering the Deceit of others, it matters much that our own Art be wound up, if I may use the Expression, in the same Key with theirs: For very artful Men sometimes miscarry by fancying others wiser, or in other Words, greater Knaves than they really are. As this Observation is pretty deep, I will illustrate it by the following short Story. Three Countrymen were pursuing a *Wiltshire* Thief through *Brentford*. The simplest of them seeing the *Wiltshire House* written under a Sign, advised his Companions to enter it, for there most probably they would find their Countryman. The second, who was wiser, laughed at this Simplicity; but the third, who was wiser still, answered, 'Let us go in, however, for he may think we should not suspect him of going amongst his own Countrymen.' They accordingly went in and searched the House, and by that Means missed over-taking the Thief, who was at that Time, but a little ways before them; and who, as they all knew, but had never once reflected, could not read.

The Reader will pardon a Digression in which so invaluable a Secret is communicated, since every Gamester will agree how necessary it is to know exactly the Play of another, in order to countermine him. This will, moreover, afford a Reason why the wiser Man, as is often seen, is the Bubble of the weaker, and why many simple and innocent Characters are so generally misunderstood and misrepresented; but what is most material, this will account for the Deceit which *Sophia* put on her politic Aunt.

Dinner being ended, and the Company retired into the Garden,

Mr. *Western*, who was thoroughly convinced of the Certainty of what his Sister had told him, took Mr. *Allworthy* aside, and very bluntly proposed a Match between *Sophia* and young Mr. *Blifil*.

Mr. *Allworthy* was not one of those Men, whose Hearts flutter at any unexpected and sudden Tidings of worldly Profit. His Mind was, indeed, tempered with that Philosophy which becomes a Man and a Christian. He affected no absolute Superiority to all Pleasure and Pain, to all Joy and Grief; but was not at the same time to be discomposed and ruffled by every accidental Blast; by every Smile or Frown of Fortune. He received, therefore, Mr. *Western's* Proposal without any visible Emotion, or without any Alteration of Countenance. He said, the Alliance was such as he sincerely wished; then launched forth into a very just Encomium on the young Lady's Merit; acknowledged the Offer to be advantageous in Point of Fortune; and after thanking Mr. *Western* for the good Opinion he had profess'd of his Nephew, concluded, that if the young People liked each other, he should be very desirous to complete the Affair.

*Western* was a little disappointed at Mr. *Allworthy's* Answer; which was not so warm as he expected. He treated the Doubt whether the young People might like one another with great Contempt; saying, 'That Parents were the best Judges of proper Matches for their Children; that, for his Part, he should insist on the most resigned Obedience from his Daughter; and if any young Fellow could refuse such a Bedfellow, he was his humble Servant, and hoped there was no Harm done.'

*Allworthy* endeavoured to soften this Resentment by many Elogiums on *Sophia*; declaring, he had no doubt but that Mr. *Blifil* would very gladly receive the Offer; but all was ineffectual, he could obtain no other Answer from the Squire but—'I say no more—I humbly hope there's no Harm done—that's all.' Which Words he repeated, at least, a hundred Times before they parted.

*Allworthy* was too well acquainted with his Neighbour to be offended at this Behaviour; and tho' he was so averse to the Rigour which some Parents exercise on their Children in the Article of Marriage, that he had resolved never to force his Nephew's Inclinations, he was nevertheless much pleased with the Prospect of this Union: For the whole Country resounded the Praises of *Sophia*, and he had himself greatly admired the uncommon Endowments of both her Mind and Person. To which, I believe we may add, the Consideration of her vast Fortune, which, tho' he was too sober to be intoxicated with it, he was too sensible to despise.

And here, in Defiance of all the barking Critics in the World, I must and will introduce a Digression concerning true Wisdom,[1] of which Mr. *Allworthy* was in Reality as great a Pattern as he was of Goodness.

True Wisdom then, notwithstanding all which Mr. *Hogarth's* poor Poet[2] may have writ against Riches, and in Spite of all which any rich, well-fed Divine may have preached against Pleasure, consists not in the Contempt of either of these. A Man may have as much Wisdom in the Possession of an affluent Fortune, as any Beggar in the Streets; or may enjoy a handsome Wife or a hearty Friend, and still remain as wise as any sour Popish Recluse, who buries all his social Faculties, and starves his Belly while he well lashes his Back.

To say Truth, the wisest Man is the likeliest to possess all worldly Blessings in an eminent Degree: For as that Moderation which Wisdom prescribes is the surest Way to useful Wealth; so can it alone qualify us to taste many Pleasures. The wise Man gratifies every Appetite and every Passion, while the Fool sacrifices all the rest to pall and satiate one.

[1] In developing the argument that true wisdom comprehends the temperate enjoyment of both riches and pleasure, Fielding owes most to Seneca, *De Vita Beata*, esp. xxi. 3 ff. With the remarks to follow, compare also *The Champion* (24 January 1739/40), where Fielding had insisted that 'Virtue is not that coy, nor that cruel Mistress she is represented. Nor is she of that morose and rigid Nature, which some mistake her to be':

'Virtue forbids not the satisfying our Appetites, Virtue forbids us only to glut and destroy them. The temperate Man tastes and relishes Pleasure in a Degree infinitely superior to that of the voluptuous. . . . The Sot soon ceases to enjoy his Wine, the Glutton his Dainties, and the Libertine his Women. The temperate Man enjoys all in the highest Degree, and indeed with the greatest Variety: For human nature will not suffice for an Excess in every Passion, and wherever one runs away with a Man, we may generally observe him sacrificing all the rest to the Enjoyment of that alone. The virtuous and temperate Man only hath Inclination, hath Strength; and . . . hath Opportunity to enjoy all his Passions.

'Poverty is so far from being enjoined us by Virtue, that Parsimony, which she expresly prescribes, is a certain Way to Wealth.'

[2] See Hogarth's *The Distressed Poet*, in the revised version of which (1740) the poet, in the midst of abject poverty, is shown composing a work entitled, 'Riches: a Poem'. Fielding was particularly amused by this piece of irony, to which he also refers in a footnote to *The Vernoniad* (1741) and in *The Jacobite's Journal* (9 July 1748, under 'Domestic News'). For other refrences to Hogarth, see above, p. 66, n. 1.

It may be objected, that very wise Men have been notoriously avaricious. I answer, not wise in that Instance. It may likewise be said, that the wisest Men have been in their Youth, immoderately fond of Pleasure. I answer, they were not wise then.

Wisdom, in short, whose Lessons have been represented as so hard to learn by those who never were at her School, only teaches us to extend a simple Maxim universally known and followed even in the lowest Life, a little farther than that Life carries it. And this is not to buy at too dear a Price.

Now, whoever takes this Maxim abroad with him into the grand Market of the World, and constantly applies it to Honours, to Riches, to Pleasures, and to every other Commodity which that Market affords, is, I will venture to affirm, a wise Man; and must be so acknowledged in the worldly Sense of the Word: For he makes the best of Bargains, since in Reality he purchases every Thing at the Price only of a little Trouble, and carries home all the good Things I have mentioned, while he keeps his Health, his Innocence, and his Reputation, the common Prices which are paid for them by others, entire and to himself.

From this Moderation, likewise, he learns two other Lessons, which complete his Character. First, never to be intoxicated when he hath made the best Bargain, nor dejected when the Market is empty, or when its Commodities are too dear for his Purchase.

But I must remember on what Subject I am writing, and not trespass too far on the Patience of a good-natured Critic. Here therefore I put an End to the Chapter.

## CHAPTER IV

*Containing sundry curious Matters.*

AS soon as Mr. *Allworthy* returned home, he took Mr. *Blifil* apart, and after some Preface, communicated to him the Proposal which had been made by Mr. *Western*, and, at the same Time, informed him how agreeable this Match would be to himself.

The Charms of *Sophia* had not made the least Impression on *Blifil*; not that his Heart was pre-engaged; neither was he totally insensible of Beauty, or had any Aversion to Women; but his Appetites were, by Nature, so moderate, that he was able by Philosophy or by Study, or by some other Method, easily to subdue them; and as to that Passion which we have treated of in the first Chapter of this Book, he had not the least Tincture of it in his whole Composition.

But tho' he was so entirely free from that mixed Passion, of which we there treated, and of which the Virtues and Beauty of *Sophia* formed so notable an Object; yet was he altogether as well furnished with some other Passions, that promised themselves very full Gratification in the young Lady's Fortune. Such were Avarice and Ambition, which divided the Dominion of his Mind between them.[1] He had more than once considered the Possession of this Fortune as a very desirable Thing, and had entertained some distant Views concerning it: But his own Youth and that of the young Lady, and indeed principally a Reflection that Mr. *Western* might marry again, and have more Children, had restrained him from too hasty or eager a Pursuit.

This last and most material Objection was now in great Measure removed, as the Proposal came from Mr. *Western* himself. *Blifil*, therefore, after a very short Hesitation, answered Mr. *Allworthy*, that Matrimony was a Subject on which he had not yet thought: But that he was so sensible of his friendly and fatherly Care, that he should in all Things submit himself to his Pleasure.

*Allworthy* was naturally a Man of Spirit, and his present Gravity arose from true Wisdom and Philosophy, not from any original Phlegm in his Disposition: For he had possessed much Fire in his Youth, and had married a beautiful Woman for Love. He was not, therefore, greatly pleased with this cold Answer of his Nephew; nor could he help launching forth into the Praises of *Sophia*, and expressing some Wonder that the Heart of a young Man could be impregnable to the force of such Charms, unless it was guarded by some prior Affection.

*Blifil* assured him he had no such Guard; and then proceeded

---

[1] In the humanist tradition, avarice and ambition were regarded as the summarizing vices of human nature, complementary passions exemplifying negative and positive excess: e.g. Aristotle, *Politics*, II. vi. 19, and Horace, *Satires*, I. iv. 25–6. Discussing worldly wisdom in *The Covent-Garden Journal* (4 November 1752), Fielding quotes the verses from Horace and declares that 'Avarice and Ambition' are 'the two great Characteristics of this Wisdom'.

to discourse so wisely and religiously on Love and Marriage, that he would have stopt the Mouth of a Parent much less devoutly inclined than was his Uncle. In the End, the good Man was satisfied, that his Nephew, far from having any Objections to *Sophia*, had that Esteem for her, which in sober and virtuous Minds is the sure Foundation of Friendship and Love. And as he doubted not but the Lover would, in a little Time, become altogether as agreeable to his Mistress, he foresaw great Happiness arising to all Parties by so proper and desirable a Union. With Mr. *Blifil's* Consent, therefore, he wrote the next Morning to Mr. *Western*, acquainting him that his Nephew had very thankfully and gladly received the Proposal, and would be ready to wait on the young Lady, whenever she should be pleased to accept his Visit.

*Western* was much pleased with this Letter, and immediately returned an Answer; in which, without having mentioned a Word to his Daughter, he appointed that very Afternoon for opening the Scene of Courtship.

As soon as he had dispatched this Messenger, he went in Quest of his Sister, whom he found reading and expounding the Gazette[1] to Parson *Supple*. To this Exposition he was obliged to attend near a Quarter of an Hour, tho' with great Violence to his natural Impetuosity, before he was suffered to speak. At length, however, he found an Opportunity of acquainting the Lady, that he had Business of great Consequence to impart to her; to which she answered, 'Brother, I am entirely at your Service. Things look so well in the North[2] that I was never in a better Humour.'

[1] Established in 1666, *The London Gazette* was the official government newspaper, published three times a week with extraordinary issues for important news. From 1741 until his death the editor was Edward Weston (1703–70). Despite the paper's official connection with the Pelham administration, which he himself supported, Fielding in *The True Patriot* repeatedly denounced the editors of the *Gazette* for incompetency and for the selfish exploitation, during a time of national crisis, of the office entrusted to them. The reasons for his disapproval are set forth by a correspondent to *The True Patriot* (24 December 1745); the letter, though asserting the innocence of the Administration itself, roundly condemns the editors of the *Gazette* for their corrupt practices: 'A Paper said to be *published by Authority* has of late been so *prolix*, so *unintelligible*, so *excessive dear* [price 2d.], the *Publication* of it so *unreasonably retarded*, and in short been so much made a JOB of, as the Phrase is, that it gives just Offence to every honest Man'. See also *The True Patriot* (7, 21 January, 28 January–4 February, 15–22 April 1746).

[2] In the political jargon of the age, 'the North' signified Sweden, Denmark, Prussia, and Russia. In *The True Patriot* (18–25 March 1746, under 'Foreign History') Fielding was

The Parson then withdrawing, *Western* acquainted her with all which had passed, and desired her to communicate the Affair to *Sophia*, which she readily and chearfully undertook; tho' perhaps her Brother was a little obliged to that agreeable Northern Aspect which had so delighted her, that he heard no Comment on his Proceedings: for they were certainly somewhat too hasty and violent.

## CHAPTER V

*In which is related what passed between* Sophia *and her Aunt.*

$S$*OPHIA* was in her Chamber reading, when her Aunt came in. The Moment she saw Mrs. *Western*, she shut the Book with so much Eagerness, that the good Lady could not forbear asking her, What Book that was which she seemed so much afraid of shewing. 'Upon my Word, Madam,' answered *Sophia*, 'it is a Book which I am neither ashamed nor afraid to own I have read. It is the Production of a young Lady of Fashion,[1] whose good Understanding, I think, doth Honour to her Sex, and whose good Heart is an Honour to Human Nature.' Mrs. *Western* then took up the Book, and immediately after threw it down, saying—'Yes, the Author is of a very good Family; but she is not much among People one knows. I have never read it; for the best Judges say, there is not much in it.' 'I dare not, Madam, set up my own Opinion,' says *Sophia*, 'against the best Judges, but there appears to me a great deal of human Nature in it; and in many Parts, so much true Tenderness and Delicacy, that it hath cost me many a Tear.' 'Ay, and do you love to cry then?' says the Aunt. 'I love a tender Sensation,' answered the Niece, 'and would pay the Price of a Tear for it at any Time.' 'Well, but

encouraged by the fact that internal disputes among these countries prevented them from combining their forces, and thereby upsetting the balance of power.

[1] The book is very probably *The Adventures of David Simple* (1744) by Fielding's sister Sarah (1710–68). In the Preface he contributed to the second edition (July 1744) Fielding remarked that the novel had been unjustly criticized by those who thereby only revealed their own 'Folly, Meanness and Malevolence'. Like Sophia he praised the work for 'a vast Penetration into human Nature' and for the 'Sentiments', which 'are in general extremely delicate'. And like Sophia he further observed that 'a short Communication with her own Heart, will leave the Author of this Book very little to seek abroad of all the Good which is to be found in Human Nature'.

shew me,' said the Aunt, 'what was you reading when I came in; there was something very tender in that, I believe, and very loving too. You blush, my dear *Sophia*. Ah! Child, you should read Books, which would teach you a little Hypocrisy, which would instruct you how to hide your Thoughts a little better.' 'I hope, Madam,' answered *Sophia*, 'I have no Thoughts which I ought to be ashamed of discovering.' 'Ashamed! no,' cries the Aunt, 'I don't think you have any Thoughts which you ought to be ashamed of, and yet, Child, you blushed just now when I mentioned the Word *Loving*. Dear *Sophy*, be assured you have not one Thought which I am not well acquainted with; as well, Child, as the *French* are with our Motions, long before we put them in Execution. Did you think, Child, because you have been able to impose upon your Father, that you could impose upon me? Do you imagine I did not know the Reason of your over-acting all that Friendship for Mr. *Blifil* yesterday? I have seen a little too much of the World, to be so deceived. Nay, nay, do not blush again. I tell you it is a Passion you need not be ashamed of. —It is a Passion I myself approve, and have already brought your Father into the Approbation of it. Indeed, I solely consider your Inclination; for I would always have that gratified, if possible, though one may sacrifice higher Prospects. Come, I have News which will delight your very Soul. Make me your Confident, and I will undertake you shall be happy to the very Extent of your Wishes.' 'La, Madam,' says *Sophia*, looking more foolishly than ever she did in her Life, 'I know not what to say—— Why, Madam, should you suspect?'—'Nay, no Dishonesty,' returned Mrs. *Western*. 'Consider, you are speaking to one of your own Sex, to an Aunt, and I hope you are convinced you speak to a Friend. Consider, you are only revealing to me what I know already, and what I plainly saw yesterday through that most artful of all Disguises, which you had put on, and which must have deceived any one who had not perfectly known the World. Lastly, consider it is a Passion which I highly approve.' 'La, Madam,' says *Sophia*, 'you come upon one so unawares, and on a sudden. To be sure, Madam, I am not blind—and certainly, if it be a Fault to see all human Perfections assembled together—— But is it possible my Father and you, Madam, can see with my Eyes?' 'I tell you,' answered the Aunt, 'we do entirely approve; and this very Afternoon your Father hath appointed for you to receive your Lover.' 'My Father, this Afternoon!' cries *Sophia*, with the Blood starting from her Face.'—'Yes, Child,' said the Aunt, 'this Afternoon. You know the Impetuosity of my Brother's Temper. I acquainted him with the Passion which I first discovered in you that Evening when you fainted away in the Field. I saw it in your Fainting. I saw it immediately upon your Recovery. I saw it that Evening at Supper, and the next Morning at Breakfast: (you know, Child, I have seen the World). Well, I no sooner acquainted my Brother; but he immediately wanted to propose it to *Allworthy*. He proposed it Yesterday, *Allworthy* consented, (as to be sure he must with Joy) and this Afternoon, I tell you, you are to put on all your best Airs.' 'This Afternoon!' cries *Sophia*. 'Dear Aunt, you frighten me out of my Senses.' 'O, my Dear,' said the Aunt, 'you will soon come to yourself again; for he is a charming young Fellow, that's the Truth on't.' 'Nay, I will own,' says *Sophia*, 'I know none with such Perfections. So brave, and yet so gentle; so witty, yet so inoffensive; so humane, so civil, so genteel, so handsome! What signifies his being base born, when compared with such Qualifications as these?' 'Base born! what do you mean,' said the Aunt, 'Mr. *Blifil* base born!' *Sophia* turned instantly pale at this Name, and faintly repeated it. Upon which the Aunt cried, 'Mr. *Blifil*, ay Mr. *Blifil*, of whom else have we been talking?' 'Good Heavens,' answered *Sophia*, ready to sink, 'of Mr. *Jones*, I thought; I am sure I know no other who deserves——' 'I protest,' cries the Aunt, 'you frighten me in your Turn. Is it Mr. *Jones*, and not Mr. *Blifil*, who is the Object of your Affection?' 'Mr. *Blifil*!' repeated *Sophia*. 'Sure it is impossible you can be in earnest; if you are, I am the most miserable Woman alive.' Mrs. *Western* now stood a few Moments silent, while Sparks of fiery Rage flashed from her Eyes. At length, collecting all her Force of Voice, she thundered forth in the following articulate Sounds:

'And is it possible you can think of disgracing your Family by allying yourself to a Bastard? Can the Blood of the *Westerns* submit to such Contamination! If you have not Sense sufficient to restrain such monstrous Inclinations, I thought the Pride of our Family would have prevented you from giving the least Encouragement to so base an Affection; much less did I imagine you would ever have had the Assurance to own it to my Face.'

'Madam,' answered *Sophia*, trembling, 'what I have said you have extorted from me. I do not remember to have ever mentioned the Name of Mr. *Jones*, with Approbation, to any one before; nor should I now, had I not conceived he had had your Approbation. Whatever were my Thoughts of that poor unhappy young Man, I intended to have carried them with me to my Grave.— To that Grave where only now, I find, I am to seek Repose.'— Here she sunk down in her Chair, drowned in her Tears, and, in all the moving Silence of unutterable Grief, presented a Spectacle which must have affected almost the hardest Heart.

All this tender Sorrow, however, raised no Compassion in her Aunt. On the contrary, she now fell into the most violent Rage.— 'And I would rather,' she cried, in a most vehement Voice, 'follow you to your Grave, than I would see you disgrace yourself and your Family by such a Match. O Heavens! could I have ever suspected that I should live to hear a Niece of mine declare a Passion for such a Fellow? You are the first—yes, Miss *Western*, you are the first of your Name who ever entertained so groveling a Thought. A Family so noted for the Prudence of its Women——' Here she run on a full Quarter of an Hour, till having exhausted her Breath rather than her Rage, she concluded with threatening to go immediately and acquaint her Brother.

*Sophia* then threw herself at her Feet, and laying hold of her Hands, begged her, with Tears, to conceal what she had drawn from her; urging the Violence of her Father's Temper, and protesting that no Inclinations of hers should ever prevail with her to do any thing which might offend him.

Mrs. *Western* stood a Moment looking at her, and then having recollected herself, said, 'that on one Consideration only she would keep the Secret from her Brother; and this was, that *Sophia* should promise to entertain Mr. *Blifil* that very Afternoon as her Lover, and to regard him as the Person who was to be her Husband.'

Poor *Sophia* was too much in her Aunt's Power to deny her any thing positively; she was obliged to promise that she would see Mr. *Blifil*, and be as civil to him as possible; but begged her Aunt that the Match might not be hurried on. She said, 'Mr. *Blifil* was by no means agreeable to her, and she hoped her Father would be prevailed on not to make her the most wretched of Women.'

Mrs. *Western* assured her, 'that the Match was entirely agreed upon, and that nothing could or should prevent it.' 'I must own,' said she, 'I looked on it as on a Matter of Indifference; nay, perhaps, had some Scruples about it before, which were actually got over by my thinking it highly agreeable to your own Inclinations; but now I regard it as the most eligible Thing in the World; nor shall there be, if I can prevent it, a Moment of Time lost on the Occasion.'

*Sophia* replied, 'Delay at least, Madam, I may expect from both your Goodness and my Father's. Surely you will give me Time to endeavour to get the better of so strong a Disinclination as I have at present to this Person.'

The Aunt answered, 'She knew too much of the World to be so deceived; that as she was sensible another Man had her Affections, she should persuade Mr. *Western* to hasten the Match as much as possible. It would be bad Politics indeed,' added she, 'to protract a Siege when the Enemy's Army is at Hand, and in Danger of relieving it. No, no, *Sophy*,' said she, 'as I am convinced you have a violent Passion, which you can never satisfy with Honour, I will do all I can to put your Honour out of the Care of your Family: For when you are married those Matters will belong only to the Consideration of your Husband. I hope, Child, you will always have Prudence enough to act as becomes you; but if you should not, Marriage hath saved many a Woman from Ruin.'

*Sophia* well understood what her Aunt meant; but did not think proper to make her an Answer. However, she took a Resolution to see Mr. *Blifil*, and to behave to him as civilly as she could: For on that Condition only she obtained a Promise from her Aunt to keep secret the Liking which her ill Fortune, rather than any Scheme of Mrs. *Western*, had unhappily drawn from her.

## CHAPTER VI

*Containing a Dialogue between* Sophia *and Mrs.* Honour*, which may a little relieve those tender Affections which the foregoing Scene may have raised in the Mind of a good-natur'd Reader.*

MRS. *Western* having obtained that Promise from her Niece which we have seen in the last Chapter, withdrew, and presently after arrived Mrs. *Honour*. She was at Work in a

neighbouring Apartment, and had been summoned to the Key-
hole by some Vociferation in the preceding Dialogue, where she
had continued during the remaining Part of it. At her Entry
into the Room, she found *Sophia* standing motionless, with the
Tears trickling from her Eyes. Upon which she immediately
ordered a proper Quantity of Tears into her own Eyes, and then
began, 'O Gemini, my dear Lady, what is the Matter?' 'Nothing,'
cries *Sophia*. 'Nothing! O dear Madam,' answers Mrs. *Honour*,
'you must not tell me that, when your Ladyship is in this Taking,
and when there hath been such a *Preamble* between your Ladyship and Madam *Western*.' 'Don't teaze me,' cries *Sophia*, 'I tell
you nothing is the Matter.—Good Heavens! Why was I born!'—
'Nay, Madam,' says Mrs. *Honour*, 'you shall never persuade me,
that your La'ship can lament yourself so for nothing. To be sure,
I am but a Servant; but to be sure I have been always faithful to
your Ladyship, and to be sure I would serve your La'ship with
my Life.' 'My dear *Honour*,' says *Sophia*, ''tis not in thy Power to
be of any Service to me. I am irretrievably undone.' 'Heaven
forbid,' answered the Waiting-woman; 'but if I can't be of any
Service to you, pray tell me, Madam, it will be some Comfort to
me to know; Pray, dear Ma'am, tell me what's the Matter.'
'My Father,' cries *Sophia*, 'is going to marry me to a Man I
both despise and hate.' 'O, dear Ma'am,' answered the other,
'Who is this wicked Man? for to be sure he is very bad, or your
La'ship would not despise him.' 'His Name is Poison to my
Tongue,' replied *Sophia*, 'thou wilt know it too soon.' Indeed,
to confess the Truth, she knew it already, and therefore was not
very inquisitive as to that Point. She then proceeded thus: 'I
don't pretend to give your La'ship Advice, *whereof* your La'ship
knows much better than I can pretend to, being but a Servant;
but, i-fackins! no Father in *England* should marry me against
my Consent. And to be sure, the Squire is so good, that if he did
but know your La'ship despises and hates the young Man, to
be sure he would not desire you to marry him. And if your La'ship
would but give me Leave to tell my Master so—— To be sure,
it would be more properer to come from your own Mouth; but
as your La'ship doth not care to foul your Tongue with his nasty
Name.' 'You are mistaken, *Honour*,' says *Sophia*, 'my Father was
determined before he ever thought fit to mention it to me.'
'More Shame for him,' cries *Honour*, 'you are to go to Bed to

him, and not Master. And thof a Man may be a very proper Man, yet every Woman mayn't think him handsome alike. I am sure my Master would never act in this Manner of his own Head. I wish some People would trouble themselves only with what belongs to them; they would not, I believe, like to be served so, if it was their own Case: For tho' I am a Maid, I can easily believe as how all Men are not equally agreeable. And what signifies your La'ship having so great a Fortune, if you can't please yourself with the Man you think most handsomest? Well, I say nothing, but to be sure it is Pity some Folks had not been better born; nay, as for that Matter, I should not mind it my self: But then there is not so much Money, and what of that, your La'ship hath Money enough for both; and where can your La'ship bestow your Fortune better? For to be sure every one must allow, that he is the most handsomest, charmingest, finest, tallest, properest Man in the World.' 'What do you mean by running on in this Manner to me?' cries *Sophia*, with a very grave Countenance. 'Have I ever given any Encouragement for these Liberties?' 'Nay, Ma'am, I ask Pardon, I meant no Harm,' answered she, 'but to be sure the poor Gentleman hath run in my Head ever since I saw him this Morning.—To be sure, if your Ladyship had but seen him just now, you must have pitied him. Poor Gentleman! I wishes some Misfortune hath not happened to him: For he hath been walking about with his Arms a-cross, and looking so melancholy[1] all this Morning; I vow and protest it made me almost cry to see him.' 'To see whom?' says *Sophia*. 'Poor Mr. *Jones*,' answered *Honour*. 'See him! Why, where did you see him?' cries *Sophia*. 'By the Canal, Ma'am,' says *Honour*. 'There

---

[1] Walking about alone with his arms folded, Jones expresses his melancholy according to stylized Renaissance conventions depicting the 'Inamorato' or 'Malcontent'. The iconographic tradition appears in a panel representing the 'Inamorato' from the frontispiece of Burton's *Anatomy of Melancholy* (1621). On the stage, several of Shakespeare's love-sick heroes strike a similar attitude—Valentine, for instance, whose passion is therefore easily recognized by Speed (*Two Gentlemen of Verona*, II. i):

*Val.* Why, how know you that I am in love?

*Speed.* Marry, sir, by these special old marks; first, you have learned, like Sir Protheus, to wreath your arms like a malecontent—to walk alone like one that had the pestilence....

Cf. also *Love's Labour's Lost* (III. i), where Berowne describes Cupid as 'Regent of love-rimes, Lord of folded arms'. This conventional posture of the melancholy man is attributed to Ferdinand in *The Tempest* (I. ii) and to Brutus in *Julius Caesar* (II. i). Portia's description of Brutus' behaviour in his grief is especially close to Honour's representation of Jones: 'You ... walk'd about, / Musing, and sighing, with your arms across ....'

he hath been walking all this Morning, and at last there he laid himself down; I believe he lies there still. To be sure, if it had not been for my Modesty, being a Maid as I am, I should have gone and spoke to him. Do, Ma'am, let me go and see, only for a Fancy, whether he is there still.' 'Pugh!' says *Sophia*, 'There! no, no, what should he do there? He is gone before this Time to be sure. Besides, why—what—why should you go to see?— Besides, I want you for something else. Go, fetch me my Hat and Gloves. I shall walk with my Aunt in the Grove before Dinner.' *Honour* did immediately as she was bid, and *Sophia* put her Hat on; when looking in the Glass, she fancied the Ribbon with which her Hat was tied, did not become her, and so sent her Maid back again for a Ribbon of a different Colour; and then giving Mrs. *Honour* repeated Charges not to leave her Work on any Account, as she said it was in violent Haste, and must be finished that very Day, she muttered something more about going to the Grove, and then sallied out the contrary Way, and walked as fast as her tender trembling Limbs could carry her, directly towards the Canal.

*Jones* had been there, as Mrs. *Honour* had told her: He had indeed spent two Hours there that Morning in melancholy Contemplation on his *Sophia*, and had gone out from the Garden at one Door, the Moment she entered it at another. So that those unlucky Minutes which had been spent in changing the Ribbons, had prevented the Lovers from Meeting at this Time. A most unfortunate Accident, from which my fair Readers will not fail to draw a very wholesome Lesson. And here I strictly forbid all Male Critics to intermeddle with a Circumstance, which I have recounted only for the Sake of the Ladies, and upon which they only are at Liberty to comment.

## CHAPTER VII

*A Picture of formal Courtship in Miniature, as it always ought to be drawn, and a Scene of a tenderer Kind, painted at full Length.*

IT was well remarked by one, (and perhaps by more) that Misfortunes do not come single. This wise Maxim was now verified by *Sophia*, who was not only disappointed of seeing the

Man she loved; but had the Vexation of being obliged to dress
herself out, in order to receive a Visit from the Man she hated.

That Afternoon, Mr. *Western*, for the first Time, acquainted
his Daughter with his Intention; telling her, he knew very well
that she had heard it before from her Aunt. *Sophia* looked very
grave upon this, nor could she prevent a few Pearls from stealing
into her Eyes. 'Come, come,' says *Western*, 'none of your Maidenish Airs; I know all; I assure you, Sister hath told me all.'

'Is it possible,' says *Sophia*, 'that my Aunt can have betrayed
me already?' 'Ay, ay,' says *Western*, 'betrayed you! ay. Why,
you betrayed yourself yesterday at Dinner. You shewed your
Fancy very plainly, I think. But you young Girls never know what
you would be at. So you cry because I am going to marry you to
the Man you are in Love with! Your Mother, I remember,
whimpered and whined just in the same Manner; but it was all
over within twenty-four Hours after we were married: Mr.
*Blifil* is a brisk young Man, and will soon put an End to your
Squeamishness. Come, chear up, chear up, I expect un every
Minute.'

*Sophia* was now convinced that her Aunt had behaved honourably to her; and she determined to go through that disagreeable Afternoon with as much Resolution as possible, and without
giving the least Suspicion in the World to her Father.

Mr. *Blifil* soon arrived; and Mr. *Western* soon after withdrawing, left the young Couple together.

Here a long Silence of near a Quarter of an Hour ensued:
For the Gentleman who was to begin the Conversation had all
that unbecoming Modesty which consists in Bashfulness. He
often attempted to speak, and as often suppressed his Words
just at the very Point of Utterance. At last out they broke in a
Torrent of far-fetched and high-strained Compliments, which
were answered, on her Side, by downcast Looks, half Bows and
civil Monosyllables. *Blifil* from his Inexperience in the Ways of
Women, and from his Conceit of himself, took this Behaviour
for a modest Assent to his Courtship; and when to shorten a
Scene which she could no longer support, *Sophia* rose up and left
the Room, he imputed that too, merely to Bashfulness, and comforted himself, that he should soon have enough of her Company.

He was indeed perfectly well satisfied with his Prospect of
Success: For as to that entire and absolute Possession of the

Heart of his Mistress, which romantic Lovers require, the very Idea of it never entered his Head. Her Fortune and her Person were the sole Objects of his Wishes, of which he made no Doubt soon to obtain the absolute Property; as Mr. *Western's* Mind was so earnestly bent on the Match; and as he well knew the strict Obedience which *Sophia* was always ready to pay to her Father's Will, and the greater still which her Father would exact, if there was Occasion. This Authority, therefore, together with the Charms which he fancied in his own Person and Conversation, could not fail, he thought, of succeeding with a young Lady, whose Inclinations, were, he doubted not, entirely disengaged.

Of *Jones* he certainly had not even the least Jealousy; and I have often thought it wonderful that he had not. Perhaps he imagined the Character which *Jones* bore all over the Country, (how justly let the Reader determine) of being one of the wildest Fellows in *England*, might render him odious to a Lady of the most exemplary Modesty. Perhaps his Suspicions might be laid asleep by the Behaviour of *Sophia*, and of *Jones* himself, when they were all in Company together. Lastly, and indeed principally, he was well assured there was not another Self in the Case. He fancied that he knew *Jones* to the Bottom, and had in reality a great Contempt for his Understanding, for not being more attached to his own Interest. He had no Apprehension that *Jones* was in Love with *Sophia*; and as for any lucrative Motives, he imagined they would sway very little with so silly a Fellow. *Blifil*, moreover, thought the Affair of *Molly Seagrim* still went on, and indeed believed it would end in Marriage: For *Jones* really loved him from his Childhood, and had kept no Secret from him, till his Behaviour on the Sickness of Mr. *Allworthy* had entirely alienated his Heart; and it was by means of the Quarrel which had ensued on this Occasion, and which was not yet reconciled, that Mr. *Blifil* knew nothing of the Alteration which had happened in the Affection which *Jones* had formerly borne towards *Molly*.

From these Reasons, therefore, Mr. *Blifil* saw no Bar to his Success with *Sophia*. He concluded, her Behaviour was like that of all other young Ladies on a first Visit from a Lover, and it had indeed entirely answered his Expectations.

Mr. *Western* took Care to way-lay the Lover at his Exit from his Mistress. He found him so elevated with his Success, so enamoured with his Daughter, and so satisfied with her Reception of him, that the old Gentleman began to caper and dance about his Hall, and by many other antic Actions, to express the Extravagance of his Joy: For he had not the least Command over any of his Passions; and that which had at any Time the Ascendant in his Mind, hurried him to the wildest Excesses.

As soon as *Blifil* was departed, which was not till after many hearty Kisses and Embraces bestowed on him by *Western*, the good Squire went instantly in Quest of his Daughter, whom he no sooner found than he poured forth the most extravagant Raptures, bidding her chuse what Clothes and Jewels she pleased; and declaring that he had no other Use for Fortune but to make her happy. He then caressed her again and again with the utmost Profusion of Fondness, called her by the most endearing Names, and protested she was his only Joy on Earth.

*Sophia* perceiving her Father in this Fit of Affection, which she did not absolutely know the Reason of, (for Fits of Fondness were not unusual to him, tho' this was rather more violent than ordinary) thought she should never have a better Opportunity of disclosing herself than at present; as far at least, as regarded Mr. *Blifil*; and she too-well foresaw the Necessity which she should soon be under of coming to a full Explanation. After having thanked the Squire, therefore, for all his Professions of Kindness, she added, with a Look full of inexpressible Softness, 'And is it possible my Papa can be so good to place all his Joy in his *Sophy*'s Happiness?' which *Western* having confirmed by a great Oath, and a Kiss; she then laid hold of his Hand, and falling on her Knees, after many warm and passionate Declarations of Affection and Duty, she begged him 'not to make her the most miserable Creature on Earth, by forcing her to marry a Man whom she detested.' 'This I entreat of you, dear Sir,' said she, 'for your Sake as well as my own, since you are so very kind to tell me your Happiness depends on mine.' 'How! what!' says *Western*, staring wildly. 'O Sir,' continued she, 'not only your poor *Sophy*'s Happiness; her very Life, her Being depends upon your granting her Request. I cannot live with Mr. *Blifil*. To force me into this Marriage, would be killing me.' 'You can't live with Mr. *Blifil*!' says *Western*. 'No, upon my Soul I can't,' answered *Sophia*. 'Then die and be d—ned,' cries he, spurning her from him. 'Oh! Sir,' cries *Sophia*, catching hold of the Skirt of his

Coat, 'take Pity on me, I beseech you. Don't look, and say such
cruel—— Can you be unmoved while you see your *Sophy* in this
dreadful Condition? Can the best of Fathers break my Heart?
Will he kill me by the most painful, cruel, lingering Death?'
'Pooh! Pooh!' cries the Squire, 'all Stuff and Nonsense, all
maidenish Tricks. Kill you indeed! Will Marriage kill you?'—
'Oh! Sir,' answered *Sophia*, 'such a Marriage is worse than
Death.— He is not even indifferent, I hate and detest him.'—
'If you detest un never so much,' cries *Western*, 'you shall ha' un.'
This he bound by an Oath too shocking to repeat, and after many
violent Asseverations, concluded in these Words. 'I am resolved
upon the Match, and unless you consent to it, I will not give you
a Groat, not a single Farthing; no, tho' I saw you expiring with
Famine in the Street, I would not relieve you with a Morsel of
Bread. This is my fixed Resolution, and so I leave you to con-
sider on it.' He then broke from her with such Violence, that her
Face dashed against the Floor, and he burst directly out of the
Room, leaving poor *Sophia* prostrate on the Ground.

When *Western* came into the Hall, he there found *Jones*;
who seeing his Friend looking wild, pale, and almost breathless,
could not forbear enquiring the Reason of all these melancholy
Appearances. Upon which the Squire immediately acquainted
him with the whole Matter, concluding with bitter Denunciations
against *Sophia*, and very pathetic Lamentations of the Misery
of all Fathers who are so unfortunate to have Daughters.

*Jones*, to whom all the Resolutions which had been taken in
Favour of *Blifil* were yet a Secret, was at first almost struck dead
with this Relation; but recovering his Spirits a little, mere
Despair, as he afterwards said, inspired him to mention a Matter
to Mr. *Western*, which seemed to require more Impudence than a
human Forehead was ever gifted with. He desired Leave to go
to *Sophia*, that he might endeavour to obtain her Concurrence
with her Father's Inclinations.

If the Squire had been as quick-sighted, as he was remarkable
for the contrary, Passion might at present very well have blinded
him. He thanked *Jones* for offering to undertake the Office, and
said, '*Go, go*, prithee, try what can'st do;' and then swore many
execrable Oaths that he would turn her out of Doors unless she
consented to the Match.

## CHAPTER VIII

*The Meeting between* Jones *and* Sophia.

*JONES* departed instantly in Quest of *Sophia*, whom he found just risen from the Ground where her Father had left her, with the Tears trickling from her Eyes, and the Blood running from her Lips. He presently ran to her, and with a Voice full at once of Tenderness and Terrour, cried, 'O my *Sophia*, what means this dreadful Sight!'—She looked softly at him for a Moment before she spoke, and then said, 'Mr. *Jones*, for Heaven's Sake, how came you here?—Leave me, I beseech you, this Moment.' 'Do not,' says he, 'impose so harsh a Command upon me—my Heart bleeds faster than those Lips. O *Sophia*, how easily could I drain my Veins to preserve one Drop of that dear Blood.' 'I have too many Obligations to you already,' answered she, 'for sure you meant them such.'—Here she looked at him tenderly almost a Minute, and then bursting into an Agony, cried,—'O Mr. *Jones*,—why did you save my Life?—my Death would have been happier for us both.'—'Happier for us both!' cried he, 'Could Racks or Wheels kill me so painfully as *Sophia's*! —I cannot bear the dreadful Sound.—Do I live but for her?'— Both his Voice and Look were full of inexpressible Tenderness when he spoke these Words, and at the same Time he laid gently hold on her Hand, which she did not withdraw from him; to say the Truth, she hardly knew what she did or suffered. A few Moments now passed in Silence between these Lovers, while his Eyes were eagerly fixed on *Sophia*, and hers declining towards the Ground; at last she recovered Strength enough to desire him again to leave her; for that her certain Ruin would be the Consequence of their being found together; adding,—'O Mr. *Jones*, you know not, you know not what hath passed this cruel Afternoon.' 'I know all, my *Sophia*,' answered he; 'your cruel Father hath told me all, and he himself hath sent me hither to you.' 'My Father sent you to me!' replied she, 'sure you dream.' 'Would to Heaven,' cries he, 'it was but a Dream. O *Sophia*, your Father hath sent me to you, to be an Advocate for my odious Rival, to solicite you in his Favour.—I took any Means to get Access to you.—O speak to me, *Sophia*, comfort my bleeding Heart. Sure no one ever loved, ever doated like me. Do not unkindly with-hold this dear, this soft, this gentle Hand.—One Moment, perhaps, tears you for ever from me.— Nothing less than this cruel Occasion could, I believe, have ever conquered the Respect and Awe, with which you have inspired me.' She stood a Moment silent and covered with Confusion, then lifting up her Eyes gently towards him, she cried, 'What would Mr. *Jones* have me say?' 'O do but promise,' cries he, 'that you never will give yourself to *Blifil.*' 'Name not,' answered she, 'the detested Sound. Be assured I never will give him what is in my Power to with-hold from him.' 'Now then,' cries he, 'while you are so perfectly kind, go a little farther, and add that I may hope.'— 'Alas,' says she, 'Mr. *Jones*, whither will you drive me? What Hope have I to bestow? You know my Father's Intentions.'— 'But I know,' answered he, 'your Compliance with them cannot be compelled.' 'What,' says she, 'must be the dreadful Consequence of my Disobedience? My own Ruin is my least Concern. I cannot bear the Thoughts of being the Cause of my Father's Misery.' 'He is himself the Cause,' cries *Jones*, 'by exacting a Power over you which Nature hath not given him. Think on the Misery which I am to suffer, if I am to lose you, and see on which Side Pity will turn the Ballance.' 'Think of it!' replied she, 'can you imagine I do not feel the Ruin which I must bring on you, should I comply with your Desire?—It is that Thought which gives me Resolution to bid you fly from me for ever, and avoid your own Destruction.' 'I fear no Destruction,' cries he, 'but the Loss of *Sophia*; if you would save me from the most bitter Agonies, recall that cruel Sentence.—Indeed, I can never part with you, indeed I cannot.'

The Lovers now stood both silent and trembling, *Sophia* being unable to with-draw her Hand from *Jones*, and he almost as unable to hold it; when the Scene, which I believe some of my Readers will think had lasted long enough, was interrupted by one of so different a Nature, that we shall reserve the Relation of it for a different Chapter.

## CHAPTER IX

*Being of a much more tempestuous Kind than the former.*

BEFORE we proceed with what now happened to our Lovers, it may be proper to recount what had past in the Hall, during their tender Interview.

Soon after *Jones* had left Mr. *Western* in the Manner above-mentioned, his Sister came to him; and was presently informed of all that had past between her Brother and *Sophia*, relating to *Blifil*.

This Behaviour in her Niece, the good Lady construed to be an absolute Breach of the Condition, on which she had engaged to keep her Love for Mr. *Jones* a Secret. She considered herself, therefore, at full Liberty to reveal all she knew to the Squire, which she immediately did in the most explicit Terms, and without any Ceremony or Preface.

The Idea of a Marriage between *Jones* and his Daughter, had never once entered into the Squire's Head, either in the warmest Minutes of his Affection towards that young Man, or from Suspicion, or on any other Occasion. He did indeed consider a Parity of Fortune and Circumstances, to be physically as necessary an ingredient in Marriage, as Difference of Sexes, or any other Essential; and had no more Apprehension of his Daughter's falling in Love with a poor Man, than with any Animal of a different Species.

He became, therefore, like one Thunder-struck at his Sister's Relation. He was, at first, incapable of making any Answer, having been almost deprived of his Breath by the Violence of the Surprize. This, however, soon returned, and, as is usual in other Cases after an Intermission, with redoubled Force and Fury.

The first Use he made of the Power of Speech, after his Recovery from the sudden Effects of his Astonishment, was to discharge a round Volley of Oaths and Imprecations. After which he proceeded hastily to the Apartment, where he expected to find the Lovers, and murmured, or indeed, rather roared forth Intentions of Revenge every Step he went.

As when two Doves, or two Wood-pigeons, or as when *Strephon* and *Phillis* (for that comes nearest to the Mark) are retired into some pleasant solitary Grove, to enjoy the delightful Conversation of Love; that bashful Boy who cannot speak in

Public, and is never a good Companion to more than two at a Time. Here while every Object is serene, should hoarse Thunder burst suddenly through the shattered Clouds, and rumbling roll along the Sky, the frightened Maid starts from the mossy Bank or verdant Turf; the pale Livery of Death succeeds the red Regimentals in which Love had before drest her Cheeks; Fear shakes her whole Frame, and her Lover scarce supports her trembling, tottering Limbs.

Or as when two Gentlemen, Strangers to the wonderous Wit of the Place, are cracking a Bottle together at some Inn or Tavern at *Salisbury*, if the great *Dowdy*[1] who acts the Part of a Madman, as well as some of his Setters-on do that of a Fool, should rattle his Chains, and dreadfully hum forth the grumbling Catch along the Gallery; the frighted Strangers stand aghast, scared at the horrid Sound, they seek some Place of Shelter from the approaching Danger, and if the well-barred Windows did admit their Exit, would venture their Necks to escape the threatning Fury now coming upon them.

So trembled poor *Sophia*, so turned she pale at the Noise of her Father, who in a Voice most dreadful to hear, came on swearing, cursing and vowing the Destruction of *Jones*. To say the Truth, I believe the Youth himself would, from some prudent Considerations, have preferred another Place of Abode at this Time, had his Terrour on *Sophia's* Account given him Liberty to reflect a Moment on what any otherways concerned himself, than as his Love made him partake whatever affected her.

---

[1] Daniel Pearce (d. 1762), one of the Corporation mace-bearers in Salisbury. An obituary appearing in *Lloyd's Evening Post, and British Chronicle* (18–20 January 1762) identifies Fielding's allusion and supplies the following account of Pearce's antics as a practical joker:

'The Demerit of this man, known by the name of *Dowdy*, consisted in assuming the tatter'd garment, decorations of straw, rattling chains, visage stained with blood, and deportment of the most desperate lunatic; in which he was assisted by a frightful tone of voice and articulation (which he could modulate, for the pastime of those who put him on this barbarous sport, to increase or decrease, at pleasure, the terror of its object): he had a peculiar genius for this part, so as to fill the boldest with real fear, and hunt them to and fro, thro' windows, up chimneys, and even over the tops of houses, to escape the fury of a supposed raving, mischievous Bedlamite, intent on their destruction. . . . Mr. Pearce (except in the exercise of this piece of false humour) was a pacifick and civil man; and, it is said, has sometimes, after he had thrown off his disguise, and the person attacked has been made sensible of the cruel joke put upon him, officiously tendered his service, and gone about with him in pretended search after the madman, in order to correct his insolence, or bring him to justice.'

And now the Squire having burst open the Door, beheld an Object which instantly suspended all his Fury against *Jones*; this was the ghastly Appearance of *Sophia*, who had fainted away in her Lover's Arms. This tragical Sight Mr. *Western* no sooner beheld, than all his Rage forsook him, he roared for Help with his utmost Violence; ran first to his Daughter, then back to the Door, calling for Water, and then back again to *Sophia*, never considering in whose Arms she then was, nor, perhaps, once re-collecting that there was such a Person in the World as *Jones*: For, indeed, I believe, the present Circumstances of his Daughter were now the sole Consideration which employed his Thoughts.

Mrs. *Western* and a great Number of Servants soon came to the Assistance of *Sophia*, with Water, Cordials, and every Thing necessary on those Occasions. These were applied with such Success, that *Sophia* in a very few Minutes began to recover, and all the Symptoms of Life to return. Upon which she was presently led off by her own Maid and Mrs. *Western*; nor did that good Lady depart without leaving some wholsome Admonitions with her Brother, on the dreadful Effects of his Passion, or, as she pleased to call it, Madness.

The Squire, perhaps, did not understand this good Advice, as it was delivered in obscure Hints, Shrugs, and Notes of Ad-miration; at least, if he did understand it, he profited very little by it: For no sooner was he cured of his immediate Fears for his Daughter, than he relapsed into his former Frenzy, which must have produced an immediate Battle with *Jones*, had not Parson *Supple*, who was a very strong Man, been present, and by mere Force restrained the Squire from Acts of Hostility.

The Moment *Sophia* was departed, *Jones* advanced in a very suppliant Manner to Mr. *Western*, whom the Parson held in his Arms, and begged him to be pacify'd; for that while he continued in such a Passion it would be impossible to give him any Satis-faction.

'I wull have Satisfaction o' thee,' answered the Squire, 'so doff thy Clothes. *At unt* half a Man, and I'll lick thee as well as wast ever licked in thy Life.' He then bespattered the Youth with Abundance of that Language, which passes between Country Gentlemen who embrace opposite Sides of the Question; with frequent Applications to him to salute that Part which is generally introduced into all Controversies, that arise among the lower

Orders of the *English* Gentry, at Horse-races, Cock-matches, and other public Places. Allusions to this Part are likewise often made for the Sake of the Jest. And here, I believe, the Wit is generally misunderstood. In Reality, it lies in desiring another to kiss your A— for having just before threatened to kick his: For I have observed very accurately, that no one ever desires you to kick that which belongs to himself, nor offers to kiss this Part in another.

It may likewise seem surprizing, that in the many thousand kind Invitations of this Sort, which every one who hath conversed with Country Gentlemen, must have heard, no one, I believe, hath ever seen a single Instance where the Desire hath been complied with. A great Instance of their Want of Politeness: For in Town, nothing can be more common than for the finest Gentlemen to perform this Ceremony every Day to their Superiors, without having that Favour once requested of them.

To all such Wit, *Jones* very calmly answered, 'Sir, this Usage, may, perhaps, cancel every other Obligation you have conferred on me; but there is one you can never cancel; nor will I be provoked by your Abuse, to lift my Hand against the Father of *Sophia*.'

At these Words, the Squire grew still more outrageous than before; so that the Parson begged *Jones* to retire, saying, 'You behold, Sir, how he waxeth Wroth at your Abode here; therefore, let me pray you not to tarry any longer. His Anger is too much kindled for you to commune with him at present. You had better, therefore, conclude your Visit, and refer what Matters you have to urge in your Behalf, to some other Opportunity.'

*Jones* accepted this Advice with Thanks, and immediately departed. The Squire now regained the Liberty of his Hands, and so much Temper as to express some Satisfaction in the Restraint which had been laid upon him; declaring that he should certainly have beat his Brains out; and adding, 'It would have vexed one confoundedly to have been hanged for such a Rascal.'

The Parson now began to triumph in the Success of his Peace-making Endeavours, and proceeded to read a Lecture against Anger, which might, perhaps, rather have tended to raise than to quiet that Passion in some hasty Minds. This Lecture he enriched with many valuable Quotations from the Antients, particularly from *Seneca*;[1] who hath, indeed, so well handled this

---

[1] Cf. Seneca's *Moral Essays*, iii ('Ad Novatum de Ira').

Passion, that none but a very angry Man can read him without great Pleasure and Profit. The Doctor concluded this Harangue with the famous Story of *Alexander* and *Clytus*;[1] but as I find that entered in my Common-Place under Title Drunkenness, I shall not insert it here.

The Squire took no Notice of this Story, nor, perhaps, of any Thing he said: For he interrupted him before he had finished by calling for a Tankard of Beer; observing (which is, perhaps, as true as any Observation on this Fever of the Mind) *that Anger makes a Man dry.*

No sooner had the Squire swallowed a large Draught than he renewed the Discourse on *Jones*, and declared a Resolution of going the next Morning early to acquaint Mr. *Allworthy*. His Friend would have dissuaded him from this, from the mere Motive of Good-nature; but his Dissuasion had no other Effect, than to produce a large Volley of Oaths and Curses, which greatly shocked the pious Ears of *Supple*; but he did not dare to remonstrate against a Privilege, which the Squire claimed as a free-born *Englishman*. To say Truth, the Parson submitted to please his Palate at the Squire's Table, at the Expence of suffering now and then this Violence to his Ears. He contented himself with thinking he did not promote this evil Practice, and that the Squire would not swear an Oath the less if he never entered within his Gates. However, tho' he was not guilty of ill Manners by rebuking a Gentleman in his own House, he paid him off obliquely in the Pulpit; which had not, indeed, the good Effect of working a Reformation in the Squire himself, yet it so far operated on his Conscience, that he put the Laws[2] very severely in Execution against others, and the Magistrate was the only Person in the Parish who could swear with Impunity.

---

[1] Cf. Plutarch's *Life of Alexander*, l–li; and Arrian, *Anabasis of Alexander*, IV. viii. Alexander killed his friend Cleitus for insulting him during a drunken quarrel (328 B.C.).

[2] That Fielding deplored what he called the 'detestable Crime' of 'profane Cursing and Swearing' is clear from *A Charge Delivered to the Grand Jury* (1749), in which he discusses the statutes designed to punish offenders and exhorts magistrates and peace-officers to enforce them. The most recent of these laws had been passed in 1746.

## CHAPTER X

### *In which Mr.* Western *visits Mr.* Allworthy.

MR. *Allworthy* was now retired from Breakfast with his Nephew, well satisfied with the Report of the young Gentleman's successful Visit to *Sophia* (for he greatly desired the Match, more on Account of the young Lady's Character than of her Riches) when Mr. *Western* broke abruptly in upon them, and without any Ceremony began as follows.

'There, you have done a fine Piece of Work truly. You have brought up your Bastard to a fine Purpose; not that I believe you have had any Hand in it neither, that is, as a Man may say, designedly; but there is a fine Kettle of Fish made on't up at our House.' 'What can be the Matter, Mr. *Western?*' said *Allworthy*. 'O Matter *enow* of all Conscience; my Daughter hath fallen in Love with your Bastard, that's all, but I won't *ge* her a *Hapenny*, not the Twentieth Part of a Brass *Varden*. I always thought what would come o' breeding up a Bastard like a Gentleman, and letting *un* come about to *Vok's* Houses. It's well *vor un* I could not get *at un*, I'd *a licked un*, I'd a spoil'd his Caterwauling, I'd a taught the Son of a Whore to meddle with Meat for his Master. He shan't ever have a Morsel of Meat of mine, or a *Varden* to buy it: If she will *ha un*, one Smock shall be her Portion. I'll sooner *ge* my *Esteate* to the *zinking* Fund,[1] that it may be sent to *Hannover* to corrupt our Nation with.' 'I am heartily sorry,' cries *Allworthy*. 'Pox o' your Sorrow,' says *Western*, 'it will do me Abundance of Good, when I have lost my only Child, my poor *Sophy*, that was the Joy of my Heart, and all the Hope and Comfort of my Age; but I am resolved I will turn her out o' Doors, she shall beg and starve and rot in the Streets. Not one *Hapenny*, not a *Hapenny* shall she ever *hae* o' mine. The Son of a Bitch was always good at finding a Hare sitting; an' be rotted to'n, I little thought what Puss he was looking after; but it shall be the worst he ever *vound* in his Life. She shall be no better than

---

[1] Established by Walpole in 1717, the Sinking Fund was created from 'the *Surplusses* of the *Aggregate, South-Sea,* and *general Funds*' and was originally intended 'to *sink* or discharge the *National Debts*' (see *An Essay on the Sinking Fund* [1736], p. 9). As the expense of government rose, however, this money was appropriated for other purposes. Since 1742 the Opposition had made a special issue of the use of the fund to maintain the Hanoverian troops (see below, p. 321, n. 2).

Carrion; the Skin o'er is all he shall *ha*, and *zu* you may tell *un*.' 'I am in Amazement,' cries *Allworthy*, 'at what you tell me, after what passed between my Nephew and the young Lady no longer ago than Yesterday.' 'Yes, Sir,' answered *Western*, 'it was after what passed between your Nephew and she that the whole Matter came out. Mr. *Blifil* there was no sooner gone than the Son of a Whore came lurching about the House. Little did I think when I used to love him for a Sportsman, that he was all the while a poaching after my Daughter.' 'Why, truly,' says *Allworthy*, 'I could wish you had not given him so many Opportunities with her; and you will do me the Justice to acknowledge, that I have always been averse to his staying so much at your House, tho' I own I had no Suspicion of this Kind.' 'Why, Zounds!' cries *Western*, 'who could have thought it? What the Devil had she to do wi'n? He did not come there a courting to her, he came there a hunting with me.' 'But was it possible,' says *Allworthy*, 'that you should never discern any Symptoms of Love between them, when you have seen them so often together?' 'Never in my Life, as I hope to be saved,' cries *Western*. 'I never so much as seed him kiss her in all my Life; and so far from courting her, he used rather to be more silent when she was in Company than at any other Time: And as for the Girl, she was always less civil to'n than to any young Man that came to the House. As to that Matter, I am not more easy to be deceived than another, I would not have you think I am, Neighbour.' *Allworthy* could scarce refrain Laughter at this; but he resolved to do a Violence to himself: For he perfectly well knew Mankind, and had too much good Breeding and good Nature to offend the Squire in his present Circumstances. He then asked *Western* what he would have him do upon this Occasion. To which the other answered, 'That he would have him keep the Rascal away from his House, and that he would go and lock up the Wench: For he was resolved to make her marry Mr. *Blifil* in Spite of her Teeth.' He then shook *Blifil* by the Hand, and swore he would have no other Son-in-law. Presently after which he took his Leave, saying, his House was in such Disorder, that it was necessary for him to make Haste home, to take care his Daughter did not give him the Slip; and as for *Jones*, he swore if he caught him at his House, he would qualify him to run for the Gelding's Plate.

When *Allworthy* and *Blifil* were again left together, a long

Silence ensued between them; all which Interval the young Gentleman filled up with Sighs, which proceeded partly from Disappointment, but more from Hatred: For the Success of *Jones* was much more grievous to him, than the Loss of *Sophia*.

At length his Uncle asked him what he was determined to do, and he answered in the following Words. 'Alas, Sir, can it be a Question what Step a Lover will take, when Reason and Passion point different Ways? I am afraid it is too certain he will, in that Dilemma, always follow the latter. Reason dictates to me, to quit all Thoughts of a Woman who places her Affections on another; my Passion bids me hope she may, in Time, change her Inclinations in my Favour. Here, however, I conceive an Objection may be raised, which if it could not fully be answered, would totally deter me from any further Pursuit. I mean the Injustice of endeavouring to supplant another, in a Heart of which he seems already in Possession; but the determined Resolution of Mr. *Western* shews, that in this Case, I shall by so doing, promote the Happiness of every Party; not only that of the Parent, who will thus be preserved from the highest Degree of Misery, but of both the others, who must be undone by this Match. The Lady, I am sure, will be undone in every Sense: For besides the Loss of most Part of her own Fortune, she will be not only married to a Beggar, but the little Fortune which her Father cannot with-hold from her, will be squandered on that Wench, with whom I know he yet converses.—Nay, that is a Trifle: For I know him to be one of the worst Men in the World: For had my dear Uncle known what I have hitherto endeavoured to conceal, he must have long since abandoned so profligate a Wretch.' 'How,' said *Allworthy*, 'hath he done any Thing worse than I already know? Tell me, I beseech you.' 'No,' replied *Blifil*, 'it is now past, and perhaps he may have repented of it.' 'I command you on your Duty,' said *Allworthy*, 'to tell me what you mean.' 'You know, Sir,' says *Blifil*, 'I never disobeyed you; but I am sorry I mentioned it, since it may now look like Revenge, whereas, I thank Heaven, no such Motive ever entered my Heart; and if you oblige me to discover it, I must be his Petitioner to you for your Forgiveness.' 'I will have no Conditions,' answered *Allworthy*, 'I think I have shewn Tenderness enough towards him, and more, perhaps, than you ought to thank me for.' 'More, indeed, I fear than he deserved,' cries *Blifil*, 'for in the very Day of your utmost Danger, when myself and all the Family were in Tears, he filled the House with Riot and Debauchery. He drank and sung and roared, and when I gave him a gentle Hint of the Indecency of his Actions, he fell into a violent Passion, swore many Oaths, called me Rascal, and struck me.' 'How!' cries *Allworthy*, 'did he dare to strike you?' 'I am sure,' cries *Blifil*, 'I have forgiven him that long ago. I wish I could so easily forget his Ingratitude to the best of Benefactors; and yet, even that, I hope you will forgive him, since he must have certainly been possessed with the Devil: For that very Evening, as Mr. *Thwackum* and myself were taking the Air in the Fields, and exulting in the good Symptoms which then first began to discover themselves, we unluckily saw him engaged with a Wench in a Manner not fit to be mentioned. Mr. *Thwackum*, with more Boldness than Prudence, advanced to rebuke him, when, (I am sorry to say it) he fell upon the worthy Man, and beat him so outragiously, that I wish he may have yet recovered the Bruises. Nor was I without my Share of the Effects of his Malice, while I endeavoured to protect my Tutor: But that I have long forgiven, nay I prevailed with Mr. *Thwackum* to forgive him too, and not to inform you of a Secret which I feared might be fatal to him. And now, Sir, since I have unadvisedly dropped a Hint of this Matter, and your Commands have obliged me to discover the whole, let me intercede with you for him.' 'O Child,' said *Allworthy*, 'I know not whether I should blame or applaud your Goodness, in concealing such Villany a Moment; but where is Mr. *Thwackum*? Not that I want any Confirmation of what you say; but I will examine all the Evidence of this Matter, to justify to the World the Example I am resolved to make of such a Monster.'

*Thwackum* was now sent for, and presently appeared. He corroborated every Circumstance which the other had deposed. Nay, he produced the Record upon his Breast, where the Handwriting of Mr. *Jones* remained very legible in black and blue. He concluded with declaring to Mr. *Allworthy*, that he should have long since informed him of this Matter, had not Mr. *Blifil*, by the most earnest Interpositions, prevented him. 'He is,' says he, 'an excellent Youth; though such Forgiveness of Enemies is carrying the Matter too far.'

In reality, *Blifil* had taken some Pains to prevail with the Parson, and to prevent the Discovery at that Time; for which he had many Reasons. He knew that the Minds of Men are apt to be softened and relaxed from their usual Severity by Sickness. Besides, he imagined that if the Story was told when the Fact was so recent, and the Physician about the House, who might have unravelled the real Truth, he should never be able to give it the malicious Turn which he intended. Again, he resolved to hoard up this Business, till the Indiscretion of *Jones* should afford some additional Complaints; for he thought the joint Weight of many Facts falling upon him together, would be the most likely to crush him; and he watched therefore some such Opportunity as that, with which Fortune had now kindly presented him. Lastly, by prevailing with *Thwackum* to conceal the Matter for a Time, he knew he should confirm an Opinion of his Friendship to *Jones*, which he had greatly laboured to establish in Mr. *Allworthy*.

## CHAPTER XI

*A short Chapter; but which contains sufficient Matter to affect the good-natured Reader.*

IT was Mr. *Allworthy's* Custom never to punish any one, not even to turn away a Servant, in a Passion.[1] He resolved, therefore, to delay passing Sentence on *Jones* till the Afternoon.

The poor young Man attended at Dinner, as usual; but his Heart was too much loaded to suffer him to eat. His Grief too was a good deal aggravated by the unkind Looks of Mr. *Allworthy*; whence he concluded that *Western* had discovered the whole Affair between him and *Sophia*: But as to Mr. *Blifil's* Story, he had not the least Apprehension; for of much the greater Part he was entirely innocent, and for the Residue, as he had forgiven and forgotten it himself, so he suspected no Remembrance on the other Side. When Dinner was over, and the Servants departed,

---

[1] In his temperate refusal to inflict punishment when he is angry, Allworthy imitates the example of Plato, about whom Diogenes Laertius records the following anecdote: 'One day, when Xenocrates had come in, Plato asked him to chastise his slave, since he was unable to do it himself because he was in a passion. Further, it is alleged that he said to one of his slaves, "I would have given you a flogging, had I not been in a passion"' (*Lives of Eminent Philosophers*, iii. 38–9; trans. R. D. Hicks, Loeb Classical Library, 1925). Cf. also Cicero, *De Officiis*, I. xxv. 89, and Seneca, *De Ira*, I. xv. 3, where the story is told of Socrates.

Mr. *Allworthy* began to harangue. He set forth, in a long Speech, the many Iniquities of which *Jones* had been guilty, particularly those which this Day had brought to light, and concluded by telling him, 'that unless he could clear himself of the Charge, he was resolved to banish him from his Sight for ever.'

Many Disadvantages attended poor *Jones* in making his Defence; nay, indeed he hardly knew his Accusation: For as Mr. *Allworthy*, in recounting the Drunkenness, *&c.* while he lay ill, out of Modesty sunk every thing that related particularly to himself, which indeed principally constituted the Crime, *Jones* could not deny the Charge. His Heart was, besides, almost broken already, and his Spirits were so sunk, that he could say nothing for himself; but acknowledged the whole, and, like a Criminal in Despair, threw himself upon Mercy; concluding, 'That tho' he must own himself guilty of many Follies and Inadvertencies, he hoped he had done nothing to deserve what would be to him the greatest Punishment in the World.'

*Allworthy* answered, 'that he had forgiven him too often already, in Compassion to his Youth, and in Hopes of his Amendment: That he now found he was an abandoned Reprobate, and such as it would be criminal in any one to support and encourage. Nay,' said Mr. *Allworthy* to him, 'your audacious Attempt to steal away the young Lady, calls upon me to justify my own Character in punishing you. The World, who have already censured the Regard I have shewn for you, may think, with some Colour at least of Justice, that I connive at so base and barbarous an Action. An Action of which you must have known my Abhorrence, and which, had you had any Concern for my Ease and Honour, as well as for my Friendship, you would never have thought of undertaking. Fie upon it, young Man! indeed there is scarce any Punishment equal to your Crimes, and I can scarce think myself justifiable in what I am now going to bestow on you. However, as I have educated you like a Child of my own, I will not turn you naked into the World. When you open this Paper, therefore, you will find something which may enable you, with Industry, to get an honest Livelihood; but if you employ it to worse Purposes, I shall not think myself obliged to supply you farther, being resolved, from this Day forward, to converse no more with you on any Account. I cannot avoid saying, There is no Part of your Conduct which I resent more than your ill

Treatment of that good young Man (meaning *Blifil*) who hath behaved with so much Tenderness and Honour towards you.'

These last Words were a Dose almost too bitter to be swallowed. A Flood of Tears now gushed from the Eyes of *Jones*, and every Faculty of Speech and Motion seemed to have deserted him. It was some Time before he was able to obey *Allworthy's* peremptory Commands of departing; which he at length did, having first kissed his Hands with a Passion difficult to be affected, and as difficult to be described.

The Reader must be very weak, if when he considers the Light in which *Jones* then appeared to Mr. *Allworthy*, he should blame the Rigour of his Sentence. And yet all the Neighbourhood, either from this Weakness, or from some worse Motive, condemned this Justice and Severity as the highest Cruelty. Nay, the very Persons who had before censured the good Man for the Kindness and Tenderness shewn to a Bastard (his own, according to the general Opinion) now cried out as loudly against turning his own Child out of Doors. The Women especially were unanimous in taking the Part of *Jones*, and raised more Stories on the Occasion, than I have room, in this Chapter, to set down.

One thing must not be omitted, that in their Censures on this Occasion, none ever mentioned the Sum contained in the Paper which *Allworthy* gave *Jones*, which was no less than Five hundred Pounds; but all agreed that he was sent away Pennyless, and some said, naked from the House of his inhuman Father.

## CHAPTER XII

### *Containing Love Letters, &c.*

JONES was commanded to leave the House immediately, and told, that his Clothes and every thing else should be sent to him whithersoever he should order them.

He accordingly set out, and walked above a Mile, not regarding, and indeed scarce knowing whither he went. At length a little Brook obstructing his Passage, he threw himself down by the Side of it; nor could he help muttering with some little Indignation, 'Sure my Father will not deny me this Place to rest in?'

Here he presently fell into the most violent Agonies, tearing his Hair from his Head, and using most other Actions which generally accompany Fits of Madness, Rage, and Despair.

When he had in this Manner vented the first Emotions of Passion, he began to come a little to himself. His Grief now took another Turn, and discharged itself in a gentler Way, till he became at last cool enough to reason with his Passion, and to consider what Steps were proper to be taken in his deplorable Condition.

And now the great Doubt was how to act with regard to *Sophia.* The Thoughts of leaving her almost rent his Heart asunder; but the Consideration of reducing her to Ruin and Beggary still racked him, if possible, more; and if the violent Desire of possessing her Person could have induced him to listen one Moment to this Alternative, still he was by no means certain of her Resolution to indulge his Wishes at so high an Expence. The Resentment of Mr. *Allworthy,* and the Injury he must do to his Quiet, argued strongly against this latter; and lastly, the apparent Impossibility of his Success, even if he would sacrifice all these Considerations to it, came to his Assistance; and thus Honour at last, backed with Despair, with Gratitude to his Benefactor, and with real Love to his Mistress, got the better of burning Desire, and he resolved rather to quit *Sophia,* than to pursue her to her Ruin.

It is difficult for any who have not felt it, to conceive the glowing Warmth which filled his Breast, on the first Contemplation of this Victory over his Passion. Pride flattered him so agreeably, that his Mind perhaps enjoyed perfect Happiness; but this was only momentary, *Sophia* soon returned to his Imagination, and allayed the Joy of his Triumph with no less bitter Pangs than a good-natured General must feel when he surveys the bleeding Heaps, at the Price of whose Blood he hath purchased his Laurels; for thousands of tender Ideas lay murdered before our Conqueror.

Being resolved, however, to pursue the Paths of this Giant Honour, as the gigantic Poet *Lee* calls it,[1] he determined to

[1] Nathaniel Lee (1653 ?–92), whose bombastic dramas Fielding had earlier burlesqued in *The Tragedy of Tragedies* (1731). The phrase is from Varanes's speech in *Theodosius: or, The Force of Love* (1680), II. i: 'As to the World thy Judgment soars above me, / And I am dar'd with this Gigantick Honour' (1725 ed.).

write a farewel Letter to *Sophia*; and accordingly proceeded to a
House not far off, where, being furnished with proper Materials,
he wrote as follows:

MADAM,

'WHEN you reflect on the Situation in which I write, I am
sure your Good-nature will pardon any Inconsistency or
Absurdity which my Letter contains; for every thing here flows
from a Heart so full, that no Language can express its Dictates.

'I have resolved, Madam, to obey your Commands, in flying
for ever from your dear, your lovely Sight. Cruel indeed those
Commands are; but it is a Cruelty which proceeds from Fortune,
not from my *Sophia*. Fortune hath made it necessary, necessary to
your Preservation, to forget there ever was such a Wretch as I am.

'Believe me, I would not hint all my Sufferings to you, if I
imagined they could possibly escape your Ears. I know the Goodness and Tenderness of your Heart, and would avoid giving you
any of those Pains which you always feel for the Miserable. O
let nothing which you shall hear of my hard Fortune cause
a Moment's Concern; for after the Loss of you, every thing is to
me a Trifle.

'O my *Sophia*! it is hard to leave you; it is harder still to desire
you to forget me; yet the sincerest Love obliges me to both.
Pardon my conceiving that any Remembrance of me can give
you Disquiet; but if I am so gloriously wretched, sacrifice me
every Way to your Relief. Think I never loved you; or think
truly how little I deserve you; and learn to scorn me for a Presumption which can never be too severely punished.—I am unable to say more.—May Guardian Angels protect you for ever.'

He was now searching his Pockets for his Wax, but found
none, nor indeed any thing else, therein; for in Truth he had,
in his frantic Disposition, tossed every thing from him, and,
amongst the rest, his Pocket-book, which he had received from
Mr. *Allworthy*, which he had never opened, and which now first
occurred to his Memory.

The House supplied him with a Wafer for his present Purpose,
with which having sealed his Letter, he returned hastily towards the Brook Side, in order to search for the Things which
he had there lost. In his Way he met his old Friend *Black George*,
who heartily condoled with him on his Misfortune; for this had

already reached his Ears, and indeed those of all the Neighbour-hood.

*Jones* acquainted the Game-keeper with his Loss, and he as readily went back with him to the Brook, where they searched every Tuft of Grass in the Meadow, as well where *Jones* had not been, as where he had been; but all to no Purpose, for they found nothing: For indeed, though the Things were then in the Meadow, they omitted to search the only Place where they were deposited; to wit, in the Pockets of the said *George*; for he had just before found them, and being luckily apprized of their Value, had very carefully put them up for his own Use.

The Game-keeper having exerted as much Diligence in Quest of the lost Goods, as if he had hoped to find them, desired Mr. *Jones* to recollect if he had been in no other Place; 'For sure,' said he, 'if you had lost them here so lately, the Things must have been here still; for this is a very unlikely Place for any one to pass by;' and indeed it was by great Accident that he himself had passed through that Field, in order to lay Wires for Hares, with which he was to supply a Poulterer at *Bath* the next Morning.

*Jones* now gave over all Hopes of recovering his Loss, and almost all Thoughts concerning it, and turning to *Black George*, asked him earnestly, If he would do him the greatest Favour in the World.

*George* answered, with some Hesitation, 'Sir, you know you may command me whatever is in my Power, and I heartily wish it was in my Power to do you any Service.' In fact, the Question staggered him; for he had, by selling Game, amassed a pretty good Sum of Money in Mr. *Western's* Service, and was afraid that *Jones* wanted to borrow some small Matter of him; but he was presently relieved from his Anxiety, by being desired to convey a Letter to *Sophia*, which with great Pleasure he promised to do. And indeed, I believe there are few Favours which he would not have gladly conferred on Mr. *Jones*; for he bore as much Gratitude towards him as he could, and was as honest as Men who love Money better than any other Thing in the Universe generally are.

Mrs. *Honour* was agreed by both to be the proper Means by which this Letter should pass to *Sophia*. They then separated; the Game-keeper returned home to Mr. *Western's*, and *Jones* walked to an Alehouse at half a Mile's Distance, to wait for his Messenger's Return.

*George* no sooner came home to his Master's House, than he met with Mrs. *Honour*; to whom, having first sounded her with a few previous Questions, he delivered the Letter for her Mistress, and received at the same Time another from her for Mr. *Jones*; which *Honour* told him she had carried all that Day in her Bosom, and began to despair of finding any Means of delivering it.

The Game-keeper returned hastily and joyfully to *Jones*, who having received *Sophia's* Letter from him, instantly withdrew, and eagerly breaking it open, read as follows:

SIR,

'It is impossible to express what I have felt since I saw you. Your submitting, on my Account, to such cruel Insults from my Father, lays me under an Obligation I shall ever own. As you know his Temper, I beg you will, for my Sake, avoid him. I wish I had any Comfort to send you; but believe this, that nothing but the last Violence shall ever give my Hand or Heart where you would be sorry to see them bestowed.'

*Jones* read this Letter a hundred Times over, and kissed it a hundred Times as often. His Passion now brought all tender Desires back into his Mind. He repented that he had writ to *Sophia* in the Manner we have seen above; but he repented more that he had made use of the Interval of his Messenger's Absence to write and dispatch a Letter to Mr. *Allworthy*, in which he had faithfully promised and bound himself to quit all Thoughts of his Love. However, when his cool Reflections returned, he plainly perceived that his Case was neither mended nor altered by *Sophia's* Billet, unless to give him some little Glimpse of Hope from her Constancy, of some favourable Accident hereafter. He therefore resumed his Resolution, and taking leave of *Black George*, set forward to a Town about five Miles distant,[1] whither he had desired Mr. *Allworthy*, unless he pleased to revoke his Sentence, to send his Things after him.

1 Probably Wells.

## CHAPTER XIII

*The Behaviour of* Sophia *on the present Occasion; which none of her Sex will blame, who are capable of behaving in the same Manner. And the Discussion of a knotty Point in the Court of Conscience.*

*SOPHIA* had passed the last twenty-four Hours in no very desirable Manner. During a large Part of them she had been entertained by her Aunt, with Lectures of Prudence, recommending to her the Example of the polite World, where Love (so the good Lady said) is at present entirely laughed at, and where Women consider Matrimony, as Men do Offices of public Trust, only as the Means of making their Fortunes, and of advancing themselves in the World. In commenting on which Text Mrs. *Western* had displayed her Eloquence during several Hours.

These sagacious Lectures, though little suited either to the Taste or Inclination of *Sophia*, were, however, less irksome to her than her own Thoughts, that formed the Entertainment of the Night, during which she never once closed her Eyes.

But though she could neither sleep nor rest in her Bed, yet, having no Avocation from it, she was found there by her Father at his Return from *Allworthy*'s, which was not till past Ten o' Clock in the Morning. He went directly up to her Apartment, opened the Door, and seeing she was not up—cried—'Oh! you are safe then, and I am resolved to keep you so.' He then locked the Door, and delivered the Key to *Honour*, having first given her the strictest Charge, with great Promises of Rewards for her Fidelity, and most dreadful Menaces of Punishment, in case she should betray her Trust.

*Honour*'s Orders were not to suffer her Mistress to come out of her Room without the Authority of the Squire himself, and to admit none to her but him and her Aunt; but she was herself to attend her with whatever *Sophia* pleased, except only Pen, Ink, and Paper, of which she was forbidden the Use.

The Squire ordered his Daughter to dress herself and attend him at Dinner; which she obeyed; and having sat the usual Time, was again conducted to her Prison.

In the Evening, the Goaler *Honour* brought her the Letter

which she received from the Game-keeper.¹ *Sophia* read it very
attentively twice or thrice over, and then threw herself upon the
Bed, and burst into a Flood of Tears. Mrs. *Honour* expressed
great Astonishment at this Behaviour in her Mistress; nor could
she forbear very eagerly begging to know the Cause of this
Passion. *Sophia* made her no Answer for some Time, and then
starting suddenly up, caught her Maid by the Hand, and cried,
'O *Honour*! I am undone.' 'Marry forbid,' cries *Honour*, 'I
wish the Letter had been burnt before I had brought it to your
La'ship. I'm sure I thought it would have comforted your
La'ship, or I would have seen it at the Devil before I would have
touch'd it.' '*Honour*,' says *Sophia*, 'you are a good Girl, and it is
vain to attempt concealing longer my Weakness from you; I
have thrown away my Heart on a Man who hath forsaken me.'
'And is Mr. *Jones*,' answered the Maid, 'such a Perfidy Man?'
'He hath taken his Leave of me,' says *Sophia*, 'for ever in that
Letter. Nay, he hath desired me to forget him. Could he have
desired that, if he had loved me? Could he have borne such a
Thought? could he have written such a Word?' 'No certainly,
Ma'am,' cries *Honour*, 'and to be sure, if the best Man in *England*
was to desire me to forget him, I'd take him at his Word. Marry
come up! I am sure your La'ship hath done him too much Honour
ever to think on him. A young Lady who may take her Choice
of all the young Men in the Country. And to be sure, if I may
be so presumptious as to offer my poor Opinion, there is young
Mr. *Blifil*, who besides that he is come of honest Parents, and will
be one of the greatest Squires all hereabouts, he is to be sure, in
my poor Opinion, a more handsomer, and a more politer Man by
half; and besides, he is a young Gentleman of a sober Character,
and who may defy any of the Neighbours to say black is his
Eye:² He follows no dirty Trollops, nor can any Bastards be
laid at his Door. Forget him indeed! I thank Heaven I myself

¹ Sophia's situation at this point in the novel recalls that of Shakespeare's heroine in
*Romeo and Juliet*. As Juliet loves Romeo but is intended by her family for Paris, so Sophia
loves Jones while her family arranges her marriage to Blifil. With the present scene between
Honour and Sophia compare, in particular, *Romeo and Juliet* (III. ii): when the Nurse
brings news that Romeo has been banished for killing Tybalt, Juliet at first condemns her
faithless lover, then reproves her companion for echoing her sentiments (see below, p. 318,
n. 1).
² A proverbial expression meaning to find fault with. (See W. G. Smith and P. Harvey,
*Oxford Dictionary of English Proverbs*, 2nd ed. [Oxford, 1948], p. 48.)

am not so much at my last Prayers, as to suffer any Man to bid
me forget him twice. If the best He that wears a Head was for to
go for to offer for to say such an affronting Word to me, I would
never give him my Company afterwards, if there was another
young Man in the Kingdom. And as I was a saying, to be sure,
there is young Mr. *Blifil*——' 'Name not his detested Name,'
cries *Sophia*. 'Nay, Ma'am,' says *Honour*, 'if your La'ship doth
not like him, there be more jolly handsome young Men that
would court your La'ship, if they had but the least Encouragement. I don't believe there is arrow young Gentleman in this
Country, or in the next to it, that if your La'ship was but to
look as if you had a Mind to him, would not come about to make
his Offers directly.' 'What a Wretch dost thou imagine me,'
cries *Sophia*, 'by affronting my Ears with such Stuff! I detest all
Mankind.' 'Nay, to be sure, Ma'am,' answered *Honour*, 'your
La'ship hath had enough to give you a Surfeit of them. To be
used ill by such a poor beggarly bastardly Fellow.' 'Hold your
blasphemous Tongue,'[1] cries *Sophia*, 'how dare you mention his
Name with Disrespect before me? He use me ill? No, his poor
bleeding Heart suffered more when he writ the cruel Words,
than mine from reading them. O! he is all heroic Virtue, and
angelic Goodness. I am ashamed of the Weakness of my own
Passion, for blaming what I ought to admire.—O *Honour*! it is
my Good only which he consults. To my Interest he sacrifices
both himself and me.—The Apprehension of ruining me hath
driven him to Despair.' 'I am very glad,' says *Honour*, 'to hear
your La'ship takes that into your Consideration: for to be sure,
it must be nothing less than Ruin, to give your Mind to one that
is turned out of Doors, and is not worth a Farthing in the World.'
'Turned out of Doors!' cries *Sophia* hastily, 'how! what dost thou
mean?' 'Why, to be sure, Ma'am, my Master no sooner told
Squire *Allworthy* about Mr. *Jones* having offered to make Love
to your Ladyship, than the Squire stripped him stark naked, and
turned him out of Doors.' 'Ha!' says *Sophia*, 'have I been the

---

[1] Cf. Juliet to the Nurse, *Romeo and Juliet* (III. ii):

> Blistered be thy tongue
> For such a wish! He was not born to shame.
> Upon his brow shame is asham'd to sit;
> For 'tis a throne where honour may be crown'd
> Sole monarch of the universal earth.
> O, what a beast was I to chide at him!

cursed, wretched Cause of his Destruction?—Turn'd naked out of Doors! Here, *Honour*, take all the Money I have; take the Rings from my Fingers.—Here my Watch, carry him all.—Go, find him immediately.' 'For Heaven's Sake, Ma'am,' answered Mrs. *Honour*, 'do but consider, if my Master should miss any of these Things, I should be made to answer for them. Therefore let me beg your Ladyship not to part with your Watch and Jewels. Besides the Money, I think, is enough of all Conscience; and as for that, my Master can never know any thing of the Matter.' 'Here then,' cries *Sophia*, 'take every Farthing I am worth, find him out immediately and give it him. Go, go, lose not a Moment.'

Mrs. *Honour* departed according to Orders, and finding *Black George* below Stairs, delivered him the Purse which contained Sixteen Guineas, being indeed the whole Stock of *Sophia*: For tho' her Father was very liberal to her, she was much too generous herself to be rich.

*Black George* having received the Purse, set forward towards the Alehouse; but in the Way a Thought occurred to him, whether he should not detain this Money likewise. His Conscience, however, immediately started at this Suggestion, and began to upbraid him with Ingratitude to his Benefactor. To this his Avarice answered, 'That his Conscience should have considered that Matter before, when he deprived poor *Jones* of his 500 *l.* That having quietly acquiesced in what was of so much greater Importance, it was absurd, if not downright Hypocrisy, to affect any Qualms at this Trifle.' In return to which, Conscience, like a good Lawyer, attempted to distinguish between an absolute Breach of Trust, as here where the Goods were delivered, and a bare Concealment of what was found, as in the former Case.[1] Avarice presently treated this with Ridicule, called it a Distinction without a Difference, and absolutely insisted, that when once all Pretensions of Honour and Virtue were given up in any one Instance, that there was no Precedent for resorting to them upon a second Occasion. In short, poor Conscience had certainly been defeated in the

[1] A casuist might thus distinguish between these points in a 'court of conscience'. In a court of law, however, if an 'action of trover' were brought against Black George by the rightful owners, he would be compelled to restore to the plaintiffs both the bank-notes and the guineas. (See below, p. 632, n. 2, and p. 947, where Lawyer Dowling advises Allworthy to prosecute George in this way.)

Argument, had not Fear stept in to her Assistance, and very strenuously urged, that the real Distinction between the two Actions, did not lie in the different Degrees of Honour, but of Safety: For that the secreting the 500 *l.* was a Matter of very little Hazard; whereas the detaining the Sixteen Guineas was liable to the utmost Danger of Discovery.

By this friendly Aid of Fear, Conscience obtained a compleat Victory in the Mind of *Black George*, and after making him a few Compliments on his Honesty, forced him to deliver the Money to *Jones*.

## CHAPTER XIV

*A short Chapter, containing a short Dialogue between Squire* Western
*and his Sister.*

MRS. *Western* had been engaged abroad all that Day. The Squire met her at her Return home; and when she enquired after *Sophia*, he acquainted her that he had secured her safe enough. 'She is locked up in Chamber,' cries he, 'and *Honour* keeps the Key.' As his Looks were full of prodigious Wisdom and Sagacity when he gave his Sister this Information, it is probable he expected much Applause from her for what he had done; but how was he disappointed, when with a most disdainful Aspect, she cry'd, 'Sure, Brother, you are the weakest of all Men. Why will you not confide in me for the Management of my Niece? Why will you interpose? You have now undone all that I have been spending my Breath in order to bring about. While I have been endeavouring to fill her Mind with Maxims of Prudence, you have been provoking her to reject them. *English* Women, Brother, I thank Heaven, are no Slaves. We are not to be locked up like the *Spanish* and *Italian* Wives. We have as good a Right to Liberty as yourselves. We are to be convinced by Reason and Persuasion only, and not governed by Force. I have seen the World, Brother, and know what Arguments to make Use of; and if your Folly had not prevented me, should have prevailed with her to form her Conduct by those Rules of Prudence and Discretion which I formerly taught her.' 'To be sure,' said the Squire, 'I am always in the Wrong.' 'Brother,' answered the

Lady, 'you are not in the Wrong, unless when you meddle with
Matters beyond your Knowledge. You must agree, that I have
seen most of the World; and happy had it been for my Niece,
if she had not been taken from under my Care. It is by living at
home with you that she hath learnt romantic Notions of Love and
Nonsense.' 'You don't imagine, I hope,' cries the Squire, 'that
I have taught her any such Things.' 'Your Ignorance, Brother,'
returned she, 'as the great *Milton* says, almost subdues my
Patience.'* 'D——n *Milton*,' answered the Squire, 'if he had the
Impudence to say so to my Face, I'd lend him a Douse, thof he
was never so great a Man. Patience! an you come to that, Sister,
I have more Occasion of Patience, to be used like an over-grown
School-boy as I am by you. Do you think no one hath any
Understanding, unless he hath been about at Court? Pox! the
World is come to a fine Pass indeed, if we are all Fools, except a
Parcel of Roundheads and *Hannover* Rats. Pox! I hope the Times
are a coming that we shall make Fools of them, and every Man
shall enjoy his own. That's all, Sister, and every Man shall enjoy
his own.[1] I hope to *zee* it, Sister, before the *Hannover* Rats have
eat up all our Corn,[2] and left us nothing but Turneps[3] to feed

---

* The Reader may perhaps subdue his own Patience, if he searches for this in *Milton*.

[1] 'The King shall enjoy his own again' was a Jacobite song.

[2] Formulated in July 1742, the government's policy of subsidizing large numbers of
Hanoverian troops to fight in the Pragmatic army soon became the most controversial issue
of the period. While in Opposition, Fielding's friends Lyttelton, Pitt, Dodington, and
Chesterfield were outspoken critics of the measure, and, ironically enough, in November
1744 Fielding himself had anticipated Squire Western's strictures in the satirical pamphlet,
*An Attempt towards a Natural History of the Hanover Rat*: these 'Vermin', he declared, 'are
become the Plague and Terror of the Nation'; 'they are now to be found in every Man's
Ground in the Kingdom, seeking what they can devour.' When, however, on the strength
of such criticism his friends rose to power the following month, their attitude toward the
Hanoverian question changed completely; from opposing the policy, they became its
staunchest advocates. (See J. B. Owen, *The Rise of the Pelhams* [1957], chs. iv–vii.) Thereafter, as the principal spokesman for the new administration, Fielding undertook to defend
the very measures he had formerly ridiculed. In *The Jacobite's Journal* (13 February 1748),
for instance, he anticipated the satire of Western by printing a letter from 'Humphry
Gubbins', a blustering, illiterate Tory squire who urges the editor to give the Ministry
'zum *Stingers* about *Forreners*; and don't forget HANNOVER RATS; for I promise you I've a
zeed um, and larger Rats they be than ever were a zeed in *England*, till of late Years'. (See
the similar letter from 'George Trott' in the *Journal* for 30 January 1748.)

[3] In the political satires of this period, Hanover was often referred to as the 'Turnip
garden'. Occasioned by Parliament's decision in 1742 to retain the Hanoverian troops in
British pay, one print, entitled 'The H[anove]r T[urni]p Man come again', depicts one of
these soldiers holding a bunch of turnips and exclaiming, 'By G-d these Turnips are dear'.

upon.' 'I protest, Brother,' cries she, 'you are now got beyond my Understanding. Your Jargon of Turneps and *Hannover* Rats, is to me perfectly unintelligible.' 'I believe,' cries he, 'you don't care to hear o'em; but the Country Interest[1] may succeed one Day or other for all that.' 'I wish,' answered the Lady, 'you would think a little of your Daughter's Interest: For believe me, she is in greater Danger than the Nation.' 'Just now,' said he, 'you chid me for thinking on her, and would ha' her left to you.' 'And if you will promise to interpose no more,' answered she, 'I will, out of my Regard to my Niece, undertake the Charge.' 'Well, do then,' said the Squire, 'for you know I always agreed, that Women are the properest to manage Women.'

Mrs. *Western* then departed, muttering something with an Air of Disdain, concerning Women and the Management of the Nation. She immediately repaired to *Sophia's* Apartment, who was now, after a Day's Confinement released again from her Captivity.

*The End of the* Second Volume.

(See Print No. 2578, *Catalogue of Prints and Drawings in the British Museum*, Division I, Political and Personal Satires, iii [1734–*c.* 1750], edd. F. G. Stephens and E. Hawkins, 1877.)
  [1] See above, p. 272, n. 1.

# BOOK VII

*Containing three Days.*

## CHAPTER I

*A Comparison between the World and the Stage.*

THE World hath been often compared to the Theatre;[1] and
many grave Writers, as well as the Poets, have considered
human Life as a great Drama, resembling, in almost every
Particular, those scenical Representations, which *Thespis*[2] is first
reported to have invented, and which have been since received
with so much Approbation and Delight in all polite Countries.

This Thought hath been carried so far, and is become so
general, that some Words proper to the Theatre, and which were,
at first, metaphorically applied to the World, are now indiscriminately and literally spoken of both: Thus Stage and Scene
are by common Use grown as familiar to us, when we speak
of Life in general, as when we confine ourselves to dramatic
Performances; and when Transactions behind the Curtain are

---

[1] For a discussion of this commonplace and its significance within the Christian humanist tradition, see Aubrey L. Williams, *Pope's 'Dunciad': A Study of its Meaning* (1955), ch.
iv, esp. pp. 94 ff., and his article, 'Poetical Justice, the Contrivances of Providence, and the
Works of William Congreve', *ELH*, xxxv (1968), 540–65, esp. pp. 547–53. The *locus
classicus* is Epictetus: 'Remember, that the World is a Theatre, and that your Part in this
Play of Life is determined by the Poet: Upon him it must depend, whether you shall act a
long or a short one; whether your Character shall be high or low: If therefore he assign you
that of a Beggar, take care to humour it well; if a Cripple, or a Prince, or a private obscure
Man, or whatever it be, make the best of it: For consider, that the playing of the Part
assigned you commendably, depends upon your self. This is your Business; but the giving
out of the Parts, and choosing the Actors, is not yours, but another Person's.' (George
Stanhope, trans. *Epictetus His Morals, With Simplicius His Comment* [1694], p. 193.) The
point of this comparison, as Simplicius remarks, is to enforce the lesson that man's duty is to
accept the part that Providence has assigned him and to act it well. To a degree anticipating
Fielding's later development of the metaphor in this chapter, Simplicius points out that,
like the audience in the theatre, those who behold this spectacle of life reserve their applause
not for the part assigned us but for the manner of our acting it.

In *The Champion* (19 August 1740) Fielding, at some length, had presented a similar
analogy between the world and the stage. For a contemporary treatment of this figure with
which he was certainly acquainted, see James Harris, 'Concerning Happiness', *Three
Treatises* (1744), pp. 210–11, 333–4 (Note liii).

[2] See Horace, *Ars Poetica*, 275–7.

mentioned, *St. James's* is more likely to occur to our Thoughts than *Drury-Lane*.

It may seem easy enough to account for all this, by reflecting that the theatrical Stage is nothing more than a Representation, or, as *Aristotle* calls it,[1] an Imitation of what really exists; and hence, perhaps, we might fairly pay a very high Compliment to those, who by their Writings or Actions have been so capable of imitating Life, as to have their Pictures, in a Manner confounded with, or mistaken for the Originals.

But, in Reality, we are not so fond of paying Compliments to these People, whom we use as Children frequently do the Instruments of their Amusement; and have much more Pleasure in hissing and buffeting them, than in admiring their Excellence. There are many other Reasons which have induced us to see this Analogy between the World and the Stage.

Some have considered the larger Part of Mankind in the Light of Actors, as personating Characters no more their own, and to which, in Fact, they have no better Title, than the Player hath to be in Earnest thought the King or Emperor whom he represents. Thus the Hypocrite may be said to be a Player; and indeed the *Greeks* called them both by one and the same Name.[2]

The Brevity of Life hath likewise given Occasion to this Comparison. So the immortal *Shakespear*:[3]

> ——*Life's a poor Player,*
> *That struts and frets his Hour upon the Stage,*
> *And then is heard no more.*

For which hackneyed Quotation, I will make the Reader Amends by a very noble one, which few, I believe, have read. It is taken from a Poem called the DEITY,[4] published about nine Years ago, and long since buried in Oblivion. A Proof that good Books no more than good Men do always survive the bad.

---

[1] Cf. *Poetics*, i. 2, xxv. 2.

[2] The Greek word ὑποκριτής signifies both a dissembler and an actor on the stage.

[3] *Macbeth*, v. v.

[4] *Deity* by Samuel Boyse (1708–May 1749), a poem on the attributes of God done vaguely in the manner of Pope's *Essay on Man*. It is pleasant to note that Fielding's 'puff' in *Tom Jones*, together with James Hervey's praise in his *Meditations and Contemplations* (1746), was instrumental in rescuing *Deity* from 'Oblivion'—as one may infer from the advertisements announcing publication of a second edition on 6 March 1749 (see *The*

> *From thee\* all human Actions take their Springs,*
> *The Rise of Empires, and the Fall of Kings!*
> *See the* VAST THEATRE OF TIME *display'd,*
> *While o'er the Scene succeeding Heroes tread!*
> *With Pomp the shining Images succeed,*
> *What Leaders triumph, and what Monarchs bleed!*
> *Perform the Parts thy Providence assign'd,*
> *Their Pride, their Passions to thy Ends inclin'd:*
> *A while they glitter in the Face of Day,*
> *Then at thy Nod the Phantoms pass away;*
> *No Traces left of all the busy Scene,*
> *But that Remembrance says*—THE THINGS HAVE BEEN!

In all these, however, and in every other Similitude of Life to the Theatre, the Resemblance hath been always taken from the Stage only. None, as I remember, have at all considered the Audience at this great Drama.

But as Nature often exhibits some of her best Performances to a very full House; so will the Behaviour of her Spectators no less admit the above-mentioned Comparison than that of her Actors. In this vast Theatre of Time are seated the Friend and the Critic; here are Claps and Shouts, Hisses and Groans; in short, every Thing which was ever seen or heard at the Theatre Royal.

Let us examine this in one Example: For Instance, in the Behaviour of the great Audience on that Scene which Nature was pleased to exhibit in the 12th Chapter of the preceding Book, where she introduced *Black George* running away with the 500 *l.* from his Friend and Benefactor.

\* The DEITY.

---

*General Advertiser*, 6–8 March 1749). A third edition appeared in 1752 and thereafter the poem was frequently anthologized.

 Fielding, in fact, had admired Boyse's poem when it was originally published in February 1740 (the title-page reads 1739). In a 'Literary Article' in *The Champion* (12 February 1739/40) he wrote: 'Last Week a Poem was publish'd, with the simple but all-comprehensive Title of *Deity*; which, 'tis presum'd, will excite but little Curiosity, and therefore, will be but little read: Not that it does not deserve a Reading, or will not afford a serious Mind a very elevated Entertainment,—but because few Readers can be entertain'd with what is serious, or care to be made so themselves. 'Tis divided into as many Sections, as we ascribe attributes to the Godhead: is wrote in a clear and elegant Stile, the versification smooth and flowing, but by being cramp'd within almost perpetual Distichs, allows very little Variety of Cadence, and Period: And that it is not void of the Sublime, let the following Passage demonstrate.' He then quotes from *Deity*, section viii ('Providence'), 615–26—the identical passage reprinted in *Tom Jones*.

Those who sat in the World's upper Gallery,[1] treated that Incident, I am well convinced, with their usual Vociferation; and every Term of scurrilous Reproach was most probably vented on that Occasion.

If we had descended to the next Order of Spectators, we should have found an equal Degree of Abhorrence, tho' less of Noise and Scurrility; yet here the good Women gave *Black George* to the Devil, and many of them expected every Minute that the cloven-footed Gentleman would fetch his own.

The Pit, as usual, was no doubt divided: Those who delight in heroic Virtue and perfect Character, objected to the producing such Instances of Villainy, without punishing them very severely for the Sake of Example.[2] Some of the Author's Friends, cry'd— 'Look'e, Gentlemen, the Man is a Villain; but it is Nature for all that.' And all the young Critics of the Age, the Clerks, Apprentices, &c. called it Low, and fell a Groaning.

As for the Boxes, they behaved with their accustomed Politeness. Most of them were attending to something else. Some of those few who regarded the Scene at all, declared he was a bad Kind of Man; while others refused to give their Opinion till they had heard that of the best Judges.

---

[1] A useful gloss on Fielding's characterization of the four classes of theatre-goers is the following passage from *The Tricks of the Town laid open: or, A Companion for Country Gentlemen*, 2nd ed. (1747), letter vii: 'In our Playhouses at *London*, besides an Upper-Gallery for Footmen, Coachmen, Mendicants, &c. we have three other different and distinct Classes; the first is called the *Boxes*, where there is one peculiar to the King and Royal Family, and the rest for the Persons of Quality, and for the Ladies and Gentlemen of the highest Rank.... The second is call'd the *Pit*, where sit the *Judges*, *Wits* and *Censurers*, or rather the *Censurers without either Wit or Judgment*. These are the *Bully-Judges*, that *damn and sink the Play at a venture*; 'tis no matter whether it be good or bad, but 'tis a *Play*, and *they are the Judges*, and so it must be *damn'd, curs'd, and censur'd* in Course; in common with these sit the *Squires, Sharpers, Beaus, Bullies* and *Whores*, and here and there an extravagant *Male* and *Female Cit*. The third is distinguished by the Title of the *Middle Gallery*, where the Citizens Wives and Daughters, together with the *Abigails*, Serving-men, Journey-men and Apprentices commonly take their Places; and now and then some desponding Mistresses and superannuated Poets' (pp. 27–8). In 1748 the prices for the four seating areas were: boxes 5s., pit 3s., first [or middle] gallery 2s., upper gallery 1s.

[2] On the differing attitudes toward the dramatic rule of poetic justice in the period, see Richard H. Tyre, 'Versions of Poetic Justice in the Early Eighteenth Century', *SP*, liv (1957), 29–44. Those who believed that in drama virtue should be invariably rewarded and vice punished for the sake of the moral lesson included Dryden's Eugenius, Rymer, Tate, Temple, Dennis, and Blackmore. Fielding, however, would seem here to side with Addison in considering this an unnatural and 'ridiculous Doctrine in modern Criticism' (*Spectator*, No. 40 [16 April 1711]).

Now we, who are admitted behind the Scenes of this great
Theatre of Nature, (and no Author ought to write any Thing
besides Dictionaries and Spelling-Books[1] who hath not this
Privilege) can censure the Action, without conceiving any
absolute Detestation of the Person, whom perhaps Nature may
not have designed to act an ill Part in all her Dramas: For in this
Instance, Life most exactly resembles the Stage, since it is often
the same Person who represents the Villain and the Heroe; and
he who engages your Admiration To-day, will probably attract
your Contempt To-Morrow. As *Garrick*,[2] whom I regard in
Tragedy to be the greatest Genius the World hath ever produced,
sometimes condescends to play the Fool; so did *Scipio* the Great
and *Lælius* the Wise, according to *Horace*,[3] many Years ago: nay,
*Cicero* reports them to have been 'incredibly childish.'[4]—These,
it is true play'd the Fool, like my Friend *Garrick*, in Jest only; but

---

[1] If a specific reference is intended, it is doubtless to Nathan Bailey (see below, p. 333,
n. 2), author of *Dictionarium Britannicum: or a more Compleat Universal Etymological
English Dictionary* (1721, 1736, and many other editions), *An Orthographical Dictionary*
(1727), and *An Introduction to the English Tongue: Being a Spelling Book . . . For the Use of
Schools* (1726). For other allusions to Bailey in Fielding's writings, see *The Champion* (14
February 1739/40, 17 May 1740) and *The Covent-Garden Journal* (18 February 1752). In
1755 Bailey's dictionary, of course, would be superseded by Johnson's, the *Plan* of which,
addressed to Lord Chesterfield, was published in August 1747. With Fielding's low opinion
of the abilities of lexicographers, compare Johnson's introductory remarks, regretting that
the work in which he was engaged 'is generally considered as drudgery for the blind, as the
proper toil of artless industry; a task that requires neither the light of learning, nor the
activity of genius, but may be successfully performed without any higher quality than that
of bearing burthens with dull patience, and beating the track of the alphabet with sluggish
resolution'. Of 'all the candidates for literary praise', Johnson continued, 'the unhappy
lexicographer holds the lowest place'.

[2] David Garrick (1717–79), the brilliant actor who in 1747 became patentee of the
Drury-Lane Theatre. Fielding and Garrick were the closest of friends. From the *Miscellanies* (1743) to *The Covent-Garden Journal* (1752) Fielding's writings abound in extravagant
compliments to the man he esteemed 'the best Actor the World could have ever produced'
(see the *Journal* for 11 January 1752). Garrick's most popular comic roles included Bayes,
Abel Drugger, Costar Pearmain, Fondlewife, and Sir John Brute. Some critics, however,
were sufficiently dour to object to his donning the sock. On 18 January 1742 the Rev. Mr.
Newton wrote to Garrick complaining: 'You . . . strangely demean yourself in acting any
thing that is low and little. . . . If I was an actor surely I would rather wish to be a Raphael
than a Hogarth; or if I was a poet, I would choose infinitely rather to be a Milton than
Hudibras' (quoted in A. H. Scouten, *The London Stage, 1660–1800*, Part III: 1729–47
[Carbondale, Ill., 1961], p. 959). For other allusions to Garrick in *Tom Jones*, see below,
pp. 493, 853.

[3] *Satires*, II. i. 71–4. Scipio Africanus Minor (*c.* 185–129 B.C.) and Caius Laelius
Sapiens (b. *c.* 186 B.C.).

[4] *De Oratore*, II. vi. See also *Joseph Andrews* (1742; III. vii).

several eminent Characters have, in numberless Instances of their Lives, played the Fool egregiously in Earnest; so far as to render it a Matter of some Doubt, whether their Wisdom or Folly was predominant; or whether they were better intitled to the Applause or Censure, the Admiration or Contempt, the Love or Hatred of Mankind.

Those Persons, indeed, who have passed any Time behind the Scenes of this great Theatre, and are thoroughly acquainted not only with the several Disguises which are there put on, but also with the fantastic and capricious Behaviour of the Passions[1] who are the Managers and Directors of this Theatre, (for as to Reason the Patentee, he is known to be a very idle Fellow, and seldom to exert himself) may most probably have learned to understand the famous *Nil admirari* of *Horace*,[2] or in the *English* Phrase, *To stare at nothing*.

A single bad Act no more constitutes a Villain in Life, than a single bad Part on the Stage. The Passions, like the Managers of

---

[1] To explain the actions of men and the apparent variety in their characters, Fielding resorted to the familiar psychological theory of the passions—a theory most memorably expressed in Pope's *Epistle to Cobham* (1734) and in Epistle II of the *Essay on Man* (1733-4). (See Bertrand A. Goldgar, 'Pope's Theory of the Passions: The Background of Epistle II of the *Essay on Man*', *PQ*, xli [1962], 730-43.) Accordingly, in the poem 'To John Hayes, Esq;' (1743) Fielding remarked in individual men

> How Passions blended on each other fix,
> How Vice with Virtues, Faults with Graces mix;
> How Passions opposite, as sour to sweet,
> Shall in one Bosom at one Moment meet.

Yet in Fielding's view, as in Pope's, a man's actions are generally determined by the impulses of one master passion that dominates the rest: thus Black George, the example of the present chapter, is said to be 'honest' enough when his better nature is not subdued by his love of money (VI. xii), and Fielding's other characters—from Lady Booby and Peter Pounce to Miss Matthews and Colonel James—similarly reveal the dominion of Lust or Avarice or Vanity in their minds. Both the cogency of this theory and its dangerous consequences to the moralist who embraces it too casually and uncritically are presented at length in the story of Captain Booth in *Amelia* (1751), whose belief that men act solely from the impulses of a dominant passion betrays him into the philosophical error of fatalism. The lesson that Booth finally learns had been stated earlier in *The Champion* (2 February 1739/40), where Fielding recommended 'that glorious Precept *vince teipsum*', the necessity for the individual, by reason and the will, to direct and order the passions. As he put it in the introductory chapter to *Amelia* (1751), only by the proper exercise of 'Prudence' (see above, p. 36, n. 1) may we escape the miseries in which we involve ourselves by 'following the blind Guidance of a predominant Passion'. (For discussions of Fielding's theory of the passions, see Battestin, *The Moral Basis of Fielding's Art* [1959], pp. 58-60, and Miller, *Essays on Fielding's 'Miscellanies'* [1961], pp. 113-18.)

[2] *Epistles*, I. vi. 1.

a Playhouse, often force Men upon Parts, without consulting their Judgement, and sometimes without any Regard to their Talents. Thus the Man, as well as the Player, may condemn what he himself acts; nay, it is common to see Vice sit as awkwardly on some Men, as the Character of *Iago* would on the honest Face of Mr. *William Mills*.[1]

Upon the whole then, the Man of Candour, and of true Understanding, is never hasty to condemn. He can censure an Imperfection, or even a Vice, without Rage against the guilty Party. In a Word, they are the same Folly, the same Childishness, the same Ill-breeding, and the same Ill-nature, which raise all the Clamours and Uproars both in Life, and on the Stage. The worst of Men generally have the Words *Rogue* and *Villain* most in their Mouths, as the lowest of all Wretches are the aptest to cry out *low* in the Pit.

---

[1] Fielding was especially fond of '*Honest Billy Mills*' (d. 17 April 1750), a good man if no very good actor. He paid him an early compliment in *Joseph Andrews* (1742; I. viii), and later, when Mills and his family had fallen upon hard times, Fielding devoted space in *The Jacobite's Journal* (23 April 1748) to urging attendance at a benefit performance for him at Drury Lane. Perhaps, as Oliver Ferguson has proposed (*PQ*, xliii [1964], 73–8), Mills in the role of Claudius is the victim of Partridge's 'vile encomium' in *Tom Jones* (XVI. v; see below, p. 855, n. 2).

Implicit in the present passage, moreover, may well be a facetious allusion to another actor friend of Fielding's, Charles Macklin (1697–1797). Macklin's 'good long, dismal, mercy-begging Face', as he himself called it in the Prologue to *The Wedding Day* (1743), was a standing jest in theatrical circles; to the player in *Joseph Andrews* (III. x), for example, he is an 'ill-looked Dog'. Early in 1747 Macklin became the focus of a critical controversy concerning his facial qualifications to play the role of Iago—not that, like Mills, his face was too 'honest', but that, on the contrary, the marks of the villain were so indelibly stamped on his countenance that the audience could not believe in him as 'honest Iago', the fair-seeming hypocrite. In *A Treatise on the Passions, So far as they regard the Stage* (February 1747), Samuel Foote defended Macklin against his detractors: 'Let us now proceed to examine whether Mr. *Macklin* is happy in looking this Character [i.e. Iago]. I think it is generally agreed that his Muscles are luckily formed for marking the Villain; but it has been objected, that Nature has denied him the Advantage of expressing the open, sincere, honest Man; or, in other Words, of playing the Hypocrite well in this Part'; but, Foote generously noted, 'let *Macklin*'s Visage be ever so unfortunate, I am sure he has the Art of looking more like a Rogue at one Time than another' (p. 38). Unconvinced, one 'J. T.' replied: '*M[acklin]* has such a strong Stamp of the Villian [*sic*] imprinted in his Countenance, even when he endeavours to appear honest; that we can't help thinking it a Weakness in *Othello* to have any Concerns with him at all' (*A Letter of Compliment to the ingenious Author of a Treatise on the Passions* [March 1747], p. 27).

## CHAPTER II

*Containing a Conversation which Mr.* Jones *had with himself.*

*JONES* received his Effects from Mr. *Allworthy's* early in the
Morning, with the following Answer to his Letter.

SIR,

'I am commanded by my Uncle to acquaint you, that as he did
not proceed to those Measures he had taken with you, without
the greatest Deliberation, and after the fullest Evidence of your
Unworthiness, so will it be always out of your Power to cause the
least Alteration in his Resolution. He expresses great Surprize
at your Presumption in saying, you have resigned all Pretensions
to a young Lady, to whom it is impossible you should ever have
had any, her Birth and Fortune having made her so infinitely your
superior. Lastly, I am commanded to tell you, that the only
Instance of your Compliance with my Uncle's Inclinations,
which he requires, is, your immediately quitting this Country. I
cannot conclude this without offering you my Advice, as a
Christian, that you would seriously think of amending your Life;
that you may be assisted with Grace so to do, will be always the
Prayer of

*Your Humble Servant,*
W. BLIFIL.'

Many contending Passions were raised in our Heroe's Mind
by this Letter; but the Tender prevailed at last over the Indig-
nant and Irascible, and a Flood of Tears came seasonably to his
Assistance, and possibly prevented his Misfortunes from either
turning his Head, or bursting his Heart.

He grew, however, soon ashamed of indulging this Remedy;
and starting up, he cried, 'Well then, I will give Mr. *Allworthy*
the only Instance he requires of my Obedience. I will go this
Moment—but whither?—why, let Fortune direct; since there is
no other who thinks it of any Consequence what becomes of this
wretched Person, it shall be a Matter of equal Indifference to
myself. Shall I alone regard what no other?—Ha! have I not
Reason to think there is another?—One whose Value is above
that of the whole World!—I may, I must imagine my *Sophia* is
not indifferent to what becomes of me. Shall I then leave this only

Friend—and such a Friend? Shall I not stay with her?—Where? How can I stay with her? Have I any Hopes of ever seeing her, tho' she was as desirous as myself, without exposing her to the Wrath of her Father? And to what Purpose? Can I think of soliciting such a Creature to consent to her own Ruin? Shall I indulge any Passion of mine at such a Price?—Shall I lurk about this Country like a Thief, with such Intentions?—No, I disdain, I detest the Thought. Farewel, *Sophia*; farewel most lovely, most beloved——' Here Passion stopped his Mouth, and found a Vent at his Eyes.

And now, having taken a Resolution to leave the Country, he began to debate with himself whither he should go. *The World*, as *Milton* phrases it,[1] *lay all before him*; and *Jones*, no more than *Adam*, had any Man to whom he might resort for Comfort or Assistance. All his Acquaintance were the Acquaintance of Mr. *Allworthy*, and he had no reason to expect any Countenance from them, as that Gentleman had with-drawn his Favour from him. Men of great and good Characters should indeed be very cautious how they discard their Dependents; for the Consequence to the unhappy Sufferer is being discarded by all others.

What Course of Life to pursue, or to what Business to apply himself, was a second Consideration; and here the Prospect was all a melancholy Void. Every Profession, and every Trade, required Length of Time, and what was worse, Money; for Matters are so constituted, that 'Nothing out of Nothing'[2] is not a truer Maxim in Physics than in Politics; and every Man who is greatly destitute of Money, is on that Account entirely excluded from all Means of acquiring it.

At last the Ocean, that hospitable Friend to the Wretched, opened her capacious Arms to receive him; and he instantly resolved to accept her kind Invitation. To express myself less figuratively, he determined to go to Sea.

This Thought indeed no sooner suggested itself, than he eagerly embraced it; and having presently hired Horses, he set out for *Bristol* to put it in Execution.

[1] *Paradise Lost*, xii. 646–7. Adam and Eve having been banished from Eden, Milton writes: 'The World was all before them, where to choose'/ Thir place of rest, and Providence thir guide.'

[2] *Ex nihilo nihil fit*—a maxim found in Aristotle, *Physica* (I. iv. 2–3) and *Metaphysica* (III. iv. 4), Lucretius *De Rerum Natura* (i. 155–6), and elsewhere. Fielding plays with the idea in his 'Essay on Nothing' (1743), section i.

But before we attend him on this Expedition, we shall resort a while to Mr. *Western's*, and see what farther happened to the charming *Sophia*.

## CHAPTER III

*Containing several Dialogues.*

THE Morning in which Mr. *Jones* departed, Mrs. *Western* summoned *Sophia* into her Apartment, and having first acquainted her that she had obtained her Liberty of her Father, she proceeded to read her a long Lecture on the Subject of Matrimony; which she treated not as a romantic Scheme of Happiness arising from Love, as it hath been described by the Poets; nor did she mention any of those Purposes for which we are taught by Divines to regard it as instituted by sacred Authority; she considered it rather as a Fund in which prudent Women deposite their Fortunes to the best Advantage, in order to receive a larger Interest for them, than they could have elsewhere.

When Mrs. *Western* had finished, *Sophia* answered, 'that she was very incapable of arguing with a Lady of her Aunt's superior Knowledge and Experience, especially on a Subject which she had so very little considered, as this of Matrimony.'

'Argue with me, Child!' replied the other, 'I do not indeed expect it. I should have seen the World to very little Purpose truly, if I am to argue with one of your Years. I have taken this Trouble, in order to instruct you. The ancient Philosophers, such as *Socrates*, *Alcibiades*,[1] and others, did not use to argue with their Scholars. You are to consider me, Child, as *Socrates*, not asking your Opinion, but only informing you of mine.' From which last Words the Reader may possibly imagine, that this Lady had read no more of the Philosophy of *Socrates*, than she had of that of *Alcibiades*; and indeed we cannot resolve his Curiosity as to this Point.

'Madam,' cries *Sophia*, 'I have never presumed to controvert

---

[1] Though he appears with Socrates in the *Symposium* and in the dialogue which bears his name, Alcibiades (b. *c.* 450 B.C.) was of course not a philosopher, but an Athenian general and politician. Nor is Mrs. Western any better acquainted with the Socratic method, in which a series of easily answered questions leads to a foregone conclusion.

any Opinion of yours, and this Subject, as I said, I have never yet thought of, and perhaps never may.'

'Indeed, *Sophy*,' replied the Aunt, 'this Dissimulation with me is very foolish. The *French* shall as soon persuade me, that they take foreign Towns in Defence only of their own Country, as you can impose on me to believe you have never yet thought seriously of Matrimony. How can you, Child, affect to deny that you have considered of contracting an Alliance, when you so well know I am acquainted with the Party with whom you desire to contract it. An Alliance as unnatural, and contrary to your Interest, as a separate League with the *French* would be to the Interest of the *Dutch*![1] But however, if you have not hitherto considered of this Matter, I promise you it is now high Time; for my Brother is resolved immediately to conclude the Treaty with Mr. *Blifil*; and indeed I am a sort of Guarantee in the Affair, and have promised your Concurrence.'

'Indeed, Madam,' cries *Sophia*, 'this is the only Instance in which I must disobey both yourself and my Father. For this is a Match which requires very little Consideration in me to refuse.'

'If I was not as great a Philosopher as *Socrates* himself,' returned Mrs. *Western*, 'you would overcome my Patience. What Objection can you have to the young Gentleman?'

'A very solid Objection, in my Opinion,' says *Sophia*,—'I hate him.'

'Will you never learn a proper Use of Words?' answered the Aunt. 'Indeed Child, you should consult *Bailey's Dictionary*.[2] It is

---

[1] Until France actually invaded Flanders in April 1747—an event which led to the election of William as Stadtholder of the United Provinces and to a stiffening of their resistance in the war—the Dutch had been openly negotiating toward a separate peace with France that would allow them to withdraw from the conflict. The French had made overtures to this purpose as early as July 1742, and in the autumn of 1745 a congress was proposed to arrange the treaty. (See Jean Rousset, *Relation historique de la grande révolution arrivée dans la république des Provinces-Unies* [Amsterdam, 1747]; also the anonymous work, *Considerations on the Conduct of the Dutch* [1745].) In England, naturally, the Dutch neutralist policy was regarded with a mixture of resentment and apprehension. In *The True Patriot* it was the subject of several articles, the intent of which was to advise the Dutch that their own interest and self-respect should dissuade them from purchasing a temporary peace at the price of becoming a mere province of France (see, for example, the numbers for 18–25 March, 25 March–1 April 1746, under 'Foreign History').

[2] Nathan or Nathaniel Bailey (d. 1742), author of *Dictionarium Britannicum: Or a Compleat Universal Etymological English Dictionary* (1721). (See above, p. 327, n. 1.) In her insistence on the 'proper Use of Words' Mrs. Western may recall Bailey's Preface: 'Words are those Vehicles or Channels by the which the Knowledge of Things is convey'd to our

impossible you should hate a Man from whom you have received no Injury. By Hatred, therefore, you mean no more than Dislike, which is no sufficient Objection against your marrying of him. I have known many Couples, who have entirely disliked each other, lead very comfortable, genteel Lives. Believe me, Child, I know these Things better than you. You will allow me, I think, to have seen the World, in which I have not an Acquaintance who would not rather be thought to dislike her Husband, than to like him. The contrary is such out-of-Fashion romantic Nonsense, that the very Imagination of it is shocking.'

'Indeed Madam,' replied *Sophia*, 'I shall never marry a Man I dislike. If I promise my Father never to consent to any Marriage contrary to his Inclinations, I think I may hope he will never force me into that State contrary to my own.'

'Inclinations!' cries the Aunt, with some Warmth. 'Inclinations! I am astonished at your Assurance. A young Woman of your Age, and unmarried, to talk of Inclinations! But whatever your Inclinations may be, my Brother is resolved; nay, since you talk of Inclinations, I shall advise him to hasten the Treaty. Inclinations!'

*Sophia* then flung herself upon her Knees, and Tears began to trickle from her shining Eyes. She entreated her Aunt 'to have Mercy upon her, and not to resent so cruelly her Unwillingness to make herself miserable;' often urging, 'that she alone was concerned, and that her Happiness only was at Stake.'

As a Bailiff, when well authorised by his Writ, having possessed himself of the Person of some unhappy Debtor, views all his Tears without Concern: In vain the wretched Captive attempts to raise Compassion; in vain the tender Wife bereft of her Companion, the little prattling Boy, or frighted Girl, are mentioned as Inducements to Reluctance. The noble Bumtrap, blind

Understandings and therefore, upon a right Apprehension of the Meaning of them, depends the Rectitude of those Ideas or Notions that we receive by hearing or reading. Therefore in Order to furnish our Minds with just and adequate Ideas, either of the Things, Matters, or Facts; Words must be apprehended in their proper Sense and Meaning, either in receiving from or communicating to others: For if the Words either of a Speaker or Writer, tho' ever so Apposite to the Matter be taken or understood in a wrong Sense, they will necessarily form wrong Conceptions concerning the Thing spoken or written of; and if we our selves use Words in an improper Sense, this will cause a Confusion in the Understanding of the Hearer and render our Discourse both unintelligible and useless' (2nd ed., 1736; Sig. a1$^r$). In this edition Bailey defines 'A HATELING' as 'a hated Person, or one who deserves to be hated'.

and deaf to every Circumstance of Distress, greatly rises above all
the Motives to Humanity, and into the Hands of the Goaler
resolves to deliver his miserable Prey.

Not less blind to the Tears, or less deaf to every Entreaty of
*Sophia* was the politic Aunt, nor less determined was she to
deliver over the trembling Maid into the Arms of the Goaler
*Blifil*. She answered with great Impetuosity, 'So far, Madam,
from your being concerned alone, your Concern is the least, or
surely the least important. It is the Honour of your Family
which is concerned in this Alliance; you are only the Instrument.
Do you conceive, Mistress, that in an Intermarriage between
Kingdoms, as when a Daughter of *France* is married into *Spain*,[1]
the Princess herself is alone considered in the Match? No, it is a
Match between two Kingdoms, rather than between two Persons.
The same happens in great Families, such as ours. The Alliance
between the Families is the principal Matter. You ought to have
a greater Regard for the Honour of your Family, than for your
own Person; and if the Example of a Princess cannot inspire you
with these noble Thoughts, you cannot surely complain at being
used no worse than all Princesses are used.'

'I hope, Madam,' cries *Sophia*, with a little Elevation of Voice,
'I shall never do any Thing to dishonour my Family; but as for
Mr. *Blifil*, whatever may be the Consequence, I am resolved
against him, and no Force shall prevail in his Favour.'

*Western*, who had been within hearing during the greater Part
of the preceding Dialogue, had now exhausted all his Patience;
he therefore entered the Room in a violent Passion, crying,
'D—n me then if *shatunt* ha' un, d—n me if *shatunt*, that's all—
that's all—— D—n me if *shatunt*.'

Mrs. *Western* had collected a sufficient Quantity of Wrath for
the Use of *Sophia*; but she now transferred it all to the Squire.
'Brother,' said she, 'it is astonishing that you will interfere in a
Matter which you had totally left to my Negotiation. Regard to
my Family hath made me take upon myself to be the mediating
Power, in order to rectify those Mistakes in Policy which you

---

[1] In August 1739, shortly after her twelfth birthday, Louise Elizabeth, daughter of
Louis XV, was married by proxy to Don Philip, son of Philip V of Spain. Commenting on
this political marriage, a correspondent in *The General Advertiser* (3 February 1748) noted
that 'a Daughter of France is little set by, if a Provision for her any Way interferes with the
Aggrandizement of the Monarchy. To this single Point, all the Maxims taught at Versailles
have a Tendency, either directly or indirectly, openly or covertly'.

have committed in your Daughter's Education. For, Brother, it is you; it is your preposterous Conduct which hath eradicated all the Seeds that I had formerly sown in her tender Mind.—It is you yourself who have taught her Disobedience.'—'Blood!' cries the Squire, foaming at the Mouth, 'you are enough to conquer the Patience of the Devil! Have I ever taught my Daughter Disobedience?—Here she stands; Speak honestly, Girl, did ever I bid you be disobedient to me? Have not I done every thing to humour, and to gratify you, and to make you obedient to me? And very obedient to me she was when a little Child, before you took her in Hand and spoiled her, by filling her Head with a Pack of Court Notions.—Why—why—why—did not I overhear you telling her she must behave like a Princess? You have made a Whig of the Girl; and how should her Father, or any body else, expect any Obedience from her?' 'Brother,' answered Mrs. *Western*, with an Air of great Disdain, 'I cannot express the Contempt I have for your Politics of all Kinds; but I will appeal likewise to the young Lady herself, whether I have ever taught her any Principles of Disobedience. On the contrary, Niece, have I not endeavoured to inspire you with a true Idea of the several Relations in which a human Creature stands in Society? Have I not taken infinite Pains to shew you, that the Law of Nature hath injoined a Duty on Children to their Parents? Have I not told you what *Plato* says on that Subject?[1]—A Subject on which you was so notoriously ignorant when you came first under my Care, that I verily believe you did not know the Relation between a Daughter and a Father.' ' 'Tis a Lie,' answered *Western*. 'The Girl is no such Fool, as to live to eleven Years old without knowing that she was her Father's Relation.' 'O more than Gothic Ignorance,' answered the Lady.—'And as for your Manners, Brother, I must tell you, they deserve a Cane.' 'Why then you may gi' it me, if you think you are able,' cries the Squire; 'nay, I suppose your Niece there will be ready enough to help you.' 'Brother,' said Mrs. *Western*, 'tho' I despise you beyond Expression, yet I shall

---

[1] Cf. *Laws*, iv. 717b–e. Pufendorf, along with Grotius the principal modern authority on the 'law of nature' (see above, p. 161, n. 1), quotes this passage when discussing 'paternal Power ' in *Of the Law of Nature and Nations* (1672), VI. ii (see B. Kennett, trans., 4th ed. [1729], p. 609). In sec. xiv, Pufendorf states that, after carefully weighing the advice of their parents concerning a marriage partner, children who are of age have the right to marry against their parents' wishes, at the risk, however, of being disowned and disinherited (ibid., pp. 612–13).

endure your Insolence no longer; so I desire my Coach may be got ready immediately, for I am resolved to leave your House this very Morning.' 'And a good Riddance too,' answered he; 'I can bear your Insolence no longer, an you come to that. Blood! it is almost enough of itself, to make my Daughter undervalue my Sense, when she hears you telling me every Minute you despise me.' 'It is impossible, it is impossible,' cries the Aunt, 'no one can undervalue such a Boor.' 'Boar,' answered the Squire, 'I am no Boar; no, nor Ass; no, nor Rat neither, Madam. Remember that —I am no Rat. I am a true *Englishman*, and not of your *Hannover* Breed, that have eat up the Nation.'[1] 'Thou art one of those wise Men,' cries she, 'whose nonsensical Principles have undone the Nation; by weakening the Hands of our Government at home, and by discouraging our Friends, and encouraging our Enemies abroad.' 'Ho! are you come back to your Politics,' cries the Squire, 'as for those I despise them as much as I do a F—t.' Which last Word he accompanied and graced with the very Action, which, of all others, was the most proper to it. And whether it was this Word, or the Contempt exprest for her Politics, which most affected Mrs. *Western*, I will not determine; but she flew into the most violent Rage, uttered Phrases improper to be here related, and instantly burst out of the House. Nor did her Brother or her Niece think proper either to stop or to follow her: For the one was so much possessed by Concern, and the other by Anger, that they were rendered almost motionless.

The Squire, however, sent after his Sister the same Holla which attends the Departure of a Hare, when she is first started before the Hounds. He was indeed a great Master of this Kind of Vociferation, and had a Holla proper for most Occasions in Life.

Women who, like Mrs. *Western*, know the World, and have applied themselves to Philosophy and Politics, would have immediately availed themselves of the present Disposition of Mr. *Western's* Mind; by throwing in a few artful Compliments to his Understanding at the Expence of his absent Adversary; but poor *Sophia* was all Simplicity. By which Word we do not intend to insinuate to the Reader, that she was silly, which is generally understood as a synonimous Term with simple: For she was indeed a most sensible Girl, and her Understanding was of the first Rate; but she wanted all that useful Art which Females

[1] See above, p. 321, n. 2.

convert to so many good Purposes in Life, and which, as it rather arises from the Heart, than from the Head, is often the Property of the silliest of Women.


## CHAPTER IV

*A Picture of a Country Gentlewoman taken from the Life.*

MR. *Western* having finished his Holla, and taken a little Breath, began to lament, in very pathetic Terms, the unfortunate Condition of Men, who are, says he, always *whipt in* by the Humours of some d—nd B—— or other. I think I was *hard run* enough by your Mother for one Man; but after giving her a *Dodge*, here's another B—— follows me upon the *Foil*;[1] but curse my Jacket if I will be *run down* in this Manner by any o'um.

*Sophia* never had a single Dispute with her Father, till this unlucky Affair of *Blifil*, on any Account, except in Defence of her Mother, whom she had loved most tenderly, though she lost her in the eleventh Year of her Age. The Squire, to whom that poor Woman had been a faithful upper Servant all the Time of their Marriage, had returned that Behaviour, by making what the World calls a good Husband. He very seldom swore at her (perhaps not above once a Week) and never beat her: She had not the least Occasion for Jealousy, and was perfect Mistress of her Time: for she was never interrupted by her Husband, who was engaged all the Morning in his Field Exercises, and all the Evening with Bottle Companions. She scarce indeed ever saw him but at Meals; where she had the Pleasure of carving those Dishes which she had before attended at the Dressing. From these Meals she retired about five Minutes after the other Servants, having only stayed to drink the King over the Water.[2] Such were, it seems, Mr. *Western's* Orders: For it was a Maxim with him, that Women should come in with the first Dish, and go out after the first Glass. Obedience to these Orders was perhaps no difficult Task: For the Conversation (if it may be called so) was

---

[1] The track of a hunted animal.

[2] A favourite Jacobite toast—in reference to the Old Pretender, James Francis Edward Stuart (1688–1766), in exile in France.

seldom such as could entertain a Lady. It consisted chiefly of Hollowing, Singing, Relations of sporting Adventures, B——d–y, and Abuse of Women and of the Government.

These, however, were the only Seasons when Mr. *Western* saw his Wife: For when he repaired to her Bed, he was generally so drunk that he could not see; and in the sporting Season he always rose from her before it was light. Thus was she perfect Mistress of her Time; and had besides a Coach and four usually at her Command; tho' unhappily indeed the Badness of the Neighbourhood, and of the Roads, made this of little Use: For none who had set much Value on their Necks would have passed through the one, or who had set any Value on their Hours, would have visited the other. Now to deal honestly with the Reader, she did not make all the Return expected to so much Indulgence: For she had been married against her Will, by a fond Father, the Match having been rather advantageous on her Side: For the Squire's Estate was upwards of 3000 *l.* a Year, and her Fortune no more than a bare 8000 *l.* Hence perhaps she had contracted a little Gloominess of Temper: For she was rather a good Servant than a good Wife; nor had she always the Gratitude to return the extraordinary Degree of roaring Mirth, with which the Squire received her, even with a good-humoured Smile. She would, moreover, sometimes interfere with Matters which did not concern her, as the violent Drinking of her Husband, which in the gentlest Terms she would take some of the few Opportunities he gave her of remonstrating against. And once in her Life she very earnestly entreated him to carry her for two Months to *London*, which he peremptorily denied; nay, was angry with his Wife for the Request ever after, being well assured, that all the Husbands in *London* are Cuckolds.

For this last, and many other good Reasons, *Western* at length heartily hated his Wife; and as he never concealed this Hatred before her Death, so he never forgot it afterwards; but when any Thing in the least soured him, as a bad scenting Day, or a Distemper among his Hounds, or any other such Misfortune, he constantly vented his Spleen by Invectives against the Deceased; saying,—'If my Wife was alive now, she would be glad of this.'

These Invectives he was especially desirous of throwing forth before *Sophia*: For as he loved her more than he did any other, so he was really jealous that she had loved her Mother better than him. And this Jealousy *Sophia* seldom failed of heightening on these Occasions: For he was not contented with violating her Ears with the Abuse of her Mother; but endeavoured to force an explicit Approbation of all this Abuse, with which Desire he never could prevail upon her by any Promise or Threats to comply.

Hence some of my Readers will, perhaps, wonder that the Squire had not hated *Sophia* as much as he had hated her Mother; but I must inform them, that Hatred is not the Effect of Love, even through the Medium of Jealousy. It is, indeed, very possible for jealous Persons to kill the Objects of their Jealousy, but not to hate them. Which Sentiment being a pretty hard Morsel, and bearing something of the Air of a Paradox, we shall leave the Reader to chew the Cud upon it to the End of the Chapter.

## CHAPTER V

*The generous Behaviour of* Sophia *towards her Aunt.*

*SOPHIA* kept Silence during the foregoing Speech of her Father, nor did she once answer otherwise than with a Sigh; but as he understood none of the Language, or as he called it, Lingo of the Eyes, so he was not satisfied without some further Approbation of his Sentiments; which he now demanded of his Daughter; telling her, in the usual Way, 'he expected she was ready to take the Part of every Body against him, as she had always done that of the B—— her Mother.' *Sophia* remaining still silent, he cry'd out, 'What art dumb? why dost unt speak. Was not thy Mother a d—d B—— to me? Answer me that. What, I suppose, you despise your Father too, and don't think him good enough to speak to?'

'For Heaven's Sake, Sir,' answered *Sophia*, 'do not give so cruel a Turn to my Silence. I am sure I would sooner die than be guilty of any Disrespect towards you; but how can I venture to speak, when every Word must either offend my dear Papa, or convict me of the blackest Ingratitude as well as Impiety to the Memory of the best of Mothers: For such, I am certain my Mamma was always to me?'

'And your Aunt, I suppose, is the best of Sisters too!' replied

the Squire. 'Will you be so kind as to allow that she is a B——?
I may fairly insist upon that, I think.'

'Indeed, Sir,' says *Sophia*, 'I have great Obligations to my
Aunt. She hath been a second Mother to me.'

'And a second Wife to me too,' returned *Western*; 'so you will
take her Part too! You won't confess that she hath acted the
Part of the vilest Sister in the World?'

'Upon my Word, Sir,' cries *Sophia*, 'I must belie my Heart
wickedly if I did. I know my Aunt and you differ very much in
your Ways of thinking; but I have heard her a thousand Times
express the greatest Affection for you; and I am convinced so far
from her being the worst Sister in the World, there are very few
who love a Brother better.'

'The *English* of all which is,' answered the Squire, 'that I am
in the wrong. Ay, certainly. Ay, to be sure the Woman is in the
Right, and the Man in the Wrong always.'

'Pardon me, Sir,' cries *Sophia*, 'I do not say so.'

'What don't you say?' answered the Father, 'you have the
Impudence to say she's in the Right; doth it not follow then of
Course that I'm in the wrong? And perhaps I am in the wrong to
suffer such a Presbyterian *Hannoverian* B—— to come into my
House. She may 'dite me of a Plot for any Thing I know, and
give my Estate to the Government.'[1]

'So far, Sir, from injuring you or your Estate,' says *Sophia*, 'if
my Aunt had died Yesterday, I am convinced she would have
left you her whole Fortune.'

Whether *Sophia* intended it or no, I shall not presume to assert;
but certain it is, these last Words penetrated very deep into the
Ears of her Father, and produced a much more sensible Effect
than all she had said before. He received the Sound with much
the same Action as a Man receives a Bullet in his Head. He
started, staggered and turned pale. After which he remained
silent above a Minute, and then began in the following hesitating
Manner. 'Yesterday! she would have left me her Esteate Yesterday! would she? Why Yesterday of all the Days in the Year? I

[1] The forfeiture of one's estate had long been the penalty for high treason. (See Wood,
*Institutes*, 7th ed. [1745], p. 679.) In April 1744, however—war with France having been
declared and the nation fearing an invasion in support of the Jacobites—Parliament passed
a bill making it treasonable to correspond with the sons of the Pretender and, according to
the terms of an amendment proposed by Lord Hardwicke (see above, p. 172, n. 2), making
forfeiture the penalty for such correspondence.

suppose if she dies To-morrow she will leave it to somebody else, and perhaps out of the Vamily!' 'My Aunt, Sir,' cries *Sophia*, 'hath very violent Passions, and I can't answer what she may do under their Influence.'

'You can't!' returned the Father, 'and pray who hath been the Occasion of putting her into those violent Passions? Nay, who hath actually put her into them? Was not you and she hard at it before I came into the Room? Besides, was not all our Quarrel about you? I have not quarreled with Sister this many Years but upon your Account; and now you would throw the whole Blame upon me, as thof I should be the Occasion of her leaving the Esteate out o' the Vamily. I could have expected no better indeed, this is like the Return you make to all the rest of my Fondness.'

'I beseech you then,' cries *Sophia*, 'upon my Knees I beseech you, if I have been the unhappy Occasion of this Difference, that you will endeavour to make it up with my Aunt, and not suffer her to leave your House in this violent Rage of Anger: She is a very good-natured Woman, and a few civil Words will satisfy her.—Let me intreat you, Sir.'

'So I must go and ask Pardon for your Fault, must I?' answered *Western*. 'You have lost the Hare, and I must draw every Way to find her again? Indeed if I was certain——' Here he stopt, and *Sophia* throwing in more Entreaties, at length prevailed upon him; so that after venting two or three bitter sarcastical Expressions against his Daughter, he departed as fast as he could to recover his Sister, before her Equipage could be gotten ready.

*Sophia* then returned to her Chamber of Mourning, where she indulged herself (if the Phrase may be allowed me) in all the Luxury of tender Grief. She read over more than once the Letter which she had received from *Jones*; her Muff too was used on this Occasion; and she bathed both these, as well as herself, with her Tears. In this Situation, the friendly Mrs. *Honour* exerted her utmost Abilities to comfort her afflicted Mistress. She ran over the Names of many young Gentlemen; and having greatly commended their Parts and Persons, assured *Sophia* that she might take her Choice of any. These Methods must have certainly been used with some Success in Disorders of the like Kind, or so skilful a Practitioner as Mrs. *Honour* would never have ventured to apply them; nay, I have heard that the College of Chambermaids hold them to be as sovereign Remedies as any in the female Dispensary; but whether it was that *Sophia's* Disease differed inwardly, from those Cases with which it agreed in external Symptoms, I will not assert; but, in Fact, the good Waiting-woman did more Harm than Good, and at last so incensed her Mistress (which was no easy Matter) that with an angry Voice she dismissed her from her Presence.

## CHAPTER VI

*Containing great Variety of Matter.*

THE Squire overtook his Sister just as she was stepping into the Coach, and partly by Force and partly by Solicitations, prevailed upon her to order her Horses back into their Quarters. He succeeded in this Attempt without much Difficulty: For the Lady was, as we have already hinted, of a most placable Disposition, and greatly loved her Brother, tho' she despised his Parts, or rather his little Knowledge of the World.

Poor *Sophia*, who had first set on Foot this Reconciliation, was now made the Sacrifice to it. They both concurred in their Censures on her Conduct; jointly declared War against her; and directly proceeded to Counsel, how to carry it on in the most vigorous Manner. For this Purpose, Mrs. *Western* proposed not only an immediate Conclusion of the Treaty with *Allworthy*; but as immediately to carry it into Execution; saying, 'That there was no other Way to succeed with her Niece but by violent Methods, which she was convinced *Sophia* had not sufficient Resolution to resist. By violent,' says she, 'I mean rather, hasty Measures: For as to Confinement or absolute Force, no such Things must or can be attempted. Our Plan must be concerted for a Surprize, and not for a Storm.'

These Matters were resolved on, when Mr. *Blifil* came to pay a Visit to his Mistress. The Squire no sooner heard of his Arrival, than he stept aside, by his Sister's Advice, to give his Daughter Orders for the proper Reception of her Lover; which he did with the most bitter Execrations and Denunciations of Judgment on her Refusal.

The Impetuosity of the Squire bore down all before him; and *Sophia*, as her Aunt very wisely foresaw, was not able to resist him. She agreed, therefore, to see *Blifil*, tho' she had scarce

Spirits or Strength sufficient to utter her Assent. Indeed, to give a peremptory Denial to a Father whom she so tenderly loved, was no easy Task. Had this Circumstance been out of the Case, much less Resolution than what she was really Mistress of, would, perhaps, have served her; but it is no unusual Thing to ascribe those Actions entirely to Fear, which are in a great Measure produced by Love.

In Pursuance, therefore, of her Father's peremptory Command, *Sophia* now admitted Mr. *Blifil's* Visit. Scenes, like this, when painted at large, afford, as we have observed, very little Entertainment to the Reader. Here, therefore, we shall strictly adhere to a Rule of *Horace*;[1] by which Writers are directed to pass over all those Matters, which they despair of placing in a shining Light. A Rule, we conceive, of excellent Use as well to the Historian as to the Poet; and which, if followed, must, at least, have this good Effect, that many a great Evil (for so all great Books are called) would thus be reduced to a small one.

It is possible the great Art used by *Blifil* at this Interview, would have prevailed on *Sophia* to have made another Man in his Circumstances her Confident, and to have revealed the whole Secret of her Heart to him; but she had contracted so ill an Opinion of this young Gentleman, that she was resolved to place no Confidence in him: For Simplicity, when set on its Guard, is often a Match for Cunning. Her Behaviour to him, therefore, was entirely forced, and indeed such as is generally prescribed to Virgins upon the second formal Visit from one who is appointed for their Husband.

But tho' *Blifil* declared himself to the Squire perfectly satisfied with his Reception; yet that Gentleman, who in Company with his Sister had overheard all, was not so well pleased. He resolved, in Pursuance of the Advice of the sage Lady, to push Matters as forward as possible; and addressing himself to his intended Son-in-Law in the hunting Phrase, he cry'd after a loud Holla, 'Follow her, Boy, follow her; run in, run in, that's it, Honeys. Dead, dead, dead.—Never be bashful, nor stand shall I, shall I? —*Allworthy* and I can finish all Matters between us this Afternoon, and let us ha' the Wedding To-morrow.'

*Blifil* having conveyed the utmost Satisfaction into his Countenance, answered, 'As there is nothing, Sir, in this World, which

[1] See above, p. 208, n. 1.

I so eagerly desire as an Alliance with your Family, except my Union with the most amiable and deserving *Sophia*, you may easily imagine how impatient I must be to see myself in Possession of my two highest Wishes. If I have not therefore importuned you on this Head, you will impute it only to my Fear of offending the Lady, by endeavouring to hurry on so blessed an Event, faster than a strict Compliance with all the Rules of Decency and Decorum will permit. But if by your Interest, Sir, she might be induced to dispence with any Formalities——'

'Formalities! with a Pox!' answered the Squire, 'Pooh, all Stuff and Nonsense. I tell thee, she shall ha' thee To-morrow; you will know the World better hereafter, when you come to my Age. Women never gi' their Consent, Man, if they can help it, 'tis not the Fashion. If I had staid for her Mother's Consent, I might have been a Batchelor to this Day.——To her, to her, co to her, that's it, you jolly Dog. I tell thee shat ha' her To-morrow Morning.'

*Blifil* suffered himself to be overpowered by the forcible Rhetoric of the Squire; and it being agreed that *Western* should close with *Allworthy* that very Afternoon, the Lover departed home, having first earnestly begged that no Violence might be offered to the Lady by this Haste, in the same Manner as a Popish Inquisitor begs the Lay Power to do no Violence to the Heretic, delivered over to it, and against whom the Church hath passed Sentence.

And to say the Truth, *Blifil* had passed Sentence against *Sophia*; for however pleased he had declared himself to *Western*, with his Reception, he was by no means satisfied, unless it was that he was convinced of the Hatred and Scorn of his Mistress; and this had produced no less reciprocal Hatred and Scorn in him. It may, perhaps, be asked, Why then did he not put an immediate End to all further Courtship? I answer, for that very Reason, as well as for several others equally good, which we shall now proceed to open to the Reader.

Tho' Mr. *Blifil* was not of the Complexion of *Jones*, nor ready to eat every Woman he saw, yet he was far from being destitute of that Appetite which is said to be the common Property of all Animals. With this, he had likewise that distinguishing Taste, which serves to direct Men in their Choice of the Objects, or Food of their several Appetites; and this taught him to consider

*Sophia* as a most delicious Morsel, indeed to regard her with the same Desires which an Ortolan inspires into the Soul of an Epicure. Now the Agonies which affected the Mind of *Sophia* rather augmented than impaired her Beauty; for her Tears added Brightness to her Eyes, and her Breasts rose higher with her Sighs. Indeed no one hath seen Beauty in its highest Lustre, who hath never seen it in Distress. *Blifil* therefore looked on this human Ortolan with greater Desire than when he viewed her last; nor was his Desire at all lessened by the Aversion which he discovered in her to himself. On the contrary, this served rather to heighten the Pleasure he proposed in rifling her Charms, as it added Triumph to Lust; nay, he had some further Views, from obtaining the absolute Possession of her Person, which we detest too much even to mention; and Revenge itself was not without its Share in the Gratifications which he promised himself. The rivalling poor *Jones*, and supplanting him in her Affections, added another Spur to his Pursuit, and promised another additional Rapture to his Enjoyment.

Besides all these Views, which to some scrupulous Persons may seem to savour too much of Malevolence, he had one Prospect, which few Readers will regard with any great Abhorrence. And this was the Estate of Mr. *Western*; which was all to be settled on his Daughter and her Issue; for so extravagant was the Affection of that fond Parent, that provided his Child would but consent to be miserable with the Husband he chose, he cared not at what Price he purchased him.

For these Reasons Mr. *Blifil* was so desirous of the Match, that he intended to deceive *Sophia*, by pretending Love to her; and to deceive her Father and his own Uncle, by pretending he was beloved by her. In doing this, he availed himself of the Piety of *Thwackum*, who held, that if the End proposed was religious (as surely Matrimony is) it mattered not how wicked were the Means. As to other Occasions, he used to apply the Philosophy of *Square*, which taught, that the End was immaterial, so that the Means were fair and consistent with moral Rectitude. To say Truth, there were few Occurrences in Life on which he could not draw Advantage from the Precepts of one or other of those great Masters.

Little Deceit was indeed necessary to be practised on Mr. *Western*; who thought the Inclinations of his Daughter of as little Consequence, as *Blifil* himself conceived them to be; but as the Sentiments of Mr. *Allworthy* were of a very different Kind, so it was absolutely necessary to impose on him. In this, however, *Blifil* was so well assisted by *Western*, that he succeeded without Difficulty: For as Mr. *Allworthy* had been assured by her Father, that *Sophia* had a proper Affection for *Blifil*, and that all which he had suspected concerning *Jones*, was entirely false, *Blifil* had nothing more to do, than to confirm these Assertions; which he did with such Equivocations, that he preserved a Salvo for his Conscience; and had the Satisfaction of conveying a Lie to his Uncle, without the Guilt of telling one. When he was examined touching the Inclinations of *Sophia*, by *Allworthy*, who said, 'he would, on no Account, be accessary to forcing a young Lady into a Marriage contrary to her own Will,' he answered, 'That the real Sentiments of young Ladies were very difficult to be understood; that her Behaviour to him was full as forward as he wished it, and that if he could believe her Father, she had all the Affection for him which any Lover could desire. As for *Jones*,' said he, 'whom I am loth to call Villain, tho' his Behaviour to you, Sir, sufficiently justifies the Appellation, his own Vanity, or perhaps some wicked Views, might make him boast of a Falshood; for if there had been any Reality in Miss *Western's* Love to him, the Greatness of her Fortune would never have suffered him to desert her, as you are well informed he hath. Lastly, Sir, I promise you I would not myself, for any Consideration, no not for the whole World, consent to marry this young Lady, if I was not persuaded she had all the Passion for me which I desire she should have.'

This excellent Method of conveying a Falshood with the Heart only, without making the Tongue guilty of an Untruth, by the Means of Equivocation and Imposture, hath quieted the Conscience of many a notable Deceiver; and yet when we consider that it is Omniscience on which these endeavour to impose, it may possibly seem capable of affording only a very superficial Comfort; and that this artful and refined Distinction between communicating a Lie, and telling one, is hardly worth the Pains it costs them.

*Allworthy* was pretty well satisfied with what Mr. *Western* and Mr. *Blifil* told him; and the Treaty was now, at the End of two Days, concluded. Nothing then remained previous to the Office of the Priest, but the Office of the Lawyers, which threatened to take up so much Time, that *Western* offered to bind himself by all Manner of Covenants, rather than defer the Happiness of the young Couple. Indeed he was so very earnest and pressing, that an indifferent Person might have concluded he was more a Principal in this Match than he really was: But this Eagerness was natural to him on all Occasions; and he conducted every Scheme he undertook in such a Manner, as if the Success of that alone was sufficient to constitute the whole Happiness of his Life.

The joint Importunities of both Father and Son-in-law would probably have prevailed on Mr. *Allworthy*, who brooked but ill any Delay of giving Happiness to others, had not *Sophia* herself prevented it, and taken Measures to put a final End to the whole Treaty, and to rob both Church and Law of those Taxes[1] which these wise Bodies have thought proper to receive from the Propagation of the human Species, in a lawful Manner. Of which in the next Chapter.

## CHAPTER VII

*A strange Resolution of* Sophia, *and a more strange Stratagem of* Mrs. Honour.

THO' Mrs. *Honour* was principally attached to her own Interest, she was not without some little Attachment to *Sophia*. To say Truth, it was very difficult for any one to know that young Lady without loving her. She no sooner, therefore, heard a Piece of News, which she imagined to be of great Importance to her Mistress, than quite forgetting the Anger which she had conceived two Days before, at her unpleasant Dismission from *Sophia's* Presence, she ran hastily to inform her of this News.

The Beginning of her Discourse was as abrupt as her Entrance into the Room. 'O dear Ma'am,' says she, 'what doth your La'ship think? To be sure, I am frightened out of my Wits; and yet I thought it my Duty to tell your La'ship, tho' perhaps it may

---

[1] Fielding refers to the lawyer's charges for drawing up the jointure (or settlement of property upon the woman in consideration of marriage) and to the cost of the marriage licence, for which the King received a tax of five shillings levied on the parchment and the Church a fee of one shilling.

make you angry, for we Servants don't always know what will
make our Ladies angry; for to be sure, every thing is always laid
to the Charge of a Servant. When our Ladies are out of Humour,
to be sure, we must be scolded; and to be sure I should not
wonder if your La'ship should be out of Humour; nay, it must
surprize you certainly, ay, and shock you too.'—'Good *Honour*!
let me know it without any longer Preface,' says *Sophia*; 'there are
few Things, I promise you, which will surprize, and fewer which
will shock me.' 'Dear Ma'am,' answered *Honour*, 'to be sure, I
overheard my Master talking to Parson *Supple* about getting a
Licence this very Afternoon; and to be sure I heard him say your
La'ship should be married To-morrow Morning.' *Sophia* turned
pale at these Words, and repeated eagerly, 'To-morrow Morning!'
—'Yes, Madam,' replied the trusty Waiting-woman, 'I will
take my Oath I heard my Master say so.' '*Honour*,' says *Sophia*,
'you have both surprized and shocked me to such a Degree, that
I have scarce any Breath or Spirits left. What is to be done in my
dreadful Situation?' 'I wish I was able to advise your La'ship,' says
she. 'Do, advise me,' cries *Sophia*, 'pray, dear *Honour* advise me.
Think what you would attempt if it was your own Case.' 'Indeed,
Ma'am,' cries *Honour*, 'I wish your La'ship and I could change
Situations; that is, I mean, without hurting your La'ship, for to
be sure I don't wish you so bad as to be a Servant; but because
that if so be it was my Case, I should find no Manner of Difficulty
in it; for in my poor Opinion, young Squire *Blifil* is a charming,
sweet, handsome Man.'—'Don't mention such Stuff,' cries
*Sophia*.—'Such Stuff,' repeated *Honour*, 'why there—— Well,
to be sure, what's one Man's Meat is another Man's Poison, and
the same is altogether as true of Women.' '*Honour*,' says *Sophia*,
'rather than submit to be the Wife of that contemptible Wretch,
I would plunge a Dagger into my Heart.' 'O lud, Ma'm,'
answered the other, 'I am sure you frighten me out of my Wits
now. Let me beseech your La'ship not to suffer such wicked
Thoughts to come into your Head. O lud, to be sure I tremble
every Inch of me. Dear Ma'm, consider—that to be denied
Christian Burial, and to have your Corpse buried in the Highway,
and a Stake drove through you, as Farmer *Halfpenny* was served
at *Ox-Cross*,¹ and, to be sure, his Ghost hath walked there ever

¹ On the laws and customs relating to the treatment and burial of the bodies of suicides,
see Edmund Gibson, *Codex Juris Ecclesiastici Anglicani* (1713), i. 540–1; Giles Jacob, *New*

since; for several People have seen him. To be sure it can be
nothing but the Devil which can put such wicked Thoughts into
the Head of any body; for certainly it is less wicked to hurt all the
World than one's own dear Self, and so I have heard said by
more Parsons than one. If your La'ship hath such a violent
Aversion, and hates the young Gentleman so very bad, that you
can't bear to think of going into Bed to him; for to be sure there
may be such Antipathies in Nature, and one had lieverer touch a
Toad than the Flesh of some People——'

*Sophia* had been too much wrapped in Contemplation to pay
any great Attention to the foregoing excellent Discourse of her
Maid; interrupting her therefore, without making any Answer to
it, she said, '*Honour*, I am come to a Resolution. I am determined
to leave my Father's House this very Night; and if you have
the Friendship for me which you have often professed, you will
keep me Company.' 'That I will, Ma'm, to the World's End,'
answered *Honour*; 'but I beg your La'ship to consider the Consequence before you undertake any rash Action. Where can your
La'ship possibly go?' 'There is,' replied *Sophia*, 'a Lady of
Quality in *London*, a Relation of mine, who spent several Months
with my Aunt in the Country; during all which Time she treated
me with great Kindness, and expressed so much Pleasure in my
Company, that she earnestly desired my Aunt to suffer me to go
with her to *London*. As she is a Woman of very great Note, I shall
easily find her out, and I make no Doubt of being very well and
kindly received by her.' 'I would not have your La'ship too
confident of that,' cries *Honour*; 'for the first Lady I lived with
used to invite People very earnestly to her House; but if she
heard afterwards they were coming, she used to get out of the
Way. Besides, tho' this Lady would be very glad to see your
La'ship, as to be sure any body would be glad to see your La'ship,
yet when she hears your La'ship is run away from my Master——'
'You are mistaken, *Honour*,' says *Sophia*, 'she looks upon the
Authority of a Father in a much lower Light than I do; for she
pressed me violently to go to *London* with her, and when I

*Law Dictionary*, 4th ed. (1739), s.v. 'felo de se'; and Michael Dalton, *The Country Justice*
(1746), p. 327. A case very similar to that of 'Farmer *Halfpenny*' was reported in *The
General Advertiser* (Monday, 16 February 1746/7): 'Friday last in the Afternoon, a
Woman, about forty Years of Age, who was found last Tuesday to have poison'd herself at
her Lodgings at Hatton Wall, was buried, and a Stake drove thro' her Body, in the Cross-
Road at the Bottom of Hatton-Garden, leading to Hockley in the Hole'.

refused to go without my Father's Consent, she laughed me to Scorn, called me silly Country Girl, and said I should make a pure loving Wife, since I could be so dutiful a Daughter. So I have no Doubt but she will both receive me, and protect me too, till my Father, finding me out of his Power, can be brought to some Reason.'

'Well but, Ma'm,' answered *Honour*, 'how doth your La'ship think of making your Escape? Where will you get any Horses or Conveyance? for as for your own Horse, as all the Servants know a little how Matters stand between my Master and your La'ship, *Robin* will be hanged before he will suffer it to go out of the Stable without my Master's express Orders.' 'I intend to escape,' said *Sophia*, 'by walking out of the Doors when they are open. I thank Heaven my Legs are very able to carry me. They have supported me many a long Evening, after a Fiddle, with no very agreeable Partner; and surely they will assist me in running from so detestable a Partner for Life.' 'O Heavens, Ma'm, doth your La'ship know what you are saying?' cries *Honour*, 'would you think of walking about the Country by Night and alone?' 'Not alone,' answered the Lady, 'you have promised to bear me Company.' 'Yes, to be sure,' cries *Honour*, 'I will follow your La'ship through the World; but your La'ship had almost as good be alone; for I shall not be able to defend you, if any Robbers, or other Villains, should meet with you. Nay, I should be in as horrible a Fright as your La'ship; for to be certain, they would ravish us both. Besides, Ma'm, consider how cold the Nights are now,[1] we shall be frozen to Death.' 'A good brisk Pace,' answered *Sophia*, 'will preserve us from the Cold; and if you cannot defend me from a Villain, *Honour*, I will defend you; for I will take a Pistol with me. There are two always charged in the Hall.' 'Dear Ma'm, you frighten me more and more,' cries *Honour*, 'sure your La'ship would not venture to fire it off! I had rather run any Chance, than your La'ship should do that.' 'Why so?' says

[1] The first clear indication that Fielding has discarded an earlier time-scheme for his central narrative. In Book V, chapter x, Jones's amorous encounter with Molly Seagrim is said to have taken place on 'a pleasant Evening in the latter End of *June*'. According to the plan of Book VI, however, this episode occurred just three weeks before Jones was expelled from 'Paradise Hall', and on the evening of the day following that sad event Jones finds himself at Hambrook (VII. xi), where he joins the King's soldiers marching north to oppose the advance of the Jacobite rebels. At this point in the narrative, the action is clearly set in late November 1745 (see below, p. 368, n. 1).

*Sophia*, smiling; 'would not you, *Honour*, fire a Pistol at any one who should attack your Virtue?' 'To be sure, Ma'm,' cries *Honour*, 'one's Virtue is a dear Thing, especially to us poor Servants; for it is our Livelihood, as a Body may say, yet I mortally hate Fire-arms; for so many Accidents happen by them.' 'Well, well,' says *Sophia*, 'I believe I may ensure your Virtue at a very cheap Rate, without carrying any Arms with us; for I intend to take Horses at the very first Town we come to, and we shall hardly be attacked in our Way thither. Look'ee, *Honour*, I am resolved to go, and if you will attend me, I promise you I will reward you to the very utmost of my Power.'

This last Argument had a stronger Effect on *Honour* than all the preceding. And since she saw her Mistress so determined, she desisted from any further Dissuasions. They then entered into a Debate on Ways and Means of executing their Project. Here a very stubborn Difficulty occurred, and this was the Removal of their Effects, which was much more easily got over by the Mistress than by the Maid: For when a Lady hath once taken a Resolution to run to a Lover, or to run from him, all Obstacles are considered as Trifles. But *Honour* was inspired by no such Motive; she had no Raptures to expect, nor any Terrors to shun, and besides the real Value of her Clothes, in which consisted a great Part of her Fortune, she had a capricious Fondness for several Gowns, and other Things; either because they became her, or because they were given her by such a particular Person; because she had bought them lately, or because she had had them long; or for some other Reasons equally good; so that she could not endure the Thoughts of leaving the poor Things behind her exposed to the Mercy of *Western*, who, she doubted not, would in his Rage make them suffer Martyrdom.

The ingenious Mrs. *Honour* having applied all her Oratory to dissuade her Mistress from her Purpose, when she found her positively determined, at last started the following Expedient to remove her Clothes, *viz.* to get herself turned out of Doors that very Evening. *Sophia* highly approved this Method, but doubted how it might be brought about. 'Oh! Ma'm,' cries *Honour*, 'your La'ship may trust that to me; we Servants very well know how to obtain this Favour of our Masters and Mistresses; tho' sometimes indeed where they owe us more Wages than they can readily pay, they will put up with all our Affronts, and will hardly take any

Warning we can give them; but the Squire is none of those; and since your La'ship is resolved upon setting out to Night, I warrant I get discharged this Afternoon.' It was then resolved that she should pack up some Linnen, and a Night-gown for *Sophia*, with her own Things; and as for all her other Clothes, the young Lady abandoned them with no more Remorse than the Sailor feels when he throws over the Goods of others in order to save his own Life.


## CHAPTER VIII

*Containing Scenes of Altercation, of no very uncommon Kind.*

MRS. *Honour* had scarce sooner parted from her young Lady, than something, (for I would not, like the old Woman in *Quivedo*,[1] injure the Devil by any false Accusation, and possibly he might have no Hand in it) but something, I say, suggested itself to her, that by sacrificing *Sophia* and all her Secrets to Mr. *Western*, she might probably make her Fortune. Many Considerations urged this Discovery. The fair Prospect of a handsome Reward for so great and acceptable a Service to the Squire, tempted her Avarice; and again, the Danger of the Enterprize she had undertaken; the Uncertainty of its Success; Night, Cold, Robbers, Ravishers, all alarmed her Fears. So forcibly did all these operate upon her, that she was almost determined to go directly to the Squire, and to lay open the whole Affair. She was, however, too upright a Judge to decree on one Side before she had heard the other. And here, first, a Journey to *London* appeared very strongly in Support of *Sophia*. She eagerly longed to see a Place in which she fancied Charms short only of those which a raptured Saint imagines in Heaven. In the next Place, as she knew *Sophia* to have much more Generosity than her Master, so her Fidelity promised her a greater Reward than she could gain by Treachery. She then cross-examined all the Articles which had raised her Fears on the other Side, and found, on fairly

1 The well-known Spanish satirist, Francisco Gomez de Quevedo (1580–1645). The allusion may be to the seventh of Quevedo's *Visions*, in which 'an *old Bawd* of a *Gouvernante*' fans the flames of rebellion in hell, threatening, though in vain, to depose the devil. (See Sir Roger L'Estrange, trans., 10th ed. [1708].) For an earlier reference to Quevedo, see *The Champion* (27 December 1739).

sifting the Matter, that there was very little in them. And now both Scales being reduced to a pretty even Ballance, her Love to her Mistress being thrown into the Scale of her Integrity, made that rather preponderate, when a Circumstance struck upon her Imagination, which might have had a dangerous Effect, had its whole Weight been fairly put into the other Scale. This was the Length of Time which must intervene before *Sophia* would be able to fulfil her Promises; for tho' she was intitled to her Mother's Fortune, at the Death of her Father, and to the Sum of 3000 *l.* left her by an Uncle when she came of Age; yet these were distant Days, and many Accidents might prevent the intended Generosity of the young Lady, whereas the Rewards she might expect from Mr. *Western* were immediate. But while she was pursuing this Thought, the good Genius of *Sophia*, or that which presided over the Integrity of Mrs. *Honour*, or perhaps mere Chance, sent an Accident in her Way, which at once preserved her Fidelity, and even facilitated the intended Business.

Mrs. *Western's* Maid claimed great Superiority over Mrs. *Honour*, on several Accounts. First, her Birth was higher: For her great Grand-mother by the Mother's Side was a Cousin, not far removed, to an *Irish* Peer. Secondly, her Wages were greater. And lastly, she had been at *London*, and had of Consequence seen more of the World. She had always behaved, therefore, to Mrs. *Honour* with that Reserve, and had always exacted of her those Marks of Distinction, which every Order of Females preserves and requires in Conversation with those of an inferior Order. Now as *Honour* did not at all Times agree with this Doctrine; but would frequently break in upon the Respect which the other demanded, Mrs. *Western's* Maid was not at all pleased with her Company: Indeed, she earnestly longed to return home to the House of her Mistress, where she domineered at Will over all the other Servants. She had been greatly, therefore, disappointed in the Morning when Mrs. *Western* had changed her Mind on the very Point of Departure, and had been in what is vulgarly called, a glouting Humour ever since.

In this Humour, which was none of the sweetest, she came into the Room where *Honour* was debating with herself, in the Manner we have above related. *Honour* no sooner saw her, than she addressed her in the following obliging Phrase. 'Soh! Madam, I find we are to have the Pleasure of your Company longer, which

I was afraid the Quarrel between my Master and your Lady
would have robbed us of.' 'I don't know, Madam,' answered the
other, 'who you mean by We and Us. I assure you I do not look
on any of the Servants in this House to be proper Company for
me. I am Company, I hope, for their Betters every Day in the
Week. I do not speak on your Account, Mrs. *Honour*; for you are
a civilized young Woman; and when you have seen a little more
of the World, I should not be ashamed to walk with you in *St.
James's* Park.' 'Hoity! toity!' cries *Honour*, 'Madam is in her Airs,
I protest. Mrs. *Honour* forsooth! sure, Madam, you might call me
by my Sir-name;[1] for tho' my Lady calls me *Honour*, I have a Sir-
name as well as other Folks. Ashamed to walk with me, quotha!
Marry, as good as yourself I hope.' 'Since you make such a
Return to my Civility,' said the other, 'I must acquaint you, Mrs.
*Honour*, that you are not so good as me. In the Country indeed
one is obliged to take up with all kind of Trumpery, but in Town
I visit none but the Women of Women of Quality. Indeed, Mrs.
*Honour*, there is some Difference, I hope, between you and me.'
'I hope so too,' answered *Honour*, 'there is some Difference in
our Ages, and—I think in our Persons.' Upon speaking which
last Words, she strutted by Mrs. *Western's* Maid with the most
provoking Air of Contempt; turning up her Nose, tossing her
Head, and violently brushing the Hoop of her Competitor with
her own. The other Lady put on one of her most malicious
Sneers, and said, 'Creature! you are below my Anger; and it is
beneath me to give ill Words to such an audacious saucy Trollop;
but, Hussy, I must tell you, your Breeding shews the Meanness of
your Birth as well as of your Education; and both very properly
qualify you to be the mean serving Woman of a Country Girl.'
'Don't abuse my Lady,' cries *Honour*, 'I won't take that of you;
she's as much better than yours as she is younger, and ten
thousand Times more handsomer.'

Here ill Luck, or rather good Luck, sent Mrs. *Western* to
see her Maid in Tears, which began to flow plentifully at her
Approach; and of which being asked the Reason by her Mistress,
she presently acquainted her, that her Tears were occasioned by
the rude Treatment of that Creature there, meaning *Honour*.
'And, Madam,' continued she, 'I could have despised all she said
to me; but she hath had the Audacity to affront your Ladyship,

---

[1] i.e. Blackmore (see Honour's letter in xv. x).

and to call you ugly.—Yes, Madam, she called you ugly old
Cat to my Face. I could not bear to hear your Ladyship called
ugly.'—'Why do you repeat her Impudence so often?' said Mrs.
*Western*. And then turning to Mrs. *Honour*, she asked her 'how
she had the Assurance to mention her Name with Disrespect?'
'Disrespect Madam!' answered *Honour*, 'I never mentioned your
Name at all. I said somebody was not as handsome as my Mistress,
and to be sure you know that as well as I.' 'Hussy,' replied the
Lady, 'I will make such a saucy Trollop as yourself, know that
I am not a proper Subject of your Discourse. And if my Brother
doth not discharge you this Moment, I will never sleep in his
House again. I will find him out and have you discharged this
Moment.' 'Discharged!' cries *Honour*, 'and suppose I am, there
are more Places in the World than one. Thank Heaven, good
Servants need not want Places; and if you turn away all who do
not think you handsome, you will want Servants very soon, let me
tell you that.'

Mrs. *Western* spoke, or rather thundered in Answer; but as she
was hardly articulate, we cannot be very certain of the identical
Words: We shall, therefore, omit inserting a Speech, which, at best,
would not greatly redound to her Honour. She then departed in
Search of her Brother, with a Countenance so full of Rage, that
she resembled one of the Furies rather than a human Creature.

The two Chambermaids being again left alone, began a second
Bout at Altercation, which soon produced a Combat of a more
active Kind. In this the Victory belonged to the Lady of inferior
Rank, but not without some Loss of Blood, of Hair, and of Lawn
and Muslin.

## CHAPTER IX

*The wise Demeanour of Mr.* Western *in the Character of a*
*Magistrate. A Hint to Justices of Peace, concerning the necessary*
*Qualifications of a Clerk; with extraordinary Instances of*
*paternal Madness, and filial Affection.*

LOGICIANS sometimes prove too much by an Argument, and
Politicians often overreach themselves in a Scheme. Thus
had it like to have happened to Mrs. *Honour*, who instead of
recovering the rest of her Clothes, had like to have stopped even

those she had on her Back from escaping: For the Squire no
sooner heard of her having abused his Sister, than he swore
twenty Oaths he would send her to *Bridewell*.[1]

Mrs. *Western* was a very good-natured Woman, and ordinarily
of a forgiving Temper. She had lately remitted the Trespass of a
Stage-coach Man, who had overturned her Post-chaise into a
Ditch; nay, she had even broken the Law in refusing to prosecute
a High-way-man who had robbed her,[2] not only of a Sum of
Money, but of her Ear-rings; at the same Time d——ning her,
and saying, 'such handsome B——s as you, don't want Jewels to
set them off, and be d——nd to you.' But now, so uncertain are our
Tempers, and so much do we at different Times differ from our-
selves, she would hear of no Mitigation; nor could all the affected
Penitence of *Honour*, nor all the Entreaties of *Sophia* for her own
Servant, prevail with her to desist from earnestly desiring her
Brother to execute Justiceship (for it was indeed a Syllable more
than Justice) on the Wench.

But luckily the Clerk had a Qualification, which no Clerk to a
Justice of Peace ought ever to be without, namely, some Understanding in the Law of this Realm. He therefore whispered in the
Ear of the Justice, that he would exceed his Authority by committing the Girl to *Bridewell*, as there had been no Attempt to
break the Peace; 'for I am afraid, Sir,' says he, 'you cannot legally
commit any one to *Bridewell* only for Ill-breeding.'

In Matters of high Importance, particularly in Cases relating
to the Game, the Justice was not always attentive to these
Admonitions of his Clerk: For, indeed, in executing the Laws
under that Head, many Justices of Peace suppose they have a
large discretionary Power. By Virtue of which, under the Notion
of searching for, and taking away Engines for the Destruction
of the Game,[3] they often commit Trespasses, and sometimes
Felony at their Pleasure.

---

[1] See above, p. 59, n. 1.

[2] Because of the injury to both the public and the Crown, a person refusing to levy 'Hue
and Cry' against a felon who had robbed him was liable to be fined and imprisoned. (See
Jacob, *New Law-Dictionary*, 4th ed. [1739], s.v. 'Hue and Cry'; and Wood, *Institutes*, 7th
ed. [1745], p. 393.) In *An Enquiry into the Causes of the late Increase of Robbers* (1751),
section viii, Fielding put the case as follows: 'Robbery is an Offence not only against the
Party robbed, but against the Public, who are therefore entitled to Prosecution; and he who
prevents or stifles such the Prosecution, is no longer an innocent Man, but guilty of a
high Offence against the Public Good.'

[3] According to the Game Laws, only those persons having an estate valued at £100 per

But this Offence was not of quite so high a Nature, nor so dangerous to the Society. Here, therefore, the Justice behaved with some Attention to the Advice of his Clerk: For, in Fact, he had already had two Informations exhibited against him in the King's-Bench,[1] and had no Curiosity to try a third.

The Squire, therefore, putting on a most wise and significant Countenance, after a Preface of several Hum's and Ha's, told his Sister, that upon more mature Deliberation, he was of Opinion that 'as there was no breaking up of the Peace, such as the Law,' says he, 'calls breaking open a Door, or breaking a Hedge, or breaking a Head; or any such Sort of Breaking; the Matter did not amount to a felonious Kind of a Thing, nor Trespasses nor Damages, and, therefore, there was no Punishment in the Law for it.'

Mrs. *Western* said, 'she knew the Law much better; that she had known Servants very severely punished for affronting their Masters; and then named a certain Justice of the Peace in *London*, who,' she said, 'would commit a Servant to *Bridewell*, at any Time when a Master or Mistress desired it.'

'Like enough,' cries the Squire, 'it may be so in *London*; but the Law is different in the Country.' Here followed a very learned Dispute between the Brother and Sister concerning the Law, which we would insert, if we imagined many of our Readers could understand it. This was, however, at length referred by both Parties to the Clerk, who decided it in Favour of the Magistrate; and Mrs. *Western* was, in the End, obliged to content herself with the Satisfaction of having *Honour* turned away; to which *Sophia* herself very readily and chearfully consented.

Thus Fortune, after having diverted herself, according to Custom, with two or three Frolicks, at last disposed all Matters to the Advantage of our Heroine; who, indeed, succeeded admirably well in her Deceit, considering it was the first she had ever practised. And, to say the Truth, I have often concluded, that the honest Part of Mankind would be much too hard for

year were eligible to possess guns, dogs, or other 'Engines for taking of the Game'. Justices could issue warrants to game-keepers authorizing them to search the houses of those suspected of violating this law and to seize such guns, dogs, etc. (See Wood, *Institutes*, 7th ed. [1745], p. 461.)

[1] Justices of the peace were appointed by the Lord Chancellor in the King's name. Their authority, if abused, was revocable. (See Theodore Barlow, *The Justice of the Peace: A Treatise Containing the Power and Duty of that Magistrate* [1745], pp. ix–x, xv.)

the knavish, if they could bring themselves to incur the Guilt, or
thought it worth their while to take the Trouble.

*Honour* acted her Part to the utmost Perfection. She no sooner
saw herself secure from all Danger of *Bridewell*, a Word which
had raised most horrible Ideas in her Mind, than she resumed
those Airs which her Terrours before had a little abated; and laid
down her Place, with as much Affectation of Content, and indeed
of Contempt, as was ever practised at the Resignation of Places of
much greater Importance. If the Reader pleases, therefore, we
chuse rather to say she resigned—which hath, indeed, been
always held a synonimous Expression with being turned out, or
turned away.

Mr. *Western* ordered her to be very expeditious in packing:
For his Sister declared she would not sleep another Night under
the same Roof with so impudent a Slut. To work therefore she
went, and that so earnestly, that every Thing was ready early in
the Evening; when having received her Wages, away packed she
Bag and Baggage, to the great Satisfaction of every one, but of
none more than of *Sophia*; who, having appointed her Maid to
meet her at a certain Place not far from the House, exactly at the
dreadful and ghostly Hour of Twelve, began to prepare for her
own Departure.

But first she was obliged to give two painful Audiences, the one
to her Aunt, and the other to her Father. In these Mrs. *Western*
herself began to talk to her in a more peremptory Stile than
before; but her Father treated her in so violent and outragious a
Manner, that he frightened her into an affected Compliance with
his Will, which so highly pleased the good Squire, that he changed
his Frowns into Smiles, and his Menaces into Promises; he
vowed his whole Soul was wrapped in hers, that her Consent (for
so he construed the Words, *You know, Sir, I must not, nor can
refuse to obey any absolute Command of yours*) had made him the
happiest of Mankind. He then gave her a large Bank-bill to
dispose of in any Trinkets she pleased, and kissed and embraced
her in the fondest Manner, while Tears of Joy trickled from
those Eyes, which a few Moments before had darted Fire and
Rage against the dear Object of all his Affection.

Instances of this Behaviour in Parents are so common, that the
Reader, I doubt not, will be very little astonished at the whole
Conduct of Mr. *Western*. If he should, I own I am not able to

account for it; since that he loved his Daughter most tenderly, is, I think, beyond Dispute. So indeed have many others, who have rendered their Children most compleatly miserable by the same Conduct; which, tho' it is almost universal in Parents, hath always appeared to me to be the most unaccountable of all the Absurdities, which ever entered into the Brain of *that strange prodigious Creature Man.*[1]

The latter Part of Mr. *Western's* Behaviour had so strong an Effect on the tender Heart of *Sophia*, that it suggested a Thought to her, which not all the Sophistry of her politic Aunt, nor all the Menaces of her Father had ever once brought into her Head. She reverenced her Father so piously, and loved him so passion- ately, that she had scarce ever felt more pleasing Sensations, than what arose from the Share she frequently had of contributing to his Amusement; and sometimes, perhaps, to higher Gratifications; for he never could contain the Delight of hearing her commended, which he had the Satisfaction of hearing almost every Day of her Life. The Idea, therefore, of the immense Happiness she should convey to her Father by her Consent to this Match, made a strong Impression on her Mind. Again, the extreme Piety of such an Act of Obedience, worked very forcibly, as she had a very deep Sense of Religion. Lastly, when she reflected how much she herself was to suffer, being indeed to become little less than a Sacrifice, or a Martyr, to filial Love and Duty, she felt an agree- able Tickling in a certain little Passion, which tho' it bears no immediate Affinity either to Religion or Virtue, is often so kind as to lend great Assistance in executing the Purposes of both.

*Sophia* was charmed with the Contemplation of so heroic an Action, and began to compliment herself with much premature Flattery, when *Cupid*, who lay hid in her Muff, suddenly crept out, and, like *Punchinello* in a Puppet-shew,[2] kicked all out before him. In Truth (for we scorn to deceive our Reader, or to vindi-

---

[1] Cf. Rochester's *Satyr against Mankind* (1679), l. 2.

[2] Punch, the rowdy hero of the English puppet theatre, ultimately derives from the Italian Pulcinella (or Punchinello), introduced into England shortly after the Restoration. (See George Speaight, *The History of the English Puppet Theatre* [1955], ch. v and p. 219.) Fielding so much admired the droll, satiric exploits of Punch and his wife Joan that in the spring of 1748 he sought to revive interest in them by conducting his own puppet theatre under the name of 'Madame de la Nash'. (See the General Introduction, p. xxxi–xxxii.) Later in *Tom Jones* (XII. v) he constructs an entire episode around his hero's chance encounter with a travelling puppet-master.

cate the Character of our Heroine, by ascribing her Actions to supernatural Impulse) the Thoughts of her beloved *Jones*, and some Hopes (however distant) in which he was very particularly concerned, immediately destroyed all which filial Love, Piety and Pride had, with their joint Endeavours, been labouring to bring about.

But before we proceed any farther with *Sophia*, we must now look back to Mr. *Jones*.


## CHAPTER X

*Containing several Matters natural enough perhaps, but* Low.

THE Reader will be pleased to remember, that we left Mr. *Jones* in the Beginning of this Book, on his Road to *Bristol*; being determined to seek his Fortune at Sea, or rather, indeed, to fly away from his Fortune on Shore.

It happened, (a Thing not very unusual) that the Guide who undertook to conduct him on his Way, was unluckily unacquainted with the Road; so that having missed his right Track, and being ashamed to ask Information, he rambled about backwards and forwards, till Night came on, and it began to grow dark. *Jones* suspecting what had happened, acquainted the Guide with his Apprehensions; but he insisted on it, that they were in the right Road, and added, it would be very strange if he should not know the Road to *Bristol*; tho', in Reality, it would have been much stranger if he had known it, having never past through it in his Life before.

*Jones* had not such implicit Faith in his Guide; but that on their Arrival at a Village,[1] he enquired of the first Fellow he saw, whether they were in the Road to *Bristol*. 'Whence did you come?' cries the Fellow. 'No Matter,' says *Jones*, a little hastily, 'I want to know if this be the Road to *Bristol*.' 'The Road to *Bristol*!' cries the Fellow, scratching his Head, 'Why, Master, I believe you will hardly get to *Bristol* this Way to Night.' 'Prithee, Friend, then,' answered *Jones*, 'do tell us which is the Way.'—'Why, Measter,' cries the Fellow, 'you must be come out of your Road

---

[1] The village, as Fielding later reveals (p. 562), is Hambrook, about five miles northeast of Bristol on the road to Gloucester.

the Lord knows whither: For thick Way goeth to *Glocester*.'
'Well, and which Way goes to *Bristol*,' said *Jones*. 'Why, you be
going away from *Bristol*,' answered the Fellow.'—'Then,' said
*Jones*, 'we must go back again.' 'Ay, you must,' said the Fellow.
'Well, and when we come back to the Top of the Hill, which
Way must we take?' 'Why you must keep the strait Road.' 'But I
remember there are two Roads, one to the Right and the other to
the Left.' 'Why you must keep the right-hand Road, and then
gu strait vorwards; only remember to turn first to your Right, and
then to your Left again, and then to your Right; and that brings
you to the Squire's, and then you must keep strait vorwards, and
turn to the Left.'

Another Fellow now came up, and asked which Way the
Gentlemen were going?—of which being informed by *Jones*, he
first scratched his Head, and then leaning upon a Pole he had in
his Hand, began to tell him, 'That he must keep the Right-hand
Road for about a Mile or a Mile and half or zuch a Matter, and
then he must turn short to the Left, which would bring him
round by Measter *Jin Bearnes's*.' 'But which is Mr. *John
Bearnes's*,' says *Jones*. 'O Lord,' cries the Fellow, 'why don't you
know Measter *Jin Bearnes*? Whence then did you come?'

These two Fellows had almost conquered the Patience of
*Jones*, when a plain well-looking Man (who was indeed a Quaker)
accosted him thus: 'Friend, I perceive thou hast lost thy Way,
and if thou wilt take my Advice thou wilt not attempt to find it to
Night. It is almost dark, and the Road is difficult to hit; besides
there have been several Robberies committed lately between this
and *Bristol*. Here is a very creditable good House just by, where
thou may'st find good Entertainment for thyself and thy Cattle
till Morning.' *Jones*, after a little Persuasion, agreed to stay in
this Place till the Morning, and was conducted by his Friend to
the Public-House.

The Landlord, who was a very civil Fellow, told *Jones*, 'he
hoped he would excuse the Badness of his Accommodation: For
that his Wife was gone from home, and had locked up almost
every Thing, and carried the Keys along with her.' Indeed, the
Fact was, that a favourite Daughter of hers was just married, and
gone, that Morning, home with her Husband; and that she and
her Mother together, had almost stript the poor Man of all his
Goods, as well as Money: For tho' he had several Children, this

Daughter only, who was the Mother's Favourite, was the Object of her Consideration; and to the Humour of this one Child, she would, with Pleasure, have sacrificed all the rest, and her Husband into the Bargain.

Tho' *Jones* was very unfit for any Kind of Company, and would have preferred being alone, yet he could not resist the Importunities of the honest Quaker; who was the more desirous of sitting with him, from having remarked the Melancholy which appeared both in his Countenance and Behaviour; and which the poor Quaker thought his Conversation might in some Measure relieve.

After they had past some Time together, in such a Manner that my honest Friend might have thought himself at one of his Silent-Meetings, the Quaker began to be moved by some Spirit or other, probably that of Curiosity; and said, 'Friend, I perceive some sad Disaster hath befallen thee; but, pray be of Comfort. Perhaps thou hast lost a Friend. If so, thou must consider we are all mortal. And why should'st thou grieve, when thou knowest thy Grief will do thy Friend no Good. We are all born to Affliction. I myself have my Sorrows as well as thee, and most probably greater Sorrows. Tho' I have a clear Estate of a 100 *l.* a Year, which is as much as I want, and I have a Conscience, I thank the Lord, void of Offence. My Constitution is sound and strong, and there is no Man can demand a Debt of me, nor accuse me of an Injury—yet, Friend, I should be concerned to think thee as miserable as myself.'

Here the Quaker ended with a deep Sigh; and *Jones* presently answered, 'I am very sorry, Sir, for your Unhappiness, whatever is the Occasion of it.' 'Ah! Friend,' replyed the Quaker, 'one only Daughter is the Occasion. One who was my greatest Delight upon Earth, and who within this Week is run away from me, and is married against my Consent. I had provided her a proper Match, a sober Man, and one of Substance; but she, forsooth would chuse for herself, and away she is gone with a young Fellow not worth a Groat. If she had been dead, as I suppose thy Friend is, I should have been happy!' 'That is very strange, Sir,' said *Jones*. 'Why, would it not be better for her to be dead, than to be a Beggar?' replied the Quaker: 'For, as I told you, the Fellow is not worth a Groat; and surely she cannot expect that I shall ever give her a Shilling. No, as she hath married for Love, let her live on Love if she can; let her carry her Love to Market, and see whether any one will change it into Silver, or even into Halfpence.' 'You know your own Concerns best, Sir,' said *Jones*. 'It must have been,' continued the Quaker, 'a long premeditated Scheme to cheat me: For they have known one another from their Infancy; and I always preached to her against Love —and told her a thousand Times over, it was all Folly and Wickedness. Nay, the cunning Slut pretended to hearken to me, and to despise all Wantonness of the Flesh; and yet, at last, broke out at a Window two Pair of Stairs: For I began, indeed, a little to suspect her, and had locked her up carefully, intending the very next Morning to have married her up to my Liking. But she disappointed me within a few Hours, and escaped away to the Lover of her own chusing, who lost no Time: For they were married and beded, and all within an Hour.

'But it shall be the worst Hour's Work for them both that ever they did, for they may starve, or beg, or steal together for me. I will never give either of them a Farthing.' Here *Jones* starting up, cry'd, 'I really must be excused, I wish you would leave me.' 'Come, come, Friend,' said the Quaker, 'don't give Way to Concern. You see there are other People miserable, besides yourself.' 'I see there are Madmen and Fools and Villains in the World,' cries *Jones*.—'But let me give you a Piece of Advice; send for your Daughter and Son-in-law home, and don't be yourself the only Cause of Misery to one you pretend to love.' 'Send for her and her Husband home!' cries the Quaker loudly, 'I would sooner send for the two greatest Enemies I have in the World!' 'Well, go home yourself, or where you please,' said *Jones*: 'For I will sit no longer in such Company.'—'Nay, Friend,' answered the Quaker, 'I scorn to impose my Company on any one.' He then offered to pull Money from his Pocket, but *Jones* pushed him with some Violence out of the Room.

The Subject of the Quaker's Discourse had so deeply affected *Jones*, that he stared very wildly all the Time he was speaking. This the Quaker had observed, and this, added to the rest of his Behaviour, inspired honest *Broadbrim* with a Conceit, that his Companion was, in Reality, out of his Senses. Instead of resenting the Affront, therefore, the Quaker was moved with Compassion for his unhappy Circumstances; and having communicated his Opinion to the Landlord, he desired him to

take great Care of his Guest, and to treat him with the highest
Civility.

'Indeed,' says the Landlord, 'I shall use no such Civility
towards him: For it seems, for all his laced Waistcoat there, he is
no more a Gentleman than myself; but a poor Parish Bastard
bred up at a great Squire's about 30 Miles off, and now turned
out of Doors (not for any Good to be sure.) I shall get him out of
my House as soon as possible. If I do lose my Reckoning, the first
Loss is always the best. It is not above a Year ago that I lost a
Silver-spoon.'

'What, dost thou talk of a Parish Bastard, *Robin*?' answered
the Quaker. 'Thou must certainly be mistaken in thy Man.'

'Not at all,' replied *Robin*, 'the Guide, who knows him very
well, told it me.' For, indeed, the Guide had no sooner taken his
Place at the Kitchin-Fire, than he acquainted the whole Company
with all he knew, or had ever heard concerning *Jones*.

The Quaker was no sooner assured by this Fellow of the Birth
and low Fortune of *Jones*, than all Compassion for him vanished;
and the honest, plain Man went home fired with no less Indignation than a Duke would have felt at receiving an Affront from
such a Person.

The Landlord himself conceived an equal Disdain for his
Guest; so that when *Jones* rung the Bell in order to retire to Bed,
he was acquainted that he could have no Bed there. Besides
Disdain of the mean Condition of his Guest, *Robin* entertained
violent Suspicion of his Intentions, which were, he supposed, to
watch some favourable Opportunity of robbing the House. In
reality, he might have been very well eased of these Apprehensions
by the prudent Precautions of his Wife and Daughter, who had
already removed every thing which was not fixed to the Freehold;
but he was by Nature suspicious, and had been more particularly
so since the Loss of his Spoon. In short, the Dread of being
robbed, totally absorbed the comfortable Consideration that he
had nothing to lose.

*Jones* being assured that he could have no Bed, very contentedly
betook himself to a great Chair made with Rushes, when Sleep,
which had lately shunned his Company in much better Apart-
ments, generously paid him a Visit in his humble Cell.

As for the Landlord, he was prevented by his Fears from
retiring to Rest. He returned therefore to the Kitchen-Fire,

whence he could survey the only Door which opened into the Parlour, or rather Hole, where *Jones* was seated; and as for the Window to that Room, it was impossible for any Creature larger than a Cat to have made his Escape through it.

## CHAPTER XI

### *The Adventure of a Company of Soldiers.*

THE Landlord having taken his Seat directly opposite to the Door of the Parlour, determined to keep Guard there the whole Night. The Guide and another Fellow remained long on Duty with him, tho' they neither knew his Suspicions, nor had any of their own. The true Cause of their watching did indeed, at length, put an End to it; for this was no other than the Strength and Goodness of the Beer, of which having tippled a very large Quantity, they grew at first very noisy and vociferous, and afterwards fell both asleep.

But it was not in the Power of Liquor to compose the Fears of *Robin*. He continued still waking in his Chair, with his Eyes fixed stedfastly on the Door which led into the Apartment of Mr. *Jones*, till a violent Thundering at his outward Gate called him from his Seat, and obliged him to open it; which he had no sooner done, than his Kitchen was immediately full of Gentlemen in red Coats, who all rushed upon him in as tumultuous a Manner, as if they intended to take his little Castle by Storm.

The Landlord was now forced from his Post to furnish his numerous Guests with Beer, which they called for with great Eagerness; and upon his second or third Return from the Cellar, he saw Mr. *Jones* standing before the Fire in the midst of the Soldiers; for it may easily be believed, that the Arrival of so much good Company should put an End to any Sleep, unless that from which we are to be awakened only by the last Trumpet.

The Company having now pretty well satisfied their Thirst, nothing remained but to pay the Reckoning, a Circumstance often productive of much Mischief and Discontent among the inferior Rank of Gentry; who are apt to find great Difficulty in assessing the Sum, with exact Regard to distributive Justice, which directs, that every Man shall pay according to the Quantity which he drinks. This Difficulty occurred upon the present Occasion; and it was the greater, as some Gentlemen had, in their extreme Hurry, marched off, after their first Draught, and had entirely forgot to contribute any thing towards the said Reckoning.

A violent Dispute now arose, in which every Word may be said to have been deposed upon Oath; for the Oaths were at least equal to all the other Words spoken. In this Controversy, the whole Company spoke together, and every Man seemed wholly bent to extenuate the Sum which fell to his Share; so that the most probable Conclusion which could be foreseen, was, that a large Portion of the Reckoning would fall to the Landlord's Share to pay, or (what is much the same thing) would remain unpaid.

All this while Mr. *Jones* was engaged in Conversation with the Serjeant; for that Officer was entirely unconcerned in the present Dispute, being privileged, by immemorial Custom, from all Contribution.

The Dispute now grew so very warm, that it seemed to draw towards a military Decision, when *Jones* stepping forward, silenced all their Clamours at once, by declaring that he would pay the whole Reckoning, which indeed amounted to no more than three Shillings and Four-pence.

This Declaration procured *Jones* the Thanks and Applause of the whole Company. The Terms honourable, noble, and worthy Gentleman, resounded through the Room; nay, my Landlord himself began to have a better Opinion of him, and almost to disbelieve the Account which the Guide had given.

The Serjeant had informed Mr. *Jones*, that they were marching against the Rebels, and expected to be commanded by the glorious Duke of *Cumberland*.[1] By which the Reader may

---

[1] William Augustus (1726–65), Duke of Cumberland, the youngest son of George II. Before his twentieth year Cumberland, though no very brilliant strategist, had distinguished himself for courage and daring at the battles of Dettingen (1743) and Fontenoy (1745), and in April 1746 he put an end to the Jacobite uprising by defeating the rebel forces at Culloden. His severity in dealing with the rebel clansmen earned him the name of 'Billy the Butcher', but Fielding never mentions him except in the most laudatory terms: after the decisive victory at Culloden, Fielding in two numbers of *The True Patriot* (22–29 April, 29 April–6 May 1746) praises 'the Glorious Duke of CUMBERLAND, that *Fulmen Belli*' and contrasts his bravery in battle with the cowardice of his rival, Charles Edward Stuart. See also *Ovid's Art of Love Paraphrased* (1747) and *An Enquiry into the Causes of the late Increase of Robbers* (1751), section ii, where Cumberland is ranked with Edward, Henry, and Marlborough as the greatest of British generals.

perceive (a Circumstance which we have not thought necessary to communicate before) that this was the very Time when the late Rebellion was at the highest; and indeed the Banditti were now marched into *England*, intending, as it was thought, to fight the King's Forces, and to attempt pushing forward to the Metropolis.[1]

*Jones* had some Heroic Ingredients in his Composition, and was a hearty Well-wisher to the glorious Cause of Liberty, and of the Protestant Religion. It is no wonder, therefore, that in Circumstances which would have warranted a much more romantic and wild Undertaking, it should occur to him to serve as a Volunteer in this Expedition.

Our commanding Officer had said all in his Power to encourage and promote this good Disposition, from the first Moment he had been acquainted with it. He now proclaimed the noble Resolution aloud, which was received with great Pleasure by the whole Company, who all cried out, 'God bless King *George*, and your Honour;' and then added, with many Oaths, 'We will stand by you both to the last Drops of our Blood.'

The Gentleman, who had been all Night tippling at the Alehouse, was prevailed on by some Arguments which a Corporal had put into his Hand, to undertake the same Expedition. And now the Portmanteau belonging to Mr. *Jones* being put up in the Baggage-cart, the Forces were about to move forwards; when the Guide, stepping up to *Jones*, said, 'Sir, I hope you will consider that the Horses have been kept out all Night, and we have travelled a great ways out of our Way.' *Jones* was surprized at the Impudence of this Demand, and acquainted the Soldiers with the Merits of his Cause, who were all unanimous in condemning the

---

[1] Though it is questionable that Fielding intended his readers to date the events of his narrative quite so precisely, the allusions in this paragraph fix the time of Jones's brief stay in Hambrook as late November 1745. The rebel army had crossed the Tweed into England on 6 November, advancing southward, steadily and virtually unopposed, until they reached Derby on 4 December; from Derby two days later, having decided not to engage the King's forces, they began their long retreat into Scotland. Cumberland's appointment as commander of the forces was not announced, however, until 23 November; he set out for Lichfield, his headquarters, on the 26th, arriving there the following evening. (See *The London Gazette*, 19–23, 23–6, 26–30 November 1745.) Finally, if there is truth in the somewhat extravagant hypothesis that Fielding consulted an almanac before making the full moon rise at 5.00 p.m. at Gloucester (VIII. ix; see below, p. 435, n. 1), then the time of the present chapter, the events of which take place four days earlier, may be precisely fixed as 25 November 1745.

Guide for his Endeavours to put upon a Gentleman. Some said, he ought to be tied Neck and Heels; others, that he deserved to run the Gauntlope; and the Serjeant shook his Cane at him, and wished he had him under his Command, swearing heartily he would make an Example of him.

*Jones* contented himself, however, with a negative Punishment, and walked off with his new Comrades, leaving the Guide to the poor Revenge of cursing and reviling him, in which latter the Landlord joined, saying, 'Ay, ay, he is a pure one, I warrant you. A pretty Gentleman, indeed, to go for a Soldier. He shall wear a laced Waistcoat truly. It is an old Proverb and a true one, all is not Gold that glisters. I am glad my House is well rid of him.'

All that Day the Serjeant and the young Soldier marched together; and the former, who was an arch Fellow, told the latter many entertaining Stories of his Campaigns, tho' in Reality he had never made any; for he was but lately come into the Service, and had, by his own Dexterity, so well ingratiated himself with his Officers, that he had promoted himself to a Halberd,[1] chiefly indeed by his Merit in recruiting, in which he was most excellently well skilled.

Much Mirth and Festivity passed among the Soldiers during their March. In which the many Occurrences that had passed at their last Quarters were remembered, and every one, with great Freedom, made what Jokes he pleased on his Officers, some of which were of the coarser Kind, and very near bordering on Scandal. This brought to our Heroe's Mind the Custom which he had read of among the *Greeks* and *Romans*,[2] of indulging, on certain Festivals and solemn Occasions, the Liberty to Slaves, of using an uncontrouled Freedom of Speech towards their Masters.

Our little Army, which consisted of two Companies of Foot, were now arrived at the Place[3] where they were to halt that Evening. The Serjeant then acquainted his Lieutenant, who was the commanding Officer, that they had picked up two Fellows in that Day's March; one of which, he said, was as fine a Man as ever he saw (meaning the Tippler) for that he was near six Feet,

---

[1] This ancient weapon denoted the rank of sergeant.

[2] The Saturnalia, a Roman religious festival held in December, was an occasion for debauchery and licentiousness, when slaves and servants were permitted to behave disrespectfully toward their masters. Cf. Lucian, *Saturnalia*, 'A Conversation with Cronos' 5–18.

[3] Possibly Cambridge, a village about ten miles south-west of Gloucester.

well-proportioned, and strongly limbed; and the other, (meaning *Jones*) would do well enough for the rear Rank.

The new Soldiers were now produced before the Officer, who having examined the six Foot Man, he being first produced, came next to survey *Jones*; at the first Sight of whom, the Lieutenant could not help shewing some Surprize; for, besides that he was very well dressed, and was naturally genteel, he had a remarkable Air of Dignity in his Look, which is rarely seen among the Vulgar, and is indeed not inseparably annexed to the Features of their Superiors.

'Sir,' said the Lieutenant, 'my Serjeant informed me, that you are desirous of enlisting in the Company I have at present under my Command; if so, Sir, we shall very gladly receive a Gentleman who promises to do much Honour to the Company, by bearing Arms in it.'

*Jones* answered: 'That he had not mentioned any thing of enlisting himself; that he was most zealously attached to the glorious Cause for which they were going to fight, and was very desirous of serving as a Volunteer;' concluding with some Compliments to the Lieutenant, and expressing the great Satisfaction he should have in being under his Command.

The Lieutenant returned his Civility, commended his Resolution, shook him by the Hand, and invited him to dine with himself and the rest of the Officers.

## CHAPTER XII

### *The Adventure of a Company of Officers.*

THE Lieutenant, whom we mentioned in the preceding Chapter, and who commanded this Party, was now near sixty Years of Age. He had entered very young into the Army, and had served in the Capacity of an Ensign at the Battle of *Tannieres*;[1] here he had received two Wounds, and had so well

---

[1] On 11 September 1709 Marlborough won a bloody victory over the French in the Battle of Malplaquet, sometimes called the Battle of Taisnières after the wood in which the enemy's left flank was strongly entrenched. (See *Relation de la campagne de Tannières* [The Hague, 1710].)

distinguished himself, that he was by the Duke of *Marlborough*[1] advanced to be a Lieutenant, immediately after that Battle.[2]

In this Commission he had continued ever since, *viz.* near forty Years; during which Time he had seen vast Numbers preferred over his Head, and had now the Mortification to be commanded by Boys, whose Fathers were at Nurse when he first entered into the Service.

Nor was this ill Success in his Profession solely owing to his having no Friends among the Men in Power. He had the Misfortune to incur the Displeasure of his Colonel, who for many Years continued in the Command of this Regiment. Nor did he owe the implacable Ill-will which this Man bore him to any Neglect or Deficiency as an Officer, nor indeed to any Fault in himself; but solely to the Indiscretion of his Wife, who was a very beautiful Woman, and who, tho' she was remarkably fond of her Husband, would not purchase his Preferment at the Expence of certain Favours which the Colonel required of her.

The poor Lieutenant was more peculiarly unhappy in this, that while he felt the Effects of the Enmity of his Colonel, he neither knew, nor suspected, that he really bore him any; for he could not suspect an Ill-will for which he was not conscious of giving any Cause; and his Wife, fearing what her Husband's nice Regard to his Honour might have occasioned, contented herself with preserving her Virtue, without enjoying the Triumphs of her Conquest.

This unfortunate Officer (for so I think he may be called) had many good Qualities, besides his Merit in his Profession; for he was a religious, honest, good-natured Man; and had behaved so well in his Command, that he was highly esteemed and beloved, not only by the Soldiers of his own Company; but by the whole Regiment.

[1] John Churchill (1650–1722), first Duke of Marlborough, victorious commander of the British forces against France, 1702–11. In frequent references to the controversial hero of the Whigs, Fielding, whose father had served under Marlborough at Blenheim and whose mother was a distant relation of the Churchills, was adulatory. In *A Proper Answer to a late Scurrilous Libel* (1747) he summed up his feelings by referring to 'the unparalell'd [*sic*] Successes of our Arms, under the Conduct of the Great, the Protestant, the Whig Duke of *Marlborough*'. In April 1742 Fielding published his *Full Vindication of the Dutchess Dowager of Marlborough*, written in behalf of Sarah, Marlborough's widow.

[2] The honest lieutenant whose career Fielding briefly describes in these paragraphs is an adumbration of Bob Bound in *Amelia* (x. ix), though the reasons for his lack of preferment more particularly foreshadow Booth's own situation.

The other Officers who marched with him were a *French* Lieutenant, who had been long enough out of *France* to forget his own Language, but not long enough in *England* to learn ours, so that he really spoke no Language at all, and could barely make himself understood, on the most ordinary Occasions. There were likewise two Ensigns, both very young Fellows; one of whom had been bred under an Attorney, and the other was Son to the Wife of a Nobleman's Butler.

As soon as Dinner was ended, *Jones* informed the Company of the Merriment which had passed among the Soldiers upon their March; 'and yet,' says he, 'notwithstanding all their Vocifera-tion, I dare swear they will behave more like *Grecians* than *Trojans* when they come to the Enemy.' '*Grecians* and *Trojans*!' says one of the Ensigns, 'who the Devil are they? I have heard of all the Troops in *Europe*, but never of any such as these.'

'Don't pretend to more Ignorance than you have, Mr. *Norther-ton*,' said the worthy Lieutenant, 'I suppose you have heard of the *Greeks* and *Trojans*, tho', perhaps, you never read *Pope's Homer*; who, I remember, now the Gentleman mentions it, compares the March of the *Trojans* to the Cackling of Geese, and greatly commends the Silence of the *Grecians*.[1] And upon my Honour, there is great Justice in the Cadet's Observation.'

'Begar, me remember dem ver well,' said the *French* Lieuten-ant, 'me ave read dem at School in dans Madam *Daciere*,[2] des *Greek*, des *Trojan*, dey fight for von Woman—ouy, ouy, me ave read all dat.'

'D—n *Homo* with all my Heart,' says *Northerton*, 'I have the Marks of him in my A—— yet. There's *Thomas*[3] of our Regi-

---

[1] Pope's *Iliad*, iii. 1–13—though Pope compares the motions of the Trojan army to a flight of cranes, not geese.

[2] Anne Lefèvre Dacier (*c*. 1654–1720), celebrated French bluestocking and wife of the critic André Dacier (see below, pp. 396, n. 1; 569, n. 3). Her translation of the *Iliad* appeared in 1711, the *Odyssey* in 1716. Though Fielding feared that learning in women was not conducive to domestic harmony—consider the examples of Jenny Jones (I. vi) and Mrs. Bennet in *Amelia* (1751)—he was nevertheless a great admirer of Mme Dacier and her works. In *A Journey from This World to the Next* (1743; I. viii), for instance, he introduces her in Elysium sitting on Homer's lap. For other references, see *The Champion* (4 December 1739), *Joseph Andrews* (1742; III. ii), *Plutus* (1742), *Amelia* (VI. vii, VIII. v, X. i), and *The Covent-Garden Journal* (8 February, 21 October 1752).

[3] Some readers identified this literate soldier with a certain Captain Lewis Thomas (of the Fourth, or King's Own, Regiment), an avid reader who amused his fellow officers by going about with a copy of Homer in his pocket. (See Thomas's letter to Welbore Ellis, written from Carlisle, 3 April 1749; quoted by J. P. Feil, *PQ*, xxxix [1960], 508–10.)

ment, always carries a *Homo* in his Pocket: D—n me if ever I come at it, if I don't burn it. And there's *Corderius*,[1] another d—n'd Son of a Whore that hath got me many a Flogging.'

'Then you have been at School, Mr. *Northerton*?' said the Lieutenant.

'Ay d—n me have I,' answered he, 'the Devil take my Father for sending me thither. The old Put wanted to make a Parson of me, but d—n me, thinks I to myself, I'll nick you there, old Cull: The Devil a Smack of your Nonsense, shall you ever get into me. There's *Jemmy Oliver* of our Regiment, he narrowly escaped being a Pimp too; and that would have been a thousand Pities: For d—n me if he is not one of the prettiest Fellows in the whole World; but he went farther than I with the old Cull: For *Jemmy* can neither write nor read.'

'You give your Friend a very good Character,' said the Lieutenant, 'and a very deserved one, I dare say; but prithee, *Northerton*, leave off that foolish as well as wicked Custom of swearing: For you are deceived, I promise you, if you think there is Wit or Politeness in it. I wish too, you would take my Advice, and desist from abusing the Clergy. Scandalous Names and Reflections cast on any Body of Men, must be always unjustifiable;[2] but especially so, when thrown on so sacred a Function: For to abuse the Body is to abuse the Function itself; and I leave to you to judge how inconsistent such Behaviour is in Men, who are going to fight in Defence of the Protestant Religion.'

Mr. *Adderley*, which was the Name of the other Ensign, had sat hitherto kicking his Heels and humming a Tune, without seeming to listen to the Discourse; he now answered, '*O Monsieur, on ne parle pas de la Religion dans la Guerre.*'[3] 'Well said,

---

Though Thomas denied that he was 'in the least known to Mr. Fielding', the two men did have at least one acquaintance in common: Mrs. Whitefield of the Bell Inn, Gloucester (see below, p. 430, n. 1).

1 The Latin name of Mathurin Cordier (1479–1564), a French-Protestant pedagogue whose best-known work, *Colloquiorum scholasticorum libri quatuor* (1563), was translated into English by Charles Hoole (1657) and John Clarke (1718), among others. The *Colloquies* of Corderius went through numerous editions and was widely used by schoolboys.

2 Cf. Fielding's 'Apology for the Clergy' in *The Champion* (29 March, 5, 12, 19 April 1740), which begins: 'There is nothing so unjustifiable as the general Abuse of any Nation or Body of Men . . .'; also 'An Essay on Conversation' (1743).

3 That the ensign should choose to express this sentiment in French is apt enough during a time of war with France, when the perfidy of the enemy was generally deplored in England. Perhaps, however, Fielding recalls the views of such French generals as the

*Jack*,' cries *Northerton*, 'if la Religion was the only Matter, the Parsons should fight their own Battles for me.'

'I don't know, Gentlemen,' says *Jones*, 'what may be your Opinion; but I think no Man can engage in a nobler Cause than that of his Religion; and I have observed in the little I have read of History, that no Soldiers have fought so bravely, as those who have been inspired with a religious Zeal: For my own Part, tho' I love my King and Country, I hope, as well as any Man in it, yet the Protestant Interest is no small Motive to my becoming a Volunteer in the Cause.'

*Northerton* now winked on *Adderley*, and whispered to him slily, 'Smoke the Prig, *Adderley*, smoke him.' Then turning to *Jones*, said to him, 'I am very glad, Sir, you have chosen our Regiment to be a Volunteer in: For if our Parson should at any Time take a Cup too much, I find you can supply his Place. I presume, Sir, you have been at the University, may I crave the Favour to know what College?'

'Sir,' answered *Jones*, 'so far from having been at the University, I have even had the Advantage of yourself: for I was never at School.'

'I presumed,' cries the Ensign, 'only upon the Information of your great Learning.'—'Oh! Sir,' answered *Jones*, 'it is as possible for a Man to know something without having been at School; as it is to have been at School and to know nothing.'

'Well said, young Volunteer,' cries the Lieutenant, 'upon my Word, *Northerton*, you had better let him alone, for he will be too hard for you.'

*Northerton* did not very well relish the Sarcasm of *Jones*; but he thought the Provocation was scarce sufficient to justify a Blow, or a Rascal, or Scoundrel, which were the only Repartees that

Marquis of Pescayre and Cipierre, recorded in Brantome's *Les Vies des hommes illustres et grands capitaines estrangers de son temps* (Leyden, 1699), i. 132–3, and given additional currency in the notes to Bayle's *General Dictionary, Historical and Critical*, iv (1736), s.v. 'Cipierre'. Having been reproved by the papal legate for the disorderly conduct of his troops in Lombardy, Pescayre replied: 'Monsieur le Legat, il n'y a point de chose plus difficile à ceux qui exercent la guerre que de servir en un mesme temps & avec esgale discipline à Mars & à Christ, parce que l'usage de la guerre en cette corruption de Milice est du tout contraire à la justice & à la Religion.' Similarly, the Cardinal of Ferrara having objected that the troops fighting the heretics at Orleans should behave like true believers and abstain from eating meat during Lent, Cipierre answered: 'Monsieur ne pensez pas regler nos gens de guerre comme vos gens d'Eglise car autre chose est de servir Dieu & servir la guerre. . . .'

suggested themselves. He was, therefore, silent at present; but resolved to take the first Opportunity of returning the Jest by Abuse.

It now came to the Turn of Mr. *Jones* to give a Toast, as it is called; who could not refrain from mentioning his dear *Sophia*. This he did the more readily, as he imagined it utterly impossible, that any one present should guess the Person he meant.

But the Lieutenant, who was the Toast-master, was not contented with *Sophia* only. He said, he must have her Sir-name; upon which *Jones* hesitated a little, and presently after named Miss *Sophia Western*. Ensign *Northerton* declared, he would not drink her Health, in the same Round with his own Toast, unless somebody would vouch for her. 'I knew one *Sophy Western*,' says he, 'that was lain-with by Half the young Fellows at *Bath*; and, perhaps, this is the same Woman.' *Jones* very solemnly assured him of the contrary; asserting that the young Lady he named was one of great Fashion and Fortune. 'Ay, ay,' says the Ensign, 'and so she is, d——n me it is the same Woman, and I'll hold Half a Dozen of *Burgundy*, *Tom French* of our Regiment brings her into Company with us at any Tavern in *Bridges-street*.'[1] He then proceeded to describe her Person exactly, (for he had seen her with her Aunt) and concluded with saying, 'That her Father had a great Estate in *Somersetshire*.'

The Tenderness of Lovers can ill brook the least jesting with the Names of their Mistresses. However, *Jones*, tho' he had enough of the Lover and of the Heroe too in his Disposition, did not resent these Slanders as hastily as, perhaps, he ought to have done. To say the Truth, having seen but little of this Kind of Wit, he did not readily understand it, and for a long Time imagined Mr. *Northerton* had really mistaken his Charmer for some other. But now turning to the Ensign with a stern Aspect, he said, 'Pray, Sir, chuse some other Subject for your Wit: For I promise you I will bear no jesting with this Lady's Character.' 'Jesting,' cries the other, 'd——n me if ever I was more in Earnest in my Life. *Tom French* of our Regiment had both her and her

---

[1] The most notorious street in the most disreputable district of London, the Hundred of Drury, which, according to Ned Ward's calculations, contained no fewer than 107 brothels. Here were 'the Gates of *Sodom* . . . the Jakes of the Town'. (See *A View of London and Westminster: or, The Town Spy* [1725], i. 13–14, ii. 48.) Bridges Street is the scene of Jonathan Wild's amorous adventure with the prostitute, Molly Straddle (II. iii).

Aunt at *Bath.*' 'Then I must tell you in Earnest,' cries *Jones,* 'that you are one of the most impudent Rascals upon Earth.'

He had no sooner spoken these Words, than the Ensign, together with a Volley of Curses, discharged a Bottle full at the Head of *Jones,* which hitting him a little above the right Temple, brought him instantly to the Ground.

The Conqueror perceiving the Enemy to lie motionless before him, and Blood beginning to flow pretty plentifully from his Wound, began now to think of quitting the Field of Battle, where no more Honour was to be gotten; but the Lieutenant interposed, by stepping before the Door, and thus cut off his Retreat.

*Northerton* was very importunate with the Lieutenant for his Liberty; urging the ill Consequences of his Stay, asking him, what he could have done less! 'Zounds!' says he, 'I was but in Jest with the Fellow. I never heard any Harm of Miss *Western* in my Life.' 'Have not you?' said the Lieutenant, 'then you richly deserve to be hanged, as well for making such Jests, as for using such a Weapon. You are my Prisoner, Sir; nor shall you stir from hence, till a proper Guard comes to secure you.'

Such an Ascendant had our Lieutenant over this Ensign, that all that Fervency of Courage which had levelled our poor Heroe with the Floor, would scarce have animated the said Ensign to have drawn his Sword against the Lieutenant, had he then one dangling at his Side; but all the Swords being hung up in the Room, were, at the very Beginning of the Fray, secured by the *French* Officer. So that Mr. *Northerton* was obliged to attend the final Issue of this Affair.

The *French* Gentleman and Mr. *Adderley,* at the Desire of their Commanding-Officer, had raised up the Body of *Jones;* but as they could perceive but little (if any) Sign of Life in him, they again let him fall. *Adderley* damning him for having blooded his Waistcoat; and the *Frenchman* declaring, 'Begar me no tush de Engliseman de mort, me ave heard de Englise Ley, Law, what you call, hang up de Man dat tush him last.'[1]

When the good Lieutenant applied himself to the Door, he applied himself likewise to the Bell; and the Drawer immediately

---

[1] Careful search of the laws pertaining to murder and presumptive evidence has failed to disclose any such curious provision, to which the lawyer in *Joseph Andrews* (1742; I. xii) also alludes.

attending, he dispatched him for a File of Musqueteers and a Surgeon. These Commands, together with the Drawer's Report of what he had himself seen, not only produced the Soldiers, but presently drew up the Landlord of the House, his Wife and Servants, and, indeed, every one else, who happened, at that Time, to be in the Inn.

To describe every Particular, and to relate the whole Conversation of the ensuing Scene, is not within my Power, unless I had forty Pens, and could, at once, write with them all together, as the Company now spoke. The Reader must, therefore, content himself with the most remarkable Incidents, and perhaps he may very well excuse the rest.

The first Thing done, was securing the Body of *Northerton*, who being delivered into the Custody of six Men with a Corporal at their Head, was by them conducted from a Place which he was very willing to leave, but it was unluckily to a Place whither he was very unwilling to go. To say the Truth, so whimsical are the Desires of Ambition, the very Moment this Youth had attained the above-mentioned Honour, he would have been well contented to have retired to some Corner of the World, where the Fame of it should never have reached his Ears.

It surprizes us, and so, perhaps, it may the Reader, that the Lieutenant, a worthy and good Man, should have applied his chief Care, rather to secure the Offender, than to preserve the Life of the wounded Person. We mention this Observation, not with any View of pretending to account for so odd a Behaviour, but lest some Critic should hereafter plume himself on discovering it. We would have these Gentlemen know we can see what is odd in Characters as well as themselves, but it is our Business to relate Facts as they are; which when we have done, it is the Part of the learned and sagacious Reader to consult that original Book of Nature, whence every Passage in our Work is transcribed, tho' we quote not always the particular Page for its Authority.

The Company which now arrived were of a different Disposition. They suspended their Curiosity concerning the Person of the Ensign, till they should see him hereafter in a more engaging Attitude. At present, their whole Concern and Attention were employed about the bloody Object on the Floor; which being placed upright in a Chair, soon began to discover some Symptoms of Life and Motion. These were no sooner perceived by the Company (for *Jones* was, at first, generally concluded to be dead) than they all fell at once to prescribing for him: (For as none of the physical Order was present, every one there took that Office upon him.)

Bleeding was the unanimous Voice of the whole Room; but unluckily there was no Operator at hand: Every one then cry'd, 'Call the Barber;' but none stirred a Step. Several Cordials were likewise prescribed in the same ineffective Manner; till the Landlord ordered up a Tankard of strong Beer, with a Toast, which he said was the best Cordial in *England*.

The Person principally assistant on this Occasion, indeed the only one who did any Service, or seemed likely to do any, was the Landlady. She cut off some of her Hair, and applied it to the Wound to stop the Blood. She fell to chafing the Youth's Temples with her Hand; and having exprest great Contempt for her Husband's Prescription of Beer, she dispatched one of her Maids to her own Closet for a Bottle of Brandy, of which, as soon as it was brought, she prevailed upon *Jones*, who was just returned to his Senses, to drink a very large and plentiful Draught.

Soon afterwards arrived the Surgeon, who having viewed the Wound, having shaken his Head, and blamed every Thing which was done, ordered his Patient instantly to Bed; in which Place, we think proper to leave him, some Time, to his Repose, and shall here, therefore, put an End to this Chapter.

## CHAPTER XIII

*Containing the great Address of the Landlady; the great Learning of a Surgeon; and the solid Skill in Casuistry of the worthy Lieutenant.*

WHEN the wounded Man was carried to his Bed, and the House began again to clear up from the Hurry which this Accident had occasioned; the Landlady thus addressed the commanding Officer. 'I am afraid, Sir,' said she, 'this young Man did not behave himself as well as he should do to your Honours; and if he had been killed, I suppose he had had but his *Desarts*; to be sure, when Gentlemen admit inferior *Parsons* into their Company, they *oft* to keep their Distance; but, as my first Husband used to say, few of em know how to do it. For my own Part, I am sure, I should not have suffered any Fellows to *include* themselves into Gentlemen's Company: but I *thoft* he had been an Officer himself, till the Serjeant told me he was but a Recruit.'

'Landlady,' answered the Lieutenant, 'you mistake the whole Matter. The young Man behaved himself extremely well, and is, I believe, a much better Gentleman than the Ensign, who abused him. If the young Fellow dies, the Man who struck him will have most Reason to be sorry for it: For the Regiment will get rid of a very troublesome Fellow, who is a Scandal to the Army; and if he escapes from the Hands of Justice, blame me, Madam, that's all.'

'Ay! Ay! good Lack-a-day!' said the Landlady, 'who could have *thoft* it? Ay, ay, ay, I am satisfied your Honour will see Justice done; and to be sure it *oft* to be to every one. Gentlemen *oft* not to kill poor Folks without answering for it. A poor Man hath a Soul to be saved as well as his Betters.'

'Indeed, Madam,' said the Lieutenant, 'you do the Volunteer wrong; I dare swear he is more of a Gentleman than the Officer.'

'Ay,' cries the Landlady, 'why look you there now: Well, my first Husband was a wise Man; he used to say, you can't always know the Inside by the Outside. Nay, that might have been well enough too: For I never *saw'd* him till he was all over blood. Who would have *thoft* it! mayhap, some young Gentleman crossed in Love. Good Lack-a-day! if he should die, what a Concern it will be to his Parents! Why sure the Devil must possess the wicked Wretch to do such an Act. To be sure, he is a Scandal to the Army, as your Honour says: For most of the Gentlemen of the Army that ever I saw, are quite different Sort of People, and look as if they would scorn to spill any Christian Blood as much as any Men. I mean, that is, in a civil Way, as my first Husband used to say. To be sure, when they come into the Wars, there must be Blood-shed; but that they are not to be blamed for. The more of our Enemies they kill there, the better; and I wish, with all my Heart, they could kill every Mother's Son of them.'

'O fie! Madam,' said the Lieutenant smiling, 'ALL is rather too bloody-minded a Wish.'

'Not at all, Sir,' answered she, 'I am not at all bloody-minded, only to our Enemies, and there is no Harm in that. To be sure it is natural for us to wish our Enemies dead, that the Wars may be at an End, and our Taxes be lowered: For it is a dreadful Thing to pay as we do. Why now there is above forty Shillings for Window-lights,[1] and yet we have stopt up all we could; we have almost blinded the House I am sure: Says I to the Exciseman, says I, I think you *oft* to favour us, I am sure we are very good Friends to the Government; and so we are for *sartain*: For we pay a Mint of Money to 'um. And yet I often think to myself, the Government doth not imagine itself more obliged to us, than to those that don't pay 'um a Farthing. Ay, ay; it is the Way of the World.'

She was proceeding in this Manner, when the Surgeon entered the Room. The Lieutenant immediately asked how his Patient did? But he resolved him only by saying, 'Better, I believe, than he would have been by this Time, if I had not been called; and even as it is, perhaps it would have been lucky if I could have been called sooner.' 'I hope, Sir,' said the Lieutenant, 'the Skull is not fractured.' 'Hum,' cries the Surgeon, 'Fractures are not always the most dangerous Symptoms. Contusions and Lacerations are often attended with worse Phænomena, and with more fatal Consequences than Fractures. People who know nothing of the Matter conclude, if the Skull is not fractured, all is well; whereas, I had rather see a Man's Skull broke all to Pieces, than some Contusions I have met with.' 'I hope,' says the Lieutenant, 'there are no such Symptoms here.' 'Symptoms,' answered the Surgeon, 'are not always regular nor constant. I have known very unfavourable Symptoms in the Morning change to favourable ones at Noon, and return to unfavourable again at Night. Of Wounds,

---

[1] According to the time-scheme established in VII. xi (see above, p. 368, n. 1), the landlady's complaint against the window tax is anachronistic. Though a window tax had been in effect since 1696, until 25 March 1747 the maximum yearly charge to the householder had been limited to 20*s*. On that date a new law (20 George II, cap. 3) levied a tax on 'every Window or Light, in every Dwelling-house', the rates being scaled so as to fall most heavily on the rich: houses having from 10 to 14 windows paid 6*d*. per window per year; for houses having from 15 to 19 windows the rate was 9*d*.; and for those having 20 or more windows, 1*s*. For the most part public opinion approved this more equitable tax. (See the articles from *The Westminster Journal* and *The Craftsman* reprinted in *The Gentleman's Magazine*, xvi [March 1746], 150–2, and xvii [February 1747], 72–3.) But there were those who preferred to seal up their windows rather than pay it. Such is 'Humphry Gubbins', the intransigent Tory of *The Jacobite's Journal* (13 February 1748), who writes to protest against the new law: 'I put out one haf of my Windows last Year, and if there comes another Ile put out t'other haf.—D—n me a Man may drink in the Dark, and mayhap he may then be the buolder in toasting honest Healths.' See also the poem, 'On a Quaker's stopping up more than half his windows, in pursuance of the late tax on lights', *The British Magazine*, ii (April 1747), 176.

indeed, it is rightly and truly said, *Nemo repente fuit turpissimus.*[1] I
was once, I remember, called to a Patient, who had received a
violent Contusion in his Tibia, by which the exterior Cutis was
lacerated, so that there was a profuse sanguinary Discharge; and
the interior Membranes were so divellicated, that the Os or Bone
very plainly appeared through the Aperture of the Vulnus or
Wound. Some febrile Symptoms intervening at the same Time,
(for the Pulse was exuberant and indicated much Phlebotomy)
I apprehended an immediate Mortification. To prevent which I
presently made a large Orifice in the Vein of the left Arm, whence
I drew twenty Ounces of Blood; which I expected to have found
extremely sizy and glutinous, or indeed coagulated, as it is in
pleuritic Complaints; but, to my Surprize, it appeared rosy and
florid, and its Consistency differed little from the Blood of those
in perfect Health. I then applied a Fomentation to the Part,
which highly answered the Intention, and after three or four
Times dressing, the Wound began to discharge a thick Pus or
Matter, by which Means the Cohesion—but perhaps I do not
make myself perfectly well understood.' 'No really,' answered the
Lieutenant, 'I cannot say I understand a Syllable.' 'Well, Sir,'
said the Surgeon, 'then I shall not tire your Patience; in short,
within six Weeks, my Patient was able to walk upon his Legs, as
perfectly as he could have done before he received the Contusion.'
'I wish, Sir,' said the Lieutenant, 'you would be so kind only
to inform me, whether the Wound this young Gentleman hath
had the Misfortune to receive is likely to prove mortal?' 'Sir,'
answered the Surgeon, 'to say whether a Wound will prove mortal
or not at first Dressing, would be very weak and foolish Presumption: We are all mortal, and Symptoms often occur in a
Cure which the greatest of our Profession could never foresee.'—
'But do you think him in Danger?' says the other. 'In Danger!
ay, surely,' cries the Doctor, 'who is there among us, who in the
most perfect Health can be said not to be in Danger? Can a Man,
therefore, with so bad a Wound as this be said to be out of
Danger? All I can say, at present, is, that it is well I was called as
I was, and perhaps it would have been better if I had been called
sooner. I will see him again early in the Morning, and in the mean
Time let him be kept extremely quiet, and drink liberally of

[1] Juvenal, *Satires*, ii. 83: 'no one reaches the depths of turpitude all at once'—trans.
G. G. Ramsay, Loeb Classical Library, 1928.

Water-Gruel.' 'Won't you allow him Sack-whey?'[1] said the Land-lady. 'Ay, ay, Sack-whey,' cries the Doctor, 'if you will, provided it be very small.' 'And a little Chicken-broth too?' added she.— 'Yes, yes, Chicken-broth,' said the Doctor, 'is very good.' 'May'nt I make him some Jellies too?' said the Landlady. 'Ay, ay,' answered the Doctor, 'Jellies are very good for Wounds, for they promote Cohesion.' And, indeed, it was lucky she had not named Soop or high Sauces, for the Doctor would have complied, rather than have lost the Custom of the House.

The Doctor was no sooner gone, than the Landlady began to trumpet forth his Fame to the Lieutenant, who had not, from their short Acquaintance, conceived quite so favourable an Opinion of his physical Abilities, as the good Woman, and all the Neighbourhood entertained; (and perhaps very rightly) for tho' I am afraid the Doctor was a little of a Coxcomb, he might be nevertheless very much of a Surgeon.

The Lieutenant having collected from the learned Discourse of the Surgeon, that Mr. *Jones* was in great Danger, gave Orders for keeping Mr. *Northerton* under a very strict Guard, designing in the Morning to attend him to a Justice of Peace, and to commit the conducting the Troops to *Gloucester* to the *French* Lieutenant, who, tho' he could neither read, write, nor speak any Language, was, however, a good Officer.

In the Evening our Commander sent a Message to Mr. *Jones*, that if a Visit would not be troublesome he would wait on him. This Civility was very kindly and thankfully received by *Jones*, and the Lieutenant accordingly went up to his Room, where he found the wounded Man much better than he expected; nay, *Jones* assured his Friend, that if he had not received express Orders to the contrary from the Surgeon, he should have got up long ago: For he appeared to himself to be as well as ever, and felt no other Inconvenience from his Wound but an extreme Soreness on that Side of his Head.

'I should be very glad,' quoth the Lieutenant, 'if you was as well as you fancy yourself: For then you could be able to do yourself Justice immediately; for when a Matter can't be made up, as in a Case of a Blow, the sooner you take him out the better; but I am afraid you think yourself better than you are, and he would have too much Advantage over you.'

[1] A hot drink of sherry (half a glass), milk (half a pint), and sugar. See also below, p. 536.

'I'll try, however,' answered *Jones*, 'if you please, and will be so kind to lend me a Sword: For I have none here of my own.'

'My Sword is heartily at your Service, my dear Boy,' cries the Lieutenant, kissing him, 'you are a brave Lad, and I love your Spirit; but I fear your Strength: For such a Blow, and so much Loss of Blood, must have very much weakened you; and tho' you feel no Want of Strength in your Bed, yet you most probably would after a Thrust or two. I can't consent to your taking him out To-night; but I hope you will be able to come up with us before we get many Days March advance; and I give you my Honour you shall have Satisfaction, or the Man who hath injured you shan't stay in our Regiment.'

'I wish,' said *Jones*, 'it was possible to decide this Matter To-night; now you have mentioned it to me, I shall not be able to rest.'

'O never think of it,' returned the other, 'a few Days will make no Difference. The Wounds of Honour are not like those in your Body. They suffer nothing by the Delay of Cure. It will be altogether as well for you, to receive Satisfaction a Week hence as now.'

'But suppose,' says *Jones*, 'I should grow worse, and die of the Consequences of my present Wound.'

'Then your Honour,' answered the Lieutenant, 'will require no Reparation at all. I myself will do Justice to your Character, and testify to the World your Intention to have acted properly, if you had recovered.'

'Still,' replied *Jones*, 'I am concerned at the Delay. I am almost afraid to mention it to you who are a Soldier; but tho' I have been a very wild young Fellow, still in my most serious Moments, and at the Bottom, I am really a Christian.'

'So am I too, I assure you,' said the Officer: 'And so zealous a one, that I was pleased with you at Dinner for taking up the Cause of your Religion; and I am a little offended with you now, young Gentleman, that you should express a Fear of declaring your Faith before any one.'

'But how terrible must it be,' cries *Jones*, 'to any one who is really a Christian, to cherish Malice in his Breast, in Opposition to the Command of him who hath expressly forbid it?[1] How can I

---

[1] See above, p. 52, n. 1. Like Steele and Richardson, Fielding condemned what he called 'the present abominable Custom of Duelling' (*The Covent-Garden Journal*,

bear to do this on a sick Bed? Or how shall I make up my Account, with such an Article as this in my Bosom against me?'

'Why I believe there is such a Command,' cries the Lieutenant; 'but a Man of Honour can't keep it. And you must be a Man of Honour, if you will be in the Army. I remember I once put the Case to our Chaplain over a Bowl of Punch, and he confessed there was much Difficulty in it; but he said, he hoped there might be a Latitude granted to Soldiers in this one Instance; and to be sure it is our Duty to hope so: For who would bear to live without his Honour? No, no, my dear Boy, be a good Christian as long as you live; but be a Man of Honour too, and never put up an Affront; not all the Books, nor all the Parsons in the World, shall ever persuade me to that. I love my Religion very well, but I love my Honour more. There must be some Mistake in the wording the Text, or in the Translation, or in the understanding it, or somewhere or other. But however that be, a Man must run the Risque, for he must preserve his Honour. So compose yourself To-night, and I promise you, you shall have an Opportunity of doing yourself Justice.' Here he gave *Jones* a hearty Buss, shook him by the Hand, and took his Leave.

But tho' the Lieutenant's Reasoning was very satisfactory to himself, it was not entirely so to his Friend. *Jones* therefore having revolved this Matter much in his Thoughts, at last came to a Resolution, which the Reader will find in the next Chapter.

## CHAPTER XIV

*A most dreadful Chapter indeed; and which few Readers ought to venture upon in an Evening, especially when alone.*

*J*ONES swallowed a large Mess of Chicken, or rather Cock, Broth, with a very good Appetite, as indeed he would have done the Cock it was made of, with a Pound of Bacon into the

7 January 1752; see Dudden, ii. 833, n. 1). Absurdly and in direct defiance of the precepts of morality and religion, *honour* in the 'Modern Glossary' had become synonymous with *duelling* (*The Covent-Garden Journal*, 14 January 1752)—a fact demonstrated at length in the character of Colonel Bath in *Amelia* (1751). Indeed, the irreconcilable opposition between Christian principles and the modern code of honour is a recurrent theme of that novel (see esp. IX. iii, XII. iii). See also the exchange between Valentine and Veromil in *The Temple Beau* (1730), II. xii. For the treatment of this theme by a divine whom Fielding greatly admired, see Robert South's sermon, 'The Fatal Influence of Words and Names Falsely Applied' (*Sermons Preached upon Several Occasions* [1865], i. 554–5).

Bargain; and now, finding in himself no Deficiency of either Health or Spirit, he resolved to get up and seek his Enemy.

But first he sent for the Serjeant, who was his first Acquaintance among these military Gentlemen. Unluckily that worthy Officer having, in a literal Sense, taken his Fill of Liquor, had been some Time retired to his Bolster, where he was snoring so loud, that it was not easy to convey a Noise in at his Ears capable of drowning that which issued from his Nostrils.

However, as *Jones* persisted in his Desire of seeing him, a vociferous Drawer at length found Means to disturb his Slumbers, and to acquaint him with the Message. Of which the Serjeant was no sooner made sensible, than he arose from his Bed, and having his Clothes already on, immediately attended. *Jones* did not think fit to acquaint the Serjeant with his Design, tho' he might have done it with great Safety; for the Halberdier was himself a Man of Honour, and had killed his Man. He would therefore have faithfully kept this Secret, or indeed any other which no Reward was published for discovering. But as *Jones* knew not those Virtues in so short an Acquaintance, his Caution was perhaps prudent and commendable enough.

He began therefore by acquainting the Serjeant, that as he was now entered into the Army, he was ashamed of being without what was perhaps the most necessary Implement of a Soldier, namely, a Sword; adding, that he should be infinitely obliged to him if he could procure one. 'For which,' says he, 'I will give you any reasonable Price. Nor do I insist upon its being Silver-hilted, only a good Blade, and such as may become a Soldier's Thigh.'

The Serjeant, who well knew what had happened, and had heard that *Jones* was in a very dangerous Condition, immediately concluded, from such a Message, at such a Time of Night, and from a Man in such a Situation, that he was light-headed. Now as he had his Wit (to use that Word in its common Signification) always ready, he bethought himself of making his Advantage of this Humour in the sick Man. 'Sir,' says he, 'I believe I can fit you. I have a most excellent Piece of Stuff by me. It is not indeed Silver-hilted, which, as you say, doth not become a Soldier; but the Handle is decent enough, and the Blade one of the best in *Europe*.—It is a Blade that—a Blade that—— In short, I will fetch it you this Instant, and you shall see it and handle it.—I am glad to see your Honour so well with all my Heart.'

Being instantly returned with the Sword, he delivered it to
*Jones*, who took it and drew it; and then told the Serjeant it
would do very well, and bid him name his Price.

The Serjeant now began to harangue in Praise of his Goods.
He said (nay he swore very heartily) 'that the Blade was taken
from a *French* Officer of very high Rank, at the Battle of *Dettingen*.[1]
I took it myself,' says he, 'from his Side, after I had knocked him
o' the Head. The Hilt was a golden one. That I sold to one of our
fine Gentlemen; for there are some of them, an't please your
Honour, who value the Hilt of a Sword more than the Blade.'

Here the other stopped him, and begged him to name a Price.
The Serjeant, who thought *Jones* absolutely out of his Senses,
and very near his End, was afraid, lest he should injure his
Family by asking too little.—However, after a Moment's
Hesitation, he contented himself with naming twenty Guineas,
and swore he would not sell it for less to his own Brother.

'Twenty Guineas!' says *Jones*, in the utmost Surprize, 'sure
you think I am mad, or that I never saw a Sword in my Life.
Twenty Guineas indeed! I did not imagine you would endeavour
to impose upon me.—Here, take the Sword—— No, now I
think on't, I will keep it myself, and shew it your Officer in the
Morning, acquainting him, at the same Time, what a Price you
asked me for it.'

The Serjeant, as we have said, had always his Wit (*in sensu
prædicto*)[2] about him, and now plainly saw that *Jones* was not in
the Condition he had apprehended him to be; he now, therefore,
counterfeited as great Surprize as the other had shewn, and said,
'I am certain, Sir, I have not asked you so much out of the way.
Besides, you are to consider, it is the only Sword I have, and I
must run the Risque of my Officer's Displeasure, by going without one myself. And truly, putting all this together, I don't
think twenty Shillings was so much out of the Way.'

'Twenty Shillings!' cries *Jones*, 'why you just now asked me
twenty Guineas.' 'How!' cries the Serjeant.—'Sure your Honour
must have mistaken me; or else I mistook myself—and indeed
I am but half awake.—Twenty Guineas indeed! no wonder your
Honour flew into such a Passion. I say twenty Guineas too.—No,

---

[1] The Battle of Dettingen (15 June 1743), in which George II led the Pragmatic Army
to victory over the French, marked the zenith of British fortunes in the Continental war.
[2] 'In the sense aforementioned'.

no, I meant twenty Shillings, I assure you. And when your Honour comes to consider every thing, I hope you will not think that so extravagant a Price. It is indeed true, you may buy a Weapon which looks as well for less Money. But——'

Here *Jones* interrupted him, saying, 'I will be so far from making any Words with you, that I will give you a Shilling more than your Demand.' He then gave him a Guinea, bid him return to his Bed, and wished him a good March; adding, he hoped to overtake them before the Division reached *Worcester*.

The Serjeant very civilly took his Leave, fully satisfied with his Merchandize, and not a little pleased with his dextrous Recovery from that false Step into which his Opinion of the Sick Man's Light-headedness had betrayed him.

As soon as the Serjeant was departed, *Jones* rose from his Bed, and dressed himself entirely, putting on even his Coat, which, as its Colour was white, shewed very visibly the Streams of Blood which had flowed down it; and now, having grasped his new-purchased Sword in his Hand, he was going to issue forth, when the Thought of what he was about to undertake laid suddenly hold of him, and he began to reflect that in a few Minutes he might possibly deprive a human Being of Life, or might lose his own. 'Very well,' said he, 'and in what Cause do I venture my Life? Why, in that of my Honour. And who is this human Being? A Rascal who hath injured and insulted me without Provocation. But is not Revenge forbidden by Heaven?—Yes, but it is enjoined by the World. Well, but shall I obey the World in Opposition to the express Commands of Heaven? Shall I incur the divine Displeasure rather than be called—Ha—Coward—Scoundrel?—I'll think no more, I am resolved and must fight him.'

The Clock had now struck Twelve, and every one in the House were in their Beds, except the Centinel who stood to guard *Northerton*, when *Jones* softly opening his Door, issued forth in Pursuit of his Enemy, of whose Place of Confinement he had received a perfect Description from the Drawer. It is not easy to conceive a much more tremendous Figure than he now exhibited. He had on, as we have said, a light-coloured Coat, covered with Streams of Blood. His Face, which missed that very Blood, as well as twenty Ounces more drawn from him by the Surgeon, was pallid. Round his Head was a Quantity of Bandage, not unlike a

Turban. In the right Hand he carried a Sword, and in the left a Candle. So that the bloody *Banquo*[1] was not worthy to be compared to him. In Fact, I believe a more dreadful Apparition was never raised in a Church-yard, nor in the Imagination of any good People met in a Winter Evening over a Christmas Fire in *Somersetshire*.

When the Centinel first saw our Heroe approach, his Hair began gently to lift up his Grenadier Cap; and in the same Instant his Knees fell to Blows with each other. Presently his whole Body was seized with worse than an Ague Fit. He then fired his Piece, and fell flat on his Face.

Whether Fear or Courage was the Occasion of his Firing, or whether he took Aim at the Object of his Terror, I cannot say. If he did, however, he had the good Fortune to miss his Man.

*Jones* seeing the Fellow fall, guessed the Cause of his Fright, at which he could not forbear smiling, not in the least reflecting on the Danger from which he had just escaped. He then passed by the Fellow, who still continued in the Posture in which he fell, and entered the Room where *Northerton*, as he had heard, was confined. Here, in a solitary Situation, he found—an empty Quart Pot standing on the Table, on which some Beer being spilt, it looked as if the Room had lately been inhabited; but at present it was entirely vacant.

*Jones* then apprehended it might lead to some other Apartment; but, upon searching all round it, he could perceive no other Door than that at which he entered, and where the Centinel had been posted. He then proceeded to call *Northerton* several Times by his Name; but no one answered; nor did this serve to any other Purpose than to confirm the Centinel in his Terrors, who was now convinced that the Volunteer was dead of his Wounds, and that his Ghost was come in Search of the Murtherer: He now lay in all the Agonies of Horror, and I wish, with all my Heart, some of those Actors, who are hereafter to represent a Man frighted out of his Wits, had seen him, that they might be taught to copy Nature instead of performing several antic Tricks and Gestures, for the Entertainment and Applause of the Galleries.

Perceiving the Bird was flown, at least despairing to find him, and rightly apprehending that the Report of the Firelock would alarm the whole House, our Heroe now blew out his Candle, and

[1] *Macbeth*, III. iv, IV. i.

gently stole back again to his Chamber, and to his Bed: Whither he would not have been able to have gotten undiscovered, had any other Person been on the same Stair-case, save only one Gentleman who was confined to his Bed by the Gout; for before he could reach the Door to his Chamber, the Hall where the Centinel had been posted was half full of People. Some in their Shirts, and others not half drest, all very earnestly enquiring of each other, what was the Matter?

The Soldier was now found lying in the same Place and Posture in which we just now left him. Several immediately applied themselves to raise him, and some concluded him dead: But they presently saw their Mistake; for he not only struggled with those who laid their Hands on him, but fell a roaring like a Bull. In reality, he imagined so many Spirits or Devils were handling him; for his Imagination being possessed with the Horror of an Apparition, converted every Object he saw or felt, into nothing but Ghosts and Spectres.

At length he was overpowered by Numbers, and got upon his Legs; when Candles being brought, and seeing two or three of his Comrades present, he came a little to himself; but when they asked him what was the Matter? he answered, 'I am a dead Man, that's all, I'm a dead Man. I can't recover it. I have seen him.' 'What hast thou seen, *Jack*,' says one of the Soldiers. 'Why, I have seen the young Volunteer that was killed Yesterday.' He then imprecated the most heavy Curses on himself, if he had not seen the Volunteer, all over Blood, vomiting Fire out of his Mouth and Nostrils, pass by him into the Chamber where Ensign *Northerton* was, and then seizing the Ensign by the Throat, fly away with him in a Clap of Thunder.

This Relation met with a gracious Reception from the Audience. All the Women present believed it firmly, and prayed Heaven to defend them from Murther. Amongst the Men too, many had Faith in the Story; but others turned it into Derision and Ridicule; and a Serjeant who was present, answered very coolly: 'Young Man, you will hear more of this for going to sleep, and dreaming on your Post.'

The Soldier replied, 'You may punish me if you please; but I was as broad awake as I am now; and the Devil carry me away, as he hath the Ensign, if I did not see the dead Man, as I tell you, with Eyes as big and as fiery as two large Flambeaux.'

The Commander of the Forces, and the Commander of the House, were now both arrived: For the former being awake at the Time, and hearing the Centinel fire his Piece, thought it his Duty to rise immediately, tho' he had no great Apprehensions of any Mischief; whereas the Apprehensions of the latter were much greater, lest her Spoons and Tankards should be upon the March, without having received any such Orders from her.

Our poor Centinel, to whom the Sight of this Officer was not much more welcome than the Apparition, as he thought it, which he had seen before, again related the dreadful Story, and with many Additions of Blood and Fire: But he had the Misfortune to gain no Credit with either of the last-mentioned Persons; for the Officer, tho' a very religious Man, was free from all Terrors of this Kind; besides, having so lately left *Jones* in the Condition we have seen, he had no Suspicion of his being dead. As for the Landlady, tho' not over religious, she had no kind of Aversion to the Doctrine of Spirits; but there was a Circumstance in the Tale which she well knew to be false, as we shall inform the Reader presently.

But whether *Northerton* was carried away in Thunder or Fire, or in whatever other Manner he was gone; it was now certain, that his Body was no longer in Custody. Upon this Occasion, the Lieutenant formed a Conclusion not very different from what the Serjeant is just mentioned to have made before, and immediately ordered the Centinel to be taken Prisoner. So that, by a strange Reverse of Fortune (tho' not very uncommon in a military Life) the Guard became the guarded.

## CHAPTER XV

*The Conclusion of the foregoing Adventure.*

BESIDES the Suspicion of Sleep, the Lieutenant harboured another, and worse Doubt, against the poor Centinel, and this was that of Treachery: For as he believed not one Syllable of the Apparition, so he imagined the whole to be an Invention, formed only to impose upon him, and that the Fellow had, in Reality, been bribed by *Northerton* to let him escape. And this he imagined the rather, as the Fright appeared to him, the more unnatural in one who had the Character of as brave and bold a Man as any in the Regiment, having been in several Actions, having received several Wounds, and, in a Word, having behaved himself always like a good and valiant Soldier.

That the Reader, therefore, may not conceive the least ill Opinion of such a Person, we shall not delay a Moment in rescuing his Character from the Imputation of this Guilt.

Mr. *Northerton* then, as we have before observed, was fully satisfied with the Glory which he had obtained from this Action. He had, perhaps, seen, or heard, or guessed, that Envy is apt to attend Fame. Not that I would here insinuate, that he was heathenishly inclined to believe in, or to worship, the Goddess *Nemesis*; for, in fact, I am convinced he never heard of her Name. He was, besides, of an active Disposition, and had a great Antipathy to those close Winter Quarters in the Castle of *Gloucester*, for which a Justice of Peace might possibly give him a Billet. Nor was he moreover free from some uneasy Meditations on a certain wooden Edifice, which I forbear to name, in Conformity to the Opinion of Mankind, who, I think, rather ought to honour than to be ashamed of this Building, as it is, or at least might be made, of more Benefit to Society than almost any other public Erection. In a Word, to hint at no more Reasons for his Conduct, Mr. *Northerton* was desirous of departing that Evening, and nothing remained for him but to contrive the *Quomodo*, which appeared to be a Matter of some Difficulty.

Now this young Gentleman, tho' somewhat crooked in his Morals, was perfectly strait in his Person, which was extremely strong and well made. His Face too was accounted handsome by the Generality of Women, for it was broad and ruddy, with tolerably good Teeth. Such Charms did not fail making an Impression on my Landlady, who had no little Relish for this kind of Beauty. She had, indeed, a real Compassion for the young Man; and hearing from the Surgeon that Affairs were like to go ill with the Volunteer, she suspected they might hereafter wear no benign Aspect with the Ensign. Having obtained, therefore, leave to make him a Visit, and finding him in a very melancholy Mood, which she considerably heightened, by telling him there were scarce any Hopes of the Volunteer's Life, she proceeded to throw forth some Hints, which the other readily and eagerly taking up, they soon came to a right Understanding; and it was at length agreed, that the Ensign should, at a certain Signal, ascend the Chimney, which communicating very soon with that of the Kitchen, he might there again let himself down; for which she would give him an Opportunity, by keeping the Coast clear.

But lest our Readers, of a different Complexion, should take this Occasion of too hastily condemning all Compassion as a Folly, and pernicious to Society, we think proper to mention another Particular, which might possibly have some little Share in this Action. The Ensign happened to be at this Time possessed of the Sum of fifty Pounds, which did indeed belong to the whole Company: For the Captain having quarreled with his Lieutenant, had entrusted the Payment of his Company to the Ensign. This Money, however, he thought proper to deposite in my Landlady's Hand, possibly by way of Bail or Security that he would hereafter appear and answer to the Charge against him; but whatever were the Conditions, certain it is, that she had the Money, and the Ensign his Liberty.

The Reader may, perhaps, expect, from the compassionate Temper of this good Woman, that when she saw the poor Centinel taken Prisoner for a Fact of which she knew him innocent, she should immediately have interposed in his Behalf; but whether it was that she had already exhausted all her Compassion in the above-mentioned Instance, or that the Features of this Fellow, tho' not very different from those of the Ensign, could not raise it, I will not determine; but far from being an Advocate for the present Prisoner, she urged his Guilt to his Officer, declaring with uplifted Eyes and Hands, that she would not have had any Concern in the Escape of a Murderer for all the World.

Every thing was now once more quiet; and most of the Company returned again to their Beds; but the Landlady, either from the natural Activity of her Disposition, or from her Fear for her Plate, having no Propensity to sleep, prevailed with the Officers, as they were to march within little more than an Hour, to spend that Time with her over a Bowl of Punch.

*Jones* had lain awake all this while, and had heard great Part of the Hurry and Bustle that had passed, of which he had now some Curiosity to know the Particulars. He therefore applied to his Bell, which he rung at least twenty Times without any Effect; for my Landlady was in such high Mirth with her Company, that no Clapper could be heard there but her own, and the Drawer and

Chambermaid, who were sitting together in the Kitchen, (for neither durst he sit up, nor she lie in Bed alone) the more they heard the Bell ring, the more they were frightened, and, as it were, nailed down in their Places.

At last, at a lucky Interval of Chat, the Sound reached the Ears of our good Landlady, who presently sent forth her Summons, which both her Servants instantly obeyed. '*Joo*,' says the Mistress, 'don't you hear the Gentleman's Bell ring? why don't you go up?' 'It is not my Business,' answered the Drawer, 'to wait upon the Chambers. It is *Betty* Chambermaid's!' 'If you come to that,' answered the Maid, 'it is not my Business to wait upon Gentlemen. I have done it, indeed, sometimes; but the Devil fetch me if ever I do again, since you make your Preambles about it.' The Bell still ringing violently, their Mistress fell into a Passion, and swore, if the Drawer did not go up immediately, she would turn him away that very Morning. 'If you do, Madam,' says he, 'I can't help it. I won't do another Servant's Business.' She then applied herself to the Maid, and endeavoured to prevail by gentle Means; but all in vain, *Betty* was as inflexible as *Joo*. Both insisted it was not their Business, and they would not do it.

The Lieutenant then fell a laughing, and said, 'Come, I will put an End to this Contention;' and then turning to the Servants, commended them for their Resolution, in not giving up the Point; but added, he was sure, if one would consent to go, the other would. To which Proposal they both agreed in an Instant, and accordingly went up very lovingly and close together. When they were gone, the Lieutenant appeased the Wrath of the Landlady, by satisfying her why they were both so unwilling to go alone.

They returned soon after, and acquainted their Mistress, that the sick Gentleman was so far from being dead, that he spoke as heartily as if he was well; and that he gave his Service to the Captain, and should be very glad of the Favour of seeing him before he marched.

The good Lieutenant immediately complied with his Desires, and sitting down by his Bed-side, acquainted him with the Scene which had happened below, concluding with his Intentions to make an Example of the Centinel.

Upon this, *Jones* related to him the whole Truth, and earnestly begged him not to punish the poor Soldier, 'who, I am confident,' says he, 'is as innocent of the Ensign's Escape, as he is of forging any Lie, or of endeavouring to impose on you.'

The Lieutenant hesitated a few Moments, and then answered: 'Why, as you have cleared the Fellow of one Part of the Charge, so it will be impossible to prove the other; because he was not the only Centinel. But I have a good mind to punish the Rascal for being a Coward. Yet who knows what Effect the Terror of such an Apprehension may have; and to say the Truth, he hath always behaved well against an Enemy. Come, it is a good Thing to see any Sign of Religion in these Fellows; so I promise you he shall be set at liberty when we march. But hark, the General beats. My dear Boy, give me another Buss. Don't discompose nor hurry yourself; but remember the Christian Doctrine of Patience, and I warrant you will soon be able to do yourself Justice, and to take an honourable Revenge on the Fellow who hath injured you.' The Lieutenant then departed, and *Jones* endeavoured to compose himself to Rest.

# BOOK VIII

*Containing above two Days.*

## CHAPTER I

*A wonderful long Chapter concerning the Marvellous; being much the longest of all our introductory Chapters.*

AS we are now entering upon a Book, in which the Course of our History will oblige us to relate some Matters of a more strange and surprizing Kind than any which have hitherto occurred, it may not be amiss in the prolegomenous, or introductory Chapter, to say something of that Species of Writing which is called the Marvellous[1]. To this we shall, as well for the

---

[1] Throughout this chapter Fielding applies to his own 'new species of writing' the familiar assumptions and arguments of neoclassical criticism of the epic. Drawing upon Aristotle (*Poetics*, ix, xxiv. 15–17, 19), the French critics had distinguished two contrary elements in 'the Fable' of the heroic poem: these were 'the Probable' ('la Vraisemblance')—the representation of such characters and actions as conform to the commonly received notions of human behaviour and therefore do not strain the credulity of the reader; and 'the Marvellous' ('l'Admirable')—the representation of such characters, actions and circumstances as contradict normal human experience and the ordinary course of nature. (Among the chief expositors of this distinction were Rapin, *Reflections on Aristotle's Treatise of Poesie*, trans. Rymer [1674], Pt. I, sec. xxii–xxiv and Pt. II, sec. xii; Le Bossu, *Traité du poëme épique* [Paris, 1675], Bk. III, chs. vii–viii; and André Dacier in the remarks to his translation of the *Poetics* [Paris, 1692].) By adhering to the rule of probability alone, a fable becomes worthy of the reader's belief, but it is likely to be dull; by containing too much of the marvellous, it may surprise and entertain, but it will do so to no purpose, since the reader will dismiss the performance as mere fantasy.

The province of the poet, moreover, differs from that of the historian or the romance writer. Truth, the recording of things as they actually are, is the business of the historian, who on occasion must therefore deal in matters stranger than fiction, relating what is possible to occur but not probable. The marvellous, freely indulged, is the stuff of romance. But the probable is the special concern of the poet, whose aim is to represent not what *did* happen or what possibly *might* happen, but what *should* happen; the poet deals not in particular facts, but in universal and general truths, and he prefers, as Aristotle expressed it, 'what is convincing though impossible' to 'what is possible and unconvincing' (*Poetics*, xxiv. 19). The theory and the ideal were summarized by Addison in *The Spectator*, no. 315 (1 March 1712):

'. . . the Fable of an Epic Poem should abound in Circumstances that are both credible and astonishing; or as the *French* Critics chuse to phrase it, the Fable should be filled with the Probable and the Marvellous. . . . If the Fable is only Probable, it differs

Sake of ourselves, as of others, endeavour to set some certain
Bounds; and indeed nothing can be more necessary, as Criticks*
of different Complexions are here apt to run into very different
Extremes; for while some are, with M. *Dacier*,¹ ready to allow,
that the same Thing which is impossible may be yet probable,†
others have so little Historic or Poetic Faith, that they believe
nothing to be either possible or probable, the like to which hath
not occurred to their own Observation.

First then, I think, it may very reasonably be required of every

* By this Word here, and in most other Parts of our Work, we mean every Reader
in the World.

† It is happy for M. *Dacier* that he was not an *Irishman*.²

---

nothing from a true History; if it is only Marvellous, it is no better than a Romance.
The great Secret therefore of Heroic Poetry is to relate such Circumstances, as may
produce in the Reader at the same time both Belief and Astonishment.'
For a comprehensive discussion of the subject, see H. T. Swedenberg, Jr., *The Theory of the
Epic in England, 1650–1800* (Berkeley and Los Angeles, Cal., 1944), ch. x.

¹ André Dacier (1651–1722), husband of Mme Dacier (see above, p. 372, n. 2), in *La
Poëtique d'Aristote traduite en françois avec des remarques* (Paris, 1692), commenting upon
*Poetics*, xxv. 31 (xxiv. 19 in the Loeb Classical Library edition). In his 'Observations on the
Tenth Book' of the *Odyssey*—to which Fielding alludes in the following paragraph (see
below, p. 397, n. 1)—Broome explains the passage in Dacier as follows: 'How are these
incredible stories to be reduc'd into the bounds of probability ? 'tis true, the Marvellous
ought to be used in Epic Poetry; but ought it to transgress all power of belief ? *Aristotle* in
his *Art of Poetry* lays down a rule to justifie these incidents: *A Poet*, says that Author, *ought
to prefer things impossible, provided they are probable, before things possible, that are nevertheless incredible.* . . . This rule is not without obscurity; but Monsieur *Dacier* has explain'd
it in his Annotations upon that Author: A thing may be impossible, and yet probable:
Thus when the Poet introduces a Deity, any incident humanly impossible receives a full
probability by being ascribed to the skill and power of a God' (Pope's *Odyssey* [1725]).
Fielding compliments Dacier later in *Tom Jones*, p. 569.

² The Irish were noted for the sort of self-contradictory assertion (later called an 'Irish
bull') which Fielding here remarks in Dacier. (See A. M. Hyamson, *Dictionary of English
Phrases* [1922], s.v. 'Bull', and E. Partridge, *Dictionary of Slang and Unconventional
English* [1961].) Thus in x. ii, Mr. Fitzpatrick declares that he would have caught up with
his errant wife, 'if I had not found her gone just as I came up with her'; and in the same
chapter, Mr. MacLachlan is equally muddled as he assures his compatriot that Mrs.
Waters is not his wife: 'don't I see that the Lady, whom the Gentleman who stands here in
his Shirt is lying in Bed with, is none of her ?' The point of Fielding's footnote seems to be
that, if Dacier had been an Irishman, his paradox would have been dismissed as such another
logical blunder. It may also be worth noting that in *The Champion* (29 January 1739/40)
Fielding had associated Irishmen with French pedagogues for the reason that they were
both adepts in the 'Science' of 'Impudence', the latter pretending to more knowledge than
they possessed. For a discussion of contemporary opinions of the Irish character, see *A
Modest Argument, Pro and Con, Enquiring into the Causes Why Base and Mean Actions should
be Committed by the Irish in particular, more than any other Nation* (1731). See also below,
pp. 601, n. 1; 828.

Writer, that he keeps within the Bounds of Possibility; and still remembers that what it is not possible for Man to perform, it is scarce possible for Man to believe he did perform. This Conviction, perhaps, gave Birth to many Stories of the antient Heathen Deities (for most of them are of poetical Original). The Poet, being desirous to indulge a wanton and extravagant Imagination, took Refuge in that Power, of the Extent of which his Readers were no Judges, or rather which they imagined to be infinite, and consequently they could not be shocked at any Prodigies related of it. This hath been strongly urged in Defence of *Homer's* Miracles; and it is, perhaps, a Defence; not, as Mr. *Pope* would have it,[1] because *Ulysses* told a Set of foolish Lies to the *Phæacians*, who were a very dull Nation; but because the Poet himself wrote to Heathens, to whom poetical Fables were Articles of Faith.[2] For my own Part, I must confess, so compassionate is my Temper, I wish *Polypheme*[3] had confined himself to his Milk Diet, and preserved his Eye; nor could *Ulysses* be much more concerned than myself, when his Companions were turned into Swine by *Circe*,[4] who shewed, I think, afterwards, too much Regard for Man's Flesh to be supposed capable of converting it into Bacon. I wish, likewise, with all my Heart, that *Homer* could have known the Rule prescribed by *Horace*,[5] to introduce

[1] Though found in Pope's *Odyssey*, the passage to which Fielding alludes is by William Broome (1689–1745), who merely repeated Dacier's interpretation (see *La Poëtique d'Aristote* [Paris, 1692], p. 408). In his 'Observations on the Tenth Book' of the *Odyssey*, Broome explains how Homer shrewdly brought such marvellous episodes as those of Circe and Polyphemus 'within the degrees' of probability: 'he makes *Ulysses* relate them before a credulous and ignorant assembly; he lets us into the character of the *Phæacians*, by saying they were a very dull nation, in the sixth book,

*Where never Science rear'd her laurel'd Head.*

It is thus the Poet gives probability to his fables, by reciting them to a people who believ'd them, and who thro' a laziness of life were fond of romantic stories; he adapts himself to his audience. . . .'

[2] According to Aristotle (cf. *Poetics*, xxiv. 19), the inclusion of fabulous episodes in a fiction could be justified if the poet's audience believed them to be true. Thus Addison observed that 'a *well chosen* Fable' must relate 'such things as have really happened, or at least . . . such things as have happen'd according to the received Opinions of Mankind', and he proceeded to illustrate this principle by reference to the extraordinary episodes of *Paradise Lost*, which, 'though they are very astonishing in themselves, are not only credible, but actual Points of Faith'. (*Spectator*, No. 315 [1 March 1712].)

[3] *Odyssey*, ix.                                                     [4] Ibid., x.

[5] *Ars Poetica*, 191–2: 'nec deus intersit, nisi dignus vindice nodus/ inciderit' ('And let no god intervene, unless a knot come worthy of such a deliverer'—trans. H. R. Fairclough, Loeb Classical Library, 1929). See *Jonathan Wild* (1743), II. xii, where Fielding quotes this passage and comments upon it. See also *Tom Jones*, pp. 512; 876, n. 1.

supernatural Agents as seldom as possible. We should not then have seen his Gods coming on trivial Errands, and often behaving themselves so as not only to forfeit all Title to Respect, but to become the Objects of Scorn and Derision.[1] A Conduct which must have shocked the Credulity of a pious and sagacious Heathen; and which could never have been defended, unless by agreeing with a Supposition to which I have been sometimes almost inclined, that this most glorious Poet, as he certainly was, had an Intent to burlesque the superstitious Faith of his own Age and Country.

But I have rested too long on a Doctrine which can be of no Use to a Christian Writer: For as he cannot introduce into his Works any of that heavenly Host which make a Part of his Creed;[2] so is it horrid Puerility to search the Heathen Theology for any of those Deities who have been long since dethroned from their Immortality.[3] Lord *Shaftesbury* observes,[4] that nothing

---

[1] Cf. Longinus' complaint that Homer's representation of the pranks and passions of the gods was 'utterly irreligious' and a violation of poetic decorum (*On the Sublime*, ix. 7— trans. W. H. Fyfe, Loeb Classical Library, 1927). Later critics, such as Sir Richard Blackmore, similarly regretted that in his irreverent treatment of the gods Homer had debased the dignity of the epic by admitting into his poem 'such Strains as have an Air of Raillery and Burlesque': 'And as by introducing into Heaven Farce and Buffoonery, an improper Place for such Diversion, he has broken in upon the Congruity and Decency which should always be preserv'd in the Characters, so he transgresses the Rule, that banishes in general from Heroick Works, all comick Manners, witty Conceits and Ridicule . . .' (*Essays upon Several Subjects*, i [1716], 75–6).

[2] A majority of critics followed Boileau (*L'Art poétique* [1674], iii. 199–204) in opposing the use of Christian 'machines' in the epic, despite the formidable example of Milton and the authority of those such as Dryden and Addison who approved his practice. Dennis was particularly adamant on this point, invoking Boileau's argument: 'That the Terrible Mysteries of the Christian Faith are not capable of delightful Ornaments. That the Gospel offers nothing to us but Repentance on the one side, or Eternal Torments on the other, and that the Criminal mixture of Poetical Fictions gives a Fabulous Air, even to its most Sacred Truths.' ('Remarks on *Prince Arthur*' [1696], in *Critical Works*, ed. E. N. Hooker, i [1939], 53; and 'Observations on the *Paradise Lost* of Milton' [1721], ibid., ii [1943], 228–9.) For a thorough discussion of the subject, see H. T. Swedenberg, op. cit., ch. xi.

[3] Though the critics disagreed about the propriety of Christian machinery in a modern epic, they were unanimous in condemning the use of mythological deities. With Fielding's phrasing, compare Addison's in *Spectator*, No. 523 (30 October 1712): '*Virgil* and *Homer* might compliment their Heroes, by interweaving the Actions of Deities with their Atchievements; but for a Christian Author to write in the Pagan Creed . . . would be downright Puerility, and unpardonable in a Poet that is past Sixteen.'

[4] In 'A Letter concerning Enthusiasm', section 1. On the poetic practice of invoking the Muse, Shaftesbury (see above, p. 217, n. 2) addresses Lord Somers: 'You must certainly have observ'd our Poets under a remarkable Constraint, when oblig'd to assume this

is more cold than the Invocation of a Muse by a Modern; he might have added that nothing can be more absurd. A modern may with much more Elegance invoke a Ballad, as some have thought *Homer* did,[1] or a Mug of Ale with the Author of *Hudibras*;[2] which latter may perhaps have inspired much more Poetry as well as Prose, than all the Liquors of *Hippocrene* or *Helicon*.

The only supernatural Agents which can in any Manner be allowed to us Moderns are Ghosts;[3] but of these I would advise an Author to be extremely sparing. These are indeed like Arsenic, and other dangerous Drugs in Physic, to be used with the utmost Caution; nor would I advise the Introduction of them at all in those Works, or by those Authors to which, or to whom a Horse-Laugh in the Reader, would be any great Prejudice or Mortification.

Character: and you have wonder'd, perhaps, why that Air of *Enthusiasm*, which sits so gracefully with an Antient, shou'd be so spiritless and aukard [*sic*] in a Modern' (*Characteristicks*, 5th ed. [1732], i. 4). In *Ovid's Art of Love Paraphrased* (1747) Fielding had expressed the view that his author's invocation of Venus was 'a manifest Burlesque' of a silly convention. Referring to this same passage from Shaftesbury, he continued: 'For my own part, I must confess, I cannot perceive *that graceful Air of Enthusiasm* which a noble Author observes in the Invocation of the Antients; many of them indeed seem to have been too apparently in jest, to endeavour to impose on their Readers, and in reality to apply to the Muses with less Devotion than our modern Poets, many of whom perhaps believe as much in those Deities as in any other.'

[1] Richard Bentley (1662–1742), the brilliant if controversial classicist, was the principal advocate of the view that Homer 'wrote a sequel of Songs and Rhapsodies, to be sung by himself for small earnings and good cheer, at Festivals and other days of Merriment; the *Ilias* he made for the Men, and the *Odysseis* for the other Sex. These loose Songs were not collected together in the form of an Epic Poem till *Pisistratus's* Time, above 500 years after.' (Bentley, 'Remarks upon a Late Discourse of Free-Thinking' [1713], in *Enchiridion Theologicum* [Oxford, 1792], v. 94.) Fielding had earlier ridiculed the theory in *Joseph Andrews* (1742; II. i), and in *A Journey from This World to the Next* (1743; I. viii) Homer himself finds it preposterous.

[2] See above, p. 151, n. 1.

[3] In his essay 'Of Heroique Playes' prefixed to *The Conquest of Granada* (1672), Dryden had defended the use of 'Spirits, or Spectres' in heroic poetry, citing the examples of Virgil, Ariosto, Tasso, and Spenser:

'. . . I dare farther affirm that the whole Doctrine of separated beings, whether those Spirits are incorporeal substances, (which Mr. *Hobbs*, with some reason thinks to imply a contradiction,) or that they are a thinner and more Aerial sort of bodies (as some of the Fathers have conjectur'd) may better be explicated by Poets, than by Philosophers or Divines. . . .

'Some men think they have rais'd a great argument against the use of Spectres and Magique in Heroique Poetry, by saying, They are unnatural: but, whether they or I believe there are such things, is not material, 'tis enough that, for ought we know, they may be in Nature: and what ever is or may be, is not, properly, unnatural.' (Sig. a4)

As for Elves and Fairies, and other such Mummery,[1] I purposely omit the Mention of them, as I should be very unwilling to confine within any Bounds those surprizing Imaginations, for whose vast Capacity the Limits of human Nature are too narrow; whose Works are to be considered as a new Creation; and who have consequently just Right to do what they will with their own. Man therefore is the highest Subject (unless on very extraordinary Occasions indeed) which presents itself to the Pen of our Historian, or of our Poet; and in relating his Actions, great Care is to be taken, that we do not exceed the Capacity of the Agent we describe.

Nor is Possibility alone sufficient to justify us, we must keep likewise within the Rules of Probability. It is, I think, the Opinion of *Aristotle*; or if not, it is the Opinion of some wise Man, whose Authority will be as weighty, when it is as old; 'that it is no Excuse for a Poet who relates what is incredible, that the thing related is really Matter of Fact.'[2] This may perhaps be allowed true with regard to Poetry, but it may be thought impracticable to extend it to the Historian: For he is obliged to record Matters as he finds them;[3] though they may be of so extraordinary a Nature, as will require no small Degree of historical Faith to swallow them. Such was the successless Armament of *Xerxes*, described by *Herodotus*,[4] or the successful

---

[1] Fielding's disdainful repudiation of the fantastic and preternatural as proper subjects for fiction reflects the usual critical response to the epic narratives of Ariosto, Tasso, and Spenser, who, straining to astonish their readers with marvellous adventures, entirely disregarded the rules of probability. Spenser, Rymer had complained, 'suffer'd himself to be misled by *Ariosto*; with whom blindly rambling on *marvellous* Adventures, he makes no Conscience of *Probability*. All is fanciful and chimerical, without any Uniformity, without any Foundation in Truth; his Poem is perfect *Fairy-Land*' (Preface to Rapin's *Reflexions on Aristotle's Treatise of Poesy*, in *The Whole Critical Works of Monsieur Rapin*, 3rd ed. [1731], ii. 114). See also Davenant, *Discourse upon Gondibert* (1650), pp. 10–13; Shaftesbury, 'Advice to an Author', in *Characteristicks*, 5th ed. (1732), i. 344–7; and Blackmore, *Essays upon Several Subjects*, i (1716), 31–3. With the language of the present paragraph, compare *Joseph Andrews* (1742; III. i), where Fielding satirizes 'those Persons of surprising Genius, the Authors of immense Romances, or the modern Novel and *Atalantis* Writers; who without any Assistance from Nature or History, record Persons who never were, or will be, and Facts which never did nor possibly can happen: Whose Heroes are of their own Creation, and their Brains the Chaos whence all their Materials are collected'.

[2] Cf. *Poetics*, xxiv. 19: 'What is convincing though impossible should always be preferred to what is possible and unconvincing' (trans. W. H. Fyfe, Loeb Classical Library, 1927). [3] Cf. *Poetics*, ix. 1–3.

[4] Herodotus, *History*, vii. 20–1 and *passim*—relating the preparations of Xerxes' armies for the invasion of Greece.

Expedition of *Alexander* related by *Arrian*.[1] Such of later Years
was the Victory of *Agincourt* obtained by *Harry* the Fifth,[2] or that
of *Narva*, won by *Charles* the Twelfth of *Sweden*.[3] All which
Instances, the more we reflect on them, appear still the more
astonishing.

Such Facts, however, as they occur in the Thread of the Story;
nay, indeed, as they constitute the essential Parts of it, the
Historian is not only justifiable in recording as they really
happened; but indeed would be unpardonable, should he omit or
alter them. But there are other Facts not of such Consequence
nor so necessary, which tho' ever so well attested, may nevertheless be sacrificed to Oblivion in Complaisance to the Scepti-
cism of a Reader. Such is that memorable Story of the Ghost of
*George Villers*,[4] which might with more Propriety have been
made a Present of to Dr. *Drelincourt*,[5] to have kept the Ghost of
Mrs. *Veale* Company, at the Head of his Discourse upon Death,
than have been introduced into so solemn a Work as the History
of the Rebellion.

To say the Truth, if the Historian will confine himself to what
really happened, and utterly reject any Circumstance, which, tho'
never so well attested, he must be well assured is false, he will

---

[1] Arrian's *Anabasis* recounts the campaigns of Alexander in seven books.

[2] The battle of Agincourt (1415), in which the English bowmen defeated a much larger
force of French knights.

[3] On 20 November 1700, Charles XII defeated a powerful Russian army that had laid
siege to Narva. For an account of this battle, 'which will be always famous in history', see
Gustavus Adlerfeld, *The Military History of Charles XII. King of Sweden* (1740), i. 50–7—
a translation from the French in which Fielding assisted.

[4] The story is told in *The True Historical Narrative of the Rebellion and Civil Wars in
England* (1702–4), Book I, by Edward Hyde (1609–74), Earl of Clarendon—a work which
Fielding had earlier ridiculed for its 'Tory' bias (see *Joseph Andrews* [1742; III. i]).
Clarendon relates that some six months before the Duke of Buckingham was assassinated in
1628, the ghost of his father, Sir George Villiers, appeared three times to a royal officer at
Windsor Castle, telling the man to warn Buckingham that unless he courted popular
favour, he would soon die. With the present passage, compare Hogarth's 'Credulity,
Superstition, and Fanaticism' (1762), in which two of the three ghostly figures decorating
the pulpit of the enthusiastical preacher are those of George Villiers and Mrs. Veale (see
below, n. 5).

[5] Charles Drelincourt (1595–1669), a French Protestant clergyman and author of
several pious works. His *Consolations* (1669) was translated into English in 1675 under the
title, *The Christian's Defence Against the Fears of Death*. To the fourth edition (1706) was
prefixed Defoe's 'True Relation of the Apparition of one Mrs. Veale, the next Day after her
Death, to one Mrs. Bargrave, at Canterbury, the 8th of September, 1705'—the ghost of
Mrs. Veale having recommended Drelincourt's book as 'the best . . . on that Subject, ever
wrote'.

sometimes fall into the Marvellous, but never into the Incredible. He will often raise the Wonder and Surprize of his
Reader, but never that incredulous Hatred mentioned by *Horace*.¹
It is by falling into Fiction therefore, that we generally offend
against this Rule, of deserting Probability, which the Historian
seldom if ever quits, till he forsakes his Character, and com-
mences a Writer of Romance. In this, however, those Historians
who relate publick Transactions, have the Advantage of us who
confine ourselves to Scenes of private Life. The Credit of the
former is by common Notoriety supported for a long Time; and
public Records, with the concurrent Testimony of many Authors
bear Evidence to their Truth in future Ages. Thus a *Trajan* and
an *Antoninus*, a *Nero* and a *Caligula*,² have all met with the Belief
of Posterity; and no one doubts but that Men so very good, and
so very bad, were once the Masters of Mankind.

But we who deal in private Character, who search into the
most retired Recesses, and draw forth Examples of Virtue and
Vice, from Holes and Corners of the World, are in a more
dangerous Situation. As we have no publick Notoriety, no concurrent Testimony, no Records to support and corroborate what
we deliver, it becomes us to keep within the Limits not only of
Possibility, but of Probability too; and this more especially in
painting what is greatly good and amiable. Knavery and Folly,
though never so exorbitant, will more easily meet with Assent;
for Ill-nature adds great Support and Strength to Faith.

Thus we may, perhaps, with little Danger relate the History of
*Fisher*;³ who having long owed his Bread to the Generosity of Mr.

---

¹ *Ars Poetica*, 188: 'incredulus odi.'

² Trajan (ruled A.D. 98–117) and either Antoninus Pius (138–61) or Marcus Aurelius
Antoninus (161–80)—probably the latter (see below, p. 406.1)—are mentioned as
excellent Roman emperors, in contrast to Nero (54–68) and Caligula (37–41).

³ On the night of 10 April 1727 Henry Fisher (b. *c*. 1704), an attorney, murdered and
robbed his benefactor, one Widdrington Darby, clerk of the Prothonotary's Office in Hare-
Court, the Inner Temple. Though arrested some three weeks later and committed to
Newgate, Fisher escaped on 17 May, the day before his trial, in the company of the notori-
ous criminal, Roger Johnson. He fled to the Continent, where he remained at large.
Fisher's villainy was not soon forgotten (see, for example, the facetious item in *The General
Advertiser* [4 February 1746/7], listing him among the Pretender's retinue in Scotland); but
Fielding's circumstantial knowledge of a crime committed more than twenty years earlier
may be owing to his friendship with Richard Willoughby (see below, p. 458, n. 1), who
was living at the time in Southampton Buildings, where Fisher, too, resided. Fisher's guilt
was discovered when 'Mr. Willoughby, his Landlord, a Gentleman of Worth and Reputation', became suspicious and caused his apartment to be searched. (For details of the

*Derby*, and having one Morning received a considerable Bounty from his Hands, yet in order to possess himself of what remained in his Friend's Scrutore, concealed himself in a public Office of the Temple, through which there was a Passage into Mr. *Derby's* Chambers. Here he overheard Mr. *Derby* for many Hours solacing himself at an Entertainment which he that Evening gave his Friends, and to which *Fisher* had been invited. During all this Time, no tender, no grateful Reflections arose to restrain his Purpose; but when the poor Gentleman had let his Company out through the Office, *Fisher* came suddenly from his lurking Place, and walking softly behind his Friend into his Chamber, discharged a Pistol Ball into his Head. This may be believed, when the Bones of *Fisher* are as rotten as his Heart. Nay, perhaps, it will be credited that the Villain went two Days afterwards with some young Ladies to the Play of *Hamlet*;[1] and with an unaltered Countenance heard one of the Ladies, who little suspected how near she was to the Person, cry out, Good God! if the Man that murdered Mr. *Derby* was now present! Manifesting in this a more seared and callous Conscience than even *Nero* himself; of whom we are told by *Suetonius*, 'that the Consciousness of his Guilt after the Death of his Mother became immediately intolerable, and so continued; nor could all the Congratulations of the Soldiers, of the Senate, and the People, allay the Horrors of his Conscience.'[2]

But now, on the other hand, should I tell my Reader, that I had known a Man[3] whose penetrating Genius had enabled him to raise a large Fortune in a Way where no Beginning was chaulked out to him: That he had done this with the most perfect Preservation of his Integrity, and not only without the least Injustice or Injury to any one individual Person, but with the highest Advantage to Trade, and a vast Increase of the public Revenue: That he had expended one Part of the Income of this Fortune in

crime, which Fielding accurately describes, see the accounts in *The Weekly Journal: or, The British Gazetteer*, 15, 29 April, 6, 13, 20 May 1727; also *The British Journal* and *The London Journal* for these dates; and *The London Gazette*, 11–15, 25–9 April, 16–20 May 1727. See also *A Full and Particular Account of the Life and Notorious Transactions of Roger Johnson* [1740], pp. 20–1.)

[1] The only performance of *Hamlet* between the time of the murder and Fisher's arrest was at Drury Lane, 15 April 1727.
[2] Suetonius, *The Lives of the Cæsars*, VI. xxxiv. 4.
[3] Ralph Allen (see above, p. 4, n. 1).

discovering a Taste superior to most, by Works where the highest Dignity was united with the purest Simplicity, and another Part in displaying a Degree of Goodness superior to all Men, by Acts of Charity to Objects whose only Recommendations were their Merits, or their Wants: That he was most industrious in searching after Merit in Distress, most eager to relieve it, and then as careful (perhaps too careful) to conceal what he had done: That his House, his Furniture, his Gardens, his Table, his private Hospitality, and his public Beneficence all denoted the Mind from which they flowed, and were all intrinsically rich and noble, without Tinsel, or external Ostentation: That he filled every Relation in Life with the most adequate Virtue: That he was most piously religious to his Creator, most zealously loyal to his Sovereign; a most tender Husband to his Wife, a kind Relation, a munificent Patron, a warm and firm Friend, a knowing and a chearful Companion, indulgent to his Servants, hospitable to his Neighbours, charitable to the Poor, and benevolent to all Mankind. Should I add to these the Epithets of wise, brave, elegant, and indeed every other amiable Epithet in our Language, I might surely say,

———*Quis credet? nemo Hercule! nemo;*
*Vel duo, vel nemo.*[1]

And yet I know a Man who is all I have here described. But a single Instance (and I really know not such another) is not sufficient to justify us, while we are writing to thousands who never heard of the Person, nor of any Thing like him. Such *Raræ Aves*[2] should be remitted to the Epitaph-Writer,[3] or to some Poet, who may condescend to hitch him in a Distich, or to slide him into a Rhime with an Air of Carelessness and Neglect, without giving any Offence to the Reader.[4]

---

[1] 'Who will believe it? No one, by Hercules! no one; maybe one or two, maybe no one'— slightly altered from Persius, *Satires*, i. 2–3.

[2] See above, p. 188, n. 2.

[3] See above, p. 114, n. 1.

[4] The phrasing echoes Pope in *The First Satire of the Second Book of Horace Imitated* (1733), 77–9: 'Who-e'er offends, at some unlucky Time/ Slides into Verse, and hitches in a Rhyme,/ Sacred to Ridicule!' Thus Pope had protested that his satire was discriminating and judicious, punishing only those who deserved castigation. But, Fielding here implies, when Pope came to praise his good friend Ralph Allen, his method was similarly 'to hitch him in a Distich'—the famous, but almost insultingly inadequate tribute of the *Epilogue to the Satires. Dialogue I* (1738), 135–6: 'Let humble ALLEN, with an aukward Shame,/ Do good by stealth, and blush to find it Fame.' (See the Dedication, p. 6, where Fielding

In the last Place, the Actions should be such as may not only be within the Compass of human Agency, and which human Agents may probably be supposed to do; but they should be likely for the very Actors and Characters themselves to have performed: For what may be only wonderful and surprizing in one Man, may become improbable, or indeed impossible, when related of another.

This last Requisite is what the dramatic Critics call Conservation of Character,¹ and it requires a very extraordinary Degree of Judgment, and a most exact Knowledge of human Nature.

It is admirably remarked by a most excellent Writer,² That Zeal can no more hurry a Man to act in direct Opposition to itself, than a rapid Stream can carry a Boat against its own Current. I will venture to say, that for a Man to act in direct Contradiction to the Dictates of his Nature, is, if not impossible, as improbable and as miraculous as any Thing which can well be conceived.

quotes from this couplet.) Prompted by Pope's condescension to Allen, the sarcasm in this passage is a rare exception to the laudatory tenor of Fielding's other public allusions to the poet, whom he greatly admired. For the most part, he regarded Pope as 'a Genius of the highest Rank' (see below, p. 406), yet it is clear from his early unpublished verses that Fielding sometimes found the poet's spitefulness and pride offensive. (See I. Grundy, 'New Verse by Henry Fielding', *PMLA*, lxxxvii [1972], 213–45.)

¹ Cf. Aristotle, *Poetics*, xv. 4, and Horace, *Ars Poetica*, 119–27. The rule stipulated that a dramatic character, if drawn from history or tradition, must be represented throughout in a manner consistent with the expectations of the audience; if invented by the author, the character must be self-consistent or, according to Horace, must be 'kept to the end even as it came forth at the first' (trans. H. R. Fairclough, Loeb Classical Library, 1929). Fielding's phrase echoes Boileau: 'Conservez à chacun son propre caractère' (*L'Art poétique*, ed. D. N. Smith [Cambridge, 1931], iii. 112). In *Jonathan Wild* (1743; IV. xiv) Fielding designed the final act of his hero's life—Wild on the gallows having picked the parson's pocket of a bottle-screw—'to shew the most admirable Conservation of Character . . . to the last moment'.

² George Lyttelton (see above, p. 3, n. 1) in *Observations on the Conversion and Apostleship of St. Paul* (May 1747): 'The power of imagination in enthusiastical minds is no doubt very strong, but always acts in conformity to the opinions imprinted upon it at the time of its working, and can no more act against them, than a rapid river can carry a boat against the current of its own stream' (*Works*, ed. G. E. Ayscough [1774], p. 316). In context this is Lyttelton's crucial argument to prove that St. Paul's conversion on the road to Damascus was a true miracle and, consequently, that Christianity itself is a divine revelation: since, Lyttelton maintains, Paul set out on his journey not only disbelieving the Christian faith but intending to persecute its followers, his sudden transformation from infidel to believer cannot be explained by reference to natural causes. For another compliment to Lyttelton as 'a Master of Style, as of every other Excellence', see Fielding's Preface to his sister's *Familiar Letters between the Principal Characters in David Simple* (1747). Later in *Tom Jones* (XVIII. iv) Lyttelton's *Observations* is part of the background of Square's conversion (see below, p. 952, n. 2).

Should the best Parts of the Story of *Marcus Antoninus* be ascribed to *Nero*, or should the worst Incidents of *Nero's* Life be imputed to *Antoninus*, what would be more shocking to Belief than either Instance; whereas both these being related of their proper Agent, constitute the Truly Marvellous.

Our modern Authors of Comedy have fallen almost universally into the Error here hinted at: Their Heroes generally are notorious Rogues, and their Heroines abandoned Jades, during the first four Acts; but in the fifth, the former become very worthy Gentlemen, and the latter, Women of Virtue and Discretion: Nor is the Writer often so kind as to give himself the least Trouble, to reconcile or account for this monstrous Change and Incongruity. There is, indeed, no other Reason to be assigned for it, than because the Play is drawing to a Conclusion; as if it was no less natural in a Rogue to repent in the last Act of a Play, than in the last of his Life; which we perceive to be generally the Case at *Tyburn*,[1] a Place which might, indeed, close the Scene of some Comedies with much Propriety, as the Heroes in these are most commonly eminent for those very Talents which not only bring Men to the Gallows, but enable them to make an heroic Figure when they are there.

Within these few Restrictions, I think, every Writer may be permitted to deal as much in the Wonderful as he pleases; nay, if he thus keeps within the Rules of Credibility, the more he can surprize the Reader, the more he will engage his Attention, and the more he will charm him. As a Genius of the highest Rank observes in his 5th Chapter of the *Bathos*, 'The great Art of all Poetry is to mix Truth with Fiction; in order to join the Credible with the Surprizing.'[2]

For though every good Author will confine himself within the

---

[1] The place of public execution in London. Until 1759 the gallows was a permanent structure situated on Tyburn Road near what is now Marble Arch. Fielding's comparison between the theatre and the scene at Tyburn (see also below, p. 875) was not as far-fetched as it may seem. 'Hanging days', which occurred eight times a year, were rowdy and festive occasions. Stands were erected and large crowds gathered to witness the spectacle and to hear the last confessions of the condemned. For a contemporary description of a typical hanging-day at Tyburn—'The Tragic-Comedy of the *Dark Leap*', as the writer calls it—see *A Trip from St. James's to the Royal Exchange* (1744), pp. 42–50. In *An Enquiry into the Causes of the Late Increase of Robbers* (1751), section xi, Fielding condemned this custom of turning so serious an occasion into an entertaining holiday for the mob.

[2] Pope's *Peri Bathous: or, Martinus Scriblerus His Treatise of the Art of Sinking in Poetry* (1728), ch. v.

Bounds of Probability, it is by no means necessary that his Characters, or his Incidents, should be trite, common, or vulgar; such as
happen in every Street, or in every House, or which may be met
with in the home Articles of a News-paper. Nor must he be
inhibited from shewing many Persons and Things, which may
possibly have never fallen within the Knowledge of great Part of
his Readers. If the Writer strictly observes the Rules above-
mentioned, he hath discharged his Part; and is then intitled to
some Faith from his Reader, who is indeed guilty of critical
Infidelity if he disbelieves him. For want of a Portion of such
Faith, I remember the Character of a young Lady of Quality,[1]
which was condemned on the Stage for being unnatural, by
the unanimous Voice of a very large Assembly of Clerks and
Apprentices; tho' it had the previous Suffrages of many Ladies of
the first Rank; one of whom very eminent for her Understanding,
declared it was the Picture of half the young People of her
Acquaintance.

## CHAPTER II

*In which the Landlady pays a Visit to Mr.* Jones.

WHEN *Jones* had taken Leave of his Friend the Lieutenant,
he endeavoured to close his Eyes, but all in vain; his
Spirits were too lively and wakeful to be lulled to Sleep. So having
amused, or rather tormented himself with the Thoughts of his
*Sophia*, till it was open Day-light, he called for some Tea; upon
which Occasion my Landlady herself vouchsafed to pay him a
Visit.

This was indeed the first Time she had seen him, or at least
had taken any Notice of him; but as the Lieutenant had assured
her that he was certainly some young Gentleman of Fashion, she
now determined to shew him all the Respect in her Power: for, to
speak truly, this was one of those Houses where Gentlemen, to
use the Language of Advertisements, meet with civil Treatment
for their Money.

[1] Probably Lady Charlotte in Fielding's own play, *The Modern Husband* (1732), which
was hissed the night of its first performance at Drury Lane. The person who approved the
characterization is likely to have been Fielding's cousin, Lady Mary Wortley Montagu
(1689–1762), to whom he had submitted the manuscript for criticism.

She had no sooner begun to make his Tea, than she likewise began to discourse. 'La! Sir,' said she, 'I think it is great Pity that such a pretty young Gentleman should undervalue himself so, as to go about with these Soldier Fellows. They call themselves Gentlemen, I warrant you; but, as my first Husband used to say, they should remember it is we that pay them. And to be sure it is very hard upon us to be obliged to pay them, and to keep 'em too, as we Publicans are.[1] I had twenty of 'um last Night, besides Officers; nay, for matter o' that, I had rather have the Soldiers than Officers: For nothing is ever good enough for those Sparks; and I am sure if you was to see the Bills; La, Sir, it is nothing. I have had less Trouble, I warrant you, with a good Squire's Family, where we take forty or fifty Shillings of a Night, besides Horses. And yet I warrants me, there is *narrow* a one of all those Officer Fellows, but looks upon himself to be as good as *arrow* a Squire of 500 *l.* a Year. To be sure it doth me Good to hear their Men run about after 'um, crying your Honour, and your Honour. Marry come up with such Honour, and an Ordinary at a Shilling a Head. Then there's such Swearing among 'um, to be sure, it frightens me out o' my Wits, I thinks nothing can ever prosper with such wicked People. And here one of 'um has used you in so barbarous a Manner. I thought indeed how well the rest would secure him; they all hang together; for if you had been in Danger of Death, which I am glad to see you are not, it would have been all as one to such wicked People. They would have let the Murderer go. Laud have Mercy upon 'um, I would not have such a Sin to answer for, for the whole World. But tho' you are likely, with the Blessing to recover, there is Laa for him yet, and if you will employ Lawyer *Small*, I darest be sworn he'll make the Fellow fly the Country for him; tho' perhaps he'll have fled the Country before; for it is here To-day and gone To-morrow with such Chaps. I hope, however, you will learn more Wit for the future, and return back to your Friends; I warrant they are all miserable for your Loss; and if they was but to know what had happened. La, my seeming! I would not for the World they should. Come, come, we know very well what all the Matter is;

---

[1] According to the annual statute against Mutiny and Desertion, the keepers of inns and ale-houses were required to provide food and lodging for the Army at a rate *per diem* of 4*d.* for a foot-soldier and 1*s.* for a commissioned officer below the rank of captain. (See Barlow, *The Justice of the Peace* [1745], s.v. 'Soldiers'.)

but if one won't, another will, so pretty a Gentleman need never
want a Lady. I am sure if I was as you, I would see the finest She
that ever wore a Head hanged, before I would go for a Soldier for
her.—Nay, don't blush so; (for indeed he did to a violent
Degree) why, you thought, Sir, I knew nothing of the Matter,
I warrant you, about Madam *Sophia*.' 'How,' says *Jones*, starting
up, 'do you know my *Sophia*?' 'Do I? ay marry,' cries the Landlady, 'many's the Time hath she laid in this House.' 'With her
Aunt, I suppose,' says *Jones*.—'Why there it is now,' cries the
Landlady. 'Ay, ay, ay, I know the old Lady very well. And a
sweet young Creature is Madam *Sophia*, that's the Truth on't.'
'A sweet Creature!' cries *Jones*, 'Oh Heavens!

> *Angels are painted fair to look like her.*
> *There's in her all that we believe of Heaven,*
> *Amazing Brightness, Purity and Truth,*
> *Eternal Joy, and everlasting Love.*[1]

'And could I ever have imagined that you had known my
*Sophia*.' 'I wish,' says the Landlady, 'you knew half so much of
her. What would you have given to have sat by her Bed-side?
What a delicious Neck she hath! Her lovely Limbs have stretched
themselves in that very Bed you now lie in.' 'Here!' cries *Jones*,
'hath *Sophia* ever lain here?'—'Ay, ay, here; there; in that very
Bed,' says the Landlady, 'where I wish you had her this Moment;
and she may wish so too, for any thing I know to the contrary:
For she hath mentioned your Name to me.'—'Ha,' cries he, 'did
she ever mention her poor *Jones*?—You flatter me now, I can
never believe so much.' 'Why then,' answered she, 'as I hope to
be sav'd, and may the Devil fetch me, if I speak a Syllable more
than the Truth. I have heard her mention Mr. *Jones*; but in a
civil and modest Way, I confess; yet I could perceive she thought
a great deal more than she said.' 'O my dear Woman,' cries *Jones*,
'her Thoughts of me I shall never be worthy of. O she is all
Gentleness, Kindness, Goodness. Why was such a Rascal as I
born, ever to give her soft Bosom a Moment's Uneasiness? Why
am I cursed? I, who would undergo all the Plagues and Miseries
which any Dæmon ever invented for Mankind, to procure her
any Good; nay, Torture itself could not be Misery to me, did I

---

[1] Jones applies to Sophia, Jaffeir's apostrophe to woman in Otway's *Venice Preserv'd*
(1682), I. i.

but know that she was happy.' 'Why look you there now,' says the Landlady, 'I told her you was a constant Lovier.' 'But pray, Madam, tell me when or where you knew any thing of me; for I never was here before, nor do I remember ever to have seen you.' 'Nor is it possible you should,' answered she, 'for you was a little Thing when I had you in my Lap at the Squire's.'—'How, the Squire's,' says *Jones*, 'what do you know that great and good Mr. *Allworthy* then?' 'Yes, marry do I,' says she; 'Who in the Country doth not?'—'The Fame of his Goodness indeed,' answered *Jones*, 'must have extended farther than this; but Heaven only can know him, can know that Benevolence which it copied from itself, and sent upon Earth as its own Pattern. Mankind are as ignorant of such divine Goodness, as they are unworthy of it; but none so unworthy of it as myself. I who was raised by him to such a Height; taken in, as you must well know, a poor base-born Child, adopted by him, and treated as his own Son to dare by my Follies to disoblige him, to draw his Vengeance upon me. Yes, I deserve it all: For I will never be so ungrateful as ever to think he hath done an Act of Injustice by me. No, I deserve to be turned out of Doors, as I am. And now, Madam,' says he, 'I believe you will not blame me for turning Soldier, especially with such a Fortune as this in my Pocket.' At which Words he shook a Purse which had but very little in it, and which still appeared to the Landlady to have less.

My good Landlady was, (according to vulgar Phrase) struck all of a Heap by this Relation. She answered coldly, 'That to be sure People were the best Judges what was most proper for their Circumstances.—But hark,' says she, 'I think I hear some body call. Coming! coming! the Devil's in all our Volk, nobody hath any Ears. I must go down Stairs, if you want any more Breakfast, the Maid will come up. Coming!' At which Words, without taking any Leave, she flung out of the Room: For the lower Sort of People are very tenacious of Respect; and tho' they are contented to give this *gratis* to Persons of Quality, yet they never confer it on those of their own Order, without taking Care to be well paid for their Pains.

## CHAPTER III

*In which the Surgeon makes his second Appearance.*

BEFORE we proceed any farther, that the Reader may not be mistaken in imagining the Landlady knew more than she did, nor surprized that she knew so much, it may be necessary to inform him, that the Lieutenant had acquainted her that the Name of *Sophia* had been the Occasion of the Quarrel; and as for the rest of her Knowledge, the sagacious Reader will observe how she came by it in the preceding Scene. Great Curiosity was indeed mixed with her Virtues; and she never willingly suffered any one to depart from her House without enquiring as much as possible into their Names, Families and Fortunes.

She was no sooner gone, than *Jones*, instead of animadverting on her Behaviour, reflected that he was in the same Bed, which he was informed had held his dear *Sophia*. This occasioned a thousand fond and tender Thoughts, which we would dwell longer upon, did we not consider that such kind of Lovers will make a very inconsiderable Part of our Readers.

In this Situation the Surgeon found him, when he came to dress his Wound. The Doctor, perceiving, upon Examination, that his Pulse was disordered, and hearing that he had not slept, declared that he was in great Danger: For he apprehended a Fever was coming on; which he would have prevented by Bleeding, but *Jones* would not submit, declaring he would lose no more Blood; and 'Doctor,' says he, 'if you will be so kind only to dress my Head, I have no Doubt of being well in a Day or two.'

'I wish,' answered the Surgeon, 'I could assure your being well in a Month or two. Well, indeed! No, no, People are not so soon well of such Contusions; but, Sir, I am not at this Time of Day to be instructed in my Operations by a Patient, and I insist on making a Revulsion[1] before I dress you.'

*Jones* persisted obstinately in his Refusal, and the Doctor at last yielded; telling him at the same Time, that he would not be answerable for the ill Consequence, and hoped he would do him the Justice to acknowledge that he had given him a contrary Advice; which the Patient promised he would.

---

[1] In medicine, the withdrawal of an inflammation from a diseased part of the body by operating upon another part—in this instance, by bleeding.

The Doctor retired into the Kitchen, where, addressing himself to the Landlady, he complained bitterly of the undutiful Behaviour of his Patient, who would not be blooded, though he was in a Fever.

'It is an eating Fever then,' says the Landlady: 'For he hath devoured two swinging buttered Toasts this Morning for Breakfast.'

'Very likely,' says the Doctor, 'I have known People eat in a Fever; and it is very easily accounted for; because the Acidity occasioned by the febrile Matter, may stimulate the Nerves of the Diaphragm, and thereby occasion a Craving, which will not be easily distinguishable from a natural Appetite; but the Aliment will not be concreted, nor assimilated into Chyle, and so will corrode the vascular Orifices, and thus will aggravate the febrific Symptoms. Indeed I think the Gentleman in a very dangerous Way, and, if he is not blooded, I am afraid will die.'

'Every Man must die some Time or other,' answered the good Woman; 'it is no Business of mine. I hope, Doctor, you would not have me hold him while you bleed him.——But, harkee, a Word in your Ear, I would advise you before you proceed too far, to take care who is to be your Paymaster.'

'Paymaster!' said the Doctor, staring, 'why, I've a Gentleman under my Hands, have I not?'

'I imagined so as well as you,' said the Landlady; 'but as my first Husband used to say, every Thing is not what it looks to be. He is an arrant Scrub, I assure you. However, take no Notice that I mentioned any thing to you of the Matter; but I think People in Business *oft* always to let one another know such Things.'

'And have I suffered such a Fellow as this,' cries the Doctor, in a Passion, 'to instruct me? Shall I hear my Practice insulted by one who will not pay me! I am glad I have made this Discovery in Time. I will see now whether he will be blooded or no.' He then immediately went up Stairs, and flinging open the Door of the Chamber with much Violence, awaked poor *Jones* from a very sound Nap, into which he was fallen, and what was still worse, from a delicious Dream concerning *Sophia*.

'Will you be blooded or no?' cries the Doctor, in a Rage. 'I have told you my Resolution already,' answered *Jones*, 'and I wish with all my Heart you had taken my answer: For you have awaked me out of the sweetest Sleep which I ever had in my Life.'

'Ay, ay,' cries the Doctor, 'many a Man hath dosed away his Life. Sleep is not always good, no more than Food; but remember I demand of you, for the last Time, will you be blooded?' 'I answer you for the last Time,' said *Jones*, 'I will not.' 'Then I wash my Hands of you,' cries the Doctor, 'and I desire you to pay me for the Trouble I have had already. Two Journeys at 5s. each, two Dressings at 5s. more, and half a Crown for Phlebotomy.' 'I hope,' said *Jones*, 'you don't intend to leave me in this Condition.' 'Indeed but I shall,' said the other. 'Then,' said *Jones*, 'you have used me rascally, and I will not pay you a Farthing.' 'Very well,' cries the Doctor, 'the first Loss is the best. What a Pox did my Landlady mean by sending for me to such Vagabonds?' At which Words he flung out of the Room, and his Patient turning himself about, soon recovered his Sleep; but his Dream was unfortunately gone.

## CHAPTER IV

*In which is introduced one of the pleasantest Barbers that was ever recorded in History, the Barber of* Bagdad,[1] *or he in* Don Quixotte[2] *not excepted.*

THE Clock had now struck Five, when *Jones* awaked from a Nap of seven Hours, so much refreshed, and in such perfect Health and Spirits, that he resolved to get up and dress himself: for which Purpose he unlocked his Portmanteau, and took out clean Linnen, and a Suit of Cloaths; but first he slipt on a Frock, and went down into the Kitchen to bespeak something that might pacify certain Tumults he found rising within his Stomach.

Meeting the Landlady, he accosted her with great Civility, and asked 'what he could have for Dinner.' 'For Dinner!' says she, 'it is an odd Time a Day to think about Dinner. There is nothing drest in the House, and the Fire is almost out.' 'Well but,' says he, 'I must have something to eat, and it is almost indifferent to

---

[1] The barber of Baghdad is introduced in Vol. ii of *The Arabian Nights* (English trans. 1706, from the French of Antoine Galland). Though an incessant prattler and a boaster who represents himself as something of a universal genius, he goes by 'the honourable Title of Silent'.

[2] Nicholas, introduced in *Don Quixote* (Motteux-Ozell version), Pt. i, Bk. i, ch. 5. For Fielding's opinion of Cervantes, see below, p. 686, n. 1.

me what: For to tell you the Truth, I was never more hungry in my Life.' 'Then,' says she, 'I believe there is a Piece of cold Buttock and Carrot, which will fit you.'—'Nothing better,' answered *Jones*, 'but I should be obliged to you, if you would let it be fried.' To which the Landlady consented, and said smiling, 'she was glad to see him so well recovered:' For the Sweetness of our Heroe's Temper was almost irresistable; besides, she was really no ill-humoured Woman at the Bottom; but she loved Money so much, that she hated every Thing which had the Semblance of Poverty.

*Jones* now returned in order to dress himself, while his Dinner was preparing, and was, according to his Orders, attended by the Barber.

This Barber, who went by the Name of little *Benjamin*, was a Fellow of great Oddity and Humour, which had frequently led him into small Inconveniencies, such as Slaps in the Face, Kicks in the Breech, broken Bones, &c. For every one doth not understand a Jest; and those who do, are often displeased with being themselves the Subjects of it. This Vice was, however, incurable in him; and though he had often smarted for it, yet if ever he conceived a Joke, he was certain to be delivered of it, without the least Respect of Persons, Time, or Place.

He had a great many other Particularities in his Character, which I shall not mention, as the Reader will himself very easily perceive them, on his farther Acquaintance with this extraordinary Person.

*Jones* being impatient to be drest, for a Reason which may easily be imagined, thought the Shaver was very tedious in preparing his Suds, and begged him to make Haste; to which the other answered, with much Gravity: For he never discomposed his Muscles on any Account. '*Festina lente*[1] is a Proverb which I learnt long before I ever touched a Razor.' 'I find, Friend, you are a Scholar,' replied *Jones*. 'A poor one,' said the Barber, '*non omnia possumus omnes*.'[2] 'Again!' said *Jones*; 'I fancy you are good at capping Verses.'[3] 'Excuse me, Sir,' said the Barber, '*non tanto*

---

[1] 'Make haste slowly'—a favourite maxim of Augustus Caesar, according to Suetonius, and also of Erasmus. (See King's *Classical Quotations*, 1887.)

[2] See above, p. 178, n. 3.

[3] A contest in which each participant tries to 'cap' a classical verse quoted by his opponent with another beginning with the last letter of the verse his rival has used. For an example, see *Joseph Andrews* (1742; II. xi).

*me dignor honore.*'¹ And then proceeding to his Operation, 'Sir,' said he, 'since I have dealt in Suds, I could never discover more than two Reasons for shaving, the one is to get a Beard, and the other to get rid of one. I conjecture, Sir, it may not be long since you shaved, from the former of these Motives. Upon my Word you have had good Success, for one may say of your Beard, that it is *Tondenti gravior.*'² 'I conjecture,' says *Jones*, 'that thou art a very comical Fellow.' 'You mistake me widely, Sir,' said the Barber, 'I am too much addicted to the Study of Philosophy, *Hinc illæ Lacrymæ,*³ Sir, that's my Misfortune. Too much Learning hath been my Ruin.' 'Indeed,' says *Jones*, 'I confess, Friend, you have more Learning than generally belongs to your Trade; but I can't see how it can have injured you.' 'Alas, Sir,' answered the Shaver, 'my Father disinherited me for it. He was a Dancing-Master; and because I could read, before I could dance, he took an Aversion to me, and left every Farthing among his other Children.—Will you please to have your Temples—— O la! I ask your Pardon, I fancy there is *Hiatus in manuscriptis.* I heard you was going to the Wars: but I find it was a Mistake.' 'Why do you conclude so?' says *Jones*. 'Sure, Sir,' answered the Barber, 'you are too wise a Man to carry a broken Head thither; for that would be carrying Coals to *Newcastle.*'

'Upon my Word,' cries *Jones*, 'thou art a very odd Fellow, and I like thy Humour extremely; I shall be very glad if thou wilt come to me after Dinner, and drink a Glass with me; I long to be better acquainted with thee.'

'O dear Sir,' said the Barber, 'I can do you twenty times as great a Favour, if you will accept of it.' 'What is that, my Friend,' cries *Jones*. 'Why, I will drink a Bottle with you, if you please; for I dearly love Good-nature, and as you have found me out to be a comical Fellow, so I have no Skill in Physiognomy, if you are not one of the best-natured Gentlemen in the Universe.' *Jones* now walked down Stairs neatly drest, and perhaps the fair *Adonis* was not a lovelier Figure; and yet he had no Charms for my Land-lady: For as that good Woman did not resemble *Venus* at all in her

---

¹ 'I do not deem myself worthy of so much honour.' Cf. Virgil, *Aeneid*, i. 335: 'haud equidem tali me dignor honore.' See below, p. 419, n. 2.

² 'Troublesome to the one shaving.'

³ 'Hence proceed all those tears'—a proverbial expression found, for example, in Terence *Andria* (i. i) and Horace, *Epistles* (i. xix. 41).

Person, so neither did she in her Taste.[1] Happy had it been for *Nancy* the Chambermaid, if she had seen with the Eyes of her Mistress; for that poor Girl fell so violently in love with *Jones* in five Minutes, that her Passion afterwards cost her many a Sigh. This *Nancy* was extremely pretty, and altogether as coy; for she had refused a Drawer, and one or two young Farmers in the Neighbourhood, but the bright Eyes of our Heroe thawed all her Ice in a Moment.

When *Jones* returned to the Kitchen, his Cloth was not yet laid; nor indeed was there any Occasion it should, his Dinner remaining in *Statu quo*, as did the Fire which was to dress it. This Disappointment might have put many a philosophical Temper into a Passion; but it had no such Effect on *Jones*. He only gave the Landlady a gentle Rebuke, saying, 'Since it was so difficult to get it heated, he would eat the Beef cold.' But now the good Woman, whether moved by Compassion, or by Shame, or by whatever other Motive, I cannot tell, first gave her Servants a round Scold for disobeying the Orders which she had never given, and then bidding the Drawer lay a Napkin in the Sun, she set about the Matter in good earnest, and soon accomplished it.

This Sun, into which *Jones* was now conducted, was truly named as *Lucus a non lucendo*;[2] for it was an Apartment into which the Sun had scarce ever looked. It was indeed the worst Room in the House; and happy was it for *Jones* that it was so. However, he was now too hungry to find any Fault; but having once satisfied his Appetite, he ordered the Drawer to carry a Bottle of Wine into a better Room, and expressed some Resentment at having been shewn into a Dungeon.

The Drawer having obeyed his Commands, he was, after some Time, attended by the Barber; who would not indeed have suffered him to wait so long for his Company, had he not been listening in the Kitchen to the Landlady, who was entertaining a Circle that she had gathered round her with the History of poor *Jones*, Part of which she had extracted from his own Lips, and the other Part was her own ingenious Composition; 'for,' she said, 'he was a poor Parish Boy, taken into the House of Squire

---

[1] Cf. Ovid, *Metamorphoses*, x. 520–59, 708–39.

[2] 'A grove is so called from its not giving light'—found in Quintilian as an example of 'the derivation of certain words from their opposites' (*Institutio Oratoria*, I. vi. 34—trans. H. E. Butler, Loeb Classical Library, 1920). See also *The Covent-Garden Journal* (9 May 1752).

*Allworthy,* where he was bred up as an Apprentice, and now turned out of Doors for his Misdeeds, particularly for making Love to his young Mistress, and probably for robbing the House; for how else should he come by the little Money he hath. And this,' says she, 'is your Gentleman, forsooth.' 'A Servant of Squire *Allworthy*!' says the Barber, 'what's his Name?' —'Why he told me his Name was *Jones*,' says she, 'perhaps he goes by a wrong Name. Nay, and he told me too, that the Squire had maintained him as his own Son, *thof* he had quarrelled with him now.' 'And if his Name be *Jones,* he told you the Truth,' said the Barber; 'for I have Relations who live in that Country, nay, and some People say he is his Son.' 'Why doth he not go by the Name of his Father?' 'I can't tell that,' said the Barber, 'many People's Sons don't go by the Name of their Father.' 'Nay,' said the Landlady, 'if I thought he was a Gentleman's Son, *thof* he was a Bye Blow, I should behave to him in anotherguess Manner; for many of these Bye Blows come to be great Men; and, as my poor first Husband used to say, Never affront any Customer that's a Gentleman.'

## CHAPTER V

### *A Dialogue between Mr.* Jones *and the Barber.*

THIS Conversation passed partly while *Jones* was at Dinner in his Dungeon, and partly while he was expecting the Barber in the Parlour. And, as soon as it was ended, Mr. *Benjamin,* as we have said, attended him, and was very kindly desired to sit down. *Jones* then filling out a Glass of Wine, drank his Health by the Appellation of *Doctissime Tonsorum.*[1] *'Ago tibi Gratias, Domine,'*[2] said the Barber, and then looking very stedfastly at *Jones,* he said, with great Gravity, and with a seeming Surprize, as if he had recollected a Face he had seen before, 'Sir, may I crave the Favour to know if your Name is not *Jones*?' To which the other answered, That it was. *'Proh Deum atque Hominum Fidem,'*[3]

---

[1] 'Most learned of barbers.'
[2] 'I give you thanks, master.'
[3] Terence, *Andria,* I. v: 'O, by the faith of gods and men!' See below, p. 419, n. 2.

says the Barber, 'how strangely Things come to pass. Mr. *Jones*, I am your most obedient Servant. I find you do not know me, which indeed is no Wonder, since you never saw me but once, and then you was very young. Pray, Sir, how doth the good Squire *Allworthy*? How doth *Ille optimus omnium Patronus*?'[1] 'I find,' said *Jones*, 'you do indeed know me; but I have not the like Happiness of recollecting you.'—'I do not wonder at that,' cries *Benjamin*; 'but I am surprized I did not know you sooner, for you are not in the least altered. And pray, Sir, may I without Offence enquire whither you are travelling this Way?' 'Fill the Glass, Mr. Barber,' said *Jones*, 'and ask no more Questions.' 'Nay, Sir,' answered *Benjamin*, 'I would not be troublesome; and I hope you don't think me a Man of an impertinent Curiosity, for that is a Vice which nobody can lay to my Charge; but I ask Pardon, for when a Gentleman of your Figure travels without his Servants, we may suppose him to be, as we say, in *Casu incognito*,[2] and perhaps I ought not to have mentioned your Name.' 'I own,' says *Jones*, 'I did not expect to have been so well known in this Country as I find I am, yet, for particular Reasons, I shall be obliged to you if you will not mention my Name to any other Person, till I am gone from hence.' '*Pauca Verba*,'[3] answered the Barber; 'and I wish no other here knew you but myself; for some People have Tongues; but I promise you I can keep a Secret. My Enemies will allow me that Virtue.' 'And yet that is not the Characteristic of your Profession, Mr. Barber,' answered *Jones*. 'Alas, Sir,' replied *Benjamin*, '*Non si male nunc et olim sic erit*.[4] I was not born nor bred a Barber, I assure you. I have spent most of my Time among Gentlemen, and tho' I say it, I understand something of Gentility. And if you had thought me as worthy of your Confidence as you have some other People, I should have shewn you I could have kept a Secret better. I should not have degraded your Name in a public Kitchen; for indeed, Sir, some People have not used you well; for besides making a public Proclamation of what you told them of a Quarrel between your-

[1] 'That best patron of all.' Cf. Catullus, *Poems* xlix, 7. See below, p. 419, n. 2.

[2] 'Some unknown misfortune', with a pun perhaps—since Partridge was once a school-master—on *casus* in the grammatical sense of *case*.

[3] 'Few words.' Cf. Lucan, *Pharsalia*, ix. 188-9, and Sir Hugh Evans in *The Merry Wives of Windsor*, I. i: 'Pauca verba, Sir John; goot worts.'

[4] Horace, *Odes*, II. x. 17-18: 'If we fare ill today, 'twill not be ever so' (trans. C. E. Bennett, Loeb Classical Library, 1914).

self and Squire *Allworthy*, they added Lies of their own, Things which I knew to be Lies.' 'You surprize me greatly,' cries *Jones*. 'Upon my Word, Sir,' answered *Benjamin*, 'I tell the Truth, and I need not tell you my Landlady was the Person. I am sure it moved me to hear the Story, and I hope it is all false; for I have a great Respect for you, I do assure you I have, and have had, ever since the Good-nature you shewed to *Black George*, which was talked of all over the Country, and I received more than one Letter about it. Indeed it made you beloved by every body. You will pardon me, therefore; for it was real Concern at what I heard made me ask any Questions; for I have no impertinent Curiosity about me; but I love Good-nature, and thence became *Amoris abundantia ergo Te.*'[1]

Every Profession of Friendship easily gains Credit with the Miserable; it is no wonder, therefore, if *Jones*, who, besides his being miserable, was extremely open-hearted, very readily believed all the Professions of *Benjamin*, and received him into his Bosom. The Scraps of *Latin*, some of which *Benjamin* applied properly enough, tho' it did not savour of profound Literature,[2] seemed yet to indicate something superior to a common Barber, and so indeed did his whole Behaviour. *Jones* therefore believed the Truth of what he had said, as to his Original and Education, and at length, after much Entreaty, he said, 'Since you have heard, my Friend, so much of my Affairs, and seem so desirous to know the Truth, if you will have Patience to hear it, I will inform you of the whole.' 'Patience,' cries *Benjamin*, 'that I will, if the Chapter was never so long, and I am very much obliged to you for the Honour you do me.'

*Jones* now began, and related the whole History, forgetting only a Circumstance or two, namely, every thing which passed on that Day in which he had fought with *Thwackum*, and ended with his Resolution to go to Sea, till the Rebellion in the North had

---

[1] 'An abundance of love towards you'—cf. Cicero, *Ad Familiares*, I. ix. I.

[2] For the most part, Partridge's 'Scraps of *Latin*' are either proverbial expressions or they were used as illustrative examples in William Lily's grammar, the standard textbook of the period. The verses from Virgil (p. 415, n. 1) and Terence (p. 417, n. 3), for instance, may be found in *A Short Introduction to Grammar* [1720], pp. 154, 171, and *Lily's Rules Construed* [1720], pp. 64, 88. These verses, together with the quotation from Catullus (p. 418, n. 1), also appear in the Eton Latin grammar, based on Lily, with which Fielding would have been thoroughly acquainted (see *An Introduction to the Latin Tongue, for the Use of Youth* [Eton, 1758], pp. 88 and 153, 96, 106, and 175).

made him change his Purpose, and had brought him to the Place where he then was.

Little *Benjamin*, who had been all Attention, never once inter-rupted the Narrative; but when it was ended, he could not help observing, that there must be surely something more invented by his Enemies, and told Mr. *Allworthy* against him, or so good a Man would never have dismissed one he had loved so tenderly, in such a Manner. To which *Jones* answered, 'He doubted not but such villanous Arts had been made use of to destroy him.'

And surely it was scarce possible for any one to have avoided making the same Remark with the Barber; who had not, indeed, heard from *Jones* one single Circumstance upon which he was condemned; for his Actions were not now placed in those injurious Lights, in which they had been misrepresented to *Allworthy*: Nor could he mention those many false Accusations which had been from time to time preferred against him to *Allworthy*; for with none of these he was himself acquainted. He had likewise, as we have observed, omitted many material Facts in his present Relation. Upon the whole, indeed, every thing now appeared in such favourable Colours to *Jones*, that Malice itself would have found it no easy Matter to fix any Blame upon him.

Not that *Jones* desired to conceal or to disguise the Truth; nay, he would have been more unwilling to have suffered any Censure to fall on Mr. *Allworthy* for punishing him, than on his own Actions for deserving it; but, in Reality, so it happened, and so it always will happen: For let a Man be never so honest, the Account of his own Conduct will, in Spite of himself, be so very favour-able, that his Vices will come purified through his Lips, and, like foul Liquors well strained, will leave all their Foulness behind. For tho' the Facts themselves may appear, yet so different will be the Motives, Circumstances, and Consequences, when a Man tells his own Story, and when his Enemy tells it, that we scarce can recognize the Facts to be one and the same.

Tho' the Barber had drank down this Story with greedy Ears, he was not yet satisfied. There was a Circumstance behind, which his Curiosity, cold as it was, most eagerly longed for. *Jones* had mentioned the Fact of his Amour, and of his being the Rival of *Blifil*, but had cautiously concealed the Name of the young

Lady. The Barber therefore, after some Hesitation, and many Hums and Ha's, at last begged Leave to crave the Name of the Lady, who appeared to be the principal Cause of all this Mischief. *Jones* paused a Moment, and then said, 'Since I have trusted you with so much, and since, I am afraid, her Name is become too public already on this Occasion, I will not conceal it from you. Her Name is *Sophia Western*.'

'*Proh Deum atque Hominum Fidem*!¹ Squire *Western* hath a Daughter grown a Woman!' 'Ay, and such a Woman,' cries *Jones*, 'that the World cannot match. No Eye ever saw any thing so beautiful; but that is her least Excellence. Such Sense, such Goodness! O I could praise her for ever, and yet should omit half her Virtues.' 'Mr. *Western* a Daughter grown up!' cries the Barber, 'I remember the Father a Boy; well, *Tempus edax Rerum*.'²

The Wine being now at an End, the Barber pressed very eagerly to be his Bottle; but *Jones* absolutely refused, saying, 'He had already drank more than he ought; and that he now chose to retire to his Room, where he wished he could procure himself a Book.' 'A Book!' cries *Benjamin*, 'what Book would you have? *Latin* or *English*? I have some curious Books in both Languages. Such as *Erasmi Colloquia, Ovid de Tristibus, Gradus ad Parnassum*;³ and in *English* I have several of the best Books, tho' some of them are a little torn; but I have a great Part of *Stowe's* Chronicle;⁴ the sixth Volume of *Pope's Homer*;⁵ the third Volume of the Spectator; the second Volume of *Echard's Roman* History;⁶ the Craftsman;⁷

¹ See above, p. 417, n. 3.
² Ovid, *Metamorphoses*, xv. 234: 'O Time, devourer of things.' An example in *A Short Introduction to Grammar* [1720], p. 141; *Lily's Rules Construed* [1720], p. 43; and the Eton Latin grammar (1758), p. 84. See also below, p. 471.
³ These three Latin works were widely used as texts for schoolboys. Erasmus's *Colloquia* was first published in 1516. *Gradus ad Parnassum* (1686) is a collection of synonyms, epithets, and phrases from the classical poets; the young Jonathan Wild pilfers a copy of this book while at school (1743; I. iii).
⁴ *The Chronicles of England from Brute unto this present yeare of Christ, 1580*, by the well-known historian and antiquary, John Stow (1525 ?–1605).
⁵ This would be the final volume of the *Iliad*, originally published in 1720.
⁶ See above, p. 273, n. 2. Vol. ii of this work related the history of Rome 'from the Settlement of the Empire by Augustus Cæsar, to the Removal of the Imperial Seat by Constantine the Great'.
⁷ Founded originally to oppose Walpole, *The Craftsman* (1726–50) was the principal 'Tory' journal of the period. The earlier numbers were reprinted in book form in 14 vols. (1731–7).

*Robinson Crusoe*;¹ *Thomas a Kempis*,² and two Volumes of *Tom Brown's* Works.'³

'Those last,' cries *Jones*, 'are Books I never saw, so if you please to lend me one of those Volumes.' The Barber assured him he would be highly entertained; for he looked upon the Author to have been one of the greatest Wits that ever the Nation produced. He then stepped to his House, which was hard by, and immediately returned, after which, the Barber having received very strict Injunctions of Secrecy from *Jones*, and having sworn inviolably to maintain it, they separated; the Barber went home, and *Jones* retired to his Chamber.

## CHAPTER VI

*In which more of the Talents of Mr.* Benjamin *will appear, as well as who this extraordinary Person was.*

IN the Morning *Jones* grew a little uneasy at the Desertion of his Surgeon, as he apprehended some Inconvenience, or even Danger, might attend the not Dressing his Wound; he enquired therefore of the Drawer what other Surgeons were to be met with in that Neighbourhood. The Drawer told him there was one not far off; but he had known him often refuse to be concerned after another had been sent for before him; 'but, Sir,' says he, 'if you will take my Advice, there is not a Man in the Kingdom can do your Business better than the Barber who was with you last Night.

¹ Though he remarked on its great vogue, Fielding seems to have considered Defoe's *Robinson Crusoe* (1719) an inferior form of popular literature. (See *The Jacobite's Journal*, 27 February 1748; also *The Champion*, 20 March 1739/40.)

² Thomas à Kempis—Thomas Haemmerlein or Hemercker of Kempen (1380–1471)—was an Augustinian monk and the supposed author of the *Imitation of Christ* (1441). He was also a favourite of Joseph Andrews (1742; I. iii).

³ Tom Brown (1663–1704), hackney journalist, satirist, and translator. Three volumes of his *Works* appeared in 1707; two more were added in 1720. In dedicating Brown's works to the Duke of Ormonde, Dr. James Drake flatly declared that '*all men of sense and learning admir'd the comic stile of Mr.* BROWN, *in which no man yet has equall'd him*', and he concluded this modest appraisal by asserting that his author, if not 'one of our best poets . . . was undeniably one of our greatest genius's' (*Works*, 8th ed. [1744], i. iv, xii). For the most part, however, Brown's admirers were limited to the likes of Dr. Drake, Swift's Simon Wagstaff, and Partridge. To Fielding, Brown was in a class with Tom D'Urfey—mere 'Scriblers' whose popularity attested to the lack of literary judgement in '*this tasteless, silly Town*' (*The Covent-Garden Journal*, 4 February 1752).

We look upon him to be one of the ablest Men at a Cut in all this Neighbourhood. For tho' he hath not been here above three Months, he hath done several great Cures.'

The Drawer was presently dispatched for little *Benjamin*, who being acquainted in what Capacity he was wanted, prepared himself accordingly, and attended; but with so different an Air and Aspect from that which he wore when his Bason was under his Arm, that he could scarce be known to be the same Person.

'So, Tonsor,' says *Jones*, 'I find you have more Trades than one; how came you not to inform me of this last Night?' 'A Surgeon,' answered *Benjamin*, with great Gravity, 'is a Profession, not a Trade. The Reason why I did not acquaint you last Night that I professed this Art, was that I then concluded you was under the Hands of another Gentleman, and I never love to interfere with my Brethren in their Business. *Ars omnibus communis*;[1] but now, Sir, if you please, I will inspect your Head, and when I see into your Skull, I will give my Opinion of your Case.'

*Jones* had no great Faith in this new Professor; however he suffered him to open the Bandage, and to look at his Wound, which as soon as he had done, *Benjamin* began to groan and shake his Head violently. Upon which *Jones*, in a peevish Manner, bid him not play the Fool, but tell him in what Condition he found him. 'Shall I answer you as a Surgeon, or a Friend?' said *Benjamin*. 'As a Friend, and seriously,' said *Jones*. 'Why then, upon my Soul,' cries *Benjamin*, 'it would require a great deal of Art to keep you from being well after a very few Dressings; and if you will suffer me to apply some Salve of mine, I will answer for the Success.' *Jones* gave his Consent, and the Plaister was applied accordingly.

'There, Sir,' cries *Benjamin*, 'now I will, if you please, resume my former Self; but a Man is obliged to keep up some Dignity in his Countenance whilst he is performing these Operations, or the World will not submit to be handled by him. You can't imagine, Sir, of how much Consequence a grave Aspect is to a grave Character. A Barber may make you laugh, but a Surgeon ought rather to make you cry.'

'Mr. *Barber*, or Mr. *Surgeon*, or Mr. *Barber-Surgeon*,' said *Jones*.—'O dear Sir,' answered *Benjamin*, interrupting him,

[1] 'The art is common to all'—perhaps a play on '*mors omnibus communis*' (see below, p. 629, n. 2).

'*Infandum Regina jubes renovare Dolorem.*[1] You recal to my Mind
that cruel Separation of the united Fraternities,[2] so much to the
Prejudice of both Bodies, as all Separations must be, according to
the old Adage, *Vis unita fortior*;[3] which to be sure there are not
wanting some of one or of the other Fraternity who are able to
construe. What a Blow was this to me who unite both in my own
Person.'—'Well, by whatever Name you please to be called,'
continued *Jones*, 'you certainly are one of the oddest, most
comical Fellows I ever met with, and must have something very
surprizing in your Story, which you must confess I have a Right
to hear.' 'I do confess it,' answered *Benjamin*, 'and will very
readily acquaint you with it, when you have sufficient Leisure;
for I promise you it will require a good deal of Time.' *Jones* told
him, He could never be more at Leisure than at present. 'Well
then,' said *Benjamin*, 'I will obey you; but first I will fasten the
Door, that none may interrupt us.' He did so, and then advancing
with a solemn Air to *Jones*, said; 'I must begin by telling you,
Sir, that you yourself have been the greatest Enemy I ever had.'
*Jones* was a little startled at this sudden Declaration. 'I your
Enemy, Sir!' says he, with much Amazement, and some Sternness in his Look. 'Nay, be not angry,' said *Benjamin*, 'for I
promise you I am not. You are perfectly innocent of having intended me any Wrong; for you was then an Infant; but I shall,
I believe, unriddle all this the Moment I mention my Name. Did
you never hear, Sir, of one *Partridge*, who had the Honour of
being reputed your Father, and the Misfortune of being ruined
by that Honour?' 'I have indeed heard of that *Partridge*,' says
*Jones*, 'and have always believed myself to be his Son.' 'Well,
Sir,' answered *Benjamin*, 'I am that *Partridge*; but I here absolve
you from all filial Duty; for I do assure you you are no Son of
mine.' 'How,' replied *Jones*, 'and is it possible that a false
Suspicion should have drawn all the ill Consequences upon you,

---

[1] Virgil, *Aeneid*, ii. 3: 'Beyond all words, O queen, is the grief thou bidst me revive'
(trans. H. R. Fairclough, Loeb Classical Library, 1916)—Aeneas to Dido, as he begins
the story of the destruction of Troy. This is Partridge's favourite quotation; see also
pp. 438, 628, 752.

[2] The barbers and surgeons of London had been united in one corporation since the time
of Henry VIII. By 18 George II, cap. 15 ('An Act for making the Surgeons of *London* and
the Barbers of *London* Two Separate and Distinct Corporations'), this union was dissolved,
effective 24 June 1745. Fielding's friend John Ranby (see pp. 112, n. 2; 468, n. 1; 911,
n. 1) was appointed governor of the new Company of Surgeons.

[3] 'Strength united is more powerful'—a proverbial expression.

with which I am too well acquainted?' 'It is possible,' cries *Benjamin*, 'for it is so; but tho' it is natural enough for Men to hate even the innocent Causes of their Sufferings, yet I am of a different Temper. I have loved you ever since I heard of your Behaviour to *Black George*, as I told you; and I am convinced, from this extraordinary Meeting, that you are born to make me Amends for all I have suffered on that Account. Besides, I dreamt, the Night before I saw you, that I stumbled over a Stool without hurting myself; which plainly shewed me something good was towards me; and last Night I dreamt again, that I rode behind you on a Milk white Mare, which is a very excellent Dream,[1] and betokens much good Fortune, which I am resolved to pursue, unless you have the Cruelty to deny me.'

'I should be very glad, Mr. *Partridge*,' answered *Jones*, 'to have it in my Power to make you Amends for your Sufferings on my Account; tho' at present I see no Likelihood of it; however, I assure you I will deny you nothing which is in my Power to grant.'

'It is in your Power sure enough,' replied *Benjamin*, 'for I desire nothing more than Leave to attend you in this Expedition. Nay, I have so entirely set my Heart upon it, that if you should refuse me, you will kill both a Barber and a Surgeon in one Breath.'

*Jones* answered smiling, That he should be very sorry to be the Occasion of so much Mischief to the Public. He then advanced many prudential Reasons, in order to dissuade *Benjamin* (whom we shall hereafter call *Partridge*) from his Purpose; but all were in vain. *Partridge* relied strongly on his Dream of the milk-white Mare. 'Besides, Sir,' says he, 'I promise you, I have as good an Inclination to the Cause, as any Man can possibly have; and go I will, whether you admit me to go in your Company or not.'

*Jones*, who was as much pleased with *Partridge*, as *Partridge* could be with him, and who had not consulted his own Inclination, but the Good of the other in desiring him to stay behind;

---

[1] A number of fortune-telling manuals purporting to explain the significance of dreams were circulating in the mid-eighteenth century: e.g. *The High German Fortune-Teller; Dreams and Moles with their Interpretation and Signification . . . by a Fellow of the Royal Society, and a true Lover of Learning*; and the *New and Well Experienced Fortune Book*. Appropriately enough, the authors of this last pamphlet were 'Partridge and Flamsted'. The omens in Partridge's dreams are among those explained in a twentieth-century descendant of such compilations, *The Mystic Dream Book* [1933].

when he found his Friend so resolute, at last gave his Consent; but then recollecting himself, he said, 'Perhaps, Mr. *Partridge*, you think I shall be able to support you, but I really am not;' and then taking out his Purse, he told out nine Guineas, which he declared were his whole Fortune.

*Partridge* answered, 'that his Dependance was only on his future Favour: For he was thoroughly convinced he would shortly have enough in his Power. At present, Sir,' said he, 'I believe I am rather the richer Man of the two; but all I have is at your Service, and at your Disposal. I insist upon your taking the whole, and I beg only to attend you in the Quality of your Servant, *Nil desperandum est Teucro duce et auspice Teucro*;'[1] But to this generous Proposal concerning the Money, *Jones* would by no means submit.

It was resolved to set out the next Morning; when a Difficulty arose concerning the Baggage, for the Portmanteau of Mr. *Jones* was too large to be carried without a Horse.

'If I may presume to give my Advice,' says *Partridge*, 'this Portmanteau, with every Thing in it, except a few Shirts, should be left behind. Those I shall be easily able to carry for you, and the rest of your Clothes will remain very safely locked up in my House.'

This Method was no sooner proposed than agreed when the Barber departed, in order to prepare every Thing for his intended Expedition.

## CHAPTER VII

*Containing better Reasons than any which have yet appeared for the Conduct of* Partridge; *an Apology for the Weakness of* Jones; *and some farther Anecdotes concerning my Landlady.*

THOUGH *Partridge* was one of the most superstitious of Men, he would hardly, perhaps, have desired to accompany *Jones* on his Expedition merely from the Omens of the Joint-stool, and white Mare, if his Prospect had been no better than to have shared the Plunder gained in the Field of Battle. In Fact, when *Partridge* came to ruminate on the Relation he had heard

---

[1] Slightly altered (Partridge adds *est*) from Horace, *Odes*, I. vii. 27: 'Nothing is to be despaired of under Teucer's leadership and Teucer's auspices.'

from *Jones*, he could not reconcile to himself, that Mr. *Allworthy* should turn his Son (for so he most firmly believed him to be) out of Doors, for any Reason which he had heard assigned. He concluded therefore, that the whole was a Fiction, and that *Jones*, of whom he had often from his Correspondents heard the wildest Character, had in reality run away from his Father. It came into his Head, therefore, that if he could prevail with the young Gentleman to return back to his Father, he should by that Means render a Service to *Allworthy*, which would obliterate all his former Anger; nay, indeed he conceived that very Anger was counterfeited, and that *Allworthy* had sacrificed him to his own Reputation. And this Suspicion, indeed, he well accounted for, from the tender Behaviour of that excellent Man to the Foundling Child; from his great Severity to *Partridge*, who knowing himself to be innocent, could not conceive that any other should think him guilty; lastly, from the Allowance which he had privately received long after the Annuity had been publickly taken from him; and which he looked upon as a kind of Smart-money, or rather by way of Atonement for Injustice: For it is very uncommon, I believe, for Men to ascribe the Benefactions they receive to pure Charity, when they can possibly impute them to any other Motive. If he could by any Means, therefore, persuade the young Gentleman to return home, he doubted not but that he should again be received into the Favour of *Allworthy*, and well rewarded for his Pains; nay, and should be again restored to his native Country; a Restoration which *Ulysses* himself never wished more heartily than poor *Partridge*.

As for *Jones*, he was well satisfied with the Truth of what the other had asserted, and believed that *Partridge* had no other Inducements but Love to him, and Zeal for the Cause. A blameable Want of Caution, and Diffidence in the Veracity of others, in which he was highly worthy of Censure. To say the Truth, there are but two Ways by which Men become possessed of this excellent Quality. The one is from long Experience, and the other is from Nature; which last, I presume, is often meant by Genius, or great natural Parts; and it is infinitely the better of the two, not only as we are Masters of it much earlier in Life, but as it is much more infallible and conclusive: For a Man who hath been imposed on by ever so many, may still hope to find others more honest; whereas he who receives certain necessary

Admonitions from within, that this is impossible, must have very little Understanding indeed, if he ever renders himself liable to be once deceived. As *Jones* had not this Gift from Nature, he was too young to have gained it by Experience; for at the diffident Wisdom which is to be acquired this Way, we seldom arrive till very late in Life; which is perhaps the Reason why some old Men are apt to despise the Understandings of all those who are a little younger than themselves.

*Jones* spent most Part of the Day in the Company of a new Acquaintance. This was no other than the Landlord of the House, or rather the Husband of the Landlady. He had but lately made his Descent down Stairs, after a long Fit of the Gout, in which Distemper he was generally confined to his Room during one half of the Year; and during the rest, he walked about the House, smoaked his Pipe, and drank his Bottle with his Friends, without concerning himself in the least with any Kind of Business. He had been bred, as they call it, a Gentleman, that is, bred up to do nothing, and had spent a very small Fortune, which he inherited from an industrious Farmer his Uncle, in Hunting, Horse-racing, and Cock-fighting, and had been married by my Landlady for certain Purposes which he had long since desisted from answering: for which she hated him heartily. But as he was a surly Kind of Fellow, so she contented herself with frequently upbraiding him by disadvantageous Comparisons with her first Husband, whose Praise she had eternally in her Mouth; and as she was for the most part Mistress of the Profit, so she was satisfied to take upon herself the Care and Government of the Family, and after a long successless Struggle, to suffer her Husband to be Master of himself.

In the Evening when *Jones* retired to his Room, a small Dispute arose between this fond Couple concerning him. 'What,' says the Wife, 'you have been tipling with the Gentleman! I see.' 'Yes,' answered the Husband, 'we have cracked a Bottle together, and a very Gentleman-like Man he is, and hath a very pretty Notion of Horse-flesh. Indeed he is young, and hath not seen much of the World: For I believe he hath been at very few Horse-races.' 'O ho! he is one of your Order, is he?' replies the Landlady, 'he must be a Gentleman to be sure, if he is a Horse-racer. The Devil fetch such Gentry, I am sure I wish I had never seen any of them. I have Reason to love Horse-racers truly.'

'That you have,' says the Husband; 'for I was one you know.'
'Yes,' answered she, 'You are a pure one indeed. As my first
Husband used to say, I may put all the Good I have ever got by
you in my Eyes, and see never the worse.' 'D—n your first
Husband,' cries he.—'Don't d—n a better Man than yourself,'
answered the Wife, 'if he had been alive, you durst not have
done it.' 'Then you think,' says he, 'I have not so much Courage as
yourself: For you have d—n'd him often in my Hearing.' 'If I
did,' says she, 'I have repented of it many's the good Time and
oft. And if he was so good to forgive me a Word spoken in Haste,
or so, it doth not become such a one as you to *twitter* me. He was
a Husband to me, he was; and if ever I did make use of an ill
Word or so in a Passion; I never called him Rascal, I should
have told a Lie, if I had called him Rascal.' Much more she said,
but not in his Hearing: For having lighted his Pipe, he staggered
off as fast as he could. We shall therefore transcribe no more of
her Speech, as it approached still nearer and nearer to a Subject
too indelicate to find any Place in this History.

Early in the Morning, *Partridge* appeared at the Bedside of
*Jones*, ready equipped for the Journey, with his Knapsack at his
Back. This was his own Workmanship; for besides his other
Trades, he was no indifferent Taylor. He had already put up his
whole Stock of Linnen in it, consisting of four Shirts, to which he
now added eight for Mr. *Jones*, and then packing up the Portmanteau, he was departing with it towards his own House, but
was stopt in his Way by the Landlady, who refused to suffer any
Removals till after the Payment of the Reckoning.

The Landlady was, as we have said, absolute Governess in
these Regions; it was therefore necessary to comply with her
Rules, so the Bill was presently writ out, which amounted to a
much larger Sum than might have been expected, from the
Entertainment which *Jones* had met with; but here we are obliged to disclose some Maxims, which Publicans hold to be the
grand Mysteries of their Trade. The first is, if they have any
Thing good in their House (which indeed very seldom happens)
to produce it only to Persons who travel with great Equipages.
Secondly, To charge the same for the very worst Provisions, as if
they were the best. And, lastly, if any of their Guests call but for
little, to make them pay a double Price for every Thing they
have; so that the Amount by the Head may be much the same.

The Bill being made and discharged, *Jones* set forward with *Partridge* carrying his Knapsack; nor did the Landlady condescend to wish him a good Journey: for this was, it seems, an Inn frequented by People of Fashion; and I know not whence it is, but all those who get their Livelihood by People of Fashion, contract as much Insolence to the rest of Mankind, as if they really belonged to that Rank themselves.

## CHAPTER VIII

Jones *arrives at* Gloucester, *and goes to the* Bell; *the Character of that House, and of a Petty-fogger, which he there meets with.*

MR. *Jones*, and *Partridge*, or *Little Benjamin*, (which Epithet of *Little* was perhaps given him ironically, he being in reality near six Feet high) having left their last Quarters in the Manner before described, travelled on to *Gloucester* without meeting any Adventure worth relating.

Being arrived here, they chose for their House of Entertainment the Sign of the *Bell*, an excellent House indeed, and which I do most seriously recommend to every Reader who shall visit this ancient City. The Master of it is Brother to the great Preacher *Whitefield*;[1] but is absolutely untainted with the pernicious Principles of Methodism, or of any other heretical Sect. He is indeed a very honest plain Man, and in my Opinion,

---

[1] For Fielding's views on George Whitefield and Methodism, see pp. 63, n. 1; 79, n. 4; 93, n. 1; 96, n. 2; 929, n. 1. Whitefield grew up in the Bell—'an excellent House indeed', as Fielding calls it, which continues to prosper at the present day—and until shortly after his brother Richard's marriage in 1729, he had intended to help manage the inn; but he quarrelled with his new sister-in-law and left the household. (See *A Short Account of God's Dealings with the Reverend Mr. George Whitefield* [1740].) Not everyone who knew her shared Fielding's fondness for this woman, Elizabeth Whitefield (d. 7 August 1755). Having read the passage in *Tom Jones*—a book which he otherwise very much admired—Captain Lewis Thomas (see above, p. 372, n. 3) wrote to Welbore Ellis on 3 April 1749, expressing his own opinion of Mrs. Whitefield's character:

'I breakfasted two or three times with Mrs Whitfield, we talk'd of nothing but gayety & Assemblies; she let me into a Short History of her Lovers, & told me ye conquests she had made when Younger, & if I might put any faith in her own Commentaries, she had had as many occasions of triumph as Julius Caesar; in short I went away extremely disgusted with the Folly & behaviour of my Coquet Landlady.

'How ye Devil came it into Fielding's head to praise this Woman so exuberantly? If I was Master of the Bell Inn, I vow I should be absolutely Jealous.' (See J. P. Feil, *PQ*, xxxix [1960], 508–10.)

not likely to create any Disturbance either in Church or State. His Wife hath, I believe, had much Pretension to Beauty, and is still a very fine Woman. Her Person and Deportment might have made a shining Figure in the politest Assemblies; but though she must be conscious of this, and many other Perfections, she seems perfectly contented with, and resigned to that State of Life to which she is called; and this Resignation is entirely owing to the Prudence and Wisdom of her Temper: For she is at present as free from any methodistical Notions as her Husband. I say at present: For she freely confesses that her Brother's Documents made at first some Impression upon her, and that she had put herself to the Expence of a long Hood, in order to attend the extraordinary Emotions of the Spirit; but having found during an Experiment of three Weeks, no Emotions, she says, worth a Farthing, she very wisely laid by her Hood, and abandoned the Sect. To be concise, she is a very friendly, good-natured Woman, and so industrious to oblige, that the Guests must be of a very morose Disposition who are not extremely well satisfied in her House.

Mrs. *Whitefield* happened to be in the Yard when *Jones* and his Attendant marched in. Her Sagacity soon discovered in the Air of our Heroe something which distinguished him from the Vulgar. She ordered her Servants, therefore, immediately to shew him into a Room, and presently afterwards invited him to Dinner with herself; which Invitation he very thankfully accepted: For indeed much less agreeable Company than that of Mrs. *Whitefield*, and a much worse Entertainment than she had provided, would have been welcome, after so long fasting, and so long a Walk.

Besides Mr. *Jones* and the good Governess of the Mansion, there sat down at Table an Attorney of *Salisbury*, indeed the very same who had brought the News of Mrs. *Blifil's* Death to Mr. *Allworthy*, and whose Name, which, I think, we did not before mention, was *Dowling*; there was likewise present another Person, who stiled himself a Lawyer, and who lived somewhere near *Lidlinch*[1] in *Somersetshire*. This Fellow, I say, stiled himself a Lawyer, but was indeed a most vile Petty-fogger, without Sense or Knowledge of any Kind; one of those who may be termed Train-bearers to the Law; a Sort of Supernumeraries in the

---

[1] The village of Lydlinch is actually situated in Dorset, four miles from the Somerset border.

Profession, who are the Hackneys of Attornies, and will ride more Miles for half a Crown, than a Post-boy.

During the time of Dinner, the *Somersetshire* Lawyer recollected the Face of *Jones*, which he had seen at Mr. *Allworthy's*: For he had often visited in that Gentleman's Kitchen. He therefore took Occasion to enquire after the good Family there, with that Familiarity which would have become an intimate Friend or Acquaintance of Mr. *Allworthy*; and indeed he did all in his Power to insinuate himself to be such, though he had never had the Honour of speaking to any Person in that Family higher than the Butler. *Jones* answered all his Questions with much Civility, though he never remembered to have seen the Pettyfogger before, and though he concluded from the outward Appearance and Behaviour of the Man, that he usurped a Freedom with his Betters, to which he was by no means intitled.

As the Conversation of Fellows of this Kind, is of all others the most detestable to Men of any Sense, the Cloth was no sooner removed than Mr. *Jones* withdrew, and a little barbarously left poor Mrs. *Whitefield* to do a Pennance, which I have often heard Mr. *Timothy Harris*,[1] and other Publicans of good Taste, lament as the severest Lot annexed to their Calling, namely, that of being obliged to keep Company with their Guests.

*Jones* had no sooner quitted the Room, than the Petty-fogger, in a whispering Tone, asked Mrs. *Whitefield*, 'if she knew who that fine Spark was?' She answered, 'she had never seen the Gentleman before.' 'The Gentleman, indeed!' replied the Pettyfogger, 'a pretty Gentleman truly! Why, he's the Bastard of a Fellow who was hanged for Horse-stealing. He was dropt at Squire *Allworthy's* Door, where one of the Servants found him in a Box so full of Rain-water, that he would certainly have been drowned, had he not been reserved for another Fate.' 'Ay, ay, you need not mention it, I protest, we understand what that Fate is very well,' cries *Dowling*, with a most facetious Grin. 'Well,' continued the other, 'the Squire ordered him to be taken in: For he is a timborsome Man every Body knows, and was afraid of drawing himself into a Scrape, and there the Bastard was bred up,

---

[1] Timothy Harris (d. October 1748), keeper of the Red Lion at Egham, Surrey, whom Fielding had earlier complimented in *Joseph Andrews* (I. xi). (See his death notice, 20 October 1748: Roll for the Manor of Staines in the County of Middlesex, 1743–8. Acc. 801. And his will, proved 16 November 1748: Prerogative Court of Canterbury. Strahan, Folio 329.)

and fed and cloathified all to the World like any Gentleman; and there he got one of the Servant Maids with Child, and persuaded her to swear it to the Squire himself; and afterwards he broke the Arm of one Mr. *Thwackum* a Clergyman, only because he reprimanded him for following Whores; and afterwards he snapt a Pistol at Mr. *Blifil* behind his Back; and once when Squire *Allworthy* was sick, he got a Drum, and beat it all over the House, to prevent him from sleeping: And twenty other Pranks he hath played, for all which, about four or five Days ago, just before I left the Country, the Squire strip'd him stark naked, and turned him out of Doors.'

'And very justly too, I protest,' cries *Dowling*, 'I would turn my own Son out of Doors, if he was guilty of half as much. And pray what is the Name of this pretty Gentleman?'

'The Name o'un!' answered Petty-fogger, 'why, he is a called *Thomas Jones.*'

'*Jones!*' answered *Dowling*, a little eagerly, 'what, Mr. *Jones* that lived at Mr. *Allworthy's!* was that the Gentleman that dined with us?' 'The very same,' said the other. 'I have heard of the Gentleman,' cries *Dowling*, 'often; but I never heard any ill Character of him.' 'And I am sure,' says Mrs. *Whitefield*, 'if half what this Gentleman hath said be true, Mr. *Jones* hath the most deceitful Countenance I ever saw; for sure his Looks promise something very different; and I must say, for the little I have seen of him, he is as civil a well-bred Man as you would wish to converse with.'

Petty-fogger calling to mind that he had not been sworn, as he usually was, before he gave his Evidence, now bound what he had declared with so many Oaths and Imprecations, that the Lady's Ears were shocked, and she put a Stop to his swearing, by assuring him of her Belief. Upon which he said, 'I hope, Madam, you imagine I would scorn to tell such Things of any Man, unless I knew them to be true. What Interest have I in taking away the Reputation of a Man who never injured me? I promise you every Syllable of what I have said is Fact, and the whole Country knows it.'

As Mrs. *Whitefield* had no Reason to suspect that the Petty-fogger had any Motive or Temptation to abuse *Jones*, the Reader cannot blame her for believing what he so confidently affirmed with many Oaths. She accordingly gave up her Skill in

Physiognomy, and henceforwards conceived so ill an Opinion of her Guest, that she heartily wished him out of her House.

This Dislike was now farther encreased by a Report which Mr. *Whitefield* made from the Kitchen, where *Partridge* had informed the Company, 'That tho' he carried the Knapsack, and contented himself with staying among Servants, while *Tom Jones* (as he called him) was regaling in the Parlour, he was not his Servant, but only a Friend and Companion, and as good a Gentleman as Mr. *Jones* himself.'

*Dowling* sat all this while silent, biting his Fingers, making Faces, grinning, and looking wonderfully arch; at last he opened his Lips, and protested that the Gentleman looked like another Sort of Man. He then called for his Bill with the utmost Haste, declared he must be at *Hereford* that Evening, lamented his great Hurry of Business, and wished he could divide himself into twenty Pieces, in order to be at once in twenty Places.

The Petty-fogger now likewise departed, and then *Jones* desired the Favour of Mrs. *Whitefield's* Company to drink Tea with him; but she refused, and with a Manner so different from that with which she had received him at Dinner, that it a little surprized him. And now he soon perceived her Behaviour totally changed; for instead of that natural Affability which we have before celebrated, she wore a constrained Severity on her Countenance, which was so disagreeable to Mr. *Jones*, that he resolved, however late, to quit the House that Evening.

He did indeed account somewhat unfairly for this sudden Change; for besides some hard and unjust Surmises concerning female Fickleness and Mutability,[1] he began to suspect that he owed this Want of Civility to his Want of Horses, a Sort of Animals which, as they dirty no Sheets, are thought, in Inns, to pay better for their Beds than their Riders, and are therefore considered as the more desirable Company; but Mrs. *Whitefield*, to do her Justice, had a much more liberal Way of thinking. She was perfectly well-bred, and could be very civil to a Gentleman, tho' he walked on Foot: In Reality, she looked on our Heroe as a sorry Scoundrel, and therefore treated him as such, for which not even *Jones* himself, had he known as much as the Reader, could have blamed her; nay, on the contrary, he must have approved her Conduct, and have esteemed her the more for the Disrespect

[1] Cf. Virgil, *Aeneid*, iv. 569–70: 'varium et mutabile semper/ femina.'

shewn towards himself. This is indeed a most aggravating Circumstance which attends depriving Men unjustly of their Reputation; for a Man who is conscious of having an ill Character, cannot justly be angry with those who neglect and slight him; but ought rather to despise such as affect his Conversation, unless where a perfect Intimacy must have convinced them that their Friend's Character hath been falsely and injuriously aspersed.

This was not, however, the Case of *Jones*; for as he was a perfect Stranger to the Truth, so he was with good Reason offended at the Treatment he received. He therefore paid his Reckoning and departed, highly against the Will of Mr. *Partridge*, who having remonstrated much against it to no Purpose, at last condescended to take up his Knapsack, and to attend his Friend.

## CHAPTER IX

*Containing several Dialogues between* Jones *and* Partridge, *concerning Love, Cold, Hunger, and other Matters; with the lucky and narrow Escape of* Partridge, *as he was on the very Brink of making a fatal Discovery to his Friend.*

THE Shadows began now to descend larger from the high Mountains: The feather'd Creation had betaken themselves to their Rest. Now the highest Order of Mortals were sitting down to their Dinners, and the lowest Order to their Suppers. In a Word, the Clock struck five just as Mr. *Jones* took his Leave of *Gloucester*; an Hour at which (as it was now Midwinter) the dirty Fingers of Night would have drawn her sable Curtain over the Universe, had not the Moon forbid her, who now with a Face as broad and as red as those of some jolly Mortals, who, like her, turn Night into Day, began to rise from her Bed,[1] where she had

---

[1] Since the time of Tom's 'mid-winter' journey is late November 1745 (see above, p. 368, n. 1), the circumstance of the full moon's rising at Gloucester at 5.00 p.m. has led to the theory that Fielding consulted an almanac when plotting the chronology of his novel. (See F. S. Dickson, *N & Q*, 11th Ser., ix [30 May 1914], 425–6, and *The Library*, 3rd Ser., viii [1917], 218–24.) According to this hypothesis, the precise date of Tom's departure from Gloucester is 29 November 1745. From this assumption it is possible to assign specific dates to the events of the narrative from the time (22 November) Western proposes a match between Sophia and Blifil (VI. iii) to the time when Tom and Sophia marry (24 December) and, two days later, retire to the country (26 December). At least one contemporary reader

slumbred away the Day, in order to sit up all Night. *Jones* had not
travelled far before he paid his Compliments to that beautiful
Planet, and turning to his Companion, asked him, If he had ever
beheld so delicious an Evening. *Partridge* making no ready
Answer to his Question, he proceeded to comment on the Beauty
of the Moon, and repeated some Passages from *Milton*,[1] who hath
certainly excelled all other Poets in his Description of the heavenly
Luminaries. He then told *Partridge* the Story from the *Spectator*,[2]
of two Lovers who had agreed to entertain themselves when they
were at a great Distance from each other, by repairing, at a
certain fixed Hour, to look at the Moon; thus pleasing themselves
with the Thought that they were both employed in contemplating
the same Object at the same Time. 'Those Lovers,' added he,
'must have had Souls truly capable of feeling all the Tenderness
of the sublimest of all human Passions.' 'Very probably,' cries
*Partridge*, 'but I envy them more if they had Bodies incapable of
feeling cold; for I am almost frozen to Death, and am very much
afraid I shall lose a Piece of my Nose before we get to another
House of Entertainment. Nay, truly, we may well expect some
Judgment should happen to us for our Folly in running away so
by Night from one of the most excellent Inns I ever set my Foot
into. I am sure I never saw more good Things in my Life, and

seems to have sensed this chronology when, in a clumsy poem, he referred to the Christmas
season as the time when 'F[IE]LD[IN]G's *Heroes* timely *hang*—or *marry*.' (See '*At* [*sic*]
String *of* SIMILIES, *in the true* CHRISTMAS, Frigid, *or* F[IE]LDINGIAN STILE', *London
Evening-Post*, 21–3 December 1749.)

In general, however, the evidence is against Fielding's having attempted to make the
action of his central narrative conform to calendar time. If, for instance, we are meant to
understand that Tom Jones's marriage takes place on Christmas Eve, it is odd that Fielding
should avoid any mention of the fact. And there are other anomalies. Originally, it appears,
Fielding thought of Allworthy's illness as occurring in June, not in early November (V. x,
p. 255). By VII. vii, however, when Honour complains of the freezing nights, the 'mid-
winter' time-scheme is clearly suggested, and by VII. xi, as we have seen, it is firmly established (see p. 368, n. 1). Yet even from this point there is no reason to believe that Fielding
has begun to follow almanac and calendar. In IX. vii—the events of which, according to
Dickson's chronology, would be placed on 30 November—the moon is said to be shining
brightly long after it had set (see p. 521, n. 1); and in XIII. ix—according to Dickson, 15
December—Sophia is made to attend a play on a Sunday. (See also, pp. 729, n. 1; 853,
n. 1.)

[1] Cf. *Paradise Lost*, i. 286–91, iv. 605–9, viii. 140–8.

[2] In *The Spectator*, No. 241 (6 December 1711), Addison recalls the story from 'one of
*Scudery's* Romances' of a couple who, while separated, set aside a certain time each day to
think of one another. The amiable function of the moon in uniting these lovers is, however,
Fielding's own contribution.

the greatest Lord in the Land cannot live better in his own House than he may there. And to forsake such a House, and go a rambling about the Country, the Lord knows whither, *per devia rura viarum*,[1] I say nothing, for my Part; but some People might not have Charity enough to conclude we were in our sober Senses.' 'Fie upon it, Mr. *Partridge*,' says *Jones*, 'have a better Heart; consider you are going to face an Enemy, and are you afraid of facing a little Cold? I wish, indeed, we had a Guide to advise which of these Roads we should take.'[2] 'May I be so bold,' says *Partridge*, 'to offer my Advice: *Interdum Stultus opportuna loquitur.*'[3] 'Why, which of them,' cries *Jones*, 'would you recommend?' 'Truly neither of them,' answered *Partridge*. 'The only Road we can be certain of finding, is the Road we came. A good hearty Pace will bring us back to *Gloucester* in an Hour; but if we go forward, the Lord *Harry* knows when we shall arrive at any Place; for I see at least fifty Miles before me, and no House in all the Way.' 'You see, indeed, a very fair Prospect,' says *Jones*, 'which receives great additional Beauty from the extreme Lustre of the Moon. However, I will keep the Left-hand Track, as that seems to lead directly to those Hills,[4] which we were informed lie not far from *Worcester*. And here, if you are inclined to quit me, you may, and return back again; but for my Part, I am resolved to go forward.'

'It is unkind in you, Sir,' says *Partridge*, 'to suspect me of any such Intention. What I have advised hath been as much on your Account as on my own; but since you are determined to go on, I am as much determined to follow. *I præ, sequar te.*'[5]

They now travelled some Miles without speaking to each other, during which Suspence of Discourse *Jones* often sighed, and *Partridge* groaned as bitterly, tho' from a very different Reason. At length *Jones* made a full Stop, and turning about, cries, 'Who knows, *Partridge*, but the loveliest Creature in the Universe may have her Eyes now fixed on that very Moon which I behold at this Instant!' 'Very likely, Sir,' answered *Partridge*, 'and if my Eyes were fixed on a good Surloin of Roast Beef, the

---

1 'Through country by-roads.' Cf. Ovid, *Metamorphoses*, i. 676: 'per devia rura capellas'.
2 The travellers have probably reached the fork in the road at Corse, some five miles north-west of Gloucester.
3 'Sometimes a fool speaks opportunely'—proverbial.
4 The Malverns.
5 Terence, *Andria*, I. i. 172: 'you go first, I will follow you.'

Devil might take the Moon and her Horns into the Bargain.'
'Did ever *Tramontane*¹ make such an Answer?' cries *Jones*.
'Prithee, *Partridge*, wast thou never susceptible of Love in thy
Life, or hath Time worn away all the Traces of it from thy
Memory?' 'Alack-a-day,' cries *Partridge*, 'well would it have been
for me if I had never known what Love was. *Infandum Regina
jubes renovare Dolorem.*² I am sure I have tasted all the Tenderness
and Sublimities and Bitternesses of the Passion.' 'Was your
Mistress unkind then?' says *Jones*. 'Very unkind indeed, Sir,'
answered *Partridge*; 'for she married me, and made one of the
most confounded Wives in the World. However, Heaven be
praised, she's gone, and if I believed she was in the Moon,
according to a Book I once read, which teaches that to be the
Receptacle of departed Spirits,³ I would never look at it for fear of
seeing her; but I wish, Sir, that the Moon was a Looking-glass
for your Sake, and that Miss *Sophia Western* was now placed
before it.' 'My dear *Partridge*,' cries *Jones*, 'what a Thought was
there! A Thought which I am certain could never have entered
into any Mind but that of a Lover. O *Partridge*, could I hope once
again to see that Face; but, alas! all those golden Dreams are
vanished for ever, and my only Refuge from future Misery is to
forget the Object of all my former Happiness.' 'And do you really
despair of ever seeing Miss *Western* again?' answered *Partridge*;
'if you will follow my Advice, I will engage you shall not only see
her, but have her in your Arms.' 'Ha! do not awaken a Thought
of that Nature,' cries *Jones*. 'I have struggled sufficiently to
conquer all such Wishes already.' 'Nay,' answered *Partridge*, 'if
you do not wish to have your Mistress in your Arms, you are a
most extraordinary Lover indeed.' 'Well, well,' says *Jones*, 'let us
avoid this Subject; but pray what is your Advice?' 'To give it you
in the military Phrase then,' says *Partridge*, 'as we are Soldiers;
"To the Right about." Let us return the Way we came, we may
yet reach *Gloucester* to Night, tho' late; whereas if we proceed,

¹ Originally an Italian expression applied to foreigners beyond the Alps, with the
connotation 'uncouth, unpolished, barbarous' (*OED*). Steele was fond of the word (see the
epilogue to *The Tender Husband* [1703] and *Tatler*, No. 222 [9 September 1710]), and
Fielding had used it earlier in *The Miser* (1733), II. iii. See also below, p. 806, n. 2.
² See above, p. 424, n. 1.
³ Cf. Plutarch, 'Concerning the Face which Appears in the Orb of the Moon', *Moralia*,
943–4. For a thorough discussion of the subject, see Marjorie Nicolson, *A World in the
Moon*, Smith College Studies in Modern Languages, xvii (1935–6).

we are likely, for ought I see, to ramble about for ever without coming either to House or Home.' 'I have already told you my Resolution is to go on,' answered *Jones*; 'but I would have you go back. I am obliged to you for your Company hither, and I beg you to accept a Guinea as a small Instance of my Gratitude, Nay, it would be cruel in me to suffer you to go any farther; for, to deal plainly with you, my chief End and Desire is a glorious Death in the Service of my King and Country.' 'As for your Money,' replied *Partridge*, 'I beg, Sir, you will put it up; I will receive none of you at this Time; for at present I am, I believe, the richer Man of the two. And as your Resolution is to go on, so mine is to follow you if you do. Nay, now my Presence appears absolutely necessary to take Care of you, since your Intentions are so desperate, for I promise you my Views are much more prudent: As you are resolved to fall in Battle, if you can, so I am resolved as firmly to come to no Hurt if I can help it. And indeed I have the Comfort to think there will be but little Danger; for a popish Priest told me the other Day, the Business would soon be over, and he believed without a Battle.' 'A popish Priest,' cries *Jones*, 'I have heard, is not always to be believed when he speaks in Behalf of his Religion.' 'Yes, but so far,' answered the other, 'from speaking in Behalf of his Religion, he assured me, the Catholicks did not expect to be any Gainers by the Change; for that Prince *Charles* was as good a Protestant as any in *England*; and that nothing but Regard to Right made him and the rest of the popish Party to be *Jacobites*.'[1] 'I believe him to be as much a Protestant as I believe he hath any Right,' says *Jones*, 'and I make

---

[1] Like Addison before him (e.g. *Freeholder*, No. 14 [6 February 1716]), Fielding scoffed at the credulity of those who subscribed to the 'Mysteries' of the Jacobite creed, all of which were 'infinitely above the Reach of human Reason'. Partridge cherishes one of the most preposterous of these, as set forth in *The Jacobite's Journal* for 19 December 1747: namely, *'That a Popish Prince may be the Defender of a Protestant Church'*. With Partridge's views, compare the belief of 'a Female Jacobite' in the *Journal* for 2 January 1748: 'That this P[retender] is deprived of his Right in the same manner as a private Person would be, who was violently turned out of his Estate. That he is protected and assisted by all the Popish Powers in *Europe*, only out of Compassion; and that he, and all his Family, tho' born and bred at *Rome*, are true, good *Englishmen* in their Hearts, *&c., &c., &c.*' Variations on this theme are heard in most of Fielding's writings of the period: besides many other numbers of *The Jacobite's Journal*, see, for instance, *A Serious Address to the People of Great Britain* (1745), *A Dialogue between the Devil, the Pope and the Pretender* (1745), *The True Patriot* (8–15 April, 27 May–3 June 1746), *A Dialogue between a Gentleman of London . . . and an honest Alderman of the Country Party* (1747), and *A Proper Answer to a late scurrilous Libel* (1747).

no Doubt of our Success, but not without a Battle. So that I am
not so sanguine as your Friend the popish Priest.' 'Nay, to be
sure, Sir,' answered *Partridge*, 'all the Prophecies I have ever
read, speak of a great deal of Blood to be spilt in the Quarrel, and
the Miller with three Thumbs, who is now alive, is to hold the
Horses of three Kings, up to his Knees in Blood.[1] Lord have
Mercy upon us all, and send better Times!' 'With what Stuff and
Nonsense hast thou filled thy Head?' answered *Jones*. 'This too,
I suppose, comes from the popish Priest. Monsters and Prodigies
are the proper Arguments to support monstrous and absurd
Doctrines. The Cause of King *George* is the Cause of Liberty and
true Religion. In other Words, it is the Cause of common Sense,

[1] In *The Freeholder*, No. 24 (12 March 1716), Addison had ridiculed the superstitions
of the Jacobites, who, having despaired of all natural means of overthrowing the government, had been 'reduced to the poor Comfort of Prodigies and old Women's Fables. . . .
Nay, I have been lately shewn a written Prophecy that is handed among them with great
Secresy, by which it appears their chief Reliance at present is upon a *Cheshire* Miller that
was born with two Thumbs upon one hand'. After the '45, Fielding adopted a similar
strategy, describing the Jacobites as 'the most superstitious of all People': 'In the worst of
Times, and when their Hopes have seemed to lose all Foundations, a River having too much
or too little Water in it, a Man born with an extraordinary Member, an Eclipse, a Comet,
an Aurora Borealis, or any such ordinary or extraordinary Phenomenon, is sufficient to
support their drooping Spirits, and is interpreted to be a Fore-runner of him they look for'
(*Jacobite's Journal*, 21 May 1748). In the *Journal* for 27 February 1748 he had facetiously
reported several prodigies in the Jacobite county of Staffordshire, where 'there are at present
several Millars with two Thumbs'.
   As usual during times of national crisis, the '45 prompted the publication of numerous
pamphlets reporting the predictions of such woeful prognosticators as Mother Shipton,
John Saltmarsh, Thomas Rymer, 'Marvellous Merlin', Thomas Newans, and many others.
The most popular of these, to which Addison alludes in *The Freeholder*, was Robert Nixon's
*Cheshire Prophecy at Large* (15th ed., 1745), with a commentary by John Oldmixon.
Nixon, 'a kind of *Idiot*' who lived during the reign of James I, prophesied that a Cheshire
miller with two heels would deliver England from foreign invaders (p. 3), that '*A Boy shall
be born with three Thumbs, and shall hold three Kings Horses, while* England *shall three
Times be Won and Lost in one Day*' (p. 4), and that a great battle would be fought upon
London Bridge, 'which would be so Bloody, that People should ride in *London* Streets up
to their Horses Bellies in Blood' (pp. 9–10). In a letter included in this volume, one William
Ewers pointed out Addison's mistake in giving the miller two thumbs rather than the two
heels Nixon endowed him with (p. 21). A good Whig, Oldmixon of course took care to
ridicule such superstitions, turning them to the advantage of the Hanoverian cause and,
appropriately enough in the present context, comparing them with the predictions of John
Partridge, the victim of Swift's Bickerstaff papers. Though Fielding certainly knew of this
work, he may have had Partridge recall the Norfolk prophecies of Mother Shipton, one
version of which, according to Walter Rye, tells 'how a wondrous Londoner, a miller by
trade, with three thumbs on one hand, is to hold the three kings' horses' in battle, 'when the
blood is to run so thickly as to clot by the wayside . . .' (Introduction, *Tourist's Guide to the
County of Norfolk* [1879], p. 19).

my Boy, and I warrant you will succeed, tho' *Briareus* himself[1]
was to rise again with his hundred Thumbs, and to turn Miller.'
*Partridge* made no Reply to this. He was indeed cast into the
utmost Confusion by this Declaration of *Jones*. For to inform the
Reader of a Secret, which we had no proper Opportunity of
revealing before, *Partridge* was in Truth a *Jacobite*, and had concluded that *Jones* was of the same Party, and was now proceeding
to join the Rebels. An Opinion which was not without Foundation. For the tall long-sided Dame, mentioned by *Hudibras*;[2]
that many-eyed, many-tongued, many-mouthed, many-eared
Monster of *Virgil*,[3] had related the Story of the Quarrel between
*Jones* and the Officer, with her usual Regard to Truth. She had
indeed changed the Name of *Sophia* into that of the Pretender,
and had reported, that drinking his Health was the Cause for
which *Jones* was knocked down. This *Partridge* had heard, and
most firmly believed. 'Tis no Wonder, therefore, that he had
thence entertained the above-mentioned Opinion of *Jones*; and
which he had almost discovered to him before he found out his
own Mistake. And at this the Reader will be the less inclined to
wonder, if he pleases to recollect the doubtful Phrase in which
*Jones* first communicated his Resolution to Mr. *Partridge*; and,
indeed, had the Words been less ambiguous, *Partridge* might
very well have construed them as he did; being persuaded, as he
was, that the whole Nation were of the same Inclination in their
Hearts: Nor did it stagger him that *Jones* had travelled in the
Company of Soldiers; for he had the same Opinion of the Army
which he had of the rest of the People.

But however well affected he might be to *James* or *Charles*,[4] he
was still much more attached to *Little Benjamin* than to either;
for which Reason he no sooner discovered the Principles of his
Fellow-traveller, than he thought proper to conceal, and outwardly to give up his own to the Man on whom he depended for the

[1] In Greek mythology, a giant with three hundred hands who helped the gods in their
war with the Titans.

[2] *Hudibras*, II. i. 45–6: 'There is a Tall Long-sided Dame,/ (But wondrous light)
ycleped *Fame*.'

[3] *Aeneid*, iv. 181–3, describing Fame—'a monster awful and huge, who for the many
feathers in her body has as many watchful eyes below—wondrous to tell—as many tongues,
as many sounding mouths, as many pricked-up ears' (trans. H. R. Fairclough, Loeb
Classical Library, 1916).

[4] The 'Old Pretender', James Francis Edward Stuart (1688–1766), and his son Charles
(1720–88), the 'Young Pretender'.

making his Fortune, since he by no means believed the Affairs of *Jones* to be so desperate as they really were with Mr. *Allworthy*; for as he had kept a constant Correspondence with some of his Neighbours since he left that Country, he had heard much, indeed more than was true, of the great Affection Mr. *Allworthy* bore this young Man, who, as *Partridge* had been instructed, was to be that Gentleman's Heir, and whom, as we have said, he did not in the least doubt to be his Son.

He imagined, therefore, that whatever Quarrel was between them, it would be certainly made up at the Return of Mr. *Jones*; an Event from which he promised great Advantages, if he could take this Opportunity of ingratiating himself with that young Gentleman; and if he could by any Means be instrumental in procuring his Return, he doubted not, as we have before said, but it would as highly advance him in the Favour of Mr. *Allworthy*.

We have already observed, that he was a very good-natured Fellow, and he hath himself declared the violent Attachment he had to the Person and Character of *Jones*; but possibly the Views which I have just before mentioned, might likewise have some little Share in prompting him to undertake this Expedition, at least in urging him to continue it, after he had discovered, that his Master and himself, like some prudent Fathers and Sons, tho' they travelled together in great Friendship, had embraced oppo-site Parties. I am led into this Conjecture, by having remarked, that tho' Love, Friendship, Esteem, and such like, have very powerful Operations in the human Mind; Interest, however, is an Ingredient seldom omitted by wise Men, when they would work others to their own Purposes. This is indeed a most excellent Medicine, and like *Ward's* Pill,[1] flies at once to the particular Part of the Body on which you desire to operate, whether it be the Tongue, the Hand, or any other Member, where it scarce ever fails of immediately producing the desired Effect.

---

[1] Joshua 'Spot' Ward (1685–1761), the well-known empiric, claimed that his 'Pill and Drop' were universal nostrums. They were in fact virulent preparations of antinomy and arsenic which killed as many people as they cured. Nevertheless, he was a generous man who dispensed his medicine gratis to the poor and he enjoyed the favour of some of the most influential members of the aristocracy. For these reasons he was especially exempted from the act of 1748 which prohibited all but duly licensed apothecaries from preparing medi-cines. In pleading Ward's case at that time a writer in *The London Evening-Post* (3–5 May 1748) compared him to the Man of Ross as a paragon of charity.

From the time he began to practise, Ward was the target of ridicule, by Pope, for in-

## CHAPTER X

*In which our Travellers meet with a very extraordinary Adventure.*

JUST as *Jones* and his Friend came to the End of their Dialogue in the preceding Chapter, they arrived at the Bottom of a very steep Hill. Here *Jones* stopt short, and directing his Eyes upwards, stood for a while silent. At length he called to his Companion, and said, '*Partridge*, I wish I was at the Top of this Hill; it must certainly afford a most charming Prospect, especially by this Light: For the solemn Gloom which the Moon casts on all Objects, is beyond Expression beautiful, especially to an Imagination which is desirous of cultivating melancholy Ideas.' 'Very probably,' answered *Partridge*; 'but if the Top of the Hill be properest to produce melancholy Thoughts, I suppose the Bottom is the likeliest to produce merry ones, and these I take to be much the better of the two. I protest you have made my Blood run cold with the very mentioning the Top of that Mountain; which seems to me to be one of the highest in the World. No, no, if we look for any thing, let it be for a Place under Ground, to screen ourselves from the Frost.'—'Do so,' said *Jones*, 'let it be but within Hearing of this Place, and I will hallow to you at my Return back.' 'Surely, Sir, you are not mad,' said *Partridge*. 'Indeed I am,' answered *Jones*, 'if ascending this Hill be Madness: But as you complain so much of the Cold already, I would have you stay below. I will certainly return to you within an Hour.' 'Pardon me, Sir,' cries *Partridge*, 'I have determined to follow you where-ever you go.' Indeed he was now afraid to stay behind; for tho' he was Coward enough in all Respects, yet his chief Fear was that of Ghosts, with which the present Time of Night, and the Wildness of the Place, extremely well suited.

At this Instant *Partridge* espied a glimmering Light through some Trees, which seemed very near to them. He immediately

stance, in the *Imitations of Horace*, Epistles I. vi. 56 (1738), II. i. 182 (1737), and by Hogarth in Plate V of the *Harlot's Progress* (1732). After several incidental satires of Ward—e.g. *The Champion* (28 February 1739/40, 26 August 1740) and *A Journey from This World to the Next* (1743), I. iii—Fielding towards the end of his life submitted to be treated by him. There is a complimentary reference to Ward's pill in *Amelia* (1751), VIII. ix, and in *The Journal of a Voyage to Lisbon* (1755) Fielding gratefully acknowledged his 'Obligations' to the man who had cared for him during his final illness.

cried out in a Rapture, 'Oh, Sir! Heaven hath at last heard my Prayers, and hath brought us to a House; perhaps it may be an Inn. Let me beseech you, Sir, if you have any Compassion either for me or yourself, do not despise the Goodness of Providence, but let us go directly to yon Light. Whether it be a Public-house or no, I am sure if they be Christians that dwell there, they will not refuse a little House-room to Persons in our miserable Condition.' *Jones* at length yielded to the earnest Supplications of *Partridge*, and both together made directly towards the Place whence the Light issued.

They soon arrived at the Door of this House or Cottage: For it might be called either, without much Impropriety. Here *Jones* knocked several Times without receiving any Answer from within; at which *Partridge*, whose Head was full of nothing but of Ghosts, Devils, Witches, and such like, began to tremble, crying, 'Lord have Mercy upon us, sure the People must be all dead. I can see no Light neither now, and yet I am certain I saw a Candle burning but a Moment before.—Well! I have heard of such Things.'—'What hast thou heard of,' said *Jones*. 'The People are either fast asleep, or probably as this is a lonely Place, are afraid to open their Door. He then began to vociferate pretty loudly, and at last an old Woman opening an upper Casement, asked 'who they were, and what they wanted?' *Jones* answered, 'they were Travellers who had lost their Way, and having seen a Light in the Window, had been led thither in Hopes of finding some Fire to warm themselves.' 'Whoever you are,' cries the Woman, 'you have no Business here; nor shall I open the Door to any body at this Time of Night.' *Partridge*, whom the Sound of a human Voice had recovered from his Fright, fell to the most earnest Supplications to be admitted for a few Minutes to the Fire, saying, 'he was almost dead with the Cold,' to which Fear had indeed contributed equally with the Frost. He assured her, that the Gentleman who spoke to her, was one of the greatest Squires in the Country, and made use of every Argument save one, which *Jones* afterwards effectually added, and this was the Promise of Half a Crown. A Bribe too great to be resisted by such a Person, especially as the genteel Appearance of *Jones*, which the Light of the Moon plainly discovered to her, together with his affable Behaviour, had entirely subdued those Apprehensions of Thieves which she had at first conceived. She agreed, therefore, at

last to let them in, where *Partridge*, to his infinite Joy, found a
good Fire ready for his Reception.

The poor Fellow, however, had no sooner warmed himself,
than those Thoughts which were always uppermost in his Mind,
began a little to disturb his Brain. There was no Article of his
Creed in which he had a stronger Faith, than he had in Witchcraft, nor can the Reader conceive a Figure more adapted to
inspire this Idea, than the old Woman who now stood before him.
She answered exactly to that Picture drawn by *Otway* in his
Orphan.¹ Indeed if this Woman had lived in the Reign of *James*
the First,² her Appearance alone would have hanged her, almost
without any Evidence.

Many Circumstances likewise conspired to confirm *Partridge*
in his Opinion. Her living, as he then imagined, by herself in so
lonely a Place; and in a House, the Outside of which seemed much
too good for her; but its Inside was furnished in the most neat
and elegant Manner. To say the Truth, *Jones* himself was not a
little surprized at what he saw: For, besides the extraordinary
Neatness of the Room, it was adorned with a great Number of

---

¹ In *The Orphan: or, The Unhappy Marriage* (1680) by Thomas Otway (1651–85)
Chamont meets a witch who warns him of danger to his sister Monimia (see also below
p. 589):

> I spy'd a wrinkled Hagg, with Age grown double,
> Picking dry Sticks, and mumbling to her self;
> Her Eyes with scalding Rheum were gall'd and red;
> Cold Palsie shook her Head, her Hands seem'd wither'd,
> And on her crooked Shoulders had she wrapt
> The tatter'd Remnant of an old strip'd Hanging,
> Which serv'd to keep her Carkass from the Cold;
> So there was nothing of a-piece about her:
> Her lower Weeds were all o'er coursely patch'd
> With diff'rent colour'd Rags, black, red, white, yellow
> And seem'd to speak variety of Wretchedness. . . . (II. i, 1712 ed.)

The speech is quoted in *Spectator*, No. 117 (14 July 1711).

² James VI of Scotland (1566–1625) succeeded Elizabeth in 1603, becoming James I of
England. In 1597 he had written *Demonology*, a tract against witches, and immediately
upon his accession to the throne of England, Parliament passed the 'Act against Conjura-
tion, Witchcraft, and dealing with evil and wicked Spirits' (1 James I, cap. 12), by which
witches were condemned as felons without benefit of clergy. This statute was repealed by
9 George II, cap. 5 (1736). To Fielding, of course, such superstitious doctrines were
characteristic of the Stuart monarchy, whose 'tyrannical Proceedings' he deplored. (See,
for example, the *Charge Delivered to the Grand Jury* [1749] and *The Jacobite's Journal*
[20 February 1748].) In the *Journal of a Voyage to Lisbon* (1755) he contrasted the practice
of former times, when Sir Matthew Hale hanged witches, to the enlightened attitude of the
Hanoverian period, as exemplified in the Act of 1736.

Nick-nacks, and Curiosities, which might have engaged the Attention of a Virtuoso.

While *Jones* was admiring these Things, and *Partridge* sat trembling with the firm Belief that he was in the House of a Witch, the old Woman said, 'I hope, Gentlemen, you will make what Haste you can; for I expect my Master presently, and I would not for double the Money he should find you here.' 'Then you have a Master,' cries *Jones*; 'indeed you will excuse me, good Woman, but I was surprized to see all those fine Things in your House.' 'Ah, Sir!' said she, 'if the twentieth Part of these Things were mine, I should think myself a rich Woman; but pray, Sir, do not stay much longer: For I look for him in every Minute.'— 'Why sure he would not be angry with you,' said *Jones*, 'for doing a common Act of Charity.' 'Alack-a-day, Sir,' said she, 'he is a strange Man, not at all like other People. He keeps no Company with any Body, and seldom walks out but by Night, for he doth not care to be seen; and all the Country People are as much afraid of meeting him; for his Dress is enough to frighten those who are not used to it. They call him, *The Man of the Hill* (for there he walks by Night) and the Country People are not, I believe, more afraid of the Devil himself. He would be terribly angry if he found you here.' 'Pray, Sir,' says *Partridge*, 'don't let us offend the Gentleman, I am ready to walk, and was never warmer in my Life.—Do, pray Sir, let us go—here are Pistols over the Chimney; who knows whether they be charged or no, or what he may do with them.' 'Fear nothing, *Partridge*,' cries *Jones*, 'I will secure thee from Danger.'—'Nay, for Matter o' that, he never doth any Mischief,' said the Woman; 'but to be sure it is necessary he should keep some Arms for his own Safety; for his House hath been beset more than once, and it is not many Nights ago, that we thought, we heard Thieves about it: for my own Part, I have often wondered that he is not murdered by some Villain or other, as he walks out by himself at such Hours; but then, as I said, the People are afraid of him, and besides they think, I suppose, he hath nothing about him worth taking.' 'I should imagine, by this Collection of Rarities,' cries *Jones*, 'that your Master had been a Traveller.' 'Yes, Sir,' answered she, 'he hath been a very great one; there be few Gentlemen that know more of all Matters than he; I fancy he hath been crost in Love, or whatever it is, I know not, but I have lived with him above these

thirty Years, and in all that Time he hath hardly spoke to six
living People.' She then again solicited their Departure, in which
she was backed by *Partridge*; but *Jones* purposely protracted the
time: For his Curiosity was greatly raised to see this extraordinary
Person. Tho' the old Woman, therefore, concluded every one of
her Answers with desiring him to be gone, and *Partridge* proceeded so far as to pull him by the Sleeve, he still continued to
invent new Questions, till the old Woman with an affrighted
Countenance, declared she heard her Master's Signal; and at the
same Instant more than one Voice was heard without the Door,
crying, 'D——n your Blood, shew us your Money this Instant.
Your Money, you Villain, or we will blow your Brains about your
Ears.'

'O, good Heaven!' cries the old Woman. 'Some Villains, to be
sure, have attacked my Master. O la! what shall I do? what shall
I do?' 'How,' cries *Jones*, 'how—— Are these Pistols loaded?'
'O, Good Sir, there is nothing in them, indeed—O, pray don't
murder us, Gentlemen' (for in reality she now had the same
Opinion of those within, as she had of those without.) *Jones* made
her no Answer; but snatching an old Broad-sword[1] which hung
in the Room, he instantly sallied out, where he found the old
Gentleman struggling with two Ruffians, and begging for Mercy.
*Jones* asked no Questions, but fell so briskly to work with his
Broad-sword, that the Fellows immediately quitted their Hold,
and without offering to attack our Heroe, betook themselves to
their Heels, and made their Escape; for he did not attempt to
pursue them, being contented with having delivered the old
Gentleman; and indeed he concluded he had pretty well done
their Business: For both of them, as they ran off, cried out with
bitter Oaths, that they were dead Men.

*Jones* presently ran to lift up the old Gentleman, who had been
thrown down in the Scuffle, expressing at the same Time great
Concern, lest he should have received any Harm from the
Villains. The old Man stared a Moment at *Jones*, and then cried,
—'No, Sir, no, I have very little Harm, I thank you. Lord have
Mercy upon me.' 'I see, Sir,' said *Jones*, 'you are not free from
Apprehensions even of those who have had the Happiness to be
your Deliverers; nor can I blame any Suspicions which you may

[1] Fielding apparently forgets that in VII. xiv Jones had acquired his own sword, with
which he later defends himself against Fitzpatrick (XVI. x).

have; but indeed, you have no real Occasion for any; here are
none but your Friends present. Having mist our Way this cold
Night, we took the Liberty of warming ourselves at your Fire,
whence we were just departing when we heard you call for
Assistance, which I must say, Providence alone seems to have
sent you.'—'Providence indeed,' cries the old Gentleman, 'if it be
so.'—'So it is, I assure you,' cries *Jones*, 'here is your own Sword,
Sir. I have used it in your Defence, and I now return it into your
own Hand.' The old Man having received the Sword, which was
stained with the Blood of his Enemies, looked stedfastly at *Jones*
during some Moments, and then with a Sigh, cried out, 'You will
pardon me, young Gentleman, I was not always of a suspicious
Temper, nor am I a Friend to Ingratitude.' 'Be thankful then,'
cries *Jones*, 'to that Providence to which you owe your Deliverance; as to my Part, I have only discharged the common Duties
of Humanity, and what I would have done for any Fellow
Creature in your Situation.' 'Let me look at you a little longer,'
cries the old Gentleman.—'You are a human Creature then?—
Well, perhaps, you are. Come, pray walk into my little Hutt. You
have been my Deliverer indeed.'

The old Woman was distracted between the Fears which she
had of her Master, and for him; and *Partridge* was, if possible, in
a greater Fright. The former of these, however, when she heard
her Master speak kindly to *Jones*, and perceived what had
happened, came again to herself; but *Partridge* no sooner saw the
Gentleman, than the Strangeness of his Dress infused greater
Terrors into that poor Fellow, than he had before felt either from
the strange Description which he had heard, or from the Uproar
which had happened at the Door.

To say the Truth, it was an Appearance which might have
affected a more constant Mind than that of Mr. *Partridge*. This
Person was of the tallest Size, with a long Beard as white as
Snow. His Body was cloathed with the Skin of an Ass, made
something into the Form of a Coat.[1] He wore likewise Boots on
his Legs, and a Cap on his Head, both composed of the Skin of
some other Animals.

---

[1] This peculiarity of dress recalls Lucian's Timon, who also appears clothed in a coat of
skins. Like Timon, too, the Man of the Hill has fled from society, his misanthropy caused
by the treachery and ingratitude of his friends. (A. M. Harmon, trans. *Lucian*, vol. ii [Loeb
Classical Library, 1915].)

As soon as the old Gentleman came into his House, the old Woman began her Congratulations on his happy Escape from the Ruffians. 'Yes,' cried he, 'I have escaped indeed, Thanks to my Preserver.' 'O the Blessing on him,' answered she, 'he is a good Gentleman, I warrant him. I was afraid your Worship would have been angry with me for letting him in; and to be certain I should not have done it, had not I seen by the Moon-light, that he was a Gentleman, and almost frozen to Death. And to be certain it must have been some good Angel that sent him hither, and tempted me to do it.'

'I am afraid, Sir,' said the old Gentleman to *Jones*, 'that I have nothing in this House which you can either eat or drink, unless you will accept a Dram of Brandy; of which I can give you some most excellent, and which I have had by me these thirty Years.' *Jones* declined this Offer in a very civil and proper Speech, and then the other asked him 'Whither he was travelling when he mist his Way;' saying, 'I must own myself surprized to see such a Person as you appear to be journeying on Foot at this Time of Night. I suppose, Sir, you are a Gentleman of these Parts: for you do not look like one who is used to travel far without Horses.'

'Appearances,' cried *Jones*, 'are often deceitful; Men some-times look like what they are not. I assure you, I am not of this Country, and whither I am travelling, in reality I scarce know myself.'

'Whoever you are, or whithersoever you are going,' answered the old Man, 'I have Obligations to you which I can never return.'

'I once more,' replied *Jones*, 'affirm, that you have none: For there can be no Merit in having hazarded that in your Service on which I set no Value. And nothing is so contemptible in my Eyes as Life.'

'I am sorry, young Gentleman,' answered the Stranger, 'that you have any Reason to be so unhappy at your Years.'

'Indeed I am, Sir,' answered *Jones*, 'the most unhappy of Mankind.'—'Perhaps you have had a Friend, or a Mistress,' replied the other. 'How could you,' cries *Jones*, 'mention two Words sufficient to drive me to Distraction?' 'Either of them are enough to drive any Man to Distraction,' answered the old Man. 'I enquire no farther, Sir. Perhaps my Curiosity hath led me too far already.'

'Indeed, Sir,' cries *Jones*, 'I cannot censure a Passion, which I feel at this Instant in the highest Degree. You will pardon me, when I assure you, that every Thing which I have seen or heard since I first entered this House, hath conspired to raise the greatest Curiosity in me. Something very extraordinary must have determined you to this Course of Life, and I have reason to fear your own History is not without Misfortunes.'

Here the old Gentleman again sighed, and remained silent for some Minutes; at last, looking earnestly on *Jones*, he said, 'I have read that a good Countenance is a Letter of Recommendation;[1] if so, none ever can be more strongly recommended than yourself. If I did not feel some Yearnings towards you from another Consideration, I must be the most ungrateful Monster upon Earth; and I am really concerned it is no otherwise in my Power, than by Words, to convince you of my Gratitude.'

*Jones* after a Moment's Hesitation, answered, 'That it was in his Power by Words to gratify him extremely. I have confest a Curiosity,' said he, 'Sir; need I say how much obliged I should be to you, if you would condescend to gratify it? Will you suffer me therefore to beg, unless any Consideration restrains you, that you would be pleased to acquaint me what Motives have induced you thus to withdraw from the Society of Mankind, and to betake yourself to a Course of Life to which it sufficiently appears you were not born?'

'I scarce think myself at Liberty to refuse you any thing, after what hath happened,' replied the old Man, 'If you desire therefore to hear the Story of an unhappy Man, I will relate it to you. Indeed you judge rightly, in thinking there is commonly something extraordinary in the Fortunes of those who fly from Society: For however it may seem a Paradox, or even a Contradiction, certain it is that great Philanthropy chiefly inclines us to avoid and detest Mankind; not on Account so much of their private and selfish Vices, but for those of a relative Kind; such as Envy, Malice, Treachery, Cruelty, with every other Species of Malevolence. These are the Vices which true Philanthropy abhors, and

---

[1] A proverbial expression attributed to Aristotle in Diogenes Laertius, *Lives of Eminent Philosophers*, v. xviii: 'Beauty he declared to be a greater recommendation than any letter of introduction' (trans. R. D. Hicks, Loeb Classical Library, 1925). Fielding's phrasing is especially close to Addison's, *Spectator*, No. 221 (13 November 1711). See also 'An Essay on the Knowledge of the Characters of Men' (1743) and *Amelia* (1751), IX. v.

which rather than see and converse with, she avoids Society itself. However, without a Compliment to you, you do not appear to me one of those whom I should shun or detest; nay, I must say, in what little hath dropt from you, there appears some Parity in our Fortunes; I hope however yours will conclude more successfully.'

Here some Compliments passed between our Heroe and his Host, and then the latter was going to begin his History, when *Partridge* interrupted him. His Apprehensions had now pretty well left him; but some Effects of his Terrors remained; he therefore reminded the Gentleman of that excellent Brandy which he had mentioned. This was presently brought, and *Partridge* swallowed a large Bumper.

The Gentleman then, without any farther Preface, began as you may read in the next Chapter.


## CHAPTER XI

### *In which the Man of the Hill begins to relate his History.*

'I WAS born in a Village of *Somersetshire*, called *Mark*, in the Year 1657; my Father was one of those whom they call Gentlemen Farmers. He had a little Estate of about 300 *l.* a Year of his own, and rented another Estate of near the same Value. He was prudent and industrious, and so good a Husbandman, that he might have led a very easy and comfortable Life, had not an arrant Vixen of a Wife soured his domestic Quiet. But tho' this Circumstance perhaps made him miserable, it did not make him poor: For he confined her almost entirely at Home, and rather chose to bear eternal Upbraidings in his own House, than to injure his Fortune by indulging her in the Extravagancies she desired abroad.

'By this *Xantippe* (so was the Wife of *Socrates* called, said *Partridge*)—By this *Xantippe* he had two Sons, of which I was the younger. He designed to give us both good Educations; but my elder Brother, who, unhappily for him, was the Favourite of my Mother, utterly neglected his Learning; insomuch that after having been five or six Years at School with little or no Improvement, my Father being told by his Master, that it would be to no

Purpose to keep him longer there, at last complied with my Mother in taking him home from the Hands of that Tyrant, as she called his Master; though indeed he gave the Lad much less Correction than his Idleness deserved, but much more, it seems, than the young Gentleman liked, who constantly complained to his Mother of his severe Treatment, and she as constantly gave him a Hearing.'

'Yes, yes,' cries *Partridge*, 'I have seen such Mothers; I have been abused myself by them, and very unjustly; such Parents deserve Correction as much as their Children.'

*Jones* chid the Pedagogue for this Interruption, and then the Stranger proceeded. 'My Brother now at the Age of fifteen, bid adieu to all Learning, and to every Thing else but to his Dog and Gun, with which latter he became so expert, that, though perhaps you may think it incredible, he could not only hit a standing Mark with great Certainty; but hath actually shot a Crow as it was flying in the Air. He was likewise excellent at finding a Hare sitting, and was soon reputed one of the best Sportsmen in the Country. A Reputation which both he and his Mother enjoyed as much as if he had been thought the finest Scholar.

'The Situation of my Brother made me at first think my Lot the harder, in being continued at School; but I soon changed my Opinion; for as I advanced pretty fast in Learning, my Labours became easy, and my Exercise so delightful, that Holidays were my most unpleasant Time: For my Mother, who never loved me, now apprehending that I had the greater Share of my Father's Affection, and finding, or at least thinking, that I was more taken Notice of by some Gentlemen of Learning, and particularly by the Parson of the Parish, than my Brother, she now hated my Sight, and made Home so disagreeable to me, that what is called by Schoolboys Black Monday, was to me the whitest in the whole Year.

'Having, at length, gone through the School at *Taunton*, I was thence removed to *Exeter* College in *Oxford*,[1] where I remained

---

[1] The mention of these institutions may well be meant as a compliment to Fielding's academic friends, the Uptons. James Upton (1670–1749), master at Eton during the period of Fielding's education there, became headmaster of the Taunton grammar school in 1730. His son John (1707–60) was born at Taunton and was a Fellow of Exeter College, Oxford. For a probable allusion to the latter's *Critical Observations on Shakespeare* (1746), see below, p. 524, n. 1. Although Fielding nowhere explicitly refers to the Uptons in his published writings, they had a close mutual friend in James Harris of Salisbury (see

four Years; at the End of which an Accident took me off entirely
from my Studies, and hence I may truly date the Rise of all
which happened to me afterwards in Life.

'There was at the same College with myself one Sir *George
Gresham*, a young Fellow who was intitled to a very considerable
Fortune; which he was not, by the Will of his Father, to come
into full Possession of till he arrived at the Age of Twenty-five.
However, the Liberality of his Guardians gave him little Cause to
regret the abundant Caution of his Father: for they allowed him
Five hundred Pound a Year while he remained at the University,
where he kept his Horses and his Whore, and lived as wicked and
as profligate a Life, as he could have done, had he been never so
entirely Master of his Fortune; for besides the Five hundred a
Year which he received from his Guardians, he found Means to
spend a thousand more. He was above the Age of Twenty-one,
and had no Difficulty in gaining what Credit he pleased.

'This young Fellow, among many other tolerable bad Qualities,
had one very diabolical. He had a great Delight in destroying and
ruining the Youth of inferior Fortune, by drawing them into
Expences which they could not afford so well as himself; and the
better, and worthier, and soberer, any young Man was, the greater
Pleasure and Triumph had he in his Destruction. Thus acting
the Character which is recorded of the Devil, and going about
seeking whom he might devour.[1]

'It was my Misfortune to fall into an Acquaintance and
Intimacy with this Gentleman. My Reputation of Diligence in
my Studies made me a desirable Object of his mischievous
Intention; and my own Inclination made it sufficiently easy for
him to effect his Purpose; for tho' I had applied myself with much
Industry to Books, in which I took great Delight, there were other
Pleasures in which I was capable of taking much greater; for I was
high-mettled, had a violent Flow of animal Spirits, was a little
ambitious, and extremely amorous.

'I had not long contracted an Intimacy with Sir *George*, before
I became a Partaker of all his Pleasures; and when I was once

Harris's *Three Treatises* [1744], p. 286, and *Upon the Rise and Progress of Criticism* [1752],
pp. 20–1 n.); moreover, the friendship between the Uptons and the Fieldings may be
inferred from Ursula Fielding's letter of 25 October 1748 (see J. P. de Castro, *N & Q*,
clxxviii [9 March 1940], 164–7).

[1] 1 Peter 5: 8: 'Be sober, be vigilant; because your adversary the devil, as a roaring lion,
walketh about, seeking whom he may devour'.

entered on that Scene, neither my Inclination, nor my Spirit, would suffer me to play an Under-Part. I was second to none of the Company in any Acts of Debauchery; nay, I soon distinguished myself so notably in all Riots and Disorders, that my Name generally stood first in the Roll of Delinquents, and instead of being lamented as the unfortunate Pupil of Sir *George*, I was now accused as the Person who had misled and debauched that hopeful young Gentleman; for tho' he was the Ring-leader and Promoter of all the Mischief, he was never so considered. I fell at last under the Censure of the Vice-Chancellor, and very narrowly escaped Expulsion.

'You will easily believe, Sir, that such a Life as I am now describing must be incompatible with my further Progress in Learning; and that in Proportion as I addicted myself more and more to loose Pleasure, I must grow more and more remiss in Application to my Studies. This was truly the Consequence; but this was not all. My Expences now greatly exceeded not only my former Income, but those Additions which I extorted from my poor generous Father, on Pretences of Sums being necessary for preparing for my approaching Degree of Batchelor of Arts. These Demands, however, grew at last so frequent and exorbitant, that my Father, by slow Degrees, opened his Ears to the Accounts which he received from many Quarters of my present Behaviour, and which my Mother failed not to eccho very faithfully and loudly; adding, "Ay, this is the fine Gentleman, the Scholar who doth so much Honour to his Family, and is to be the Making of it. I thought what all this Learning would come to. He is to be the Ruin of us all, I find, after his elder Brother hath been denied Necessaries for his Sake, to perfect his Education forsooth, for which he was to pay us such Interest; I thought what the Interest would come to;" with much more of the same Kind; but I have, I believe, satisfied you with this Taste.

'My Father, therefore, began now to return Remonstrances, instead of Money, to my Demands, which brought my Affairs, perhaps a little sooner to a Crisis; but had he remitted me his whole Income, you will imagine it could have sufficed a very short Time to support one who kept Pace with the Expences of Sir *George Gresham*.

'It is more than possible, that the Distress I was now in for

Money, and the Impracticability of going on in this Manner, might have restored me at once to my Senses, and to my Studies, had I opened my Eyes, before I became involved in Debts, from which I saw no Hopes of ever extricating myself. This was indeed the great Art of Sir *George*, and by which he accomplished the Ruin of many, whom he afterwards laughed at as Fools and Coxcombs, for vying, as he called it, with a Man of his Fortune. To bring this about, he would now and then advance a little Money himself, in order to support the Credit of the unfortunate Youth with other People; till, by Means of that very Credit, he was irretrievably undone.

'My Mind being, by these Means, grown as desperate as my Fortune, there was scarce a Wickedness which I did not meditate, in order for my Relief. Self-murder itself became the Subject of my serious Deliberation; and I had certainly resolved on it, had not a more shameful, tho' perhaps less sinful, Thought, expelled it from my Head.' Here he hesitated a Moment, and then cried out, 'I protest, so many Years have not washed away the Shame of this Act, and I shall blush while I relate it.' *Jones* desired him to pass over any thing that might give him Pain in the Relation; but *Partridge* eagerly cried out, 'O pray, Sir, let us hear this, I had rather hear this than all the rest; as I hope to be saved, I will never mention a Word of it.' *Jones* was going to rebuke him, but the Stranger prevented it by proceeding thus. 'I had a Chum, a very prudent, frugal young Lad, who, tho' he had no very large Allowance, had by his Parsimony heaped up upwards of forty Guineas, which I knew he kept in his Escritore. I took therefore an Opportunity of purloining his Key from his Breeches Pocket while he was asleep, and thus made myself Master of all his Riches. After which I again conveyed his Key into his Pocket, and counterfeiting Sleep, tho' I never once closed my Eyes, lay in Bed till after he arose and went to Prayers, an Exercise to which I had long been unaccustomed.

'Timorous Thieves, by extreme Caution, often subject themselves to Discoveries, which those of a bolder Kind escape. Thus it happened to me; for had I boldly broke open his Escritore, I had, perhaps, escaped even his Suspicion; but as it was plain that the Person who robbed him had possessed himself of his Key, he had no Doubt, when he first missed his Money, but that his Chum was certainly the Thief. Now as he was of a fearful Disposition, and much my Inferior in Strength, and, I believe, in Courage, he did not dare to confront me with my Guilt, for fear of worse bodily Consequences which might happen to him. He repaired therefore immediately to the Vice-Chancellor, and, upon swearing to the Robbery, and to the Circumstances of it, very easily obtained a Warrant against one who had now so bad a Character through the whole University.

'Luckily for me I lay out of the College the next Evening; for that Day I attended a young Lady in a Chaise to *Whitney*, where we staid all Night; and in our Return the next Morning to *Oxford*, I met one of my Cronies, who acquainted me with sufficient News concerning myself to make me turn my Horse another Way.'

'Pray Sir, did he mention any thing of the Warrant?' said *Partridge*. But *Jones* begged the Gentleman to proceed without regarding any impertinent Questions; which he did as follows.

'Having now abandoned all Thoughts of returning to *Oxford*, the next Thing which offered itself was a Journey to *London*. I imparted this Intention to my female Companion, who at first remonstrated against it, but upon producing my Wealth, she immediately consented. We then struck across the Country into the great *Cirencester* Road,[1] and made such Haste, that we spent the next Evening (save one) in *London*.

'When you consider the Place where I now was, and the Company with whom I was, you will, I fancy, conceive that a very short Time brought me to an End of that Sum of which I had so iniquitously possessed myself.

'I was now reduced to a much higher Degree of Distress than before; the Necessaries of Life began to be numbred among my Wants; and what made my Case still the more grievous, was, that my Paramour, of whom I was now grown immoderately fond, shared the same Distresses with myself. To see a Woman you love in Distress; to be unable to relieve her, and at the same Time to reflect that you have brought her into this Situation, is, perhaps, a Curse of which no Imagination can represent the Horrors to those who have not felt it.' 'I believe it from my Soul,' cries *Jones*, 'and I pity you from the Bottom of my Heart.' He then took two or three disorderly Turns about the Room, and at last begged

[1] This road ran between Gloucester and London, passing through Cirencester, Abingdon, Dorchester, Henley, Maidenhead, and Brentford. (See John Ogilby, *Britannia* [1675].)

Pardon, and flung himself into his Chair, crying, 'I thank Heaven I have escaped that.'

'This Circumstance,' continued the Gentleman, 'so severely aggravated the Horrors of my present Situation, that they became absolutely intolerable. I could with less Pain endure the raging of my own natural unsatisfied Appetites, even Hunger or Thirst, than I could submit to leave ungratified the most whimsical Desires of a Woman, on whom I so extravagantly doated, that tho' I knew she had been the Mistress of half my Acquaintance, I firmly intended to marry her. But the good Creature was unwilling to consent to an Action which the World might think so much to my Disadvantage. And as, possibly, she compassionated the daily Anxieties which she must have perceived me suffer on her Account, she resolved to put an End to my Distress. She soon, indeed, found Means to relieve me from my troublesome and perplexed Situation: For while I was distracted with various Inventions to supply her with Pleasures, she very kindly— betrayed me to one of her former Lovers at *Oxford*, by whose Care and Diligence I was immediately apprehended and committed to Goal.

'Here I first began seriously to reflect on the Miscarriages of my former Life; on the Errors I had been guilty of; on the Misfortunes which I had brought on myself; and on the Grief which I must have occasioned to one of the best of Fathers. When I added to all these the Perfidy of my Mistress, such was the Horror of my Mind, that Life, instead of being longer desirable, grew the Object of my Abhorrence, and I could have gladly embraced Death, as my dearest Friend, if it had offered itself to my Choice unattended by Shame.

'The Time of the Assizes soon came, and I was removed by *Habeas Corpus* to *Oxford*, where I expected certain Conviction and Condemnation; but, to my great Surprize, none appeared against me, and I was, at the End of the Sessions, discharged for Want of Prosecution. In short, my Chum had left *Oxford*, and whether from Indolence, or from what other Motive, I am ignorant, had declined concerning himself any farther in the Affair.'

'Perhaps,' cries *Partridge*, 'he did not care to have your Blood upon his Hands, and he was in the right on't. If any Person was to be hanged upon my Evidence, I should never be able to lie alone afterwards, for Fear of seeing his Ghost.'

'I shall shortly doubt, *Partridge*,' says *Jones*, 'whether thou art more brave or wise.' 'You may laugh at me, Sir, if you please,' answered *Partridge*, 'but if you will hear a very short Story which I can tell, and which is most certainly true, perhaps you may change your Opinion. In the Parish where I was born——' Here *Jones* would have silenced him, but the Stranger interceded that he might be permitted to tell his Story, and in the mean time promised to recollect the Remainder of his own.

*Partridge* then proceeded thus. 'In the Parish where I was born, there lived a Farmer whose Name was *Bridle*, and he had a Son named *Francis*, a good hopeful young Fellow; I was at the Grammar School with him, where I remember he was got into *Ovid's Epistles*, and he could construe you three Lines together sometimes without looking into a Dictionary. Besides all this, he was a very good Lad, never missed Church o' Sundays, and was reckoned one of the best Psalm-Singers in the whole Parish. He would indeed now and then take a Cup too much, and that was the only Fault he had.'—'Well, but come to the Ghost,' cries *Jones*. 'Never fear, Sir, I shall come to him soon enough,' answered *Partridge*. 'You must know then, that Farmer *Bridle* lost a Mare, a sorrel one to the best of my Remembrance, and so it fell out, that this young *Francis* shortly afterward being at a Fair at *Hindon*, and as I think it was on—I can't remember the Day; and being as he was, what should he happen to meet, but a Man upon his Father's Mare. *Frank* called out presently, Stop Thief; and it being in the Middle of the Fair, it was impossible, you know, for the Man to make his Escape. So they apprehended him, and carried him before the Justice, I remember it was Justice *Willoughby* of *Noyle*,[1] a very worthy good Gentleman, and he committed him to Prison, and bound *Frank* in a Recognizance,[2] I think they call it, a hard Word compounded of *re* and

---

[1] Richard Willoughby (c. 1703–62) of West Knoyle, Wilts.—a village about three miles west of Hindon. His family, many of whom were lawyers, had long resided in West Knoyle, but Willoughby sold the estate soon after he inherited it in 1731. At that time he was living at Southampton Buildings, London (see *The Gentleman's Magazine*, i [January 1731], 32) —a circumstance which, four years earlier, seems to have involved him as a principal witness in the Darby murder case (see above, p. 402, n. 3). Willoughby's name appears among the subscribers to Fielding's *Miscellanies* (1743). For the tradition (which is certainly correct) that Richard Willoughby is the person Fielding meant to compliment in the present passage, see Sir Richard Colt Hoare, *The History of Modern Wiltshire. Hundred of Mere* (1822), p. 41.

[2] '*A Recognizance* is a Bond of Record acknowledged to the King, upon Condition to

*cognosco*, but it differs in its Meaning from the Use of the Simple, as many other Compounds do. Well, at last, down came my Lord Justice *Page*[1] to hold the Assizes, and so the Fellow was had up, and *Frank* was had up for a Witness. To be sure I shall never forget the Face of the Judge, when he began to ask him what he had to say against the Prisoner. He made poor *Frank* tremble and shake in his Shoes. "Well, you Fellow," says my Lord, "what have you to say? Don't stand humming and hawing, but speak out;" but however he soon turned altogether as civil to *Frank*, and began to thunder at the Fellow; and when he asked him, if he had any Thing to say for himself, the Fellow said he had found the Horse. "Ay!" answered the Judge, "thou art a lucky Fellow; I have travelled the Circuit these forty Years, and never found a Horse in my Life; but I'll tell thee what, Friend, thou wast more lucky than thou didst know of: For thou didst not only find a Horse; but a Halter too, I promise thee." To be sure I shall never forget the Word. Upon which every Body fell a laughing, as how could they help it. Nay, and twenty other Jests he made which I can't remember now. There was something about his Skill in Horse-Flesh, which made all the Folks laugh. To be certain the Judge must have been a very brave Man, as well as a Man of much Learning. It is indeed charming Sport to hear Trials upon Life and Death. One Thing I own I thought a little hard, that the Prisoner's Counsel was not suffered to speak for him, though he desired only to be heard one very short Word; but my Lord would not hearken to him, though he suffered a Counsellor to talk against him for above half an Hour. I thought it hard, I own, that there should be so many of them; my Lord,

pay a certain Sum of Money if the Condition is not performed; as to appear at the Assises or Quarter-Sessions, to be of the Good Behaviour, &c.' (Wood's *Institutes*, 7th ed. [1745], p. 84). As a commissioner of the peace, Willoughby's function was only to commit the prisoner to stand trial and to bind over the witness. The actual trial would have taken place at the Salisbury Assizes. (See J. P. de Castro, *N & Q*, 11th Ser., x [26 September 1914], 253.)

[1] Sir Francis Page (1661 ?–1741), known as 'the hanging judge', was notorious for his coarseness and brutality while on the bench. Pope satirized him in several poems: e.g. *Imitations of Horace, Satires II. i* (1733), 82, and *The Dunciad*, iv (1742), 30. The last time Page presided over the Western Circuit during the Summer Assizes was in 1739. Bishop Douglas of Salisbury was once present when an innocent man was brought before Page to stand trial for horsestealing. As soon as he saw the prisoner, the judge exclaimed: 'A very ill-looking Fellow; I have no doubt of his guilt'. Happily, however, the trial ended in an acquittal. (See John Butt, ed. Pope's *Imitations of Horace*, Twickenham Edition, 2nd ed., iv [1953], 376.)

and the Court, and the Jury, and the Counsellors, and the Witnesses all upon one poor Man, and he too in Chains. Well, the Fellow was hanged, as to be sure it could be no otherwise, and poor *Frank* could never be easy about it. He never was in the dark alone, but he fancied he saw the Fellow's Spirit.' 'Well, and is this thy Story?' cries *Jones*. 'No, no,' answer'd *Partridge*, 'O Lord have Mercy upon me,—I am just now coming to the Matter; for one Night, coming from the Alehouse in a long narrow dark Lane, there he ran directly up against him, and the Spirit was all in white and fell upon *Frank*, and *Frank* who is a sturdy Lad, fell upon the Spirit again, and there they had a Tussel together, and poor *Frank* was dreadfully beat; indeed he made a shift at last to crawl Home, but what with the beating, and what with the Fright, he lay ill above a Fortnight; and all this is most certainly true, and the whole Parish will bear Witness to it.'

The Stranger smiled at this Story, and *Jones* burst into a loud Fit of Laughter, upon which *Partridge* cried, 'Ay, you may laugh, Sir, and so did some others, particularly a Squire, who is thought to be no better than an Atheist; who forsooth, because there was a Calf with a white Face found dead in the same Lane the next Morning, would fain have it, that the Battle was between *Frank* and that, as if a Calf would set upon a Man. Besides, *Frank* told me he knew it to be a Spirit, and could swear to him in any Court in Christendom, and he had not drank above a Quart or two, or such a Matter of Liquor at the time. Lud have Mercy upon us, and keep us all from dipping our Hands in Blood, I say.'

'Well, Sir,' said *Jones* to the Stranger, 'Mr. *Partridge* hath finished his Story, and I hope will give you no future Interruption, if you will be so kind to proceed.' He then resumed his Narration; but as he hath taken Breath for a while, we think proper to give it to our Reader, and shall therefore put an End to this Chapter.


## CHAPTER XII

*In which the Man of the Hill continues his History.*

'I HAD now regained my Liberty,' said the Stranger,'but I had lost my Reputation; for there is a wide Difference between the Case of a Man who is barely acquitted of a Crime in a Court of

Justice, and of him who is acquitted in his own Heart, and in the Opinion of the People. I was conscious of my Guilt, and ashamed to look any one in the Face, so resolved to leave *Oxford* the next Morning, before the Daylight discovered me to the Eyes of any Beholders.

'When I had got clear of the City, it first entered into my Head to return Home to my Father, and endeavour to obtain his *Saved* Forgiveness; but as I had no Reason to doubt his Knowledge of all which had past, and as I was well assured of his great Aversion to all Acts of Dishonesty, I could entertain no Hopes of being received by him, especially since I was too certain of all the good Offices in the Power of my Mother: Nay, had my Father's Pardon been as sure, as I conceived his Resentment to be, I yet question whether I could have had the Assurance to behold him, or whether I could, upon any Terms, have submitted to live and converse with those, who, I was convinced, knew me to have been guilty of so base an Action.

'I hastened therefore back to *London*, the best Retirement of either Grief or Shame, unless for Persons of a very public Character; for here you have the Advantage of Solitude without its Disadvantage, since you may be alone and in Company at the same Time; and while you walk or sit unobserved, Noise, Hurry, and a constant Succession of Objects, entertain the Mind, and prevent the Spirits from preying on themselves, or rather on Grief or Shame, which are the most unwholesome Diet in the World; and on which (though there are many who never taste either but in public) there are some who can feed very plentifully, and very fatally when alone.

'But as there is scarce any human Good without its concomitant Evil, so there are People who find an Inconvenience in this unobserving Temper of Mankind; I mean Persons who have no Money; for as you are not put out of Countenance, so neither are you cloathed or fed by those who do not know you. And a Man may be as easily starved in *Leadenhall* Market[1] as in the Desarts of *Arabia*.

'It was at present my Fortune to be destitute of that great Evil, as it is apprehended to be by several Writers, who I suppose were overburthened with it, namely, Money.' 'With Submission,

---

[1] Located in the City of London, Leadenhall was one of the largest provision markets in Europe.

Sir,' said *Partridge*, 'I do not remember any Writers who have called it *Malorum*; but *Irritamenta Malorum. Essodiuntur opes irritamenta Malorum.*'[1] 'Well, Sir,' continued the Stranger, 'whether it be an Evil, or only the Cause of Evil, I was entirely void of it, and at the same Time of Friends, and as I thought of Acquaintance; when one Evening as I was passing through the *Inner Temple*, very hungry and very miserable, I heard a Voice on a sudden haling me with great Familiarity by my Christian Name; and upon my turning about, I presently recollected the Person who so saluted me, to have been my Fellow Collegiate, one who had left the University above a Year, and long before any of my Misfortunes had befallen me. This Gentleman, whose Name was *Watson*, shook me heartily by the Hand, and expressing great Joy at meeting me, proposed our immediately drinking a Bottle together. I first declined the Proposal, and pretended Business; but as he was very earnest and pressing, Hunger at last overcame my Pride, and I fairly confessed to him I had no Money in my Pocket; yet not without framing a Lie for an Excuse, and imputing it to my having changed my Breeches that Morning. Mr. *Watson* answered, "I thought, *Jack*, you and I had been too old Acquaintance for you to mention such a Matter." He then took me by the Arm and was pulling me along; but I gave him very little Trouble, for my own Inclinations pulled me much stronger than he could do.

'We then went into the Friars,[2] which you know is the Scene of all Mirth and Jollity. Here when we arrived at the Tavern,[3] Mr. *Watson* applied himself to the Drawer only, without taking the least Notice of the Cook; for he had no Suspicion but that I

[1] Ovid, *Metamorphoses*, i. 140: 'riches, the incitement to crime, are sought by digging'.

[2] The familiar name for the Blackfriars, the precinct situated between Ludgate Hill and the Thames, a few minutes' walk eastward from the Inner Temple. The district had been formerly occupied by the Dominicans or Black Friars, but after the dissolution of the monasteries by Henry VIII it became a retreat for disreputable persons of all kinds—thieves, sharpers, fences, prostitutes.

[3] The story of the Man of the Hill's experiences among the gamblers and confidence men of London should be viewed in the context of an extensive contemporary literature exposing the follies and vices of the town, many of these fugitive works being designed as cautionary guides for the naïve visitor from the country. Ned Ward's *London Spy* (1698–1709) is perhaps the best-known example, but with the present chapter compare, in particular, *The Tricks of the Town Laid Open; or, a Companion for Country Gentlemen* (1747), esp. letter xi, 'In which the Humours of the *Groom Porter's*, and the Tricks and Cheats of *Ordinaries*, and other *Gaming-houses* are briefly exposed'.

had dined long since. However, as the Case was really otherwise,
I forged another Falshood, and told my Companion, I had been
at the further End of the City on Business of Consequence, and
had snapt up a Mutton Chop in Haste, so that I was again hungry,
and wished he would add a Beef Steak to his Bottle.' 'Some
People,' cries *Partridge*, 'ought to have good Memories, or did
you find just Money enough in your Breeches to pay for the
Mutton Chop?' 'Your Observation is right,' answered the
Stranger, 'and I believe such Blunders are inseparable from all
dealing in Untruth.—But to proceed—I began now to feel
myself extremely happy. The Meat and Wine soon revived my
Spirits to a high Pitch, and I enjoyed much Pleasure in the Conversation of my old Acquaintance, the rather, as I thought him
entirely ignorant of what had happened at the University since
his leaving it.

'But he did not suffer me to remain long in this agreeable
Delusion; for taking a Bumper in one Hand, and holding me by
the other, "Here, my Boy," cries he, "here's wishing you Joy of
your being so honourably acquitted of that Affair laid to your
Charge." I was Thunderstruck with Confusion at those Words,
which *Watson* observing, proceeded thus—"Nay, never be
ashamed, Man; thou hast been acquitted, and no one now dares
call thee guilty; but prithee do tell me, who am thy Friend, I hope
thou didst really rob him; for rat me if it was not a meritorious
Action to strip such a sneaking pitiful Rascal, and instead of the
Two hundred Guineas, I wish you had taken as many thousand.
Come, come, my Boy, don't be shy of confessing to me, you are
not now brought before one of the Pimps. D—n me, if I don't
honour you for it; for, as I hope for Salvation, I would have made
no manner of Scruple of doing the same Thing."

'This Declaration a little relieved my Abashment, and as
Wine had now somewhat opened my Heart, I very freely acknowledged the Robbery, but acquainted him that he had been
misinformed as to the Sum taken, which was little more than a
fifth Part of what he had mentioned.

' "I am sorry for it with all my Heart," quoth he, "and I wish
thee better Success another Time. Tho' if you will take my
Advice, you shall have no Occasion to run any such Risque.
Here," said he, (taking some Dice out of his Pocket) "here's
the Stuff. Here are the Implements; here are the little

Doctors[1] which cure the Distempers of the Purse. Follow but my Counsel, and I will shew you a Way to empty the Pockets of a *Queer Cull*,[2] without any Danger of the *Nubbing Cheat*." [3]

'*Nubbing Cheat*,' cries *Partridge*, 'Pray, Sir, what is that?'

'Why that, Sir,' says the Stranger, 'is a Cant Phrase for the Gallows; for as Gamesters differ little from Highwaymen in their Morals, so do they very much resemble them in their Language.

'We had now each drank our Bottle, when Mr. *Watson* said, the Board was sitting, and that he must attend, earnestly pressing me, at the same Time, to go with him and try my Fortune. I answered, He knew that was at present out of my Power, as I had informed him of the Emptiness of my Pocket. To say the Truth, I doubted not, from his many strong Expressions of Friendship, but that he would offer to lend me a small Sum for that Purpose; but he answered, "Never mind that, Man, e'en boldly run a Levant;[4] (*Partridge* was going to enquire the Meaning of that Word; but *Jones* stopped his Mouth) but be circumspect as to the Man. I will tip you the proper Person, which may be necessary, as you do not know the Town, nor can distinguish a Rum Cull[5] from a Queer one."

'The Bill was now brought, when *Watson* paid his Share, and was departing. I reminded him, not without blushing, of my having no Money. He answered, "That signifies nothing, score it behind the Door, or make a bold Brush,[6] and take no Notice.— Or—stay," says he, "I will go down Stairs first, and then do you take up my Money, and score the whole Reckoning at the Bar, and I will wait for you at the Corner." I expressed some Dislike at this, and hinted my Expectations that he would have deposited

---

1 Watson's low-life jargon, like that of Jonathan Wild (I. v, xiii), may be illustrated from *A New Canting Dictionary: Comprehending All the Terms, Antient and Modern, Used in the Several Tribes of Gypsies, Beggars, Shoplifters, Highwaymen, Foot-Pads, and all other Clans of Cheats and Villains* (1725). An 'Implement' is a 'Tool' or 'Property' which may be 'easily engag'd in any (tho' difficult and dangerous) Enterprize'. A 'Doctor' is 'a false Die that will run but two or three Chances'.

2 'Cull' is the cant word for 'a Man, either Honest, or otherwise'. A 'queer cull', however, is 'a Fop, or Fool, a Codshead' (*New Canting Dictionary*).

3 As Fielding explains in a footnote to *Jonathan Wild* (IV. ii), these are cant terms for 'hanging' and the 'gallows'.

4 To make a bet with the intention of absconding if it is lost. (See *OED*, which cites this passage in *Tom Jones*.)

5 According to the *New Canting Dictionary*, 'a rich Fool, that can be easily *bit*, or cheated by any body'.

6 To 'brush' is 'to flee, or run away' (*New Canting Dictionary*).

the whole; but he swore he had not another Sixpence in his Pocket.

'He then went down, and I was prevailed on to take up the Money and follow him, which I did close enough to hear him tell the Drawer the Reckoning was upon the Table. The Drawer passed by me up Stairs; but I made such Haste into the Street, that I heard nothing of his Disappointment, nor did I mention a Syllable at the Bar, according to my Instructions.

'We now went directly to the Gaming-Table, where Mr. *Watson*, to my Surprize, pulled out a large Sum of Money, and placed it before him, as did many others; all of them, no doubt, considering their own Heaps as so many decoy Birds, which were to entice and draw over the Heaps of their Neighbours.

'Here it would be tedious to relate all the Freaks which Fortune, or rather the Dice, played in this her Temple. Mountains of Gold were in a few Moments reduced to nothing at one Part of the Table, and rose as suddenly in another. The Rich grew in a Moment poor, and the Poor as suddenly became rich; so that it seemed a Philosopher could no where have so well instructed his Pupils in the Contempt of Riches, at least he could no where have better inculcated the Incertainty of their Duration.

'For my own Part, after having considerably improved my small Estate, I at last entirely demolished it. Mr. *Watson* too, after much Variety of Luck, rose from the Table in some Heat, and declared he had lost a cool hundred, and would play no longer. Then coming up to me, he asked me to return with him to the Tavern; but I positively refused, saying, I would not bring myself a second Time into such a Dilemma, and especially as he had lost all his Money, and was now in my own Condition.' "Pooh," says he, "I have just borrowed a couple of Guineas of a Friend; and one of them is at your Service." He immediately put one of them into my Hand, and I no longer resisted his Inclination.

'I was at first a little shocked at returning to the same House whence we had departed in so unhandsome a Manner; but when the Drawer, with very civil Address, told us, "he believed we had forgot to pay our Reckoning," I became perfectly easy, and very readily gave him a Guinea, bid him pay himself, and acquiesced in the unjust Charge which had been laid on my Memory.

'Mr. *Watson* now bespoke the most extravagant Supper he could well think of, and tho' he had contented himself with simple Claret before, nothing now but the most precious Burgundy would serve his Purpose.

'Our Company was soon encreased by the Addition of several Gentlemen from the Gaming-Table; most of whom, as I afterwards found, came not to the Tavern to drink, but in the Way of Business: For the true Gamesters pretended to be ill, and refused their Glass, while they plied heartily two young Fellows, who were to be afterwards pillaged, as indeed they were without Mercy. Of this Plunder I had the good Fortune to be a Sharer, tho' I was not yet let into the Secret.

'There was one remarkable Accident attended this Tavern Play; for the Money, by Degrees, totally disappeared, so that tho' at the Beginning the Table was half covered with Gold, yet before the Play ended, which it did not till the next Day, being *Sunday*, at Noon, there was scarce a single Guinea to be seen on the Table; and this was the stranger, as every Person present except myself declared he had lost; and what was become of the Money, unless the Devil himself carried it away, is difficult to determine.'

'Most certainly he did,' says *Partridge*, 'for evil Spirits can carry away any thing without being seen, tho' there were never so many Folk in the Room; and I should not have been surprized if he had carried away all the Company of a Set of wicked Wretches, who were at play in Sermon-time. And I could tell you a true Story, if I would, where the Devil took a Man out of Bed from another Man's Wife, and carried him away through the Key-hole of the Door. I've seen the very House where it was done, and no Body hath lived in it these thirty Years.'

Tho' *Jones* was a little offended by the Impertinence of *Partridge*, he could not however avoid smiling at his Simplicity. The Stranger did the same, and then proceeded with his Story, as will be seen in the next Chapter.

## CHAPTER XIII

*In which the foregoing Story is farther continued.*

'MY Fellow Collegiate had now entered me in a new Scene of Life. I soon became acquainted with the whole Fraternity of Sharpers, and was let into their Secrets. I mean into the Knowledge of those gross Cheats which are proper to impose upon the raw and unexperienced: For there are some Tricks of a finer Kind, which are known only to a few of the Gang, who are at the Head of their Profession; a Degree of Honour beyond my Expectation; for Drink, to which I was immoderately addicted, and the natural Warmth of my Passions, prevented me from arriving at any great Success in an Art, which requires as much Coolness as the most austere School of Philosophy.

'Mr. *Watson*, with whom I now lived in the closest Amity, had unluckily the former Failing to a very great Excess; so that instead of making a Fortune by his Profession, as some others did, he was alternately rich and poor, and was often obliged to surrender to his cooler Friends over a Bottle which they never tasted, that Plunder that he had taken from Culls at the public Table.

'However, we both made a Shift to pick up an uncomfortable Livelihood, and for two Years I continued of the Calling, during which Time I tasted all the Varieties of Fortune; sometimes flourishing in Affluence, and at others being obliged to struggle with almost incredible Difficulties. To-day wallowing in Luxury, and To-morrow reduced to the coarsest and most homely Fare. My fine Clothes being often on my Back in the Evening, and at the Pawnshop the next Morning.

'One Night as I was returning Pennyless from the Gaming-table, I observed a very great Disturbance, and a large Mob gathered together in the Street. As I was in no Danger from Pick-pockets, I ventured into the Croud, where, upon Enquiry, I found that a Man had been robbed and very ill used by some Ruffians. The wounded Man appeared very bloody, and seemed scarce able to support himself on his Legs. As I had not therefore been deprived of my Humanity by my present Life and Conversation, tho' they had left me very little of either Honesty or Shame, I immediately offered my Assistance to the unhappy Person, who thankfully accepted it, and putting himself under my Conduct, begged me to convey him to some Tavern, where he might send for a Surgeon, being, as he said, faint with Loss of Blood. He seemed indeed highly pleased at finding one who appeared in the Dress of a Gentleman: For as to all the rest of the Company present, their Outside was such that he could not wisely place any Confidence in them.

'I took the poor Man by the Arm, and led him to the Tavern where we kept our Rendezvous, as it happened to be the nearest at Hand. A Surgeon happening luckily to be in the House, immediately attended, and applied himself to dressing his Wounds, which I had the Pleasure to hear were not likely to be mortal.

'The Surgeon having very expeditiously and dextrously finished his Business, began to enquire in what Part of the Town the wounded Man lodged; who answered, "That he was come to Town that very Morning; that his Horse was at an Inn in *Piccadilly*, and that he had no other Lodging, and very little or no Acquaintance in Town."

'This Surgeon, whose Name I have forgot, tho' I remember it began with an *R*,[1] had the first Character in his Profession, and was Serjeant-Surgeon to the King. He had moreover many good Qualities, and was a very generous, good-natured Man, and ready to do any Service to his Fellow-Creatures. He offered his Patient the Use of his Chariot to carry him to his Inn, and at the same Time whispered in his Ear, "That if he wanted any Money, he would furnish him."

'The poor Man was not now capable of returning Thanks for this generous Offer: For having had his Eyes for some Time stedfastly on me, he threw himself back in his Chair, crying, O, my Son! my Son! and then fainted away.

'Many of the People present imagined this Accident had happened through his Loss of Blood; but I, who at the same Time began to recollect the Features of my Father, was now confirmed in my Suspicion, and satisfied that it was he himself who

---

[1] Though an anachronism, Fielding here certainly means to compliment his friend John Ranby (1703–73), who had been appointed Sergeant-Surgeon to George II in 1740 and Principal Sergeant-Surgeon in 1742. In 1745, the year in which he became involved in the medical controversy concerning the cause of Walpole's death (see above, p. 112, n. 2), Ranby was named governor of the newly created Company of Surgeons (see above, p. 424, n. 2). In *Amelia* (1751; v. vi) it is doubtless Ranby who is complimented as 'the most eminent Surgeon in the Kingdom, or perhaps in the World'. He advised Fielding during his final illness (see the *Journal of a Voyage to Lisbon*, 1755) and after the novelist's death in 1754, succeeded him as tenant of the farm at Fordhook, Ealing (see J. P. de Castro, *N & Q*, 12th Ser., ii [1 July 1916], 11). Later in *Tom Jones* (p. 911) Ranby attends Fitzpatrick after the latter has been wounded in his duel with Jones.

It has been proposed that the present passage alludes to Etienne Ronjat, who became Sergeant-Surgeon to William III in the 1690s. (See B. L. Greenberg, *N & Q*, N.S., ix [December 1962], 456–7.) But there is no evidence that Fielding knew of Ronjat, and, since this episode in the Man of the Hill's narrative is set some four years before Monmouth's Rebellion in 1685, this identification would in no way rectify the anachronism.

appeared before me. I presently ran to him, raised him in my Arms, and kissed his cold Lips with the utmost Eagerness. Here I must draw a Curtain over a Scene which I cannot describe: For though I did not lose my Being, as my Father for a while did, my Senses were however so overpowered with Affright and Surprize, that I am a Stranger to what past during some Minutes, and indeed till my Father had again recovered from his Swoon, and I found myself in his Arms, both tenderly embracing each other, while the Tears trickled a-pace down the Cheeks of each of us.

'Most of those present seemed affected by this Scene, which we, who might be considered as the Actors in it, were desirous of removing from the Eyes of all Spectators, as fast as we could; my Father therefore accepted the kind Offer of the Surgeon's Chariot, and I attended him in it to his Inn.

'When we were alone together, he gently upbraided me with having neglected to write to him during so long a Time, but entirely omitted the Mention of that Crime which had occasioned it. He then informed me of my Mother's Death, and insisted on my returning Home with him, saying, "That he had long suffered the greatest Anxiety on my Account; that he knew not whether he had most feared my Death, or wished it; since he had so many more dreadful Apprehensions for me. At last," he said, "a neighbouring Gentleman, who had just recovered a Son from the same Place, informed him where I was, and that to reclaim me from this Course of Life, was the sole Cause of his Journey to *London*." He thanked Heaven he had succeeded so far as to find me out by Means of an Accident which had like to have proved fatal to him; and had the Pleasure to think he partly owed his Preservation to my Humanity, with which he profest himself to be more delighted than he should have been with my filial Piety, if I had known that the Object of all my Care was my own Father.

'Vice had not so depraved my Heart, as to excite in it an Insensibility of so much paternal Affection, tho' so unworthily bestowed. I presently promised to obey his Commands in my return Home with him as soon as he was able to travel, which indeed he was in a very few Days, by the Assistance of that excellent Surgeon who had undertaken his Cure.

'The Day preceding my Father's Journey (before which Time I scarce ever left him) I went to take my Leave of some of my most intimate Acquaintance, particularly of Mr. *Watson*, who dissuaded me from burying myself, as he called it, out of a simple Compliance with the fond Desires of a foolish old Fellow. Such Solicitations, however, had no Effect, and I once more saw my own Home. My Father now greatly solicited me to think of Marriage; but my Inclinations were utterly averse to any such Thoughts. I had tasted of Love already, and perhaps you know the extravagant Excesses of that most tender and most violent Passion.' Here the old Gentleman paused, and looked earnestly at *Jones*; whose Countenance within a Minute's Space displayed the Extremities of both red and white. Upon which the old Man, without making any Observations, renewed his Narrative.

'Being now provided with all the Necessaries of Life, I betook myself once again to Study, and that with a more inordinate Application that I had ever done formerly. The Books which now employed my Time solely, were those, as well ancient as modern, which treat of true Philosophy, a Word, which is by many thought to be the Subject only of Farce and Ridicule. I now read over the Works of *Aristotle* and *Plato*, with the rest of those inestimable Treasures which ancient *Greece* had bequeathed to the World.

'These Authors, though they instructed me in no Science by which Men may promise to themselves to acquire the least Riches, or worldly Power, taught me, however, the Art of despising the highest Acquisitions of both. They elevate the Mind, and steel and harden it against the capricious Invasions of Fortune. They not only instruct in the Knowledge of Wisdom, but confirm Men in her Habits, and demonstrate plainly, that this must be our Guide, if we propose ever to arrive at the greatest worldly Happiness; or to defend ourselves with any tolerable Security against the Misery which every where surrounds and invests us.

'To this I added another Study, compared to which all the Philosophy taught by the wisest Heathens is little better than a Dream, and is indeed as full of Vanity as the silliest Jester ever pleased to represent it.[1] This is that divine Wisdom which is

[1] The Man of the Hill's insistence on the superior wisdom of Christian to heathen philosophy, the former being infallibly based upon divine revelation, has a place in a long tradition of Christian apologetics which, in the seventeenth and eighteenth centuries, came to be directed chiefly against the threat of deism. See, for example, Swift's sermon, 'The Excellency of Christianity, in Opposition to Heathen Philosophy' (upon 1 Corinthians 3: 19: 'The wisdom of this world is foolishness with God'), and the discussion by Louis Landa, ed. Swift's *Irish Tracts, 1720–1723, and Sermons* (Oxford, 1948), pp. 111–14. Fielding returns to this theme in XVIII. iv, as he presents the conversion of the deist Square.

alone to be found in the Holy Scriptures: for they impart to us
the Knowledge and Assurance of Things much more worthy our
Attention, than all which this World can offer to our Acceptance.
Of Things which Heaven itself hath condescended to reveal to us,
and to the smallest Knowledge of which the highest human Wit
unassisted could never ascend. I began now to think all the Time
I had spent with the best Heathen Writers, was little more than
Labour lost: For however pleasant and delightful their Lessons
may be, or however adequate to the right Regulation of our
Conduct with Respect to this World only, yet when compared
with the Glory revealed in Scripture, their highest Documents
will appear as trifling, and of as little Consequence as the Rules by
which Children regulate their childish little Games and Pastime.
True it is, that Philosophy makes us wiser, but Christianity makes
us better Men. Philosophy elevates and steels the Mind, Christianity softens and sweetens it. The Former makes us the
Objects of human Admiration, the Latter of Divine Love. That
insures us a temporal, but this an eternal Happiness.—But I am
afraid I tire you with my Rhapsody.'

'Not at all,' cries *Partridge*, 'Lud forbid we should be tired
with good Things.'

'I had spent,' continued the Stranger, 'about four Years in the
most delightful Manner to myself, totally given up to Contemplation, and entirely unembarrassed with the Affairs of the
World, when I lost the best of Fathers, and one whom I so
entirely loved, that my Grief at his Loss exceeds all Description.
I now abandoned my Books, and gave myself up for a whole
Month to the Efforts of Melancholy and Despair. Time, however, the best Physician of the Mind, at length brought me
Relief.' 'Ay, ay, *Tempus edax Rerum*,'[1] said *Partridge*. 'I then,'
continued the Stranger, 'betook myself again to my former
Studies, which I may say perfected my Cure: For Philosophy
and Religion may be called the Exercises of the Mind, and when
this is disordered they are as wholesome as Exercise can be to a
distempered Body. They do indeed produce similar Effects with
Exercise: For they strengthen and confirm the Mind; till Man
becomes, in the noble Strain of *Horace*,

*Fortis, et in seipso totus teres atque rotundus,*

[1] See above, p. 421, n. 2.

*Externi ne quid valeat per læve morari:*
*In quem manca ruit semper Fortuna.——*¹

Here *Jones* smiled at some Conceit which intruded itself into
his Imagination; but the Stranger, I believe, perceived it not, and
proceeded thus.

'My Circumstances were now greatly altered by the Death of
that best of Men: For my Brother, who was now become Master
of the House, differed so widely from me in his Inclinations, and
our Pursuits in Life had been so very various, that we were the
worst of Company to each other; but what made our living
together still more disagreeable, was the little Harmony which
could subsist between the few who resorted to me, and the numerous Train of Sportsmen who often attended my Brother from the
Field to the Table: For such Fellows, besides the Noise and
Nonsense with which they persecute the Ears of sober Men,
endeavour always to attack them with Affronts and Contempt.
This was so much the Case, that neither I myself, nor my
Friends, could ever sit down to a Meal with them, where we were
not treated with Derision, because we were unacquainted with
the Phrases of Sportsmen. For Men of true Learning, and almost universal Knowledge, always compassionate the Ignorance
of others. But Fellows who excel in some little, low, contemptible
Art, are always certain to despise those who are unacquainted
with that Art.

'In short, we soon separated, and I went by the Advice of a
Physician to drink the *Bath* Waters: For my violent Affliction,

---

\* Firm in himself, who on himself relies,
  Polish'd and round, who runs his proper Course,
  And breaks Misfortunes with superior Force.
                              Mr. FRANCIS.²

---

¹ *Satires*, II. vii. 86–8. Later in the novel (pp. 760–1) Fielding's own ironic paraphrase of
this passage reveals the reason for Jones's good-humoured disapproval of the Man of the
Hill's stoical self-sufficiency. Jones, Fielding remarks, 'had all that Weakness which is
called Compassion, and which distinguishes this imperfect Character from that noble
Firmness of Mind, which rolls a Man, as it were, within himself, and, like a polished Bowl,
enables him to run through the World, without once being stopped by the Calamities
which happen to others'. Cf. also 'Of the Remedy of Affliction for the Loss of Our
Friends' (1743).
² Philip Francis (c. 1708–73), whose verse translation of Horace began to be published
by Andrew Millar in 1746. Fielding frequently quotes from this work: e.g. *Tom Jones*
(pp. 489, 570, 660) and *The Jacobite's Journal* (12 March, 15 October 1748).

added to a sedentary Life, had thrown me into a kind of paralytic Disorder, for which those Waters are accounted an almost certain Cure.[1] The second Day after my Arrival, as I was walking by the River, the Sun shone so intensely hot (tho' it was early in the Year) that I retired to the Shelter of some Willows, and sat down by the River-side. Here I had not been seated long before I heard a Person on the other Side the Willows, sighing and bemoaning himself bitterly. On a sudden, having uttered a most impious Oath, he cried, "I am resolved to bear it no longer," and directly threw himself into the Water. I immediately started, and ran towards the Place, calling at the same Time as loudly as I could for Assistance. An Angler happened luckily to be a fishing a little below me, tho' some very high Sedge had hid him from my Sight. He immediately came up, and both of us together, not without some Hazard of our Lives, drew the Body to the Shore. At first we perceived no Sign of Life remaining; but having held the Body up by the Heels (for we soon had Assistance enough) it discharged a vast Quantity of Water at the Mouth, and at length began to discover some Symptoms of Breathing, and a little afterwards to move both its Hands and its Legs.

'An Apothecary, who happened to be present among others, advised that the Body, which seemed now to have pretty well emptied itself of Water, and which began to have many convulsive Motions, should be directly taken up, and carried into a warm Bed. This was accordingly performed, the Apothecary and myself attending.

'As we were going towards an Inn, for we knew not the Man's Lodgings, luckily a Woman met us, who, after some violent Screaming, told us, that the Gentleman lodged at her House.

'When I had seen the Man safely deposited there, I left him to the Care of the Apothecary, who, I suppose, used all the right Methods with him; for the next Morning I heard he had perfectly recovered his Senses.

'I then went to visit him, intending to search out as well as I could the Cause of his having attempted so desperate an Act, and

---

[1] On the supposed efficacy of the Bath waters in curing such muscular disorders as 'Palsies, and the nervous *Atrophy* of the Limbs', see Dr. George Cheyne's *Account of the Nature and Quality of Bath-Waters*, 8th ed. (1737), sec. xliv. On Cheyne, see below, p. 605, n. 1.

to prevent, as far as I was able, his pursuing such wicked Intentions for the future. I was no sooner admitted into his Chamber, than we both instantly knew each other; for who should this
Person be, but my good Friend Mr. *Watson*! Here I will not
trouble you with what past at our first Interview: For I would
avoid Prolixity as much as possible.' 'Pray let us hear all,' cries
*Partridge*, 'I want mightily to know what brought him to *Bath*.'

'You shall hear every Thing material,' answered the Stranger;
and then proceeded to relate what we shall proceed to write, after
we have given a short breathing Time to both ourselves and the
Reader.

CHAPTER XIV

*In which the Man of the Hill concludes his History.*

'MR. *Watson*,' continued the Stranger, 'very freely acquainted me, that the unhappy Situation of his Circumstances, occasioned by a Tide of Ill-Luck, had in a Manner
forced him to a Resolution of destroying himself.

'I now began to argue very seriously with him, in Opposition
to this Heathenish, or indeed Diabolical Practice; and said every
Thing which occurred to me on the Subject; but to my great
Concern, it seemed to have very little Effect on him. He seemed
not at all to repent of what he had done, and gave me Reason to
fear, he would soon make a second Attempt of the like horrible
kind.

'When I had finished my Discourse, instead of endeavouring
to answer my Arguments, he looked me stedfastly in the Face,
and with a Smile said, "You are strangely altered, my good
Friend, since I remember you. I question whether any of our
Bishops could make a better Argument against Suicide than you
have entertained me with, but unless you can find Somebody who
will lend me a cool Hundred, I must either hang, or drown, or
starve; and in my Opinion the last Death is the most terrible of
the three."

'I answered him very gravely, that I was indeed altered since
I had seen him last. That I had found Leisure to look into my
Follies, and to repent of them. I then advised him to pursue the

same Steps; and at last concluded with an Assurance, that I
myself would lend him a hundred Pound, if it would be of any
Service to his Affairs, and he would not put it into the Power of a
Die to deprive him of it.

'Mr. *Watson*, who seemed almost composed in Slumber by the
former Part of my Discourse, was roused by the latter. He seized
my Hand eagerly, gave me a thousand Thanks, and declared
I was a Friend indeed; adding, that he hoped I had a better
Opinion of him, than to imagine he had profited so little by
Experience, as to put any Confidence in those damned Dice,
which had so often deceived him. "No, no," cries he, "let me but
once handsomely be set up again, and if ever Fortune makes a
broken Merchant of me afterwards, I will forgive her."

'I very well understood the Language of *setting up*, and *broken
Merchant*. I therefore said to him with a very grave Face, "Mr.
*Watson*, you must endeavour to find out some Business, or
Employment, by which you may procure yourself a Livelihood;
and I promise you, could I see any Probability of being repaid
hereafter, I would advance a much larger Sum than what you
have mentioned, to equip you in any fair and honourable Calling;
but as to Gaming, besides the Baseness and Wickedness of making
it a Profession, you are really, to my own Knowledge, unfit for it,
and it will end in your certain Ruin."

' "Why now, that's strange," answered he, "neither you, nor
any of my Friends, would ever allow me to know any Thing of
the Matter, and yet, I believe, I am as good a Hand at every
Game as any of you all; and I heartily wish I was to play with you
only for your whole Fortune; I should desire no better Sport, and
I would let you name your Game into the Bargain; but come, my
dear Boy, have you the Hundred in your Pocket?"

'I answered, I had only a Bill for 50 *l*. which I delivered him,
and promised to bring him the rest next Morning; and after
giving him a little more Advice, took my Leave.

'I was indeed better than my Word: For I returned to him that
very Afternoon. When I entered the Room, I found Mr. *Watson*
sitting up in his Bed at Cards with a notorious Gamester. This
Sight, you will imagine, shocked me not a little; to which I may
add the Mortification of seeing my Bill delivered by Mr. *Watson*
to his Antagonist, and thirty Guineas only given in Exchange
for it.

'The other Gamester presently quitted the Room, and then *Watson* declared he was ashamed to see me; "but," says he, "I find Luck runs so damnably against me, that I will resolve to leave off Play for ever. I have thought of the kind Proposal you made me ever since, and I promise you there shall be no Fault in me, if I do not put it in Execution."

'Though I had no great Faith in his Promises, I produced him the Remainder of the hundred in Consequence of my own; for which he gave me a Note, and which Note was all I ever expected to see in Return for my Money.

'We were prevented from any further Discourse at present, by the Arrival of the Apothecary, who with much Joy in his Countenance, and without even asking his Patient how he did, proclaimed there was great News arrived in a Letter to himself, which he said would shortly be public, "that the Duke of *Monmouth*[1] was landed in the West with a vast Army of *Dutch*, and that another vast Fleet hovered over the Coast of *Norfolk*, and was to make a Descent there, in order to favour the Duke's Enterprize with a Diversion on that Side."

'This Apothecary was one of the greatest Politicians of his Time. He was more delighted with the most paultry Packet, than with the best Patient; and the highest Joy he was capable of, he received from having a Piece of News in his Possession an Hour or two sooner than any other Person in the Town. His Advices, however, were seldom authentic; for he would swallow almost any thing as a Truth, a Humour which many made use of to impose upon him.

'Thus it happened with what he at present communicated; for it was known within a short Time afterwards, that the Duke was

---

[1] James Scott (1649–85), Duke of Monmouth and Buccleuch, was the natural son of Charles II. He hoped to become King of England upon the death of his father and to this end associated himself with the Whig-Protestant interest which in 1679 and 1680, under the leadership of the first Earl of Shaftesbury, attempted unsuccessfully to pass a bill excluding the Catholic Duke of York from the throne. When York succeeded Charles as James II in 1685, Monmouth returned from exile in Holland intending to seize the throne by force. With 150 attendants he landed at Lyme, Dorset, on 11 June; his army soon grew to several thousand, drawing strength from the large nonconformist population of the West Country. After some early successes the rebels were crushed at Sedgemoor, near Bridgwater, and in the following days the fugitives were ruthlessly hunted down and executed. Monmouth himself was beheaded. In Fielding's opinion, the severity with which James suppressed the rebellion was 'inhuman and unparallel'd', the action of 'a Bigot and . . . a Tyrant' (see *A Serious Address to the People of Great Britain* [1745]).

really landed; but that his Army consisted only of a few Attendants; and as to the Diversion in *Norfolk*, it was entirely false.

'The Apothecary staid no longer in the Room, than while he acquainted us with his News; and then, without saying a Syllable to his Patient on any other Subject, departed to spread his Advices all over the Town.

'Events of this Nature in the Public are generally apt to eclipse all private Concerns. Our Discourse, therefore, now became entirely political. For my own Part, I had been for some Time very seriously affected with the Danger to which the Protestant Religion was so visibly exposed, under a Popish Prince; and thought the Apprehension of it alone sufficient to justify that Insurrection: For no real Security can ever be found against the persecuting Spirit of Popery, when armed with Power, except the depriving it of that Power, as woeful Experience presently shewed. You know how King *James* behaved after getting the better of this Attempt; how little he valued either his Royal Word, or Coronation-Oath, or the Liberties and Rights of his People. But all had not the Sense to foresee this at first; and therefore the Duke of *Monmouth* was weakly supported; yet all could feel when the Evil came upon them; and therefore all united, at last, to drive out that King, against whose Exclusion a great Party among us had so warmly contended, during the Reign of his Brother, and for whom they now fought with such Zeal and Affection.'

'What you say,' interrupted *Jones*, 'is very true; and it has often struck me, as the most wonderful thing I ever read of in History, that so soon after this convincing Experience, which brought our whole Nation to join so unanimously in expelling King *James*, for the Preservation of our Religion and Liberties, there should be a Party among us mad enough to desire the placing his Family again on the Throne.' 'You are not in Earnest!' answered the old Man; 'there can be no such Party. As bad an Opinion as I have of Mankind, I cannot believe them infatuated to such a Degree! There may be some hot-headed Papists led by their Priests to engage in this desperate Cause, and think it a Holy War; but that Protestants, that Members of the Church of *England* should be such Apostates, such *Felos de se*,[1] I cannot

---

[1] 'Felons to themselves', the legal phrase for suicides. Cf. *The True Patriot* (27 May–3 June 1746), where Fielding declares that, after having experienced the tyranny of

believe it; no, no, young Man, unacquainted as I am with what has past in the World for these last thirty Years, I cannot be so imposed upon as to credit so foolish a Tale: But I see you have a Mind to sport with my Ignorance.' 'Can it be possible,' replied *Jones*, 'that you have lived so much out of the World as not to know,' that during that Time there have been two Rebellions in favour of the Son of King *James*,[1] one of which is now actually raging in the very Heart of this Kingdom?' At these Words the old Gentleman started up, and, in a most solemn Tone of Voice conjured *Jones* by his Maker to tell him, if what he said was really true: Which the other as solemnly affirming, he walked several Turns about the Room, in a profound Silence, then cried, then laughed, and, at last, fell down on his Knees, and blessed God, in a loud Thanksgiving-Prayer, for having delivered him from all Society with Human Nature, which could be capable of such monstrous Extravagances. After which being reminded by *Jones*, that he had broke off his Story, he resumed it again, in this Manner.

'As Mankind, in the Days I was speaking of, was not yet arrived to that Pitch of Madness which I find they are capable of now, and which, to be sure, I have only escaped by living alone, and at a Distance from the Contagion, there was a considerable Rising in favour of *Monmouth*, and my Principles strongly inclining me to take the same Part, I determined to join him, and Mr. *Watson*, from different Motives concurring in the same Resolution, (for the Spirit of a Gamester will carry a Man as far upon such an Occasion as the Spirit of Patriotism) we soon provided ourselves with all Necessaries, and went to the Duke at *Bridgwater*.

'The unfortunate Event of this Enterprize you are, I conclude, as well acquainted with as myself. I escaped, together with Mr. *Watson*, from the Battle at *Sedgemore*, in which Action I received a slight Wound. We rode near forty Miles together on the *Exeter* Road, and then abandoning our Horses, scrambled as well as we could through the Fields and Bye-Roads, till we arrived at a

James II, any Protestant who supports the Pretender's cause is guilty of idiocy: 'Nay, such Men may be said to participate of the Guilt to which they become the Objects. They are in a manner *Felo's de se*, and may more properly be said to impose on themselves, than to be imposed on by others'.

[1] The Jacobite uprisings in 1715 and 1745.

little wild Hut on a Common, where a poor old Woman took all the Care of us she could, and dressed my Wound with Salve, which quickly healed it.'

'Pray, Sir, where was the Wound,' says *Partridge*. The Stranger satisfied him it was in his Arm, and then continued his Narrative. 'Here, Sir,' said he, 'Mr. *Watson* left me the next Morning, in order, as he pretended, to get us some Provision from the Town of *Cullumpton*;[1] but—can I relate it? or can you believe it?—This Mr. *Watson*, this Friend, this base, barbarous, treacherous Villain, betrayed me to a Party of Horse belonging to King *James*, and, at his Return, delivered me into their Hands.

'The Soldiers, being six in Number, had now seized me, and were conducting me to *Taunton* Goal; but neither my present Situation, nor the Apprehensions of what might happen to me, were half so irksome to my Mind, as the Company of my false Friend, who, having surrendered himself, was likewise considered as a Prisoner, tho' he was better treated, as being to make his Peace at my Expence. He at first endeavoured to excuse his Treachery; but when he received nothing but Scorn and Upbraiding from me, he soon changed his Note, abused me as the most atrocious and malicious Rebel, and laid all his own Guilt to my Charge, who, as he declared, had solicited, and even threatened him, to take up Arms against his gracious, as well as lawful, Sovereign.

'This false Evidence, (for, in Reality, he had been much the forwarder of the two) stung me to the Quick, and raised an Indignation scarce conceivable by those who have not felt it. However, Fortune at length took Pity on me; for as we were got a little beyond *Wellington*,[2] in a narrow Lane, my Guards received a false Alarm, that near fifty of the Enemy were at hand, upon which they shifted for themselves, and left me and my Betrayer to do the same. That Villain immediately ran from me, and I am glad he did, or I should have certainly endeavoured, though I had no Arms, to have executed Vengeance on his Baseness.

'I was now once more at Liberty, and immediately withdrawing from the Highway into the Fields, I travelled on, scarce knowing which Way I went, and making it my chief Care to avoid all public Roads, and all Towns, nay, even the most

---

[1] A market town in Devon, twelve miles north-east of Exeter.
[2] A market town in Somerset, six miles from Taunton on the Exeter road.

homely Houses; for I imagined every human Creature whom I saw, desirous of betraying me.

'At last, after rambling several Days about the Country, during which the Fields afforded me the same Bed, and the same Food, which Nature bestows on our Savage Brothers of the Creation, I at length arrived in this Place, where the Solitude and Wildness of the Country invited me to fix my Abode. The first Person with whom I took up my Habitation was the Mother of this old Woman, with whom I remained concealed, till the News of the glorious Revolution[1] put an End to all my Apprehensions of Danger, and gave me an Opportunity of once more visiting my own Home, and of enquiring a little into my Affairs, which I soon settled as agreeably to my Brother as to myself; having resigned every thing to him, for which he paid me the Sum of a thousand Pound, and settled on me an Annuity for Life.

'His Behaviour in this last Instance, as in all others, was selfish and ungenerous. I could not look on him as my Friend, nor indeed did he desire that I should; so I presently took my Leave of him, as well as of my other Acquaintance; and from that Day to this my History is little better than a Blank.'

'And is it possible, Sir,' said *Jones*, 'that you can have resided here, from that Day to this?' 'O no, Sir,' answered the Gentleman, 'I have been a great Traveller, and there are few Parts of *Europe* with which I am not acquainted.' 'I have not, Sir,' cried *Jones*, 'the Assurance to ask it of you now. Indeed it would be cruel, after so much Breath as you have already spent. But you will give me Leave to wish for some further Opportunity of hearing the excellent Observations, which a Man of your Sense and Knowledge of the World must have made in so long a Course of Travels.' 'Indeed, young Gentleman,' answered the Stranger, 'I will endeavour to satisfy your Curiosity on this Head likewise, as far as I am able.' *Jones* attempted fresh Apologies, but was prevented; and while he and *Partridge* sat with greedy and impatient Ears, the Stranger proceeded as in the next Chapter.

---

[1] The deposition of James II in 1688 was precipitated both by his own absolutist policies in the interest of re-establishing Catholicism as the national religion and by the birth of his son and heir on 20 June. William of Orange landed in England with his army in November.

## CHAPTER XV

*A brief History of* Europe. *And a curious Discourse between Mr.* Jones *and the Man of the Hill.*

'IN *Italy* the Landlords are very silent. In *France* they are more talkative, but yet civil. In *Germany* and *Holland* they are generally very impertinent. And as for their Honesty, I believe it is pretty equal in all those Countries. The *Valets a Louage*¹ are sure to lose no Opportunity of cheating you: And as for the Postilions, I think they are pretty much alike all the World over. These, Sir, are the Observations on Men which I made in my Travels. My Design, when I went abroad, was to divert myself by seeing the great Variety with which God hath been pleased to enrich the several Parts of this Globe.² A Variety, which as it must give great Pleasure to a contemplative Beholder, so doth it greatly

¹ Manservants for hire by travellers.

² Throughout this chapter the Man of the Hill—like Pope in the *Essay on Man* (1733–4)— echoes the orthodox cosmological theories of the period. Such works as Ralph Cudworth's *True Intellectual System of the Universe* (1678), John Ray's *The Wisdom of God Manifested in the Works of the Creation* (1691), and William Derham's *Physico-* (1713) *and Astro-Theology* (1715) attempted to demonstrate the being and attributes of the Deity by analysing the order apparent in the universe, its fullness and variety, its nice gradations and coherency. Barrow, Tillotson, Clarke, and many other rationalist divines expounded this doctrine from the pulpit, and it was popularized by Addison in *The Spectator* (No. 519 [20 October 1712]) and by such poets as Blackmore, Thomson, Boyse (see above, p. 324, n. 4), Young, and Smart. The classic study of this idea is A. O. Lovejoy, *The Great Chain of Being* (Cambridge, Mass., 1936); see also W. P. Jones, *The Rhetoric of Science* (Berkeley, Cal., 1966). Like Pope—who, Fielding remarked, *'taught me a System of Philosophy in* English *Numbers'* (see the Preface to *Plutus* [1742])—the Man of the Hill, 'Expatiate[s] free o'er all this scene of Man' (i. 5), contemplating the 'Vast chain of being' from the heavens to the lower creation: 'Beast, bird, fish, insect! what no eye can see' (i. 239). (Cf. the phrasing of this passage in the first edition of *Tom Jones*.) But whereas Pope concludes that 'Heav'n's design' is not broken by the turpitude even of 'a Borgia, or a Catiline' (i. 155–6), the Man of the Hill asserts that the Creator is dishonoured by the immorality of mankind. In this respect the lesson of the *Essay on Man* is one to which Fielding would have subscribed:

> From pride, from pride, our very reas'ning springs;
> Account for moral as for nat'ral things:
> Why charge we Heav'n in those, in these acquit?
> In both, to reason right is to submit.
> Better for Us, perhaps, it might appear,
> Were there all harmony, all virtue here;
> That never air or ocean felt the wind;
> That never passion discomposed the mind:
> But ALL subsists by elemental strife;
> And Passions are the elements of Life.
> The gen'ral ORDER, since the whole began,
> Is kept in Nature, and is kept in Man. (i. 161–72)

display the vast Powers of its omnipotent Author. Indeed, to say
the Truth, there is but one Work in his whole Creation that doth
him any Dishonour, and with that I have long since avoided
holding any Conversation.'

'You will pardon me,' cries *Jones*, 'but I have always imagined,
that there is in this very Work you mention, as great Variety as in
all the rest; for besides the Difference of Inclination, Customs and
Climates have, I am told, introduced the utmost Diversity into
Human Nature.' 'Very little indeed,' answered the other; 'those
who travel in order to acquaint themselves with the different
Manners of Men, might spare themselves much Pains, by going
to a Carnival at *Venice*; for here they will see at once all which
they can discover in the several Courts of *Europe*. The same
Hypocrisy, the same Fraud; in short, the same Follies and Vices,
dressed in different Habits. In *Spain* these are equipped with
much Gravity; and in *Italy*, with vast Splendor. In *France*, a
Knave is dressed like a Fop; and in the Northern Countries, like a
Sloven. But Human Nature is every where the same, every
where the Object of Detestation and Avoidance.'

'As for my own Part, I past through all these Nations, as you
perhaps may have done through a Croud at a Shew, jostling to
get by them, holding my Nose with one Hand, and defending my
Pockets with the other, without speaking a Word to any of
them, while I was pressing on to see what I wanted to see, which,
however entertaining it might be in itself, scarce made me
Amends for the Trouble the Company gave me.'

'Did not you find some of the Nations among which you
travelled, less troublesome to you than others?' said *Jones*. 'O yes,'
replied the old Man, 'the *Turks* were much more tolerable to me
than the *Christians*. For they are Men of profound Taciturnity,
and never disturb a Stranger with Questions. Now and then
indeed they bestow a short Curse upon him, or spit in his Face as
he walks the Streets, but then they have done with him, and a
Man may live an Age in their Country without hearing a Dozen
Words from them. But of all the People I ever saw, Heaven
defend me from the *French*. With their damned Prate and
Civilities, and doing the Honour of their Nation to Strangers,
(as they are pleased to call it)[1] but indeed setting forth their own

---

[1] An idiom meaning to receive a guest or visitor according to the rules of politeness, as in
Molière's *L'Avare*, III: 'Je vais faire pour vous, mon père, les honneurs de votre logis'.

Vanity; they are so troublesome, that I had infinitely rather pass my Life with the *Hottentots*, than set my Foot in *Paris* again. They are a nasty People, but their Nastiness is mostly *without*, whereas in *France*, and some other Nations that I won't name, it is all *within*, and makes them stink much more to my Reason than that of *Hottentots* does to my Nose.

'Thus, Sir, I have ended the History of my Life; for as to all that Series of Years, in which I have retired here, they afford no Variety to entertain you, and may almost be considered as one Day. The Retirement has been so compleat, that I could hardly have enjoyed a more absolute Solitude in the Deserts of the *Thebais*,[1] than here in the midst of this populous Kingdom. As I have no Estate, I am plagued with no Tenants or Stewards; my Annuity is paid me pretty regularly, as indeed it ought to be, for it is much less than what I might have expected, in Return for what I gave up. Visits I admit none, and the old Woman who keeps my House knows, that her Place entirely depends upon her saving me all the Trouble of buying the Things that I want, keeping off all Sollicitation or Business from me, and holding her Tongue whenever I am within hearing. As my Walks are all by Night, I am pretty secure in this wild, unfrequented Place from meeting any Company. Some few Persons I have met by Chance, and sent them Home heartily frighted, as from the Oddness of my Dress and Figure they took me for a Ghost or a Hobgoblin. But what has happened to Night shews, that even here I cannot be safe from the Villany of Men; for without your Assistance I had not only been robbed, but very probably murdered.'

*Jones* thanked the Stranger for the Trouble he had taken in relating his Story, and then expressed some Wonder how he could possibly endure a Life of such Solitude; 'in which,' says he, 'you may well complain of the Want of Variety. Indeed I am astonished how you have filled up, or rather killed, so much of your Time.'

'I am not at all surprized,' answered the other, 'that to one whose Affections and Thoughts are fixed on the World, my Hours shall appear to have wanted Employment in this Place; but there is one single Act, for which the whole Life of Man is infinitely short. What Time can suffice for the Contemplation and

---

[1] In ancient geography, the domain of Thebes in Upper Egypt and the place of origin of Christian monasticism.

Worship of that glorious, immortal, and eternal Being, among the Works of whose stupendous Creation, not only this vast Globe, but even those numberless Luminaries which we may here behold spangling all the Sky, tho' they should many of them be Suns lighting different Systems of Worlds,[1] may possibly appear but as a few Atoms, opposed to the whole Earth which we inhabit? Can a Man who, by Divine Meditations, is admitted, as it were, into the Conversation of this ineffable, incomprehensible Majesty, think Days, or Years, or Ages, too long, for the Continuance of so ravishing an Honour? Shall the trifling Amusements, the palling Pleasures, the silly Business of the World, roll away our Hours too swiftly from us; and shall the Pace of Time seem sluggish to a Mind exercised in Studies so high, so important, and so glorious! And as no Time is sufficient, so neither is any Place improper for this great Concern. On what Object can we cast our Eyes, which may not inspire us with Ideas of his Power, of his Wisdom, and of his Goodness? It is not necessary, that the rising Sun should dart his fiery Glories over the Eastern Horizon; nor that the boisterous Winds should rush from their Caverns, and shake the lofty Forest; nor that the opening Clouds should pour their Deluges on the Plains: It is not necessary, I say, that any of these should proclaim his Majesty; there is not an Insect, not a Vegetable, of so low an Order in the Creation, but it is honoured with bearing Marks of the Attributes of its great Creator; Marks not only of his Power, but of his Wisdom and Goodness. Man alone, the King of this Globe, the last and greatest Work of the Supreme Being, below the Sun; Man alone hath basely dishonoured his own Nature, and by Dishonesty, Cruelty, Ingratitude, and accursed Treachery, hath called his Maker's Goodness in Question, by puzzling us to account how a benevolent Being should form so imperfect, and so vile an Animal. Yet this is the Being from whose Conversation you think, I suppose, that I have been unfortunately restrained;

---

[1] Fontenelle's influential treatise, *Entretiens sur la pluralité des mondes* (1686), helped to disseminate the belief that the universe contained innumerable planetary systems and inhabited worlds. In his *Astro-Theology* (1715) Derham explained this 'New Systeme', which 'supposeth that there are many other Systemes of Suns and Planets, besides that in which we have our residence: namely, that every Fixt Star is a Sun, and encompassed with a Systeme of Planets, both Primary and Secondary, as well as ours'. Addison accepts this theory in *The Spectator* (No. 519 [20 October 1712]), as does Pope in the *Essay on Man* (i. 21–7). For a full discussion see Lovejoy, *The Great Chain of Being* (1936), pp. 130–42.

and without whose blessed Society, Life, in your Opinion, must be tedious and insipid.'

'In the former Part of what you said,' replied *Jones*, 'I most heartily and readily concur; but I believe, as well as hope, that the Abhorrence which you express for Mankind, in the Conclusion, is much too general. Indeed you here fall into an Error, which, in my little Experience, I have observed to be a very common one, by taking the Character of Mankind from the worst and basest among them; whereas indeed, as an excellent Writer observes,[1] nothing should be esteemed as characteristical of a Species, but what is to be found among the best and most perfect Individuals of that Species. This Error, I believe, is generally committed by those who, from Want of proper Caution in the Choice of their Friends and Acquaintance, have suffered Injuries from bad and worthless Men; two or three Instances of which are very unjustly charged on all the Human Race.'

'I think I had Experience enough of them,' answered the other. 'My first Mistress, and my first Friend, betrayed me in the basest Manner, and in Matters which threatened to be of the worst of Consequences, even to bring me to a shameful Death.'

'But you will pardon me,' cries *Jones*, 'if I desire you to reflect who this Mistress, and who that Friend was. What better, my good Sir, could be expected in Love derived from the Stews, or in Friendship first produced and nourished at the Gaming-Table! To take the Characters of Women from the former Instance, or of Men from the latter, would be as unjust as to assert, that Air is a nauseous and unwholesome Element, because we find it so in a Jakes. I have lived but a short Time in the World, and yet have known Men worthy of the highest Friendship, and Women of the highest Love.'

'It is possible,' answered the Stranger; 'but you have lived, you confess, a very short Time only in the World; I was somewhat older than you when I was of the same Opinion.'

'You might have remained so still,' replies *Jones*, 'if you had not been unfortunate, I will venture to say incautious in the placing your Affections. If there was indeed much more

[1] Cf. Cicero, *Tusculan Disputations*, I. xiv. 32: 'num dubitas quin specimen naturae capi deceat ex optima quaque natura?' ('Can you doubt that properly our ideal of human nature should be formed from the finest natures we meet with?'—trans. J. E. King, Loeb Classical Library, 1927). In a general way, this assumption also underlies the ethical philosophy of Shaftesbury and the Latitudinarian divines.

Wickedness in the World than there is, it would not prove such general Assertions against human Nature, since much of this arrives by mere Accident, and many a Man who commits Evil, is not totally bad and corrupt in his Heart. In Truth, none seem to have any Title to assert Human Nature to be necessarily and universally evil, but those whose own Minds afford them one Instance of this natural Depravity;[1] which is not, I am convinced, your Case.'

'And such,' said the Stranger, 'will be always the most backward to assert any such thing. Knaves will no more endeavour to persuade us of the Baseness of Mankind, than a Highwayman will inform you that there are Thieves on the Road. This would indeed be a Method to put you on your Guard, and to defeat their own Purposes. For which Reason tho' Knaves, as I remember, are very apt to abuse particular Persons; yet they never cast any Reflection on Human Nature in general.' The old Gentleman spoke this so warmly, that as *Jones* despaired of making a Convert, and was unwilling to offend, he returned no Answer.

The Day now began to send forth its first Streams of Light, when *Jones* made an Apology to the Stranger for having staid so long, and perhaps detained him from his Rest. The Stranger answered, 'He never wanted Rest less than at present; for that Day and Night were indifferent Seasons to him, and that he commonly made use of the former for the Time of his Repose, and of the latter for his Walks and Lucubrations. However,' said he, 'it is now a most lovely Morning, and if you can bear any longer to be without your own Rest or Food, I will gladly entertain you with the Sight of some very fine Prospects, which I believe you have not yet seen.'

*Jones* very readily embraced this Offer, and they immediately set forward together from the Cottage. As for *Partridge,* he had fallen into a profound Repose, just as the Stranger had finished his Story; for his Curiosity was satisfied, and the subsequent Discourse was not forcible enough in its Operation to conjure down the Charms of Sleep. *Jones* therefore left him to enjoy his Nap; and as the Reader may perhaps be, at this Season, glad of the same Favour, we will here put an End to the Eighth Book of our History.

[1] See above, p. 269, n. 2.

# BOOK IX

*Containing twelve Hours.*

## CHAPTER I

*Of those who lawfully may, and of those who may not write such Histories as this.*

AMONG other good Uses for which I have thought proper to institute these several introductory Chapters, I have considered them as a Kind of Mark or Stamp, which may hereafter enable a very indifferent Reader to distinguish, what is true and genuine in this historic Kind of Writing, from what is false and counterfeit. Indeed it seems likely that some such Mark may shortly become necessary, since the favourable Reception which two or three Authors have lately procured for their Works of this Nature from the Public,[1] will probably serve as an Encouragement to many others to undertake the like. Thus a Swarm of foolish Novels, and monstrous Romances will be produced, either to the great impoverishing of Booksellers, or to the great Loss of Time, and Depravation of Morals in the Reader; nay, often to the spreading of Scandal and Calumny, and to the Prejudice of the Characters of many worthy and honest People.

I question not but the ingenious Author of the Spectator[2] was principally induced to prefix *Greek* and *Latin* Mottos to every

---

[1] Probably an allusion to Richardson's *Clarissa*, which began to be published in December 1747, and to Smollett's first novel, *Roderick Random*, which appeared in January 1748 with a second edition in April. Though Fielding had earlier ridiculed *Pamela* (1740), he had a high regard for Richardson's second novel: in *The Jacobite's Journal* (2 January, 5 March 1748) he published two letters in praise of *Clarissa*, and before the year was out he had written personally to congratulate Richardson on his book (see the letter of 15 October 1748). That his admiration for the novel was not unqualified, however, is suggested later in *Tom Jones* (see pp. 793, 850) where he implicitly invites the reader to compare the sentiments and conduct of Sophia with those of Clarissa. Fielding's opinion of Smollett's novel is recorded in *The Covent-Garden Journal* (7 January 1752): 'This Rodorick, in a former Skirmish with the People called Critics, had owed some slight Success more to the Weakness of the Critics, than to any Merit of his own.'

[2] In *Spectator*, No. 221 (13 November 1711), Addison discusses the mottoes to his papers, but he does not give Fielding's explanation for them.

Paper from the same Consideration of guarding against the Pursuit of those Scribblers, who, having no Talents of a Writer but what is taught by the Writing-master, are yet nowise afraid nor ashamed to assume the same Titles with the greatest Genius, than their good Brother in the Fable was of braying in the Lion's Skin.[1]

By the Device therefore of his Motto, it became impracticable for any Man to presume to imitate the Spectators, without understanding at least one Sentence in the learned Languages. In the same Manner I have now secured myself from the Imitation of those who are utterly incapable of any Degree of Reflection, and whose Learning is not equal to an Essay.

I would not be here understood to insinuate, that the greatest Merit of such historical Productions can ever lie in these introductory Chapters; but, in Fact, those Parts which contain mere Narrative only, afford much more Encouragement to the Pen of an Imitator, than those which are composed of Observation and Reflection. Here I mean such Imitators as *Rowe* was of *Shakespear*,[2] or as *Horace* hints[3] some of the *Romans* were of *Cato*, by bare Feet and sour Faces.

To invent good Stories, and to tell them well, are possibly very rare Talents, and yet I have observed few Persons who have scrupled to aim at both; and if we examine the Romances and Novels with which the World abounds, I think we may fairly conclude, that most of the Authors would not have attempted to shew their Teeth (if the Expression may be allowed me) in any other Way of Writing; nor could indeed have strung together a dozen Sentences on any other Subject whatever. *Scribimus*

---

[1] The fable of the ass who disguised himself in a lion's skin only to be discovered by his voice and ears is included in Sir Roger L'Estrange, *Fables of Æsop and Other Eminent Mythologists,* 5th ed. (1708), No. 224. It is there attributed to Avianus. In the present context Fielding may wish to recall the lion's head that Addison erected at Button's Coffeehouse to serve as a depository for contributions to *The Guardian.* In No. 134 (14 August 1713) Addison lamented that by pouring ribaldry and scandal down the lion's throat, his correspondents 'have made a very Ass of him' (1747 ed., ii. 275).

[2] Nicholas Rowe (1674–1718), poet laureate, dramatist, and editor of Shakespeare's plays (1709). His tragedy of *Jane Shore* (1714), according to the title-page, was 'Written in Imitation of Shakespear's Style', but in Fielding's opinion Rowe produced only 'Fustian'. (See letter xl of Sarah Fielding's *Familiar Letters* [1747].)

[3] In discussing the subject of literary imitation in *Epistles,* I. xix, Horace, by way of analogy, asks: 'What if a man were to ape Cato with grim and savage look, with bare feet and the cut of a scanty gown, would he thus set before us Cato's virtue and morals?' (lines 12–14—trans. H. R. Fairclough, Loeb Classical Library, 1926).

*indocti doctique passim,*\*[1] may be more truly said of the Historian
and Biographer, than of any other Species of Writing: For all the
Arts and Sciences (even Criticism itself) require some little
Degree of Learning and Knowledge. Poetry indeed may perhaps
be thought an Exception; but then it demands Numbers, or
something like Numbers; whereas to the Composition of Novels
and Romances, nothing is necessary but Paper, Pens and Ink,
with the manual Capacity of using them. This, I conceive, their
Productions shew to be the Opinion of the Authors themselves;
and this must be the Opinion of their Readers, if indeed there be
any such.

Hence we are to derive that universal Contempt, which the
World, who always denominate the Whole from the Majority,
have cast on all historical Writers, who do not draw their Materials
from Records.[2] And it is the Apprehension of this Contempt, that
hath made us so cautiously avoid the Term Romance, a Name
with which we might otherwise have been well enough contented.
Though as we have good Authority for all our Characters, no less
indeed than the vast authentic Doomsday-Book of Nature, as is
elsewhere hinted, our Labours have sufficient Title to the Name
of History. Certainly they deserve some Distinction from those
Works, which one of the wittiest of Men regarded only as proceeding from a Pruritus,[3] or indeed rather from a Looseness of
the Brain.

> \*    ——Each desperate Blockhead dares to write,
>         Verse is the Trade of every living Wight.
>                                                     FRANCIS.

[1] Horace, *Epistles*, II. i. 117: 'scribimus indocti doctique poemata passim' ('but, skilled or
unskilled, we scribble poetry, all alike'—trans. H. R. Fairclough, Loeb Classical Library,
1926). On Francis and his translation, see above, p. 472, n. 2.

[2] To distinguish his own 'Species of Writing' from the scandal-mongering novels of
Mrs. Manley or the fantastic productions of the French romance-writers, Fielding had
earlier defined *Joseph Andrews* as a kind of biography or history, or as 'a Comic Romance'
or 'Comic Epic-Poem in Prose' (see the Preface and I. i, III. i). In III. i of that work he
developed the distinction between himself and Cervantes, who were historians 'of the World
in general', and the authors of the histories of particular eras and countries, whom he
preferred to call 'Chorographers' or 'Topographers'.

[3] Cf. Martinus Scriblerus, *Peri Bathous: The Art of Sinking in Poetry*, ch. iii ('*The
Necessity of the* Bathos, *Physically consider'd*'): 'Therefore is the Desire of Writing properly
term'd *Pruritus*, the *Titillation of the Generative Faculty of the Brain* . . .' This work, which
comprised the final volume of *Miscellanies* (1727) by Swift, Pope, and Arbuthnot, is now
generally attributed to Pope; but Fielding may have supposed Swift to be the author.

But besides the Dishonour which is thus cast on one of the most useful as well as entertaining of all Kinds of Writing, there is just Reason to apprehend, that by encouraging such Authors, we shall propagate much Dishonour of another Kind; I mean to the Characters of many good and valuable Members of Society: For the dullest Writers, no more than the dullest Companions, are always inoffensive. They have both enough of Language to be indecent and abusive. And surely if the Opinion just above cited be true, we cannot wonder, that Works so nastily derived should be nasty themselves, or have a Tendency to make others so.

To prevent therefore for the future, such intemperate Abuses of Leisure, of Letters, and of the Liberty of the Press, especially as the World seems at present to be more than usually threatned with them, I shall here venture to mention some Qualifications, every one of which are in a pretty high Degree necessary to this Order of Historians.

The first is Genius, without a full Vein of which, no Study, says *Horace*,[1] can avail us. By Genius I would understand that Power, or rather those Powers of the Mind, which are capable of penetrating into all Things within our Reach and Knowledge, and of distinguishing their essential Differences.[2] These are no other

---

[1] *Ars Poetica*, 409–10: 'ego nec studium sine divite vena, / nec rude quid prosit video ingenium.'

[2] Fielding's synthesis of *invention* (or what others among his contemporaries often called 'wit') and *judgment* as the correlative attributes of genius places him on the side of such critics as Quintilian and La Rochefoucauld. Quintilian, for example, disagreed with those who would separate judgement from invention in the creative process 'on the ground that it is necessary first to *invent* and then to *exercise our judgment*. For my part,' he asserts, 'I do not believe that *invention* can exist apart from *judgment*, since we do not say that a speaker has *invented* inconsistent, two-edged or foolish arguments, but merely that he has failed to avoid them' (*Institutio Oratoria*, III. iii. 5–6; trans. H. E. Butler, Loeb Classical Library, 1921–2). This, too, is the view of La Rochefoucauld, whose phrasing recalls Fielding's own: 'The making a Difference between Wit and Judgment, is a Vulgar Error. Judgment is nothing else but the exceeding Brightness of Wit, which, like Light, pierces [i.e., *penetre*] into the very Bottom of Things, observes all that ought to be observed there, and discovers what seemed to be past any bodies finding out: From whence we must conclude, that the Energy and Extension of this Light of the Wit, is the very Thing that produces all those Effects, usually ascribed to the Judgment' (*Moral Maxims and Reflections*, 2nd ed. [1706], Maxim 98). The following discussions of the relationship between wit and judgement in Pope are useful in the present context: E. N. Hooker, 'Pope on Wit: The *Essay on Criticism*', in *The Seventeenth Century: Studies in the History of English Thought and Literature from Bacon to Pope*, by R. F. Jones, *et al.* (Stanford, Cal., 1951), pp. 225–46; and the Introduction to the Twickenham Edition of Pope's *Essay on Criticism*, edd. E. Audra and A. Williams (1961). Cf. Fielding's earlier account of the complementary functions of 'Judgment' and 'Sagacity' in *The True Patriot* (24 December 1745).

than Invention and Judgment; and they are both called by the
collective Name of Genius, as they are of those Gifts of Nature
which we bring with us into the World. Concerning each of
which many seem to have fallen into very great Errors: For by
Invention, I believe, is generally understood a creative Faculty;
which would indeed prove most Romance-Writers to have the
highest Pretensions to it; whereas by Invention is really meant no
more, (and so the Word signifies) than Discovery, or finding
out; or to explain it at large, a quick and sagacious Penetration
into the true Essence of all the Objects of our Contemplation.
This, I think, can rarely exist without the Concomitancy of
Judgment: For how we can be said to have discovered the true
Essence of two Things, without discerning their Difference,
seems to me hard to conceive; now this last is the undisputed
Province of Judgment,[1] and yet some few Men of Wit[2] have
agreed with all the dull Fellows in the World, in representing
these two to have been seldom or never the Property of one and
the same Person.

But tho' they should be so, they are not sufficient for our
Purpose without a good Share of Learning; for which I could
again cite the Authority of *Horace*,[3] and of many others, if any
was necessary to prove that Tools are of no Service to a Workman, when they are not sharpened by Art, or when he wants
Rules to direct him in his Work, or hath no Matter to work upon.
All these Uses are supplied by Learning: For Nature can only
furnish us with Capacity, or, as I have chose to illustrate it, with

---

[1] Cf. Locke's *Essay concerning Human Understanding*, II. xi. 2—a passage from which
Fielding had quoted in *The True Patriot* (24 December 1745): 'If in having our *Ideas* in the
Memory ready at hand, consists Quickness of Parts; in this of having them unconfused,
and being able nicely to distinguish one Thing from another, where there is but the least
Difference, consists, in a great measure, the Exactness of Judgment, and Clearness of
Reason, which is to be observed in one Man above another. And hence, perhaps, may be
given some Reason of that common Observation, That Men who have a great deal of Wit,
and prompt Memories, have not always the clearest Judgment, or deepest Reason. For
*Wit* lying most in the Assemblage of *Ideas*, and putting those together with Quickness and
Variety, wherein can be found any Resemblance or Congruity, thereby to make up pleasant
Pictures, and agreeable Visions in the Fancy: *Judgment* on the contrary, lies quite on the
other Side, in separating carefully, one from another, *Ideas* wherein can be found the least
Difference, thereby to avoid being misled by Similitude, and by Affinity to take one Thing
for another' (12th ed. [1741], i. 117).

[2] Locke, for one (see preceding note), and for another, Addison, who in *The Spectator*,
No. 62 (11 May 1711), agrees with his opinion that wit and judgement 'are not always the
Talents of the same Person'.                              [3] Cf. *Ars Poetica*, 408–18.

the Tools of our Profession; Learning must fit them for Use, must direct them in it; and lastly, must contribute, Part at least, of the Materials. A competent Knowledge of History and of the *Belles Lettres*, is here absolutely necessary; and without this Share of Knowledge at least, to affect the Character of an Historian, is as vain as to endeavour at building a House without Timber or Mortar, or Brick or Stone. *Homer* and *Milton*,[1] who, though they added the Ornament of Numbers to their Works, were both Historians of our Order, were Masters of all the Learning of their Times.

Again, there is another Sort of Knowledge beyond the Power of Learning to bestow, and this is to be had by Conversation.[2] So necessary is this to the understanding the Characters of Men, that none are more ignorant of them than those learned Pedants, whose Lives have been entirely consumed in Colleges, and among Books: For however exquisitely Human Nature may have been described by Writers, the true practical System can be learnt only in the World. Indeed the like happens in every other Kind of Knowledge. Neither Physic, nor Law, are to be practically known from Books. Nay, the Farmer, the Planter, the Gardener, must perfect by Experience what he hath acquired the Rudiments of by Reading. How accurately soever the ingenious Mr. *Miller*[3]

---

[1] On Homer's reputation for learning, see, for example, 'An Essay on the Life, Writings and Learning, of Homer', section iii, prefixed to Pope's *Iliad* (1715). According to Rapin, Homer was 'the first Founder of all Arts and Sciences, and the Pattern of the wise Men in all Ages' ('Reflections on Aristotle's Treatise of Poesie', trans. Thomas Rymer, in Rapin's *Whole Critical Works*, 3rd ed. [1731], ii. 138). For Fielding's similar opinion, see *The True Patriot* (24 December 1745). In that journal for 5 November 1745 he described *Paradise Lost* as 'the best Poem which perhaps [the World] hath ever seen'.

[2] Cf. *Ars Poetica*, 156–7, 317–18.

[3] Philip Miller (1691–1771), F.R.S., gardener to the Company of Apothecaries at the Botanic Garden, Chelsea, and author of *The Gardeners Dictionary*, 2 vols. (1731, 1739). He was the best horticulturalist of his time and his *Dictionary* went through eight editions during his lifetime. To Fielding, Miller's work, which is an exhaustive description of the various species and uses of plants with a prefatory account of the history of gardening from Eden, may have seemed to comprise an amusing analogue to his own fictional anatomy of 'Human Nature'. In Miller's Preface, at least, Fielding would have found two passages relevant to his own themes in the present chapter. Miller, too, emphasized the need for practical experience in the art of gardening: 'to what Purpose is it, to a Person who wants to know the exact Method of propagating any particular Plant, to read over a fine Theory of *Gardening*, without ever entering into the necessary Instructions how he must proceed: And this is too often the Fault in many Books on this Subject; most of which have been wrote by Persons only skilful in the *Theory*, and therefore can't be suppos'd capable of instructing others in the *Practice*, that being what they themselves are unacquainted with' (I. x). And like Fielding, who began this chapter with reflections on incompetent imitators

may have described the Plant, he himself would advise his
Disciple to see it in the Garden. As we must perceive, that after
the nicest Strokes of a *Shakespear*, or a *Johnson*, of a *Wycherly*, or
an *Otway*, some Touches of Nature will escape the Reader,
which the judicious Action of a *Garrick*, of a *Cibber*, or a *Clive*,*¹
can convey to him; so on the real Stage, the Character shews
himself in a stronger and bolder Light, than he can be described.
And if this be the Case in those fine and nervous Descriptions,
which great Authors themselves have taken from Life, how much
more strongly will it hold when the Writer himself takes his
Lines not from Nature, but from Books! Such Characters are

* There is a peculiar Propriety in mentioning this great Actor, and these two most
justly celebrated Actresses in this Place; as they have all formed themselves on the Study
of Nature only; and not on the Imitation of their Predecessors.² Hence they have been
able to excel all who have gone before them; a Degree of Merit which the servile Herd
of Imitators can never possibly arrive at.

of the novelist's art, applying the fable of the ass in the lion's skin, so Miller castigated those
authors on gardening who were no better than ignorant plagiarists of their predecessors:
these impostors, however, have 'manifested, how unable the assum'd Skin of the Lyon, has
been to conceal those Ears, which are the peculiar Diagnostic of a much more servile and
ignoble Creature' (I. xi). For another allusion to Miller, see the notes to *Ovid's Art of Love
Paraphrased* (1747).

   ¹ With the new theatrical season of 1747, these three fine performers were together for the
first time at Drury Lane, Mrs. Cibber having joined the company after Garrick became
patentee. On Garrick, see above, pp. 327, n. 2, and 853. Susannah Arne Cibber (1714–66)
was unhappily married to Colley Cibber's son Theophilus. Handel admired her singing
voice and as an actress she distinguished herself in tragedy. For Fielding's compliments to
her, see *The Jacobite's Journal* (6, 13 February 1748), *Amelia* (1751), v. viii. and *The
Covent-Garden Journal* (11 January 1752). Catherine 'Kitty' Clive (1711–85) was also a
pleasing singer and in comedy the finest actress of her time—such, at least, was the opinion
of Samuel Foote (*The Roman and English Comedy Consider'd and Compar'd* [1747], p. 41)
and of Fielding himself (letter xl of Sarah Fielding's *Familiar Letters* [1747] and *The
Jacobite's Journal* [30 January 1748]). In the late 1740s, however, Mrs. Clive's fortunes
appear to have declined. One writer observed that she, though once 'esteem'd the Phænix
[*sic*] of the Age, seems now to be of little Consequence; her Laurels are all wither'd; her
Friends grown cold; and the repeated Acclamations that us'd to welcome her Appearance,
are now no more' (J. T., *A Letter of Compliment to the ingenious Author of a Treatise on the
Passions* [1747 ?], p. 33). Fielding, at least, who had been among the first to recognize her
abilities and who had dedicated to her the published version of *The Intriguing Chambermaid*
(1734), never ceased to praise her: besides the complimentary references already cited, see,
for example, *Joseph Andrews* (1742), III. x; *Amelia*, I. vi, where she is said to be to acting
what Shakespeare is to poetry and Hogarth to painting; and *The Covent-Garden Journal*
(11 January 1752).
   ² Cf. *The Jacobite's Journal* (6 February 1748), where Fielding similarly declares 'That
the Business of an Actor, as well as of a Writer, is to copy Nature, and not to imitate
the Excellencies of their Predecessors: That Mr. *Garrick*, Mr. *Quin*, Mrs. *Cibber*, Mrs.
*Clive*, and Mrs. *Woffington*, are all, in their several Capacities, Examples of this Merit'.

only the faint Copy of a Copy, and can have neither the Justness nor Spirit of an Original.

Now this Conversation in our Historian must be universal, that is, with all Ranks and Degrees of Men: For the Knowledge of what is called High-Life, will not instruct him in low, nor *e converso*, will his being acquainted with the inferior Part of Mankind, teach him the Manners of the superior. And though it may be thought that the Knowledge of either may sufficiently enable him to describe at least that in which he hath been conversant; yet he will even here fall greatly short of Perfection: for the Follies of either Rank do in reality illustrate each other. For Instance, the Affectation of High-life appears more glaring and ridiculous from the Simplicity of the Low; and again the Rudeness and Barbarity of this latter, strikes with much stronger Ideas of Absurdity, when contrasted with, and opposed to the Politeness which controuls the former. Besides, to say the Truth, the Manners of our Historian will be improved by both these Conversations: For in the one he will easily find Examples of Plainness, Honesty, and Sincerity; in the other of Refinement, Elegance, and a Liberality of Spirit; which last Quality I myself have scarce ever seen in Men of low Birth and Education.

Nor will all the Qualities I have hitherto given my Historian avail him, unless he have what is generally meant by a good Heart, and be capable of feeling. The Author who will make me weep, says *Horace*,[1] must first weep himself. In reality, no Man can paint a Distress well, which he doth not feel while he is painting it; nor do I doubt, but that the most pathetic and affecting Scenes have been writ with Tears. In the same Manner it is with the Ridiculous. I am convinced I never make my Reader laugh heartily, but where I have laughed before him, unless it should happen at any Time, that instead of laughing with me, he should be inclined to laugh at me. Perhaps this may have been the Case at some Passages in this Chapter, from which Apprehension I will here put an End to it.

[1] *Ars Poetica*, 102–3: 'si vis me flere, dolendum est/ primum ipsi tibi.' On the requirement that a good author must first be a good man, see also Quintilian, *Institutio Oratoria*, i (Preface), 9–14.

## CHAPTER II

*Containing a very surprizing Adventure indeed, which Mr.* Jones
*met with in his Walk with the Man of the Hill.*

*AURORA* now first opened her Casement, *anglicè*, the Day
began to break, when *Jones* walked forth in Company with
the Stranger, and mounted *Mazard-Hill*;[1] of which they had no
sooner gained the Summit, than one of the most noble Prospects
in the World presented itself to their View, and which we would
likewise present to the Reader; but for two Reasons. *First*, We
despair of making those who have seen this Prospect, admire our
Description. *Secondly*, We very much doubt whether those, who
have not seen it, would understand it.

*Jones* stood for some Minutes fixed in one Posture, and directing his Eyes towards the South; upon which the old Gentleman
asked, What he was looking at with so much Attention? 'Alas,
Sir,' answered he, with a Sigh, 'I was endeavouring to trace out
my own Journey hither. Good Heavens! what a Distance is
*Gloucester* from us! What a vast Tract of Land must be between
me and my own Home.' 'Ay, ay, young Gentleman,' cries the
other, 'and, by your Sighing, from what you love better than your
own Home, or I am mistaken. I perceive now the Object of your
Contemplation is not within your Sight, and yet I fancy you have
a Pleasure in looking that Way.' *Jones* answered with a Smile, 'I
find, old Friend, you have not yet forgot the Sensations of your
Youth.—I own my Thoughts were employed as you have guessed.'

They now walked to that Part of the Hill which looks to the
North West, and which hangs over a vast and extensive Wood.
Here they were no sooner arrived, than they heard at a Distance
the most violent Skreams of a Woman, proceeding from the
Wood below them. *Jones* listened a Moment, and then, without
saying a Word to his Companion (for indeed the Occasion seemed
sufficiently pressing) ran, or rather slid, down the Hill, and
without the least Apprehension or Concern for his own Safety,
made directly to the Thicket whence the Sound had issued.

---

[1] Apparently a fictitious name, but Fielding probably has in mind the Worcestershire
Beacon, the highest peak (1,394 ft.) of the Malverns and famous for its prospect of fourteen
counties. From this vantage point Gloucester is in full view to the south and, in the
eighteenth century, the dense woods of Malvern Chace extended to the north-west.

He had not entered far into the Wood before he beheld a most shocking Sight indeed, a Woman stript half naked, under the Hands of a Ruffian, who had put his Garter round her Neck, and was endeavouring to draw her up to a Tree. *Jones* asked no Questions at this Interval; but fell instantly upon the Villain, and made such good Use of his trusty Oaken Stick, that he laid him sprawling on the Ground, before he could defend himself, indeed almost before he knew he was attacked; nor did he cease the Prosecution of his Blows, till the Woman herself begged him to forbear, saying, She believed he had sufficiently done his Business.

The poor Wretch then fell upon her Knees to *Jones*, and gave him a thousand Thanks for her Deliverance: He presently lifted her up, and told her he was highly pleased with the extraordinary Accident which had sent him thither for her Relief, where it was so improbable she should find any; adding, that Heaven seemed to have designed him as the happy Instrument of her Protection. 'Nay,' answered she, 'I could almost conceive you to be some good Angel; and to say the Truth, you look more like an Angel than a Man, in my Eye.' Indeed he was a charming Figure, and if a very fine Person, and a most comely Set of Features, adorned with Youth, Health, Strength, Freshness, Spirit and Good-Nature, can make a Man resemble an Angel, he certainly had that Resemblance.

The redeemed Captive had not altogether so much of the human-angelic Species; she seemed to be, at least, of the middle Age, nor had her Face much Appearance of Beauty; but her Cloaths being torn from all the upper Part of her Body, her Breasts, which were well formed, and extremely white, attracted the Eyes of her Deliverer, and for a few Moments they stood silent, and gazing at each other; till the Ruffian on the Ground beginning to move, *Jones* took the Garter which had been intended for another Purpose, and bound both his Hands behind him. And now, on contemplating his Face, he discovered, greatly to his Surprize, and perhaps not a little to his Satisfaction, this very Person to be no other than Ensign *Northerton*. Nor had the Ensign forgotten his former Antagonist, whom he knew the Moment he came to himself. His Surprize was equal to that of *Jones*; but I conceive his Pleasure was rather less on this Occasion.

*Jones* helped *Northerton* upon his Legs, and then looking him stedfastly in the Face, 'I fancy, Sir,' said he, 'you did not expect to meet me any more in this World, and I confess I had as little Expectation to find you here. However, Fortune, I see, hath brought us once more together, and hath given me Satisfaction for the Injury I have received, even without my own Knowledge.'

'It is very much like a Man of Honour indeed,' answered *Northerton*, 'to take Satisfaction by knocking a Man down behind his Back. Neither am I capable of giving you Satisfaction here, as I have no Sword; but if you dare behave like a Gentleman, let us go where I can furnish myself with one, and I will do by you as a Man of Honour ought.'

'Doth it become such a Villain as you are,' cries *Jones*, 'to contaminate the Name of Honour by assuming it? But I shall waste no Time in Discourse with you—Justice requires Satisfaction of you now, and shall have it.' Then turning to the Woman, he asked her, if she was near her Home, or if not, whether she was acquainted with any House in the Neighbourhood, where she might procure herself some decent Cloaths, in order to proceed to a Justice of the Peace.

She answered, She was an entire Stranger in that Part of the World. *Jones* then recollecting himself, said he had a Friend near, who would direct them; indeed he wondered at his not following; but, in Fact, the Good Man of the Hill, when our Heroe departed, sat himself down on the Brow, where, tho' he had a Gun in his Hand, he with great Patience and Unconcern, had attended the Issue.

*Jones* then stepping without the Wood, perceived the old Man sitting as we have just described him; he presently exerted his utmost Agility, and with surprizing Expedition ascended the Hill.

The old Man advised him to carry the Woman to *Upton*,[1] which, he said, was the nearest Town, and there he would be sure of furnishing her with all manner of Conveniencies. *Jones* having received his Direction to the Place, took his Leave of the Man of the Hill, and desiring him to direct *Partridge* the same Way, returned hastily to the Wood.

Our Heroe, at his Departure to make this Enquiry of his

[1] From the Worcestershire Beacon, the nearest settlement would have been Great Malvern; the nearest 'Town', however, was Upton-upon-Severn, some six miles to the south-east. And clearly for the purposes of his narrative, Fielding wished to bring Jones to Upton, where the threads of the plot could converge more naturally.

Friend, had considered, that as the Ruffian's Hands were tied behind him, he was incapable of executing any wicked Purposes on the poor Woman. Besides, he knew he should not be beyond the Reach of her Voice, and could return soon enough to prevent any Mischief. He had moreover declared to the Villain, that if he attempted the least Insult, he would be himself immediately the Executioner of Vengeance on him. But *Jones* unluckily forgot that tho' the Hands of *Northerton* were tied, his Legs were at Liberty; nor did he lay the least Injunction on the Prisoner, that he should not make what use of these he pleased. *Northerton* therefore having given no Parole of that Kind, thought he might, without any Breach of Honour, depart, not being obliged, as he imagined, by any Rules, to wait for a formal Discharge. He therefore took up his Legs, which were at Liberty, and walked off thro' the Wood, which favoured his Retreat; nor did the Woman, whose Eyes were perhaps rather turned towards her Deliverer, once think of his Escape, or give herself any Concern or Trouble to prevent it.

*Jones* therefore, at his Return, found the Woman alone. He would have spent some Time in searching for *Northerton*; but she would not permit him; earnestly entreating that he would accompany her to the Town whither they had been directed. 'As to the Fellow's Escape,' said she, 'it gives me no Uneasiness: For Philosophy and Christianity both preach up Forgiveness of Injuries. But for you, Sir, I am concerned at the Trouble I give you, nay indeed my Nakedness may well make me ashamed to look you in the Face; and if it was not for the Sake of your Protection, I should wish to go alone.'

*Jones* offered her his Coat; but, I know not for what Reason, she absolutely refused the most earnest Solicitations to accept it. He then begged her to forget both the Causes of her Confusion. 'With Regard to the former,' says he, 'I have done no more than my Duty in protecting you; and as for the latter, I will entirely remove it, by walking before you all the Way; for I would not have my Eyes offend you, and I could not answer for my Power of resisting the attractive Charms of so much Beauty.'

Thus our Heroe and the redeemed Lady walked in the same Manner as *Orpheus* and *Eurydice* marched heretofore:[1] But tho' I

---

[1] See Ovid, *Metamorphoses*, x. 1–63. To redeem his dead wife Eurydice, Orpheus descended to Hades and by his music so charmed Persephone that he was permitted to lead

cannot believe that *Jones* was designedly tempted by his Fair
One to look behind him, yet as she frequently wanted his
Assistance to help her over Stiles, and had besides many Trips
and other Accidents, he was often obliged to turn about. However, he had better Fortune than what attended poor *Orpheus*; for
he brought his Companion, or rather Follower, safe into the
famous Town of *Upton*.

## CHAPTER III

*The Arrival of Mr.* Jones, *with his Lady, at the Inn, with a very full
Description of the Battle of* Upton.

THO' the Reader, we doubt not, is very eager to know who
this Lady was, and how she fell into the Hands of Mr.
*Northerton*; we must beg him to suspend his Curiosity for a short
Time, as we are obliged, for some very good Reasons, which
hereafter perhaps he may guess, to delay his Satisfaction a little
longer.

Mr. *Jones* and his fair Companion no sooner entered the Town,
than they went directly to that Inn[1] which, in their Eyes, presented
the fairest Appearance to the Street. Here *Jones*, having ordered
a Servant to shew a Room above Stairs, was ascending, when the
dishevelled Fair hastily following, was laid hold on by the
Master of the House, who cried, 'Hey day, where is that Beggar
Wench going? stay below Stairs, I desire you;' but *Jones* at that
Instant thundered from above, 'Let the Lady come up,' in so
authoritative a Voice, that the good Man instantly withdrew his
Hands, and the Lady made the best of her Way to the Chamber.

---

Eurydice from the underworld upon condition that he not look back. He forgot his promise and Eurydice was lost to him for ever.

[1] Situated on the river and along the main road, Upton was an important communications point between Gloucester and Worcester and a prosperous trading town in its own
right. It abounded with inns and ale-houses, but according to a tradition well established
by the mid-nineteenth century (see Lascelles's *Directory and Gazetteer of the City of Worcester
and Neighbourhood* [1851], p. 118), the particular hostel in which the central books of *Tom
Jones* are set is to be identified with the White Lion, a comfortable inn that still stands. (See
Mildred Berkeley, 'Some Old Worcestershire Inns', *Transactions of the Worcestershire
Archæological Society, 1924–5* [Worcester, 1925], ii. 108.) Advertisements in *The Weekly
Worcester Journal* reveal that the innkeeper was one John Hurst (see the numbers for 4–11
April 1746, 20–7 March 1747, 30 March 1749).

500 *The History of Tom Jones* Bk. IX

Here *Jones* wished her Joy of her safe Arrival, and then departed, in order, as he promised, to send the Landlady up with some Cloaths. The poor Woman thanked him heartily for all his Kindness, and said, She hoped she should see him again soon, to thank him a thousand Times more. During this short Conversation, she covered her white Bosom as well as she could possibly with her Arms: For *Jones* could not avoid stealing a sly Peep or two, tho' he took all imaginable Care to avoid giving any Offence.

Our Travellers had happened to take up their Residence at a House of exceeding good Repute, whither *Irish* Ladies of strict Virtue, and many Northern Lasses of the same Predicament, were accustomed to resort in their Way to *Bath*. The Landlady therefore would by no Means have admitted any Conversation of a disreputable Kind to pass under her Roof. Indeed so foul and contagious are all such Proceedings, that they contaminate the very innocent Scenes where they are committed, and give the Name of a bad House, or of a House of ill Repute, to all those where they are suffered to be carried on.

Not that I would intimate, that such strict Chastity as was preserved in the Temple of *Vesta* can possibly be maintained at a public Inn. My good Landlady did not hope for such a Blessing, nor would any of the Ladies I have spoken of, or indeed any others of the most rigid Note, have expected or insisted on any such Thing. But to exclude all vulgar Concubinage, and to drive all Whores in Rags from within the Walls, is within the Power of every one. This my Landlady very stiffly adhered to, and this her virtuous Guests, who did not travel in Rags, would very reasonably have expected of her.

Now it required no very blameable Degree of Suspicion, to imagine that Mr. *Jones* and his ragged Companion had certain Purposes in their Intention, which, tho' tolerated in some Christian Countries, connived at in others, and practised in all; are however as expressly forbidden as Murder, or any other horrid Vice, by that Religion which is universally believed in those Countries. The Landlady therefore had no sooner received an Intimation of the Entrance of the abovesaid Persons, than she began to meditate the most expeditious Means for their Expulsion. In order to do this, she had provided herself with a long and deadly Instrument, with which, in Times of Peace, the Chambermaid was wont to demolish the Labours of the industrious

Spider. In vulgar Phrase, she had taken up the Broomstick, and was just about to sally from the Kitchen, when *Jones* accosted her with a Demand of a Gown, and other Vestments, to cover the half-naked Woman above Stairs.

Nothing can be more provoking to the human Temper, nor more dangerous to that cardinal Virtue, Patience, than Solicitations of extraordinary Offices of Kindness, on Behalf of those very Persons with whom we are highly incensed. For this Reason *Shakespear* hath artfully introduced[1] his *Desdemona* soliciting Favours for *Cassio* of her Husband, as the Means of enflaming not only his Jealousy, but his Rage, to the highest Pitch of Madness; and we find the unfortunate Moor less able to command his Passion on this Occasion, than even when he beheld his valued Present to his Wife in the Hands of his supposed Rival. In Fact, we regard these Efforts as Insults on our Understanding, and to such the Pride of Man is very difficultly brought to submit.

My Landlady, though a very good-tempered Woman, had, I suppose, some of this Pride in her Composition; for *Jones* had scarce ended his Request, when she fell upon him with a certain Weapon, which, tho' it be neither long, nor sharp, nor hard, nor indeed threatens from its Appearance with either Death or Wound, hath been however held in great Dread and Abhorrence by many wise Men; nay, by many brave ones; insomuch that some who have dared to look into the Mouth of a loaded Cannon, have not dared to look into a Mouth where this Weapon was brandished; and rather than run the Hazard of its Execution, have contented themselves with making a most pitiful and sneaking Figure in the Eyes of all their Acquaintance.

To confess the Truth, I am afraid Mr. *Jones* was one of these; for tho' he was attacked and violently belaboured with the aforesaid Weapon, he could not be provoked to make any Resistance; but in a most cowardly Manner applied, with many Entreaties, to his Antagonist to desist from pursuing her Blows; in plain *English*, he only begged her with the utmost Earnestness to hear him; but before he could obtain his Request, my Landlord himself entered into the Fray, and embraced that Side of the Cause which seemed to stand very little in need of Assistance.

There are a Sort of Heroes who are supposed to be determined

[1] Cf. *Othello*, III. iii–IV. i.

in their chusing or avoiding a Conflict by the Character and Behaviour of the Person whom they are to engage. These are said to know their Man, and *Jones*, I believe, knew his Woman; for tho' he had been so submissive to her, he was no sooner attacked by her Husband, than he demonstrated an immediate Spirit of Resentment, and enjoined him Silence under a very severe Penalty; no less than that, I think, of being converted into Fuel for his own Fire.

The Husband, with great Indignation, but with a Mixture of Pity, answered, 'You must pray first to be made able; I believe I am a better Man than yourself; ay, every Way, that I am;' and presently proceeded to discharge half a dozen Whores at the Lady above Stairs, the last of which had scarce issued from his Lips, when a swinging Blow from the Cudgel that *Jones* carried in his Hand assaulted him over the Shoulders.

It is a Question whether the Landlord or the Landlady was the most expeditious in returning this Blow. My Landlord, whose Hands were empty, fell to with his Fist, and the good Wife, up-lifting her Broom, and aiming at the Head of *Jones*, had probably put an immediate End to the Fray, and to *Jones* likewise, had not the Descent of this Broom been prevented,—not by the miracu-lous Intervention of any Heathen Deity, but by a very natural, tho' fortunate Accident; *viz.* by the Arrival of *Partridge*; who entered the House at that Instant (for Fear had caused him to run every Step from the Hill) and who, seeing the Danger which threatned his Master, or Companion, (which you chuse to call him) prevented so sad a Catastrophe, by catching hold of the Landlady's Arm, as it was brandished aloft in the Air.

The Landlady soon perceived the Impediment which pre-vented her Blow; and being unable to rescue her Arm from the Hands of *Partridge*, she let fall the Broom, and then leaving *Jones* to the Discipline of her Husband, she fell with the utmost Fury on that poor Fellow, who had already given some Inti-mation of himself, by crying, 'Zounds! do you intend to kill my Friend?'

*Partridge*, though not much addicted to Battle, would not however stand still when his Friend was attacked; nor was he much displeased with that Part of the Combat which fell to his Share: He therefore returned my Landlady's Blows as soon as he received them; and now the Fight was obstinately maintained on all Parts, and it seemed doubtful to which Side Fortune would incline, when the naked Lady, who had listened at the Top of the Stairs to the Dialogue which preceded the Engagement, descended suddenly from above, and without weighing the unfair Inequality of two to one, fell upon the poor Woman who was boxing with *Partridge*; nor did that great Champion desist, but rather redoubled his Fury, when he found fresh Succours were arrived to his Assistance.

Victory must now have fallen to the Side of the Travellers (for the bravest Troops must yield to Numbers) had not *Susan* the Chambermaid come luckily to support her Mistress. This *Susan* was as two-handed a Wench (according to the Phrase) as any in the Country, and would, I believe, have beat the famed *Thalestris* herself,[1] or any of her subject *Amazons*; for her Form was robust and manlike, and every way made for such Encounters. As her Hands and Arms were formed to give Blows with great Mischief to an Enemy, so was her Face as well contrived to receive Blows without any great Injury to herself: Her Nose being already flat to her Face; her Lips were so large, that no Swelling could be perceived in them, and moreover they were so hard, that a Fist could hardly make any Impression on them. Lastly, her Cheek-Bones stood out, as if Nature had intended them for two Bastions to defend her Eyes in those Encounters for which she seemed so well calculated, and to which she was most wonderfully well inclined.

This fair Creature entering the Field of Battle, immediately filed to that Wing where her Mistress maintained so unequal a Fight with one of either Sex. Here she presently challenged *Partridge* to single Combat. He accepted the Challenge, and a most desperate Fight began between them.

Now the Dogs of War being let loose,[2] began to lick their bloody Lips; now Victory with Golden Wings hung hovering in the Air. Now Fortune taking her Scales from her Shelf, began to weigh the Fates of *Tom Jones*, his Female Companion, and *Partridge*, against the Landlord, his Wife, and Maid; all which hung in exact Ballance before her; when a good-natured Accident

---

[1] Queen of the Amazons, who travelled to meet Alexander hoping to raise a race of heroes. (See Strabo, *Geography*, XI. v. 4.) In *Jonathan Wild* (1743), II. iii, she is said to be a popular character in the drolls at Bartholomew Fair. See also below, p. 846.

[2] Cf. *Julius Caesar*, III. i.

put suddenly an End to the bloody Fray, with which half of the Combatants had already sufficiently feasted. This Accident was the Arrival of a Coach and four; upon which my Landlord and Landlady immediately desisted from fighting, and at their Entreaty obtained the same Favour of their Antagonists; but *Susan* was not so kind to *Partridge*, for that *Amazonian* Fair having overthrown and bestrid her Enemy, was now cuffing him lustily with both her Hands, without any Regard to his Request of a Cessation of Arms, or to those loud Exclamations of Murder which he roared forth.

No sooner, however, had *Jones* quitted the Landlord, than he flew to the Rescue of his defeated Companion, from whom he with much Difficulty drew off the enraged Chambermaid; but *Partridge* was not immediately sensible of his Deliverance; for he still lay flat on the Floor, guarding his Face with his Hands, nor did he cease roaring till *Jones* had forced him to look up, and to perceive that the Battle was at an End.

The Landlord who had no visible Hurt, and the Landlady hiding her well scratched Face with her Handkerchief, ran both hastily to the Door to attend the Coach, from which a young Lady and her Maid now alighted. These the Landlady presently ushered into that Room where Mr. *Jones* had at first deposited his fair Prize, as it was the best Apartment in the House. Hither they were obliged to pass through the Field of Battle, which they did with the utmost Haste, covering their Faces with their Handkerchiefs, as desirous to avoid the Notice of any one. Indeed their Caution was quite unnecessary: For the poor unfortunate *Helen*, the fatal Cause of all the Bloodshed, was entirely taken up in endeavouring to conceal her own Face, and *Jones* was no less occupied in rescuing *Partridge* from the Fury of *Susan*; which being happily effected, the poor Fellow immediately departed to the Pump to wash his Face, and to stop that bloody Torrent which *Susan* had plentifully set a flowing from his Nostrils.

## CHAPTER IV

*In which the Arrival of a Man of War puts a final End to Hostilities,*
*and causes the Conclusion of a firm and lasting Peace between all*
*Parties.*

A SERJEANT and a File of Musqueteers, with a Deserter in
their Custody, arrived about this Time. The Serjeant presently enquired for the principal Magistrate of the Town, and
was informed by my Landlord, that he himself was vested in that
Office. He then demanded his Billets, together with a Mug of
Beer, and complaining it was cold, spread himself before the
Kitchen Fire.

Mr. *Jones* was at this Time comforting the poor distressed
Lady, who sat down at a Table in the Kitchen, and leaning her
Head upon her Arm, was bemoaning her Misfortunes; but lest
my fair Readers should be in Pain concerning a particular
Circumstance, I think proper here to acquaint them, that before
she had quitted the Room above Stairs, she had so well covered
herself with a Pillowbere which she there found, that her Regard
to Decency was not in the least violated by the Presence of so
many Men as were now in the Room.

One of the Soldiers now went up to the Serjeant, and whispered
something in his Ear; upon which he stedfastly fixed his Eyes on
the Lady, and having looked at her for near a Minute, he came
up to her, saying, 'I ask Pardon, Madam, but I am certain I am
not deceived, you can be no other Person than Captain *Waters's*
Lady.'

The poor Woman, who in her present Distress had very little
regarded the Face of any Person present, no sooner looked at the
Serjeant, than she presently recollected him, and calling him by
his Name, answered, 'That she was indeed the unhappy Person he
imagined her to be;' but added, 'I wonder any one should know
me in this Disguise.' To which the Serjeant replied, 'he was very
much surprized to see her Ladyship in such a Dress, and was
afraid some Accident had happened to her.' 'An Accident hath
happened to me, indeed,' says she, 'and I am highly obliged to
this Gentleman (pointing to *Jones*) that it was not a fatal one,
or that I am now living to mention it.' 'Whatever the Gentleman
hath done,' cries the Serjeant, 'I am sure the Captain will make him

Amends for it; and if I can be of any Service, your Ladyship may command me, and I shall think myself very happy to have it in my Power to serve your Ladyship; and so indeed may any one, for I know the Captain will well reward them for it.'

The Landlady who heard from the Stairs all that past between the Serjeant and Mrs. *Waters*, came hastily down, and running directly up to her, began to ask Pardon for the Offences she had committed, begging that all might be imputed to Ignorance of her Quality: For, 'Lud! Madam,' says she, 'how should I have imagined that a Lady of your Fashion would appear in such a Dress? I am sure, Madam, if I had once suspected that your Ladyship was your Ladyship, I would sooner have burnt my Tongue out, than have said what I have said: And I hope your Ladyship will accept of a Gown, till you can get your own Cloaths.'

'Prithee Woman,' says Mrs. *Waters*, 'cease your Impertinence: How can you imagine I should concern myself about any thing which comes from the Lips of such low Creatures as yourself. But I am surprized at your Assurance in thinking, after what is past, that I will condescend to put on any of your dirty Things. I would have you know, Creature, I have a Spirit above that.'

Here *Jones* interfered, and begg'd Mrs. *Waters* to forgive the Landlady, and to accept her Gown: 'For I must confess,' cries he, 'our Appearance was a little suspicious when first we came in; and I am well assured, all this good Woman did, was, as she professed, out of Regard to the Reputation of her House.'

'Yes, upon my truly was it,' says she; 'the Gentleman speaks very much like a Gentleman, and I see very plainly is so; and to be certain the House is well known to be a House of as good Reputation as any on the Road, and tho' I say it, is frequented by Gentry of the best Quality, both *Irish* and *English*. I defy any Body to say black is my Eye,[1] for that Matter. And, as I was saying, if I had known your Ladyship to be your Ladyship, I would as soon have burnt my Fingers as have affronted your Ladyship; but truly where Gentry come and spend their Money, I am not willing that they should be scandalized by a Set of poor shabby Vermin, that wherever they go, leave more Lice than Money behind them; such Folks never raise my Compassion: For to be certain, it is foolish to have any for them, and if our

[1] See above, p. 317, n. 2.

Justices did as they ought, they would be all whipt out of the
Kingdom; for to be certain it is what is most fitting for them. But
as for your Ladyship, I am heartily sorry your Ladyship hath had
a Misfortune, and if your Ladyship will do me the Honour to
wear my Cloaths till you can get some of your Ladyship's own, to
be certain the best I have is at your Ladyship's Service.'

Whether Cold, Shame, or the Persuasions of Mr. *Jones*
prevailed most on Mrs. *Waters*, I will not determine; but she
suffered herself to be pacified by this Speech of my Landlady, and
retired with that good Woman, in order to apparel herself in a
decent Manner.

My Landlord was likewise beginning his Oration to *Jones*, but
was presently interrupted by that generous Youth, who shook
him heartily by the Hand; and assured him of entire Forgiveness,
saying, 'If you are satisfied, my worthy Friend, I promise you I
am;' and indeed in one Sense the Landlord had the better Reason
to be satisfied; for he had received a Bellyfull of Drubbing,
whereas *Jones* had scarce felt a single Blow.

*Partridge*, who had been all this Time washing his bloody Nose
at the Pump, returned into the Kitchen at the Instant when his
Master and the Landlord were shaking Hands with each other.
As he was of a peaceable Disposition, he was pleased with
those Symptoms of Reconciliation; and tho' his Face bore some
Marks of *Susan's* Fist, and many more of her Nails, he rather
chose to be contented with his Fortune in the last Battle, than to
endeavour at bettering it in another.

The heroic *Susan* was likewise well contented with her Victory,
tho' it had cost her a Black-Eye, which *Partridge* had given her
at the first Onset. Between these two, therefore, a League was
struck, and those Hands which had been the Instruments of
War, became now the Mediators of Peace.

Matters were thus restored to a perfect Calm, at which the
Serjeant, tho' it may seem so contrary to the Principles of his
Profession, testified his Approbation. 'Why now, that's friendly,'
said he; 'D—n me, I hate to see two People bear Ill-will to one
another, after they have had a Tussel. The only Way when
Friends quarrel, is to see it out fairly in a friendly Manner, as a
Man may call it, either with a Fist, or Sword, or Pistol, according as they like, and then let it be all over: For my own Part,
d—n me if ever I love my Friend better than when I am fighting

with him. To bear Malice is more like a *Frenchman* than an *Englishman*.'

He then proposed a Libation[1] as a necessary Part of the Ceremony at all Treaties of this Kind. Perhaps the Reader may here conclude that he was well versed in antient History; but this, tho' highly probable, as he cited no Authority to support the Custom, I will not affirm with any Confidence. Most likely indeed it is, that he founded his Opinion on very good Authority, since he confirmed it with many violent Oaths.

*Jones* no sooner heard the Proposal, than immediately agreeing with the learned Serjeant, he ordered a Bowl, or rather a large Mug, filled with the Liquor used on these Occasions to be brought in, and then began the Ceremony himself. He placed his Right Hand in that of the Landlord, and seizing the Bowl with his Left, uttered the usual Words, and then made his Libation. After which the same was observed by all present. Indeed there is very little Need of being particular in describing the whole Form, as it differed so little from those Libations of which so much is recorded in ancient Authors, and their modern Transcribers. The principal Difference lay in two Instances: For first, the present Company poured the Liquor only down their Throats; and, secondly, The Serjeant, who officiated as Priest, drank the last; but he preserved, I believe, the antient Form in swallowing much the largest Draught of the whole Company, and in being the only Person present who contributed nothing towards the Libation, besides his good Offices in assisting at the Performance.

The good People now ranged themselves round the Kitchin Fire, where good Humour seemed to maintain an absolute Dominion, and *Partridge* not only forgot his shameful Defeat, but converted Hunger into Thirst, and soon became extremely facetious. We must, however, quit this agreeable Assembly for a while, and attend Mr. *Jones* to Mrs. *Waters's* Apartment, where the Dinner which he had now bespoke was on the Table. Indeed it took no long Time in preparing, having been all drest three Days before, and required nothing more from the Cook than to warm it over again.

[1] The Greek word for treaty or truce is σπονδαί, literally 'libations'. In the following passage Fielding parodies this ceremony as described, for instance, in the *Iliad*, xvi. 268 ff., where Achilles makes a libation to Zeus, pouring wine from the δέπας or 'Bowl' on to the ground. See also below, p. 546.25.

## CHAPTER V

*An Apology for all Heroes who have good Stomachs, with a Description of a Battle of the amorous Kind.*

HEROES, notwithstanding the high Ideas, which by the Means of Flatterers they may entertain of themselves, or the World may conceive of them, have certainly more of mortal than divine about them. However elevated their Minds may be, their Bodies at least (which is much the major Part of most) are liable to the worst Infirmities and subject to the vilest Offices of human Nature. Among these latter the Act of Eating, which hath by several wise Men been considered as extremely mean and derogatory from the Philosophic Dignity, must be in some Measure performed by the greatest Prince, Heroe, or Philosopher upon Earth; nay, sometimes Nature hath been so frolicksome as to exact of these dignified Characters, a much more exorbitant Share of this Office, than she hath obliged those of the lowest Order to perform.

To say the Truth, as no known Inhabitant of this Globe is really more than Man, so none need be ashamed of submitting to what the Necessities of Man demand; but when those great Personages I have just mentioned, condescend to aim at confining such low Offices to themselves; as when by hoarding or destroying, they seem desirous to prevent any others from eating, they then surely become very low and despicable.

Now after this short Preface, we think it no Disparagement to our Heroe to mention the immoderate Ardour with which he laid about him at this Season. Indeed it may be doubted, whether *Ulysses*, who by the Way seems to have had the best Stomach of all the Heroes in that eating Poem of the Odyssey, ever made a better Meal. Three Pounds at least of that Flesh which formerly had contributed to the Composition of an Ox, was now honoured with becoming Part of the individual Mr. *Jones*.

This Particular we thought ourselves obliged to mention, as it may account for our Heroe's temporary Neglect of his fair Companion; who eat but very little, and was indeed employed in Considerations of a very different Nature, which passed unobserved by *Jones*, till he had entirely satisfied that Appetite which a Fast of twenty-four Hours had procured him; but his

Dinner was no sooner ended, than his Attention to other Matters revived; with these Matters therefore we shall now proceed to acquaint the Reader.

Mr. *Jones*, of whose personal Accomplishments we have hitherto said very little, was in reality, one of the handsomest young Fellows in the World. His Face, besides being the Picture of Health, had in it the most apparent Marks of Sweetness and Good-Nature. These Qualities were indeed so characteristical in his Countenance, that while the Spirit and Sensibility in his Eyes, tho' they must have been perceived by an accurate Observer, might have escaped the Notice of the less discerning, so strongly was this Good-nature painted in his Look, that it was remarked by almost every one who saw him.

It was, perhaps, as much owing to this, as to a very fine Complection, that his Face had a Delicacy in it almost inexpressible, and which might have given him an Air rather too effeminate, had it not been joined to a most masculine Person and Mein; which latter had as much in them of the *Hercules*, as the former had of the *Adonis*. He was besides active, genteel, gay and good-humoured, and had a Flow of Animal Spirits, which enlivened every Conversation where he was present.

When the Reader hath duly reflected on these many Charms which all centered in our Heroe, and considers at the same Time the fresh Obligations which Mrs. *Waters* had to him, it will be a Mark more of Prudery than Candour to entertain a bad Opinion of her, because she conceived a very good Opinion of him.

But whatever Censures may be passed upon her, it is my Business to relate Matters of Fact with Veracity. Mrs. *Waters* had, in Truth, not only a good Opinion of our Heroe, but a very great Affection for him. To speak out boldly at once, she was in Love, according to the present universally received Sense of that Phrase, by which Love is applied indiscriminately to the desirable Objects of all our Passions, Appetites, and Senses, and is understood to be that Preference which we give to one Kind of Food rather than to another.

But tho' the Love to these several Objects may possibly be one and the same in all Cases, its Operations however must be allowed to be different; for how much soever we may be in Love with an excellent Surloin of Beef, or Bottle of *Burgundy*; with a

Damask Rose, or *Cremona* Fiddle;[1] yet do we never smile, nor ogle, nor dress, nor flatter, nor endeavour by any other Arts or Tricks to gain the Affection of the said Beef, &c. Sigh indeed we sometimes may; but it is generally in the Absence, not in the Presence of the beloved Object. For otherwise we might possibly complain of their Ingratitude and Deafness, with the same Reason as *Pasiphae* doth of her Bull,[2] whom she endeavoured to engage by all the Coquetry practised with good Success in the Drawing Room, on the much more sensible, as well as tender, Hearts of the fine Gentlemen there.

The contrary happens, in that Love which operates between Persons of the same Species, but of different Sexes. Here we are no sooner in Love, than it becomes our principal Care to engage the Affection of the Object beloved. For what other Purpose indeed are our Youth instructed in all the Arts of rendering themselves agreeable? If it was not with a View to this Love, I question whether any of those Trades which deal in setting off and adorning the Human Person would procure a Livelihood. Nay, those great Polishers of our Manners, who are by some thought to teach what principally distinguishes us from the Brute Creation, even Dancing-Masters themselves, might possibly find no Place in Society. In short, all the Graces which young Ladies and young Gentlemen too learn from others; and the many Improvements which, by the Help of a Looking-glass, they add of their own, are in Reality those very *Spicula et Faces Amoris*, so often mentioned by *Ovid*;[3] or, as they are sometimes called in our own Language, *The whole Artillery of Love.*

Now Mrs. *Waters* and our Heroe had no sooner sat down together, than the former began to play this Artillery upon the latter. But here, as we are about to attempt a Description hitherto unessayed either in Prose or Verse,[4] we think proper to invoke the Assistance of certain Aerial Beings, who will, we doubt not, come kindly to our Aid on this Occasion.

[1] The town in Lombardy where the violins of Amati, Stradivari and Guarneri were made.

[2] Cf. Ovid, *Metamorphoses*, viii. 131–7, 152–6, ix. 735–43. In order to satisfy her unnatural passion for a bull, Pasiphaë had Daedalus fashion her a wooden cow, in which she disguised herself.

[3] 'The stings and flames of love'—not a direct quotation, but these are among the effects of love mentioned in Ovid's amatory verse (e.g. *Ars Amatoria*, ii. 520, 708; *Remedia Amoris*, 140).

[4] Cf. *Paradise Lost*, i. 16: 'Things unattempted yet in prose or rhyme.'

'Say then, ye Graces, you that inhabit the heavenly Mansions of *Seraphina's* Countenance; for you are truly Divine, are always in her Presence, and well know all the Arts of charming, Say, what were the Weapons now used to captivate the Heart of Mr. *Jones*.'

'First, from two lovely blue Eyes, whose bright Orbs flashed Lightning at their Discharge, flew forth two pointed Ogles. But happily for our Heroe, hit only a vast Piece of Beef which he was then conveying into his Plate, and harmless spent their Force. The fair Warrior perceived their Miscarriage, and immediately from her fair Bosom drew forth a deadly Sigh. A Sigh, which none could have heard unmoved, and which was sufficient at once to have swept off a dozen Beaus; so soft, so sweet, so tender, that the insinuating Air must have found its subtle Way to the Heart of our Heroe, had it not luckily been driven from his Ears by the coarse Bubbling of some bottled Ale, which at that Time he was pouring forth. Many other Weapons did she assay; but the God of Eating (if there be any such Deity; for I do not confidently assert it) preserved his Votary; or perhaps it may not be *Dignus vindice nodus*,[1] and the present Security of *Jones* may be accounted for by natural Means: For as Love frequently preserves from the Attacks of Hunger, so may Hunger possibly, in some Cases, defend us against Love.

'The Fair One, enraged at her frequent Disappointments, determined on a short Cessation of Arms. Which Interval she employed in making ready every Engine of Amorous Warfare for the renewing of the Attack, when Dinner should be over.

'No sooner then was the Cloth removed, than she again began her Operations. First, having planted her Right Eye side-ways against Mr. *Jones*, she shot from its Corner a most penetrating Glance; which, tho' great Part of its Force was spent before it reached our Heroe, did not vent itself absolutely without Effect. This the Fair One perceiving, hastily withdrew her Eyes, and leveled them downwards as if she was concerned for what she had done: Tho' by this Means she designed only to draw him from his Guard, and indeed to open his Eyes, through which she intended to surprize his Heart. And now, gently lifting up those two bright Orbs which had already begun to make an Impression on poor *Jones*, she discharged a Volley of small Charms at

[1] See above, p. 397, n. 5.

once from her whole Countenance in a Smile. Not a Smile of
Mirth, nor of Joy; but a Smile of Affection, which most Ladies
have always ready at their Command, and which serves them to
show at once their Good-Humour, their pretty Dimples, and
their white Teeth.

'This Smile our Heroe received full in his Eyes, and was
immediately staggered with its Force. He then began to see the
Designs of the Enemy, and indeed to feel their Success. A
Parley now was set on Foot between the Parties; during which
the artful Fair so slily and imperceptibly carried on her Attack,
that she had almost subdued the Heart of our Heroe, before she
again repaired to Acts of Hostility. To confess the Truth, I am
afraid Mr. *Jones* maintained a Kind of *Dutch* Defence, and
treacherously delivered up the Garrison[1] without duly weighing
his Allegiance to the fair *Sophia*. In short, no sooner had the
amorous Parley ended, and the Lady had unmasked the Royal
Battery, by carelessly letting her Handkerchief drop from her
Neck, than the Heart of Mr. *Jones* was entirely taken, and the
fair Conqueror enjoyed the usual Fruits of her Victory.'

Here the Graces think proper to end their Description, and
here we think proper to end the Chapter.

## CHAPTER VI

*A friendly Conversation in the Kitchen, which had a very common,
tho' not very friendly Conclusion.*

WHILE our Lovers were entertaining themselves in the
Manner which is partly described in the foregoing Chapter; they were likewise furnishing out an Entertainment for their
good Friends in the Kitchen. And this in a double Sense, by
affording them Matter for their Conversation, and, at the same
Time, Drink to enliven their Spirits.

[1] Throughout the war the English had complained of 'Towns given up and lost by
*Dutch* Governors' (*Considerations on the Conduct of the Dutch* [1745], p. 47). In 1747 this
became a constant theme in the newspapers, which accused the Dutch commanders of
taking bribes to surrender their fortresses to the enemy. In this way, it was alleged, General
La Roque had delivered up Hulst to the French, and Sluys, Axel, and Bergen-op-Zoom
had fallen. (See, for example, *The General Advertiser*, 9, 13, 28 May, 17 August,
12 September 1747.) See also above, p. 240, n. 3.

There were now assembled round the Kitchen Fire, besides my
Landlord and Landlady, who occasionally went backward and
forward, Mr. *Partridge*, the Serjeant, and the Coachman who
drove the young Lady and her Maid.

*Partridge* having acquainted the Company with what he had
learnt from the Man of the Hill, concerning the Situation in
which Mrs. *Waters* had been found by *Jones*, the Serjeant
proceeded to that Part of her History which was known to him.
He said, she was the Wife of Mr. *Waters*, who was a Captain in
their Regiment, and had often been with him at Quarters. 'Some
Folks,' says he, 'used indeed to doubt whether they were lawfully married in a Church or no. But, for my Part, that's no
Business of mine; I must own, if I was put to my Corporal Oath,
I believe she is little better than one of us, and I fancy the
Captain may go to Heaven when the Sun shines upon a rainy
Day. But if he does, that is neither here nor there, for he won't
want Company. And the Lady, to give the Devil his Due, is a
very good Sort of Lady, and loves the Cloth, and is always
desirous to do strict Justice to it; for she hath begged off many a
poor Soldier, and, by her Good-will, would never have any of
them punished. But yet, to be sure, Ensign *Northerton* and she
were very well acquainted together, at our last Quarters, that is
the very Right and Truth of the Matter. But the Captain he knows
nothing about it; and as long as there is enough for him too,
what does it signify! He loves her not a bit the worse, and I am
certain would run any Man through the Body that was to abuse
her, therefore I won't abuse her, for my Part. I only repeat what
other Folks say; and to be certain, what every body says, there
must be some Truth in.' 'Ay, ay, a great deal of Truth, I warrant
you,' cries *Partridge*, '*Veritas odium parit*.'[1] 'All a Parcel of
scandalous Stuff,' answered the Mistress of the House. 'I am
sure now she is drest, she looks like a very good Sort of Lady,
and she behaves herself like one; for she gave me a Guinea for the
Use of my Cloaths.' 'A very good Lady indeed,' cries my Landlord, 'and if you had not been a little too hasty, you would not
have quarrelled with her as you did at first.' 'You need mention
that with my truly,' answered she, 'if it had not been for your
Nonsense, nothing had happened. You must be meddling with

[1] Terence, *Andria*, I. i: 'Truth begets hatred.' Cf. Ausonius, *Ludus Septem Sapientum*,
viii.

what did not belong to you, and throw in your Fool's Discourse.'
'Well, well,' answered he, 'what's past cannot be mended, so
there's an End of the Matter.' 'Yes,' cries she, 'for this once, but
will it be mended ever the more hereafter? This is not the first
Time I have suffered for your Numscull's Pate. I wish you would
always hold your Tongue in the House, and meddle only in
Matters without Doors which concern you. Don't you remember
what happened about seven Years ago?'—'Nay, my Dear,'
returned he, 'don't rip up old Stories. Come, come, all's well, and
I am sorry for what I have done.' The Landlady was going to
reply, but was prevented by the Peace-making Serjeant, sorely to
the Displeasure of *Partridge*, who was a great Lover of what is
called Fun, and a great Promoter of those harmless Quarrels
which tend rather to the Production of comical than tragical
Incidents.

The Serjeant asked *Partridge* whither he and his Master were
travelling. 'None of your Magisters,' answered *Partridge*, 'I am
no Man's Servant, I assure you; for tho' I have had Misfortunes
in the World, I write Gentleman after my Name; and as poor and
simple as I may appear now, I have taught Grammar School in
my Time. *Sed hei mihi non sum quod fui.*[1] 'No Offence, I hope,
Sir,' said the Serjeant, 'where then, if I may venture to be so
bold, may you and your Friend be travelling?'—'You have now
denominated us right,' says *Partridge*. '*Amici Sumus.*[2] And I
promise you my Friend is one of the greatest Gentlemen in the
Kingdom,' (at which Words both Landlord and Landlady
pricked up their Ears). 'He is the Heir of Squire *Allworthy*.'
'What, the Squire who doth so much Good all over the Country?'
cries my Landlady. 'Even he,' answered *Partridge*. 'Then I
warrant,' says she, 'he'll have a swinging great Estate hereafter.'
'Most certainly,' answered *Partridge*. 'Well,' replied the Landlady, 'I thought the first Moment I saw him he looked like a good
Sort of Gentleman; but my Husband here, to be sure, is wiser
than any body.' 'I own, my Dear,' cries he, 'it was a Mistake.'
'A Mistake indeed!' answered she; 'but when did you ever know
me to make such Mistakes?'—'But how comes it, Sir,' cries the
Landlord, 'that such a great Gentleman walks about the Country
afoot?' 'I don't know,' returned *Partridge*, 'great Gentlemen have
Humours sometimes. He hath now a dozen Horses and Servants

[1] 'But woe to me! I am not what I was.'          [2] 'We are friends.'

at *Gloucester*, and nothing would serve him, but last Night, it being very hot Weather, he must cool himself with a Walk to yon high Hill, whither I likewise walked with him to bear him Company; but if ever you catch me there again: For I was never so frightened in all my Life. We met with the strangest Man there.' 'I'll be hanged,' cries the Landlord, 'if it was not the Man of the Hill, as they call him; if indeed he be a Man; but I know several People who believe it is the Devil that lives there.' 'Nay, nay, like enough,' says *Partridge*, 'and now you put me in the Head of it, I verily and sincerely believe it was the Devil; tho' I could not perceive his cloven Foot; but perhaps he might have the Power given him to hide that, since evil Spirits can appear in what Shapes they please.' 'And pray, Sir,' says the Serjeant, 'no Offence I hope; but pray what Sort of a Gentleman is the Devil? For I have heard some of our Officers say, There is no such Person, and that it is only a Trick of the Parsons, to prevent their being broke; for if it was publickly known that there was no Devil, the Parsons would be of no more Use than we are in Time of Peace.' 'Those Officers,' says *Partridge*, 'are very great Scholars, I suppose.' 'Not much of Schollards neither,' answered the Serjeant, 'they have not half your Learning, Sir, I believe; and to be sure, I thought there must be a Devil, notwithstanding what they said, tho' one of them was a Captain; for methought, thinks I to myself, if there be no Devil, how can wicked People be sent to him, and I have read all that upon a Book.' 'Some of your Officers,' quoth the Landlord, 'will find there is a Devil, to their Shame, I believe. I don't question but he'll pay off some old Scores, upon my Account. Here was one quartered upon me half a Year, who had the Conscience to take up one of my best Beds, tho' he hardly spent a Shilling a Day in the House, and suffered his Men to roast Cabbages at the Kitchen Fire, because I would not give them a Dinner on a *Sunday*. Every good Christian must desire there should be a Devil for the Punishment of such Wretches.' 'Harkee, Landlord,' said the Serjeant, 'don't abuse the Cloth, for I won't take it.' 'D——n the Cloth,' answered the Landlord, 'I have suffered enough by them.' 'Bear Witness, Gentlemen,' says the Serjeant, 'he curses the King, and that's High Treason.' 'I curse the King! you Villain,' said the Landlord. 'Yes you did,' cries the Serjeant, 'you cursed the Cloth, and that's cursing the King. It's all one and the same; for every Man who curses the Cloth, would curse the King if he durst; so for Matter o' that, it's all one and the same Thing.' 'Excuse me there, Mr. Serjeant,' quoth *Partridge*, 'that's a *Non Sequitur*.' 'None of your outlandish Linguo,' answered the Serjeant, leaping from his Seat, 'I will not sit still and hear the Cloth abused.'— 'You mistake me, Friend,' cries *Partridge*, 'I did not mean to abuse the Cloth; I only said your Conclusion was a *Non Sequitur*.'\* 'You are another,' cries the Serjeant, 'an you come to that. No more a *Sequitur* than yourself. You are a Pack of Rascals, and I'll prove it; for I will fight the best Man of you all for twenty Pound.' This Challenge effectually silenced *Partridge*, whose Stomach for drubbing did not so soon return, after the hearty Meal which he had lately been treated with; but the Coachman, whose Bones were less sore, and whose Appetite for Fighting was somewhat sharper, did not so easily brook the Affront, of which he conceived some Part at least fell to his Share. He started therefore from his Seat, and advancing to the Serjeant, swore he looked on himself to be as good a Man as any in the Army, and offered to box for a Guinea. The military Man accepted the Combat, but refused the Wager; upon which both immediately stript and engaged, till the Driver of Horses was so well mauled by the Leader of Men, that he was obliged to exhaust his small Remainder of Breath in begging for Quarter.

The young Lady was now desirous to depart, and had given Orders for her Coach to be prepared; but all in vain; for the Coachman was disabled from performing his Office for that Evening. An antient Heathen would perhaps have imputed this Disability to the God of Drink, no less than to the God of War; for, in Reality, both the Combatants had sacrificed as well to the former Deity as to the latter. To speak plainly, they were both dead drunk, nor was *Partridge* in a much better Situation. As for my Landlord, drinking was his Trade, and the Liquor had no more Effect on him, than it had on any other Vessel in his House.

The Mistress of the Inn being summoned to attend Mr. *Jones* and his Companion, at their Tea, gave a full Relation of the latter Part of the foregoing Scene; and at the same Time expressed great Concern for the young Lady, 'who,' she said, 'was under the utmost Uneasiness at being prevented from pursuing her

---

\* This Word, which the Serjeant unhappily mistook for an Affront, is a Term in Logic, and means that the Conclusion doth not follow from the Premises.

Journey. She is a sweet pretty Creature,' added she, 'and I am certain I have seen her Face before. I fancy she is in Love, and running away from her Friends. Who knows but some young Gentleman or other may be expecting her, with a Heart as heavy as her own.'

*Jones* fetched a hearty Sigh at those Words; of which, tho' Mrs. *Waters* observed it, she took no Notice while the Landlady continued in the Room; but after the Departure of that good Woman, she could not forbear giving our Heroe certain Hints of her suspecting some very dangerous Rival in his Affections. The aukward Behaviour of Mr. *Jones* on this Occasion convinced her of the Truth, without his giving her a direct Answer to any of her Questions; but she was not nice enough in her Amours to be greatly concerned at the Discovery. The Beauty of *Jones* highly charmed her Eye; but, as she could not see his Heart, she gave herself no concern about it. She could feast heartily at the Table of Love, without reflecting that some other already had been, or hereafter might be, feasted with the same Repast. A Sentiment which, if it deals but little in Refinement, deals however much in Substance; and is less capricious, and perhaps less ill-natured and selfish than the Desires of those Females who can be contented enough to abstain from the Possession of their Lovers, provided they are sufficiently satisfied that no one else possesses them.


## CHAPTER VII

*Containing a fuller Account of Mrs.* Waters, *and by what Means she came into that distressful Situation from which she was rescued by* Jones.

THOUGH Nature hath by no Means mixed up an equal Share either of Curiosity or Vanity in every human Composition, there is perhaps no Individual to whom she hath not allotted such a Proportion of both, as requires much Art, and Pains too, to subdue and keep under. A Conquest, however, absolutely necessary to every one who would in any Degree deserve the Characters of Wisdom or Good-Breeding.

As *Jones* therefore might very justly be called a well-bred Man, he had stifled all that Curiosity which the extraordinary Manner in which he had found Mrs. *Waters*, must be supposed to have occasioned. He had indeed at first thrown out some few Hints to the Lady; but when he perceived her industriously avoiding any Explanation, he was contented to remain in Ignorance, the rather as he was not without Suspicion, that there were some Circumstances which must have raised her Blushes, had she related the whole Truth.

Now, since it is possible that some of our Readers may not so easily acquiesce under the same Ignorance, and as we are very desirous to satisfy them all, we have taken uncommon Pains to inform ourselves of the real Fact, with the Relation of which we shall conclude this Book.

This Lady then had lived some Years with one Captain *Waters*, who was a Captain in the same Regiment to which Mr. *Northerton* belonged. She past for that Gentleman's Wife, and went by his Name; and yet, as the Serjeant said, there were some Doubts concerning the Reality of their Marriage, which we shall not at present take upon us to resolve.

Mrs. *Waters*, I am sorry to say it, had for some Time contracted an Intimacy with the above mentioned Ensign, which did no great Credit to her Reputation. That she had a remarkable Fondness for that young Fellow is most certain; but whether she indulged this to any very criminal Lengths, is not so extremely clear, unless we will suppose that Women never grant every Favour to a Man but one, without granting him that one also.

The Division of the Regiment to which Captain *Waters* belonged, had two Days preceded the March of that Company to which Mr. *Northerton* was the Ensign; so that the former had reached *Worcester*, the very Day after the unfortunate Rencounter between *Jones* and *Northerton*, which we have before recorded.

Now it had been agreed between Mrs. *Waters* and the Captain, that she should accompany him in his March as far as *Worcester*, where they were to take their Leave of each other, and she was thence to return to *Bath*, where she was to stay till the End of the Winter's Campaign against the Rebels.

With this Agreement Mr. *Northerton* was made acquainted. To say the Truth, the Lady had made him an Assignation at this very Place, and promised to stay at *Worcester* till his Division came thither; with what View, and for what Purpose must be left to the Reader's Divination: For though we are obliged to relate Facts, we are not obliged to do a Violence to our Nature by any Comments to the Disadvantage of the loveliest Part of the Creation.

*Northerton* no sooner obtained a Release from his Captivity, as we have seen, than he hasted away to overtake Mrs. *Waters*; which, as he was a very active nimble Fellow, he did at the last mentioned City, some few Hours after Captain *Waters* had left her: At his first Arrival he made no Scruple of acquainting her with the unfortunate Accident, which he made appear very unfortunate indeed: For he totally extracted every Particle of what could be called Fault, at least in a Court of Honour, though he left some Circumstances which might be questionable in a Court of Law.

Women, to their Glory be it spoken, are more generally capable of that violent and apparently disinterested Passion of Love, which seeks only the Good of its Object, than Men. Mrs. *Waters*, therefore, was no sooner apprized of the Danger to which her Lover was exposed, than she lost every Consideration besides that of his Safety; and this being a Matter equally agreeable to the Gentleman, it became the immediate Subject of Debate between them.

After much Consultation on this Matter, it was at length agreed, that the Ensign should go a-cross the Country to *Hereford*, whence he might find some Conveyance to one of the Sea-Ports in *Wales*, and thence might make his Escape abroad. In all which Expedition Mrs. *Waters* declared she would bear him Company; and for which she was able to furnish him with Money, a very material Article to Mr. *Northerton*, she having then in her Pocket three Bank Notes to the Amount of 90 *l.* besides some Cash, and a Diamond Ring of pretty considerable Value on her Finger. All which she, with the utmost Confidence, revealed to this wicked Man, little suspecting she should by these Means inspire him with a Design of robbing her. Now as they must, by taking Horses from *Worcester*, have furnished any Pursuers with the Means of hereafter discovering their Rout, the Ensign proposed, and the Lady presently agreed to make their first Stage on Foot; for which Purpose the Hardness of the Frost was very seasonable.

The main Part of the Lady's Baggage was already at *Bath*, and she had nothing with her at present besides a very small Quantity of Linnen, which the Gallant undertook to carry in his own Pockets. All Things, therefore, being settled in the Evening, they arose early the next Morning, and at Five o'Clock departed from *Worcester*, it being then above two Hours before Day. But the Moon which was then at the full, gave them all the Light she was capable of affording.[1]

Mrs. *Waters* was not of that delicate Race of Women who are obliged to the Invention of Vehicles for the Capacity of removing themselves from one Place to another, and with whom consequently a Coach is reckoned among the Necessaries of Life. Her Limbs were indeed full of Strength and Agility, and as her Mind was no less animated with Spirit, she was perfectly able to keep Pace with her nimble Lover.

Having travelled on for some Miles in a High Road, which *Northerton* said he was informed led to *Hereford*, they came at the Break of Day to the Side of a large Wood, where he suddenly stopped, and affecting to meditate a Moment with himself, expressed some Apprehensions from travelling any longer in so public a Way. Upon which he easily persuaded his fair Companion to strike with him into a Path which seemed to lead directly through the Wood, and which at length brought them both to the Bottom of *Mazard-Hill*.

Whether the execrable Scheme which he now attempted to execute, was the Effect of previous Deliberation, or whether it now first came into his Head, I cannot determine. But being arrived in this lonely Place, where it was very improbable he should meet with any Interruption; he suddenly slipped his Garter from his Leg, and laying violent Hands on the poor Woman, endeavoured to perpetrate that dreadful and detestable Fact, which we have before commemorated, and which the providential Appearance of *Jones* did so fortunately prevent.

Happy was it for Mrs. *Waters*, that she was not of the weakest Order of Females; for no sooner did she perceive by his tying a Knot in his Garter, and by his Declarations, what his Hellish

---

[1] If, as seems unlikely, Fielding had earlier troubled to consult an almanac when plotting the time-scheme of his narative (see above, p. 435, n. 1), at this point he was no longer doing so. The moon which had risen over Gloucester at 5.00 p.m., presumably on 29 November 1745, set the following morning at 3.05 (Greenwich time), some five hours before daybreak. (See Nathanael Culpepper, *The Family Almanack, for 1745*.)

Intentions were, than she stood stoutly to her Defence, and so strongly struggled with her Enemy, screaming all the while for Assistance, that she delayed the Execution of the Villain's Purpose several Minutes, by which Means Mr. *Jones* came to her Relief, at that very Instant when her Strength failed, and she was totally overpowered, and delivered her from the Ruffian's Hands, with no other Loss than that of her Cloaths, which were torn from her Back, and of the Diamond Ring, which during the Contention either dropped from her Finger, or was wrenched from it by *Northerton*.

Thus, Reader, we have given thee the Fruits of a very painful Enquiry, which for thy Satisfaction we have made into this Matter. And here we have opened to thee a Scene of Folly, as well as Villainy, which we could scarce have believed a human Creature capable of being guilty of; had we not remembered that this Fellow was at that Time firmly persuaded, that he had already committed a Murther, and had forfeited his Life to the Law. As he concluded therefore that his only Safety lay in Flight, he thought the possessing himself of this poor Woman's Money and Ring, would make him Amends for the additional Burthen he was to lay on his Conscience.

And here, Reader, we must strictly caution thee, that thou dost not take any Occasion from the Misbehaviour of such a Wretch as this, to reflect on so worthy and honourable a Body of Men, as are the Officers of our Army in general. Thou wilt be pleased to consider, that this Fellow, as we have already informed thee, had neither the Birth nor Education of a Gentleman, nor was a proper Person to be enrolled among the Number of such. If therefore his Baseness can justly reflect on any besides himself, it must be only on those who gave him his Commission.

*The End of the* Third Volume.